HANDBOOK OF
Whales, Dolphins, and Porpoises
OF THE WORLD

HANDBOOK OF
Whales, Dolphins, and Porpoises
OF THE WORLD

Mark Carwardine

Illustrated by
Martin Camm

With additional illustrations by
Rebecca Robinson
Toni Llobet

PRINCETON UNIVERSITY PRESS
PRINCETON AND OXFORD

Published in the United States, Canada, and the Philippines in 2020 by Princeton University Press

Princeton University Press
41 William Street
Princeton, New Jersey 08540
press.princeton.edu

First published by Bloomsbury Publishing Plc in 2019

Library of Congress Control Number 2019945377

ISBN 978-0-691-20210-5

2 4 6 8 10 9 7 5 3 1

Maps and scale drawings by Julie Dando, Fluke Art
Design by Julie Dando, Fluke Art
Printed and bound in India by Replika Press Pvt. Ltd.

CONTENTS

HOW TO USE THIS BOOK

SPECIES NAMES

The currently accepted common name of the species is given in English. Many have alternative names – some in common usage, many rare or regional and others historical – and these are all provided as well. Names in other languages are not given, purely for reasons of space (each species has lots of different names in almost every language, so the number of possibilities is huge). Common names can vary but each species has only one scientific name, which is given in italics. The authority (the person credited with first publishing the name of the species) is also provided. If a species has been transferred to a new genus – not the one in which it was originally described – the original author's name and date are put in parentheses, for example: (Linnaeus, 1758). If it is not in parentheses, it is still in the original genus. There is also information on the origins of the various common and scientific names and what they mean.

CLASSIFICATION AND TAXONOMY

The guide follows the taxonomic arrangement, and the scientific names of species and subspecies, recommended by the Society for Marine Mammalogy's Committee on Taxonomy (with one exception, the dwarf Baird's beaked whale, which has been included as a separate species in anticipation of formal recognition). This authoritative list is updated annually. It is in a constant state of flux, with species being combined and split as more information comes to light. Notes about the taxonomy of each species are given as background information and to point out any possible future changes.

SIZE

The species silhouette shows the typical size of an adult to scale against a human diver (all human silhouettes represent 1.8m). L = length, WT = weight. Size ranges for adult males, adult females and calves are given, together with the maximum lengths and weights recorded to date. All measurements are in metric, but there is a conversion chart at the back of the book for those who prefer imperial.

AT A GLANCE

An abbreviated list of key features is provided for quick reference – outlining the main features to concentrate on to achieve a correct identification – including distribution, size and key physical and behavioural features. Size is based on a simple scale: small (up to 3m), medium (4–10m), large (11–15m), and extra large (more than 15m).

ILLUSTRATIONS

The main illustration for each species shows a typical side view (if males and females look different they are illustrated separately). Other images show the opposite side view (if it is different), the upperside and underside, any subspecies, regional variations or age variations, and any relevant close-ups of dorsal fins, beaks, flippers or other features (sometimes including comparisons with similar species). Each illustration has its own annotations, pointing out the main distinguishing features useful for identification and any other interesting characteristics. See Cetacean Topography on page 20 for a breakdown of the names of the various parts of a cetacean. There are additional illustrations showing the shape and size of the blow or spout from behind (for the larger species) and a typical dive sequence.

CONFUSING SPECIES

It is useful to know which species within the range are similar, and could therefore cause identification problems, so abbreviated information is provided on how to tell them apart.

DISTRIBUTION

The distribution maps show the known and/or presumed range of each species. For many, there is very little information and putting together a distribution map is like putting together a jigsaw with a few or many parts missing. The accompanying text explains in more detail what is known about the distribution and where there are gaps in our knowledge, as well as providing more information on habitat and depth preferences (within the mapped range, each species occurs only in appropriate habitats and depths), migrations and other movements, and extralimital records.

BEHAVIOUR

Behaviour such as breaching, spyhopping, lobtailing and reaction to boats can provide valuable clues in cetacean identification, and details are given in this section. Bear in mind, though, that behaviour can vary enormously between individuals, from one region to another, with the seasons and according to many other factors.

TEETH/BALEEN PLATES

The number of teeth is normally given as a count for each row (i.e. two rows in the upper jaw and two in the lower jaw). However, for simplicity, the figures in this guide show the range in total number of teeth in the upper and the same for the lower jaw. Baleen plates are present only in the upper jaw and the figure gives the total range.

FOOD AND FEEDING

This section includes short notes on the main prey species, foraging behaviour, dive depth and dive times (with the maximum recorded to date).

LIFE HISTORY

This includes short notes on the age at sexual maturity (for males and females, i.e. the age at which a male first mates successfully and a female has her first calf), the mating system and breeding behaviour, the length of gestation, calving intervals, breeding season, age at weaning and average lifespan (with the oldest recorded to date).

GROUP SIZE AND STRUCTURE

There is a great deal of variation in cetacean groupings, between individuals, regions and seasons, but the most commonly observed group sizes and structures are given, together with further information on variability. There are also details on the social organisation of the groups.

PREDATORS

Killer whales and large sharks are the most common predators of cetaceans, but there is further information on specific evidence for predation on each species, and any other known predators.

PHOTO-IDENTIFICATION

This section lists the key features that scientists photograph – for example, nicks on the trailing edge of the dorsal fin – in order to tell one individual from another.

POPULATION

Counting cetaceans is notoriously difficult and, inevitably, estimates are of variable accuracy (and, of course, some are more recent than others). However, while most population figures should be viewed cautiously, this section provides what is known and gives a guide to the estimated abundance of the species.

CONSERVATION

This gives a review of historical and current conservation issues. Global warming is generally not listed in species accounts, because it is assumed that it will ultimately affect them all to varying degrees (something that is notoriously difficult to forecast). The IUCN status is given for each species (together with the year of assessment). This is the official status on the International Union for Conservation of Nature Red List of Threatened Species, which is the most authoritative, objective and comprehensive list of species that have been rigorously evaluated for their risk of extinction. There are eight categories: Extinct (no reasonable doubt that the last individual has died); Extinct in the Wild (known only to survive in captivity or as a naturalised population well outside its historical range); Critically Endangered (extremely high risk of extinction in the wild); Endangered (very high risk of extinction in the wild); Vulnerable (high risk of extinction in the wild); Near Threatened (likely to qualify for a threatened category in the future); Least Concern (does not qualify for a more at-risk category); and Data Deficient (not enough data to make an assessment). A ninth category – Not Evaluated – is for species not yet assessed.

VOCALISATIONS

Vocalisations are described for some species – mostly the baleen whales – but not for all, simply for reasons of space.

SOURCES AND RESOURCES

Countless thousands of scientific papers were consulted during research for this book and there simply isn't room to list them all. However, general references and sources of further information are given at the end of the book.

THE CHALLENGES OF IDENTIFICATION

Identifying whales, dolphins and porpoises at sea can be enormously satisfying, but also quite challenging. In fact, it can be so difficult that even the world's experts are unable to identify every species they encounter – on most official surveys, at least some sightings have to be logged as 'unidentified'.

The trick is to use a relatively simple process of elimination, running through a mental checklist of 14 key features every time a new animal is encountered at sea. It is not often possible to use all of these features together and one alone is rarely enough for a positive identification. The best approach is to gather information on as many as possible before drawing any firm conclusions.

1. Geographical location There is not a single place in the world where every cetacean species has been recorded. In fact, there are not many places with records of more than a few dozen, so this immediately helps to cut down on the number of possibilities.

2. Habitat Just as cheetahs live on open plains rather than in jungles, and snow leopards prefer mountains to wetlands, most whales, dolphins and porpoises are adapted to specific marine or freshwater habitats. In this respect, marine charts can be surprisingly useful identification aids. Knowing the underwater topography could help to tell the difference between a minke whale (normally found over the continental shelf) and a superficially similar northern bottlenose whale (more likely to be seen over submarine canyons or in deep waters offshore).

3. Size It is difficult to estimate size accurately at sea, unless a direct comparison can be made with the length of the boat, a passing bird or an object in the water.

Remember that only a small portion of the animal (the top of the head and back, for example) may be visible at any one time. Larger species don't necessarily show more of themselves than smaller species, so size can be quite deceptive. It is therefore better to use four simple categories: small (up to 3m), medium (4–10m), large (11–15m), and extra large (more than 15m).

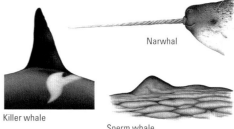

Narwhal

Killer whale

Sperm whale

4. Unusual features Some cetaceans have very unusual features, which can be used for a quick identification. These include the extraordinary long tusk of the male narwhal, the enormous dorsal fin of the male killer whale and the wrinkly skin of the sperm whale.

5. Dorsal fin The size, shape and position of the dorsal fin varies greatly between species and is a particularly useful aid to identification. Don't forget to look for any distinctive colours or markings on the fin.

Pacific white-sided dolphin

Spectacled porpoise

Pygmy beaked whale

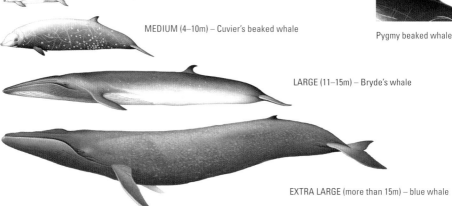

SMALL (up to 3m) – vaquita

MEDIUM (4–10m) – Cuvier's beaked whale

LARGE (11–15m) – Bryde's whale

EXTRA LARGE (more than 15m) – blue whale

6. Flippers The length, colour and shape of the flippers, as well as their position on the animal's body, vary greatly from one species to another. It is not always possible to see them, but flippers can be useful for identification in some species – in the humpback whale, for example, they are unmistakable.

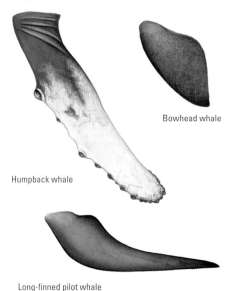

Bowhead whale

Humpback whale

Long-finned pilot whale

7. Body shape Much of the time, whales, dolphins and porpoises do not show enough of themselves to provide an overall impression of their shape. Sometimes, however, this can be a useful feature. Is the animal stocky or slim, for example? The shape of the melon (forehead) can also be distinctive.

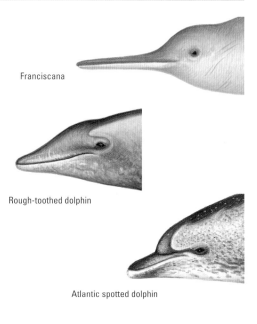

Franciscana

Rough-toothed dolphin

Atlantic spotted dolphin

8. Beak The presence or absence of a prominent beak is a particularly useful identification feature in toothed whales. Broadly speaking, river dolphins, beaked whales and half the oceanic dolphins have prominent beaks, while porpoises, belugas and narwhals, killer whales and their allies, and the remaining oceanic dolphins do not. There is also great variation in the beak length from one species to another. And try to see if there is a smooth transition from the top of the head to the end of the snout (as in rough-toothed dolphins, for example) or a distinct crease (as in Atlantic spotted dolphins).

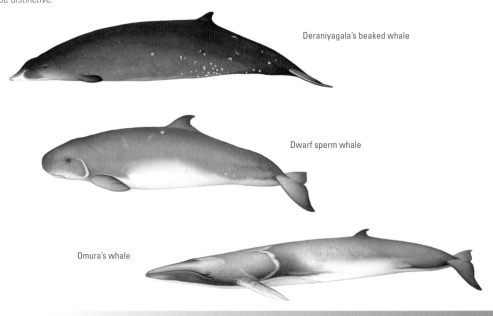

Deraniyagala's beaked whale

Dwarf sperm whale

Omura's whale

9. Colour and markings Many cetaceans are surprisingly colourful and have distinctive markings such as body stripes or eye patches. Bear in mind that colours at sea vary according to water clarity and light conditions, and the animal can appear much darker than normal if viewed against the sun.

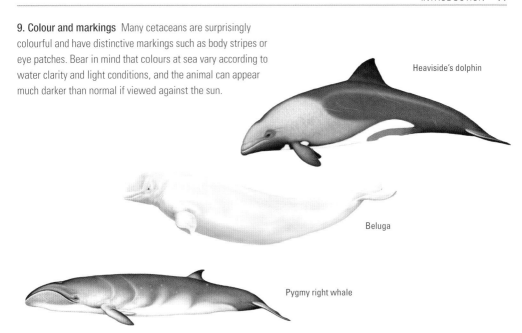

Heaviside's dolphin

Beluga

Pygmy right whale

10. Flukes The flukes can be important in identifying larger whales. Some species lift their flukes high into the air before they dive, while others do not, and that alone can help to tell one from another. It is also worth checking the shape of the flukes, looking for any distinctive markings and noticing whether or not there is a notch between the trailing edges.

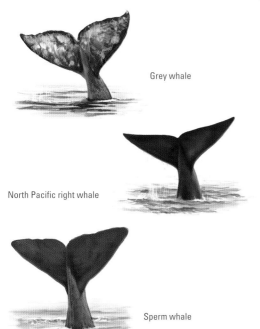

Grey whale

North Pacific right whale

Sperm whale

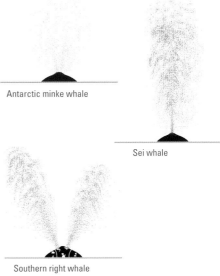

Antarctic minke whale

Sei whale

Southern right whale

11. Blow or spout The blow is particularly distinctive in larger whales. It varies in height, shape and visibility between species and can be extremely useful for identification, especially on calmer days. But identifying a blow is not easy – if it is raining or windy, the blow can be bent out of shape, and there are variations between individuals – and the first blow after a deep dive tends to be stronger than the rest. However, experienced observers can often tell one species from another just by the blow, even from a considerable distance.

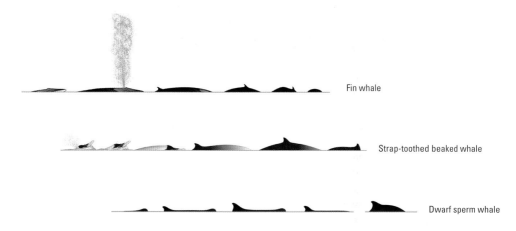

Fin whale

Strap-toothed beaked whale

Dwarf sperm whale

12. Dive sequence The dive sequence can be surprisingly distinct in many species. Variations include: the angle at which the head breaks the surface; how much of the head and beak (if present) is visible; whether or not the dorsal fin and blowhole are visible at the same time; whether the animal arches its back to dive (and how much it arches) or whether it merely sinks below the surface; the time interval between breaths; and the number of breaths before a deep dive.

13. Behaviour Some species are more active at the surface than others, so any unusual behaviour can sometimes be useful for identification purposes. Did it leap out of the water, for example, or was its behaviour quite cryptic? The reaction to boats can also be helpful: common bottlenose dolphins may race over and bow-ride, while the similar-looking Atlantic humpback dolphins tend to be more shy and will not bow-ride.

Spinner dolphin

14. Group size Since some species are highly gregarious, while others tend to live alone or in small groups, it is worth noting the number of animals seen together. Estimating group size is notoriously difficult, because the animals are mobile and frequently change direction and, at the time of counting, any number of them can be hidden beneath the surface. Estimating the size of a large school of active dolphins is especially challenging – the tendency is usually to underestimate.

It is often tempting to guess the identification of an unusual whale, dolphin or porpoise that you have not seen very clearly. However, working hard at identification – and then enjoying the satisfaction of knowing that an animal has been identified correctly – is what makes a real expert in the long term. It is perfectly acceptable to record simply 'unidentified dolphin', 'unidentified whale' or 'unidentified beaked whale' if a more accurate identification is not possible. If you write detailed notes at the time, and then see the same species again in the future, it may be possible to turn a sighting previously recorded as 'unidentified' into a positive identification, days, weeks, months or even years later.

It does get easier with practice. After a while, you look at a whale and it triggers a switch in your brain. You know what it is likely to be – a single species or, perhaps, several possibilities – from its 'jizz' (the overall impression). At a glance, you get an overall impression that is more instinctive than something that can easily be put into words.

Part of the fun is that cetaceans are unpredictable. Never say 'never' on a whale-watching trip: just because the distribution maps suggest you're unlikely to see a particular species in a particular area, it doesn't mean to say it couldn't pop up anywhere at any time; and just because the guidebooks say that one species of whale doesn't fluke, it doesn't mean to say the particular individual next to your boat won't prove everyone wrong by lifting its tail high into the air.

INTRODUCTION TO
THE 14 CETACEAN FAMILIES

There are currently 90 recognised species of whales, dolphins and porpoises (including the dwarf Baird's beaked whale – yet to be formally accepted), in 14 families (although one species – the Yangtze river dolphin – is now possibly extinct). The precise number is in a constant state of flux as new species are discovered or split from existing species, and two or more are combined to form a single species.

They belong to the order Cetacea (although the taxonomic status of 'Cetacea' is under review and it may slip down the ranks); the name comes from the Latin *cetus* or *cetos* and the Greek *ketos*, for 'whale'. Cetaceans share many common features: a streamlined body, flattened foreflippers, no hindlimbs (sometimes present as vestiges), boneless tail flukes, an elongated skull, nasal openings on the top of the head, a dorsal fin or ridge (secondarily lost in some species), a thick layer of blubber and internal reproductive organs.

Modern cetaceans are divided into the mysticetes and odontocetes (traditionally considered sub-orders, though their taxonomic status is also under review).

MYSTICETES – humpback whale

MYSTICETES
Baleen whales, or whalebone whales (14 species in four families and six genera)
The name 'mysticete' is believed to come from the Greek *mystakos*, meaning 'moustache', and the Greek *ketos* for 'huge fish' or 'sea monster' (effectively 'moustached whale', referring to the baleen plates). Instead of teeth, mysticetes have hundreds of tightly packed baleen plates or 'whalebone' – dense, comb-like structures hanging down from their upper jaws. These form a giant sieve for filter-feeding large numbers of small prey (mostly fish and crustaceans). Filter-feeding is an efficient system that allows some of the largest animals on the planet to feed on some of the smallest. They tend to feed at shallower depths than many odontocetes. They also have a double blowhole and a symmetrical skull. Unlike odontocetes, they do not have a melon and are not capable of echolocation (although there is limited evidence that they might use some form of sonar to navigate ocean basins or,

in the case of the bowhead whale, under ice). However, songs and other vocalisations – for communication and display, for example – are well developed. Most mysticetes are large (with females growing bigger than males) and long lived, and most make substantial annual north–south migrations between warm-water winter breeding grounds and cold-water summer feeding grounds. They tend to live in smaller groups than odontocetes and have a simpler social organisation.

ODONTOCETES – killer whale

ODONTOCETES
Toothed whales (76 species in 10 diverse families and 34 genera)
The name 'odontocete' comes from the Greek *odous* or *odontos*, meaning 'tooth', and *ketos*, for 'huge fish' or 'sea monster' (effectively 'toothed whale'). Odontocetes are characterised by the presence of teeth rather than baleen. They have highly variable numbers of mostly identical teeth, although these do not erupt in some species (or sexes), form peculiar shapes in others, and can be broken or worn. In some species there has evolved a secondary reduction in the number of teeth, mostly as an adaptation for feeding on squid. Odontocetes chase, capture and swallow individual prey (mostly fish and squid, but also large crustaceans, marine mammals and other species) and tend to feed at greater depths than mysticetes. They have a single crescent-shaped blowhole (the open side faces forward in all but three species) and an asymmetrical skull. A bulging fatty area in the forehead, called the melon, is believed to be used in most (if not all) to focus and modulate sounds for echolocation (the process of sending out high-frequency sounds and interpreting the returning echoes to navigate, find food and avoid predators). Most odontocetes are small to medium sized (the sperm whale is a notable exception – males can reach lengths of at least 19m), with variable sexual dimorphism (in some species, males are much larger than females, in others females are larger than males). Lifespans vary enormously between

species, from about 10 to 200 years or more. They tend to live in larger groups than most mysticetes and have a more complex social organisation.

A third group, called the **ARCHAEOCETES**, or ancient whales, has been extinct for millions of years. A primitive assemblage of cetaceans – including the initial amphibious stages in cetacean evolution – these are the ancestors of all modern baleen and toothed whales. They lived in the Eocene epoch, about 55–34 million years ago. There are currently six recognised families: Pakicetidae (four genera), Ambulocetidae (three genera), Remingtonocetidae (five genera), Protocetidae (16 genera), Basilosauridae (11 genera), and Kekenodontidae (one genus).

THE 14 CETACEAN FAMILIES

BALAENIDAE – North Atlantic right whale

BALAENIDAE
Right and bowhead whales (four species in two genera: *Eubalaena* and *Balaena*)
The three species of right whale and one species of bowhead whale are distinctive. They have large rotund bodies, enormous heads (up to one-third of their body length), a strongly arched rostrum, no dorsal fin or trace of a dorsal ridge, and none of the throat grooves or pleats that characterise the rorquals (in the family Balaenopteridae). Their baleen plates – which are covered by enormous lower lips when the mouth is shut – are the longest of all the whales. They tend to skim-feed at or near the water's surface by swimming slowly with their mouths open, rather than lunging forward towards their prey. The three right whale species are the only cetaceans to have callosities – areas of thick, irregular, calcified skin scattered about their heads. They are found in temperate and polar waters, with one right whale in the southern hemisphere, and two right whales and a bowhead whale in the northern hemisphere. All four species have suffered from tragic commercial overexploitation and all have, at some point, been close to extinction. The North Atlantic and North Pacific right whales are the world's most endangered baleen whales.

NEOBALAENIDAE
Pygmy right whale (one species in one genus: *Caperea*)
The pygmy right whale is the smallest baleen whale and is poorly known. Living in the temperate and sub-polar

NEOBALAENIDAE – pygmy right whale

southern hemisphere, it is in some ways intermediate between the Balaenopteridae (rorquals) and the Balaenidae (right and bowhead whales). It is a slender whale with a moderately arched rostrum, a head only about a quarter of the total length, a short falcate dorsal fin set two-thirds of the way along its back and a pair of shallow throat depressions. Recent evidence suggests that it may be a surviving member of the otherwise extinct family Cetotheriidae.

ESCHRICHTIIDAE – grey whale

ESCHRICHTIIDAE
Grey whale (one species in one genus: *Eschrichtius*)
In some ways intermediate between the Balaenopteridae (rorquals) and the Balaenidae (right and bowhead whales), the grey whale has a moderately stocky body, a slightly arched rostrum, a hump instead of a true dorsal fin (followed by a series of knobs or knuckles along the dorsal surface of the tailstock) and two to seven (usually two or three) throat grooves. It also has the shortest and coarsest baleen of all mysticete whales. Adults are usually covered with patches of barnacles and whale lice. Once present in both the North Atlantic and North Pacific oceans, it was exterminated in the North Atlantic in the past few hundred years.

BALAENOPTERIDAE – blue whale

BALAENOPTERIDAE
Rorquals (eight species in two genera: *Balaenoptera* and *Megaptera*)
The name 'rorqual' comes from the Norwegian word *rørval*, meaning 'the whale with pleats'. This refers to the variable number of pleats or throat grooves that run longitudinally from the chin towards the navel in

all members of this family (although, strictly speaking, the term should not be applied to the rather different humpback whale); the pleats expand during feeding to take in huge mouthfuls of food and water. Balaenopterids, as these whales are often known, are mostly fast lunge-feeders, able to open their jaws very widely (by more than 90 degrees in some species). Their baleen plates are of moderate length. Most are large and slender bodied (the humpback is stockier), with females being a little larger than males in all species. Unlike members of the Balaenidae and Eschrichtiidae families, they do have dorsal fins, which vary in size and shape according to the species, and are set behind the midpoint of the back. This is a diverse family, including the largest animal on the planet (blue whale), the animal with the longest and most complex song (humpback whale), and the most recently discovered baleen whale (Omura's whale). Most make long north–south migrations between warm-water winter breeding grounds and cold-water summer feeding grounds.

PHYSETERIDAE – sperm whale

PHYSETERIDAE

Sperm whale (one species in one genus: *Physeter*)

The sperm whale – the only member of this family – gets its name from a large oil-filled reservoir, called the spermaceti organ, which is enclosed in a muscular 'case' inside its highly modified head. 'Spermaceti' literally means 'sperm of the whale', and it is believed that whalers either misinterpreted the function of the oil or simply noticed its physical resemblance (when cooled) to mammalian sperm. The principal function of the spermaceti organ, and its associated structures, appears to be to form and focus the clicks used in the sperm whale's extremely powerful echolocation system. Only dwarf and pygmy sperm whales (which used to be members of the Physeteridae family but are now placed in a family of their own) share this otherwise unique characteristic.

With its huge squarish head, narrow underslung lower jaw, low dorsal hump (followed by a series of bumps or crenulations along the tailstock) and wrinkled skin, the sperm whale is unmistakable. The largest of the odontocetes, or toothed whales, it also has the highest degree of sexual dimorphism among all cetaceans, with adult males much larger and heavier than adult females. Herman Melville's classic tale *Moby Dick* helped to make the sperm whale the archetypal whale.

KOGIIDAE – pygmy sperm whale

KOGIIDAE

Dwarf and pygmy sperm whales (two species in one genus: *Kogia*)

Like their larger and better-known namesake, the two members of the family Kogiidae also have a spermaceti organ inside their heads. All three species prefer deep waters, where they feed primarily on squid, and are only encountered close to shore where there is sufficient depth. But despite these common characteristics – and the fact that they were once all placed in the family Physeteridae – they share only a superficial resemblance to one another. The head of the two Kogiidae species is much smaller relative to body size, the dorsal fin is relatively larger and the blowhole is not located at the front of the head (as it is in the sperm whale). Dwarf and pygmy sperm whales employ a 'squid tactic' when startled or distressed, releasing a reddish-brown liquid from a sac in the lower intestine, which forms an opaque cloud in the water and may hide the whale or distract a predator. With an underslung lower jaw, gill-like markings on either side of the head and long, sharp teeth, these two small whales are often mistaken for sharks when they strand. Their appearance may be a form of mimicry, to help avoid predation.

MONODONTIDAE – narwhal

MONODONTIDAE

Narwhal and beluga (two species in two genera: *Monodon* and *Delphinapterus*)

The family name Monodontidae – meaning 'one tooth' – refers to the narwhal's extraordinarily long tusk. It is not such an appropriate name for the beluga, which has up to 40 teeth. However, the teeth do not seem to serve a critical function for feeding in either species and the beluga's teeth are often worn down to the gums in older animals. The monodontids live in high-latitude regions of the northern hemisphere – belugas in the sub-Arctic north and narwhals in the High Arctic – and both are often found in dense ice. They are medium-sized toothed whales with stocky bodies; blunt, bulbous heads; broad, rounded flippers; and fleshy dorsal ridges rather than dorsal fins (an adaptation to living among ice). They are gregarious and often travel together in small groups. Their skulls are unusually flat in profile.

ZIPHIIDAE – Perrin's beaked whale

ZIPHIIDAE

Beaked whales (22–23 species in six genera: *Mesoplodon*, *Ziphius*, *Hyperoodon*, *Berardius*, *Tasmacetus* and *Indopacetus*)

This is the second-largest cetacean family, after the Delphinidae, and one of Ziphiidae's genera, *Mesoplodon*, is far and away the largest genus. Yet beaked whales are among the least known of all large animals: some have never been seen alive and are known only from a few dead animals washed ashore, others are seen only rarely, and most are unobtrusive and spend long periods deep underwater far from land. These medium- to large-sized whales are found worldwide, in every major ocean and from the poles to the tropics, although some appear to have quite restricted ranges.

Beaked whales share a number of features. They have spindle-shaped bodies, relatively small dorsal fins set about two-thirds of the way along their backs, pronounced beaks of various shapes and sizes, V-shaped throat grooves, no significant notch on the trailing edge of their flukes, and short flippers that tuck into slight depressions on the sides of their bodies (called 'flipper pockets') to reduce drag when diving.

But it is their teeth that are most distinctive. Most males have dramatically reduced dentition, with only one or two pairs of erupted teeth in the lower jaw and none in the upper jaw, while most females have no erupted teeth at all. They do not use their teeth for feeding (they eat mostly squid, using suction) but do use them to fight one another (which is why males are often extensively scarred). There are a few exceptions: Arnoux's and Baird's beaked whales, in which both males and females have two pairs of exposed teeth; and Shepherd's beaked whale, in which both sexes have long rows of slender functional teeth. The number, position, size and shape of the males' teeth are usually the best clues to their identification; it is virtually impossible to tell most females and juveniles apart at sea, because many species look so alike.

The name Ziphiidae seems to be derived from an erroneous form of the Latin *xiphias*, for 'swordfish', or Greek *xiphos* for 'sword' (referring to the long, sharply pointed rostrum of many species).

DELPHINIDAE – Chilean dolphin

DELPHINIDAE

Marine dolphins (37 species in 17 genera: *Orcinus*, *Globicephala*, *Pseudorca*, *Feresa*, *Peponocephala*, *Orcaella*, *Sotalia*, *Sousa*, *Steno*, *Lagenorhynchus*, *Grampus*, *Tursiops*, *Stenella*, *Delphinus*, *Lagenodelphis*, *Lissodelphis* and *Cephalorhynchus*)

This is the largest and most morphologically and taxonomically diverse family of cetaceans. Indeed, in the past it has been called a 'taxonomic trash basket', because it contains so many dissimilar species. It includes all the marine dolphins (including some partly riverine species) and the so-called blackfish (a colloquial term for a group of six superficially similar members of the Delphinidae – killer whale, false killer whale, pygmy killer whale, melon-headed whale, short-finned pilot whale and long-finned pilot whale). There is great variation in coloration; in size (1.2–9.8m); in the shapes of their bodies, beaks, dorsal fins and flippers; and in the number of teeth (tooth counts range from fewer than 14 to more than 240). With some exceptions, most have a noticeable beak and a prominent dorsal fin set near the centre of the back (though the shape of the fin varies considerably between species and between individuals). They differ from porpoises in a number of ways: in particular, their teeth are conical (not spade-shaped) and they tend to be more gregarious, living in complex and sometimes very large social groups. Few delphinids seem to undertake regular long-distance migrations, though they can move considerable distances according to food supply and other local conditions.

PLATANISTIDAE – South Asian river dolphin

PLATANISTIDAE

South Asian river dolphin (one species in one genus: *Platanista*)

The four currently recognised species of river dolphins live in large river systems in Asia and South America. Despite their name, they are not all exclusively riverine animals, nor are they the only cetaceans living in rivers. They share many common features (such as narrow, elongated beaks and small eyes with poor vision) and have broadly similar habits, but they are not closely related and each species belongs to a different family. The Platanistidae (from the Greek *platanistes*, meaning 'flat' or 'broad' – referring to the relatively flattened beak) includes the Ganges river dolphin, or susu, and the Indus river dolphin, or bhulan. Currently classified as a single species, the south Asian river dolphin, these were originally considered to be two species and may be split again, since recent studies reveal significant differences in their DNA and skull morphology. Restricted to a few river systems in South Asia, the South Asian river dolphin is nearly blind and relies largely on echolocation to navigate and find food.

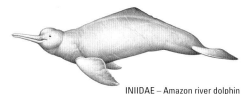

INIIDAE – Amazon river dolphin

INIIDAE
Amazon river dolphin (one species in one genus: *Inia*)
Currently, there is just one accepted species in this family – the Amazon river dolphin, boto or pink dolphin – but morphological and genetic differences between populations may justify splitting it into two or three subspecies or even species in the future. It is a slow but extremely manoeuvrable dolphin that spends much of the year weaving between the trees and roots of flooded forests in its vast, complex and fragmented range in northern South America. The largest of the river dolphins, it is often bright pink in colour.

LIPOTIDAE – Yangtze river dolphin

LIPOTIDAE
Yangtze river dolphin (one species in one genus: *Lipotes*)
The only member of this family – the Yangtze river dolphin, or baiji – was declared 'functionally extinct' in 2007. The last confirmed sighting was in 2002 and there have been no verified sightings since, leaving little doubt that it is the first cetacean species known to have been driven to extinction by human activity. It was endemic to a 1,700km stretch of the Yangtze River in China, in a region that is home to nearly 10 per cent of the entire human population.

PONTOPORIIDAE
Franciscana (one species in one genus: *Pontoporia*)
The sole member of this family – the franciscana or La

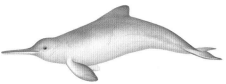

PONTOPORIIDAE – Franciscana

Plata river dolphin – is unique among river dolphins in inhabiting saltwater estuaries and coastal marine habitats rather than rivers. The smallest of the river dolphins, and one of the smallest of all cetaceans, it has an extremely long beak – proportionately, the longest of any cetacean – and a low, triangular dorsal fin. It lives along the central east coast of South America.

PHOCOENIDAE – Dall's porpoise

PHOCOENIDAE
Porpoises (seven species in three genera: *Neophocaena*, *Phocoenoides* and *Phocoena*)
'Porpoise' tends to be a general term used, particularly in North America, to mean any small cetacean. But it is the correct name for the small, rather stocky, generally shy members of this family (Phocoenidae is a variant of the Latin *phocaena* or Greek *phokaina*, meaning 'porpoise'). They are all less than 2.5m long and, since they rarely perform the acrobatic feats of many oceanic dolphins, are often overlooked. With the noticeable exception of Dall's porpoise – which produces a distinctive spray of water when it surfaces to breathe and will often ride the bow-waves of boats – a brief glimpse of the dorsal fin and a small portion of the back is all that is normally seen. Patience, perseverance and a certain amount of luck are prerequisites for watching most porpoises.

Porpoises differ from dolphins in a number of ways: in particular, their teeth are spade-shaped (not conical), but they also lack the distinctive beak that characterises many dolphins and they tend not to be as gregarious, typically living alone or in small groups. They occur in both hemispheres in pelagic, coastal and riverine habitats, but there is little overlap in range – nowhere has more than two porpoise species – so geography can help to distinguish one from another. The family includes the Critically Endangered vaquita, which occupies the smallest geographic range of any marine mammal species.

INFORMATION FOR WORKING AT SEA

RECOGNISING THE SEA STATE

'Sea state' is the term used to describe sea conditions. A sea state of three or less, when there are no or few whitecaps, is best for whale watching. As the sea state increases, it becomes increasingly difficult to spot anything among the waves and spray.

Sea state	Official term	Forecast description	Specification
0	Calm	Calm	Sea like a mirror
1	Calm	Light air	Small ripples; no crests or whitecaps
2	Smooth	Light breeze	Small wavelets; glassy crests; no whitecaps
3	Smooth	Gentle breeze	Large wavelets; crests begin to break; a few scattered whitecaps
4	Slight	Moderate breeze	Small waves; fairly frequent whitecaps
5	Moderate	Fresh breeze	Moderate; longer waves; many whitecaps; some spray
6	Rough	Strong breeze	Large waves; many whitecaps; frequent spray
7	Very rough	Near gale	Sea heaps up; white foam from breaking waves blows in streaks
8	High	Gale	Long; moderately high waves; edges of crests breaking; foam blows in streaks
9	Very high	Severe gale	High waves; dense streaks of foam; crests of waves topple; tumble and roll over; sea begins to roll; spray may affect visibility
10	Very high	Storm	Very high waves with long, overhanging crests; dense streaks of foam make sea appear mostly white
11	Phenomenal	Violent storm	Exceptionally high waves; sea covered in patches of foam; crests of waves blown into froth; visibility affected
12	Phenomenal	Hurricane	Air filled with foam and spray; sea completely white with driving spray; visibility seriously affected

READING A WIND CHART

Wind is illustrated on a weather chart using 'wind barbs', which are a convenient way to represent both wind speed and direction. The barbs point in the direction from which the wind is blowing (north is always 'up'). They also show the wind speed in knots: each short barb represents 5 knots, and each long barb 10 knots. Simply add the value of all the barbs to find the wind speed – a long barb and a short barb, for example, is 15 knots. If there are no barbs (or simply a dot) the wind speed is less than 2 knots, and a flag or triangle is used to show winds of 50 knots.

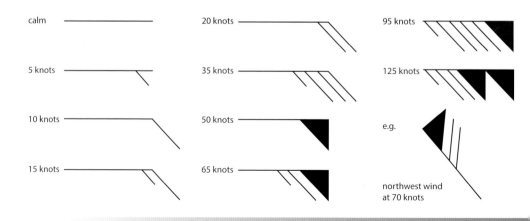

calm

5 knots

10 knots

15 knots

20 knots

35 knots

50 knots

65 knots

95 knots

125 knots

e.g.

northwest wind at 70 knots

CROSS SECTION OF THE OCEAN FLOOR

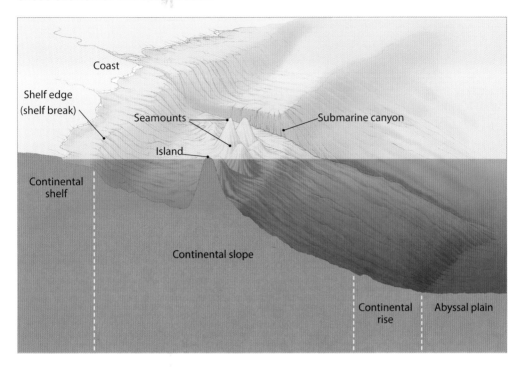

CLIMATE ZONES

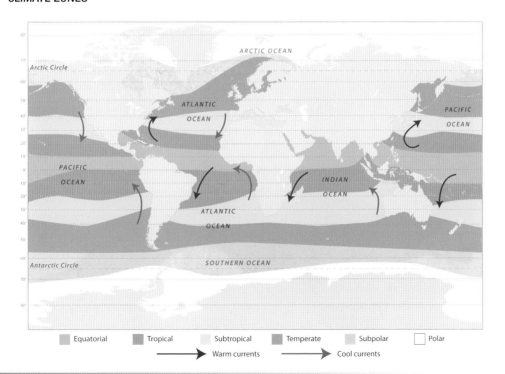

CETACEAN TOPOGRAPHY

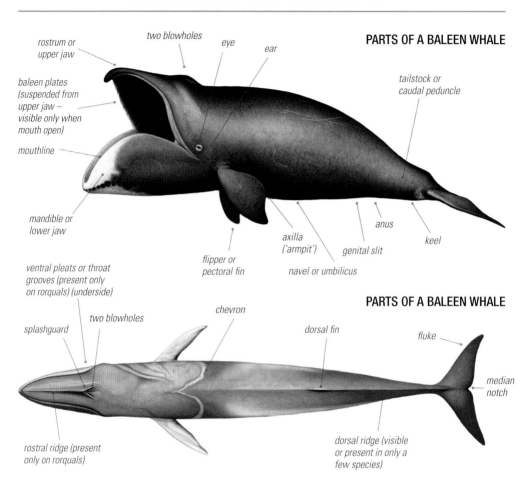

PARTS OF A BALEEN WHALE

rostrum or upper jaw

two blowholes

eye

ear

tailstock or caudal peduncle

baleen plates (suspended from upper jaw – visible only when mouth open)

mouthline

mandible or lower jaw

anus

axilla ('armpit')

genital slit

keel

flipper or pectoral fin

navel or umbilicus

PARTS OF A BALEEN WHALE

ventral pleats or throat grooves (present only on rorquals) (underside)

splashguard

two blowholes

chevron

dorsal fin

fluke

median notch

rostral ridge (present only on rorquals)

dorsal ridge (visible or present in only a few species)

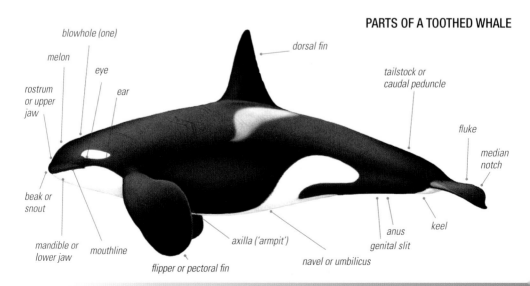

PARTS OF A TOOTHED WHALE

blowhole (one)

melon

eye

rostrum or upper jaw

ear

dorsal fin

tailstock or caudal peduncle

fluke

median notch

beak or snout

keel

mandible or lower jaw

mouthline

flipper or pectoral fin

axilla ('armpit')

navel or umbilicus

anus

genital slit

PARTS OF A TOOTHED WHALE

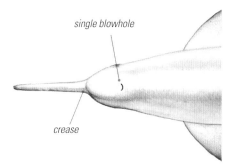

single blowhole

crease

DORSAL FIN

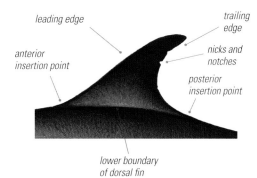

leading edge

trailing edge

anterior insertion point

nicks and notches

posterior insertion point

lower boundary of dorsal fin

HOW TO SEX A CETACEAN

female

male

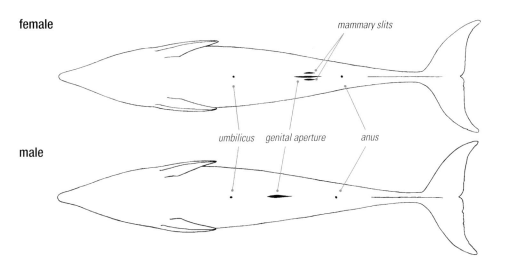

mammary slits

umbilicus genital aperture anus

PARTS OF A CETACEAN SKELETON

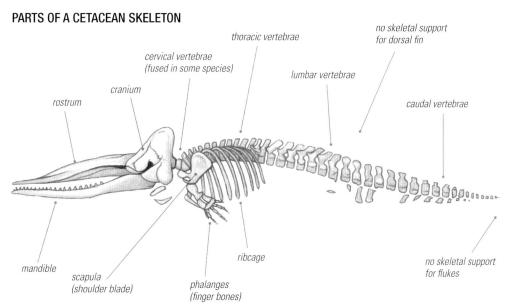

thoracic vertebrae

cervical vertebrae (fused in some species)

no skeletal support for dorsal fin

cranium

lumbar vertebrae

rostrum

caudal vertebrae

mandible

scapula (shoulder blade)

phalanges (finger bones)

ribcage

no skeletal support for flukes

BARNACLES TO WHALE LICE

An introduction to the ectoparasites and other creatures living on cetaceans.

BARNACLES

Barnacles are crustaceans that as adults permanently attach themselves to a variety of inanimate and animate objects. They occur everywhere from the tropics to the poles and from the seashore to the ocean depths. There are more than 1,000 species altogether, but only eight live on cetaceans. They settle in the greatest numbers on large baleen whales, but also occur on some toothed whales.

Barnacles are not true parasites, because they do not obtain nourishment from their hosts and do not appear to cause infection or inflammation. They are hitch-hikers, getting a free ride as they filter their planktonic food out of the water that passes over them. However, heavy infestations of barnacles can create drag, reducing swimming efficiency, and may cause irritations. In some cases, they may actually be beneficial to the whales – humpbacks, for example, use their barnacle-encrusted flippers as weapons (like 'knuckledusters') in competition with other males and to fight off attacks by tiger sharks, false killer whales and other species. Most barnacles are hermaphroditic (individuals possess the reproductive structures of both sexes) and their life cycle usually includes six free-swimming stages; the final larval stage searches for a place to settle and anchors itself with a specially secreted cement. The breeding season of barnacles that cling to whales is probably synchronous with the breeding season of their hosts.

There are three main types of whale barnacle:

ACORN BARNACLE *Cryptolepas rhachianecti*

Acorn barnacles Four species in three genera live on cetaceans: *Coronula diadema* (found in large numbers on most humpback whales – one individual had 450kg of this species attached to its body – and in very small numbers on some other baleen whales and sperm whales); *Coronula reginae* (common on humpback whales and found in very small numbers on blue, fin, sei, right and sperm whales);

Cryptolepas rhachianecti (found in large numbers on most grey whales); and *Cetopirus complanatus* (found on right whales). Named for their superficial resemblance to the acorns of oak trees, acorn barnacles are mound-shaped, and most often occur on the head, flippers and flukes.

RABBIT-EAR BARNACLE (*Conchoderma auritum*) attached to an acorn barnacle on a humpback whale's flipper

Stalked, goose or gooseneck barnacles Two species in one genus live on cetaceans (though there are isolated records of *Lepas* and *Pollicepes* species on whales). Stalked barnacles require a hard surface for attachment and frequently connect to other barnacles rather than directly onto a cetacean's skin. The rabbit-ear barnacle *Conchoderma auritum* is common worldwide on humpback whales – it usually attaches to the acorn barnacle *Coronula diadema* rather than the whale itself – and is found in very small numbers on blue, fin and sperm whales. Up to 7cm across, it also sometimes attaches to the teeth of adult male beaked whales and occasionally occurs on baleen plates. The much smaller *Conchoderma virgatum* – no more than 3.5mm across – is found mainly in the tropics and sub-tropics. It usually occurs on inanimate objects, such as driftwood or ships' hulls, but also attaches to sea snakes, ocean sunfish and some marine mammals (including, rarely, baleen whales). It occasionally settles directly onto a cetacean's skin, but normally attaches to a parasitic copepod or whale louse.

Pseudo-stalked barnacles Two species in two genera live on cetaceans. *Xenobalanus globicipitis* is unusual because it superficially resembles a stalked barnacle (it has developed an aberrant pseudo stalk). This curious dark, worm-like animal – which can be up to 5cm long – hangs from the trailing edges of the tails, dorsal fins and flippers of at least 34 cetacean species in tropical, sub-tropical and temperate waters worldwide. It is sometimes on the rostrum, and even on baleen plates and teeth. Pseudo-

PSEUDO-STALKED BARNACLES (*Xenobalanus globicipitis*)

stalked barnacles settle in the greatest numbers on the larger baleen whales, but are also found on killer whales, common bottlenose dolphins, Indo-Pacific finless porpoises and many other species. There can be just one or as many as 100 in a cluster. They burrow into the skin (and blubber) to various depths and, once attached with the shell base embedded in the host, do not move. *Tubicinella major* is found among the callosities on southern right whales. *Xenobalanus* still protrudes significantly, but *Tubicinella* is so deeply embedded that only the tip is exposed for feeding.

REMORAS

Remoras (otherwise known as suckerfish or diskfish) occur mostly in tropical to warm temperate waters worldwide. Elongate and round in cross section, they use a flat, oval-shaped suction disc on the top of their head – which makes them look as if they are upside down – to stick onto cetaceans, sirenians, sharks, sea turtles and any other large marine object (including ships, submarines and even occasionally human divers). A modified dorsal fin, the disc resembles venetian-blind slats and, when the slats are lifted, they create a strong vacuum, enabling the fish to suck onto its host. There are also tooth-like projections, called spinules, that help to prevent slippage. The disc is so effective that, with fine control, a remora can slide quickly around the host's body without falling off (although they are capable of free-swimming).

Benefits to the remoras include hitching a free ride, protection from predators, a surface for meeting of males and females, and a swift passage of water over their gills (they cannot survive in still water). They opportunistically feed on parasitic copepods (which account for most of their diet), zooplankton and smaller nekton in the passing water, scraps from their hosts' meals, sloughing whale skin and whale faeces. Cetaceans are rarely harmed by remoras, which do not normally hurt or leave scars (although they may leave temporary marks). However, at least in the case of some spinner, pantropical spotted and bottlenose dolphins, they can cause persistent damage – usually large raw patches just below the dorsal fin – that potentially could become infected. They can also cause hydrodynamic drag (they have been dubbed hydrodynamic parasites for reducing swimming efficiency) and may be irritating. It is unknown why cetaceans generally tolerate them – there may be as yet unknown benefits – but some dolphin species have been seen biting off remoras from each other, and may leap and spin to dislodge them from uncomfortable positions.

WHALESUCKER (*Remora australis*) adult on dolphin

There are eight species altogether in the family Echeneidae, and only one of them is known to attach regularly to cetaceans. The whalesucker (*Remora australis* – formerly *Remilegia australis*) occurs only on cetaceans (although, if it falls off, it may attach to any passing animal or object until a preferred host passes nearby); pale sky blue, it is found in warm pelagic waters worldwide and grows to a length of 62cm. Different sizes probably

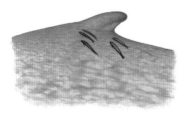

WHALESUCKER (*Remora australis*)

WHALESUCKER (*Remora australis*) young on blue whale

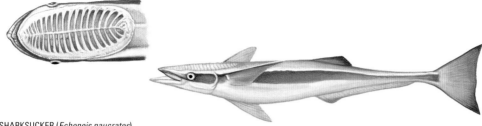

SHARKSUCKER (*Echeneis naucrates*)

represent different life-history stages of this species (possibly with different diets – e.g. small individuals on blue whales could be young remora feeding on sloughed whale skin, larger individuals on common dolphins could be older remora feeding on larger food items). The sharksucker (*Echeneis naucrates*), which reaches about 90cm, has been found only on common bottlenose dolphins, but may occur on other cetaceans (identification in the field is difficult).

Remora larvae do not appear to be free-living in the plankton layer, but may hang onto the baleen plates of whales until they develop a disc.

LAMPREYS

Lampreys belong to a primitive class of cartilaginous jawless fish, the Agnatha. Eel-shaped and lacking the scales, paired fins and jaws of true fish, they have a disc-shaped suction-cup around their mouth – which is wider than the mouth itself – ringed with sharp, horny teeth. They latch onto their unfortunate host and use their rough tongue to rasp away the animal's flesh, in order to feed on the blood and body fluids. Rather like leeches, they produce anti-coagulants to prevent the blood from clotting and increase the flow. After spending several years at sea, lampreys stop feeding and migrate to fresh water to spawn.

There are 43 species altogether, ranging from 15cm to 1.2m in length and living in coastal, cool temperate waters worldwide (except Africa). Thirty-two of these are almost always confined to fresh water and 18 are parasitic. Few lamprey–cetacean interactions have been described in detail, but two species in particular are known to attack cetaceans: the Pacific lamprey (*Lampetra tridentata* – formerly *Entosphenus tridentatus*), which is found in the North Pacific; and the sea lamprey (*Petromyzon marinus*), found in the North Atlantic, which is the largest lamprey species.

COOKIECUTTER SHARK

The cigar-shaped cookiecutter shark is a strange-looking member of the family Dalatiidae. Reaching a maximum length of only about 50cm, but armed with large, serrated teeth on the lower jaw and tiny, spike-like teeth on the upper jaw, it is a menace to other marine animals. Its name comes from its nasty habit of biting neat, round, cookiecutter-shaped chunks of flesh from a variety of marine megafauna – especially cetaceans, but probably any other marine megafauna, including seals, dugongs, tuna and sharks (and a human on one verified occasion in Hawaii in 2003). An ambush predator, with very large eyes for better vision in the dark depths, it attaches itself to its prey with its lips, then inserts its hook-like upper teeth and proportionately massive lower teeth, and spins its body to remove a plug of flesh. It leaves behind an oval or round hole or 'pit' up to *c.* 10cm across and *c.* 4cm deep (though usually narrower and shallower).

Cookiecutter sharks usually spend the day in deep waters – sometimes down to 3.5km – then migrate

PACIFIC LAMPREY (*Lampetra tridentata*)

NORTH ATLANTIC LAMPREY (*Petromyzon marinus*).

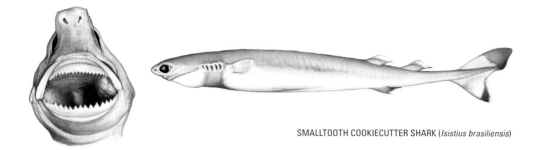

SMALLTOOTH COOKIECUTTER SHARK (*Isistius brasiliensis*)

to surface waters at night to feed. Light-emitting photophores, scattered on the belly and other parts of the body, lure would-be predators close enough to attack and then the predators become the prey.

There are three known species: smalltooth cookiecutter (*Isistius brasiliensis*), which is probably responsible for most cetacean attacks; the apparently rare bigtooth cookiecutter (*I. plutodus*); and the poorly known South China cookiecutter (*I. labialis*). The smalltooth cookiecutter occurs at water depths of at least 1,000m during the day, and is believed to migrate towards surface waters at night (when most attacks on cetaceans presumably occur). It lives in temperate to tropical seas, most commonly between 20°N and 20°S (though on occasion to 35°), which suggests that cetaceans pockmarked with the tell-tale oval or round scars of their bites have been in warmer waters at some point (species that live year-round in colder waters generally do not have cookiecutter shark bites).

Cookiecutter shark bites – which are much deeper than lamprey bites – have been recorded on at least 49 species of cetacean. They are harmful and painful, but do not normally cause death (except, possibly, when the sharks attack young calves or bite through the stomach wall). It can take several months for the bites to heal, though the scars may remain for many years (or even for life). In addition to their unique 'hit-and-run' feeding behaviour, cookiecutter sharks also eat free-living squid, small fish and crustaceans.

WHALE LICE

Whale lice belong to an order of crustaceans called amphipods and are all in the family Cyamidae (their correct name is 'cyamid amphipods'). They are not 'lice' (which are insects) and were named incorrectly by whalers in the 1800s, who thought they looked and moved like human lice.

Seven genera and 28 species have been positively identified living on cetaceans: *Cyamus* (14 species), *Isocyamus* (5), *Neocyamus* (1), *Platycyamus* (2), *Orcinocyamus* (1), *Scutocyamus* (2) and *Syncyamus* (3). They tend to be host-specific on mysticetes and generalists on odontocetes. Some species of whale louse live exclusively on a single species of whale: e.g. *Cyamus boopis* lives on humpback whales (although there is one case of this species on a southern right whale) and *Cyamus scammoni*, *C. kessleri* and *C. eschrichtii* live on grey whales; *C. catodontis* lives exclusively on medium-sized and large male sperm whales; and *Neocyamus physeteris* lives exclusively on female and small-sized male sperm whales. They usually spend their entire lives on their whale of birth, but some do risk transferring to other whales when they come into direct physical contact with one another. There can be as many as 7,500 whale lice on a single whale (in some species, at least, exceptionally large numbers are a diagnostic indicator of poor health).

Measuring 3–30mm long (females are generally broader but shorter than males), they have no free-swimming larval stage and spend their entire lives clinging to their hosts with stout, grasping appendages tipped with exceedingly sharp, recurved claws. They have small heads and flattened bodies and require shelter to avoid being swept into the sea – if they fall off they are doomed – and usually aggregate in areas of reduced water flow, such

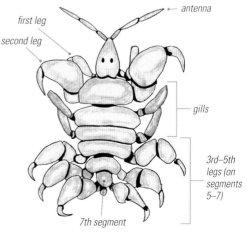

LOUSE anatomy

antenna

first leg

second leg

gills

3rd–5th legs (on segments 5–7)

7th segment

Whale lice and their known hosts

Cyamus balaenopterae	Common minke whale, blue whale, fin whale	
Cyamus boopis	Humpback whale; also recorded on single southern right whale in Brazil	
Cyamus ceti	Bowhead whale, grey whale	
Cyamus erraticus	Southern right whale, North Atlantic right whale, North Pacific right whale	
Cyamus gracilis	Southern right whale, North Atlantic right whale, North Pacific right whale	
Cyamus ovalis	Southern right whale, North Atlantic right whale, North Pacific right whale, sperm whale	
Cyamus eschrichtii	Grey whale	
Cyamus kessleri	Grey whale	
Cyamus scammoni	Grey whale	
Cyamus catodontis	Sperm whale (medium-sized and large males only)	
Cyamus mesorubraedon	Sperm whale	
Cyamus nodosus	Narwhal, beluga	
Cyamus monodontis	Narwhal, beluga	
Cyamus orubraedon	Baird's beaked whale	
Isocyamus antarcticensis	Killer whale	
Isocyamus deltobranchium	Killer whale, long-finned pilot whale, short-finned pilot whale	
Isocyamus delphinii	False killer whale, melon-headed whale, short-finned pilot whale, long-finned pilot whale, Risso's dolphin, common dolphin, rough-toothed dolphin, Gervais' beaked whale, white-beaked dolphin, harbour porpoise	

Whale lice and their known hosts

Isocyamus indopacetus	Longman's beaked whale	
Isocyamus kogiae	Pygmy sperm whale	
Neocyamus physeteris	Sperm whale (females and small males), Dall's porpoise	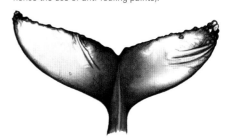
Orcinocyamus orcini	Killer whale	
Platycyamus flaviscutatus	Baird's beaked whale	
Platycyamus thompsoni	Northern bottlenose whale, southern bottlenose whale, Gray's beaked whale	
Scutocyamus antipodensis	Hector's dolphin, dusky dolphin	
Scutocyamus parvus	White-beaked dolphin	
Syncyamus aequus	Striped dolphin, spinner dolphin, common dolphin, common bottlenose dolphin	
Syncyamus ilheusensis	Short-finned pilot whale, melon-headed whale, Clymene dolphin	
Syncyamus pseudorcae	False killer whale, Clymene dolphin	

as the deep ventral grooves of many baleen whales, the callosities of right whales or among the barnacles on the heads of grey whales. Females have a pouch, or marsupium, in which they protect their eggs, embryos and juveniles until they are old enough to cling onto the skin themselves.

Cyamids eat sloughed whale skin (and possibly other foods that adhere to the skin, such as bacteria and algae) and feed on damaged tissue. Though usually considered parasites, they might be more accurately described as cleaning symbionts. They are eaten by some fish (such as topsmelt silversides which often accompany grey whales in their breeding lagoons).

DIATOMS

Many cetacean species often have a thin yellowish, brownish, greenish or orangish film – or irregular patches – of microscopic single-celled algae called diatoms over their skin. There are countless tens or even hundreds of thousands of species of diatoms – they are the key primary producers in the ocean – but only four genera and a small number of species have been found on cetacean skin. The cold-water *Bennettella* (formerly *Cocconeis*) *ceticola* is the most common species on baleen whales and killer whales in particular, and can cover their bodies after an extended stay in polar waters; it has never been found free-living.

In the Antarctic, the diatom layer takes about a month to develop, so its extent can be used to judge the length of time an animal has been in the region. Normally, whales slough and regenerate their skin continually (it needs to be regenerated to repair scars, sunburn, etc.), but the build-up of diatoms strongly indicates that this is not happening in cold waters (probably to limit heat loss). Indeed, it is believed that Antarctic killer whales make rapid migrations into tropical waters, where they incidentally shed the diatoms when they regenerate their skin tissue. Round trips typically last 5–7 weeks, and they return to the cold waters of the Antarctic looking much 'cleaner'. Otherwise, the diatom layer can get so thick that it may cause significant drag, slowing the animals down (diatoms are a big problem for ships – reducing speed by up to 5 per cent – hence the use of anti-fouling paints).

DIATOMS on the flukes of a humpback whale

QUICK ID GUIDES

BOW-RIDING DOLPHINS AND PORPOISES

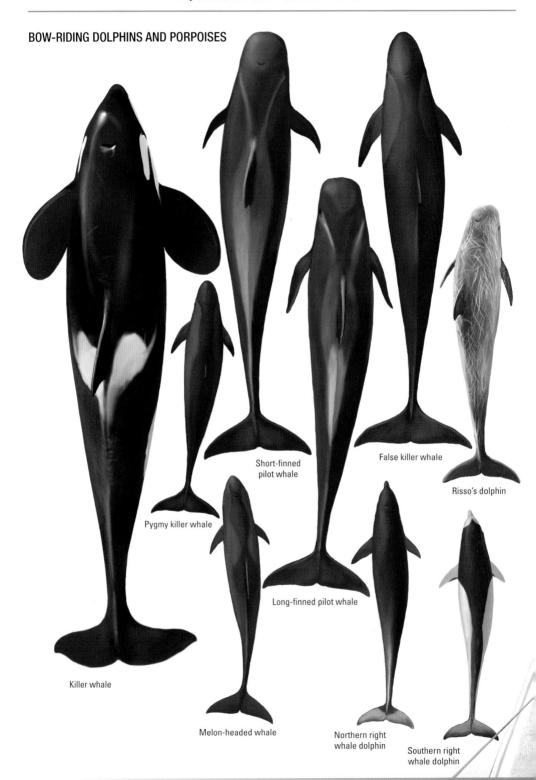

Short-finned
pilot whale

False killer whale

Risso's dolphin

Pygmy killer whale

Long-finned pilot whale

Killer whale

Melon-headed whale

Northern right
whale dolphin

Southern right
whale dolphin

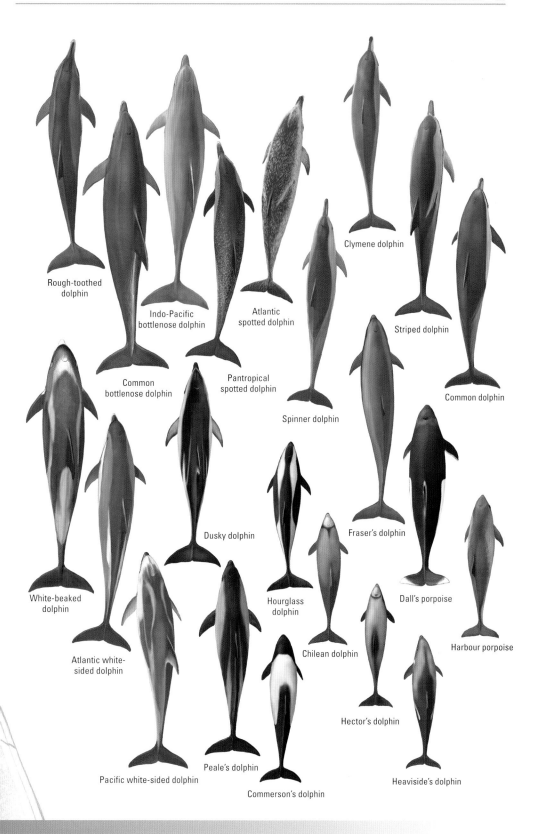

Rough-toothed dolphin

Indo-Pacific bottlenose dolphin

Atlantic spotted dolphin

Clymene dolphin

Striped dolphin

Common bottlenose dolphin

Pantropical spotted dolphin

Common dolphin

Spinner dolphin

Dusky dolphin

Fraser's dolphin

White-beaked dolphin

Hourglass dolphin

Dall's porpoise

Atlantic white-sided dolphin

Chilean dolphin

Harbour porpoise

Hector's dolphin

Pacific white-sided dolphin

Peale's dolphin

Commerson's dolphin

Heaviside's dolphin

IDENTIFYING WHALES BY THEIR FLUKES

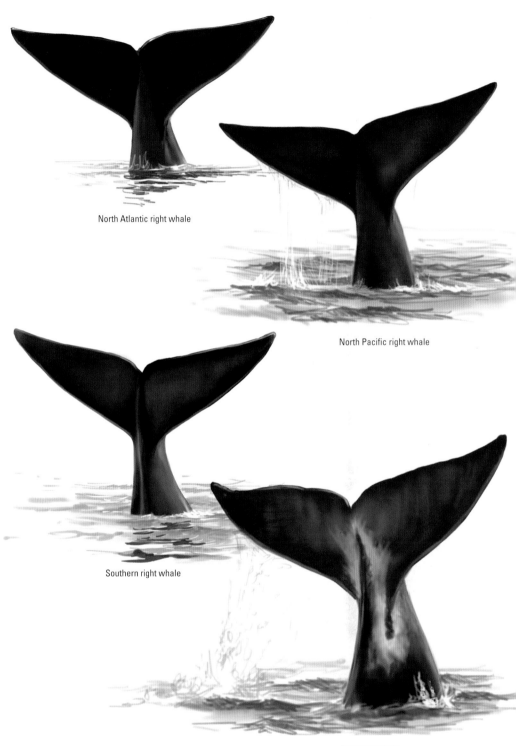

North Atlantic right whale

North Pacific right whale

Southern right whale

Bowhead whale

Blue whale

Grey whale

Humpback whale

Killer whale

Sperm whale

IDENTIFYING WHALES BY THEIR BLOWS

The height and intensity of a whale's blow, or spout, depends on many factors, including behaviour, the size of the individual, when it occurs during the surfacing sequence, air temperature, the quality of the light and wind conditions. It is therefore important to bear in mind that a single whale's blow can vary from virtually invisible to tall and dramatic. Indeed, blow heights have been seriously underestimated in the past, not least because they largely disappear against a pale sea or sky background.

These illustrations show picture-perfect blows (from behind the whales) on the first surfacing after a long dive – in ideal conditions – and represent the maximum heights. Not all cetaceans have clearly visible blows, but these are the ones that are most distinctive and most useful for identification purposes.

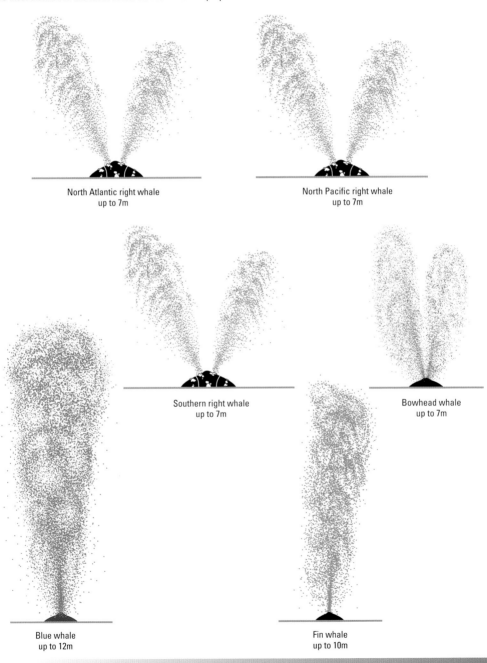

North Atlantic right whale
up to 7m

North Pacific right whale
up to 7m

Southern right whale
up to 7m

Bowhead whale
up to 7m

Blue whale
up to 12m

Fin whale
up to 10m

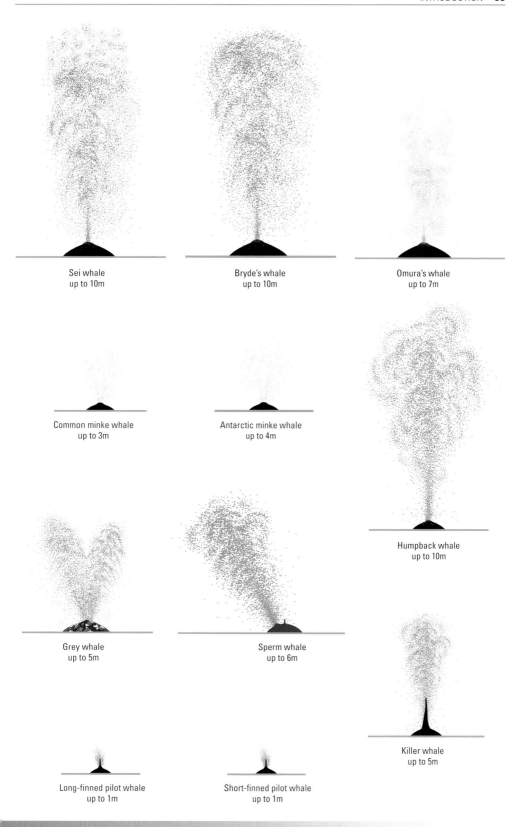

Sei whale
up to 10m

Bryde's whale
up to 10m

Omura's whale
up to 7m

Common minke whale
up to 3m

Antarctic minke whale
up to 4m

Humpback whale
up to 10m

Grey whale
up to 5m

Sperm whale
up to 6m

Killer whale
up to 5m

Long-finned pilot whale
up to 1m

Short-finned pilot whale
up to 1m

QUICK ID GUIDE: NORTH ATLANTIC OCEAN
(including the Caribbean Sea, Gulf of Mexico, Mediterranean Sea, Black Sea, Baltic Sea)

Please note: many species on this spread have very restricted ranges within this broad region, and it is not impossible to see species from other parts of the world outside their normal range. Relative sizes (for average-length males) are correct for the region.

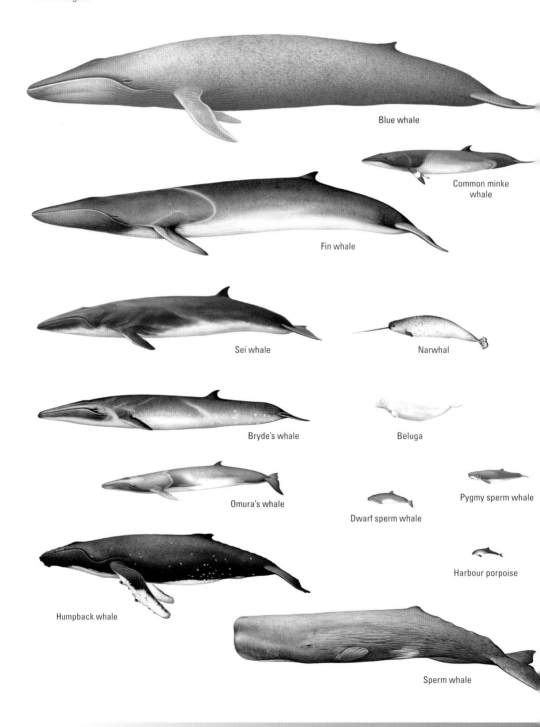

Blue whale

Common minke whale

Fin whale

Sei whale

Narwhal

Bryde's whale

Beluga

Omura's whale

Dwarf sperm whale

Pygmy sperm whale

Harbour porpoise

Humpback whale

Sperm whale

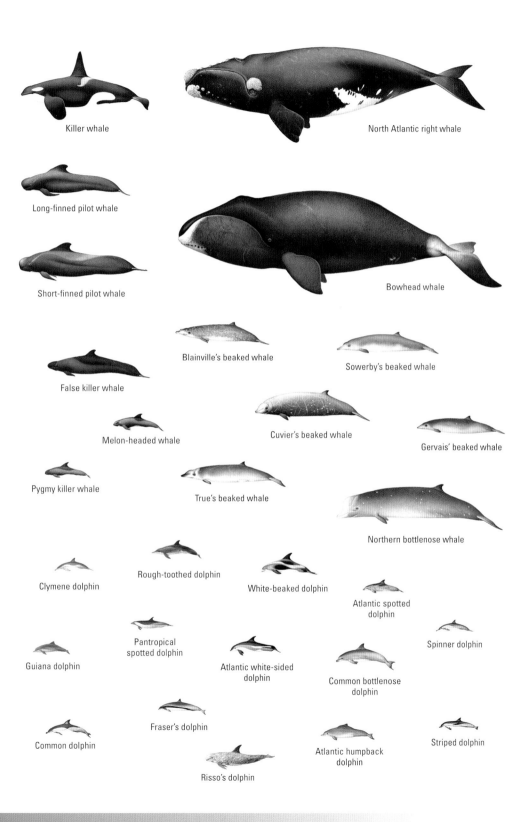

Killer whale

North Atlantic right whale

Long-finned pilot whale

Short-finned pilot whale

Bowhead whale

Blainville's beaked whale

Sowerby's beaked whale

False killer whale

Melon-headed whale

Cuvier's beaked whale

Gervais' beaked whale

Pygmy killer whale

True's beaked whale

Northern bottlenose whale

Clymene dolphin

Rough-toothed dolphin

White-beaked dolphin

Atlantic spotted dolphin

Spinner dolphin

Guiana dolphin

Pantropical spotted dolphin

Atlantic white-sided dolphin

Common bottlenose dolphin

Fraser's dolphin

Common dolphin

Atlantic humpback dolphin

Striped dolphin

Risso's dolphin

QUICK ID GUIDE: SOUTH ATLANTIC OCEAN

Please note: many species on this spread have very restricted ranges within this broad region, and it is not impossible to see species from other parts of the world outside their normal range. Relative sizes (for average-length males) are correct for the region.

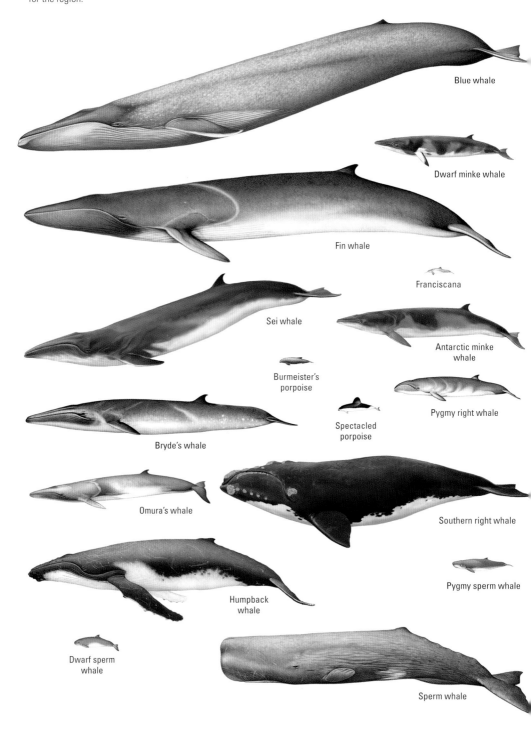

Blue whale

Dwarf minke whale

Fin whale

Franciscana

Sei whale

Antarctic minke whale

Burmeister's porpoise

Pygmy right whale

Bryde's whale

Spectacled porpoise

Omura's whale

Southern right whale

Pygmy sperm whale

Humpback whale

Dwarf sperm whale

Sperm whale

Southern bottlenose whale

Arnoux's beaked whale

Killer whale

Shepherd's beaked whale

Gray's beaked whale

Hector's beaked whale

Andrew's beaked whale

Long-finned pilot whale

Spade-toothed whale

Strap-toothed beaked whale

Short-finned pilot whale

True's beaked whale

Blainville's beaked whale

False killer whale

Spinner dolphin

Cuvier's beaked whale

Gervais' beaked whale

Melon-headed whale

Hourglass dolphin

Southern right whale dolphin

Risso's dolphin

Pygmy killer whale

Peale's dolphin

Commerson's dolphin

Rough-toothed dolphin

Clymene dolphin

Heaviside's dolphin

Dusky dolphin

Chilean dolphin

Pantropical spotted dolphin

Guiana dolphin

Atlantic spotted dolphin

Common bottlenose dolphin

Common dolphin

Fraser's dolphin

Atlantic humpback dolphin

Striped dolphin

QUICK ID GUIDE: NORTH PACIFIC OCEAN
(including the Gulf of California, Gulf of Alaska, Bering Sea, Sea of Okhotsk, Sea of Japan, Philippine Sea, Yellow Sea, East China Sea, South China Sea)

Please note: many species on this spread have very restricted ranges within this broad region, and it is not impossible to see species from other parts of the world outside their normal range. Relative sizes (for average-length males) are correct for the region.

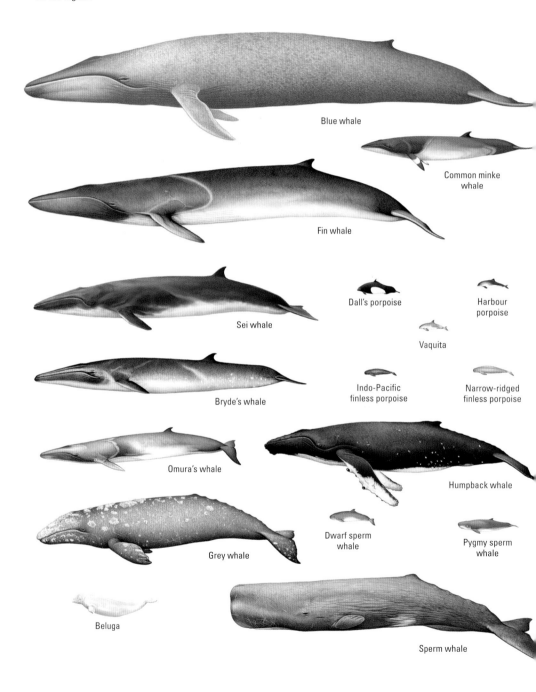

Blue whale

Common minke whale

Fin whale

Sei whale

Dall's porpoise

Harbour porpoise

Vaquita

Bryde's whale

Indo-Pacific finless porpoise

Narrow-ridged finless porpoise

Omura's whale

Humpback whale

Grey whale

Dwarf sperm whale

Pygmy sperm whale

Beluga

Sperm whale

North Pacific right whale

Cuvier's beaked whale

Killer whale

Bowhead whale

Melon-headed whale

Baird's beaked whale

Short-finned pilot whale

Pygmy killer whale

False killer whale

Blainville's beaked whale

Dwarf Baird's beaked whale

Perrin's beaked whale

Hubbs' beaked whale

Ginkgo-toothed beaked whale

Deraniyagala's beaked whale

Stejneger's beaked whale

Peruvian beaked whale

Longman's beaked whale

Risso's dolphin

Rough-toothed dolphin

Indo-Pacific humpback dolphin

Common bottlenose dolphin

Irrawaddy dolphin

Indo-Pacific bottlenose dolphin

Pantropical spotted dolphin

Spinner dolphin

Striped dolphin

Common dolphin

Fraser's dolphin

Pacific white-sided dolphin

Northern right whale dolphin

QUICK ID GUIDE: SOUTH PACIFIC OCEAN

Please note: many species on this spread have very restricted ranges within this broad region, and it is not impossible to see species from other parts of the world outside their normal range. Relative sizes (for average-length males) are correct for the region.

Omura's whale

Blue whale

Dwarf minke whale

Fin whale

Sei whale

Antarctic minke whale

Indo-Pacific finless porpoise

Burmeister's porpoise

Pygmy right whale

Spectacled porpoise

Bryde's whale

Southern right whale

Humpback whale

Pygmy sperm whale

Dwarf sperm whale

Sperm whale

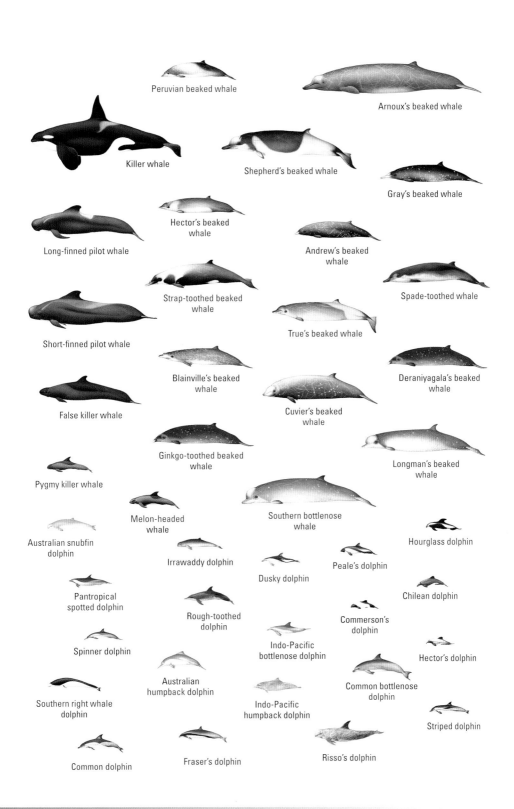

Peruvian beaked whale

Arnoux's beaked whale

Killer whale

Shepherd's beaked whale

Gray's beaked whale

Hector's beaked whale

Long-finned pilot whale

Andrew's beaked whale

Spade-toothed whale

Strap-toothed beaked whale

True's beaked whale

Short-finned pilot whale

Blainville's beaked whale

Deraniyagala's beaked whale

Cuvier's beaked whale

False killer whale

Ginkgo-toothed beaked whale

Longman's beaked whale

Pygmy killer whale

Melon-headed whale

Southern bottlenose whale

Hourglass dolphin

Australian snubfin dolphin

Irrawaddy dolphin

Peale's dolphin

Dusky dolphin

Chilean dolphin

Pantropical spotted dolphin

Rough-toothed dolphin

Commerson's dolphin

Spinner dolphin

Indo-Pacific bottlenose dolphin

Hector's dolphin

Australian humpback dolphin

Common bottlenose dolphin

Southern right whale dolphin

Indo-Pacific humpback dolphin

Striped dolphin

Common dolphin

Fraser's dolphin

Risso's dolphin

QUICK ID GUIDE: INDIAN OCEAN
(including the Mozambique Channel, Red Sea, Persian Gulf, Arabian Sea, Bay of Bengal)

Please note: many species on this spread have very restricted ranges within this broad region, and it is not impossible to see species from other parts of the world outside their normal range. Relative sizes (for average-length males) are correct for the region.

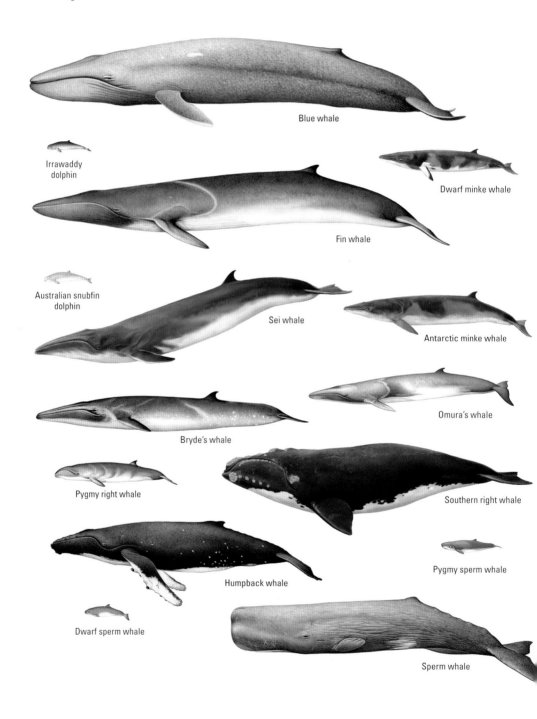

Blue whale

Irrawaddy dolphin

Dwarf minke whale

Fin whale

Australian snubfin dolphin

Sei whale

Antarctic minke whale

Omura's whale

Bryde's whale

Pygmy right whale

Southern right whale

Humpback whale

Pygmy sperm whale

Dwarf sperm whale

Sperm whale

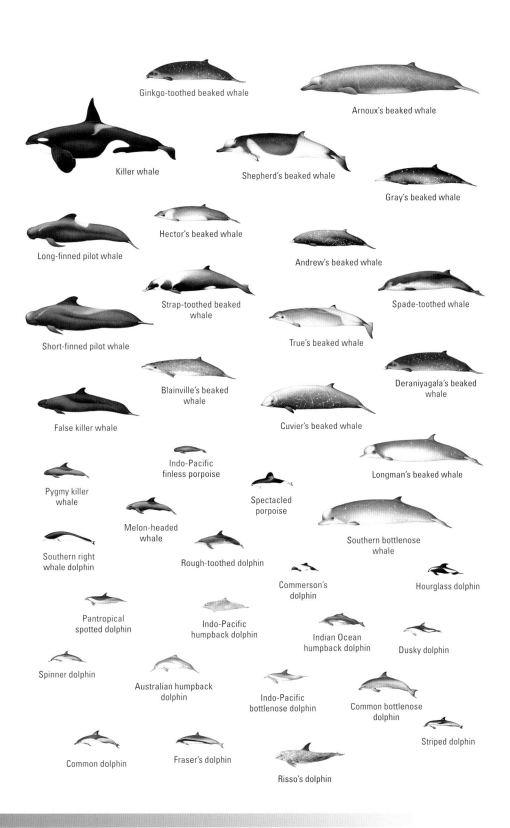

Ginkgo-toothed beaked whale

Arnoux's beaked whale

Killer whale

Shepherd's beaked whale

Gray's beaked whale

Hector's beaked whale

Long-finned pilot whale

Andrew's beaked whale

Strap-toothed beaked whale

Spade-toothed whale

Short-finned pilot whale

True's beaked whale

Blainville's beaked whale

Deraniyagala's beaked whale

False killer whale

Cuvier's beaked whale

Indo-Pacific finless porpoise

Longman's beaked whale

Pygmy killer whale

Spectacled porpoise

Melon-headed whale

Southern bottlenose whale

Southern right whale dolphin

Rough-toothed dolphin

Commerson's dolphin

Hourglass dolphin

Pantropical spotted dolphin

Indo-Pacific humpback dolphin

Indian Ocean humpback dolphin

Dusky dolphin

Spinner dolphin

Australian humpback dolphin

Indo-Pacific bottlenose dolphin

Common bottlenose dolphin

Striped dolphin

Common dolphin

Fraser's dolphin

Risso's dolphin

QUICK ID GUIDE: ARCTIC OCEAN
(including the Greenland Sea, Barents Sea, White Sea, Kara Sea, Laptev Sea, East Siberian Sea, Chukchi Sea, Beaufort Sea, Davis Strait, Baffin Bay, Hudson Bay)

Please note: many species on this spread have very restricted ranges within this broad region, and it is not impossible to see species from other parts of the world outside their normal range. Relative sizes (for average-length males) are correct for the region.

Blue whale

Harbour porpoise

Common minke whale

Fin whale

Beluga

Sei whale

Humpback whale

Sowerby's beaked whale

Narwhal

Grey whale

Northern bottlenose whale

Common bottlenose dolphin

Killer whale

Baird's beaked whale

Long-finned pilot whale

Sperm whale

Bowhead whale

White-beaked dolphin

Atlantic white-sided dolphin

QUICK ID GUIDE: SOUTHERN OCEAN
(including the Weddell Sea and the Ross Sea)

Please note: many species on this spread have very restricted ranges within this broad region (south of 60°S), and it is not impossible to see species from other parts of the world outside their normal range. Relative sizes (for average-length males) are correct for the region.

Sperm whale

Arnoux's beaked whale

Cuvier's beaked whale

Southern right whale

Southern bottlenose whale

Pygmy right whale

Spectacled porpoise

Antarctic minke whale

Humpback whale

Dwarf minke whale

Sei whale

Gray's beaked whale

Strap-toothed beaked whale

Long-finned pilot whale

Fin whale

Killer whale

Commerson's dolphin

Southern right whale dolphin

Blue whale

Hourglass dolphin

Peale's dolphin

NORTH ATLANTIC RIGHT WHALE
Eubalaena glacialis

(Müller, 1776)

The North Atlantic right whale is one of the most closely studied – and most endangered – large whales in the world. The few animals around today are the survivors of nearly 1,000 years of commercial exploitation and, although hunting has stopped, they face new human-induced threats and are widely considered to be in very real danger of extinction.

Classification Mysticeti, family Balaenidae.

Common name There are two theories: conventional wisdom holds that it was named by early English whalers for being the 'right' (i.e. correct) whale to hunt (it occurred near shore, swam slowly enough to be caught from a small boat propelled by sails or oars, floated when killed, and produced an exceedingly valuable yield of oil and baleen). However, scientists in the mid-1800s considered 'right' to mean 'true' or 'proper' (i.e. showing the characteristics typical of whales).

Other names Atlantic right whale, northern right whale; historically – black right whale, black whale, Biscayan right whale, nordcaper.

Scientific name From the Greek *eu* for 'right' or 'true', and Latin *balaena* for 'whale'; *glacialis* from the Latin for 'icy' or 'frozen' (the type locality was North Cape, northern Norway).

Taxonomy No recognised forms or subspecies, though there were two recognised populations on either side of the North Atlantic; formally split from the North Pacific right whale in 2000 due to genetic differences between both the whales and their lice (the two species were previously lumped together as the northern right whale, *Eubalaena glacialis*).

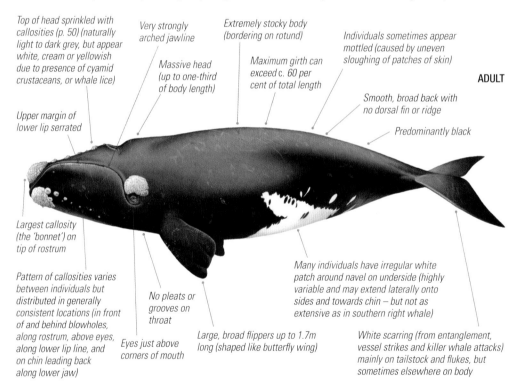

Top of head sprinkled with callosities (p. 50) (naturally light to dark grey, but appear white, cream or yellowish due to presence of cyamid crustaceans, or whale lice)

Very strongly arched jawline

Extremely stocky body (bordering on rotund)

Individuals sometimes appear mottled (caused by uneven sloughing of patches of skin)

Massive head (up to one-third of body length)

Maximum girth can exceed c. 60 per cent of total length

ADULT

Smooth, broad back with no dorsal fin or ridge

Upper margin of lower lip serrated

Predominantly black

Largest callosity (the 'bonnet') on tip of rostrum

Pattern of callosities varies between individuals but distributed in generally consistent locations (in front of and behind blowholes, along rostrum, above eyes, along lower lip line, and on chin leading back along lower jaw)

No pleats or grooves on throat

Eyes just above corners of mouth

Large, broad flippers up to 1.7m long (shaped like butterfly wing)

Many individuals have irregular white patch around navel on underside (highly variable and may extend laterally onto sides and towards chin – but not as extensive as in southern right whale)

White scarring (from entanglement, vessel strikes and killer whale attacks) mainly on tailstock and flukes, but sometimes elsewhere on body

---

AT A GLANCE
- North Atlantic
- Extra-large size
- Extremely stocky body
- Predominantly black
- Smooth back with no dorsal fin or ridge

- Low body profile at surface
- Massive head covered in light-coloured callosities
- Very strongly arched jawline
- No pleats or grooves on throat
- V-shaped blow
- Rectangular, broad, paddle-shaped flippers

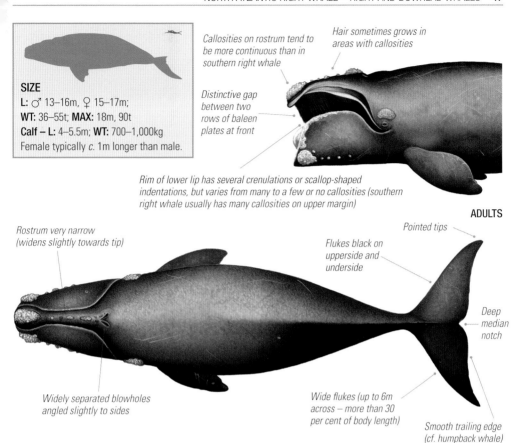

SIZE
L: ♂ 13–16m, ♀ 15–17m;
WT: 36–55t; **MAX:** 18m, 90t
Calf – L: 4–5.5m; **WT:** 700–1,000kg
Female typically *c.* 1m longer than male.

Callosities on rostrum tend to be more continuous than in southern right whale

Hair sometimes grows in areas with callosities

Distinctive gap between two rows of baleen plates at front

Rim of lower lip has several crenulations or scallop-shaped indentations, but varies from many to a few or no callosities (southern right whale usually has many callosities on upper margin)

ADULTS

Rostrum very narrow (widens slightly towards tip)

Pointed tips

Flukes black on upperside and underside

Deep median notch

Widely separated blowholes angled slightly to sides

Wide flukes (up to 6m across – more than 30 per cent of body length)

Smooth trailing edge (cf. humpback whale)

SIMILAR SPECIES

The bulky size, presence of callosities, arched mouthline, lack of a dorsal fin, predominantly black coloration and V-shaped blow should distinguish the North Atlantic right whale from all other large whales in the region. The more northerly bowhead looks similar, but there is virtually no overlap in distribution. At a distance, confusion may be possible with humpbacks, which sometimes also have a V-shaped blow (look for the humpback's stubby dorsal fin, long flippers, and black-and-white markings on the underside of the flukes). Dive sequences are also very different between the large whales. The

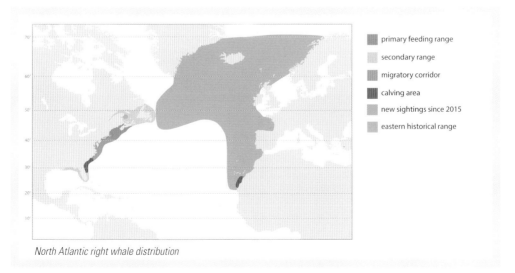

primary feeding range

secondary range

migratory corridor

calving area

new sightings since 2015

eastern historical range

North Atlantic right whale distribution

Smooth, pale grey areas on head and rostrum may be apparent on newborns (where callosities will develop)

CALF

Pale grey areas thicken and roughen during first few months after birth (callosities not fully developed and colonised by whale lice until 7–10 months old)

FLUKES

two northern hemisphere right whale species would be indistinguishable at sea, but their ranges do not overlap.

DISTRIBUTION

Historically, there were two largely isolated populations on either side of the North Atlantic. However, the eastern population is considered functionally extinct: there have been fewer than a dozen confirmed sightings since 1960

– likely wandering animals from the western population (or possibly representing a remnant stock). Western North Atlantic animals are highly mobile, but only pregnant females and a small number of other animals undertake predictable seasonal migrations. Occurs mainly in temperate and sub-polar coastal waters, including shallow basins, and in relatively deeper areas over the continental shelf.

EASTERN POPULATION

Historically, North Atlantic right whales probably ranged from the only known breeding ground, in Cintra Bay, off Western Sahara, to feeding grounds in the Bay of Biscay, off western Britain, around Iceland and across the Norwegian Sea to the North Cape in northern Norway. According to whaling records, they migrated along the coasts in between. There have been some recent confirmed resightings of individuals known from the western North Atlantic off Iceland (most recently in July 2018), northern

DIVE SEQUENCE

* Blow appears as huge head breaks surface (may lift head almost clear of water on surfacing after long dive).
* Head disappears below surface as smooth, broad, low-profile back appears.
* After last blow before long dive, head lifted much higher out of water as whale inhales deeply.
* Head pushed down and back arches at steep angle.
* Typical sequence includes four to six blows in succession, *c.* 10–30 seconds apart, before fluking dive.
* Flukes often raised quite high before deep dive.

BLOW

* Bushy V-shaped blow (when seen from in front or behind – oval and bushy from side).
* Up to 7m high (highly variable height).
* Jets often asymmetric in height.
* V more widely spaced at base than in grey or humpback (which sometimes produces V-shaped blows).
* If wind dissipates blow, it can be difficult to see (as body so low in water).

Norway and the Azores, indicating an extended range for at least some animals (or perhaps the existence of important habitat areas not currently described).

WESTERN POPULATION

There are six known critical summer feeding grounds, used by two-thirds of the population: the Great South Channel (south-east of Cape Cod); Jordan Basin (northern Gulf of Maine); Georges Basin (along the northeastern edge of Georges Bank); Cape Cod and Massachusetts Bays; the lower Bay of Fundy (between Maine and Nova Scotia); and the Roseway Basin (on the Scotian Shelf, 50km south of Nova Scotia). Traditionally, most congregated in southern feeding areas in spring and moved to the Bay of Fundy and Roseway Basin in the summer and autumn, but they have been less predictable in recent years. There is speculation that the whales are being driven north in search of food in response to warming seas. Regional movements between summer feeding grounds may be common and can be far ranging (exceeding 2,000km in some cases).

It is unclear where the remaining third of the population goes to feed (though it is probably offshore, since most of the coastal zone of eastern North America has been well surveyed over the past 25 years – and no alternative site has been found). Some have been detected in the Gulf of St Lawrence for periods of eight to nine months (increasing numbers since 2011), the Davis and Denmark Straits and, rarely, Newfoundland. There have been recent acoustic detections near the nineteenth-century whaling grounds east of southern Greenland, though the number of whales and their origin are unknown.

In November and December, pregnant females (sometimes accompanied by a small number of juveniles and non-calving females) migrate south down the eastern seaboard of North America to the only known calving ground, in the relatively sheltered, shallow coastal waters of northern Florida and southern Georgia (mainly between Savannah and St Augustine); the calving grounds may extend as far north as Cape Fear, North Carolina, at least for some individuals, and occasionally further west into the Gulf of Mexico. They return to the northern feeding grounds in March and April. Most animals (including most juveniles and adult males) do not migrate to these calving grounds and their wintering range is unknown. However, in the early 2000s, a continuous presence of North Atlantic right whales was documented in winter months in the central Gulf of Maine (from November to January), where it was thought they probably mated; there was limited evidence that others gathered at Roseway Basin. However, this seasonal aggregation has not persisted.

BEHAVIOUR

Generally slow moving and may rest at the surface for long periods. But North Atlantic right whales frequently engage in active surface behaviour and will breach, spyhop, lobtail and flipper-slap repeatedly. They frequently show little or no avoidance behaviour in the presence of boats and can be inquisitive and approachable.

BALEEN

- 205–270 plates (each side of the upper jaw).
- Long, thin plates averaging 2–2.8m long and grey-brown to black (fringed with very fine greyish bristles, reflecting small prey taken).

LIFE HISTORY

Sexual maturity Females 7–10 years, males usually do not reproduce until at least 15 years.

Mating Sexual behaviour occurs year-round, but outside winter breeding season probably has social function (or for females to assess potential mates); courtship involves 'surface-active groups' averaging five but up to 20 animals or more (usually numerous males with one or maybe two females, rolling and splashing for up to several hours); interactions between males involve little serious aggression (though plenty of active pushing to get access to female), suggesting sperm competition (females mate with multiple males and those producing most sperm have reproductive advantage); right whale testes are the largest of any animal, at 2m long and weighing 525kg each (further evidence of sperm competition).

Gestation Probably 12–13 months.

Calving Birth intervals appear to be increasing, averaging every 3.3 years in 1983–92, 5 years (as high as 5.8 years) in 1993–2003, 3.4 years in 2004–05, 5.5 years in 2015 and 10.2 years in 2017; single calf born in winter (late November–early March, with peak in early January).

Weaning Usually after 10–12 months (range of 8–17 months).

Lifespan Unknown, but likely to be at least 70 years and up to 85 years under prime conditions; significantly shorter today (c. 35 years – due to ship strikes and entanglements).

FOOD AND FEEDING

Prey Mostly calanoid copepod crustaceans (especially *Calanus finmarchicus* – roughly 2–3mm long), but will take other small invertebrates, including smaller copepods, amphipods, krill, pteropods (tiny planktonic snails) and larval barnacles.

Feeding Normally skim-feeds at about 5km/h (swimming slowly with mouth open through patches of concentrated prey, at or near surface, and closing mouth occasionally to flush out water and swallow prey); will also filter-feed at depth (up to 200m), must locate and exploit extremely dense patches of zooplankton to feed efficiently; most feeding in late winter to late autumn, but may continue in mid-winter; generally no evidence of collaboration while foraging near other

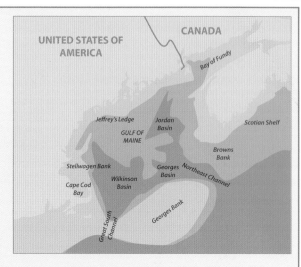

whales, though coordinated echelon skim-feeding observed in Cape Cod Bay; no feeding on winter breeding grounds.

Dive depth Often at or near surface; can easily reach near-bottom depths on continental shelf feeding grounds of 200m or more; max. possibly at least 300m.

Dive time Typical deep-feeding dives 10–20 minutes; max. 40 minutes.

GROUP SIZE AND STRUCTURE

Normally one to two, up to 12 in loose aggregations on occasion; much larger aggregations may form on temporarily rich feeding grounds or in breeding groups; will leave an area en masse in a matter of days.

CALLOSITIES

Callosities are areas of thick, irregular, calloused tissue – found only on right whales – that develop around the sparse hairs scattered about the whale's head. They are named after their resemblance to the 'callus' or thickened skin that occurs naturally in many animal species. Pockmarked with ridges and depressions, they feel like hard rubber to touch and, from a distance, look a little like barnacles. The callosity tissue is naturally light to dark grey, but it is home to colonies of thousands of creamy-white or yellowish cyamid crustaceans or 'whale lice' (p. 25), which obscure the underlying colour. Callosities occur in approximately the same places that humans have facial hair: above the eyes (eyebrows), along the rostrum, between the blowholes and the tip of the snout (moustache), and along the margins of the lower lips and jaw (beard). Their height can change throughout a whale's life (growing upwards and breaking off repeatedly), but

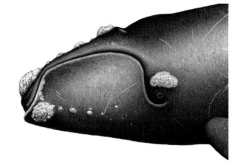

their overall size and placement on the head remains the same; consequently, their shape and size serve as 'fingerprints' or 'distinguishable faces' that enable researchers to tell one individual right whale from another. The root of each hair is highly innervated, but the function of the callosities themselves is unknown. One theory is that they are designed specifically to attract dense populations of whale lice, which stand on their hind legs to catch copepods – thus alerting the whale and helping to steer it towards denser concentrations of its tiny prey.

LICE

Right whales carry large populations of three species of cyamid crustaceans or 'whale lice'. Two of these are endemic (i.e. found on no other whale species) and one (*Cyamus ovalis*) is also found on sperm whales. Recent genetic evidence suggests that these three species should be split into nine species, because they are sufficiently

CALLOSITIES

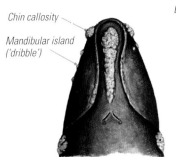

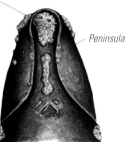

Chin callosity

Bonnet

Mandibular island ('dribble')

Peninsula

Eyebrow callosity

Rostral island

Lip patch

Coaming

Post-blowhole callosity

different on their North Atlantic, North Pacific and southern hemisphere hosts. Whale lice occur among the callosities and are common in creases and folds elsewhere on the body.

Cyamus gracilis
6mm long
Predominantly yellow
Typically *c.* 500 per whale
Mainly in pits and grooves between elevated patches of callosity tissue

Cyamus erraticus
12–15mm long
Predominantly orange
Typically *c.* 2,000 per whale
Mainly on smooth skin in genital and mammary slits, and in large concentrations in wounds
Also found in large patches on heads (where there is no callosity tissue) of young calves (disappear when calf is *c.* 2 months old)

Cyamus ovalis
12–15mm long
Predominantly white
Typically *c.* 5,000 per whale
Coat callosities at average density of one adult per cm^2 (main reason for pale colour of callosities)

PREDATORS
Killer whales are known predators, though there is not much overlap. North Atlantic right whales may actively defend themselves against killer whale attack (they are a 'fight' species, rather than a 'flight' species), hitting with their tails and ramming (the roughened callosities on the head could possibly serve as weapons or armour). There is also evidence that large sharks – great white, tiger, shortfin mako and possibly bull – occasionally attack calves and unaccompanied juveniles in the breeding grounds, as well as vulnerable adults (such as when they are entangled in fishing gear).

PHOTO-IDENTIFICATION
Primarily by the natural pattern of callosities on the head (which is unique to each individual); since callosity patterns are three-dimensional, numerous photographs from all angles are helpful in identification. Callosities get their colour from the lice living on them, so their shape can sometimes appear to shift as the lice move around, but researchers are able to account for these variations. Callosity photographs are combined with unique scars or markings on the body, head and flukes; white markings on the belly; and crenulations (unique edge patterns) along the upper margins of the lower lips (especially important in calves, when the callosity pattern has not fully developed).

POPULATION
Once common on both sides of the North Atlantic, but now one of the world's most endangered large whales.

After protection, numbers increased slowly, from fewer than 100 in the mid-1930s, to 270 in 1990, to a peak of 483 in 2010. But numbers appear to have decreased since then – the most recent estimate, in 2018, was *c.* 432. This figure includes just 100 reproductively mature females. An average of 24 calves were born each year during the period 2000–10, but since 2010 calving rates have dropped by nearly 40 per cent. No calves were born in the 2017/18 calving season – for the first time in history (unless a calf was missed by survey teams) – but at least seven were born in 2019.

CONSERVATION

IUCN status: Endangered (2017); if listed separately, the eastern population would be classified as Critically Endangered, Possibly Extinct. The North Atlantic right whale was the first species of whale to be hunted commercially, starting as early as the eleventh century with a Basque fishery in the Bay of Biscay, and it was pursued well into the twentieth century. Quantitative estimates of early catches are not available, but it has been calculated that 5,500–11,000 were killed during the period 1634–1950 in the western North Atlantic alone. At least 120 were taken around Britain and Iceland during 1881–1924; the last recorded catch was a mother–calf pair off Madeira in 1967, accompanied by a third individual that escaped. By the time the species was protected in 1935 (though some hunting did continue after then), the eastern population was functionally extinct and there were probably no more than 100 survivors in the western population.

The two major threats today – vessel strikes and entanglement in fishing gear – together have caused more than half of the documented North Atlantic right whale deaths since 1970. Entanglement appears to be taking a growing toll – nearly 85 per cent of North Atlantic right whales have been entangled in fishing gear at least once. The prime culprit is the New England lobster industry (there are an estimated 3 million lobster traps in the Gulf of Maine – and newer, stronger rope is catching and killing more whales), but crab fishing in Canadian waters is another significant cause of death. Since 2009, entanglement has been responsible for 58 per cent of deaths (a big jump from 25 per cent in 2000–08); even survivors can suffer for years and adult females are less likely to breed.

North Atlantic right whales are particularly vulnerable to ship strikes because they are large and slow, tend to feed near the surface and (with no dorsal fin) are difficult to see; worse, they aggregate in major shipping lanes. A variety of mitigation measures have been successfully introduced in both Canada and the US to reduce the number of strikes, but it is still a major problem.

In summer and autumn 2017 there was an unprecedented number of mortalities, with at least 17 dead whales altogether (the average is 3.8 whales per

North Atlantic right whales frequently engage in active surface behaviour – breaching is common.

A mother and calf photographed 16km east of Jekyll Island, Georgia.

year); initial findings suggest that most died as a result of ship strikes or entanglements. Other threats include low genetic variability, poor nutrition, chemical contaminants, biotoxins, noise pollution, disturbance by vessel traffic and fluctuating environmental conditions.

The situation is so dire that the North Atlantic right whale could become functionally (reproductively) extinct within 20 years.

VOCALISATIONS

North Atlantic right whales are highly vocal, producing a variety of low-frequency moans, groans, grunts, sighs, bellows and pulses. These appear to have social communication functions. The most common vocalisations are stereotyped 'upcalls', produced by all age classes and both sexes. These last about 1–2 seconds and are believed to function as long-distance contact calls. Recent research suggests that it is possible to identify individuals by subtle differences in their upcalls. Less common are 'downcalls', which start with a brief downward sweep before rising

North Atlantic right whale with Atlantic white-sided dolphins.

in frequency like an upcall, and constant-tonal 'moans'. The most common call recorded in surface-active groups is the 'scream call', which lasts for 0.5–2.8 seconds; it is believed to be produced by the focal female. A loud vocalisation called a 'gunshot call' – which sounds like a rifle being fired – is made by solitary adult males and may function as a threat display to other males or to attract females; recent research reveals that quiet gunshot calls are also made by females with newborn calves, apparently as emotive indicators of heightened stress and agitation. Otherwise, mother–calf pairs are mostly silent during the first six weeks of development – perhaps to avoid predators and to minimise acoustic detection or harassment by conspecifics.

Skim-feeding through a dense patch of zooplankton near the surface.

NORTH PACIFIC RIGHT WHALE
Eubalaena japonica

(Lacépède, 1818)

In 1874, whaling captain and naturalist Charles Scammon remarked that North Pacific right whales were 'scattered over the surface of the water as far as the eye can discern'. But commercial whaling was so intense that they suffered the most dramatic and rapid depletion of all the great whales.

Classification Mysticeti, family Balaenidae.

Common name There are two theories: conventional wisdom holds that it was named by early English whalers for being the 'right' (i.e. correct) whale to hunt (it occurred near shore, swam slowly enough to be caught from a small boat propelled by sails or oars, floated when killed, and produced an exceedingly valuable yield of oil and baleen). However, scientists in the mid-1800s considered 'right' to mean 'true' or 'proper' (i.e. showing the characteristics typical of whales).

Other names Pacific right whale; historically – northern right whale, black right whale, black whale.

Scientific name From the Greek *eu* for 'right' or 'true', and Latin *balaena* for 'whale'; *japonica* is feminine of the Latin *japonicus*, meaning 'Japanese' (the type locality is Japan).

Taxonomy No recognised forms or subspecies, though there are two recognised populations, on either side of the North Pacific; formally split from the North Atlantic right whale in 2000 due to genetic differences between both the whales and their lice (the two species were previously lumped together as the northern right whale, *Eubalaena glacialis*); the North Pacific right whale is more closely related to its southern counterpart than to the North Atlantic species.

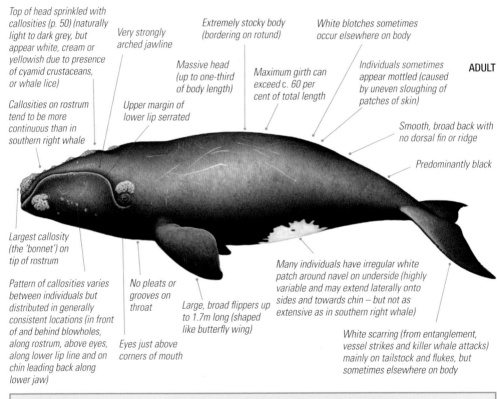

Top of head sprinkled with callosities (p. 50) (naturally light to dark grey, but appear white, cream or yellowish due to presence of cyamid crustaceans, or whale lice)

Very strongly arched jawline

Extremely stocky body (bordering on rotund)

White blotches sometimes occur elsewhere on body

Massive head (up to one-third of body length)

Maximum girth can exceed c. 60 per cent of total length

Individuals sometimes appear mottled (caused by uneven sloughing of patches of skin)

ADULT

Callosities on rostrum tend to be more continuous than in southern right whale

Upper margin of lower lip serrated

Smooth, broad back with no dorsal fin or ridge

Predominantly black

Largest callosity (the 'bonnet') on tip of rostrum

Pattern of callosities varies between individuals but distributed in generally consistent locations (in front of and behind blowholes, along rostrum, above eyes, along lower lip line and on chin leading back along lower jaw)

No pleats or grooves on throat

Large, broad flippers up to 1.7m long (shaped like butterfly wing)

Eyes just above corners of mouth

Many individuals have irregular white patch around navel on underside (highly variable and may extend laterally onto sides and towards chin – but not as extensive as in southern right whale)

White scarring (from entanglement, vessel strikes and killer whale attacks) mainly on tailstock and flukes, but sometimes elsewhere on body

---

AT A GLANCE
- Northern North Pacific
- Extra large size
- Extremely stocky body
- Predominantly black
- Smooth back with no dorsal fin or ridge

- Low body profile at surface
- Massive head covered in light-coloured callosities
- Very strongly arched jawline
- No pleats or grooves on throat
- V-shaped blow
- Rectangular, broad, paddle-shaped flippers

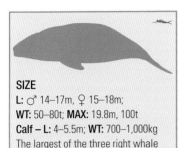

SIZE
L: ♂ 14–17m, ♀ 15–18m;
WT: 50–80t; **MAX:** 19.8m, 100t
Calf – L: 4–5.5m; **WT:** 700–1,000kg
The largest of the three right whale species, by a small margin; female typically *c.* 1m longer than male.

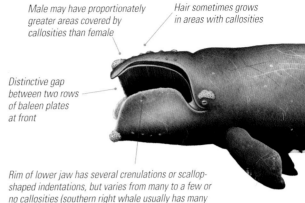

Male may have proportionately greater areas covered by callosities than female

Hair sometimes grows in areas with callosities

Distinctive gap between two rows of baleen plates at front

Rim of lower jaw has several crenulations or scallop-shaped indentations, but varies from many to a few or no callosities (southern right whale usually has many callosities on upper margin)

ADULTS

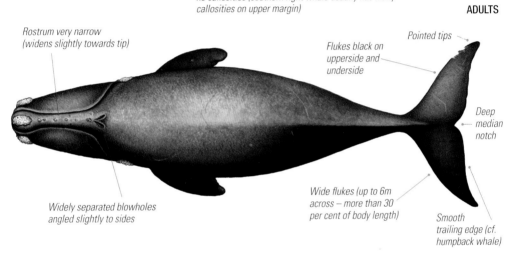

Rostrum very narrow (widens slightly towards tip)

Flukes black on upperside and underside

Pointed tips

Deep median notch

Widely separated blowholes angled slightly to sides

Wide flukes (up to 6m across – more than 30 per cent of body length)

Smooth trailing edge (cf. humpback whale)

SIMILAR SPECIES

The bulky size, arched mouthline, lack of a dorsal fin, predominantly black coloration and V-shaped blow should distinguish the North Pacific right whale from all other large whales in the region, except the bowhead (although there is little overlap in distribution and bowheads are more likely to be associated with ice). At close range, the callosities and the lack of white on the head or tailstock are distinctive. At a distance, confusion may be possible with grey whales (look for the mottled grey colour and dorsal hump with knuckles) and humpbacks (look for the humpback's stubby dorsal fin, long flippers and black-and-white markings on the undersides of the flukes); right whales and humpbacks have been observed interacting. Dive sequences are also very different between the large whales. The two northern hemisphere right whale species would be indistinguishable at sea, but their ranges do not overlap.

DISTRIBUTION

Formerly abundant in cold temperate waters across much of the North Pacific in the summer, mainly north of 40°N,

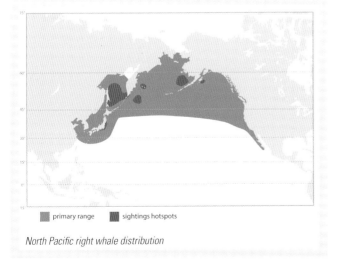

■ primary range ▨ sightings hotspots

North Pacific right whale distribution

Smooth, pale grey areas on head and rostrum may be apparent on newborns (where callosities will develop)

CALF

Pale grey areas thicken and roughen during first few months after birth (callosities not fully developed and colonised by whale lice until 7–10 months old)

FLUKES

North Pacific, found primarily in the Bering Sea and Gulf of Alaska. There appear to be seasonal migrations from summer feeding grounds in the 40°–60°N latitudinal range to potential winter breeding grounds in the 20°–30°N range (perhaps even further south). The location of calving grounds has yet to be established with certainty. It tends to be more pelagic than the North Atlantic right whale. Most sightings in the past 20 years have occurred in the southeastern Bering Sea (but this is where there has been greatest research effort). Exceptional (probably extralimital) records in recent years include: Maui, Hawaii, in March 1979 and April 1996; Baja California, Mexico, in February 1996; British Columbia, Canada, in June 2013 and October 2013; La Jolla, California, in April 2017; and near the Channel Islands, California, in May 2017. North Pacific, North Atlantic and southern right whales are separated by Arctic ice and warm equatorial waters, and it is estimated that there has been no interchange between the three populations for millions of years.

with a general shift southward to at least 30°N in winter. The North Pacific right whale currently occupies only a fraction of this former range. There appear to be two distinct populations: one of several hundred individuals in the western North Pacific, centred around the Sea of Okhotsk; and one of just tens of individuals in the eastern

DIVE SEQUENCE
- Blow appears as huge head breaks surface (may lift head almost clear of water on surfacing after long dive).
- Head disappears below surface as smooth, broad, low-profile back appears.
- After last blow before long dive, head lifted much higher out of water as whale inhales deeply.
- Head pushed down and back arches at steep angle.
- Typical sequence includes four to six blows in succession, *c.* 10–30 seconds apart, before high fluking dive.
- While at surface, water washes over back creating distinctive white water.

BLOW
- Bushy V-shaped blow (when seen from in front or behind – oval and bushy from side).
- Up to 7m high (highly variable height).
- Jets often asymmetric in height.
- V more widely spaced at base than in grey or humpback (which sometimes produces V-shaped blows).
- If wind dissipates blow, it can be difficult to see (as body so low in water).

FOOD AND FEEDING

Prey Mostly calanoid copepods (crustaceans roughly 5–10mm long), but will take other small invertebrates, including smaller copepods, amphipods, krill, pteropods (tiny planktonic snails) and larval barnacles.

Feeding Normally skim-feeds at about 5km/h (swimming slowly with mouth open through patches of concentrated prey at or near the surface, and closing mouth occasionally to flush out water); will also filter-feed at depth (up to 300m); water flows through gap between baleen plates at the front; has been at least one observation of lunge-feeding; no feeding on winter breeding grounds.

Dive depth Often at or near surface; may be deeper diver than North Atlantic right whale (as occurs in deeper water further offshore) but no quantitative data; known to descend rapidly to dense layers of zooplankton up to 300m below surface; has been observed surfacing with mud on its head (thought to be result of swimming upside down just above seafloor, feeding on layers of zooplankton).

Dive time Typical deep-feeding dives 10–20 minutes.

WESTERN POPULATION

Historical whaling records indicate that the principal summer feeding grounds were in the Sea of Okhotsk (between Sakhalin Island and Kamchatka), around the Kuril and Commander Islands, along the east coast of Kamchatka and in the central Bering Sea – north of 40°N. These regions are still considered to be important summer habitats. In the autumn, there was a southward shift in distribution to at least 30°N and possibly 25°N. Wintering grounds (and likely calving grounds) may have included the Ryukyu Islands, the Yellow Sea (west of the Korean Peninsula), the Taiwan Strait and/or the Ogasawara Islands. Current locations for calving grounds remain a mystery (there are only scattered records of lone individuals during winter, though there have been recent reports from the Ogasawara Islands). Unlike North Atlantic right whales, which are known to breed in shallow nearshore waters, the lack of evidence for coastal winter breeding grounds for North Pacific right whales suggests that they may breed in open-ocean waters offshore.

There is some historical evidence of two distinct stocks of right whales in the western North Pacific, kept apart by the Japanese islands. The 'Sea of Japan stock' migrated along the western coast of Japan, between summering grounds in the Sea of Okhotsk and unidentified wintering grounds south of Japan; and the 'Pacific stock' travelled along the eastern coast of Japan, between summering grounds around the Kuril Islands and in the western Bering Sea and unidentified (but possibly the same) wintering grounds. Surveys for large whales in offshore waters east of Hokkaido (Japan) and the Kuril Islands (Russia) during 1994–2013 resulted in 55 sightings of right whales (77 individuals) and included 10 female–calf pairs.

EASTERN POPULATION

Historical whaling records indicate that the principal summer feeding grounds were in the eastern Bering Sea and the Gulf of Alaska – north of 40°N. In the autumn, there was a southward shift in distribution to unknown wintering grounds. Since the 1990s, most sightings of the eastern population have been concentrated in two areas during summer: one in the southeastern Bering Sea, west of Bristol Bay, Alaska (c. 57–59°N), where the whales appear to select relatively shallow waters c. 70m deep over the mid-continental shelf; and, to a lesser degree, the other over the continental shelf and slope south of Kodiak Island in the Gulf of Alaska. Possible wintering grounds for the eastern population are obscure (it seems likely that calving takes place offshore).

BEHAVIOUR

There have been relatively few direct observations of living North Pacific right whales in recent decades. They are generally slow moving and may rest at the surface for long periods. But they have been observed breaching, spyhopping, lobtailing and flipper-slapping. They show little or no avoidance behaviour in the presence of boats

LIFE HISTORY

Sexual maturity Probably 9–10 years for females (occasionally as young as five years); males unknown.

Mating Poorly known (inferred from North Atlantic right whale); sexual behaviour occurs year-round, but outside winter breeding season probably has social function; courtship involves 'surface-active groups' of up to 20 or more animals (usually numerous males with single female); interactions between males involve little aggression, suggesting sperm competition (females mate with multiple males and those producing most sperm have reproductive advantage); right whale testes are the largest of any animal, at 2m long and weighing 525kg each.

Gestation 12–13 months.

Calving Every three years (occasionally two to five years); single calf born in winter.

Weaning Usually after 10–12 months (range of 8–17 months).

Lifespan Unknown, but likely to be at least 70 years.

and can be inquisitive and approachable; however, during the whaling days they became increasingly hard to approach, and some individuals may still be very sensitive to vessels.

BALEEN
- 205–270 plates (each side of the upper jaw).
- Long, thin plates averaging 2–2.8m long and grey-brown to black (fringed with very fine greyish bristles, reflecting small prey taken).

GROUP SIZE AND STRUCTURE
Normally one to two, though larger aggregations of 30 or more may form on temporarily rich feeding grounds or breeding grounds.

PREDATORS
Likely to be killer whales and large sharks (mainly attacking calves and unaccompanied juveniles). North Pacific right whales will actively defend themselves against killer whale attack (rather than fleeing), hitting with their tails and ramming (the roughened callosities on the head may serve as weapons or armour).

PHOTO-IDENTIFICATION
Primarily by the natural pattern of callosities on the head (which is unique to each individual); since callosity

patterns are three-dimensional, numerous photographs from all angles are helpful in identification. These are combined with unusual scars or markings on the body, head and flukes, as well as crenulations (unique edge patterns) along the upper margins of the lower lips.

POPULATION
The pre-whaling population is believed to have been at least 30,000, though it was never documented in detail. The current population is estimated to be *c.* 400 individuals in the western North Pacific and *c.* 30 animals (with a strong male bias) in the eastern North Pacific. Population trends are not known with any certainty, although there are no records of births in recent years and there is no evidence of a significant recovery.

CONSERVATION
IUCN status: Endangered (2017); northeastern North Pacific stock Critically Endangered (2017). First hunted by shore-based Japanese whalers in the tenth century. Large-scale whaling by Europeans and Americans began in 1835. Within 14 years, 21,000–30,000 right whales had been killed in the North Pacific and adjoining seas; the eastern population had been reduced to such an extent that whalers switched to other species. Despite legal protection since 1935, illegal hunting continued into the 1970s; the most recent accounting indicates that 681–765 North Pacific right whales were taken illegally by Soviet whalers (the majority during the period 1962–68) and this is thought to have removed the bulk of the surviving eastern population. The last commercial catch was by China, in 1977, in the Yellow Sea. Other threats are likely to include entanglement in fishing gear (which is known to occur around Japan, Russia and South Korea) and, especially in the Sea of Okhotsk, oil and gas development. No deaths have been reported from ship strikes, but this is

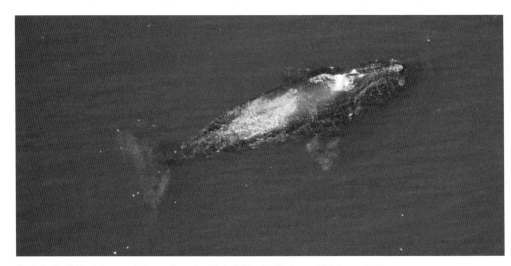

North Pacific right whale seen off the southern tip of Baja California, Mexico, on 20 February 1996.

A North Pacific right whale photographed in the Bering Sea, west of Bristol Bay, Alaska – notice the large number of callosities along the rim of the lower jaw (unusual in North Pacific right whales).

likely to be an issue, especially with increased ship traffic through Unimak Pass and in the Bering Sea. The prognosis for recovery in the east, at least, is bleak.

VOCALISATIONS

North Pacific right whales are highly vocal, producing a variety of low-frequency moans, groans, grunts, sighs, bellows and pulses. These appear to have social communication functions. The most common vocalisations are 'gunshot calls' – which sound like rifles being fired – made by solitary adult males; they may function as a threat display to other males, or to attract females. Another common call is the stereotyped 'upcall', produced by all age classes and both sexes. This lasts about 1–2 seconds and is believed to function as a long-distance contact call. Recent research suggests that it is possible to identify individuals by subtle differences in their upcalls. During a two-month period in 2016, an acoustic recording station in the northern Bering Sea registered a total of 15,575 gunshot calls and 139 upcalls. Less common are 'downcalls', which start with a brief downward sweep before rising in frequency like an upcall, and constant-tonal 'moans'. The most common call recorded in surface-active groups is the 'scream call', which lasts for 0.5–2.8 seconds; it is believed to be produced by the focal female. Recent research in the North Atlantic reveals that quiet gunshot calls are also made by females with newborn calves, apparently as emotive indicators of heightened stress and agitation. Otherwise, mother–calf pairs are mostly silent during the first six weeks of development.

The North Pacific right whale is the first right whale species known to sing. Four distinct song types have been documented, in the southeastern Bering Sea, from July to January. Each consists of up to three repeating phrases dominated by gunshot sounds, but usually also includes downsweeps, moans and low-frequency pulsive calls. Singers have all been male, and the songs do not appear to change with time. They are presumed to be reproductive displays.

A rare picture of a North Pacific right whale in the Bering Sea.

SOUTHERN RIGHT WHALE
Eubalaena australis

(Desmoulins, 1822)

The southern right whale is one of the best-known large whales in the world: research at Peninsula Valdes in Argentina has been ongoing since 1971 and is one of the longest-running studies following the lives of known individual large whales. While a long way from recovering from the ravages of whaling, the southern right is not as seriously endangered as its two northern relatives.

Classification Mysticeti, family Balaenidae.

Common name There are two theories: conventional wisdom holds that it was named by early English whalers for being the 'right' (i.e. correct) whale to hunt (it occurred near shore, swam slowly enough to be caught from a small boat propelled by sails or oars, floated when killed, and produced an exceedingly valuable yield of oil and baleen). However, scientists in the mid-1800s considered 'right' to mean 'true' or 'proper' (i.e. showing the characteristics typical of whales).

Other names Great right whale, black right whale.

Scientific name From the Greek *eu* for 'right' or 'true', and the Latin *balaena* for 'whale'; *australis* from the Latin *australis* for 'southern'.

Taxonomy No recognised forms or subspecies; separated from North Atlantic and North Pacific right whales genetically, though the three species barely differ morphologically.

Pattern of callosities varies between individuals but is distributed in consistent locations (in front of and behind blowholes, along rostrum, above eyes, on upper margin of lower lips, along sides of lower jaws and on chin)

Very strongly arched mouthline

Around 3–6 per cent of individuals have white or light grey blazes on back (uncommon in northern hemisphere right whales)

ADULT

Some individuals have varying amounts of white on upperside

Extremely stocky body (bordering on rotund)

May appear mottled pale grey (caused by uneven sloughing of patches of skin)

Top of head has raised patches of roughened skin (callosities) – naturally light to dark grey, but appear creamy or yellowish due to presence of whale lice

Massive head (c. 25–33 per cent of body length)

Maximum girth can exceed c. 60 per cent of total length

Smooth, broad back with no dorsal fin or ridge

Predominantly black

Largest callosity (the 'bonnet') on tip of rostrum

Many individuals have irregular white patch on underside around navel (highly variable and may extend laterally onto sides and towards chin – generally more extensive than in northern relatives)

Eyes just above corners of mouth (below large callosity)

Callosities often on upper margin of lower lips (cf. northern relatives)

No pleats or grooves on throat

Large, broad flippers up to 1.7m long

Extent and shape of white patch does not change with time

AT A GLANCE
- Cold temperate southern hemisphere
- Extra-large size
- Extremely stocky body
- Predominantly black with variable white on underside
- Smooth back with no dorsal fin or ridge
- No pleats or grooves on throat
- Low body profile at surface
- Massive head covered in light-coloured callosities
- Very strongly arched jawline
- V-shaped blow
- Frequently engages in active surface behaviour

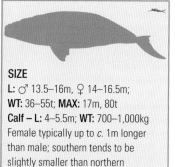

SIZE
L: ♂ 13.5–16m, ♀ 14–16.5m;
WT: 36–55t; **MAX:** 17m, 80t
Calf – L: 4–5.5m; **WT:** 700–1,000kg
Female typically up to *c.* 1m longer
than male; southern tends to be
slightly smaller than northern
hemisphere right whales; heavier than
most other baleen whales of similar
length.

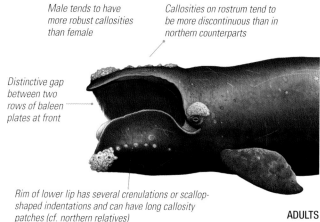

*Male tends to have
more robust callosities
than female*

*Callosities on rostrum tend to
be more discontinuous than in
northern counterparts*

*Distinctive gap
between two
rows of baleen
plates at front*

*Rim of lower lip has several crenulations or scallop-
shaped indentations and can have long callosity
patches (cf. northern relatives)*

ADULTS

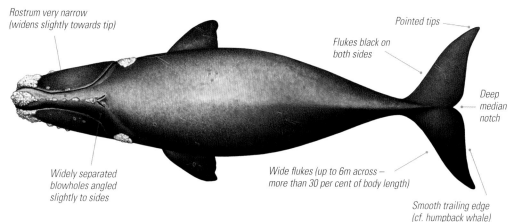

*Rostrum very narrow
(widens slightly towards tip)*

Pointed tips

*Flukes black on
both sides*

*Deep
median
notch*

*Widely separated
blowholes angled
slightly to sides*

*Wide flukes (up to 6m across –
more than 30 per cent of body length)*

*Smooth trailing edge
(cf. humpback whale)*

SIMILAR SPECIES
The bulky size, callosities, arched mouthline, lack of a
dorsal fin, predominantly black coloration and V-shaped
blow should distinguish the southern right whale from all
other large whales in the region. At a distance, confusion
may be possible with humpbacks, which sometimes also
have a V-shaped blow (look for the stubby dorsal fin, long
flippers, and black-and-white markings on the underside
of the flukes of the humpback).
There is no overlap with North
Atlantic or North Pacific right
whales.

DISTRIBUTION
Circumglobal distribution in
the southern hemisphere,
approximately between
20°S and 60°S (occasionally
to 16°S on both coasts of
South America and to at least
65°S along the Antarctic
Peninsula). Migrates between
low-latitude coastal winter
breeding grounds (typically
May–December – precise
timing varies with region) and
high-latitude predominantly

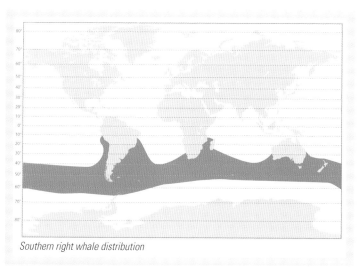

Southern right whale distribution

offshore feeding grounds. Most research has focused on the breeding grounds. One satellite-tagged individual in South Africa travelled 8,200km to its feeding grounds in the South Atlantic. There is little or no interchange with populations of North Atlantic or North Pacific right whales (they are widely separated by warm equatorial waters – though studies of whale lice DNA show that at least one southern right whale must have crossed the equator in the Pacific within the last 1–2 million years).

During the winter breeding season, the species prefers sheltered, nearshore, shallow waters and bays with sandy bottoms for calving (probably for protection from predatory killer whales and large sharks). Major mating and calving areas are:

Southern Africa Mainly South Africa, from Saint Helena Bay in the west to Port Elizabeth in the east, but also Namibia (occasionally into southern Angola) and Mozambique, with small numbers off eastern Madagascar; there is a small, separate population around Tristan da Cunha.

Southern South America Mainly Argentina (especially Peninsula Valdes) south to the Beagle Channel, but also an expanding range in southern Brazil, with very small numbers (probably forming separate populations) in Uruguay, and Peru and Chile.

Australia Mainly along the southern coasts of Western Australia (at least as far north as Exmouth) and South Australia (most between Cape Leeuwin in Western Australia and Ceduna in South Australia) and Tasmania (especially off the southeastern coast); probably forming two populations (southwestern/south-central and southeastern/eastern).

Sub-Antarctic islands of New Zealand Mainly off the Auckland and Campbell Islands – one of the few breeding grounds remaining in the South Pacific. Historically, there were winter breeding grounds around the North and South Islands of mainland New Zealand but, after extensive whaling in the nineteenth and twentieth centuries, no southern right whales were seen for nearly four decades (1928–63). However, they have been sighted every year since 1988, with 28 mother–calf pairs seen between 2003 and 2010.

There appears to be some interchange between breeding areas off the same continent (e.g. 13–15 per cent of Brazilian whales have been resighted off Argentina in alternate years) but little interchange between continents.

Feeding is predominantly offshore, mostly in the mid Southern Ocean south of 40°S (labelled I to VI by the IWC), with some individuals reaching the edge of the pack ice. Specific feeding areas include the Falkland Islands, South Georgia and Shag Rocks, and the Antarctic Peninsula.

SKIN PATTERNS

Five main colour variants are known in southern right whales:

1 'Black' or 'wild type' – whales born predominantly black, with sharp-edged white patches on the belly; their skin remains the same black and white throughout life.
2 'White-blaze' – whales born predominantly black, with sharp-edged white patches on the belly *and* on the back; their skin remains the same black and white throughout life.

DIVE SEQUENCE
- Blow appears as huge head breaks surface (may lift head almost clear of water on surfacing after long dive).
- Head disappears below surface as smooth, broad, low-profile back appears.
- Head pushed down and back arches at steep angle.
- Flukes often raised quite high before deep dive.
- Often lies motionless at surface on breeding grounds.

BLOW
- Bushy V-shaped blow (when seen from in front or behind – oval and bushy from side).
- Up to 7m high (highly variable height).
- Jets often asymmetric in height.
- V more widely spaced at base than in grey or humpback (which sometimes produces V-shaped blows).
- Can be difficult to see if wind dissipates blow (as body so low in water).

DORSAL SKIN PATTERNS

'black' or 'wild type'

'white-blaze'

'grey-morph'

'partial-grey-morph'

'partial-grey-morph with white-blaze'

3 'Grey-morph' (previously known as 'partially albinistic') – whales born predominantly white, with splatterings of black spots in lateral bands behind the blowhole and across the back (lacking the pink eyes associated with albinism); their white skin darkens to pale grey or light brown with age, but the splatterings of black remain the same.

4 'Partial-grey-morph' (previously known as 'grey-blaze') – whales born predominantly black, with splatterings of white in lateral bands across the back; the white splatterings darken to pale grey or light brown with age; in adults, partial-grey-morphs are similar to grey-morphs – except the colours are in reverse.

5 'Partial-grey-morph with white-blaze' – like partial-grey-morph whales, with sharp-edged white patches on their backs.

These colour variants are not known in northern hemisphere right whales. The southern right whale is the only cetacean species in which anomalously white individuals are relatively common.

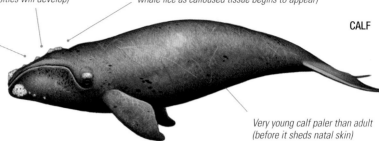

Smooth, pale grey circular areas on head and rostrum may be apparent on newborns (where callosities will develop)

Large patches of orange whale lice disappear when calf is c. 2 months old (replaced by white whale lice as calloused tissue begins to appear)

Pale grey areas begin to thicken and roughen into calloused tissue when 3 months old (callosities not fully developed and colonised by whale lice until 7–10 months old)

CALF

Very young calf paler than adult (before it sheds natal skin)

FLUKES

SAILING

BEHAVIOUR
Generally slow moving and may rest or log at the surface for long periods. But it can move surprisingly quickly, frequently engaging in surface active behaviour, including repeated breaching, spyhopping, lobtailing and flipper-slapping. Unlike its northern hemisphere counterparts, it will also 'sail' by tipping its head down, with its tail sticking out of the water (perpendicular to the wind) and being blown along for a short distance (then righting itself, swimming back upwind and doing it all again); or, especially on Abrolhos Bank off Brazil, it may simply hang upside down in the water, with its flukes suspended in the air, for minutes at a time. Tactile behaviour (touching and rubbing conspecifics) is fairly common. It will playfully poke, bump and push objects in the water, it frequently shows little or no avoidance behaviour in the presence of boats, and it can be inquisitive and approachable.

LIFE HISTORY
Sexual maturity Females probably 7–12 years (usually have first calf at 9–10 years); males unknown.
Mating Sexual behaviour occurs year-round, but outside winter breeding season probably has social function (or for females to assess potential mates); courtship involves 'surface-active groups', averaging five but up to 20 animals or more (usually numerous males with one or occasionally two females, rolling and splashing for one hour or more), usually initiated in response to vocalisations by female; males will also approach mother–calf pairs and juvenile females, which try to escape; interactions between males involve little serious aggression (though plenty of active pushing to get access to female), suggesting sperm competition (females mate with multiple males and those producing most sperm have reproductive advantage); right whale testes are the largest of any animal, at 2m long and weighing 525kg each (further evidence of sperm competition).
Gestation 12–13 months.
Calving Usually every 3.2–3.4 years (range of 2–4 years, occasionally five years when prey availability limited); single calf born June–October (peak late August).
Weaning Usually after 10–12 months (range of 7–14 months).
Lifespan Unknown, but likely to be at least 70 years under prime conditions.

FOOD AND FEEDING

Prey Exclusively zooplankton (mostly copepods, e.g. *Calanus propinquus* and *Pleuromamma robusta* north of 40°S; krill, especially Antarctic krill (*Euphausia superba*) south of 50°S; varying proportions in between); will also take squat lobster (*Munida* spp.), juvenile pelagic crabs, mysid shrimp, pteropods (tiny planktonic snails), larval barnacles, other small invertebrates; very narrow range of acceptable prey, which must be concentrated in exceptionally high densities to elicit feeding.

Feeding Normally skim-feeds at about 5km/h (swimming slowly with mouth open through dense patches of prey, near surface or at moderate depth, and closing mouth occasionally to flush out water and swallow prey); little feeding on winter breeding grounds (sometimes on spring plankton blooms).

Dive depth Often at or near surface, or shallow dives; will sometimes reach greater depths of 200m or more; max. possibly at least 300m.

Dive time Typical feeding dives 10–20 minutes; maximum recorded 50 minutes.

BALEEN

- 200–270 plates (each side of the upper jaw); average 222.
- Long, thin plates averaging 2–2.8m long and dark grey to black (fringed with very fine grey to black hairs, reflecting small prey taken).

GROUP SIZE AND STRUCTURE

Normally one to two (away from aggregation sites on the breeding grounds or on rich feeding grounds), up to 12 in loose associations; much larger loose aggregations of up to 100 may form on temporarily rich feeding grounds.

CALLOSITIES

See North Atlantic right whale (p. 50).

LICE AND BARNACLES

For lice, see North Atlantic right whale (p. 50). There is a single record of *Cyamus boopis* (considered host-specific to humpback whales) on a southern right whale in Brazil. *Tubinicella major* pseudo-stalked barnacles also occur in the callosities of southern right whales.

PREDATORS

Killer whales are known predators, particularly of adults in the open ocean. Right whales may actively defend themselves against killer whale attack (they are a 'fight' species, rather than a 'flight' species), hitting with their tails and ramming (the roughened callosities on the head could possibly serve as weapons or armour). There is

The distinctive V-shaped blow of a southern right whale.

also evidence that great whites and other large sharks may occasionally attack calves, unaccompanied juveniles and sick or injured adults on the breeding grounds. Kelp gulls will gouge skin and blubber from the backs of living whales in Argentina (see Conservation).

PHOTO-IDENTIFICATION

Primarily by the natural pattern of callosities on the head (which is unique to each individual); since callosity patterns are three-dimensional, numerous photographs from all angles are helpful in identification. These are combined with unusual scars or markings on the body, head and flukes, white and grey markings on their backs and bellies, and crenulations (unique edge patterns) along the upper margins of the lower lips.

POPULATION

The most recent global estimate is at least 12,800, including 4,006 in Argentina (2010); 3,612 in South Africa (2008); 2,900 in Australia between Cape Leeuwin and Ceduna (2009); and at least 2,306 in New Zealand's Auckland Islands (2009). Numbers have increased significantly since a 1997 estimate of *c.* 7,600 (including 2,577 in Argentina, 3,104 in South Africa and 1,197 in Australia). There were 536 cow-calf pairs in South Africa in 2018 (cf. 249 in 2015, 55 in 2016 and 183 in 2017). The main populations appear to have been increasing at *c.* 6–7.6 per cent per year (i.e. numbers are doubling approximately every 10–12 years), so the total population could now be as high as 25,000–30,000. However, the rate of increase appears to be slowing in Argentina, at least. There are likely fewer than 50 breeding adults remaining in Chile and Peru, with no sign of recovery. The pre-whaling abundance in 1770 is estimated at *c.* 55,000–70,000.

CONSERVATION

IUCN status: Least Concern (2017); Chile–Peru subpopulation Critically Endangered (2017). Heavy commercial whaling from the 1770s to the early 1970s killed at least *c.* 114,000 (*c.* 63,000 in the South Atlantic, 38,000 in the South Pacific and 13,000 in the Indian Ocean). Stocks were left severely depleted – possibly down to 0.5 per cent of pre-exploitation abundance. Officially protected from commercial hunting in 1935, but the Soviet Union illegally took at least a further 3,300, mainly off Peninsula Valdes in the 1960s. Since full protection, most populations appear to be recovering.

Current threats include vessel strikes and entanglement in fishing gear, though these are relatively rare compared with the number of cases known in North Atlantic right whales. Habitat disturbance, noise pollution from shipping and prey depletion (caused by overfishing of krill and declines in krill abundance associated with the reduction of Antarctic ice) may also present a threat. The British Antarctic Survey predicts at least a 95 per cent reduction in the biomass and abundance of krill in the Scotia Sea

A silvery-white 'grey-morph' southern right whale in South Africa.

The distinctive arched lower jaw of a southern right whale.

Mother–calf pair ('wild type').

by the end of the century if sea surface temperatures increase by 1°C.

There have been significant calf die-offs (737 between 2003 and 2015) around Peninsula Valdes, Argentina. One possible explanation is parasitism by kelp gulls, which feed by pecking skin and blubber from the backs of live southern right whales – particularly mother–calf pairs – sometimes causing extensive injuries. These attacks have increased since they were first documented in 1972, and the gulls are now targeting calves, which causes chronic stress.

Prospects for long-term survival are much better for the southern right whale than for either of the northern hemisphere right whales. However, there appears to

be a direct correlation between breeding success off Argentina and sea surface temperature at the feeding grounds around South Georgia, suggesting that the average calving rate is likely to decline with global warming.

VOCALISATIONS

Southern right whales are highly vocal, producing a variety of low-frequency (mostly below 500Hz) moans, groans, grunts, sighs, bellows and pulses. These appear to have a variety of functions, possibly including social signals, threats or signs of aggression, and contact calls between separated individuals. For further information on call types, see North Atlantic right whale (p. 52).

'Sailing' in Argentina – a behaviour that appears to be play.

BOWHEAD WHALE
Balaena mysticetus

Linnaeus, 1758

The only large whale found exclusively in the Arctic, the bowhead is well adapted to life in its freezing home. With a layer of blubber up to 28cm thick and the ability to create its own breathing holes by breaking through ice up to 60cm thick, it can live at higher latitudes than any other baleen whale.

Classification Mysticeti, family Balaenidae.
Common name After the huge, strongly arched (bow-shaped) rostrum.
Other names Greenland/Arctic whale, Greenland/Arctic right whale.
Scientific name From the Latin *Balaena* for 'whale', and the Greek *mystakos* and Latin *cetus* for 'moustached whale' (referring to the baleen plates).
Taxonomy No recognised forms or subspecies (though four separate stocks).

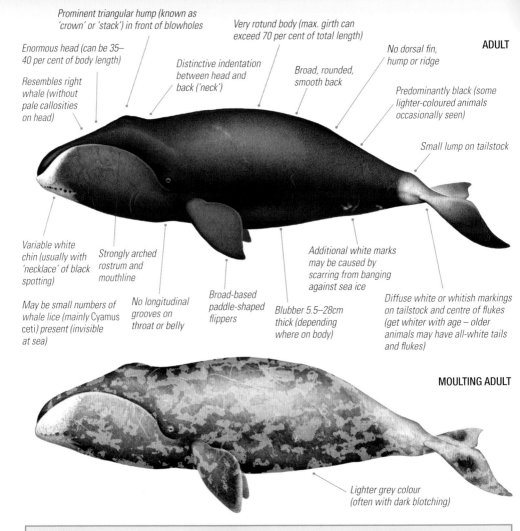

Prominent triangular hump (known as 'crown' or 'stack') in front of blowholes

Very rotund body (max. girth can exceed 70 per cent of total length)

Enormous head (can be 35–40 per cent of body length)

Distinctive indentation between head and back ('neck')

Broad, rounded, smooth back

No dorsal fin, hump or ridge

ADULT

Resembles right whale (without pale callosities on head)

Predominantly black (some lighter-coloured animals occasionally seen)

Small lump on tailstock

Variable white chin (usually with 'necklace' of black spotting)

Strongly arched rostrum and mouthline

Additional white marks may be caused by scarring from banging against sea ice

May be small numbers of whale lice (mainly Cyamus ceti) present (invisible at sea)

No longitudinal grooves on throat or belly

Broad-based paddle-shaped flippers

Blubber 5.5–28cm thick (depending where on body)

Diffuse white or whitish markings on tailstock and centre of flukes (get whiter with age – older animals may have all-white tails and flukes)

MOULTING ADULT

Lighter grey colour (often with dark blotching)

AT A GLANCE		
• Arctic and sub-Arctic	• Predominantly black	• V-shaped bushy blow
• Extra-large size	• No dorsal fin	• Two distinct humps in profile
	• Enormous head	• No callosities or barnacles

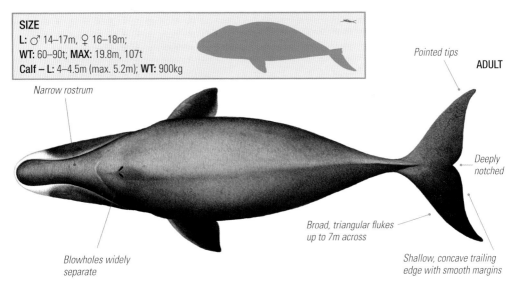

SIZE
L: ♂ 14–17m, ♀ 16–18m;
WT: 60–90t; **MAX:** 19.8m, 107t
Calf – L: 4–4.5m (max. 5.2m); **WT:** 900kg

ADULT

Pointed tips

Narrow rostrum

Deeply notched

Blowholes widely separate

Broad, triangular flukes up to 7m across

Shallow, concave trailing edge with smooth margins

SIMILAR SPECIES

The lack of a dorsal fin and predominantly black coloration distinguishes the bowhead from all other large whales entering the High Arctic. North Atlantic and North Pacific right whales are superficially similar, but there is very little overlap in range, they are unlikely to be associated with ice and their callosities are distinctive.

DISTRIBUTION

Circumpolar in the Arctic and sub-Arctic, mainly 54–85°N (it is the only baleen whale living exclusively in this region).

Closely associated with the pack ice and its seasonal movements, migrating to the High Arctic in summer (belugas often follow through leads in the ice) and retreating southward in winter with the advancing ice edge (the winter range is poorly known, but it is believed to live in areas near the ice edge, in polynyas and unconsolidated pack ice). May travel long distances (up to 200km per day) between high-productivity feeding areas. Mainly pelagic, but it does occur in coastal waters. There is some geographic segregation by sex: animals in Disko Bay are 78 per cent mature females

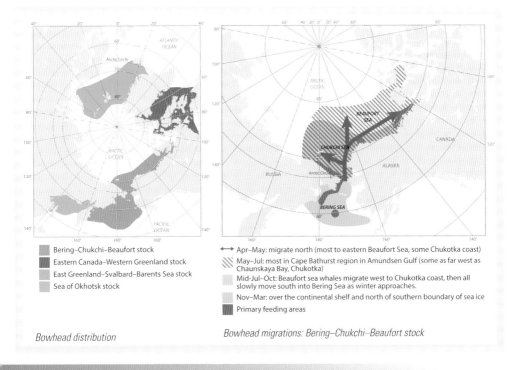

Bering–Chukchi–Beaufort stock
Eastern Canada–Western Greenland stock
East Greenland–Svalbard–Barents Sea stock
Sea of Okhotsk stock

← Apr–May: migrate north (most to eastern Beaufort Sea, some Chukotka coast)
May–Jul: most in Cape Bathurst region in Amundsen Gulf (some as far west as Chaunskaya Bay, Chukotka)
Mid-Jul–Oct: Beaufort sea whales migrate west to Chukotka coast, then all slowly move south into Bering Sea as winter approaches.
Nov–Mar: over the continental shelf and north of southern boundary of sea ice
Primary feeding areas

Bowhead distribution

Bowhead migrations: Bering–Chukchi–Beaufort stock

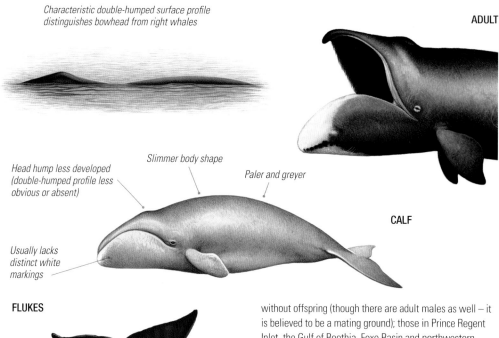

Characteristic double-humped surface profile distinguishes bowhead from right whales

ADULT

Head hump less developed (double-humped profile less obvious or absent)

Slimmer body shape

Paler and greyer

CALF

Usually lacks distinct white markings

FLUKES

without offspring (though there are adult males as well – it is believed to be a mating ground); those in Prince Regent Inlet, the Gulf of Boothia, Foxe Basin and northwestern Hudson Bay are primarily female–calf pairs and sub-adults; and Baffin Bay animals are primarily mature males and resting or pregnant females.

MAIN STOCKS

Four stocks or sub-populations are currently recognised (mainly based on geographical separation): Bering–Chukchi–Beaufort (Alaska, Canada and Russia); Sea of Okhotsk (Russia); Eastern Canada–Western Greenland

DIVE SEQUENCE

- After sounding dive, usually surfaces with head and blowhole first (with body typically oriented at 30-degree angle from horizontal).
- After shallow dive, usually head and body surface at approximately same time.
- On surface shows distinctive double-humped profile.
- Frequently flukes before deep dive (tail may tip to right).
- When travelling, typically dives for 10–20 minutes then breathes several times at surface for 2–3 minutes.

BLOW

- Tall, bushy, V-shaped blow up to 7m (typically 5m) (height highly variable).
- Jets usually different heights.
- May appear as a single blow if seen from side or in wind.

FOOD AND FEEDING

Prey Catholic diet (more than 100 prey species known) but prefers small- to medium-sized (mostly 3–30mm-long) crustaceans, especially copepods and euphausiid krill; also feeds on mysids and gammarid amphipods.

Feeding Feeds throughout water column, anywhere from surface to seabed, under ice as well as in open water (where may 'skim' through concentrated prey at surface, swimming slowly with mouth open); usually feeds alone but groups gather at productive feeding grounds and up to 14 may form echelon (V-shape) to sweep an area; may remain at surface for 30 minutes or more when skim-feeding; feeds year-round (but less frequent in winter).

Dive depth Frequently less than 30m when foraging (varies according to region, season and behaviour); dives deeper during winter and when travelling; maximum recorded 487m and 582m (West Greenland, 2003 and 2011).

Dive time Typically 1–20 minutes (depending on behaviour – foraging dives in Beaufort Sea average 3.4–12.1 minutes); tends to dive for longer under heavy pack ice than in open water; maximum documented 61 minutes under natural conditions (80 minutes when harpooned and being chased by whalers).

(formerly considered two stocks: Hudson Bay–Foxe Basin, Canada, and Baffin Bay–Davis Strait, Canada and Greenland); and East Greenland–Svalbard–Barents Sea (Greenland, Norway and Russia). There is some recent evidence of limited mixing in the extreme summer ranges between the BCB and Eastern Canada–Western Greenland stocks (due to diminishing ice in the Northwest Passage).

MIGRATIONS

Bering–Chukchi–Beaufort seas November–March: northern Bering Sea (over the continental shelf and south of the southern boundary of sea ice – south to Karaginsky Gulf, on the northern Kamchatka Peninsula and St Matthew Island, Alaska). April–June: most migrate north from the Bering Sea to the eastern Beaufort Sea (keeping relatively close to the Alaskan coast) though some turn west along the Chukotka coast, Russia, reaching as far as Chaunskaya Bay. June–August: eastern Beaufort Sea, particularly in the Cape Bathurst region, in Amundsen Gulf, Canada (with small numbers remaining on the Russian side of the Chukchi Sea all summer). Late August–October: whales in the Canadian Beaufort Sea migrate west, following the Alaskan coast to Point Barrow, and then crossing the Chukchi Sea to the Chukotka coast and slowly moving southward along the Siberian coast into the Bering Sea as winter approaches.

Eastern Canada–Western Greenland *West Greenland* February–June (mainly March–May): Disko Bay, Greenland, travelling across Baffin Bay into Arctic Canada at end of May. June–mid-October: some individuals spend summer along the east and north coasts of Baffin Island, while others move into Lancaster Sound and Prince Regent Inlet. Mid-October: starting to move south. November–February: Hudson Strait and northern Hudson Bay (where they join Canadian bowheads). Late February: travelling back across Baffin Bay into Greenland.

Canada March–September: Foxe Basin, northern Hudson Bay, in fjords along the east coast of Baffin Island and in the Canadian High Arctic. October–February: Hudson Strait and northern Hudson Bay (where they are joined by

Greenland bowheads), at the mouth of Cumberland Sound, along West Greenland and in the North Water Polynya (at the northern end of Baffin Bay).

East Greenland–Svalbard–Barents Sea Surveys in Svalbard in 2015–2018 revealed significant summer aggregations (more than 200 individuals) in Fram Strait (between Greenland and Svalbard). Limited evidence suggests other important summering grounds in the North East Water Polynya, north-east Greenland; at the so-called Southern Whaling Ground, south-east Greenland; and much further east at Franz Josef Land, Russia. Little is known about winter distribution but at least some appear to winter in Fram Strait.

Sea of Okhotsk Spring in Gizhigin and Penzhina Bays, in the Gulf of Shelikhov, in the north-east (no recent sightings later than June); summer mainly in waters south of the Shantar Islands, in Sakhalin Gulf, in the west; winter in polynyas throughout the Sea of Okhotsk (there is no evidence that bowheads in this stock ever leave the Sea of Okhotsk).

BEHAVIOUR

Generally a slow, deliberate swimmer – typically 3–6km/h – but capable of bursts of speed up to 21km/h. Frequently breaches, flipper-slaps, lobtails and spyhops, and may inspect or play with objects in the water. During breaches, up to 60 per cent of the body leaves the water and the whale usually falls back into the water on its back or side. May play with logs and other objects. Often quite approachable by boat and may closely investigate people

LIFE HISTORY

Sexual maturity Females and males 18–31 years.
Mating Poorly known, but likely March–April (though sexual activity may occur in any season); mating groups can be male–female pair or several males with single female (she mates with them all); males may cooperate during mating.
Gestation 13–14 months.

Calving Every 3–4 years; single calf born late April–early June (usually just before, or during, northern spring migration).
Weaning After 9–12 months (but may remain with mother further 3–6 months).
Lifespan At least 100 years (oldest recorded 211 years – likely one of longest-lived animals on Earth).

standing on the floe edge. It can swim beneath ice, making breathing holes by breaking through ice up to 60cm thick with the raised part of its massive head. Often seen in association with belugas and narwhal. Behaviour is poorly known during the winter, when ice conditions and polar darkness make observations difficult.

BALEEN
- 230–360 plates (each side of the upper jaw).
- Baleen plates are up to 4m (maximum 5.2m) long – the longest of any whale; they are dark grey to brownish black, usually with lighter fringes.

GROUP SIZE AND STRUCTURE
Bowheads are usually solitary, but they are sometimes seen in small groups of two to three (up to 14). There are occasional loose aggregations of as many as 60 at productive feeding grounds and during migration. In summer, groups are often segregated by sex and age. There is little stability in social organisation beyond the mother–calf pair (most associations last hours or, rarely, days); however, vocalisations can be heard over long distances, so a loose herd structure is possible.

PREDATORS
Killer whales. Rake marks are found on up to 10 per cent of adult bowheads, but it is likely that many calves and weaned juveniles succumb. The bowhead's close association with sea ice may be a way of seeking refuge from killer whales, which tend to avoid extensive sea ice in the Arctic; however, predation may increase with substantial reductions in Arctic ice due to global warming. One killer whale pod in the Sea of Okhotsk is known to specialise in hunting juvenile bowheads around the Shantar Islands. Bowheads will often fight back, rather than flee.

Bowhead whale baleen plate

PHOTO-IDENTIFICATION
Identifiable by the characteristic white patterns on the chin (visible from aircraft), the underside, around the tailstock and on the flukes, combined with dorsal scarring.

POPULATION
The best estimate is *c.* 25,000, with most in the Bering–Chukchi–Beaufort stock; the pre-whaling population was probably *c.* 71,000–113,000. Numbers have grown considerably in the past 10–15 years (primarily due to an increase in the large Bering–Chukchi–Beaufort stock but also, more recently, the Eastern Canada–Western Greenland stock). Specific stock estimates are: Bering–Chukchi–Beaufort 19,000 (2017), with an average annual growth of 3.7 per cent since the late 1980s – the pre-whaling population was *c.* 10,000–20,000; Eastern Canada–Western Greenland *c.* 7,700 (including *c.* 1,600 in Disko Bay) – the estimated pre-whaling population was *c.* 25,000; Sea of Okhotsk probably 400–500 – the pre-whaling population was at least 3,000; East Greenland–Svalbard–Barents Sea *c.* 300–400, with recent signs of a population recovery (or immigration from other increasing stocks facilitated by a reduction in sea ice) – the pre-whaling population was 33,000–65,000.

CONSERVATION
IUCN status: Least Concern (2018); Sea of Okhotsk stock Endangered (2018); East Greenland–Svalbard–Barents Sea stock Endangered (2018). The bowhead's large size, long baleen, thick blubber, slow speed and gentle disposition made it a major target for whalers. Commercial whaling began in 1611 in the North Atlantic, but was most intense during the 1800s and early 1900s, when tens of thousands were slaughtered. It has been officially protected since the inception of the IWC in 1946 (though Canada is not a member). Limited aboriginal whaling is permitted by the IWC from the Bering–Chukchi–Beaufort stock, by native peoples of Alaska, USA, and Chukotka, Russia – with no more than 67 whales struck in any given year, for the period 2019–2025 (more than 90 per cent by Alaska). Very small numbers (typically two to three per year) are also taken in Nunavut, Canada, and the IWC permits an annual strike limit of two whales for West Greenland for the period 2019–2025. The primary potential threat is believed to

CHIN VARIATIONS

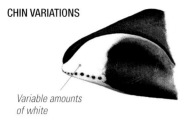

Variable amounts of white

'necklace' of black spotting variable

be disturbance from oil and gas development, which can decrease feeding efficiency and brings an increased risk of oil spills. The impact of climate change is unknown, but ship strikes and noise pollution are likely to increase with more ship traffic in the Arctic. Other threats include entanglement in fishing gear, chemical pollution and mining.

VOCALISATIONS

The bowhead has an extensive vocal repertoire, including distinctive 'upcalls' and 'downcalls' (with ascending and descending frequencies) and loud, complex songs. Songs are often sung with 'two voices' (the same whale simultaneously producing high- and low-frequency sounds); they can be heard at any time of the year (though mostly during the winter and early-spring breeding season,

before mid-May) and 24 hours a day. Songs tend to be simpler towards the end of the breeding season. There is no information on the age, sex or behaviour of singing whales, but they are presumed to be male and the song is believed to be a reproductive display. Bowhead songs are more diverse than in any other baleen whale and vary within a population, between populations, during a season and from year to year. One study in Fram Strait, in the northern North Atlantic, counted 184 distinct melodies over a three-year period. Intense feeding during the summer usually occurs in silence. Bowheads also make complex tones at higher frequencies, which are believed to be a simple form of echolocation (possibly for navigating under pack ice and around icebergs).

The distinctive, strongly arched mouthline of a bowhead.

Female bowhead with her paler calf.

Bowhead whales in Nunavat, Canada. Notice the 'necklace' of black spotting.

Female (showing the distinctive white chin).

PYGMY RIGHT WHALE
Caperea marginata

(Gray, 1846)

The smallest and least-known baleen whale, the pygmy right whale is rarely observed at sea but can be positively identified when seen well. Despite its name, it is placed in a separate family and not regarded as one of the 'true' right whales.

Classification Mysticeti, family Neobalaenidae.
Common name Denoting the similar mouthline to right whales and its smaller size.
Other names None.
Scientific name *Caperea* from the Latin *capero* for 'wrinkle' (referring to the texture of the ear bone); *marginata* from the Latin *margo* for 'within a border' (describing the dark margin of the light-coloured baleen).
Taxonomy No recognised forms or subspecies. New fossil evidence suggests that it should be moved to the family Cetotheriidae.

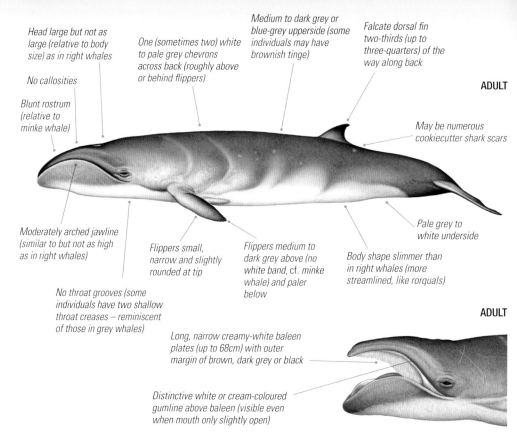

Head large but not as large (relative to body size) as in right whales

One (sometimes two) white to pale grey chevrons across back (roughly above or behind flippers)

Medium to dark grey or blue-grey upperside (some individuals may have brownish tinge)

Falcate dorsal fin two-thirds (up to three-quarters) of the way along back

ADULT

No callosities

Blunt rostrum (relative to minke whale)

May be numerous cookiecutter shark scars

Moderately arched jawline (similar to but not as high as in right whales)

Flippers small, narrow and slightly rounded at tip

Flippers medium to dark grey above (no white band, cf. minke whale) and paler below

Body shape slimmer than in right whales (more streamlined, like rorquals)

Pale grey to white underside

ADULT

No throat grooves (some individuals have two shallow throat creases – reminiscent of those in grey whales)

Long, narrow creamy-white baleen plates (up to 68cm) with outer margin of brown, dark grey or black

Distinctive white or cream-coloured gumline above baleen (visible even when mouth only slightly open)

AT A GLANCE
- Temperate waters of southern hemisphere
- Medium size
- Proportionately large head with arched jawline
- Falcate dorsal fin two-thirds of the way along back
- Light-coloured chevrons on back
- Indistinct blow
- Often 'throws' head out of water on surfacing

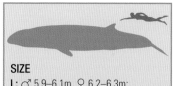

SIZE
L: ♂ 5.9–6.1m, ♀ 6.2–6.3m;
WT: 2.9–3.4t; **MAX:** 6.5m, 3.9t
Calf – L: 1.6–2.2m; **WT:** unknown

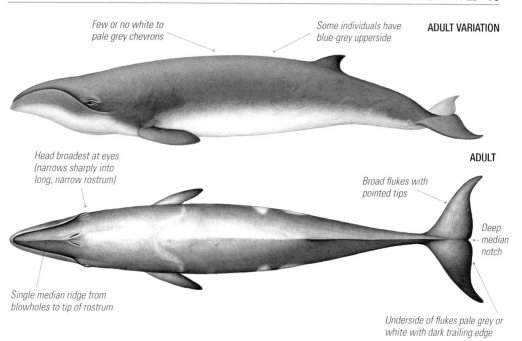

Few or no white to pale grey chevrons

Some individuals have blue-grey upperside

ADULT VARIATION

Head broadest at eyes (narrows sharply into long, narrow rostrum)

ADULT

Broad flukes with pointed tips

Deep median notch

Single median ridge from blowholes to tip of rostrum

Underside of flukes pale grey or white with dark trailing edge

SIMILAR SPECIES

Confusion is most likely with other rorqual whales of a similar size, especially minkes. At close range, the blunter rostrum, strongly arched lower jaw, lack of a white flipper band and white gumline (visible if the mouth is partly or wholly open) should help with identification. From a distance, the pygmy right whale's habit of 'throwing' its head out of the water at an angle can be distinctive. The back and dorsal fin could be confused with those of a beaked whale, but the head shape and dive sequence are very different.

DISTRIBUTION

Circumpolar in both coastal and oceanic mid-latitude temperate waters of the southern hemisphere. Mainly between 30°S and 55°S, preferring water temperatures of 5–20°C; however, if cold currents are present (such as the Benguela Current off south-west Africa), it has been known to reach 19°S. There are records from Chile, Argentina, the Falkland Islands, Crozet Islands, Namibia, South Africa, New Zealand and Australia. May be resident year-round in some parts of the range, but elsewhere there is limited evidence of inshore movements in spring and summer. The presence of numerous oval cookiecutter shark scars and wounds on some individuals suggests that at least some time is spent in tropical or warm temperate waters. Limited evidence suggests that the Subtropical Convergence (an area of high productivity) is an important feeding area. Birthing and nursery grounds are not known, though there is one possible location off the coast of Namibia; most very young animals have been observed north of 41°S. There have been no confirmed sightings south of the Antarctic Convergence.

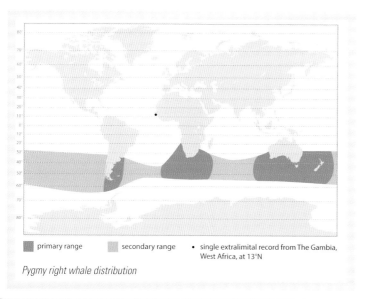

primary range   secondary range   • single extralimital record from The Gambia, West Africa, at 13°N

Pygmy right whale distribution

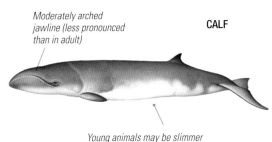

Moderately arched jawline (less pronounced than in adult)

CALF

Young animals may be slimmer and lighter than adults

LIFE HISTORY
Sexual maturity Unknown.
Mating Unknown.
Gestation *c.* 10–12 months.
Calving Little known; single calf born year-round, with possible peak April–October.
Weaning After *c.* five months.
Lifespan Unknown.

BEHAVIOUR

Relatively few confirmed sightings at sea. No records of breaching, spyhopping or lobtailing. Apparently swims slowly at the surface, but it is capable of very rapid acceleration and speed (leaving a conspicuous wake). Known to associate with other cetaceans. Reaction to vessels appears to vary according to size: smaller vessels have been approached quite closely, but larger vessels are more often avoided. In response to aircraft and ships, groups have been observed forming a tight circle and swimming in a counter-clockwise direction.

BALEEN

• 213–230 plates (each side of upper jaw).

FOOD AND FEEDING

Prey Calanoid and cyclopoid copepods, amphipods, small krill and possibly other plankton.
Feeding Believed to skim-feed (rather than gulp); presence of bird feathers in stomachs may indicate surface-feeding.
Dive depth Probably not deep diver (dives short, and heart and lungs small).
Dive time 40 seconds–4 minutes.

GROUP SIZE AND STRUCTURE

Sightings close to shore tend to be of 1–2 animals (often mother–calf pairs), but groups of up to 14 have been observed. Aggregations of 80 (590km south of Western Australia, in 1992) and more than 100 (40km south-west of Victoria, Australia, in 2007) have been reported in the open ocean.

PREDATORS

Unknown. Possibly killer whales and large sharks.

POPULATION

There are no estimates of abundance. Judging by the number of strandings it is likely to be reasonably common, at least in some parts of its range.

CONSERVATION

IUCN status: Least Concern (2018). There are currently no known threats. Chemical and noise pollution, global warming and entanglement in nets may be problems in some areas. There is no evidence that pygmy right whales are targeted by whalers (probably because they are too small to be profitable to kill and are rarely encountered at sea); they have been protected under international agreement since 1935. They are sometimes taken opportunistically (and accidentally) by inshore fishermen in South Africa, New Zealand and Australia.

DIVE SEQUENCE

• Surfaces inconspicuously and fairly quickly (rarely for more than few seconds).
• 'Throws' head out of water at an angle (often possible to see arched mouthline).
• Dorsal fin may be visible briefly just before blowhole disappears.
• Slight arching of back as dives.
• Does not raise flukes clear of water before diving.

BLOW

• Blow often inconspicuous.
• When visible, ranges from narrow and columnar to small and oval.

GREY WHALE
Eschrichtius robustus

(Lilljeborg, 1861)

The grey whale is an inveterate traveller: the round-trip distance between its winter breeding grounds and summer feeding grounds can be more than 20,000km. One of the most-watched whales in the world, it is instantly recognisable thanks to its mottled grey colouring and the small hump instead of a dorsal fin.

Classification Mysticeti, family Eschrichtiidae.

Common name No firm agreement on the origin of the common name; either from the grey colouring (the American spelling is 'gray'), in which case either 'grey' or 'gray' is appropriate; or after British zoologist John Edward Gray (1800–75), who recognised the grey whale's distinctiveness and placed it in its own genus in 1864.

Other names Gray whale, grayback, California gray whale, Pacific gray whale; historically – mussel-digger, mud-digger, scrag whale, ripsack, hardhead, devilfish (by American whalers, for its ferocity when hunted).

Scientific name *Eschrichtius* after the nineteenth-century Danish zoologist Daniel Frederick Eschricht (1798–1863), and *robustus* from Latin for 'strong' or 'robust'.

Taxonomy No recognised forms or subspecies; two possible sub-populations (eastern North Pacific and western North Pacific), though there is evidence of mixing on the Mexican breeding grounds.

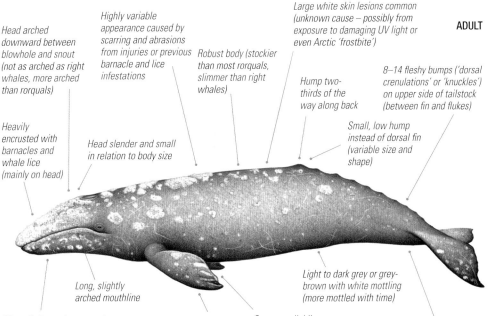

Head arched downward between blowhole and snout (not as arched as right whales, more arched than rorquals)

Highly variable appearance caused by scarring and abrasions from injuries or previous barnacle and lice infestations

Robust body (stockier than most rorquals, slimmer than right whales)

Large white skin lesions common (unknown cause – possibly from exposure to damaging UV light or even Arctic 'frostbite')

ADULT

Hump two-thirds of the way along back

8–14 fleshy bumps ('dorsal crenulations' or 'knuckles') on upper side of tailstock (between fin and flukes)

Heavily encrusted with barnacles and whale lice (mainly on head)

Head slender and small in relation to body size

Small, low hump instead of dorsal fin (variable size and shape)

Long, slightly arched mouthline

Light to dark grey or grey-brown with white mottling (more mottled with time)

More vibrissae than any other whale (widely spaced bristles emerge from small dimples mainly on upper and lower jaw; many obliterated by barnacles and scarring in older animals

Relatively short, broad, paddle-shaped flippers (usually with pointed tips – more rounded from abrasion in older individuals)

Some parallel linear scarring, especially on flippers and flukes (rake marks – tooth scars – from killer whale attacks)

Unique cyst-like structure (10–25cm diameter) on ventral surface of caudal peduncle (unknown function)

AT A GLANCE

- Coastal or shallow waters of North Pacific and adjacent seas
- Light to dark grey or grey-brown with white mottling
- Large size
- Low hump (instead of dorsal fin)
- Head (and other parts of body) encrusted with barnacles and lice
- 'Knuckles' on upper side of tailstock (between fin and flukes)
- Low V-shaped or heart-shaped bushy blow
- Frequently flukes on deep dive

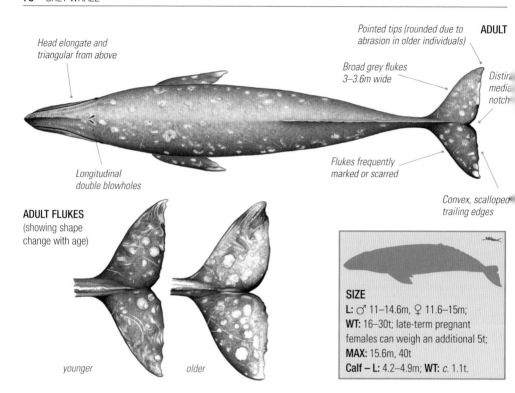

Head elongate and triangular from above

Pointed tips (rounded due to abrasion in older individuals) **ADULT**

Broad grey flukes 3–3.6m wide

Disti... media... notch

Longitudinal double blowholes

Flukes frequently marked or scarred

Convex, scalloped trailing edges

ADULT FLUKES
(showing shape change with age)

younger   *older*

SIZE
L: ♂ 11–14.6m, ♀ 11.6–15m;
WT: 16–30t; late-term pregnant females can weigh an additional 5t;
MAX: 15.6m, 40t
Calf – L: 4.2–4.9m; **WT:** *c.* 1.1t.

SIMILAR SPECIES

The mottled grey coloration and low surface profile are distinctive at close range. At a distance, there is potential confusion with other large whales lacking prominent dorsal fins: sperm, right and bowhead. Shape, colour, blow and dive sequences should enable a positive identification.

DISTRIBUTION

Mainly over shallow continental shelf waters of the North Pacific and adjacent seas. Primarily coastal, but it does feed far from shore on the shallow flats of its feeding grounds and is capable of navigating deep ocean areas on migration. Two geographical populations are recognised (albeit with no anatomical differences). The Eastern North Pacific (ENP) stock migrates between winter breeding grounds in Baja California, Mexico, and summer feeding grounds predominantly in the Bering, Chuckchi and Beaufort seas; it appears to be expanding its range north-west as the Arctic ice opens up. The Western North Pacific (WNP) stock migrates between winter breeding grounds (believed to be in the South China Sea), and summer feeding grounds in the Sea of Okhotsk and off southern

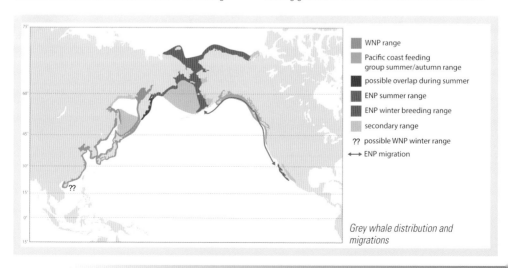

WNP range
Pacific coast feeding group summer/autumn range
possible overlap during summer
ENP summer range
ENP winter breeding range
secondary range
?? possible WNP winter range
⟷ ENP migration

Grey whale distribution and migrations

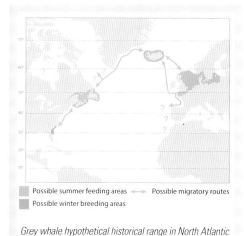

Possible summer feeding areas ←→ Possible migratory routes
Possible winter breeding areas

Grey whale hypothetical historical range in North Atlantic

return journey – between San Ignacio Lagoon, Mexico, and Unimak Pass, Alaska – is *c.* 12,000km, but some individuals may swim considerably further; the longest documented migration of any mammal was a female grey whale that completed a 22,511km round trip between Sakhalin Island, Russia, and Baja California, Mexico.

Since 2011, there has been evidence of individuals remaining in the Arctic for longer – even year-round in exceptional cases – to obtain sufficient food and energy stores. This is presumed to be the result of reduced ice cover, due to global warming, affecting distribution and availability of prey. With the retreat of sea ice, the summer distribution has also expanded in recent decades, especially to more northerly feeding areas (to at least 71°N); observations as far east as the Canadian Beaufort Sea and as far west as Wrangel Island in the Chukchi Sea (and even into the East Siberian Sea) are now common. The southernmost record in the North Pacific is an adult that stranded in July 2010 in El Salvador (*c.* 14°N).

PACIFIC COAST FEEDING GROUP

Some 200 grey whales – known as the Pacific Coast Feeding Group (Canada) or the Pacific Coast Feeding Aggregation (USA) – do not migrate all the way to the Arctic, and instead spend the summer and autumn feeding in a well-defined coastal region between northern California and south-east Alaska. Officially, they occur from 41°N to 52°N between May and November (though some range to *c.* 60°N). These whales interbreed with other eastern grey whales, but are believed to comprise a demographically distinct stock. A separate 'group' of *c.* 10–15 grey whales sometimes feeds in Puget Sound, Washington State, typically from February until May or June.

and southeastern Kamchatka. There is evidence of some mixing between these stocks during the winter breeding season (a total of 54 whales has been recorded in both the WNP and ENP); there is also mixing during the summer feeding season, in southeastern Kamchatka and possibly off Sakhalin Island. Historically, grey whales also occurred in the North Atlantic and there is one record from the South Atlantic (see Exceptional Sightings, p. 82).

MIGRATIONS

The breeding and feeding grounds are widely separated, with long coastal migrations in between (spanning up to 50° of latitude). The ENP population makes an exceptionally long migration along the length of North America – hugging the coast, usually within 10km of shore. The shortest

DIVE SEQUENCE

* On initial surfacing, head appears to slope downward from blowholes (giving appearance of shallow triangle).
* 'Knuckles' clearly visible as back arches slightly to dive.
* Many dives short and shallow (flukes rarely raised).
* Flukes raised high into air before deep dive.
* When travelling or feeding, typically remains submerged for 3–7 minutes, then surfaces and blows 3–5 times (each surfacing 15–30 seconds apart).

BLOW

* Bushy blow up to 5m (highly variable height).
* May be V-shaped, tall and bushy, tree-shaped or heart-shaped (when spray falls inward) when seen from front or rear.
* May be single bushy column.

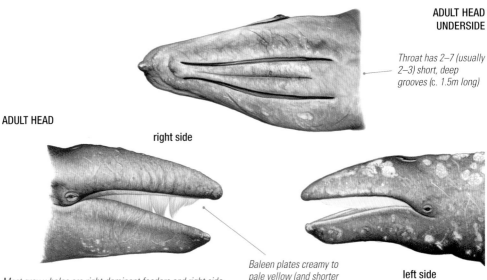

ADULT HEAD UNDERSIDE

Throat has 2–7 (usually 2–3) short, deep grooves (c. 1.5m long)

ADULT HEAD

right side

Baleen plates creamy to pale yellow (and shorter than in any other whale)

left side

Most grey whales are right-dominant feeders and right side of head often differs from left side due to abrasion during seafloor feeding: more heavily scarred, fewer barnacles and whale lice, shorter and more worn baleen plates

ANNUAL CYCLE (Eastern North Pacific population)

April–November On the feeding grounds in the Arctic.

November–February Migrating south. Prompted by the development of winter sea ice and decreasing day length, the whales start heading south. Ninety per cent leave the Bering Sea through Unimak Pass, in Alaska's Aleutian Islands, in mid-November–late December, and from there it takes about 60 days to reach Baja. There is a specific order of departure: near-term pregnant females first, followed by all other adults, immature females and, finally, immature males. The last of the migrants heading south overlap with the first of the migrants returning north. Average swimming speed is 7–9km/h.

December–April On the breeding grounds along the Pacific coast of Baja California, Mexico. There are three main aggregation and breeding lagoons: Scammon's Lagoon (or Ojo de Liebre), San Ignacio Lagoon and the Magdalena Bay complex (including Bahía Almejas). Historically, Guerrero Negro Lagoon was important, but few whales use it today. Small numbers once used several lagoons inside the Gulf of California, on 'mainland' Mexico; these included: Yavaros–Tijahui in Sonora and Bahía Navachiste, Bahía Altata and Bahía Santa María La Reforma in Sinaloa. Time spent in and around the lagoons varies by sex and reproductive condition: in San Ignacio, it averages 7–9 days (maximum 72 days) for breeding males and females; and 28–30 days (maximum 89 days) for females with young calves.

February–early June Migrating north. The departure is in two pulses. First, all whales except mothers and calves. These individuals normally swim from headland to headland and cross (rather than enter) bights and indentations in the coastline; their average swimming speed is roughly the same as on the journey south, though they tend to pick up the pace as they approach the summer feeding grounds. Second, mothers with calves, which leave 1–2 months later (when the calves are strong enough). Ninety per cent travel within 200m of shore (often within the kelp beds fringing much of this coast) and usually go round bights and indentations (rather than crossing them) to avoid predation by killer whales; their average swimming speed is 4–5km/h and they normally arrive on the summer feeding grounds in late May or June.

ANNUAL CYCLE (Western North Pacific population)

Note: this is the historical annual cycle; it is believed that a small number of western grey whales (fewer than 80) do still migrate to an Asian breeding ground.

Late May–mid-December On the feeding grounds. Historically, this population spent the summer feeding throughout the northern Sea of Okhotsk, but now it is mainly off northeastern Sakhalin Island (in shallow water along the coast adjacent to Piltun Bay and in deeper water 30–40km offshore from Chayvo Bay), with at least some individuals off southern and southeastern Kamchatka early in the season. Peak numbers off north-east Sakhalin Island are reached by late July; some 20–30 individuals may remain in the area until mid-December (depending on ice conditions).

November–February Migrating south. The current route is uncertain. Historically, it included the coastal waters of eastern Russia, both coasts of Japan, the Korean

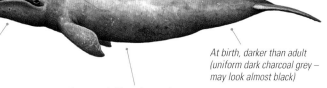

CALF

No barnacles or lice
(although obtained from
mother shortly after birth)

100–170 vibrissae (more prominent than
on adult – particularly on rostrum and
along margins of upper and lower jaws)

At birth, darker than adult
(uniform dark charcoal grey –
may look almost black)

Less mottled (may have a few
swirls of grey, black and white)

FLUKES

Peninsula and much of eastern China. Grey whales were once hunted off Korea, with peaks in December–January and March–April suggesting southbound and northbound migrations, respectively; however, despite intensive surveys, the last confirmed sighting was in 1977. There are records of only 15 strandings or sightings in Japanese waters during the period 1990–2012 (most concentrated during March–May – suggesting a northward migration – mainly along the Pacific coast, especially in Honshū).

December–April On the breeding grounds. There is limited evidence of a historical breeding ground in Japan's Seto Inland Sea (between the three islands of Honshū, Shikoku and Kyūshū). The current breeding ground is unknown, but is likely to be around Hainan Island in the coastal waters of the South China Sea (at the southwesterly end of the known range). While observations in China are infrequent (24 since 1933), they continue to occur and the few modern records are scattered along virtually the entire coast from the northern Yellow Sea south to the Hainan Strait. It is not known if WNP greys use coastal lagoons like the ENP population. In addition, some individuals summering off Sakhalin migrate to the wintering areas used by ENP grey whales, so clearly not all grey whales in the region share a common breeding ground.

February–May Migrating north. The current route is uncertain (see above).

NORTH ATLANTIC POPULATION

Grey whales once occurred on both sides of the North Atlantic (indeed, Lilljeborg's original description of the species in 1861 was from a subfossil skeleton found in

---

FOOD AND FEEDING

Prey Variety of benthic and planktonic prey; in northern seas, benthic amphipods are preferred prey and usually account for 90 per cent of diet (*Ampelisca macrocephalus*, up to 33mm long, probably most important); in feeding areas south of Aleutian Islands, main prey often planktonic mysids, but also benthic amphipods and other species. Off Sakhalin Island, will switch to most abundant benthic prey (e.g. isopods or sand lance) during low amphipod years. Will opportunistically take pelagic species such as red crabs and crab larvae, mysids, fish eggs and larvae, baitfish and squid. Over 80 species invertebrate and fish prey identified altogether. May shift foraging habits from benthic to pelagic as Arctic ecosystem changes due to climate change.

Feeding Most feeding during summer (when eats 1–1.3t food per day for *c.* six months), then fasts for remainder of year. Females with calves feed opportunistically on northerly migration, juveniles of both sexes on northerly and southerly migrations. Swims slowly along seabed and sucks up sediment (suction created by retracting its 1.4-t tongue and opening mouth – while throat creases allow its mouth to expand), then filters out prey. Usually rolls onto right side to bring head parallel to seabed (although some are left-handed feeders). Feeding behaviour creates long trails of water borne sediment ('mud plumes'), clearly visible from surface. May also skim-feed like right whales, or gulp-feed like rorquals, to exploit free-swimming prey.

Dive depth Mainly seafloor feeder (prefers 30–60m; range of 3–120m, maximum known 170m) but will feed opportunistically in mid-water and at surface.

Dive time On migration, 3–7 minutes; feeding dives typically 5–8 minutes; in breeding lagoons, 50 per cent of dives less than 1 minute; when resting, up to *c.* 26 minutes.

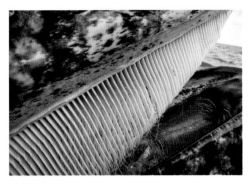

A clear view of the creamy-coloured baleen plates.

Grey whales breach frequently, and often repeatedly.

Sweden). There is very little information on their range or migratory routes, but there were possibly two discrete populations (with some overlap in Iceland). The population was predominantly extinct by the late seventeenth or early eighteenth centuries (the most recent subfossils found in the eastern North Atlantic are dated *c.* 1650, and in the western North Atlantic *c.* 1685). This is probably due to (or at least hastened by) early hunting by Basque, Icelandic and Yankee whalers. However, as ice barriers in the Northwest and Northeast passages are reduced, due to global warming, it is quite possible that we will start to see a steady trickle of grey whales arriving in the Atlantic from the Pacific. Ultimately, they could recolonise.

EXCEPTIONAL SIGHTINGS

Three sightings are noteworthy. On 8 May 2010, a single grey whale was observed near Tel Aviv, off the coast of Israel, and again on 30 May near Barcelona, in Spanish Mediterranean waters; it almost certainly came from the North Pacific via ice-free Arctic waters (Northwest Passage or Northeast Passage). On 4 May 2013, an entirely different individual appeared in Walvis Bay, Namibia – the first grey whale ever recorded in the southern hemisphere – and was seen almost every day until 9 June; its origin could be the same as the Israeli

grey, or it could have travelled around the southern tip of South America and across the South Atlantic. Two individuals were spotted to the west of the New Siberian Islands, in the Laptev Sea, in autumn 2011, extending the range of the species 500km to the west.

BEHAVIOUR

The grey whale is one of the most active large whales at the surface, frequently breaching (often several times in a row, exceptionally 40–50 times), spyhopping (with the eyes above or below the surface), and waving its tail or flippers in the air. May also appear to 'play' in the surf and will rub against pebble beaches, rocks, and even piers and boats, possibly to ease skin irritations caused by ectoparasites. Often inquisitive and may approach boats. 'Friendly' or 'curious' behaviour (allowing itself to be petted and stroked by whale watchers) is most common in the Mexican breeding lagoons (especially San Ignacio, where it was first reported in 1972) but is known elsewhere.

BALEEN
- 130–180 plates (each side of the upper jaw).
- The shortest and coarsest baleen plates of any whale – just 5–50cm long.

LIFE HISTORY
Sexual maturity Females and males 6–12 years (average eight).
Mating Mainly during short three-week period of oestrus in late November–December (while migrating south) or during second oestrus *c.* 40 days later on winter breeding grounds. Mating promiscuous (assortment of males and females mating with multiple partners – up to 20 consorting adults); no fighting between males (sperm competition more important) but courting can be energetic (group may take off in high-speed chase – dubbed 'freight-training' – presumably with female in lead).
Gestation 12–13.5 months.

Calving Every two years (sometimes every three years, especially in western population; 1 in every 45 females has a calf every year); single calf born late December–mid-Feb (25–50 per cent on southward migration, remainder in or around breeding lagoons); most births 5 January–15 February (median 27 January).
Weaning After 6–9 months, during July or August (but may remain with mother further 1–2 months, separating on summer feeding grounds).
Lifespan Possibly 70–80 years; photo-ID research in Baja California, Mexico, estimates age of some breeding females to be at least 48 years; maximum recorded 76 years (female).

HOW TO AGE A CALF

1–10 days: Uniformly dark, pronounced wrinkles (foetal folds) from mouth to blowhole, no barnacles (or very tiny barnacles), usually touching mother.

2–4 weeks: Wrinkles gone, deep dimples on head, barnacles appearing (but tiny), usually within 1–2m of mother.

4–8 weeks: Obviously larger, very curious and will approach boats without mother (though mother seldom more than 6m away), more barnacles, white scarring from mother's barnacles.

8 weeks +: Larger still, up to 50m from mother, developed mottled grey-and-white colour characteristic of adults by 12 weeks, fully grown barnacles only on whales one year or older.

GROUP SIZE AND STRUCTURE

On migration, grey whales are usually alone or in twos or threes, but up to 16 can be seen in unstable groups (inevitable given that they are all travelling in the same direction at roughly the same speed). Mother–calf pairs tend to migrate alone. More than 1,000 can congregate in a single winter aggregation area and breeding lagoon. On the summer feeding grounds, they are usually alone or in pairs, but there may be several hundred scattered across food-rich areas. Towards the end of the feeding season, recently weaned young animals may form groups of up to 12 or more.

Close-up of the barnacles and whale lice on an adult grey whale's head.

BARNACLES AND LICE

Grey whale calves are born free of external parasites, but rapidly acquire them as they grow. Adults have more than any other cetacean: on average they carry more than 180kg of acorn barnacles (one species) and whale lice (four species).

The barnacles are thought to be host-specific to grey whales (though there are isolated examples on captive bottlenose dolphins and beluga whales, and one wild killer whale) and their life cycle is synchronous with that of their hosts. They can occur anywhere, but are most prevalent on the top of the head and immediately behind (where they are exposed to maximum water flow).

Cryptolepas rhachianecti (whale barnacle)

- Up to 5.5cm diameter (fully grown after one year).
- Low profile (to avoid being torn off by water current).

Cyamus scammoni (grey whale louse – found only on greys)

- Largest and most abundant louse on grey whales.
- Male up to 2.7cm long, female to 1.7cm long.
- Two pairs of curly, branched gills coiled up against underside of thorax.

Cyamus kessleri (little grey whale louse – found only on greys)

- Two pairs of straight, unbranched gills (extensions project forward in front of head or to sides, where look like legs).
- Male up to 1.5cm long, female to 1cm.
- Rarely found on head or flippers of grey whale (usually in anal and vaginal slits).

Cyamus ceti (grey and bowhead whale amphipod – also found on bowhead whales)

- Two pairs of straight, branched gills.
- Male up to 1.2cm, female to 1.1cm.
- Many more little 'spines' on underside of rear segments than other species.

Cyamus eschrichtii (found only on greys)

- Male up to 1.4cm long, female to 0.8cm.

PREDATORS

Bigg's (transient) killer whales probably take up to 35 per cent of the grey whale calf population annually. It is possible that nearly every grey whale has been in a killer whale's jaws at some point (most have tell-tale rake mark scars); they will often fight back rather than flee. There are two major attack hotspots along the migration route – where natural features tip the balance in favour of the killer whales – Monterey Bay, California (mostly during April and May), and Unimak Pass, Alaska (mostly during May and June). Most successful attacks occur in Unimak Pass, where the calves are fatter and their mothers are tired after the long journey. Predation also takes place on the northern feeding grounds (mainly during June and July); as the season progresses, the calves grow bigger and the mothers feed and replenish their body condition – making them harder prey. There are fewer incidences of predation during the southbound migration, possibly because southbound whales are in far better condition at the end of the summer feeding season. The prevalence of killer whale rake marks on western grey whales (43 per cent) is the highest reported for any whale species. Cookiecutter sharks are also known to attack grey whales and bite out chunks of flesh. Large sharks (especially great whites) scavenge on carcasses and may kill small numbers of calves (with one reported attack on an adult in Oregon).

PHOTO-IDENTIFICATION

All grey whales are individually identifiable by natural (and permanent) pigmentation patterns on the sides of their bodies, which stabilise after their first year, combined with the profile of 'knuckles' on the dorsal ridge and scarring (though this changes with time). The underside of the flukes can also help with individual identification. While researchers target the dorsal fin region of the back (on both sides) for photo-identification, other distinguishing marks and injuries are often used as additional individual identifiers.

POPULATION

Due to whaling, the ENP population dropped to 1,000–2,000 or even the low hundreds by 1885 (one estimate at the time was 160 whales). Following protection, it has largely recovered. The most recent estimate is 26,960 (2015–16); this represents a 22 per cent increase in the five years since the 2010–11 estimate of 20,990 (consistent with four of the highest years of calf production – more than 1,000 calves per year – since calf counts began in 1994). Pre-exploitation levels are uncertain, but the most widely accepted estimate is 15,000–24,000 (although one DNA study estimated an original population size of 76,000–118,000). In 2015, the WNP population was thought to be fewer than 100 animals at least one year old; some 132–287 grey whales (depending on counting technique) feed in the Sea of Okhotsk/southern Kamchatka region regularly during summer and autumn (numbers have increased steadily since the early 2000s) but a large proportion of these migrate to coastal waters of Mexico in the winter. Pre-exploitation abundance of the western population is unknown, but guesstimates range from 1,500 to 10,000 individuals.

CONSERVATION

IUCN status: ENP population Least Concern (2017); WNP population Endangered (2018). The ENP population was reduced to near-extinction by intensive commercial whaling on the feeding grounds, on migration and around the breeding lagoons. The species was given full official protection in 1946 (although 320 were taken under scientific permit – and 138 illegally – by Soviet whalers in the 1960s). It has since made a remarkable comeback and was taken off the Endangered Species List in 1994. The IWC currently allows one aboriginal hunt: a maximum of 140 strikes per year by the Chukotka people, in the Russian Far East (during the seven-year period 2019–25). A smaller proposed hunt, by the Makah Indian tribe of Washington State, USA, to take up to five whales per year, is being considered (though the Canadian government recently declared the Pacific coast population of about 200 whales as endangered); one was harvested in Alaska in 2018.

The WNP population (if it exists as a separate population) is one of the most endangered whale populations in the world. It was hunted from the late 1500s to at least 1966 (though its drastic decline is largely attributed to modern whaling from 1890 to 1960, particularly off Korea and Japan, when about 2,000 animals were killed). It is now so rare that a very small annual mortality could push the population to extinction.

The main concerns today are oil and gas development in the Arctic (a particular concern for the WNP population) and declining sea ice (with complex but potentially severe ramifications for food source availability, new competition from other cetacean species and predator intrusions). Starvation was considered a possible cause of a widespread grey whale die-off in 1999–2001, in which at least 651 deaths were confirmed (the ENP population dropped to approximately 16,500 individuals). Entanglement in fishing gear, occasional illegal harpooning, chemical and noise pollution, disturbance from coastal development, ship collisions and the threat of expanding large-scale sea salt production in Baja California are other worries.

VOCALISATIONS

Grey whales have an extensive vocal repertoire, including rasps, croaks, snorts, moans, groans, roars, clicks, bongs and metallic 'bloink bloink' noises. The most common sounds in the breeding lagoons are bursts of metallic knocks, while there seem to be more moaning sounds on migration. Most vocalisations are low frequency, from 100Hz to 4kHz (though some are as high as 12kHz), possibly to circumvent the high levels of natural background noise in their coastal environment. They also make low-frequency clicking sounds, not unlike basic echolocation; these may be for long-range navigation, or to detect large targets such as other whales and broad topographical features.

BLUE WHALE
Balaenoptera musculus

(Linnaeus, 1758)

The largest animal known to have existed on Earth, the blue whale can be remarkably inconspicuous and difficult to see. But a close encounter with this true gargantuan is unforgettable. It was hunted relentlessly worldwide, until every population was severely depleted, and came dangerously close to extinction.

Classification Mysticeti, family Balaenopteridae.
Common name From the distinctive mottled bluish colouring (particularly when underwater).
Other names Sulphur-bottomed whale or sulphur-bottom (after the diatom film that can form on its body – especially on the underside), Sibbald's rorqual (after Scottish naturalist Robert Sibbald, who published the first scientific description of the blue whale in 1694), great blue whale, blue rorqual, great northern rorqual.
Scientific name *Balaenoptera* from the Latin *balaena* for 'whale', and the Greek *pteron* for 'wing' or 'fin'; *musculus* from the Latin *musculus*, which can mean either 'muscular' or 'little mouse' – perhaps an intentionally wry double-meaning by the great Swedish naturalist and taxonomist Carl Linnaeus; alternatively, Pliny the Elder, the first-century Roman naturalist, used *musculus* to refer to a fish having 'no teeth at all, but in place of them, the interior of the mouth is lined with bristles' (i.e. a baleen whale).
Taxonomy Five subspecies are currently recognised (though there is still debate about whether they should be subspecies or races): northern blue whale (*B. m. musculus*), Antarctic or 'true' blue whale (*B. m. intermedia*), northern Indian Ocean blue whale (*B. m. indica*), pygmy blue whale (*B. m. brevicauda*) (a remarkable oxymoron) and Chilean blue whale (unnamed subspecies). The first two share a similar external form (though they differ genetically and acoustically). It has been suggested that *indica* and *brevicauda* may belong to the same subspecies, but their geographical distribution is fairly discrete and their breeding cycle is six months out of phase.

ADULT

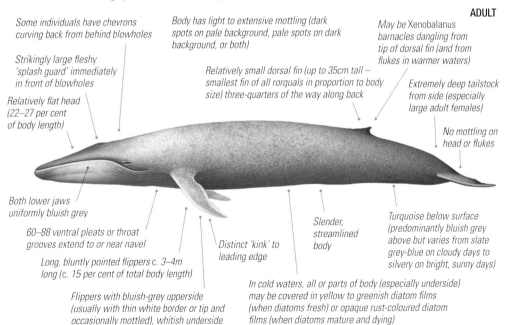

Some individuals have chevrons curving back from behind blowholes

Strikingly large fleshy 'splash guard' immediately in front of blowholes

Relatively flat head (22–27 per cent of body length)

Body has light to extensive mottling (dark spots on pale background, pale spots on dark background, or both)

Relatively small dorsal fin (up to 35cm tall – smallest fin of all rorquals in proportion to body size) three-quarters of the way along back

May be Xenobalanus barnacles dangling from tip of dorsal fin (and from flukes in warmer waters)

Extremely deep tailstock from side (especially large adult females)

No mottling on head or flukes

Both lower jaws uniformly bluish grey

60–88 ventral pleats or throat grooves extend to or near navel

Long, bluntly pointed flippers c. 3–4m long (c. 15 per cent of total body length)

Distinct 'kink' to leading edge

Slender, streamlined body

Turquoise below surface (predominantly bluish grey above but varies from slate grey-blue on cloudy days to silvery on bright, sunny days)

Flippers with bluish-grey upperside (usually with thin white border or tip and occasionally mottled), whitish underside

In cold waters, all or parts of body (especially underside) may be covered in yellow to greenish diatom films (when diatoms fresh) or opaque rust-coloured diatom films (when diatoms mature and dying)

AT A GLANCE
- Worldwide (though patchy distribution)
- Extra-large size
- Streamlined body shape
- Mottled bluish-grey colour
- Turquoise underwater (when viewed from surface)

- Small to large dorsal fin three-quarters of the way along back
- Prominent blowhole 'splash guard'
- Extremely deep tailstock
- Often raises flukes on diving

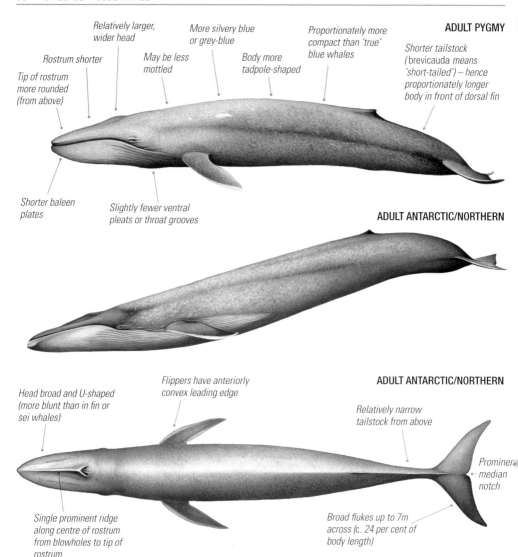

ADULT PYGMY

Tip of rostrum more rounded (from above)

Rostrum shorter

Relatively larger, wider head

May be less mottled

More silvery blue or grey-blue

Body more tadpole-shaped

Proportionately more compact than 'true' blue whales

Shorter tailstock (brevicauda means 'short-tailed') – hence proportionately longer body in front of dorsal fin

Shorter baleen plates

Slightly fewer ventral pleats or throat grooves

ADULT ANTARCTIC/NORTHERN

ADULT ANTARCTIC/NORTHERN

Head broad and U-shaped (more blunt than in fin or sei whales)

Flippers have anteriorly convex leading edge

Relatively narrow tailstock from above

Prominent median notch

Single prominent ridge along centre of rostrum from blowholes to tip of rostrum

Broad flukes up to 7m across (c. 24 per cent of body length)

SIMILAR SPECIES

Easy to identify at close range by the mottled bluish-grey colour, the blue whale generally appears paler than all other species of large whale – except the grey whale. At a distance, it could be confused with a fin or sei whale. The huge size may aid in identification, but it cannot be distinguished by size alone (there is substantial overlap with adult fin and sei whales). Blow height and shape can be useful – and blue whale blows tend to be denser – but there is great variability within species and some large fin and sei whales can also have exceptionally tall blows. There are key differences in head shape and dorsal fin shape, size and position, and many blue whales fluke (fin and sei whales virtually never do). Telling pygmy blue whales from 'true' blue whales can be difficult, except by experienced observers under ideal conditions, since the

differences are subtle. Hybrids between blue whales and fin whales are common; at least one sei–blue hybrid has been confirmed.

DISTRIBUTION

Occurs from the tropics to the edge of the pack ice in both hemispheres, though distribution is patchy and it is rare in most equatorial waters and in the centre portions of major ocean basins (such as the 35–45°S band in the South Atlantic). Most populations are migratory – moving between productive, higher-latitude feeding areas in summer and early autumn, and lower-latitude breeding and feeding areas in winter – but at least one population (in the northern Indian Ocean) is largely resident year-round. Unlike most other baleen whales, blue whales feed year-round and food availability probably dictates

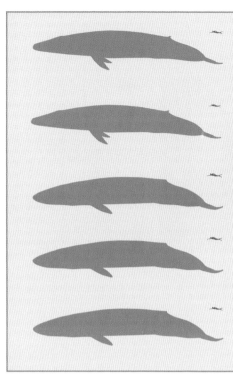

SIZE – NORTHERN
L: ♂ 23–26m, ♀ 24–27m; **WT:** 70–135t; **MAX:** 28.1m, 150t
Calf – L: 6–7m; **WT:** 2–3t
Female longer than male (in all subspecies).

SIZE – ANTARCTIC
L: ♂ 24–27m, ♀ 24–29m; **WT:** 75–150t; **MAX:** 33.58m, 190t
(though these max. sizes were estimated by non-standard
measurements at whaling stations).
Calf – L: 7–8m; **WT:** 2.7–3.6kg

SIZE – NORTHERN INDIAN OCEAN
L: ♂ 20–22m, ♀ 21–23m;
WT: 70–95t; **MAX:** 24m, 130t

SIZE – PYGMY
L: ♂ 20–22m, ♀ 21–23m; **WT:** 70–95t; **MAX:** 24m, 130t
Tends to be shorter than 'true' blues, but with a relatively
heavier body weight.

SIZE – CHILEAN
L: ♂ 22–25m, ♀ 22–25m; **WT:** unknown; **MAX:** 25.6m
Intermediate in size between pygmy and Antarctic blue
whales.

distribution for the majority of the year; they will forage
in productive areas anywhere. Seasonal movements
can be extensive, but they are complex and poorly
understood.

No specific breeding grounds have been discovered
conclusively in any ocean (they do not appear to be as
well defined as for humpback, grey and right whales)
but they are believed to be in tropical and sub-tropical
waters. One probable breeding ground is the Costa Rica
Dome (or Papagayo upwelling), in the eastern tropical
Pacific; another in the Galapagos Islands (for the Chilean
subspecies). The Gulf of California, in Mexico, is a definite
nursing area and possible calving area.

The species is mainly oceanic and associated with
waters deeper than the continental shelf, roaming widely
across ocean basins, but it also inhabits some shelf and
coastal waters (such as in the Gulf of California in Mexico,
the southern California Bight in the US, the Gulf of St
Lawrence in Canada, and Skjalfandi Bay in Iceland). It
prefers habitats marked by steep submarine topographic
features that enhance upwelling. There are still many
gaps in our knowledge of any overlap in distribution
between different subspecies, especially in the southern
hemisphere.

Northern blue whale (*B. m. musculus*)
In the North Atlantic and North Pacific oceans there are
four recognised populations:

1. North-west Atlantic – from Davis Strait and Baffin Bay
   at 60–70°N in summer, to South Carolina at *c.* 34°N
   in winter; there have been sightings as far south as
   Bermuda.
2. North-east Atlantic – from as far north as the Barents
   Sea and Svalbard at *c.* 80°N in summer (right to the
   ice edge), to Mauritania and Cape Verde Islands at
   c. 15°N in winter. Much variation: some individuals
   travel widely (e.g. one has been photo-identified in
   Mauritania, Iceland and the Azores), some push north,
   others remain south of the UK year-round. They are
   generally pushing further north with the rapid warming
   in the Arctic and resultant sea ice losses (with more
   frequent sightings in Svalbard, for example).
3. North-east Pacific – from as far north as the Aleutian
   Islands at *c.* 55°N in summer (but mostly off central
   California) to Baja California and south to the Costa
   Rica Dome at *c.*10°N in winter; some individuals
   live year-round off the central California coast and
   small numbers reach Hawaii; one individual has
   been matched between the Costa Rica Dome and the
   Galapagos Islands.
4. North-west Pacific – from Kamchatka, the Kuril Islands
   and the western Aleutian Islands at 45–60°N in
   summer, to the area south of Japan around the Bonin
   Islands at *c.* 27°N in winter (though this population is
   tiny after severe over-hunting).

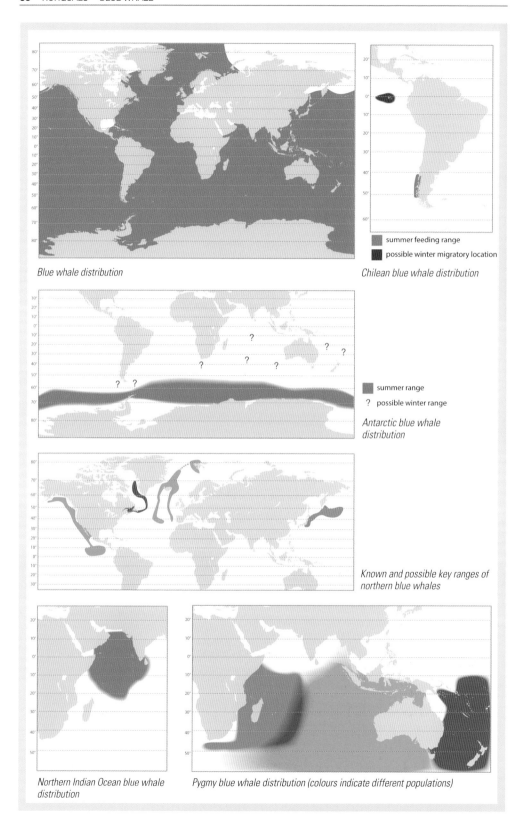

Blue whale distribution

Chilean blue whale distribution

- ■ summer feeding range
- ▮ possible winter migratory location

- ■ summer range
- ? possible winter range

Antarctic blue whale
distribution

Known and possible key ranges of
northern blue whales

Northern Indian Ocean blue whale
distribution

Pygmy blue whale distribution (colours indicate different populations)

Antarctic blue whale (*B. m. intermedia*)

During the austral summer and early autumn (mainly November–March) feeding season, Antarctic blue whales have a wide-ranging, nearly circumpolar distribution in Antarctic waters, south of 55°S. The main feeding grounds are between the Antarctic Convergence and the Antarctic pack ice (though some individuals remain in low- and mid-latitudes during the summer); calls have been detected off southern New Zealand during the southern summer.

Winter breeding grounds are unknown. Most are believed to migrate to more northerly, mid- to low-latitude locations (mainly May–October), where they are likely more clustered and localised. Possible wintering grounds include the central Indian Basin, the southern Indian Ocean, the eastern tropical Pacific Ocean, south-west of Australia, and off northern New Zealand (where there is likely overlap with pygmy blue whales); historically, the west coast of South Africa, Namibia and Angola may have been important, but this population was severely depleted by whaling and sightings are scarce today (though calls are heard May–August in the Benguela ecosystem). At least some appear to remain in Antarctic or sub-Antarctic waters year-round (such as along the western Antarctic Peninsula, in East Antarctica, in the southern Indian Ocean around the Crozet Islands and around South Georgia); they may follow the ice edge as it expands northwards in the southern winter and recedes in the southern summer.

Pygmy blue whale (*B. m. brevicauda*)

Found mainly north of 45°S in a broad area from the south-western Indian Ocean to Australia, Indonesia and New Zealand. The pygmy blue whale is ostensibly separated from the Antarctic blue whale by the Antarctic Convergence during the southern summer, but some overlap is likely (indeed, recent research reveals that the two subspecies occur sympatrically around the Crozet Islands). Current understanding is that there are three populations (which might be ranked as subspecies in the future): south-west Indian Ocean, south-east Indian Ocean and south-west Pacific Ocean.

The south-west Indian Ocean population is believed to migrate from wintering grounds predominantly over the Madagascar Plateau, south of Madagascar (but also probably around the Seychelles and off Kenya), to summering grounds in the sub-Antarctic (north of the Antarctic Convergence). Likely feeding areas include waters around Crozet, Heard and Kerguelen islands (there is probably overlap around Crozet with Antarctic blue whales, and Heard and Kerguelen with south-east Indian Ocean animals).

The south-east Indian Ocean population is believed to summer in feeding grounds that include the Subtropical Convergence Zone south of Australia, then move along the southern and western coasts of Australia (feeding in the Bonney Upwelling and Perth Canyon en route) to possible winter breeding grounds in the Banda Sea, in Indonesia.

The poorly known south-west Pacific Ocean population occurs off south-east Australia and New Zealand. It is reported in New Zealand during every month of the year, with reports concentrated in the South Taranaki Bight region.

Northern Indian Ocean blue whale (*B. m. indica*)

Year-round resident in low-latitude waters of the northern Indian Ocean, mainly between Somalia and Sri Lanka, with a small number of strandings outside the Indian Ocean as far east as Bangladesh and Burma. Showing parallels with the resident Arabian Sea population of humpback whales, these blue whales also have a northern hemisphere breeding cycle (they breed six months out of phase with conspecific populations to the south). They occur mainly north of the equator, but recent acoustic recordings show that at least a few individuals move south of the equator during the late southern summer and early autumn.

These whales are less obviously migratory – in contrast to most other populations of blue whales – but there appears to be a seasonal movement associated with monsoon upwellings. During the intense northern summer upwelling associated with the south-west monsoon (May–October), most feed in the northwestern Arabian Sea, off the coasts of Somalia and the Arabian Peninsula; some also feed in the area of upwelling off the south-west coast of India and the west coast of Sri Lanka. There appears to be a shift in distribution during the less productive north-east monsoon (December–March), when the whales disperse more widely to feed in areas with seasonally high productivity; these include the east coast of Sri Lanka, west of the Maldives and (at least historically) around the Indus Canyon off Pakistan. Many are believed to migrate eastwards past the northern Maldives and southern Sri Lanka in November–January and return westwards in April–May.

There may also be a year-round population close to the equator around Diego Garcia, an atoll in the central Indian Ocean, with small seasonal movements towards and away from the equator. These are mainly northern Indian Ocean blue whales, probably on passage, together with a few south-west Indian Ocean and Antarctic blue whales.

Chilean blue whale (unnamed subspecies)

The main summer and autumn feeding grounds (late December–early May) are in southern Chile, from the northern Los Lagos region (41°S) south to the outer coast of Isla Grande de Chiloé and to Isla Guafo (43.6°S), and east into the Golfo Corcovado (around the northern islands of the Chonos Archipelago). There is a general and wide-ranging northerly movement in late autumn, and it is likely that at least some migrate to winter breeding grounds in equatorial waters south and west of the Galapagos

CALF

Similar in appearance and shape to adult

FLUKES

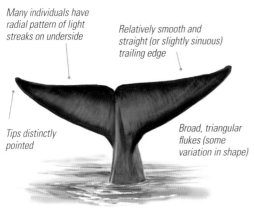

Many individuals have radial pattern of light streaks on underside

Relatively smooth and straight (or slightly sinuous) trailing edge

Tips distinctly pointed

Broad, triangular flukes (some variation in shape)

Islands. Antarctic blue whales have been recorded in southern Chile, but most of the animals here belong to the Chilean subspecies (there is a gap of 20° latitude between their southernmost distribution and most Antarctic blue whale records, they have a unique acoustic call type, and there are significant genetic and size differences).

BEHAVIOUR

Some blue whales raise their flukes when diving (*c.* 18 per cent in the north-west Atlantic and north-east Pacific, 25 per cent in the Gulf of California in Mexico and 55 per cent off Sri Lanka). Normal swimming speed is 3–6km/hr, but it is capable of burst speeds of up to 35km/hr if being chased by boats or killer whales (when swimming very fast, it sometimes almost porpoises above the surface, throwing up a large rooster-tail and pushing a mass of water in front as it flees). There have been a few observations of breaching blue whales – usually youngsters – leaping at an angle of *c.* 45° out of the water. Behaviour around boats varies from avoidance to indifference to inquisitiveness.

BALEEN

- 260–400 plates (each side of the upper jaw).
- Baleen plates are black, broad-based, and each *c.* 1m long (slightly longer in 'true' blues, cf. pygmy blue).

GROUP SIZE AND STRUCTURE

Usually alone or in pairs, though groups of 3–6 are known in some areas during summer. May be scattered in loose aggregations of 50 or more on good feeding grounds.

DIVE SEQUENCE ('true' blues)

- Surfaces slowly at shallow angle.
- Blows as soon as head begins to break surface.
- Distinctive blowhole 'splash guard' appears as rounded hump.
- Massive elongated expanse of back rolls into view.
- Dorsal fin often remains below surface until sounding dive.
- Before sounding dive, often raises blowhole and 'shoulder' region higher than other rorquals.
- Dorsal fin appears after head drops below surface.
- Arches back and tailstock.
- Many individuals raise flukes before sounding dive.

BLOW

- Slender, columnar blow can be at least 12m high (highly variable height).
- Denser and broader than that of fin or sei whale.

DORSAL FIN VARIATIONS

Highly variable dorsal fin (from small nubbin to triangular, hooked or falcate)

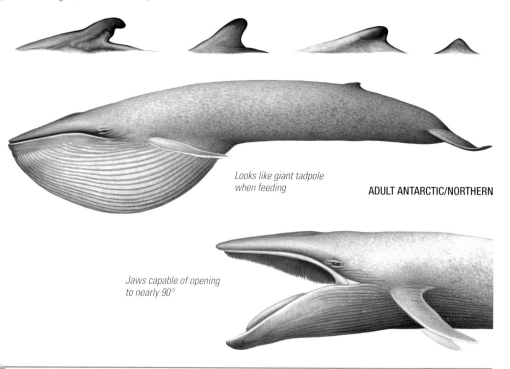

Looks like giant tadpole when feeding

ADULT ANTARCTIC/NORTHERN

Jaws capable of opening to nearly 90°

FOOD AND FEEDING

Prey Mainly euphausiid crustaceans (i.e. krill) typically 2–3cm long; some other crustaceans (including copepods, mysids and amphipods); very occasionally small schooling fish and cephalopods. In North Pacific, mainly *Euphausia pacifica, Thysanoessa inermis, T. spinifera, T. longipes, Nematoscelis megalops, Nyctiphanes symplex*; also pelagic red crabs or lobster krill (*Pleuroncodes planipes*) in southern California Current; will sometimes eat copepods (*Calanus* spp.). In North Atlantic, mainly *Meganyctiphanes norvegica, Thysanoessa inermis, T. raschii, T. longicaudata*; will sometimes eat copepods (*Temora longicornis*). In Antarctic, mainly *Euphausia superba* (up to 6cm long), *E. vallentini, E. crystallorophias, Nyctiphanes australis*. In southern Indian Ocean, mainly *Euphausia vallentini* (1.3–2.8cm long), *E. recurva*. In northern Indian Ocean, mainly sergestid shrimps.

Feeding Unlike most other baleen whales, it probably does not fast during winter (continues to feed on breeding grounds); off California, at least, most feeding during the day (at night, krill often spread out at densities too low to feed on efficiently) but in other areas (e.g. Gulf of St Lawrence) significant surface feeding at night; dives below dense layer of krill, turns upwards and lunges, rolling sideways or doing full barrel-roll and opening mouth, then drifts slowly forward as closes mouth (taking in up to 65t of seawater); lunge typically takes *c.* 10 seconds, purging water from mouth *c.* 30 seconds; typically up to 6–7 lunge-feeds per dive (maximum 15); when feeding near surface, it often surfaces slowly on one side or upside down (with one flipper and part of flukes out of water); 80t blue whale needs *c.* 1.5 million calories per day to survive (more than any other living animal); adult may eat up to 4t krill (40 million krill) on a good day.

Dive depth When foraging, dives typically to maximum 250m but probably capable of 300m or more (deepest recorded, 330m off Ecuador and 293m in Southern California Bight); dives deeper during the middle of the day – follows diel vertical movements of prey to feed at shallower depths up to surface later in day; non-foraging dives are typically shallower than *c.* 70m.

Dive time Feeding dives typically last 8–15 minutes, but 20 minutes is not uncommon during the daytime; occasionally up to 30 minutes (maximum recorded is 36 minutes); dives typically interspersed with long series of short surfacings at 15–20-second intervals lasting 2–6 minutes.

LIFE HISTORY

Sexual maturity Females and males 8–10 years (range of 5–15 years). Several reproductively active 35–40-year-old females known in the Gulf of St Lawrence, and at least two 30-year-olds in the Gulf of California, Mexico.
Mating Little known; female–male pairings seen regularly in Gulf of St Lawrence from summer to autumn, sometimes lasting up to five weeks (when approached by third whale – usually male – vigorous surface displays for 7–50 minutes as second male tries to displace first); around Costa Rica Dome, trios of whales displaying boisterous behaviour suggests courtship and mating; mating late autumn and throughout winter.
Gestation 10–12 months.
Calving Every two years (sometimes every three years); single calf born in winter.
Weaning After *c.* 6–8 months.
Lifespan Probably at least 65 years, perhaps up to 80–90 years (oldest recorded is 110 years); one male, called Nubbin, photographed as an adult of unknown age off southern California in 1970 and again in 2017 in the Gulf of California, Mexico.

PREDATORS

Killer whales are the only natural predators, though there appear to be few attacks in most parts of the world (mostly on calves and juveniles). However, *c.* 25 per cent of photo-identified blue whales in the Gulf of California, Mexico, and 42.1 per cent of pygmy blue whales off western Australia, have rake marks on their tails made by killer whale teeth – suggesting that attacks occur quite regularly but perhaps are not often successful.

PHOTO-IDENTIFICATION

Mottling is permanent and unique to each whale – researchers photograph the region around the dorsal fin to tell one individual from another. Many individuals have light striations on the underside of their tails, which can also be used for photo-identification.

WHY ARE BLUE WHALES SO BIG?

Blue whales feed on krill – small animals that swarm in mind-boggling numbers (up to 1,500 individuals per square metre – but live in patches that might be hundreds or thousands of kilometres apart. Anything that feeds on krill needs to be able to swim great distances quickly and efficiently (the relative energy cost of travelling declines as body size increases); able to store energy for days, weeks or even months at a time, to fill the gaps between krill patches (about a quarter of a blue whale's body mass consists of blubbery fat reserves); and able to ingest huge numbers of the tiny prey when it is available (feeding on a few krill at a time would be far too inefficient). Therefore, the ultimate krill-eating predator is a large-bodied, big-gulping, filter-feeding whale. And there are no size constraints thanks to the buoyancy of water.

POPULATION

Possibly 5,000–15,000 mature individuals, widely dispersed worldwide. The most recent regional estimates include: 1,650 in the eastern North Pacific; 1,000 in the western North Pacific; 2,280 in the Antarctic; *c.* 2,990 in the North Atlantic; 662–1,754 in Western Australia; 718 in New Zealand; and 570–760 in southern Chile. The worldwide pre-whaling population was about 300,000, including 239,000 Antarctic blue whales. There is some evidence of recovery in the eastern North Pacific, the central and eastern North Atlantic, and the Antarctic.

CONSERVATION

IUCN status: Endangered (2018); Antarctic blue whale Critically Endangered (2018). Commercial whaling of blue

Some (but not all) blue whales raise their flukes before a sounding dive; notice the deep tailstock.

whales began in Norway in the 1860s and had spread to all oceans (including the Antarctic) by the early twentieth century. They were highly sought after because of their large size, providing the largest yield per unit of hunting effort.

The final death toll included: 363,648 Antarctic blue whales in Antarctic waters (reduced to *c.* 360 survivors by the early 1970s); at least 20,773 northern blue whales (10,747 in the North Atlantic and 9,773 in the North Pacific), plus unknown numbers among 15,762 whales killed in 1900–39 that were not recorded or assigned to a species; 10,956 pygmy blue whales in the southern Indian Ocean and southwestern Pacific Ocean; 5,782 in Chile, Peru and Ecuador; and 1,228 in the Arabian Sea. The greatest numbers were taken between 1904 and the late 1930s (the highest toll was in the 1930–31 Antarctic season, when 30,727 were killed).

Despite rapidly declining numbers, the blue whale did not receive legal protection from whaling until 1955 in the North Atlantic (although Denmark and Iceland continued to take them under formal objection to the IWC's protection provision until 1960), 1965 in the Southern Ocean and 1966 in the North Pacific. However, there was illegal whaling (98 per cent by the former Soviet Union), especially in the northern Indian Ocean, until the early 1970s. Iceland's fin whalers killed (what they claimed to be) two blue–fin hybrids in 2018.

Major threats today include vessel strikes (especially by large cargo ships and tankers in the North Pacific, off Chile, around Sri Lanka and in the Arabian Sea), entanglement in fishing gear (scars from past encounters with fishing nets and other gear are sometimes observed on blue whales, though entanglement is not considered a significant cause of mortality) and chemical pollution (especially PCBs). Sunburn appears to be a growing problem in some areas (due to rising levels of UV radiation) and may appear as blistering. Increasing low-frequency ambient noise levels from shipping may mask the calls of blue whales, and noise from oil and gas exploration and military sonar may displace them from important habitats. If commercial exploitation of krill in the Antarctic expands in the future, or if there are any major changes in krill availability due to climate change, there could be serious consequences.

VOCALISATIONS

Vocalises regularly year-round, with exceptionally loud, low-frequency sounds (mostly 11–100Hz). Some of these are up to 189 decibels – the loudest sounds made by any animal – and, under optimal oceanographic conditions, one blue whale may be able to hear another vocalising from hundreds or even thousands of kilometres away.

Vocalisations can be classified as either calls (individual pulsed or tonal sound units produced at irregular intervals or as counter-calls between two or more individuals) or songs (stereotypical sounds produced by repeating calls in a regular sequence to form a recognisable pattern). These are related to a variety of behaviours, including navigation, mate attraction, aggression and possibly feeding. Blue whales of both sexes produce several types of calls, but only males sing.

Researchers have so far identified 13 different song types, corresponding to different geographical regions: three in the North Pacific, one in the North Atlantic and at least nine in the southern hemisphere (including a large variety in the Indian Ocean). Some song types have remained stable for more than 40 years. Most singing seems to take place as individuals travel between feeding areas – probably because a large blue whale can't afford to be singing when it could be eating.

Calls and songs from the same population show remarkably little variation: blue whales living in the same area call and sing at the same frequencies, for the same duration and in the same patterns. But these dialects, or sound signatures, are distinctly different from blue whale calls in other parts of the world – and can be used to distinguish one population from another.

In the eastern North Pacific, for example, there are four main call types. The commonest are so-called A and B calls, which are believed to be made only by males. An A call is a burst of about 20 monotone pulses less than one second apart; a B call is a downsweeping signal (20–16Hz) lasting *c.* 10–20 seconds and often given *c.* 25 seconds after an A call. A and B calls are often produced by travelling males, in a repetitive series that can last many hours. The usual calling pattern is ABABAB or ABBBABBB, with the intervals between parts and patterns both remarkably consistent. These are believed to be songs that might be part of courtship. C calls are much shorter (a brief upsweep 9–12Hz) and usually precede a B call. The D call is a highly variable downsweep (80–30Hz) some 2–5 seconds in duration and is produced by both sexes; it is believed to be a counter-call, not produced with the other call types, and often used among several individuals between feeding bouts. The D call is usually the only one audible to humans.

Blue whale mother and calf in the Gulf of California, Mexico.

FIN WHALE
Balaenoptera physalus
(Linnaeus, 1758)

The second-longest whale, after the blue, the fin whale is also one of the fastest – it has been dubbed the 'greyhound of the sea'. The distinctive asymmetrical pigmentation on its lower jaw – largely dark on the left and white on the right – is also a feature of Omura's whales, and some sei and dwarf minke whales, but is more marked on the fin whale. It has never been satisfactorily explained.

Classification Mysticeti, family Balaenopteridae.
Common name After the sharp dorsal ridge between the dorsal fin and the flukes (an alternative name is finback).
Other names Finback, finner, razorback, common rorqual, herring whale, finfish, northern fin whale, southern fin whale.
Scientific name *Balaenoptera* from the Latin *balaena* for 'whale', and the Greek *pteron* for 'wing' or 'fin'; *physalus* from the Greek *physa* for 'bellows', referring to the expandable throat pleats (alternatively, it is sometimes stated to be after *physalis* for 'a kind of toad that puffs itself up').
Taxonomy Three subspecies are recognised: northern fin whale (*B. p. physalus*) in the North Atlantic and North Pacific, southern fin whale (*B. p. quoyi*) in the southern hemisphere and pygmy fin whale (*B. p. patachonica*) off the west coast of South America (south to *c.* 55°S). It has been proposed that North Atlantic and North Pacific fin whales should also be separated into subspecies, due to genetic evidence, small differences in body proportions and coloration, and geographical isolation; there are several genetically distinct and relatively isolated sub-populations.

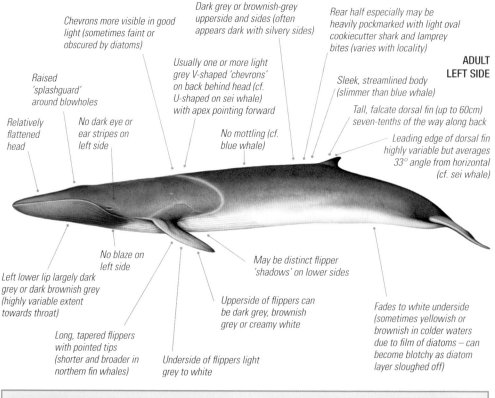

Chevrons more visible in good light (sometimes faint or obscured by diatoms)

Dark grey or brownish-grey upperside and sides (often appears dark with silvery sides)

Rear half especially may be heavily pockmarked with light oval cookiecutter shark and lamprey bites (varies with locality)

ADULT LEFT SIDE

Raised 'splashguard' around blowholes

Usually one or more light grey V-shaped 'chevrons' on back behind head (cf. U-shaped on sei whale) with apex pointing forward

Sleek, streamlined body (slimmer than blue whale)

Relatively flattened head

No dark eye or ear stripes on left side

No mottling (cf. blue whale)

Tall, falcate dorsal fin (up to 60cm) seven-tenths of the way along back

Leading edge of dorsal fin highly variable but averages 33° angle from horizontal (cf. sei whale)

No blaze on left side

May be distinct flipper 'shadows' on lower sides

Left lower lip largely dark grey or dark brownish grey (highly variable extent towards throat)

Upperside of flippers can be dark grey, brownish grey or creamy white

Fades to white underside (sometimes yellowish or brownish in colder waters due to film of diatoms – can become blotchy as diatom layer sloughed off)

Long, tapered flippers with pointed tips (shorter and broader in northern fin whales)

Underside of flippers light grey to white

AT A GLANCE
- Worldwide
- Dark grey or brownish-grey upperside
- Extra-large size
- Light grey V-shaped chevrons on back

- Asymmetrical lower lip coloration
- Single prominent ridge on rostrum
- Backward-sloping dorsal fin
- Rarely raises flukes on diving
- Alone or in pairs or small groups

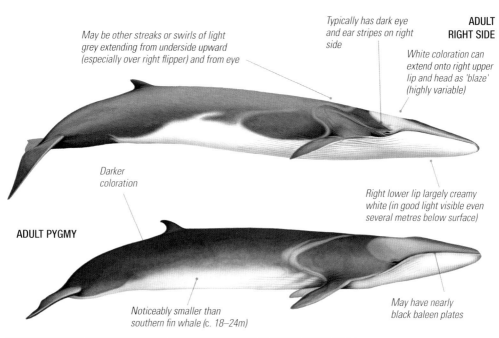

May be other streaks or swirls of light grey extending from underside upward (especially over right flipper) and from eye

Typically has dark eye and ear stripes on right side

ADULT RIGHT SIDE

White coloration can extend onto right upper lip and head as 'blaze' (highly variable)

Darker coloration

Right lower lip largely creamy white (in good light visible even several metres below surface)

ADULT PYGMY

Noticeably smaller than southern fin whale (c. 18–24m)

May have nearly black baleen plates

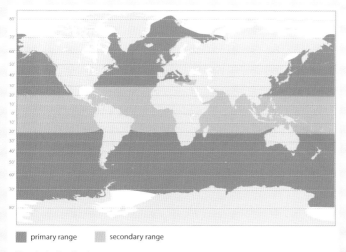

SIZE (NORTHERN)
L: ♂ 18–22m, ♀ 20–23m;
WT: 40–50t; **MAX:** 24m, 90t
Calf – L: 6–6.5m; **WT:** 1–1.7t

SIZE (SOUTHERN)
L: ♂ 23–25m, ♀ 24–26m;
WT: 60–80t; **MAX:** 27m, 120t
Calf – L: 6–7m; **WT:** 1–1.9t

Females are 5–10 per cent longer than males; northern hemisphere animals are smaller; body weight varies seasonally.

primary range   secondary range

Fin whale distribution

SIMILAR SPECIES

At a distance, confusion is possible with other medium to large balaeonopterids (blue, sei, Bryde's and Omura's). Fin whale is larger than all except the blue whale, though relative size can be difficult to judge at sea. At a distance, key features to look for are the dorsal fin shape and position and the dive sequence (e.g. the dorsal fin appears more rapidly after blowing than in the blue whale, and the fin whale is more likely to arch its tailstock than a sei whale). At close range, the fin has a single median ridge on its rostrum (take care not to be confused by rippling water making it appear like the three ridges on a Bryde's whale). The light chevrons and streaks distinguish it from all other species except Omura's whale, sei whale and some minke whales; the sei whale has a slightly arched head with a downturned tip and a tall, erect dorsal fin, and usually does not have asymmetrically coloured lower jaws; Omura's

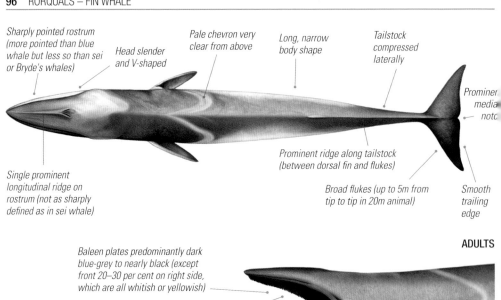

Sharply pointed rostrum (more pointed than blue whale but less so than sei or Bryde's whales)

Head slender and V-shaped

Pale chevron very clear from above

Long, narrow body shape

Tailstock compressed laterally

Prominent median notch

Single prominent longitudinal ridge on rostrum (not as sharply defined as in sei whale)

Prominent ridge along tailstock (between dorsal fin and flukes)

Broad flukes (up to 5m from tip to tip in 20m animal)

Smooth trailing edge

ADULTS

Baleen plates predominantly dark blue-grey to nearly black (except front 20–30 per cent on right side, which are all whitish or yellowish)

Often striated with grey bands and fringed with horizontal lines of yellowish white, brownish grey or olive green

50–100 longitudinal throat pleats (extend slightly beyond umbilicus)

CALF

DORSAL FIN

Leading edge usually rises at shallower angle (average c. 33°) than in other balaenopterids

Tip not hooked (cf. Omura's whale)

Less erect and lower than on sei whale or Bryde's whale

Taller, more falcate and set further forward than on blue whale

Shape varies from falcate and rounded to triangular and pointed (tip always strongly directed backward)

Underside of flukes light grey to white with dark grey border (rarely raised above surface)

FLUKES

is considerably smaller, and its dorsal fin tends to rise at a steeper angle and is usually hooked. There have been reports of hybrids between fin whales and blue whales (with at least one female hybrid being pregnant); their morphology is intermediate between the two species, so they can be confused with either of them.

DISTRIBUTION

In summer, found in cool temperate to polar waters worldwide, in all major oceans in both hemispheres. Winter breeding grounds include sub-tropical waters but appear to be more widely dispersed. It is rarely found in the tropics (except in certain cool-water areas such as off Peru) or in high latitudes near the ice edge. Movements are complex: some populations appear to be migratory, with a general shift to higher latitudes for feeding in summer and lower latitudes for breeding (and less feeding) in winter, but they do not follow a simple pattern and breeding grounds remain uncertain (assuming such areas exist). Resident or semi-resident populations occur in the Gulf of California in Mexico, the Gulf of Alaska in the USA, the East China Sea off Japan, and possibly southern California and the central and western Mediterranean Sea (where there appears to be some mixing with seasonal visitors from the North Atlantic). Absent from the Black Sea, and scarce in the Baltic Sea, the Persian Gulf, the Red Sea, the Caribbean and the Gulf of Mexico.

Density tends to be higher near or seaward of the continental shelf edge, but it is frequently seen over the shelf and close to shore where the water is deep enough. Typically, it is in water deeper than 200m (100m in some regions) wherever topographic and oceanographic conditions concentrate prey.

The warm waters of the Gulf Stream appear to moderate annual migration cycles in the North Atlantic. Movements vary from year to year but there is evidence that fin whales may occur to some extent throughout the range year-round. They are known from Cape Hatteras (35°N) and the Cape Verde Islands (14°N), north as far as Svalbard at *c.* 80°N (but rarely far into the Barents Sea), and into the Davis Strait and Baffin Bay at *c.* 69°N (but rarely into the inner Canadian Arctic).

In the North Pacific, there are some north–south movements but overall there is relatively little seasonality in distribution. They range from southern Baja California and the East China Sea, north into the Gulf of Alaska, much of the Sea of Okhotsk and into the Bering Sea (they are present year-round in the southern Bering Sea); later in the summer, they are even in the northern Chukchi Sea (though rarely into the Beaufort Sea).

In the southern hemisphere, they appear to be more migratory. In summer they occur mainly between 40°S and 60°S in the South Atlantic and southern Indian Ocean, and between 50°S and to beyond the Antarctic Circle (66°30′S) in the South Pacific. Traditional wintering areas may have included west of northern Chile and Peru, east of Brazil, off the west coast of Africa, southern Africa, off East Africa and Madagascar, north-west of Western Australia, in the Coral Sea, and in the Fiji Sea and adjacent waters; however, after decades of commercial whaling, they are now rare in many of these locations.

BEHAVIOUR

Capable of swimming exceptionally fast – the normal cruising speed is 9–15km/h and it can do 37km/h for short bursts. Rarely breaches (more when feeling harassed). Often forms mixed schools with blue whales and sometimes associates with pilot whales and dolphins; often seen in large feeding aggregations with humpback whales, minke whales, Atlantic white-sided dolphins and other species. Typically, neither avoids boats nor approaches them, but it can be quite approachable and is sometimes curious.

BALEEN

- 260–480 (average *c.* 350–390) plates (each side of the upper jaw).
- Longest plates *c.* 80cm; northern fin whales have slightly more plates on average.

GROUP SIZE AND STRUCTURE

Frequently seen alone, but often in small groups of 2–7; large, loose aggregations of several dozen (up to 100 in exceptional cases) may occur in highly productive areas.

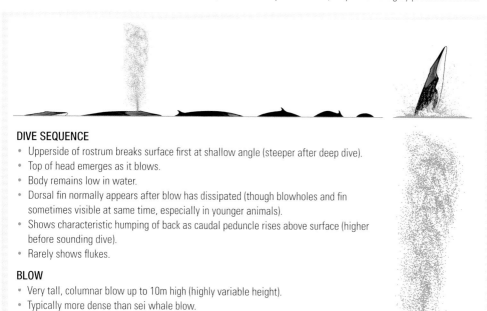

DIVE SEQUENCE

- Upperside of rostrum breaks surface first at shallow angle (steeper after deep dive).
- Top of head emerges as it blows.
- Body remains low in water.
- Dorsal fin normally appears after blow has dissipated (though blowholes and fin sometimes visible at same time, especially in younger animals).
- Shows characteristic humping of back as caudal peduncle rises above surface (higher before sounding dive).
- Rarely shows flukes.

BLOW

- Very tall, columnar blow up to 10m high (highly variable height).
- Typically more dense than sei whale blow.
- Only blue whale blow regularly taller (humpback and sei whale blows can occasionally be as tall).

FOOD AND FEEDING

Prey Opportunistic, depending on locality, season and availability. Northern hemisphere: mainly krill (especially northern krill), also copepods, schooling fish (including herring, mackerel, cod, pollock, capelin, sardines, sand lance, blue whiting), some small squid. Southern hemisphere: almost exclusively krill (especially sub-Antarctic krill), also other planktonic crustaceans.

Feeding Feeds intensively in summer (up to 1t per day), consumes much less in winter; lunge-feeder (often rolling on side – typically to the right); mouth opens to almost 90° angle; no evidence of cooperative feeding.

Dive depth Frequently dives to 100m; in Ligurian Sea, frequently to 180m; maximum 474m; some feeding at surface.

Dive time Typically 3–10 minutes; maximum 25 minutes.

Long-term bonds between individuals are rare (except mother–calf pairs) and group composition tends to be dynamic (with individuals frequently moving between groups).

PREDATORS

Killer whales. Frequently bears scars from killer whale attacks on flippers, flukes and sides. Like other rorquals, the fin whale is a 'flight species', using a combination of high speed and stamina as its main escape strategy (rather than fighting back).

PHOTO-IDENTIFICATION

Pattern of the light blaze and chevrons on the back, as well as the size and shape of the dorsal fin and scarring.

POPULATION

More than *c.* 100,000 mature individuals, and believed to be increasing in some areas. Approximate estimates include: 90,400 in the North Atlantic (including the Mediterranean Sea) and 38,200 in the Antarctic; there is no overall abundance estimate for the North Pacific (regional estimates total at least 9,300 – but the actual figure is probably several times as high). The North Atlantic population consists of: 53,600 in the Faroes, East Greenland, Iceland, Norway and Jan Mayen region; 18,100 around Portugal, Spain, France and the UK; 6,400 off East Greenland; 5,000 in the Mediterranean Sea; 7,300 off the east coast of North America and West Greenland.

CONSERVATION

IUCN status: Vulnerable (2018); Mediterranean sub-population Vulnerable (2018). Hunted relentlessly in all major oceans from the late 1860s onwards; the peak was 1935–70, when as many as 30,000 were taken annually and the fin whale formed the largest part of worldwide catches. Some 147,607 were taken in the northern hemisphere (split roughly 50:50 between the North Atlantic and North Pacific), and 726,461 in the southern hemisphere. Protected in 1976 in the North Pacific, 1976–77 in the Southern Ocean and 1987 in the North Atlantic. Some populations appear to be recovering. Still being hunted today, albeit on a much smaller scale: West Greenland has an annual strike limit of 19 per year (under the IWC's aboriginal subsistence whaling regulations 2019–25); Iceland has killed nearly 1,000 since it resumed commercial whaling in 2006 (with a self-allocated quota of 154 per year, rising to 161 in 2018); there was a short reprieve 2016–17, but fin whaling resumed in 2018; and small numbers have been taken by Japan in the Antarctic under its so-called scientific whaling (though none since 2011). There is currently no whaling for fin whales in

Fin whales rarely breach.

LIFE HISTORY

Sexual maturity Females 7–8 years, males 5–7 years (age at sexual maturity pre-1930s was 10–12 years, but dropped after whaling drastically depleted population); physical maturity *c.* 25 years in both sexes.

Mating Believed to be competition between males over females; limited evidence of mating in groups of 3–4, with two copulating and attendant males as bystanders.

Gestation 11–11.5 months.

Calving Every two years (occasionally three); single calf born with peaks in November–December (northern hemisphere), May–June (southern hemisphere); as many as six foetuses recorded, but no known cases of more than one offspring successfully reared.

Weaning After 6–7 months.

Lifespan Up to 80–90 years (oldest recorded 114 years).

the North Pacific. Other threats include entanglement in fishing nets (uncommon but not unknown), overfishing of prey species, vessel strikes (of all the great whales, the fin whale is the most frequently reported as being hit by ships), noise pollution (especially military sonar, seismic testing and heavy shipping) and possibly ingestion of microplastics.

VOCALISATIONS

Makes a variety of very loud, low-frequency moans and grunts, and higher-frequency pulses, in the range of *c.* 18–300Hz. Best known is the male's relatively simple song – dubbed the '20Hz pulse' – which consists of low-frequency, downward-sweeping pulses of 23–18Hz, each

lasting about one second. A song can be composed of single pulses repeated at fixed intervals of about 7–26 seconds (so-called 'singlets'), or with two or three different alternating intervals (known as 'doublets' and 'triplets'). Not counting rest periods between bouts of singing, a song can last as long as 32.5 hours. The fin whale's song is one of the loudest biological sounds in the ocean – up to 186 decibels – and can be heard from hundreds of kilometres away. It is sung year-round, with variations according to the season, but mostly during the winter (it probably has a reproductive function, to attract females from great distances). There is evidence of differences in song structure between populations.

When fin whales (and other rorquals) begin to exhale, there may be a lateral branch on either side in addition to the single vertical blow.

Fin whales are sleek and streamlined.

The characteristic V-shaped chevron, as well as the dark eye stripe and the white lower jaw (both features of the right-hand side), are clearly visible in these feeding fin whales.

SEI WHALE
Balaenoptera borealis

Lesson, 1828

The enigmatic sei whale is the third-longest whale, yet it is surprisingly poorly known. This is partly because in the past it was often confused in whaling records and scientific accounts with Bryde's (and possibly Omura's) whales.

Classification Mysticeti, family Balaenopteridae.

Common name From the Norwegian *seihval* after the *seje* fish (*Pollachius virens* – English names include pollock, saithe, coley and coalfish) and *hval* for 'whale'; the two species often appeared off northern Norway at the same time (presumably feeding on the same prey); pronounced 'say' or 'sigh' (the Norwegian pronunciation is halfway between the two).

Other names Coalfish whale, sardine whale, lesser fin whale, pollack whale, Japan finner, northern rorqual, Rudolphi's rorqual (after Swedish-born naturalist Karl Asmund Rudolphi, who made an early description of the type specimen).

Scientific name *Balaenoptera* from the Latin *balaena* for 'whale', and the Greek *pteron* for 'wing' or 'fin'; *borealis* from the Latin *borealis* for 'of the north'.

Taxonomy Two subspecies are recognised by some authorities: northern sei whale (*B. b. borealis*) and southern sei whale (*B. b. schlegelii*); there is currently insufficient evidence of genetic differences, but the southern grows larger and the seasonal migrations of the two groups are out of sync (i.e. they have limited opportunity to meet).

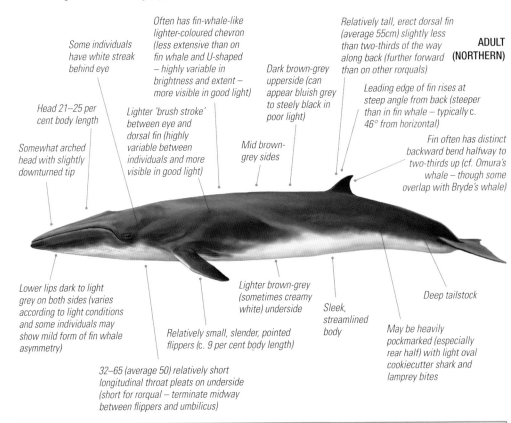

Often has fin-whale-like lighter-coloured chevron (less extensive than on fin whale and U-shaped – highly variable in brightness and extent – more visible in good light)

Some individuals have white streak behind eye

Relatively tall, erect dorsal fin (average 55cm) slightly less than two-thirds of the way along back (further forward than on other rorquals)

ADULT (NORTHERN)

Dark brown-grey upperside (can appear bluish grey to steely black in poor light)

Head 21–25 per cent body length

Lighter 'brush stroke' between eye and dorsal fin (highly variable between individuals and more visible in good light)

Leading edge of fin rises at steep angle from back (steeper than in fin whale – typically c. 46° from horizontal)

Somewhat arched head with slightly downturned tip

Mid brown-grey sides

Fin often has distinct backward bend halfway to two-thirds up (cf. Omura's whale – though some overlap with Bryde's whale)

Lower lips dark to light grey on both sides (varies according to light conditions and some individuals may show mild form of fin whale asymmetry)

Lighter brown-grey (sometimes creamy white) underside

Sleek, streamlined body

Deep tailstock

May be heavily pockmarked (especially rear half) with light oval cookiecutter shark and lamprey bites

Relatively small, slender, pointed flippers (c. 9 per cent body length)

32–65 (average 50) relatively short longitudinal throat pleats on underside (short for rorqual – terminate midway between flippers and umbilicus)

AT A GLANCE
- Sub-tropical to sub-polar offshore waters worldwide
- Large size
- Sleek body
- Dark upperside, lighter underside
- Pale 'brush strokes' on sides

- May have fin-whale-like chevron (U-shaped)
- Single prominent ridge on rostrum
- Rostrum has downturned tip
- Tall and erect dorsal fin (highly variable)
- Symmetrical head colouring
- Dorsal fin and blowholes may be visible simultaneously

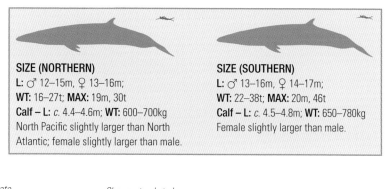

SIZE (NORTHERN)
L: ♂ 12–15m, ♀ 13–16m;
WT: 16–27t; **MAX:** 19m, 30t
Calf – L: *c.* 4.4–4.6m; **WT:** 600–700kg
North Pacific slightly larger than North
Atlantic; female slightly larger than male.

SIZE (SOUTHERN)
L: ♂ 13–16m, ♀ 14–17m;
WT: 22–38t; **MAX:** 20m, 46t
Calf – L: *c.* 4.5–4.8m; **WT:** 650–780kg
Female slightly larger than male.

Relatively narrow, fairly pointed rostrum (intermediate between broadly U-shaped blue whale rostrum and more sharply pointed fin whale rostrum)

Chevron tends to be more U-shaped (cf. V-shaped on fin whale)

Relatively small flukes (width c. 25 per cent body length)

ADULT

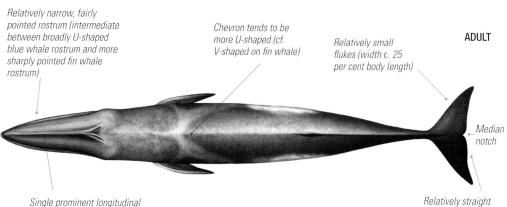

Median notch

Single prominent longitudinal ridge on rostrum

Relatively straight trailing edge

SIMILAR SPECIES

Confusion is possible with other rorquals, especially smaller fin whales and larger Bryde's, Omura's and minke whales. A combination of body size and coloration, relative height and position of the dorsal fin, the angle of the dorsal fin, head shape, symmetrical or asymmetrical lower lip coloration, number of longitudinal ridges on the rostrum and height of the blow should help to separate them. For a long time, sei whales were not distinguished from Bryde's whales (the two species overlap in mid-latitudes). However, the sei has a single median ridge on the rostrum (take care not to be confused by rippling water making it appear like the three ridges on a Bryde's whale); it also has a slightly arched head with a downturned tip and a 'brush' marking on each side, and often has a 'jointed axis' on its dorsal fin (although there is some overlap here with Bryde's whale).

DISTRIBUTION

Ranges from the tropics to the poles in both hemispheres, but most abundant in mid-latitude temperate zones. Distribution is poorly documented (especially in sub-tropical and tropical regions) and most information comes from whaling catches. Migrates between higher-latitude (cold temperate to sub-polar) summer and autumn

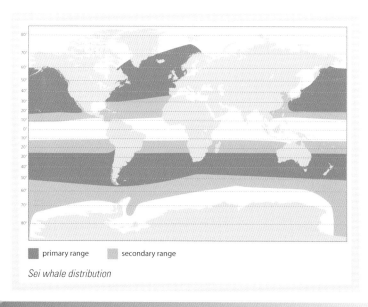

■ primary range   ■ secondary range

Sei whale distribution

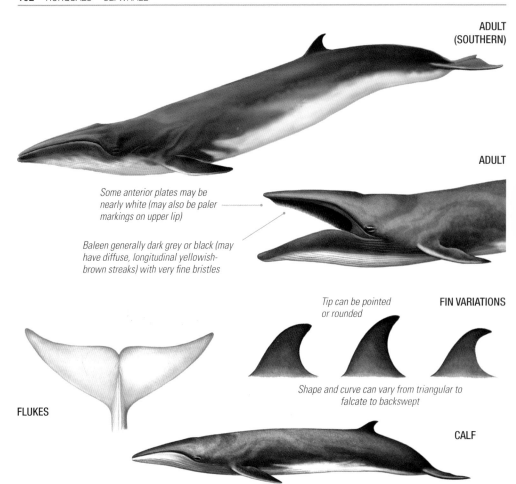

ADULT
(SOUTHERN)

ADULT

Some anterior plates may be
nearly white (may also be paler
markings on upper lip)

Baleen generally dark grey or black (may
have diffuse, longitudinal yellowish-
brown streaks) with very fine bristles

Tip can be pointed
or rounded

FIN VARIATIONS

Shape and curve can vary from triangular to
falcate to backswept

FLUKES

CALF

DIVE SEQUENCE
- Surfaces at shallow angle.
- Tip of rostrum usually just breaks the surface.
- Blowhole and dorsal fin often (but not always) visible at same time (characteristic shared with minke whales and sometimes juvenile fin and Bryde's whales).
- Tends to sink below surface (back relatively flat, though sometimes arches before deep dive).
- Fin disappears last.
- Very rarely, if ever, raises flukes.
- Sometimes dives and surfaces in predictable line (remaining visible just below surface during 20–30-second intervals between breaths) frequently leaving long series of flukeprints on surface – but often impossible to predict and can be erratic in surfacing behaviour.

BLOW
- Blow up to 9–10m high and columnar to bushy (highly variable height – typically 3–5m).
- Generally more diffuse than fin whale blow.

FOOD AND FEEDING

Prey Diverse diet varies regionally; mainly dense concentrations of minuscule copepods and krill, but also amphipods, squid, schooling fish (including sand lance, lumpfish, capelin, anchovy, herring, saury, lanternfish); in the North Atlantic it prefers pelagic copepods (especially *Calanus* spp.) in the late stage of their moulting cycle, when calorific content is highest; around the Falkland Islands, mainly lobster krill (*Munida gregaria*); in some areas, especially when feeding near the surface, often associated with large flocks of feeding seabirds.

Feeding The sei whale is unusual among baleen whales in having two modes of feeding: mainly the 'skimming' technique of right whales, but sometimes the 'lunging and gulping' technique of other rorquals; it feeds deeper during the day, shallower at night, corresponding to the vertical migrations of prey; most feeding occurs during summer (it feeds in winter but consumption is low); individuals may remain in a specific feeding area for several weeks if prey densities are sufficient; there are no reports of cooperative feeding.

Dive depth Varies according to vertical migrations of prey – limited evidence from Japan suggests averages *c.* 10–12m at night, *c.* 16–19m in day.

Dive time On feeding grounds typically 1–3 breaths at the surface over 20–30 seconds, then longer dives of up to 13 minutes.

feeding grounds and lower-latitude (warm temperate to sub-tropical) winter breeding grounds. Compared with some other rorquals, the migrations are not as extensive, the feeding and breeding grounds are less distinct, and it generally does not range as far north or south. It tends to be less predictable than other rorquals. It may abruptly disappear from areas where it had occurred regularly for years, and suddenly appear in other areas where it had been absent for years (or even decades); irruptions of sei whales are known as 'sei whale years' or 'invasion years'. One individual travelled 4,100km in 10 days (Azores to the Labrador Sea).

Generally considered a pelagic species with an offshore distribution along and beyond the continental shelf edge, especially in areas characterised by complex submarine topography such as seamounts and ridges. However, in some areas (e.g. Chile and the Falkland Islands) it regularly enters shelf waters and can be found in relatively shallow depths (less than 40m) and close to shore, including inside inlets and channels. Prefers sea surface temperatures of 8–18°C (occasionally up to 25°C).

In the North Pacific, mainly north of 40°N in summer, ranging to 62°N off Chukotka, Russia, in the west, and 59°N in the Gulf of Alaska, USA, in the east. More widely dispersed and poorly known in winter, but there are records from as far south as the Ogasawara Islands, Japan (27°N), in the west and the Revillagigedo Islands, Mexico

(18°N), in the east. Rarer in the eastern North Pacific, after heavy whaling.

In the North Atlantic, mainly north of 44°N in summer, with records up to 79°N in the east and at least 67°N in the west. Winter distribution is poorly known, but aggregations have been reported at 19°N off Mauritania; reports from the Caribbean and Gulf of Mexico are probably mostly misidentified Bryde's whales. Rarer in the eastern North Atlantic, after heavy whaling, and only an occasional visitor to the Mediterranean. Probably absent from the northern Indian Ocean.

Occurs throughout the Southern Ocean in summer, down to the Antarctic Peninsula (68°S on the west side), although it tends to remain north of the Antarctic Convergence, and the greatest concentrations are in cool temperate feeding grounds between 30°S and 50°S. Winter distribution is poorly known, and there is great confusion between sei and Bryde's whales in the whaling records; however, there is at least one reliable record of a sei landed at Cap Lopez, Gabon, on the equator (which suggests northern limits in the tropics).

BEHAVIOUR

One of the swiftest of the rorquals, capable of swimming at least 25km/h (even 55km/h in short bursts, according to some whaling records); the normal swimming speed is typically 3.7–7.4km/hr. It rarely breaches – when it does, it is usually at a low angle and ends in a belly-flop.

LIFE HISTORY

Sexual maturity Females and males *c.* eight years (age of maturity reduced by 2–3 years since populations depleted by whaling – was *c.* 11 years before 1935).

Mating Conception October–February (peak November–December) in northern hemisphere, April–August (peak June–July) in southern hemisphere.

Gestation 10.5–12.5 months.

Calving Every 2–3 years (normally two); single calf born in mid-winter; one case of conjoined twins.

Weaning After 6–8 months.

Lifespan Probably 50–60 years (oldest recorded 74 years).

Aerial view of a feeding sei whale, showing the extraordinarily long, streamlined body.

It has been seen in association with Peale's dolphins in the Falkland Islands. Most individuals will avoid boats, or are indifferent, but some can be curious and will repeatedly approach and swim alongside.

BALEEN
- 219–402 (average *c.* 350) plates (each side of the upper jaw).
- Longest plates *c.* 80cm; tend to be narrower than in other rorquals.

GROUP SIZE AND STRUCTURE
Varies according to location and season – often seen alone or in small, fluid groups of 2–5. Larger groups may travel together, and loose aggregations numbering tens of individuals can form in productive feeding areas. Sightings of apparent social groups have been recorded, perhaps engaged in courtship behaviour, involving high-speed chases and swimming on their sides with their tail flukes emerging from the water.

PREDATORS
Killer whales are the main predator and many sei whales show scarring from killer whale attacks. Large sharks may take calves.

PHOTO-IDENTIFICATION
Possible using nicks and notches on the dorsal fin, the pattern of scarring from cookiecutter shark bites, and other features such as killer whale tooth-rake scars.

POPULATION
No precise overall estimate, and few recent regional figures, but probably at least 80,000. May be in the order of 35,000 in the North Pacific, a minimum of 12,000 in the North Atlantic and 37,000 in the southern hemisphere.

CONSERVATION
IUCN status: Endangered (2018). Exploitation by commercial whalers did not begin until the late 1800s (sei whales were too fast to be caught until the advent of modern whaling techniques). The heaviest period of exploitation was between the 1950s and 1970s, following depletion of the larger blue and fin whales. Total numbers taken were: 14,000 (plus an unknown proportion of *c.* 30,000 unspecified large whales) in the North Atlantic, 74,000 in the North Pacific, and 204,589 in the southern hemisphere (including a record 17,721 taken in the 1964–65 season alone). Overall, numbers were reduced by *c.* 80 per cent. The IWC established a moratorium on killing sei whales in the North Pacific in 1975, in the southern hemisphere in 1979 and in the North Atlantic in 1986; however, Iceland took 70 in 1986–88 (under objection to the moratorium), and Japan had self-assigned 'scientific permit' quotas for the north-west Pacific of 100 per year in 2004–13, 90 per year in 2013–16, and 134 until it withdrew from the IWC in 2019; commercial whaling of 25 per year in Japanese waters resumed in June 2019. Its offshore distribution in many areas protects the sei whale from some human impacts, though threats might include ship strikes, entanglement in fishing gear and noise pollution. An unusual mass mortality of at least 343 sei whales in southern Chile in March 2015 may have been caused by a harmful algal bloom (associated with the El Niño event).

VOCALISATIONS
Vocalises at low frequencies, mainly below 1kHz. In the Southern Ocean, it produces 'growls' and 'whooshes' (100–600Hz, 1.5 seconds in duration), 'tonal' calls (100–400Hz, lasting 1 second) and 'down-sweep' calls (39–21Hz,

Sei whale mother and calf, showing the distinctive pale 'chevron' also seen on fin whales and Omura's whales.

lasting 1.3 seconds). It produces down-sweep calls in the North Atlantic (82–34Hz, lasting 1.4 seconds) and the North Pacific (39–21Hz, lasting 1.3 seconds and repeated at regular intervals of 5–25 seconds). Down-sweeps may be contact calls between widely dispersed individuals. Most vocalising is during the day.

A sei whale surfaces at a characteristically shallow angle.

The height of a whale blow can be deceptive and it is easy to underestimate. Seen properly against a dark background, these sei whale blows are easily 10m tall.

BRYDE'S WHALE
Balaenoptera edeni
Anderson, 1879

One of the least known of the large baleen whales, the 'Bryde's whale' is actually a complex of subspecies and possible species with taxonomic issues that are yet to be resolved. They all have one particular characteristic in common: three parallel longitudinal ridges on the rostrum (all other rorquals have a single ridge).

Classification Mysticeti, family Balaenopteridae.

Common name After Johan Bryde (1858–1925), a Norwegian consul and pioneering whaler, who helped to build the first modern whaling station in South Africa (in Durban, 1909). It is pronounced 'broo-dus'.

Other names Tropical whale; see taxonomy for subspecies common names.

Scientific name *Balaenoptera* from the Latin *balaena* for 'whale', and the Greek *pteron* for 'wing' or 'fin'; *edeni* in honour of Ashley Eden, Chief Commissioner of Burma, who secured the type specimen (which stranded on a beach in Burma in 1871) for John Anderson (who named the species).

Taxonomy Species-level taxonomy of the 'Bryde's whale complex' has yet to be resolved. Currently, two subspecies are recognised: the larger, pelagic Bryde's whale (*B. e. brydei*), otherwise known as the large-form Bryde's whale, the offshore Bryde's whale or the ordinary Bryde's whale; and the smaller, predominantly coastal Bryde's whale (*B. e. edeni*), otherwise known as Eden's whale or the small-form Bryde's whale. Given stro
ng genetic and morphological differences, as well as habitat partitioning, it is likely that these should be given full species status (in which case, they would likely be called Bryde's whale and Eden's whale, respectively). In addition, Bryde's whales in the northern Gulf of Mexico represent another distinct lineage, which probably justifies subspecies or, more likely, species status. The term 'pygmy Bryde's whale' was erroneously used for whales that are now known to be Omura's whale, which was described as a new species in 2003 (but was originally considered part of the Bryde's whale complex).

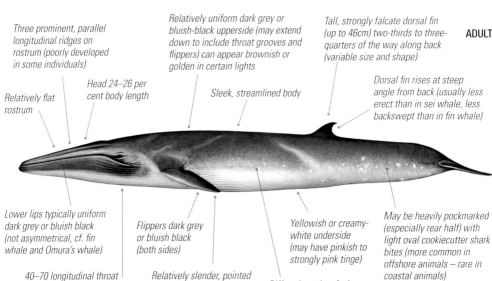

Three prominent, parallel longitudinal ridges on rostrum (poorly developed in some individuals)

Relatively uniform dark grey or bluish-black upperside (may extend down to include throat grooves and flippers) can appear brownish or golden in certain lights

Tall, strongly falcate dorsal fin (up to 46cm) two-thirds to three-quarters of the way along back (variable size and shape)

ADULT

Relatively flat rostrum

Head 24–26 per cent body length

Sleek, streamlined body

Dorsal fin rises at steep angle from back (usually less erect than in sei whale, less backswept than in fin whale)

Lower lips typically uniform dark grey or bluish black (not asymmetrical, cf. fin whale and Omura's whale)

Flippers dark grey or bluish black (both sides)

Yellowish or creamy-white underside (may have pinkish to strongly pink tinge)

May be heavily pockmarked (especially rear half) with light oval cookiecutter shark bites (more common in offshore animals – rare in coastal animals)

40–70 longitudinal throat pleats on underside (unusually long – reach to or past umbilicus – cf. sei whale)

Relatively slender, pointed flippers (c. 8–10 per cent body length)

Diffuse boundary fusing between dark upperside and light underside

AT A GLANCE
- Tropical to warm temperate waters worldwide
- Large size
- Sleek, streamlined body
- Uniform dark grey upperside, lighter underside
- Throat sometimes pinkish
- Three parallel longitudinal ridges on rostrum
- Tall, strongly falcate dorsal fin two-thirds to three-quarters of the way along back
- Dorsal fin usually visible after blowholes submerged
- Symmetrical lower lip coloration
- Typically arches back and tailstock on diving

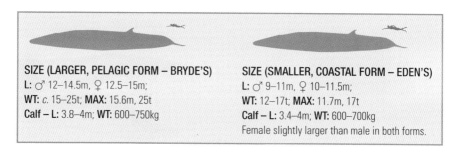

SIZE (LARGER, PELAGIC FORM – BRYDE'S)
L: ♂ 12–14.5m, ♀ 12.5–15m;
WT: *c.* 15–25t; **MAX:** 15.6m, 25t
Calf – L: 3.8–4m; **WT:** 600–750kg

SIZE (SMALLER, COASTAL FORM – EDEN'S)
L: ♂ 9–11m, ♀ 10–11.5m;
WT: 12–17t; **MAX:** 11.7m, 17t
Calf – L: 3.4–4m; **WT:** 600–700kg
Female slightly larger than male in both forms.

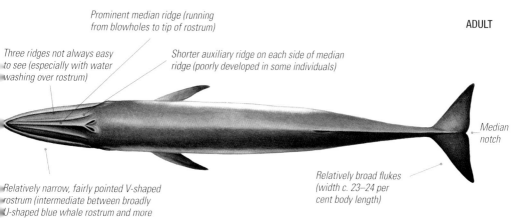

Prominent median ridge (running from blowholes to tip of rostrum)

ADULT

Three ridges not always easy to see (especially with water washing over rostrum)

Shorter auxiliary ridge on each side of median ridge (poorly developed in some individuals)

Median notch

Relatively narrow, fairly pointed V-shaped rostrum (intermediate between broadly U-shaped blue whale rostrum and more sharply pointed fin whale rostrum)

Relatively broad flukes (width c. 23–24 per cent body length)

SIMILAR SPECIES

A clear look at the distinctive three ridges on the rostrum easily identifies Bryde's whales (although some Omura's whales may also have a faint ridge on either side of the main one – and take care not to be confused by rippling water making a single ridge appear like three ridges). For a long time, Bryde's whales were not distinguished from sei whales (the two species overlap in mid-latitudes and can be difficult to tell apart). However, the sei has a single median ridge on the rostrum; it also has a slightly arched head with a downturned tip, and a 'brush' marking on each side; another useful feature is the 'jointed axis' on the sei's dorsal fin (although there is some overlap here with Bryde's whale). At a distance, confusion is possible with sei, fin, Omura's and minke whales. A combination of body size and coloration (Bryde's whale coloration is more uniform), relative height, position and angle of the dorsal fin, head shape, symmetry or asymmetry of the lower lip coloration, and height and shape of the blow should help to separate them. Field identification of different forms within the Bryde's whale complex is currently extremely difficult, if not impossible, although size and geographical location may be useful clues.

DISTRIBUTION

Circumglobal distribution in tropical, sub-tropical and some warm temperate waters in the Atlantic, Pacific and Indian oceans, roughly between 40°N and 40°S. Tends to concentrate

Bryde's whale distribution

ADULT

250–280 plates (each side of upper jaw) but up to 365 (including many rudimentary plates)

Longest plates c. 50cm

Plates tend to be yellowish or creamy white in the anterior quarter to one-third of mouth, often darkening to slate grey or dark grey (particularly on outside) in posterior three-quarters to two-thirds of mouth

Plates may be more slender in Eden's whale

Some individuals have asymmetrical coloration of throat and baleen plates

CALF

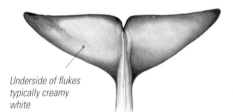

FLUKES

Underside of flukes typically creamy white

FIN VARIATIONS

Tip usually pointed

Height and strength of sickle shape variable

Often hooked at tip

Fin of some individuals may have slight backward bend halfway to two-thirds up (cf. Omura's whale – not as obvious as in sei whale)

DIVE SEQUENCE
- Surfaces at shallow angle.
- Tip of rostrum usually breaks surface first.
- Rostrum (and often mouthline) briefly visible.
- Dorsal fin usually seen after blowholes submerged (sometimes simultaneously, especially in younger individuals).
- Tends to arch back before deep dive (cf. sei whale).
- Strongly arching tailstock typically visible briefly after fin disappears.
- Does not raise flukes.
- When travelling, may blow mostly underwater, revealing very little of back or fin – disappears for several minutes before repeating same behaviour.
- Often impossible to predict and can be erratic in surfacing behaviour.
- Frequently does not leave telltale flukeprints behind on surface (cf. sei whale).

BLOW
- Blow up to 9–10m high and columnar to bushy (highly variable height – often only 3–4m).
- Often exhales underwater, then surfaces with little or no visible blow (especially if frightened by killer whales or vessel approaching too close).

FOOD AND FEEDING
Prey Mainly small schooling fish (including pilchard, anchovy, mackerel, herring, sardine, lanternfish); also squid, krill, pelagic red crabs, other zooplankton; appears to have prey preferences, but mostly opportunistic feeder, switching prey preference according to availability, geographical location, season and year.
Feeding Wide variety of foraging techniques; active lunge-feeder (often attracting seabirds and other pelagic predators); may skim-feed at surface like right whale; some observations of using bubble nets to corral prey; in Gulf of Thailand, uses passive feeding technique among schooling fish called 'trap-feeding' or 'tread-water feeding' (various subtle differences in technique include whale hanging nearly vertically for several seconds, with mouth wide open at surface, allowing fish to swim or wash inside, then lifting head up and closing mouth); in New Zealand, uses 'chin-slaps' to aggregate zooplankton prey, then side-lunges through concentrated patch.
Dive depth Often feeds at or close to surface; maximum 300m.
Dive time 5–15 minutes; maximum 20 minutes.

in water warmer than 16°C, in areas with exceptionally high productivity. It occurs in some semi-enclosed seas, such as the Red Sea and Persian Gulf, but is not found in the Mediterranean. Primarily pelagic or coastal, depending on the subspecies.

No extensive north–south migrations are known, although at least some offshore animals make shorter, general movements towards lower latitudes in winter and mid-latitudes in summer. Other populations – especially inshore in mid-latitudes – remain year-round in highly productive waters (e.g. the Gulf of California in Mexico, the Hauraki Gulf in New Zealand, and the Gulf of Thailand).

BRYDE'S WHALE COMPLEX
The so-called 'Bryde's whale complex' currently consists of two or three subspecies – or species – and the precise taxonomic status of all of these is still in dispute. There is some range overlap between Eden's and Bryde's whales.

Eden's whale
Appears to be restricted to the northern Indian Ocean and western Pacific Ocean, between 40°N and 40°S. Genetic studies confirm its presence in Oman, Bangladesh, off the south-east coast of India, near Sri Lanka, and in Pulau Sugi, Indonesia (in the northern Indian Ocean); and from southwestern Japan south-east to at least as far as the central coast of New South Wales, Australia (in the western Pacific Ocean). There are no verified records from the Atlantic Ocean. Primarily in coastal waters (with some records very close inshore) and over the continental shelf; it has not been recorded offshore. It seems to be resident year-round and there is no evidence of long-distance migrations.

Large-form Bryde's whale
Circumglobal distribution in tropical and sub-tropical waters of the Pacific, Atlantic, Caribbean and Indian oceans, primarily (though not exclusively) between 20°N and 20°S. Genetic studies confirm its presence in the north-west Pacific; in the South Pacific, south of Fiji, in

New Zealand, and off Peru; in the eastern Indian Ocean, south of Java; in the northern Indian Ocean, off Sri Lanka, Oman and the Maldives; off South Africa; in the Caribbean; and in the Atlantic. All Bryde's whales in the Atlantic Ocean are believed to be this form. Primarily offshore, but its distribution is more cosmopolitan than previously thought and appears to include some coastal habitat (the resident population in the Hauraki Gulf, New Zealand, for example, is primarily coastal). Some offshore populations are known to migrate, but these migrations appear to be relatively short for baleen whales (typically over 20°–30° latitude). Inshore populations tend to be resident year-round. Recent genetic studies demonstrate that broadly sympatric populations of migratory offshore Bryde's whales and resident inshore Bryde's whales off South Africa – which also differ in size and prey preference – are this large-form Bryde's.

Gulf of Mexico Bryde's whale
Bryde's whales are year-round residents in a small area of the northern gulf of Mexico. Historical whaling records suggest that they once had a broader distribution throughout much of the Gulf, but today they occur primarily off the Florida Panhandle, along the shelf break in waters 100–300m deep in an area known as De Soto Canyon. The current population is estimated to be just 33–44 animals. Within this population there is very little genetic diversity, yet these whales are genetically distinct from all other members of the Bryde's whale complex worldwide.

LIFE HISTORY
Sexual maturity Females and males 6–11 years.
Mating Unknown.
Gestation 11–12 months.
Calving Every two years (occasionally three); single calf born year-round, with possible peaks in spring (inshore animals) and winter (offshore animals).
Weaning After six months.
Lifespan Probably at least 40–50 years.

A rare image of a breaching Bryde's whale.

There are also size differences: based on measurements from 14 strandings, they appear to be intermediate between Eden's whale and the large-form Bryde's whale. In addition, their vocalisations are consistent with – but differ from – Bryde's whale vocalisations elsewhere in the world. The conclusion is that they represent an evolutionarily distinct unit, and warrant subspecies or species status

(in which case the Gulf of Mexico Bryde's whale would become the most endangered baleen whale in the world). There is some evidence that a small number of individuals may occasionally stray into the North Atlantic.

BEHAVIOUR

Occasionally breaches (typically coming out of the water vertically), sometimes multiple times in a row (70 times on one exceptional occasion off Ogata, Japan). When feeding, it typically makes sudden changes in direction, both underwater and at the surface. Behaviour around vessels ranges from taking flight to unconcerned, or even sometimes curious.

GROUP SIZE AND STRUCTURE

Generally seen alone, but sometimes in small groups of 2–3, and occasionally loose aggregations of 10–20 on prime feeding grounds.

PREDATORS

Killer whales are known predators. Large sharks may take calves.

PHOTO-IDENTIFICATION

Primarily using nicks and notches on the dorsal fin, sometimes combined with the pattern of scarring from cookiecutter shark bites (in offshore animals) and other features such as killer whale tooth-rake scars.

POPULATION

No overall global estimate. There have been problems of identity (earlier surveys mixed Bryde's, Omura's and sei whales). A broad guesstimate might be 50,000–100,000.

The sleeker, streamlined, uniformly dark body of a Bryde's whale.

Eden's whale trap-feeding in the Gulf of Thailand.

However, even this figure would be meaningless if the Bryde's whale complex is split into separate species.

CONSERVATION

IUCN status: Least Concern (2017). Never hunted as intensively as many larger whales, due to its small size, lower blubber yields, and absence from most cold-water whaling grounds. Prior to 1972, whaling statistics did not differentiate between Bryde's whales and sei whales, but in some cases it has been possible to infer the species by geographical location and time of year. During the period 1900–99 it is estimated that a total of 14,049 Bryde's whales were killed in the northern hemisphere and 7,913 in the southern hemisphere. Since the IWC's 1986 moratorium on commercial whaling, Japan has continued to hunt Bryde's whales in the western North Pacific: during the period 1986–2016 it killed 1,368 (734 under so-called 'scientific permit' and 634 under commercial quotas). Since leaving the IWC in 2019, it has set a self-determined annual quota of 150. Some were hunted at a few sites in the Philippines, until this was banned in 1997 (although illegal hunting may continue on a small scale); and up to five small baleen whales are still hunted from Lamakera, Indonesia, every year (although these could also be Eden's, Omura's, Antarctic minkes or dwarf minkes).

Other threats include entanglement in fishing gear, habitat modification, vessel strikes, oil pollution, agricultural runoff and noise pollution (from seismic testing and military sonar).

VOCALISATIONS

Known to make short, but loud, low-frequency moans, similar to the calls of other balaenopterids. These vary in frequency, duration, modulation and the presence or absence of harmonics, at least partly according to geographic region, but also according the group size. Most Bryde's whale calls have a fundamental frequency below 60Hz, last from one-quarter to several seconds and are produced in extended sequences. A single whale is capable of emitting two types of calls simultaneously. Different whales call back and forth.

The three longitudinal ridges on the head confirm that this is a Bryde's whale.

OMURA'S WHALE
Balaenoptera omurai

Wada, Oishi and Yamada, 2003

Omura's whale is the most recently described living species of baleen whale. Scientifically named in 2003, it was initially known from only a dozen or so specimens and a handful of probable sightings at sea. But in the past few years our knowledge of this slender, tropical whale has grown substantially.

Classification Mysticeti, family Balaenopteridae.
Common name After renowned Japanese cetologist Hideo Omura (1906–93).
Other names Often referred to in older whaling literature as small-form Bryde's whale, pygmy Bryde's whale, dwarf Bryde's whale or dwarf fin whale.
Scientific name *Balaenoptera* from the Latin *balaena* for 'whale', and the Greek *pteron* for 'wing' or 'fin'; *omurai* – see above.
Taxonomy No recognised forms or subspecies.

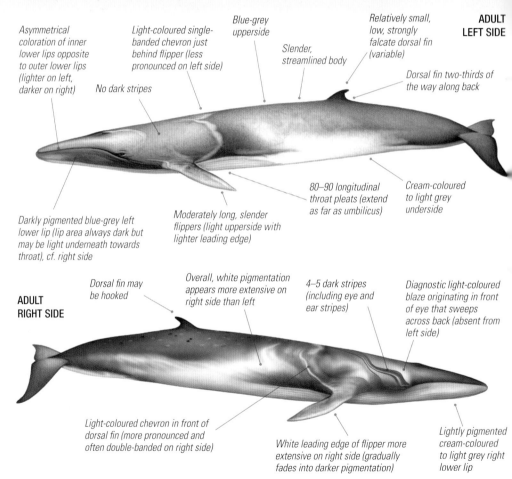

ADULT LEFT SIDE

Asymmetrical coloration of inner lower lips opposite to outer lower lips (lighter on left, darker on right)

Light-coloured single-banded chevron just behind flipper (less pronounced on left side)

No dark stripes

Blue-grey upperside

Slender, streamlined body

Relatively small, low, strongly falcate dorsal fin (variable)

Dorsal fin two-thirds of the way along back

Darkly pigmented blue-grey left lower lip (lip area always dark but may be light underneath towards throat), cf. right side

Moderately long, slender flippers (light upperside with lighter leading edge)

80–90 longitudinal throat pleats (extend as far as umbilicus)

Cream-coloured to light grey underside

ADULT RIGHT SIDE

Dorsal fin may be hooked

Overall, white pigmentation appears more extensive on right side than left

4–5 dark stripes (including eye and ear stripes)

Diagnostic light-coloured blaze originating in front of eye that sweeps across back (absent from left side)

Light-coloured chevron in front of dorsal fin (more pronounced and often double-banded on right side)

White leading edge of flipper more extensive on right side (gradually fades into darker pigmentation)

Lightly pigmented cream-coloured to light grey right lower lip

---

AT A GLANCE
- Mainly Indo-Pacific (also Atlantic)
- Shallow, nearshore tropical and sub-tropical waters
- Large size
- Distinctly counter-shaded
- Asymmetrical lower-lip coloration
- Relatively small, low, strongly falcate dorsal fin
- Body pigmentation similar to fin whale
- Single prominent ridge on rostrum
- Alone or in small, loose aggregations

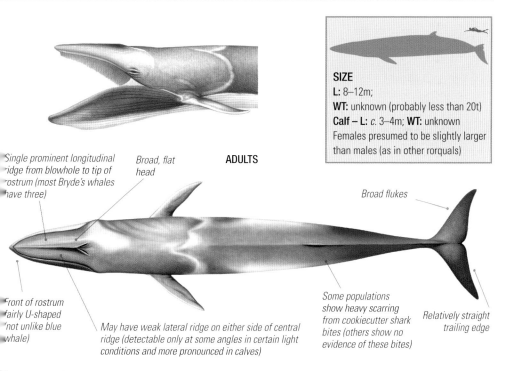

SIZE
L: 8–12m;
WT: unknown (probably less than 20t)
Calf – L: c. 3–4m; **WT:** unknown
Females presumed to be slightly larger
than males (as in other rorquals)

Single prominent longitudinal ridge from blowhole to tip of rostrum (most Bryde's whales have three)

Broad, flat head

ADULTS

Broad flukes

Front of rostrum fairly U-shaped (not unlike blue whale)

May have weak lateral ridge on either side of central ridge (detectable only at some angles in certain light conditions and more pronounced in calves)

Some populations show heavy scarring from cookiecutter shark bites (others show no evidence of these bites)

Relatively straight trailing edge

SIMILAR SPECIES

Confusion is possible with Bryde's, sei, minke and small fin whales. Bryde's has three longitudinal head ridges instead of one (though some Omura's may also have a faint ridge on either side of the main one, and rippling water on the head can be mistaken for ridges). Sei whales tend to be larger, the tip of the upper jaw is usually downturned, and the dorsal fin is taller and less falcate. Minke whales tend to be slightly smaller, have white bands on the flippers and have a more sharply pointed head, which usually breaks the surface at a steeper angle. However, the combination of a complex colour pattern, with chevrons and blazes, and asymmetrical lower jaws (light on the right side, dark on the left) can only really be confused with small fin whales. Pay attention to the dorsal fin, which tends to rise at a steeper angle and is often hooked in Omura's whale.

DISTRIBUTION

Knowledge of the distribution is limited and remains tentative; the range is likely to be broader than the current estimate as more populations are found. Most records are from the Indo-Pacific, on both sides of the equator, but it is also known from three records in the Atlantic. Whaling or stranded specimens, and confirmed or likely sightings, are from 21 range states. There are no records from the eastern Pacific – despite extensive survey effort – and this could represent a genuine gap in distribution. Three recent (and geographically distant) records from either side of the Atlantic Ocean – near Chott Boul, Mauritania, the Saint

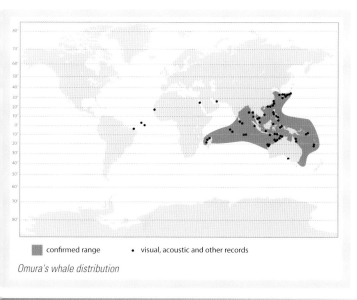

■ confirmed range   • visual, acoustic and other records

Omura's whale distribution

FLUKES

Irregular dark margins

Underside of flukes off-white

Gradually sloping front side

Often very hooked (variable)

Swept-back appearance

FIN VARIATIONS

Fin intermediate between fin whale (more graduated slope) and Bryde's and sei whales (more upright)

Fin typically strongly falcate (but varies to nearly triangular)

Peter and Saint Paul Archipelago in Brazil, and Pecém Beach, northeastern Brazil – are particularly interesting because they suggest that the distribution could be much wider. These animals could have been vagrants, but circumstances (the fact that they were juveniles, the great distances from the 'normal' range in the Indo-Pacific and the necessary inter-ocean passage through cold temperate waters) favour the hypothesis that the Omura's whale does occur in the Atlantic, but it is uncertain if it occurs regularly. Believed to be non-migratory, with resident populations. The type locality in the Sea of Japan (34°N) and the South Australia record (34°S) are the northernmost and southernmost records to date; the Australian record is probably extralimital. All records occur between 35°N and 35°S, with 83 per cent in the tropics between 23.5°N and 23.5°S. Records of 'small Bryde's whales' elsewhere may yet prove to be this species. No long-distance migrations are known.

Studies in north-west Madagascar show the species has a preference for shallow water – primarily 10–25m but ranging from 4m to 202m – with sea surface temperatures of 27.4–30.2°C. In this region, it is distributed exclusively over the continental shelf, within approximately 10–15km of the shelf break, and avoids both deep water off the shelf and very shallow coastal water and bays. There is some evidence of distribution in deeper water in the Solomon

Sea and off the Cocos Islands, and on the Mid-Atlantic Ridge, and this may be the case in other parts of the range (or at certain times of year).

BEHAVIOUR

Some information on behaviour, dive sequences, group sizes and vocalisations comes from observations since 2014 of a small population in north-west Madagascar. Breaching has been observed. Omura's whale frequently rolls at the surface when lunge-feeding, showing both a flipper and a fluke above the water.

DISCOVERY OF A NEW WHALE

For many years, Omura's whale was believed to be a small member of the 'Bryde's whale complex' – the so-called 'pygmy Bryde's whale'. But there are significant morphological differences – especially in the skull – and geneticists have confirmed that it diverged from the rest of the rorqual lineage much earlier than Bryde's or sei whales. It was described as a new species from nine specimens: eight killed by Japanese whalers (six near the Solomon Islands in 1976 and two near the Cocos Islands in 1978 – only recently identified from archived tissue) and one that died after colliding with a fishing boat near Tsunoshima Island, in the southern Sea of Japan, in 1998. The Japanese animal – an 11.03m adult female – is the type specimen.

DIVE SEQUENCE
- Head breaks surface at relatively shallow angle.
- Dorsal fin typically emerges just as head and blowholes submerge.
- Gently arches back.
- Dorsal fin clearly visible.
- Does not fluke on diving.

BLOW
- Diffuse, bushy blow, rarely conspicuous (height highly variable).

FOOD AND FEEDING

Prey Mostly krill (especially *Euphausia diomedeae* and *Pseudeuphausia latifrons*) and minuscule (as yet unidentified) zooplankton and/or fish eggs.

Feeding Frequently lunge-feeds at surface; observed feeding in areas with high densities of whale sharks (perhaps feeding on the same prey).

Dive depth Unknown, but probably typically less than 100m.

Dive time Unknown.

BALEEN

- 180–210 plates (each side of the upper jaw).
- Fewer plates than any other *Balaenoptera* species; longest plates 23–28cm.

GROUP SIZE AND STRUCTURE

Generally seen alone, in mother–calf pairs, in temporary pairings of two adults (lasting no more than 10 minutes), or in loose aggregations of up to six animals within a few to several hundred metres of each other.

PREDATORS

Unknown.

PHOTO-IDENTIFICATION

Possible using the dorsal fin shape, nicks and scars, the blaze on the right side and the chevron pigmentation patterns on both sides.

POPULATION

No estimate of global abundance.

CONSERVATION

IUCN status: Data Deficient (2017). Virtually nothing is known about its status or any threats. It was almost certainly hunted commercially – misidentified as Bryde's whale – and at least eight were killed by Japanese whalers under 'scientific permits' for Bryde's whales near the Solomon Islands and the Cocos Islands in the 1970s. There is evidence of sizeable captures by the Philippines artisanal whale fishery in the Bohol Sea and this is true of Indonesia and possibly elsewhere as well. At least eight individuals are known to have drowned in fishing nets in Japan, Thailand, Korea and Sri Lanka, and given its shallow-water habitat the species is likely to be vulnerable to bycatch throughout its range. Other potential threats include ship strikes, noise pollution (such as that from commercial shipping) and seismic surveys for oil exploration.

VOCALISATIONS

The Omura's whale is highly vocal. Its long, rumbling song is stereotyped, forming a distinct, consistent and recognisable pattern that is similar each time it is produced. Low frequency (below the range of human hearing), with an average duration of 8–9 seconds, it is repeated rhythmically every 2–3 minutes and continues uninterrupted for as long as several hours; this is believed to be a single whale repeating the song over and over again. Frequently, several whales sing together in a 'chorus'. The song is likely to be a sexual display, as in humpback whales, and is believed to be sung only by males. It has been heard year-round in Madagascar, north-west Australia and the Chagos Archipelago.

LIFE HISTORY

Sexual maturity Unknown.

Mating Unknown.

Gestation Probably *c.* 12 months.

Calving Unknown; single calf likely to be born year-round, but very limited evidence.

Weaning Unknown.

Lifespan Based on six specimens, oldest recorded is 38 years for male, 29 years for female.

An extremely rare photograph of a mother–calf pair of Omura's whales, in the Raja Ampat Islands, Indonesia.

COMMON MINKE WHALE
Balaenoptera acutorostrata

Lacépède, 1804

The common minke whale is the smallest rorqual and the second smallest of all the baleen whales (after the pygmy right whale). It has three disjunct populations: in the North Atlantic, the North Pacific and the southern hemisphere.

Classification Mysticeti, family Balaenopteridae.

Common name 'Common' to distinguish it from 'Antarctic minke whale'; 'minke' reputedly from a nineteenth-century German labourer, called Meincke, who was working as a whaler for Norwegian Svend Foyn (dubbed 'the inventor of modern whaling') and kept misidentifying minke whales as blue whales (thereafter, all small and undersized whales were mockingly called 'Meincke's whales' and, with slight changes in pronunciation and spelling, the name stuck). It is pronounced 'mink-ee'.

Other names Lesser rorqual, little piked whale, pikehead, lesser finback, sharp-headed finner, little finner (and various combinations of these); northern minke whale (for the two northern hemisphere species); nicknamed 'stinky minke' for its bad breath, or 'slinky minke' for its cryptic surfacing behaviour; see taxonomy for subspecies common names.

Scientific name *Balaenoptera* from the Latin *balaena* for 'whale' and the Greek *pteron* for 'wing' or 'fin'; *acutorostrata* from the Latin *acutus* for 'sharp' and *rostrata* for 'beaked' (referring to the sharply pointed rostrum).

Taxonomy Three subspecies are currently recognised: North Atlantic minke whale (*B. a. acutorostrata*); North Pacific minke whale (*B. a. scammoni*); and dwarf (occasionally white-shouldered) minke whale (*B. a. unnamed subspecies*).

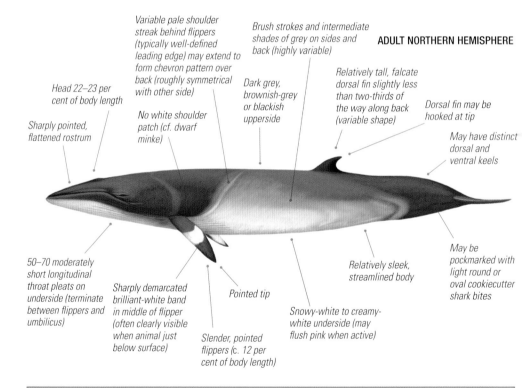

Variable pale shoulder streak behind flippers (typically well-defined leading edge) may extend to form chevron pattern over back (roughly symmetrical with other side)

Brush strokes and intermediate shades of grey on sides and back (highly variable)

ADULT NORTHERN HEMISPHERE

Head 22–23 per cent of body length

Dark grey, brownish-grey or blackish upperside

Relatively tall, falcate dorsal fin slightly less than two-thirds of the way along back (variable shape)

Dorsal fin may be hooked at tip

Sharply pointed, flattened rostrum

No white shoulder patch (cf. dwarf minke)

May have distinct dorsal and ventral keels

50–70 moderately short longitudinal throat pleats on underside (terminate between flippers and umbilicus)

Sharply demarcated brilliant-white band in middle of flipper (often clearly visible when animal just below surface)

Pointed tip

Relatively sleek, streamlined body

May be pockmarked with light round or oval cookiecutter shark bites

Slender, pointed flippers (c. 12 per cent of body length)

Snowy-white to creamy-white underside (may flush pink when active)

AT A GLANCE

- Tropics to poles worldwide
- Medium size
- Dark grey, brownish-grey or blackish upperside, white underside
- Variable swathes of lighter grey on sides and back

- Sharply pointed rostrum breaks surface first
- Single longitudinal ridge on rostrum
- Relatively tall, falcate dorsal fin two-thirds of the way along back
- Unique, bright white flipper bands
- Indistinct or invisible blow

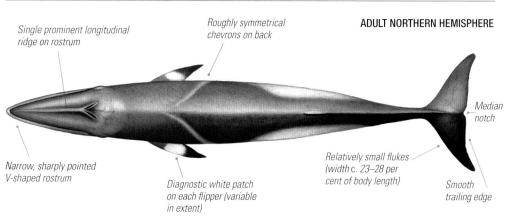

ADULT NORTHERN HEMISPHERE

Single prominent longitudinal ridge on rostrum

Roughly symmetrical chevrons on back

Median notch

Narrow, sharply pointed V-shaped rostrum

Diagnostic white patch on each flipper (variable in extent)

Relatively small flukes (width c. 23–28 per cent of body length)

Smooth trailing edge

ADULT NORTHERN HEMISPHERE FLIPPERS

Size and shape of white flipper band varies between individuals

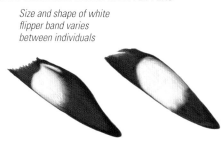

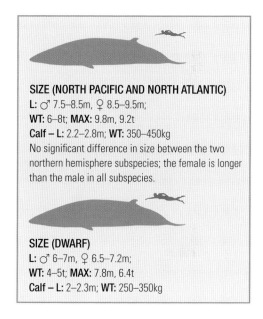

SIZE (NORTH PACIFIC AND NORTH ATLANTIC)
L: ♂ 7.5–8.5m, ♀ 8.5–9.5m;
WT: 6–8t; **MAX:** 9.8m, 9.2t
Calf – L: 2.2–2.8m; **WT:** 350–450kg
No significant difference in size between the two northern hemisphere subspecies; the female is longer than the male in all subspecies.

SIZE (DWARF)
L: ♂ 6–7m, ♀ 6.5–7.2m;
WT: 4–5t; **MAX:** 7.8m, 6.4t
Calf – L: 2–2.3m; **WT:** 250–350kg

SIMILAR SPECIES
Relatively easy to distinguish from other rorquals with a similar body form, by its smaller size, uniquely pointed head shape, white flipper bands and rather indistinct (or invisible) blow. There is some overlap between dwarf and Antarctic minke whales, at least in the southern summer, and the two look alike from a distance; the dwarf minke is about 2m shorter, has distinctive white flipper and shoulder patches (both of which are absent in the Antarctic minke), and has symmetrical dark grey throat

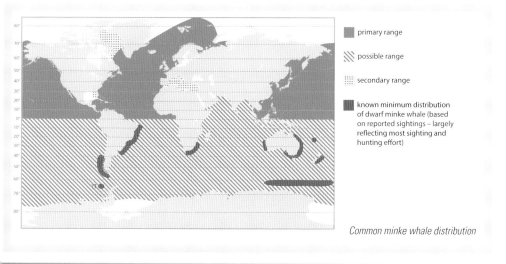

primary range

possible range

secondary range

known minimum distribution of dwarf minke whale (based on reported sightings – largely reflecting most sighting and hunting effort)

Common minke whale distribution

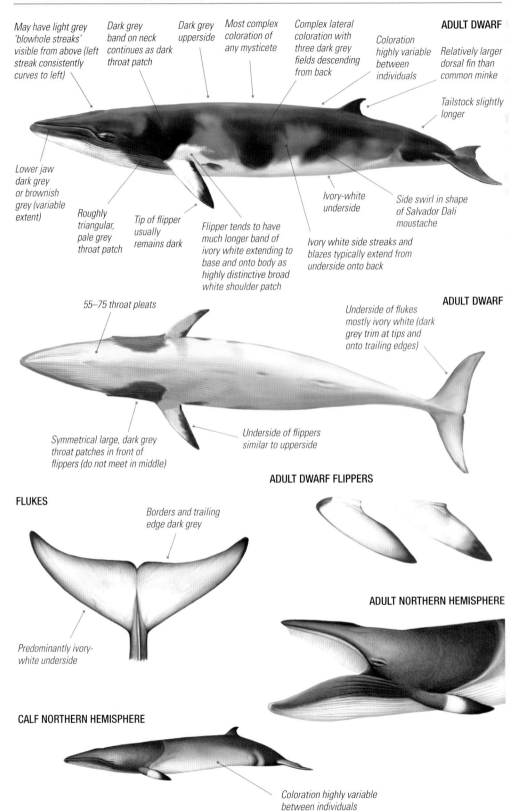

May have light grey 'blowhole streaks' visible from above (left streak consistently curves to left)

Dark grey band on neck continues as dark throat patch

Dark grey upperside

Most complex coloration of any mysticete

Complex lateral coloration with three dark grey fields descending from back

Coloration highly variable between individuals

ADULT DWARF

Relatively larger dorsal fin than common minke

Tailstock slightly longer

Lower jaw dark grey or brownish grey (variable extent)

Roughly triangular, pale grey throat patch

Tip of flipper usually remains dark

Flipper tends to have much longer band of ivory white extending to base and onto body as highly distinctive broad white shoulder patch

Ivory-white underside

Side swirl in shape of Salvador Dali moustache

Ivory white side streaks and blazes typically extend from underside onto back

55–75 throat pleats

ADULT DWARF

Underside of flukes mostly ivory white (dark grey trim at tips and onto trailing edges)

Symmetrical large, dark grey throat patches in front of flippers (do not meet in middle)

Underside of flippers similar to upperside

ADULT DWARF FLIPPERS

FLUKES

Borders and trailing edge dark grey

ADULT NORTHERN HEMISPHERE

Predominantly ivory-white underside

CALF NORTHERN HEMISPHERE

Coloration highly variable between individuals

patches. There could be confusion with the pygmy right whale and some beaked whales from a distance, but the head shape and coloration are entirely different. Probable hybrids between common and Antarctic minke whales have been reported, with evidence indicating potential for reproductive compatibility between the two species.

DISTRIBUTION (NORTHERN HEMISPHERE)

The North Atlantic minke whale ranges to *c.* 80°N during summer and is found as far north as Baffin Bay, Denmark Strait, Svalbard, Franz Josef Land and Novaya Zemlya. The wintering grounds – probably in the southern North Atlantic – are poorly known. They extend at least to the Caribbean and the Bahamas in the west, and possibly to West Africa as far as Senegal and the Cape Verde Islands in the east. Reported year-round in the Canary Islands (28°N), but rare in the Azores and the Gulf of Mexico, and only an occasional visitor to the Mediterranean.

The North Pacific minke whale ranges to at least 70°N during summer and is found as far north as the Chukchi Sea. The wintering grounds – probably in the southern North Pacific – are also poorly known. They extend to at least 15°N in the South China and Philippine Seas, and southern Baja California. Present, but rarely seen, around Hawaii.

Northern minke migrations are not as well defined as in some other baleen whales. There is a tendency for the distribution to shift from high-latitude summer feeding areas to lower-latitude winter breeding areas (although some individuals are resident in cold temperate regions year-round). During summer, they appear to be most abundant in cold temperate to polar waters (where they are known to penetrate areas with extensive ice floes and polynyas). At this time of year, they occur in inshore coastal waters more frequently than any other species of rorqual, and will enter bays, inlets, fjords and even some large rivers (such as the St Lawrence River, Canada). Winter sightings are uncommon, suggesting that when they are in lower latitudes they are mainly offshore.

Some populations – such as around the Isle of Mull, Scotland, and the San Juan Islands, Washington State – have high site fidelity, returning each year to feed in particular locations. Some also have exclusive, adjoining home ranges (which may be unique to baleen whales).

DISTRIBUTION (SOUTHERN HEMISPHERE)

The dwarf minke occurs only in the southern hemisphere, and may or may not be circumglobal (relatively little is known about its distribution, since all southern animals were lumped together as a single species until recently).

Occurs in both coastal and offshore waters off South Africa, southern Mozambique, Australia, New Zealand (North and South Islands), New Caledonia, the east coast of South America (from northern Brazil to northern Argentina), and Chilean Patagonia. These records cover most of the year (March–December), but there are strong indications that at least some populations are migratory. The only known predictable aggregation of dwarf minke whales anywhere in the world is off the northern Great Barrier Reef in Australia, predominantly in June–July. The most northerly confirmed records are from 2°S off the northern coast of Brazil and 11°S in the western Pacific off Australia.

DIVE SEQUENCE
* Surfaces at a distinct angle *c.* 20–40°.
* Tip of rostrum pointed up and distinctively breaks surface first.
* Quickly rolls forward as blows.
* Blowhole and dorsal fin generally visible at same time (characteristic shared with Antarctic minke, some sei, juvenile Bryde's and juvenile fin whales) or dorsal fin appears very quickly after blowholes submerged.
* Typically arches back and tailstock quite high before sounding dive.
* Does not raise flukes.
* Surfacing behaviour generally brief and erratic (easily 'lost' after one or a few surfacings)

BLOW
* Diffuse, upright blow up to 3m high (more bushy than columnar) (height highly variable).
* Generally less distinct than any other large whale blow (often invisible).

FOOD AND FEEDING

Prey Northern hemisphere minkes feed on wide variety of small schooling fish (including sand lance, salmon, capelin, cod, mackerel, coal fish, sprat, pollack, whiting, herring, haddock, anchovy, saury, lanternfish) and small invertebrates (including euphausiids and copepods); prey choice depends on location, prey availability, season and year. Dwarf minke prefers lanternfish, but opportunistically feeds on other fish, possibly krill.

Feeding Feeding behaviour varies significantly according to prey and location; entrapment manoeuvres include circles, gyres, ellipses, figure-of-eights, hyperbolas, head-slaps and underwater blows; engulfing manoeuvres include plunges and oblique, lateral, vertical and ventral lunges.

Dive depth Feeds mostly at or near surface; dwarf minkes observed at 20–40m.

Dive time Northern typically 3–10 minutes, maximum 20 minutes; dwarf minkes up to 12 minutes 30 seconds.

It partly overlaps with the Antarctic minke whale during summer in the sub-Antarctic, but is not as polar. Most sightings in the sub-Antarctic have been in December–March south of Australia and New Zealand – between 55°S and 60°S, with one record as far as 65°S – probably because this is where there has been most research effort. But it is also likely to occur in sub-Antarctic waters south of South America and South Africa. It is not known from the northern Indian Ocean.

BEHAVIOUR

Breaches fairly frequently, sometimes completely clearing the water, and performs other aerial behaviours such as head rises and spyhops (it frequently sphops in icy areas). Rarely lobtails or flipper-slaps. Can be quite curious towards boats in some parts of the world – including Iceland, the Gulf of St Lawrence and northeastern Australia – and will swim around stationary vessels or alongside moving vessels for minutes or even hours at a time. In other areas, it can be difficult to approach.

ADULT BALEEN

- 231–290 plates in North Pacific, 270–325 in North Atlantic, 200–300 in dwarf (each side of the upper jaw).
- Longest plates c. 21cm; in northern animals, usually white, creamy or yellowish; in dwarf minke, about half of the plates posteriorly appear dark grey or brown (due to a narrow, dark fringe); all subspecies have symmetrical plate coloration.

GROUP SIZE AND STRUCTURE

Typically solitary, sometimes in twos or threes, but there can be larger, temporary aggregations in good feeding areas. Social structure appears to be complex, with evidence for some segregation by age, sex and/or reproductive class.

PREDATORS

Killer whales are significant predators (being smaller, minke whales are more vulnerable than other baleen whales). Pursuits are often characterised by prolonged chases, on a straight heading at 15–30km/h, sometimes lasting up to an hour or more. Although killer whales are capable of faster sprinting speeds, adult minkes can maintain higher sustained speeds. Generally succumbs, especially if herded too close to shore with no way of escape. Large sharks (including tiger and great white) may take calves and possibly adult dwarf minkes.

PHOTO-IDENTIFICATION

Difficult compared with some other baleen whales, but possible using nicks and notches on the trailing edge of the dorsal fin, the shape of the dorsal fin, body pigmentation, and any other distinctive marks and scars (the precise combination varies according to population). Colour pattern variations are particularly useful in recognising individual dwarf minke whales.

POPULATION

No precise overall estimate, but at least 200,000 mature individuals. Approximate regional estimates for the North Atlantic include 90,000 in the north-east Atlantic; 48,000 in the central North Atlantic (including 28,000 in Icelandic and Faroese shelf waters); 23,300 off the eastern coasts of Canada and the US; and 17,000 off West Greenland. There are fewer estimates for the North Pacific: 25,000 off northern Japan and in the Sea of Okhotsk; 4,500 in coastal waters of the Sea of Japan and along the Pacific coast of Japan; 1,160 off the west coast of the US and British Colombia; and 2,000 in the central and southeastern Bering Sea. There are c. 342–789 off the northern Great Barrier Reef; and 1,230 in the coastal waters of the northern Gulf of Alaska and Aleutian Islands.

LIFE HISTORY

Sexual maturity Females c. 6–8 years, males c. 5–8 years.
Mating Unknown.
Gestation c. 10–11 months.
Calving Every year (sometimes every other year); single calf born year-round, with seasonal peaks.
Weaning After 4–6 months.
Lifespan Probably at least 50 years (oldest recorded c. 60 years).

Dwarf minke whale in Australia.

CONSERVATION

IUCN status: Least Concern (2018). Considered too small to hunt by commercial whalers until well into the 1930s. But as larger whales were depleted, minkes were hunted more intensively. The total number reported killed in the northern hemisphere in 1930–99 was 166,342. The dwarf minke was never hunted on a large scale, although some were taken by shore-based whalers in South Africa and a few individuals were caught in the large commercial hunt for Antarctic minke whales.

Nowadays, common minke whales are the main target of commercial whaling – in defiance of the IWC moratorium – by Norway and Iceland in the North Atlantic, and Japan in the North Pacific (see Antarctic minke whale for the Southern Ocean hunt). Combined,

they have killed an average of 970 a year in recent years: the annual average take for 2014–16 was 662 by Norway in the North Atlantic, 130 by Iceland in the North Atlantic and 178 by Japan in the North Pacific. West Greenland continues to hunt up to 164 minkes annually and East Greenland up to 20 annually from shore stations, under IWC aboriginal quotas. Some dwarf minkes carry scars apparently made by traditional harpoons, which are used by some South Pacific island nations.

Other threats include entanglement in fishing gear, pollution, vessel strikes, habitat disturbance and noise pollution (from vessel traffic, seismic exploration and naval sonar).

VOCALISATIONS

Minke whales seem to be quiet in many areas – perhaps to reduce the likelihood of being detected by mammal-hunting killer whales – but they produce a variety of vocalisations in others. These include low-frequency 'downsweep' calls in the North Atlantic and loud 'boing' calls in the North Pacific, as well as pig-like grunts, moans, belches and pulse-trains.

Dwarf minkes are renowned for producing a loud, complex and stereotyped sound sequence – known as the 'Star Wars' vocalisation – that spans a wide frequency range between 50Hz and 9.4kHz. A rather mechanical sound, it consists of three rapid pulses and a longer trailing note, repeated at regular intervals. The complexity is due, in part, to the simultaneous production of two different sounds. Its function remains unknown.

Common minke whales breach fairly frequently.

ANTARCTIC MINKE WHALE
Balaenoptera bonaerensis

Burmeister, 1867

The Antarctic minke whale was declared a new species in 1998, when it was formally split from the slightly smaller common minke whale (although the two species are believed to have diverged 4.7–7.5 million years ago). It is actually more closely related to sei and Bryde's whales than to its namesake.

Classification Mysticeti, family Balaenopteridae.

Common name 'Antarctic' for its range in cold waters around the Antarctic continent; 'minke' reputedly from a nineteenth-century German labourer, called Meincke, who was working as a whaler for Norwegian Svend Foyn (dubbed 'the inventor of modern whaling') and kept misidentifying minke whales as blue whales (thereafter, all small and undersized whales were mockingly called 'Meincke's whales' and, with slight changes in pronunciation and spelling, the name stuck). It is pronounced 'mink-ee'.

Other names Southern minke whale.

Scientific name *Balaenoptera* from the Latin *balaena* for 'whale', and the Greek *pteron* for 'wing' or 'fin'; *bonaerensis* from 'Buenos Aires', where the type specimen was found.

Taxonomy No recognised forms or subspecies.

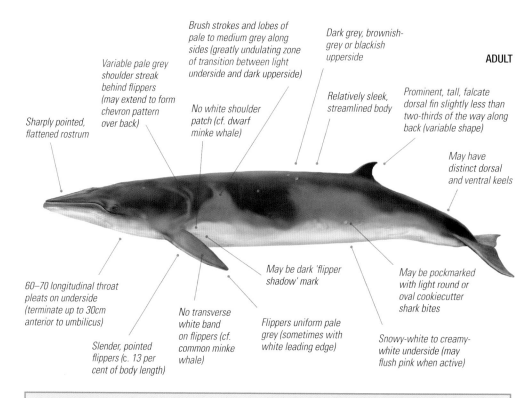

Brush strokes and lobes of pale to medium grey along sides (greatly undulating zone of transition between light underside and dark upperside)

Dark grey, brownish-grey or blackish upperside

ADULT

Variable pale grey shoulder streak behind flippers (may extend to form chevron pattern over back)

Relatively sleek, streamlined body

Prominent, tall, falcate dorsal fin slightly less than two-thirds of the way along back (variable shape)

Sharply pointed, flattened rostrum

No white shoulder patch (cf. dwarf minke whale)

May have distinct dorsal and ventral keels

60–70 longitudinal throat pleats on underside (terminate up to 30cm anterior to umbilicus)

May be dark 'flipper shadow' mark

May be pockmarked with light round or oval cookiecutter shark bites

Slender, pointed flippers (c. 13 per cent of body length)

No transverse white band on flippers (cf. common minke whale)

Flippers uniform pale grey (sometimes with white leading edge)

Snowy-white to creamy-white underside (may flush pink when active)

AT A GLANCE

- Tropics to poles in southern hemisphere
- Medium size
- Dark grey, brownish-grey or blackish upperside, white underside
- Variable undulating swathes of lighter grey on sides and back
- May be blotchy ochre with diatoms

- Sharply pointed rostrum breaks surface first
- Single longitudinal ridge on rostrum
- Tall, falcate dorsal fin two-thirds of the way along back
- Light grey chevron across back (at level of flippers)
- Often has light grey pigmentation trailing from blowholes
- Pale grey flippers (no white band)
- Distinct blow in high latitudes

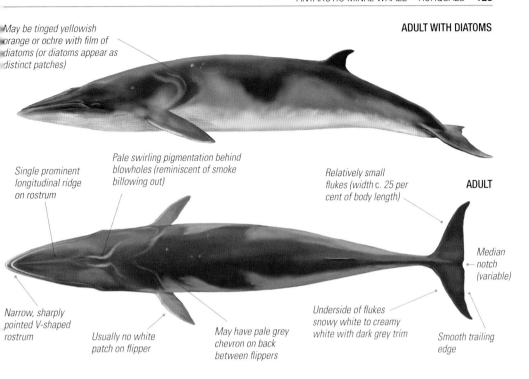

ADULT WITH DIATOMS

May be tinged yellowish orange or ochre with film of diatoms (or diatoms appear as distinct patches)

Single prominent longitudinal ridge on rostrum

Pale swirling pigmentation behind blowholes (reminiscent of smoke billowing out)

Relatively small flukes (width c. 25 per cent of body length)

ADULT

Median notch (variable)

Narrow, sharply pointed V-shaped rostrum

Usually no white patch on flipper

May have pale grey chevron on back between flippers

Underside of flukes snowy white to creamy white with dark grey trim

Smooth trailing edge

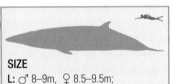

SIZE
L: ♂ 8–9m, ♀ 8.5–9.5m;
WT: 7–9t; **MAX:** 10.7m, 11t
Calf – L: 2.6–2.8m; **WT:** 350–500kg
Female is longer than the male.

SIMILAR SPECIES

Relatively easy to distinguish from other rorquals with a similar body form by its smaller size, uniquely pointed head shape, colour pattern and quicker movements. There is some overlap between Antarctic and dwarf minke whales, at least in the southern summer, and the two look alike from a distance; the Antarctic minke is about 2m longer, and does not have the distinctive white flipper and shoulder patches or the symmetrical dark grey throat patches (all of which are present in the dwarf minke). There could be confusion with the pygmy right whale and some beaked whales from a distance, but the head shape and coloration are entirely different. Probable hybrids between Antarctic and common minke whales have been reported, with evidence indicating potential for reproductive compatibility between the two species.

DISTRIBUTION

Endemic to the southern hemisphere, ranging from c. 7°S in the tropics to near the Antarctic continent. It is believed to be circumpolar, and occurs both nearshore and offshore. There have been four extralimital records in the North Atlantic: Suriname

■ primary range   • extralimital records   • hybrids with common minke whales

Antarctic minke whale distribution

ADULT

ADULT DORSAL FIN VARIATIONS

Most dorsal fins have pointed tips

on the Atlantic coast of South America, Togo in the Gulf of Guinea, Louisiana in the northern Gulf of Mexico, and north of the Arctic Circle off Jan Mayen. Two individuals identified as hybrids with common minke whales have been recorded in Svalbard.

Most abundant south of 60°S during the southern summer – south of the Antarctic Circumpolar Current – and known to reach at least 78°S in the Ross Sea. It occurs in greatest densities near the ice edge and is probably the most ice-affiliated rorqual (it is least abundant in ice-free waters). Found from the ice edge to several hundred kilometres inside the ice in anything from brash to floes – even with nearly 100% ice cover – following leads and utilising polynyas for breathing; it may even use its pointed, stout rostrum to break through newly formed or tightly packed brash ice to create breathing holes. The density decreases with growing distance from the shelf edge. High densities reported in parts of the

DIVE SEQUENCE
- Slower and more leisurely around ice.
- Surfaces at distinct angle *c.* 20–40°.
- Tip of rostrum pointed up and distinctively breaks surface first.
- Quickly rolls forward as blows.
- Blowhole and dorsal fin generally visible at same time (characteristic shared with common minke, some sei, juvenile Bryde's and juvenile fin whales) or dorsal fin appears very quickly after blowholes submerged.
- Typically arches back and tailstock quite high before sounding dive.
- Does not raise flukes.

BLOW
- Diffuse, upright blow up to 3.5–4m high (height highly variable), more bushy than columnar.
- Generally more distinct than common minke whale blow but highly variable (conspicuous in colder Antarctic waters, but can be invisible at lower latitudes).

CALF

ADULT FLIPPER VARIATIONS

Extent of pale grey and white bordering variable

Weddell and Ross Seas. It partly overlaps with the dwarf minke whale during summer in the sub-Antarctic, but tends to be much more polar.

Migrations are not as well defined as in some other baleen whales. Many Antarctic minkes appear to overwinter in the Antarctic, but others may migrate from their high-latitude feeding grounds to dispersed lower-latitude winter breeding areas. Most calving seems to take place north of the Antarctic Convergence. There may be poorly defined breeding grounds roughly from 10°S to 30°S in the Pacific (between 170°E and 100°W), as well as west of Easter Island in Chile, off northeastern and eastern Australia, off western South Africa and off the northeastern coast of Brazil. Three tagged whales left the Antarctic for temperate waters during winter; however, recent genetic and acoustic evidence sheds doubt on tropical and temperate regions being a major destination. Intriguingly, Antarctic minke whale vocalisations have been heard simultaneously during winter and spring in the eastern Weddell Sea and off Western Australia, indicating a very widespread distribution – or a seasonal migration by one segment of the population and a year-round presence in Antarctic waters by another.

BEHAVIOUR

Breaches fairly frequently, sometimes completely clearing the water, and performs other aerial behaviours such as head rises and spyhops. In dense pack ice, it frequently lifts its head right out of the water to breathe. Behaviour around vessels ranges from taking flight to unconcerned or even curious; tends to be more approachable when feeding. There appears to be a growing tendency towards curious and 'friendly' behaviour among single smaller whales around the Antarctic Peninsula, with increasing close encounters with rigid-hulled inflatable boats and kayaks.

ADULT BALEEN

- 261–359 plates (each side of the upper jaw).
- Longest plates *c.* 31cm; asymmetrical coloration: most plates are black, except for the first few on the left side and the first third on the right side (which are yellowish white).

GROUP SIZE AND STRUCTURE

On summer feeding grounds, typically solitary or in groups of 2–6; larger aggregations of up to 50 are uncommon, but are seen occasionally around the Antarctic Peninsula (socialising as well as feeding). Groups of 2–5 are common in warmer waters during winter. Groups of one male and two females, or two males and three or more females, have been reported in the western South Atlantic. There may be some segregation by age, sex and/or reproductive status.

PREDATORS

Killer whales are significant predators. One estimate suggests that Antarctic minke whales make up 85 per cent of the diet of Type A Antarctic killer whales in the Southern Ocean.

FOOD AND FEEDING

Prey Primarily Antarctic krill (*Euphausia superba*) on summer feeding grounds in offshore waters (e.g. Weddell Sea); sometimes smaller krill (*E. crystallorophias* and *E. spinifera*) in coastal shelf waters (e.g. Ross Sea); known to feed on krill under the ice; occasionally amphipods (*Themisto gaudichaudi*) and Antarctic silver fish.

Feeding Lunges into large prey aggregations (often rolling to one side); most feeding may be during southern summer, but little information; no accounts of cooperative feeding, though groups of feeding whales observed around Antarctic Peninsula; lunge-feeds up to 22–24 times per dive (cf. 6–7 for feeding blue whale).

Dive depth Generally feeds in upper 100m of water column (up to 150m); dive depths may change from day to night with vertical migration of prey.

Dive time Typically 1–5 minutes; maximum *c.* 15 minutes; typically surfaces 2–15 times between deep dives.

LIFE HISTORY

Sexual maturity Females *c.* 7–8 years, males *c.* eight years (probably older before commercial whaling, when densities of other baleen whales were higher).
Mating Probably promiscuous mating system (both males and females mate with multiple partners).
Gestation *c.* 10 months.

Calving Every 1–2 years; single calf, with seasonal peak May–August.
Weaning After 4–6 months; weaned young may remain with mother up to two years.
Lifespan Probably at least 50 years (oldest recorded 73 years).

PHOTO-IDENTIFICATION

Difficult compared with some other baleen whales, but possible using nicks and notches on the trailing edge of the dorsal fin, the shape of the dorsal fin, body pigmentation, and any other distinctive marks and scars.

POPULATION

No precise overall estimate and there is controversy about its current abundance, but it certainly numbers in the hundreds of thousands. IWC surveys show an overall decline of 30 per cent from 720,000 in 1985/86–90/91 to 515,000 in 1992/93–2003/04. It is unclear if this reflects a problem with survey methodology, differing ice conditions from year to year (affecting the total number of animals counted) or a real decline. There is an approximate estimate of 1,544 off the western Antarctic Peninsula.

CONSERVATION

IUCN status: Near Threatened (2018). Considered too small to hunt by commercial whalers until the early 1970s, when factory-ship whaling in the Antarctic turned to minke whales (as larger whales were depleted). The total number reported killed in the Antarctic in 1967–99 was 116,395; in 1964–85, a further 14,600 were killed in the wintering grounds off Brazil and 1,113 off South Africa. All commercial whaling was banned from the 1985/86 Antarctic season, but Japan continued so-called 'scientific whaling' (despised by scientists around the world as a sham for commercial whaling). It took an average of 335 Antarctic minke whales per year in 2015–2018. With its decision to leave the IWC in 2019, 'scientific' whaling will stop and be replaced by a commercial whaling programme in Japan's Exclusive Economic Zone (52 per year in 2019).

Other threats include entanglement in fishing gear, ship strikes, pollution, habitat disturbance and noise pollution (from vessel traffic, seismic exploration and naval sonar). Global warming is a particular concern – the great reduction in Antarctic sea ice expected this century is likely to cause significant shifts or reductions in prey.

An Antarctic minke whale surfaces near the Antarctic Penninsula.

The sharply pointed, flattened rostrum is clearly visible in this photograph.

VOCALISATIONS

Antarctic minke whale vocalisations are poorly known. However, a mysterious sound (dubbed the 'bio-duck') that has been registered by submariners and on passive acoustic hydrophones in the Southern Ocean since the 1960s has recently been attributed to this species. It is heard mainly during the southern winter in the Southern Ocean, but has also been recorded off Western Australia. It consists of a highly stereotyped sequence of between 3–12 downswept pulses (in the range of 50–300Hz), separated by intervals of *c.* 3.1 seconds, and with a number of variations to this basic theme. Antarctic minkes also produce low-frequency 'downsweeps', consisting of a single pulse at 130–60Hz. In one study, these were produced just before or after surfacing, while the animals were within pack ice; they may serve a social function, or to maintain spacing and contact between separated individuals.

Single smaller Antarctic minkes are showing more friendly behaviour.

HUMPBACK WHALE
Megaptera novaeangliae

(Borowski, 1781)

Renowned for its spectacular breaching, lobtailing and flipper-slapping, its complex and melodious song, and its remarkably long flippers, the humpback whale is one of the most familiar and best known of all the large whales. The black-and-white markings on the underside of its tail are distinctive and readily identifiable, enabling researchers to tell one individual from another.

Classification Mysticeti, family Balaenopteridae.

Common name From the tendency to arch its back conspicuously when diving, and because the dorsal fin sits on a 'hump' on the back.

Other names Hump-backed whale, hunchback whale.

Scientific name *Megaptera* from the Greek *mega* for 'big' or 'great', and *ptera* for 'wings' (referring to the long flippers); *novaeangliae* is a Latin derivation of the French name *baleine de la Nouvelle Angleterre* for 'of New England', because it was named from a specimen found in 1781 in New England, USA (i.e. 'big-winged New Englander').

Taxonomy Three subspecies were recently recognised: North Atlantic (*M. n. novaeangliae*); North Pacific (*M. n. kuzira*); and southern (*M. n. australis*). A fourth subspecies, the Arabian Sea humpback whale (*M. n. indica*), has been proposed (believed to be the most genetically distinct humpback whale in the world). Molecular studies show that the humpback does not represent a distinct evolutionary lineage (i.e. placing it in a separate genus from other rorquals may not be appropriate).

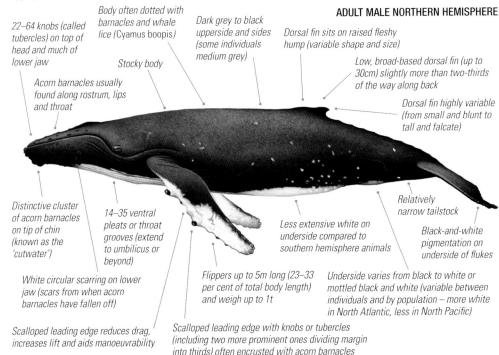

ADULT MALE NORTHERN HEMISPHERE

22–64 knobs (called tubercles) on top of head and much of lower jaw

Body often dotted with barnacles and whale lice (*Cyamus boopis*)

Stocky body

Dark grey to black upperside and sides (some individuals medium grey)

Dorsal fin sits on raised fleshy hump (variable shape and size)

Low, broad-based dorsal fin (up to 30cm) slightly more than two-thirds of the way along back

Acorn barnacles usually found along rostrum, lips and throat

Dorsal fin highly variable (from small and blunt to tall and falcate)

Distinctive cluster of acorn barnacles on tip of chin (known as the 'cutwater')

14–35 ventral pleats or throat grooves (extend to umbilicus or beyond)

Less extensive white on underside compared to southern hemisphere animals

Relatively narrow tailstock

Black-and-white pigmentation on underside of flukes

White circular scarring on lower jaw (scars from when acorn barnacles have fallen off)

Flippers up to 5m long (23–33 per cent of total body length) and weigh up to 1t

Underside varies from black to white or mottled black and white (variable between individuals and by population – more white in North Atlantic, less in North Pacific)

Scalloped leading edge reduces drag, increases lift and aids manoeuvrability

Scalloped leading edge with knobs or tubercles (including two more prominent ones dividing margin into thirds) often encrusted with acorn barnacles

---

AT A GLANCE

- Worldwide distribution
- Large size
- Predominantly dark grey to black upperside
- Variable amount of white on underside
- Stocky body
- Small dorsal fin sits on (variable) hump on back
- Exceptionally long white (or black-and-white) flippers
- Distinctive knobs on head
- Strongly arches back when diving
- Usually flukes on sounding dive
- Variable (and individually distinctive) black-and-white pigmentation on underside of flukes

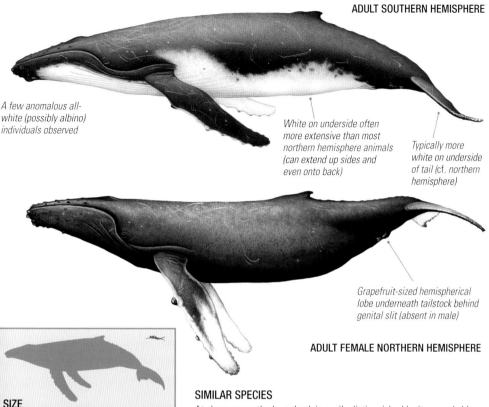

ADULT SOUTHERN HEMISPHERE

A few anomalous all-white (possibly albino) individuals observed

White on underside often more extensive than most northern hemisphere animals (can extend up sides and even onto back)

Typically more white on underside of tail (cf. northern hemisphere)

Grapefruit-sized hemispherical lobe underneath tailstock behind genital slit (absent in male)

ADULT FEMALE NORTHERN HEMISPHERE

SIZE
L: ♂ 11–15m, ♀ 12–16m;
WT: 25–35t; **MAX:** 18.6m, 40t (historically – rarely more than 16m today)
Calf – L: 4–4.6m; **WT:** 0.6–1t
Adult females typically 1–1.5m longer than males.

SIMILAR SPECIES
At close range, the humpback is easily distinguished by its remarkably long flippers, the numerous knobs or tubercles on its head and jaws, and the dorsal fin sitting on a distinctive hump. At a distance, it could be confused with other large whales that typically fluke when they dive and have no or small dorsal fins, especially grey, right and sperm whales. There are many distinguishing features, but they all have very differently shaped and patterned flukes, the grey whale is much lighter in colour, the right whale has no dorsal fin, and the sperm whale's blow is distinctive (coming from the front left corner of the head).

DISTRIBUTION
Worldwide, migrating between mid- to high-latitude summer feeding grounds and low-latitude winter breeding grounds (where it mates and calves). Coastal, continental shelf and offshore waters during summer. Breeds around oceanic islands, offshore seamounts and reef systems, and most populations migrate through deep oceanic waters. It is rare in the Mediterranean Sea, and there is no evidence

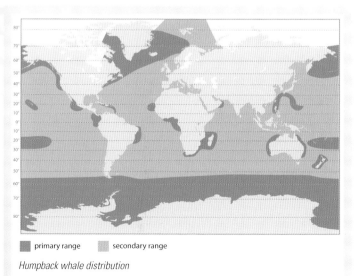

■ primary range   ▨ secondary range

Humpback whale distribution

Humpback whale North Atlantic

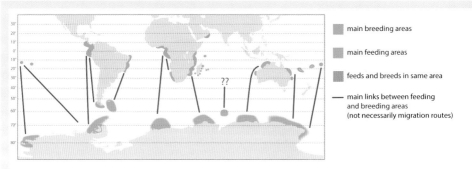

Humpback whale southern hemisphere

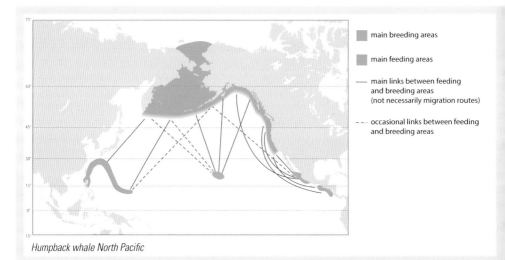

Humpback whale North Pacific

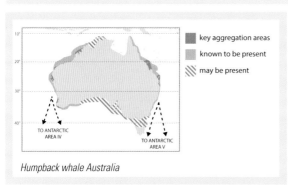

Humpback whale Australia

for a large historical presence there. Significant numbers also occur at mid- to high latitudes during winter – in British Columbia, Norway, Iceland and other locations – but it is unclear whether these are actually overwintering or simply very late migrants. Some populations are responding to climate change by expanding their range into higher polar latitudes (significant declines in sea ice are also resulting in longer feeding seasons).

The record holder for the longest documented migration of any humpback whale migrated from the Antarctic Peninsula to American Samoa and back – an 18,840km round trip. Seven humpbacks that migrated from their breeding grounds off Central America to their feeding grounds around Antarctica travelled at least 8,461km distance one way – from as far north as 11°N off Costa Rica to the Antarctic Peninsula. The breeding area in Costa Rica used by southern hemisphere humpbacks during the austral winter is also used by North Pacific humpbacks during the boreal winter (it's not clear whether the two ever overlap at the same time).

An isolated population of c. 89 individuals in the Arabian Sea (along the coast of Oman, mainly around the Gulf of Masirah and Kuria Muria Islands, but ranging from the Gulf of Aden into the southwestern Bay of Bengal) is unique in being resident. Monsoon-driven productivity in summer permits the whales to remain in tropical and sub-tropical waters year-round.

WINTER BREEDING DISTRIBUTION

There are 14 known and two suspected winter breeding grounds: two (plus one suspected) in the North Atlantic, four (plus one suspected) in the North Pacific, seven in the southern hemisphere and one in the Arabian Sea. These are all between 30°N and 40°S, and mostly centred around c. 20° latitude. They are typically in warm, relatively shallow water (less than 200m) surrounded by much deeper water. Mother–calf pairs show a strong preference for shallower waters (in some areas less than 20m deep). The preferred sea temperature on the breeding grounds is c. 25°C (in the range of 21.1–28.3°C, depending on the population, irrespective of latitude). Humpbacks that feed in widely separate regions in summer gather together and mix on the same winter breeding grounds (increasing the chances of finding each other and promoting genetic diversity). There is a high fidelity to natal breeding grounds, and a low level of interchange between these regions.

SUMMER FEEDING DISTRIBUTION

Individuals usually return to the same feeding grounds used by their mothers and there is relatively little exchange between feeding areas. Habitat preferences include the continental shelf break, areas of upwelling, submarine channels, oceanic fronts, eastern boundary currents and ice-edge zones; in the southern hemisphere, feeding habitat is often closely linked to regions of marginal sea ice. The preferred sea temperature on the feeding grounds is typically below 14°C.

NORTH ATLANTIC

The majority of North Atlantic humpbacks breed in the West Indies, primarily on the oceanic side of many Caribbean islands: in the Greater Antilles (Cuba, Haiti, Dominican Republic and Puerto Rico) and the Lesser Antilles (the island arc from the Virgin Islands east and south to Trinidad and Tobago), and northern Venezuela. The most populous areas are along the northern coast of the Dominican Republic and over the offshore reef systems of Silver, Navidad and Mouchoir banks.

Historical whaling records reveal the Cape Verde islands (possibly extending to the continental shelf of Senegal and Western Sahara) as another breeding ground, with as many as c. 4,000 whales before whaling commenced. However, it appears to be utilised by relatively few whales today – far fewer than are known to exist in the eastern North Atlantic (and unaccounted for in the West Indies). This suggests the existence of a third, as yet undetermined, breeding ground.

North Atlantic humpbacks feed in six major feeding grounds: the Gulf of Maine; the Gulf of St Lawrence; Labrador and Newfoundland; western Greenland; Iceland; and northern Norway (including the Barents Sea). Individuals from all these feeding areas have been observed on the West Indies breeding grounds, though those from more easterly feeding areas (around Iceland and northern Norway) are observed there less frequently (perhaps because they tend to arrive later in the season, when there is less research effort). Some of the eastern North Atlantic humpbacks may breed in the Cape Verde islands (there have been several matches – around Bear Island in Norway and Iceland) but most are believed to breed in an undetermined area in the eastern tropical Atlantic (which may be more geographically diffuse than the West Indies breeding ground); genetic evidence also suggests a third breeding ground.

Bermuda and the Azores are believed to be migratory stopover sites.

NORTH PACIFIC

There are six known and suspected breeding populations in the North Pacific:

1. Main Hawaiian Islands. Approximately half of these whales feed in coastal waters of northern British Columbia and south-east Alaska, the remainder mainly in the northern Gulf of Alaska and the Bering Sea.
2. Mainland Mexico, which feed mainly off California.
3. Revillagigedo Islands, which feed mostly from northern California to Alaska, with some venturing as far north as the Aleutian and Commander Islands.
4. Central America, along the Pacific coast from southern Mexico and Guatemala to Costa Rica. These feed almost exclusively in offshore waters along California and Oregon, with small numbers as far north as the US/Canada border.
5. Southern Japan (mainly the Okinawa Islands) to Taiwan and the northern Philippines, and east to the Mariana and Marshall Islands. These feed mainly along the eastern coast of Kamchatka, but also across a broad

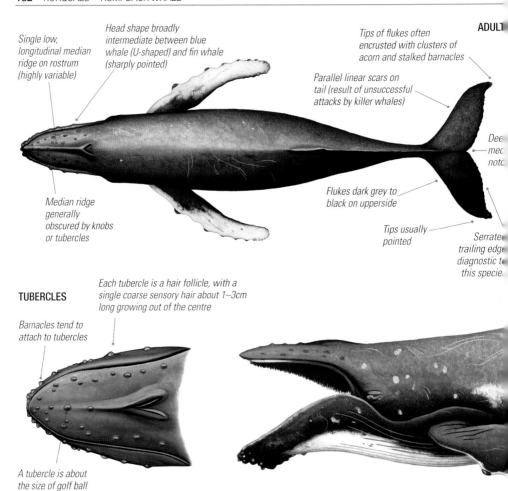

ADULT

Single low, longitudinal median ridge on rostrum (highly variable)

Head shape broadly intermediate between blue whale (U-shaped) and fin whale (sharply pointed)

Tips of flukes often encrusted with clusters of acorn and stalked barnacles

Parallel linear scars on tail (result of unsuccessful attacks by killer whales)

Dee mec notc

Median ridge generally obscured by knobs or tubercles

Flukes dark grey to black on upperside

Tips usually pointed

Serrate trailing edge diagnostic t this specie

TUBERCLES

Each tubercle is a hair follicle, with a single coarse sensory hair about 1–3cm long growing out of the centre

Barnacles tend to attach to tubercles

A tubercle is about the size of golf ball

area including the Bering Sea, the Commander Islands and western Aleutian Islands, and possibly as far north as the Chukchi and Beaufort Seas (the migratory destination of Chukchi and Beaufort humpbacks is uncertain); a small number may reach the Gulf of Alaska and northern British Columbia.

6. As yet unknown breeding ground somewhere else in the western North Pacific – possibly in the Northwestern Hawaiian Islands. This is inferred from sightings of humpbacks in the Russian Far East and around the Aleutian Islands that cannot be linked to any known breeding population, and by significant genetic differences between humpbacks in the Okinawa–Philippines breeding ground.

Baja California and the Ogasawara Islands are not believed to be primary migratory destinations, but are more likely to be transiting areas.

SOUTHERN HEMISPHERE

There are seven separate breeding populations in the southern hemisphere that migrate to feed in the Southern Ocean (in six specific areas designated by the International Whaling Commission as I–VI):

1. Pacific coasts of Central and South America, with the greatest concentration in Colombia but ranging from the Gulf of Papagayo in Costa Rica to the Gulf of Guayaquil in Ecuador, including the Galapagos Islands, with some as far south as northern Peru. They feed in Antarctic Area I – those from northern Peru, Ecuador and Colombia mainly along the western Antarctic Peninsula, those from the northern parts of the breeding range mostly in the Fuegian Archipelago (though there have been matches between Panama and the Antarctic Peninsula).

2. Atlantic coastal waters of Brazil, between Natal (3°S) and Cabo Frio (23°S), with a particular concentration around Abrolhos Bank (16°40'S–19°30'S); the range appears to be expanding as the population recovers. They feed in the Scotia Sea region of Antarctic Area II (including off South Georgia and the South Sandwich Islands).

CALF

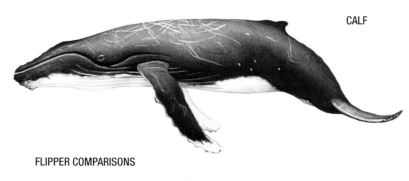

FLIPPER COMPARISONS

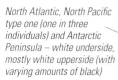

North Atlantic, North Pacific type one (one in three individuals) and Antarctic Peninsula – white underside, mostly white upperside (with varying amounts of black)

FLUKES

North Pacific type two – white underside, mostly black upperside (two in three individuals)

Western Australia – white underside, mostly black upperside (with varying amounts of white)

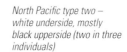

DIVE SEQUENCE
- Surfaces at shallow angle.
- Blowholes appear first and remain in view as dorsal fin appears.
- Distinctive sloping back forms shallow triangle with surface of sea.
- Body arches, forming high triangle and making hump on back especially evident.
- Dorsal fin disappears and tailstock arches as whale rolls into dive.
- Flukes lifted high on many dives.

BLOW
- Blow more variable than in any other large whale species (bushy, columnar or, very occasionally, V-shaped).
- Usually tall and columnar (may be bushier at top), up to 10m high (height highly variable – often only 4–5m).

3. Southwestern Africa, between northern Angola and Togo, and possibly as far as Ghana, centred around the Gulf of Guinea. They feed south of 18°S, in waters off Namibia and western South Africa, and in Antarctic Area III.
4. Southeastern Africa and Madagascar, in the coastal waters of eastern South Africa, Mozambique, Tanzania and southern Kenya, and around the southern Seychelles, the west coast of La Réunion, the Comoros Islands and Madagascar. They feed in Antarctic Area III.
5. Northwestern Australia, calving off Ningaloo Reef and north to the Kimberley region, with a widely expanding range along the Western Australian coast. They feed in Antarctic Area IV.
6. Northeastern Australia. They feed in Antarctic Area V.
7. Oceania, consisting of whales from the South Pacific Islands, including American Samoa, Samoa, Vanuatu, Fiji, Niue, Cook Islands, New Caledonia, Tonga, French Polynesia and Norfolk Island; there is a less regular presence in Kiribati, Solomon Islands, Nauru, Wallis and Futuna, Tuvalu, Tokelau and the Pitcairn Islands (though this may reflect research effort). They feed in Antarctic Areas V, VI and I (including the western Antarctic Peninsula).

BEHAVIOUR

More demonstrative at the surface – and probably more acrobatic – than any other large whale. Breaching, flipper-slapping and lobtailing are common. May lie on its side or back, holding one or both flippers in the air. All these activities occur at all times of year, and in a variety of contexts, and clearly perform a range of functions (probably including communication, mate attraction, parasite removal, prey corralling, expression of excitement or annoyance, and even play). Both sexes and all ages frequently breach, on both the feeding grounds and the breeding grounds, alone or in small groups, once or many times in succession. They sometimes perform full breaches that bring their entire bodies out of the water. Calves (and sometimes older whales) will play with objects in the water.

Occasionally associates with other species on the breeding grounds, including right whale, fin whale, short-finned pilot whale, rough-toothed dolphin and bottlenose dolphin. Indo-Pacific and common bottlenose dolphins often play with or harass humpbacks (it can be hard to tell the difference) – the whales make the 'trumpeting' or 'forced' blows normally associated with competitive groups; humpbacks sometimes lift dolphins out of the water on the top of their heads.

Known to intercept when mammal-eating killer whales attack other humpbacks and even other species (including grey whale, minke whale, Dall's porpoise, Steller sea lion, California sea lion, Weddell seal, crabeater seal, harbour seal, northern elephant seal, ocean sunfish). This is believed to be a mobbing behaviour, which incidentally may allow the killer whales' prey to escape (though interspecific altruism cannot be ruled out).

Generally shows little fear of boats and is frequently very inquisitive (especially juveniles).

BALEEN PLATES
- 270–400 plates (each side of the upper jaw)
- Plates dark grey to black, often with white or brownish-white longitudinal streaks (anterior-most plates may be lighter); maximum length 85–107cm.

BUBBLE-NETTING

Some humpback whales will cooperate to construct enormous circular fishing nets with bubbles – up to 45m across – to capture schooling herring or other small fish. This behaviour is most common in south-east Alaska, but to a lesser degree is observed in other parts of the world. Members of a bubble-netting group can be male and/or female, and either gender can take the leadership role. Not all humpbacks participate in this cooperative behaviour and membership appears to be fluid (there are often visitors that join for only a day or two, and some move between feeding groups from dive to dive).

It is a team effort – there can be just a few or as many as 24 whales working together – and, at least in some

A large group of humpbacks bubble-netting in south-east Alaska.

FOOD AND FEEDING

Prey Krill (including *Euphausia*, *Thysanoessa*, *Meganyctiphanes*); wide variety of schooling fish (including herring, sand lance, pollock, mackerel, sardines, anchovies, capelin); rarely squid; some mysids, copepods and benthic amphipods (probably taken incidentally); generalist in northern hemisphere (with regional preferences); Antarctic krill (*Euphausia superba*) are main prey in southern hemisphere.

Feeding Adaptable gulp- or lunge-feeder (lunges at prey patches with mouth open) using diverse techniques; uniquely among large whales, uses bubble nets (circular nets of large bubbles) or bubble clouds (single or multiple bursts of tiny bubbles) to corral and concentrate schooling prey (individually or in groups); one of few baleen whale species to group-feed, with individuals having defined roles (the larger the prey, the larger the groups); other feeding techniques (often restricted to one or a few localities) include flick-feeding (while upside down, repeatedly sweeping tail forward at surface one or more times, before surfacing and lunging through edge of splash zone with mouth open to capture krill), lobtail-feeding (slapping surface above school of fish, then diving to blow bubble screen), trap-feeding (recently observed in a growing number of individuals off Vancouver Island and southwestern Australia – whale remains at surface with mouth wide open and uses flippers to push fish into the 'trap'; may be culturally transmitted foraging innovation for feeding on small, diffuse prey patches); little or no feeding on winter breeding grounds, but opportunistic feeding during migration.

Dive depth On summer feeding grounds often follows diel movement cycle of prey (deeper dives during day, shallower dives at night); most foraging in upper 120m of water column (upper 25m during bubble-netting), but capable of at least 400m (routinely to 300m during summer feeding season along Antarctic Peninsula); on breeding grounds usually shallow, but some dives to *c.* 170m at or near seabed in Hawaii.

Dive time Depends on season, location and behaviour; singing dives up to 20 minutes; resting dives in breeding areas 15–30 minutes; foraging dives typically 3–10 minutes (up to 15 minutes); maximum *c.* 40 minutes.

---

cases, individuals appear to have a different role and favoured position. In south-east Alaska, at least, one whale is the caller, using a loud, haunting feeding call to scare the herring upwards from the deep (these feeding calls have recently been heard in northern British Columbia, as the culture spreads). Another whale (or, possibly, the same one) is the bubble blower, creating the ring of bubbles that will act as a net to contain the prey. Meanwhile, other whales in the group use their bodies to corral the fish into the 'net' (the white undersides of their flippers may be used as 'flashers' to scare the herring in the right direction). The bubbles appear at the surface in a closed circle or a figure of '9' (whales working alone frequently create figures of '9') and, when everything is ready, all the whales rapidly swim up through the net with their mouths wide open and engulf the concentrated prey. They often appear above the surface with their mouths agape.

Some humpback whale groups may feed like this for 12 hours or more, completing a bubble-net as often as every few minutes, and some of the core groups of two or three whales within these coalitions can endure for an entire summer or even years.

COMPETITIVE, ROWDY OR SURFACE-ACTIVE GROUPS

Male humpbacks have to compete for relatively few females because the operational sex ratio on the breeding grounds is 2–3 males to one female (there are equal numbers in the population overall, but not all females are receptive in any one season, and the males tend not to remain in low latitudes for as long).

Female humpbacks on the breeding grounds are frequently (by choice or coercion) accompanied by at least one male, which typically remains within a body length of her (close behind and a little to the side) and often synchronises his breathing and dive patterns with hers. This 'primary escort' fiercely takes on all challengers to defend his position – there can be as many as a dozen other males in one of these 'competitive' or 'rowdy' groups, although not all are active challengers. Larger females usually have more escorts. These competitive groups can last for a few minutes or as long as many hours, and involve lots of energetic lunging, lobtailing, tail lashing (tail thrashing), flipper-slapping, bubble-blowing, head-lifting, jaw-clapping, head-ramming, breaching and high-speed chasing. These aggressive behaviours frequently result in injury.

There is some evidence that females might convey their presence to males through the percussive sounds of flipper-slapping or lobtailing. As a group forms, the female is usually in the lead, but sometimes can be in the centre of the activity. Other males will stop whatever they are doing and travel many kilometres to join the fray (they probably hear the whistles, screeches, grunts and growls made by competing males). The group often picks up more males, and loses others, while the principal escort becomes more agitated and active as he defends his position. Most of the action takes place between the principal escort and two or three challengers, which may temporarily cooperate to outmanoeuvre him and

LIFE HISTORY

Sexual maturity Males and females 4–11 years, varying within and among populations; 9–11 years in the southern hemisphere; considerably older in the North Pacific than North Atlantic.

Mating Males compete aggressively for females; reproductive behaviour begins and ends on migration (north and south) but peaks during winter assembly; females can undergo several oestrus cycles during winter until pregnant; postpartum oestrus may occur regularly (explaining why males escort female–calf pairs in breeding season).

Gestation 11–11.5 months.

Calving Every two years, sometimes every three years, occasionally every year (for up to four sequential years), rarely every 4–5 years; single calf born in winter (though known to have occurred rarely at other times of year); twin foetuses reported from pregnant females killed by whalers (but live twin births unknown).

Weaning After 10–12 months (begins to feed independently as young as six months); usually breaks maternal bond on autumn migration or on feeding grounds.

Lifespan At least 50 years, probably nearer 75 years (oldest recorded 95 years, if ageing technique accurate).

gain access to the female, but there are usually other males following along on the periphery; young whales may also be present, observing and mimicking the adult activity. The principal escort may hold his position, or be displaced by one of the other males. The aim is presumed to be to acquire the position nearest to the female when she comes into oestrus and is ready for mating, but observations of actual copulation are extremely rare.

GROUP SIZE AND STRUCTURE (WINTER BREEDING GROUNDS)

Usually occurs singly or in small groups, with seven main groupings:

1. Singer: Usually a lone male (though he may be accompanied by another male or a female with or without a calf). They can be stationary or travelling while singing.
2. Adult female with a male escort: most common in the first half of the winter breeding season. Researchers dub these pairs 'breath-holders', because they remain submerged for up to 30 minutes at a time. They may remain together for a day or two, the male defending his position against other males.
3. Competitive or surface-active group: multiple males following a single female (presumably in oestrus, although this is unknown) and competing with one another for the position of female's primary escort. There are often juveniles observing from the periphery, and the female may or may not have a calf.
4. Lone (non-singing) whales travelling to join others.
5. Groups of juveniles.
6. Mother–calf pair: often seen in nearshore shallow waters, actively avoiding other mother–calf pairs. Early in the season, they are sometimes accompanied by a juvenile – the mother's calf from the previous year.
7. Mother–calf pair and male escort: Male escorts are found in c. 83 per cent of encounters with mothers and calves (the female may undergo post-partum oestrus). These trios are most common towards the end of the

breeding season. Some researchers speculate that the mother may accept a single male escort as a 'hired gun', which is better than being harassed by lots of males; the escort may also help to defend the calf from predators.

GROUP SIZE AND STRUCTURE (SUMMER FEEDING GROUNDS)

There are five main groupings:

1. Single individual (male or female) or pair of either sex (may remain together entire summer).
2. Mother–calf pair.
3. Small, usually temporary feeding association (the number of individuals depends on constantly varying prey and prey-patch sizes); a few feeding associations, such as in the Gulf of Maine, can be more stable and may last most of the feeding season (though they are not believed to be based upon kinship).
4. Larger (and usually very ephemeral) feeding association of up to 24 whales, working together to corral and capture prey by bubble-net feeding.
5. Super-groups of up to 200 whales, apparently feeding on krill (*Euphausia lucens*) and mantis shrimp (*Pterygosquilla armata*) – recently observed in the Benguela Upwelling System off southwestern Africa (likely the result of increasing humpback whale abundance in the region, together with highly concentrated prey). However, these are aggregations rather than associated, coordinated groups, and occur mainly during spring southerly migrations.

GROUP SIZE AND STRUCTURE (MIGRATION)

Typically small, fluid groups with individuals joining and leaving on a regular basis.

PREDATORS

Mainly killer whales. Prevalence of rake marks suggests that as many as one-quarter of humpbacks have been in a killer whale's mouth at least once (highest reported figures for individuals with killer whale rake marks include New

A humpback whale's distinctive blow.

Lobtailing in Arctic Norway.

Zealand (37 per cent), New Caledonia (31.3 per cent) and Mexico (40 per cent); it averages 15 per cent in the North Pacific and ranges from 2.7 to 17.4 per cent in the North Atlantic. Most attacks are on calves (particularly during the first year) and juveniles; adults are rarely attacked, and will fight back using their powerful tail flukes and long flippers (which, armed with barnacles, make formidable weapons – like knuckle-dusters). Tiger sharks and other large sharks have been observed attacking and killing sick or injured calves, sub-adults and sometimes adults (though it is not known if they hunt healthy animals). False killer whales are occasional predators of young calves in Hawaii.

PHOTO-IDENTIFICATION

Unique black-and-white pigmentation pattern and scarring on the underside of the flukes, combined with the serrations on the trailing edge of the flukes. The combination of shape, size and scarring of the dorsal fin is also extensively used to identify individuals. In the past 40 years, tens of thousands of individual humpback whales have been identified and catalogued all over the world, and some individuals have been tracked in this way for more than 40 years.

POPULATION

Minimum 140,000 worldwide, probably more (compared to an all-time low of fewer than 10,000 due to whaling). Most recent estimated population figures include *c.* 97,000 in the southern hemisphere (6,500 along the Pacific coasts of Central and South America (2006); 16,410 in the Atlantic coastal waters of Brazil (2008); 7,100 in south-west Africa (2005); 13,500 in south-east Africa and Madagascar (2003–04); 28,800 in Western Australia (2012); and 24,500

FLUKE COMPARISONS

Underside of flukes varies from virtually all black to virtually all white with countless combinations of black and white in between

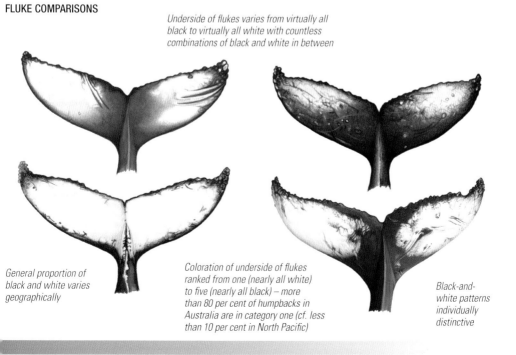

General proportion of black and white varies geographically

Coloration of underside of flukes ranked from one (nearly all white) to five (nearly all black) – more than 80 per cent of humpbacks in Australia are in category one (cf. less than 10 per cent in North Pacific)

Black-and-white patterns individually distinctive

Humpbacks are among the most acrobatic of all the large whales.

in east Australia (2015). There are also an estimated 21,808 in the North Pacific (2006); *c.* 20,000 in the North Atlantic, including 15,247 in the waters around Greenland, Iceland and the Faroe Islands (2015); and 89 in the Arabian Sea (2015).

Annual increases of 3.1 per cent to as high as 11.8 per cent (the maximum theoretically possible for the species) have been recorded in different populations around the world, so the current population sizes are likely to be significantly larger. In Hawaii, for example, numbers increased from 1,400 in 1980–83 to 10,100 in 2005–06 and, in theory, with a continued 5–6 per cent annual increase, there could be as many as 21,000 today.

CONSERVATION

IUCN status: Least Concern (2018); Arabian Sea population Endangered (2018). Hunted commercially in coastal and oceanic whaling operations in all major oceans since the seventeenth century. Some 215,848 were killed in the southern hemisphere, and 33,585 in the northern hemisphere. Many populations were seriously depleted – some by more than 95 per cent. Commercial whaling of humpbacks officially ended in 1955 (North Atlantic), 1963 (southern hemisphere) and 1966 (North Pacific). However, more than 48,000 were taken mainly illegally in 1948–73 by the Soviet Union. Small aboriginal hunts for humpbacks still take place in Greenland (annual strike limit is 10 per year) and Bequia in the Caribbean islands of St Vincent and the Grenadines (maximum

take four per year 2019–25 – none taken in 2018). Since commercial whaling ended, there has been an impressive increase in most populations.

The single biggest threat today is entanglement in fishing gear. Other modern threats include overfishing, noise pollution, ship strikes, oil and gas development, coastal habitat destruction and disturbance.

VOCALISATIONS

Humpback whales make a wide variety of vocalisations – songs, feeding calls, social sounds and trumpet blasts among them – on the breeding and feeding grounds, and on migration. Both males and females make calls on the summer feeding grounds, and on migration, that seem to have specific functions (and, in some cases, are restricted to particular social groups). For example, so-called 'wops' are used between a mother and calf (very quiet – probably to avoid attracting the attention of killer whales), 'thwops' are a more general contact call among individuals of any age or sex, and a series 'grunt trains' are used when animals come together in a group.

Males sing the longest and most complex songs in the animal kingdom (there are no records of females singing – although two females in the Antarctic were recorded producing elements of song during their feeding dives): haunting medleys of whines, grunts and squeals. Singing is presumed to start at around sexual maturity. It can be heard at any time of year, but is most prevalent in late autumn as the whales leave the feeding grounds,

Tubercles ripped off and bloodied during fighting.

continues on migration, peaks during the winter assembly, and decreases in the spring. Singers typically hang motionless in the water, at a *c.* 45° angle, with their head down, tail up and flukes 7–15m below the surface (on some breeding grounds, the tail may be above the surface). Each song usually lasts for 10–20 minutes and is repeated over and over (with the whale surfacing to breathe after singing a complete song). A song session (continuous singing) sometimes lasts for hours. Songs cover a wide range of frequencies (from 20Hz to 24kHz) and can probably be heard over distances of at least tens of kilometres.

A male usually sings alone, day and night, until it is joined by another male (or moves off to join a passing group itself). These interactions typically last a few minutes, until the whales split (it may be that the visiting male is simply checking to see if the singer is accompanying a female – and leaves fairly quickly if not);

and they are rarely aggressive (though may involve lots of flipper-slapping, lobtailing, breaching and other surface activity). Sometimes the two whales stay together for longer and are joined by other males to form a group.

All humpbacks in one area sing broadly the same highly structured and stereotyped song but, uniquely, they improvise, so the song is constantly evolving. When one male alters a few 'notes', all the other males typically incorporate his modification, so at any one time they are all singing the same version of the ever-changing song. The rate of change varies according to location – it can take 2–5 years for an entire composition to change through this cultural transmission. The next breeding season, the whales tend to pick up where they left off. Those living in other parts of world sing very different compositions.

There is much speculation about the purpose of the song. There are four main theories: it's a way to serenade females (though there is no evidence that females are attracted to particular singing males); it determines or facilitates male–male interactions (visits to singers are almost always by other lone males not singing at the time – perhaps seeking a coalition to increase the chances of winning a female, to disrupt the song or to assert dominance); it's a way for males to signify status (though this would require significant differences between the songs sung by different individuals – which is not the case); and it's used to attract females to a male aggregation (rather than to individual singers) within the context of a lekking system. The communal singing may also stimulate female receptivity. Or, of course, it may serve several or all of these functions.

The remarkably long flippers of the humpback whale are unique.

SPERM WHALE
Physeter macrocephalus

Linnaeus, 1758

The largest of the odontocetes, the iconic sperm whale – well known from the pages of *Moby Dick* – is designed for a life spent in the ocean depths. It is an animal of extremes: it shows the greatest size difference of all cetaceans between males and females, its brain is the largest on Earth, and it dives deeper, and for longer, than almost any other whale.

Classification Odontoceti, family Physeteridae.
Common name From the spermaceti oil found in the head, alluding to the fancied physical resemblance to semen; *spermaceti* literally means 'sperm of the whale'.
Other names Cachalot, great sperm whale.
Scientific name *Physeter* from the latinised Greek *physeter* for 'blower' (referring to the blowhole); *macrocephalus* from the Greek *makros* for 'big' or 'long' and *kephale* for 'head' (i.e. 'big-headed blower' – a fitting name).
Taxonomy No recognised forms or subspecies; the scientific name was highly controversial in the past – whether it should be *Physter macrocephalus* or *P. catodon* – but *macrocephalus* is now used almost universally.

ADULT MALE

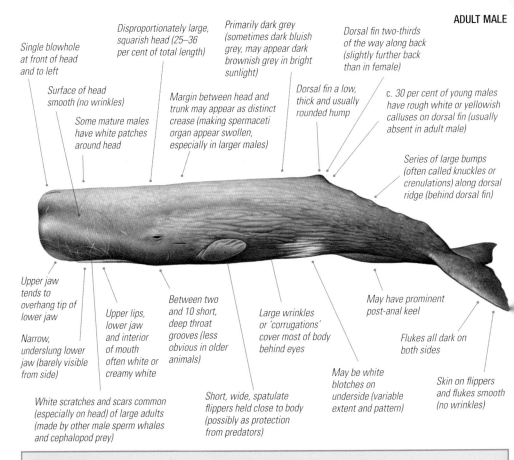

Single blowhole at front of head and to left

Surface of head smooth (no wrinkles)

Some mature males have white patches around head

Disproportionately large, squarish head (25–36 per cent of total length)

Primarily dark grey (sometimes dark bluish grey, may appear dark brownish grey in bright sunlight)

Margin between head and trunk may appear as distinct crease (making spermaceti organ appear swollen, especially in larger males)

Dorsal fin two-thirds of the way along back (slightly further back than in female)

Dorsal fin a low, thick and usually rounded hump

c. 30 per cent of young males have rough white or yellowish calluses on dorsal fin (usually absent in adult male)

Series of large bumps (often called knuckles or crenulations) along dorsal ridge (behind dorsal fin)

Upper jaw tends to overhang tip of lower jaw

Narrow, underslung lower jaw (barely visible from side)

Upper lips, lower jaw and interior of mouth often white or creamy white

Between two and 10 short, deep throat grooves (less obvious in older animals)

Large wrinkles or 'corrugations' cover most of body behind eyes

May have prominent post-anal keel

Flukes all dark on both sides

White scratches and scars common (especially on head) of large adults (made by other male sperm whales and cephalopod prey)

Short, wide, spatulate flippers held close to body (possibly as protection from predators)

May be white blotches on underside (variable extent and pattern)

Skin on flippers and flukes smooth (no wrinkles)

AT A GLANCE
- Deep, ice-free oceanic waters worldwide
- Large to extra-large size
- Primarily dark grey
- Huge squarish head
- Thick, low, rounded dorsal fin
- 'Knuckles' from dorsal fin to flukes
- Wrinkly, prune-like skin
- Bushy blow directed forwards and to left
- Often motionless (or swims leisurely) at surface
- Flukes usually raised on diving

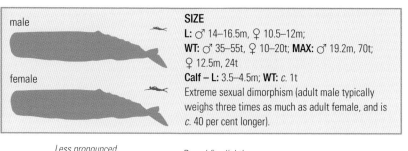

male

female

SIZE
L: ♂ 14–16.5m; ♀ 10.5–12m;
WT: ♂ 35–55t, ♀ 10–20t; **MAX:** ♂ 19.2m, 70t;
♀ 12.5m, 24t
Calf – L: 3.5–4.5m; **WT:** *c.* 1t
Extreme sexual dimorphism (adult male typically
weighs three times as much as adult female, and is
c. 40 per cent longer).

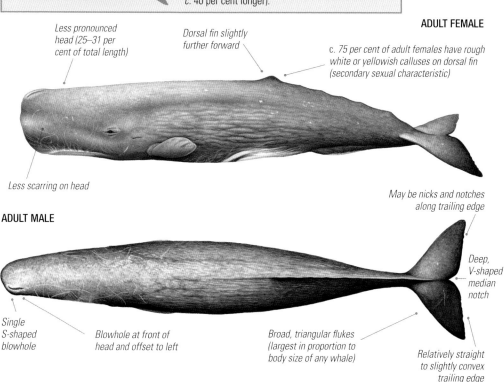

ADULT FEMALE

Less pronounced
head (25–31 per
cent of total length)

Dorsal fin slightly
further forward

*c. 75 per cent of adult females have rough
white or yellowish calluses on dorsal fin
(secondary sexual characteristic)*

Less scarring on head

May be nicks and notches
along trailing edge

ADULT MALE

Deep,
V-shaped
median
notch

Single
S-shaped
blowhole

Blowhole at front of
head and offset to left

Broad, triangular flukes
(largest in proportion to
body size of any whale)

Relatively straight
to slightly convex
trailing edge

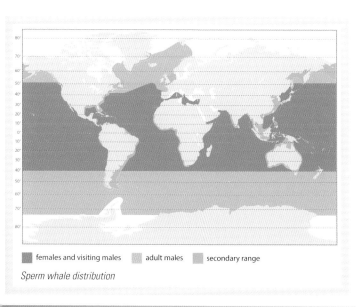

females and visiting males   adult males   secondary range

Sperm whale distribution

SIMILAR SPECIES
Unlikely to be confused with
any other cetacean. From a
distance, on a windless day, it
can be identified by its uniquely
angled blow alone; the blows
of some large baleen whales
can appear similar in windy
conditions, but theirs come
from much further back on the
head. The dive sequence is also
distinctive – after surfacing, the
sperm whale tends to remain
motionless, or moves slowly
forward, as it catches its breath
(none of the similar-sized
baleen whales tend to do this).
At close range, the square-
shaped head, rounded, hump-

ADULT MALE

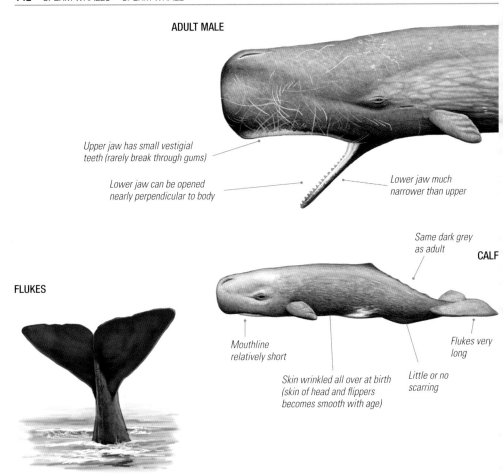

Upper jaw has small vestigial teeth (rarely break through gums)

Lower jaw can be opened nearly perpendicular to body

Lower jaw much narrower than upper

Same dark grey as adult

CALF

FLUKES

Mouthline relatively short

Flukes very long

Skin wrinkled all over at birth (skin of head and flippers becomes smooth with age)

Little or no scarring

like dorsal fin, wrinkly skin and single blowhole positioned far forward and on the left side are all unmistakable.

DISTRIBUTION

One of the most widely distributed marine mammals (after killer whales). Found in the deeper parts of the world's oceans, from the tropics to the edge of the polar pack ice in both hemispheres. Found in many deep, semi-enclosed seas, including the Mediterranean Sea, Gulf of Mexico, Caribbean Sea, Sea of Japan and Gulf of California; mostly absent from enclosed seas and semi-enclosed seas with shallow entrances (e.g. the Black Sea, Red Sea and Persian Gulf).

Generally more abundant where there is high productivity, usually from upwelling, in areas dubbed the 'grounds' by Yankee whalers; there are also grounds in apparently unproductive waters, such as the Sargasso Sea. Bathymetric and oceanographic features that can concentrate prey – including frontal boundaries, eddies, submarine canyons and steep continental shelf edges – are preferred. Daily movements depend on prey abundance: 10–20km when it is plentiful to 90–100km when feeding conditions are poor. Where there is abundant prey, there

can be hundreds or even a few thousand sperm whales in areas a few hundred kilometres across.

For most of their adult lives, male and female sperm whales are widely separated – exhibiting the largest geographical sexual segregation of any animal.

FEMALE AND YOUNG MALE DISTRIBUTION

Females and young males tend to remain in the tropics, sub-tropics and warm temperate waters year-round, usually between the equator and 40°S in the southern hemisphere, and the equator and 50°N in the northern hemisphere (sometimes ranging higher in the North Pacific). Their distribution corresponds roughly to sea surface temperatures greater than 15°C. In some areas, there is a general shift to higher latitudes during the summer, but they do not appear to follow particular migration routes or timings (their movements are likely nomadic responses to changes in food abundance). Females make latitudinal and longitudinal movements of up to c. 1,500km, typically travelling about 35,000km per year within a home range (much less than males). They are usually far from land, in waters deeper than c. 1,000m; however, they are often found around oceanic islands (which rise from deep ocean floors) and in the Gulf of California, Mexico, are regularly seen in waters less than 300m deep. When young males leave their natal groups, they gradually move to higher latitudes: the larger and older the male, the higher the average latitude.

ADULT MALE DISTRIBUTION

Large adult males are usually in waters deeper than 300m (often in shallower water than females) and they occur in sea surface temperatures as low as *c.* 0°C; however, in some areas, such as off Long Island in New York, Nova Scotia and Arctic Norway, they are regularly found in waters less than 200m deep and will approach close to shore where there is sufficiently deep water, such as in submarine canyons. They spend much of their time in more productive latitudes higher than 40°, venturing to the northern and southern extremes of the species' range, often near the edge of the polar pack ice. The largest males tend to use the highest-latitude feeding grounds. However, they do return sporadically to warm-water breeding grounds to mate (on an unknown schedule and, possibly, not every year). They move between female family units, usually spending no more than a few minutes or a few hours with each, presumably searching for receptive females. The extent to which they return to their natal grounds to mate is unknown. Over time, they range widely – often moving across entire ocean basins and sometimes from one ocean basin to another.

BEHAVIOUR

Sperm whales have two main behavioural states: foraging (*c.* 75 per cent of their time) and resting or socialising.

When foraging, they make repeated deep dives. Groups of family units spread out over distances of 1km or more, diving for extended periods and then breathing at the surface before diving again. Adult males tend to forage alone.

While resting or socialising, often in the afternoon, females and young sperm whales gather at or near the surface. Their behaviour during these periods is highly variable: they may lie still and quiet, close together and apparently resting, sometimes for hours at a time; or they may be much more active, emitting vocalisations (codas and creaks), rolling around and touching one another, and breaching and lobtailing. Large males also lie quietly at the surface, or socialise if they are with groups of females.

A breaching sperm whale typically leaves the water at an angle of 20–60°, often twisting in the air and usually (though not always) landing on its side. Breaching is most common when groups come together or split, and between bouts of foraging, and tends to occur in bouts (with individuals breaching repeatedly). Females breach more often than lone adult males.

Frequently spyhops, rising above the surface slowly and with little splash, often in the vicinity of whale-watching or research boats. Females spyhop more often when there are mature males around during the breeding season. May also spyhop in response to killer whale vocalisations, as if looking for the source of the threat.

A behaviour apparently unique to sperm whales is 'drift-diving'. They hang passively and upright in the water, with their heads up or down, just below the surface. In one study, they did this for 0.7–31.5 minutes. They are

DIVE SEQUENCE

- Between dives, logs at surface (moving slowly forward or, less often, remaining motionless) to breathe for *c.* 7–10 minutes – typically blows every 10–15 seconds (female and immature) or 15–20 seconds (male).
- While at surface, several individuals may cluster together, facing same direction.
- Before sounding dive, lifts head higher out of water for penultimate breath.
- Body straightens out and back bends in a 'stretch'.
- May drop below surface temporarily.
- Reappears and accelerates forward.
- Takes final breath.
- Back arches high out of water showing rounded hump and 'knuckles'.
- Throws flukes high into air (though usually does not fluke if disturbed).
- Drops vertically.
- Often defecates as flukes, leaving large cloud behind in water.

BLOW

- Bushy or 'puffy' blow directed forward and to left.
- Blow projects up to 6m (height highly variable).

FOOD AND FEEDING

Prey Mainly deepwater squid (more than 25 species, including giant squid and jumbo squid); more than 60 species of medium- to large-sized deep-sea fish (especially lumpsuckers and redfish); male tends to feed on larger individuals in same taxa than females, and more likely to feed on bony fish, sharks and rays; female eats *c.* 750 squid per 24 hours (averaging 37 per foraging dive), male eats *c.* 350; will also occasionally take octopuses, crustaceans, jellyfish and other marine life.

Feeding Feeds mainly in water column (water depth typically at least 200m deeper than dive depth) but some evidence of also feeding along seabed; details of how it catches prey unknown (probably draws it into mouth by suction); recent research suggests unlikely to use powerful clicks for acoustic stunning; in some areas, males take fish from longline fisheries for sable and Pacific halibut (North Pacific); Greenland halibut, Atlantic halibut, Atlantic cod and Greenland cod (North Atlantic); and toothfish (Southern Ocean).

Dive depth Renowned deep diver; adult female foraging dives typically to 200–1,200m, many adult male dives shallower than 400m (though sometimes to 2,000m or more); deepest recorded 2,035m; presence of fresh seafloor-dwelling sharks (*Scymnodon* spp.) in stomach of large male captured in water more than 3,193m deep, off South Africa in 1969, provides strong evidence they may dive deeper than 3km; will often make shallow dive (50–300m) when disturbed.

Dive time Foraging dives typically 30–50 minutes, ranging from 15 minutes to more than 60 minutes; maximum recorded 138 minutes (male, Caribbean, 1983).

probably sleeping and – since they rarely respond to approaching vessels – may be taking advantage of more efficient 'bihemispheric' sleep (in which both halves of the brain rest at the same time); other odontocetes sleep with one hemisphere of the brain at a time. This behaviour is observed most often later in the day, between about 18:00 hrs and midnight.

Generally seems to be oblivious to boats, but it will dive prematurely if a boat approaches too rapidly or too closely. Juveniles are often curious and may come close to investigate. However, there are stories of sperm whales sinking whaling ships – one famously sunk the whaleship *Essex* in the equatorial Pacific in 1820 (the inspiration for Herman Melville's classic, *Moby Dick*).

TEETH

Upper 0

Lower 36–52

Large conical teeth vary from sharply pointed in young individuals to rounded stumps in old individuals. Teeth do not seem to be necessary for feeding (they do not erupt until near puberty – and healthy sperm whales have been caught with broken teeth, no teeth or even broken lower jaws). When the mouth is closed, the teeth fit into shallow sockets in the upper jaw (teeth in the upper jaw are vestigial or rudimentary if they erupt).

GROUP SIZE AND STRUCTURE

There are five main types of social groups:

1. Family unit, or nursery group, consisting of about 10 females and their young and generally stable over decades. Females are always in the company of other females – relying on one another to help raise young, find food and defend against predators – and most spend their entire lives in the same unit. In the North Atlantic, all members of a family unit usually belong to a single matriline and are close relatives; in the North Pacific, a family unit may contain two or more matrilines and individuals occasionally switch between units. Defining a unit can be difficult – when foraging, individuals may be spread out over large distances (sometimes separated by as much as 2–3km).

2. Temporary cohesive group, consisting of two or more family units that share the same dialect (and therefore belong to the same vocal clan); these are common in the North Pacific, but rare in the North Atlantic. They may travel together as a cohesive group of about 20–40 animals for a few hours, days or even months.

3. Clan, containing many family units (hundreds or thousands of females and their calves), that can be spread over large parts of an ocean basin. Clans have distinctive cultures – recognisable sets of coda vocalisations, as well as characteristic movement, foraging, and social behaviours. Two or more clans may use the same waters, but family units form groups only with other units of their own clan.

4. Bachelor school. Young males leave their family unit on reaching sexual maturity, between four and 21 years old (usually in their mid-teens). Not yet in a position to command mating privileges, they form loose aggregations with other young males (usually of approximately the same size and age).

5. Lone adult male. As males in a bachelor school age, they move to higher latitudes and the aggregations become smaller, until the largest males in their late 20s and older are usually alone. Lone males generally avoid one another (though strandings of multiple adult males together suggests that there is still much to learn about male social behaviour).

Part of a super-pod of hundreds, or thousands, of sperm whales.

PREDATORS

Killer whales will attack sperm whales, and tend to focus on females and calves rather than the larger and more aggressive males (it is possible that females remain in relatively nutrient-poor warm seas because of the reduced risk of killer whale attack). Under attack, female sperm whales may adopt one of two circular formations at the surface: a 'marguerite' (named after a daisy), 'rosette' or 'wagon wheel' formation, with their heads pointing inwards, tails outward and bodies radiating out like spokes; or a 'heads-out' formation, to face their attackers. In both, young calves and injured adults remain protected in the centre. Females will assist other members of a family unit under attack, at risk to themselves. In one case, other sperm whales responded to what were believed to be acoustic alarms and came from afar to confront the killer whales en masse. Whalers used to take advantage of this habit of 'standing by' injured animals to kill all members of a group.

Sperm whales are very occasionally attacked, or at least harassed, by other odontocetes – including pilot whales – but these are believed to be rarely fatal. In theory, large sharks are also potential predators of calves.

PHOTO-IDENTIFICATION

Outline of the tail flukes – especially markings along the trailing edge – taken as the animal dives. These markings accumulate with age but remain relatively stable over time. Calves, which do not usually raise their flukes when diving, are identified from their dorsal fin markings.

LIFE HISTORY

Sexual maturity Females 9–10 years (range of 7–13 years), males 18–21 years (but do not take active role in breeding until at least late 20s and typically reach physical maturity at *c.* 40–50 years); very few females give birth after 40 years of age.

Mating Polygynous; adult male roves in search of receptive females on unknown schedule; males fight for access to females (but female choice of mates may also be important).

Gestation 14–16 months.

Calving Every 4–6 years (varies geographically and with age – birth rate drops to *c.* every 15 years in older females); single calf born in summer or autumn; females collectively care for offspring in their social group (even suckling calves that are not their own) and stagger their dives to provide better babysitting.

Weaning After minimum two years (highly variable – milk found in stomachs of females at least 7.5 years old and males 13 years old), though may eat solid food before one year old; duration of lactation may increase with mother's age.

Lifespan Probably at least 60–70 years, possibly longer; oldest recorded 77 years.

POPULATION

Global population is estimated to be roughly 360,000. The highest densities are in the north-west Atlantic, between the edge of the continental shelf and the Gulf Stream, and the lowest densities are believed to be in the Antarctic. It is one of the most abundant of all the great whales (despite intensive exploitation, it was not depleted to the levels of some baleen whales). However, the current population is only c. one-third of the estimated pre-whaling population of 1.1 million. It is unknown if numbers are recovering. Due to its naturally low reproductive rate, even under ideal conditions the maximum possible rate of population increase is estimated at c. 1 per cent per year.

SPERMACETI ORGAN

The spermaceti organ complex – which dominates the sperm whale's head – is the world's most powerful natural sonar or echolocation system. It consists of a complex array of soft structures, cradled above the lower jaw and in front of the skull, in the whale's

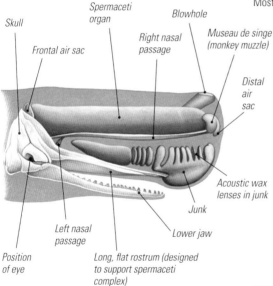

Skull
Spermaceti organ
Blowhole
Frontal air sac
Right nasal passage
Museau de singe (monkey muzzle)
Distal air sac
Acoustic wax lenses in junk
Junk
Left nasal passage
Lower jaw
Position of eye
Long, flat rostrum (designed to support spermaceti complex)

highly modified and asymmetric head. The complex is dominated by the spermaceti organ itself, but includes several other strange structures: the so-called junk, various air sacs and passages, and the curiously named museau de singe or 'monkey muzzle' (two weird lobes a bit like blackened chestnuts set flat side towards each other, which to early French biologists apparently looked like the muzzle of a monkey).

Early theories proposed that the spermaceti organ was used as a battering ram, for absorbing nitrogen under pressure or even as a buoyancy regulator. But more recent studies show that it is mainly for forming, focusing and broadcasting extremely powerful, highly directional clicks.

It may also be used in acoustic displays by males – the spermaceti organ is proportionally larger in males than females and, given that males are much larger anyway, they probably have a much more powerful sound producer.

Known by whalers as the 'case', the spermaceti organ itself is up to c. 5m long and ellipsoid in shape – somewhere between a barrel and a cone – and enclosed by a tough muscular sheath. It consists of white spongy tissue soaked in a liquid wax called spermaceti oil (which differs chemically from the oil found in the melons of most other odontocetes). Between the spermaceti organ and the rostrum is the junk – a complex arrangement of partition blocks or acoustic lenses of a slightly denser tissue – that is also soaked in spermaceti oil.

It is believed that a pulse of sound is initially produced by air being forced through the museau de singe (a pair of 'phonic lips' made of tough connective tissue). The lips open and snap shut, making the clicks. These then pass back through the spermaceti organ, until they are reflected off the air-filled cushion at the far end (the frontal air sac). Most of the click is then redirected into the junk, where it is amplified through a series of c. 20 acoustic lenses, and from there is broadcast into the ocean. The rest makes an additional transit back and forth along the spermaceti organ, before being redirected into the junk and broadcast into the ocean. Thus each click is heard as a series of pulses.

The presence of the spermaceti organ makes other parts of the skull and air passages considerably asymmetrical. In particular, the nasal passages are highly modified: the left nasal passage leads from the blowhole to the lungs and the museau de singe, while the right nasal passage has no function in breathing and is a closed system (connected at one end to an air sac and at the other end to the museau de singe). Externally, the most obvious asymmetrical feature is the blowhole, which is pointed forward and to the left.

AMBERGRIS

Sperm whales occasionally produce a rare greyish substance called ambergris. Naturally waxy and moist, but dry and brittle when exposed to air, ambergris has a pleasant earthy odour. Primarily made of ambrein (a fatty substance similar to cholesterol), it forms around the indigestible beaks of cephalopods that have passed into a sperm whale's lower intestine (and is disgorged when the whale vomits). Pieces of ambergris can weigh up to 635kg, but float in water. Dubbed 'whale gold', it was once regarded as the most valuable of whale products. Found in just 1 per cent of sperm whales killed, ambergris was originally used as a medicine and then as a fixative in perfumes.

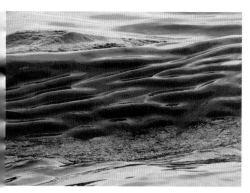

The sperm whale's skin is distinctively wrinkled.

CONSERVATION

IUCN status: Vulnerable (2008); Mediterranean sub-population Endangered (2006). Sperm whales were hunted intensively during two main waves of commercial whaling: sail-powered open-boat whaling with handheld harpoons mainly in 1712–1880 (whose dramas and dangers were depicted in Herman Melville's classic novel *Moby Dick*), and modern whaling mainly from 1946 to the late 1980s. They were highly prized for their spermaceti oil, which produced the brightest and cleanest-burning candles ever made (they illuminated much of the world for decades) and was used as an industrial lubricant.

The global catch during the nineteenth century was estimated at 271,000 and during the twentieth century at 761,000 – more than 1 million sperm whales were killed altogether. Commercial hunting of sperm whales virtually ceased with the IWC moratorium in 1986. However, Japan took 200 in 1986, 188 in 1987 and then up to 10 per year in 2000–13 under its controversial 'scientific' hunt. In small fisheries, three sperm whales were taken in the Azores in 1987, and an average of 20 (ranging from 51 in 2007 to six in 2012) are being caught every year from Lamalera, on the island of Lembata in Indonesia.

Sperm whales – females with young, sub-adult males, and sometimes adult males – are susceptible to mass

Clustered together and characteristically facing the same direction.

strandings. The reason is unknown (perplexingly, the majority appear to be healthy), but it may be that the social bonds are so strong that when a single individual comes ashore others are likely to follow.

Current threats include ingestion of marine debris (including plastic bags), vessel strikes, entanglement in fishing gear, loss of prey due to overfishing, noise pollution (from shipping, military sonar, explosives, and oil and gas exploration), chemical pollution, and habitat loss and degradation. The Mediterranean sub-population is considered to be in decline, probably due to entanglement in high-seas swordfish and tuna driftnets, and ship strikes.

VOCALISATIONS

Sperm whale vocalisations consist almost entirely of low-frequency clicks (ranging between 5kHz and 25kHz), though they also produce occasional, relatively quiet 'squeals' and 'trumpets'. Researchers have identified five distinct types of click – 'regular clicks', 'creaks' or 'buzz vocalisations', 'surface creaks', 'codas', and 'slow clicks' or 'clangs' – and these are used variously for foraging, orientation and communication.

Regular clicks are the most common. Extremely loud, they are used in echolocation to help the whales orientate and locate prey. Consisting of evenly spaced clicks strung together at intervals of 0.5–1 seconds, they can be heard for up to 16km and are typically produced during at least 80 per cent of a dive.

Creaks are best described as accelerated clicking – closely spaced clicks that resemble the sound of a rusty door opening. Audible up to 6km away, they are thought to be used in short-range sonar and are associated with prey capture. Surface creaks are shorter and have constant intervals; they may help sperm whales to locate objects in the water.

Stereotyped patterns of clicks (typically 3–20 clicks lasting 0.2–2 seconds) are called 'codas'. They are most commonly heard from groups of females, when they are socialising, as well as immediately following a dive, and generally have less directionality and power than other clicks. Codas can be characterised using the number of clicks and the pattern of inter-click intervals. Individual sperm whales sharing the same coda repertoires or 'dialects' belong to the same vocal clan: codas are like acoustic signatures, which are probably inherited culturally from other members of the family unit. Large males rarely emit codas.

Slow clicks are produced mostly or entirely by large males, particularly on the breeding grounds. Extremely loud, they can be heard up to 60km away. They are repeated every 6–8 seconds. Their function is unclear, but they are likely to be used as an acoustic display, perhaps either in competition with other males or to attract females.

PYGMY SPERM WHALE
Kogia breviceps

(Blainville, 1838)

Pygmy and dwarf sperm whales are typically seen floating on the surface, with just the top of the head and back (as far as the dorsal fin) exposed. They are very difficult to spot in anything but calm conditions and sightings of both species tend to be brief.

Classification Odontoceti, family Kogiidae.
Common name Reminiscent of a small sperm whale, with a spermaceti organ.
Other names Lesser cachalot, short-headed cachalot, lesser sperm whale, short-headed sperm whale.
Scientific name Two theories proposed for the origin of *Kogia* (Gray, who named the genus, never explained why or from where he chose it): from the Turkish naturalist Cogia Effendi, who observed whales in the Mediterranean in the early 1800s, or a Latinised form of the English word codger (meaning 'mean or miserly old fellow'); *breviceps* from the Latin *brevis* for 'short' and *cepitis* for 'head'.
Taxonomy No recognised forms or subspecies; pygmy and dwarf sperm whales were originally described as two separate species, then lumped together (as the pygmy sperm whale, *Kogia breviceps*), then recognised as genuinely distinct in 1966.

ADULT

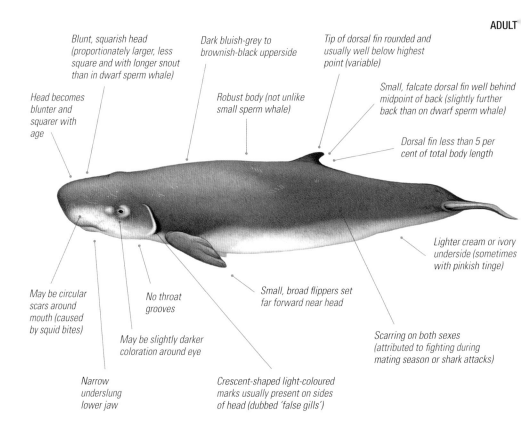

Blunt, squarish head (proportionately larger, less square and with longer snout than in dwarf sperm whale)

Dark bluish-grey to brownish-black upperside

Tip of dorsal fin rounded and usually well below highest point (variable)

Head becomes blunter and squarer with age

Robust body (not unlike small sperm whale)

Small, falcate dorsal fin well behind midpoint of back (slightly further back than on dwarf sperm whale)

Dorsal fin less than 5 per cent of total body length

Lighter cream or ivory underside (sometimes with pinkish tinge)

May be circular scars around mouth (caused by squid bites)

No throat grooves

Small, broad flippers set far forward near head

May be slightly darker coloration around eye

Scarring on both sexes (attributed to fighting during mating season or shark attacks)

Narrow underslung lower jaw

Crescent-shaped light-coloured marks usually present on sides of head (dubbed 'false gills')

AT A GLANCE
- Deep tropical to warm temperate waters worldwide
- Small size
- Generally appears dark grey at sea
- Blunt, squarish head
- Small, falcate dorsal fin slightly further back than on dwarf sperm whale
- Floats motionless on surface between dives
- Back has distinctive bulge when logging

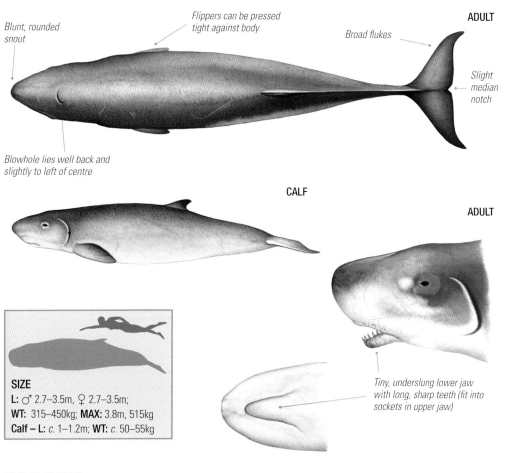

ADULT

Blunt, rounded snout

Flippers can be pressed tight against body

Broad flukes

Slight median notch

Blowhole lies well back and slightly to left of centre

CALF

ADULT

SIZE
L: ♂ 2.7–3.5m, ♀ 2.7–3.5m;
WT: 315–450kg; MAX: 3.8m, 515kg
Calf – L: *c.* 1–1.2m; WT: *c.* 50–55kg

Tiny, underslung lower jaw with long, sharp teeth (fit into sockets in upper jaw)

SIMILAR SPECIES
Difficult to tell apart from the dwarf sperm whale at sea, but possible in good conditions. The somewhat larger pygmy sperm whale has a smaller, lower, more rounded dorsal fin set further back on the body, a proportionately much larger head and a distinctive bulge on the back.

DISTRIBUTION
Tropical to warm temperate waters worldwide, in the Atlantic, Pacific and Indian Oceans. Generally inhabits waters along the outer continental shelf and beyond, particularly over and near the continental slope. In the North Atlantic, it is associated exclusively with the Gulf Stream. Prefers more temperate seas and relatively deeper, more pelagic waters than the dwarf sperm whale. There is no evidence of long-distance migrations. Most information comes from strandings.

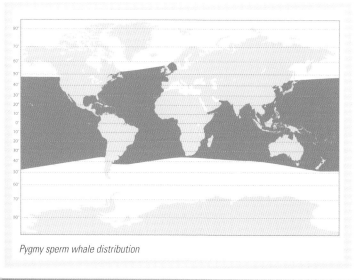

Pygmy sperm whale distribution

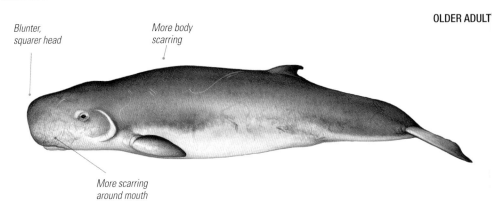

OLDER ADULT

Blunter, squarer head

More body scarring

More scarring around mouth

BEHAVIOUR

Difficult to spot, except in extremely calm seas. Surfacing patterns are hard to predict and it tends to be shy, undemonstrative and tricky to approach closely. Aerial behaviour is extremely rare, though it does sometimes breach (usually falling back into the water tail first). Between dives, it tends to raft motionless at the surface – where it looks like a piece of driftwood from a distance – with the top of the head and back and dorsal fin exposed, and the tail hanging down loosely underwater. It releases a reddish-brown liquid from a sac in the lower intestine when it is startled or distressed and, possibly, during foraging; this forms an opaque cloud in the water, which may hide the whale or distract a predator. There is no evidence of associations with dwarf sperm whales or other cetaceans.

TEETH

Upper 0
Lower 20–32

GROUP SIZE AND STRUCTURE

Usually solitary, but up to six of varying age and sex composition. Strandings usually involve single animals (maximum known was three: one male and two females).

PREDATORS

Scarring from attacks by large sharks is fairly common. The location of bite wounds on their backs suggests that they roll over as a defence mechanism if they detect a shark about to bite (perhaps to protect the more vulnerable belly – although larval elasmobranch tapeworms, which presumably complete their life cycle in sharks, are concentrated in the blubber of the pygmy

COMPARISON OF SILHOUETTES

Pygmy sperm whale
- Distinctive rounded bulge on back (between blowhole and dorsal fin) visible when logging.
- Distinct 'neck' behind relatively large head.
- Smaller, rounded dorsal fin, further back.
- Sometimes dorsal fin invisible until animal rolls out of sight.

Dwarf sperm whale
- Flatter profile in water (usually without a prominent bulge), reminiscent of an upside-down surfboard.
- Tends to float lower in water.
- Larger, pointed dorsal fin, further forward.
- Dorsal fin not unlike that of bottlenose dolphin.

DIVE SEQUENCE
- Rises to surface slowly.
- Inconspicuous blow.
- Floats motionless in same position on surface (with front of melon to dorsal fin visible).
- Usually sinks vertically out of sight but (particularly if startled) may roll forward with little arching of back.
- Does not show flukes.

FOOD AND FEEDING

Prey Mostly deepwater squid; will take some fish and shrimps; more diverse diet and averages larger prey than dwarf sperm whale.
Feeding Most feeding on or near seabed; anatomy suggests powerful suction feeding.
Dive depth Unknown but believed to forage at greater depths than dwarf sperm whale.
Dive time 12–15 minutes (based on limited evidence); maximum recorded 18 minutes.

sperm whale's lower belly). Predation by killer whales has been documented.

POPULATION

No overall abundance estimate, although frequent strandings in some areas (such as Florida, South Africa and New Zealand) implies that it is more common than the lack of sightings suggests. There are very rough estimates for dwarf and pygmy sperm whales combined of 150,000 in the eastern tropical Pacific and 395 in the western North Atlantic. A 2002 survey estimated more than 7,000 in Hawaii (but no live animals were seen during a 2010 survey).

CONSERVATION

IUCN status: Data Deficient (2008). No regular large hunts are known, but pygmy sperm whales have been taken in small numbers in harpoon fisheries in St Vincent in the Caribbean, Japan, Taiwan, Sri Lanka and Indonesia. There is growing evidence that they ingest ocean debris such as plastic bags and balloons (causing associated fatal gut blockage). Relatively small numbers are caught as bycatch in fisheries. Their habit of lying quietly at the surface seems to have led to occasional ship strikes. They appear to be vulnerable to noise pollution (including military sonar and seismic surveying).

LIFE HISTORY

Sexual maturity Females five years, males 2.5–5 years.
Mating May be some direct male–male aggression, but sperm competition may be important in male reproductive success.
Gestation 9–12 months.
Calving Every 1–2 years; single calf probably born in summer (December–March in South Africa).
Weaning After 6–12 months.
Lifespan c. 22 years (oldest recorded 23 years).

Two pygmy sperm whales lying motionless at the surface.

DWARF SPERM WHALE
Kogia sima
(Owen, 1866)

With their long, sharp teeth, underslung lower jaws and gill-like markings on either side of the head, dwarf and pygmy sperm whales are often mistaken for sharks when they strand. Their appearance may be a form of mimicry, to help avoid predation.

Classification Odontoceti, family Kogiidae.

Common name Alternative name for a small cetacean resembling a sperm whale.

Other names Owen's pygmy whale, snub-nosed cachalot.

Scientific name Two theories proposed for the origin of *Kogia* (Gray, who named the genus, never explained why or from where he chose it): from the Turkish naturalist Cogia Effendi, who observed whales in the Mediterranean in the early 1800s, or a Latinised form of the English word codger (meaning 'mean or miserly old fellow'); *sima* (formerly *simus*) from the Latin *sima* or Greek *sîmos* for 'snub-nosed'.

Taxonomy No recognised forms or subspecies; however, recent genetic studies suggest there may be two distinct species, in the Atlantic and Indo-Pacific; dwarf and pygmy sperm whales were originally described as two separate species, then lumped together (as the pygmy sperm whale, *Kogia breviceps*), then recognised as genuinely distinct in 1966.

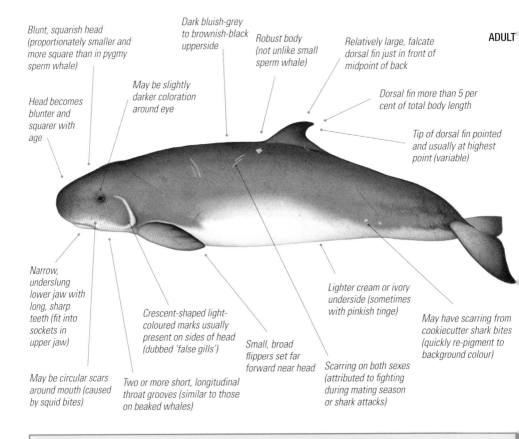

Blunt, squarish head (proportionately smaller and more square than in pygmy sperm whale)

Dark bluish-grey to brownish-black upperside

Robust body (not unlike small sperm whale)

Relatively large, falcate dorsal fin just in front of midpoint of back

ADULT

Head becomes blunter and squarer with age

May be slightly darker coloration around eye

Dorsal fin more than 5 per cent of total body length

Tip of dorsal fin pointed and usually at highest point (variable)

Narrow, underslung lower jaw with long, sharp teeth (fit into sockets in upper jaw)

Crescent-shaped light-coloured marks usually present on sides of head (dubbed 'false gills')

Lighter cream or ivory underside (sometimes with pinkish tinge)

May have scarring from cookiecutter shark bites (quickly re-pigment to background colour)

Small, broad flippers set far forward near head

Scarring on both sexes (attributed to fighting during mating season or shark attacks)

May be circular scars around mouth (caused by squid bites)

Two or more short, longitudinal throat grooves (similar to those on beaked whales)

AT A GLANCE
- Deep tropical to warm temperate waters worldwide
- Small size
- Generally appears dark grey at sea
- Blunt, squarish head
- Tall, pointed, falcate dorsal fin slightly further forward than on pygmy sperm whale
- Floats motionless on surface between dives
- Back appears flat when logging

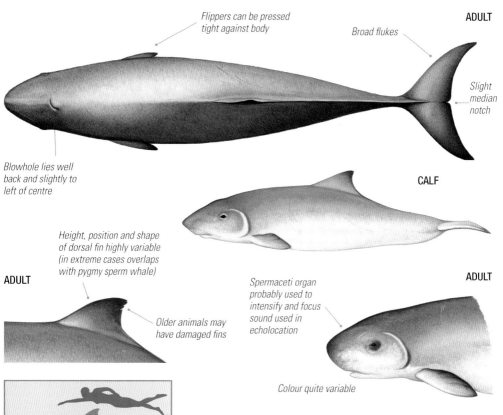

ADULT

Flippers can be pressed tight against body

Broad flukes

Slight median notch

Blowhole lies well back and slightly to left of centre

CALF

Height, position and shape of dorsal fin highly variable (in extreme cases overlaps with pygmy sperm whale)

ADULT

ADULT

Older animals may have damaged fins

Spermaceti organ probably used to intensify and focus sound used in echolocation

Colour quite variable

SIZE
L: ♂ 2.1–2.4m, ♀ 2.1–2.4m;
WT: 135–270kg; **MAX:** 2.7m, 303kg
Calf – L: c. 0.9–1.1m; **WT:** 40–50kg

SIMILAR SPECIES

Difficult to tell apart from the pygmy sperm whale at sea, but possible in good conditions. The somewhat smaller dwarf sperm whale has a larger, taller, more erect and pointed dorsal fin set further forward on the body, a proportionately much smaller head and a flatter profile in the water (without a back bulge); when logging it is reminiscent of an upside-down surfboard. The overall appearance of the dwarf sperm whale is more dolphin-like than the pygmy sperm whale.

DISTRIBUTION

Tropical to warm temperate waters worldwide, in the Atlantic, Pacific and Indian Oceans. Generally inhabits deep waters over or near the edge of the continental shelf. In the North Atlantic, it is associated exclusively with the Gulf Stream. Prefers more tropical seas and relatively shallower, less pelagic waters than the pygmy sperm whale (it sometimes occurs in more coastal areas) and probably does not range as far into high latitudes. There is no evidence of long-distance migrations,

Dwarf sperm whale distribution

although some populations show seasonal movements (e.g. in the Bahamas into deeper water during summer, perhaps to avoid sharks). Most information comes from strandings.

BEHAVIOUR

Difficult to spot, except in extremely calm seas. Surfacing patterns are hard to predict and it has a large personal space (rarely allowing a close approach). Aerial behaviour is extremely rare, though it does sometimes breach (usually falling back into the water tail first). Between dives, it tends to raft motionless at the surface – where it looks like a piece of driftwood from a distance – with the top of the head and back and dorsal fin exposed, and the tail hanging down loosely underwater. It releases a reddish-brown liquid from a sac in the lower intestine when it is startled or distressed and, possibly, during foraging; this forms an opaque cloud in the water, which may hide the whale or distract a predator. There is no evidence of associations with pygmy sperm whales or other cetaceans.

TEETH

Upper 0–6
Lower 14–26

GROUP SIZE AND STRUCTURE

Usually solitary, but up to 12 (maximum 16 recorded) of varying age and sex composition. Group size varies according to location and season: e.g. in the Bahamas

1–8 in summer, 1–12 in winter; average in Hawaii is 2.7. Individuals in a group appear to be loosely associated – when one appears, there are often others several hundred metres away. Strandings usually involve single animals (maximum known was four immatures: one male and three females).

PREDATORS

Scarring from attacks by large sharks is fairly common. The location of bite wounds on their backs suggests that they roll over as a defence mechanism if they detect a shark about to bite (perhaps to protect the more vulnerable belly – although larval elasmobranch tapeworms, which presumably complete their life cycle in sharks, are concentrated in the blubber of the dwarf sperm whale's lower belly). Predation by killer whales has been documented.

PHOTO-IDENTIFICATION

Difficult, but possible – almost all adults have distinctively shaped or damaged dorsal fins.

POPULATION

No overall abundance estimate, although frequent strandings in some areas implies that it is more common than the lack of sightings suggests. There are very rough estimates for dwarf and pygmy sperm whales combined of 150,000 in the eastern tropical Pacific and 395 in the western North Atlantic. A 2002 survey estimated more than 19,000 in Hawaii.

COMPARISON OF SILHOUETTES

Pygmy sperm whale
- Distinctive rounded bulge on back (between blowhole and dorsal fin) visible when logging.
- Distinct 'neck' behind relatively large head.
- Smaller, rounded dorsal fin, further back.
- Sometimes dorsal fin invisible until animal rolls out of sight.

Dwarf sperm whale
- Flatter profile in water (usually without a prominent bulge), reminiscent of an upside-down surfboard.
- Tends to float lower in water.
- Larger, pointed dorsal fin, further forward.
- Dorsal fin not unlike that of bottlenose dolphin.

DIVE SEQUENCE
- Rises to surface slowly.
- Inconspicuous blow.
- Floats motionless in same position on surface (with front of melon to dorsal fin visible).
- Usually sinks vertically out of sight but (particularly if startled) may roll forward with little arching of back.
- Does not show flukes.

FOOD AND FEEDING

Prey Mostly mid- and deepwater squid; will take some fish and shrimps; less diverse diet and averages smaller prey than pygmy sperm whale.

Feeding Most feeding on or near seabed; anatomy suggests powerful suction feeding.

Dive depth Unknown, but believed to forage at shallower depths than pygmy sperm whale (600–1,200m suggested).

Dive time 7–15 minutes (possibly up to 30 minutes); brief 1–3 minutes at surface in between.

CONSERVATION

IUCN status: Data Deficient (2008). No regular large hunts are known, but dwarf sperm whales have been taken in small numbers in harpoon fisheries in St Vincent in the Caribbean, Japan, Taiwan, Sri Lanka and Indonesia. There is growing evidence that they ingest ocean debris such as plastic bags and balloons (causing associated fatal gut blockage). Relatively small numbers are caught as bycatch in fisheries; deaths have been linked to dynamite fishing in the Philippines. Their habit of lying quietly at the surface seems to have led to occasional ship strikes. They appear to be vulnerable to noise pollution (including military sonar and seismic surveying).

LIFE HISTORY

Sexual maturity Females 4.5–5 years, males 2.5–3 years.

Mating May be some direct male–male aggression, but sperm competition may be important in male reproductive success.

Gestation 9–12 months.

Calving Every 1–2 years; single calf probably born in summer (December–March in South Africa).

Weaning After 6–12 months.

Lifespan c. 22 years (oldest recorded 22 years).

Two dwarf sperm whales: one logging at the surface and the other just rolling forward into a dive.

NARWHAL
Monodon monoceros

Linnaeus, 1758

The narwhal can be difficult to see: it lives in remote regions of the High Arctic and spends half the year in dense pack ice and in continuous darkness. But it does have predictable migratory patterns and the male is unmistakable, with its extraordinary long, spiralling tusk.

Classification Odontoceti, family Monodontidae.
Common name From the Old Norse *nar* for 'corpse' and *hval* for 'whale' – literally 'corpse whale' – as the skin colour was thought to resemble that of a floating corpse (and the narwhal has a habit of lying still at the surface).
Other names Narwhale, unicorn whale, sea unicorn, horned whale.
Scientific name From the Greek *monos* for 'one', *odon* for 'tooth' and *keros* for 'unicorn' or 'horn' – i.e. 'one-toothed unicorn' or 'one tooth, one horn'.
Taxonomy No recognised forms or subspecies; *c.* 11–12 sub-populations are currently recognised (depending on whether east/north-east Greenland narwhals are considered distinct), with varying degrees of genetic differentiation and geographical isolation.

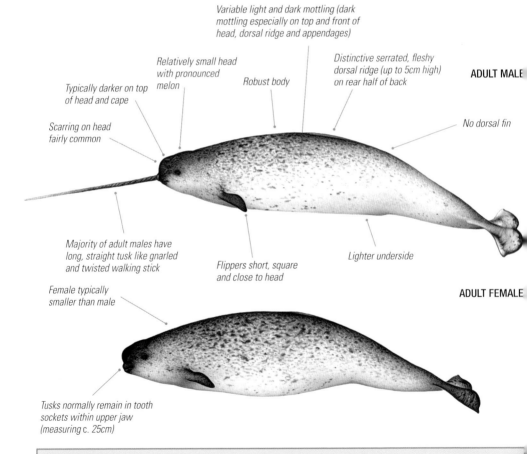

Variable light and dark mottling (dark mottling especially on top and front of head, dorsal ridge and appendages)

Relatively small head with pronounced melon

Typically darker on top of head and cape

Robust body

Distinctive serrated, fleshy dorsal ridge (up to 5cm high) on rear half of back

ADULT MALE

Scarring on head fairly common

No dorsal fin

Majority of adult males have long, straight tusk like gnarled and twisted walking stick

Flippers short, square and close to head

Lighter underside

Female typically smaller than male

ADULT FEMALE

Tusks normally remain in tooth sockets within upper jaw (measuring c. 25cm)

AT A GLANCE
- High Arctic
- Small to medium size
- Long tusk of male

- Relatively small bulbous head
- Little or no beak
- No dorsal fin (but slight dorsal ridge)
- Variable light and dark mottling

OLDER ADULT MALE

*Tusk typically to c. 2m
(maximum 3m in old males)*

*Typically remains dark on
top and front of head, along
dorsal ridge and along
borders of flippers and flukes*

*Flippers often curl
up at the tips (more
exaggerated in males)*

*Mottling becomes lighter with age
(older males, especially, can appear
almost white at a distance)*

*Right tusk usually remains
embedded in skull
(measuring c. 30cm)*

*Dark brown dorsal surface (strongest
on top and front of head, along
dorsal ridge and along borders of
flippers and flukes)*

ADULT MALE

*Erupted tusk appears on
left side of upper jaw and
angles slightly to left*

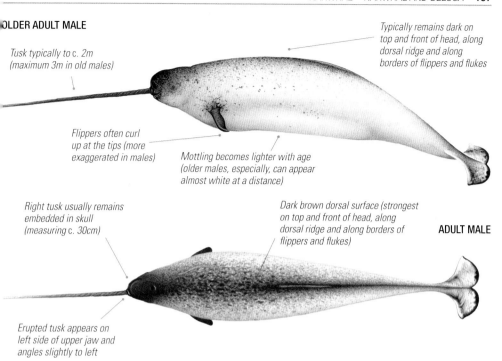

SIZE
L: ♂ 4.3–4.8m (excluding tusk of up to
3m), ♀ 3.7–4.2m;
WT: 700–1,650kg; **MAX:** 5m, 1,800kg
Calf – L: 1.5–1.7m, **WT:** *c.* 80kg

SIMILAR SPECIES

The beluga is the only similar-sized cetacean (and the only other
monodontid) overlapping in range and may be confused with female
and juvenile narwhals, or older males at a distance (if the tusk is
not visible). The narwhal's mottling should help to separate the two
species. Young belugas and narwhals are both grey and look similar. A
skull found in west Greenland was a narwhal–beluga hybrid – dubbed a
'narluga'. A ringed seal rolling at the surface may resemble a narwhal,
if glimpsed briefly.

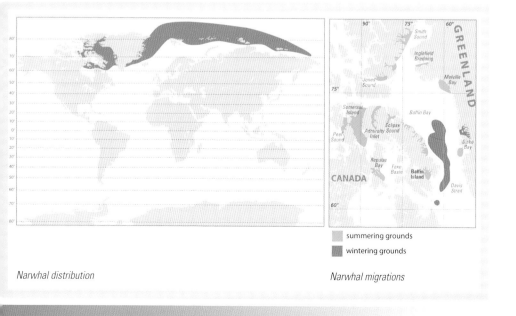

Narwhal distribution

Narwhal migrations

summering grounds
wintering grounds

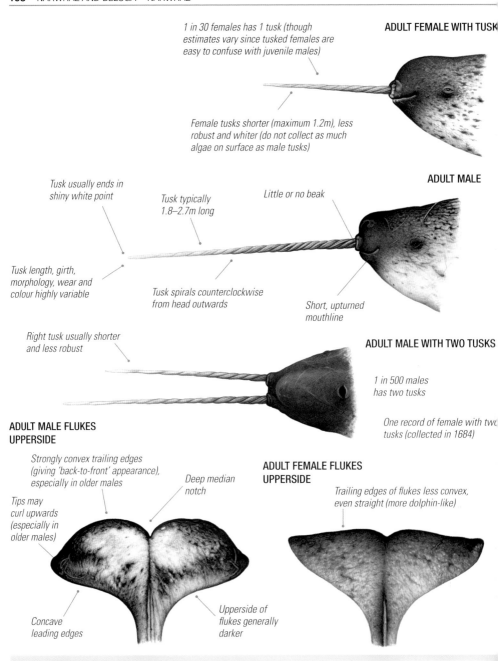

ADULT FEMALE WITH TUSK

1 in 30 females has 1 tusk (though estimates vary since tusked females are easy to confuse with juvenile males)

Female tusks shorter (maximum 1.2m), less robust and whiter (do not collect as much algae on surface as male tusks)

ADULT MALE

Tusk usually ends in shiny white point

Tusk typically 1.8–2.7m long

Little or no beak

Tusk length, girth, morphology, wear and colour highly variable

Tusk spirals counterclockwise from head outwards

Short, upturned mouthline

Right tusk usually shorter and less robust

ADULT MALE WITH TWO TUSKS

1 in 500 males has two tusks

One record of female with two tusks (collected in 1684)

ADULT MALE FLUKES UPPERSIDE

Strongly convex trailing edges (giving 'back-to-front' appearance), especially in older males

Deep median notch

ADULT FEMALE FLUKES UPPERSIDE

Trailing edges of flukes less convex, even straight (more dolphin-like)

Tips may curl upwards (especially in older males)

Concave leading edges

Upperside of flukes generally darker

DIVE SEQUENCE

- Visible but inconspicuous blow (clearly audible on calm days and at close range).
- Male's tusk sometimes (but not always) appears above surface (usually briefly).
- Alternatively, may see impression of tusk just below surface.
- Distinctive indentation at neck noticeable at surface.
- May fluke before deep dive (rarely before shallow dive).

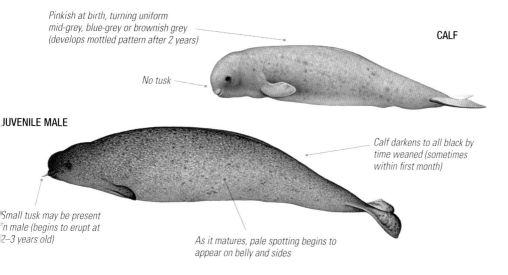

Pinkish at birth, turning uniform
mid-grey, blue-grey or brownish grey
(develops mottled pattern after 2 years)

CALF

No tusk

JUVENILE MALE

Calf darkens to all black by
time weaned (sometimes
within first month)

Small tusk may be present
in male (begins to erupt at
2–3 years old)

As it matures, pale spotting begins to
appear on belly and sides

DISTRIBUTION

Mainly in the Atlantic sector of the Arctic (60°–85°N, most commonly 70°–80°N). Occasional stragglers in the Pacific sector. Relatively rare in Svalbard, the western Canadian Arctic, Alaska and south of the Arctic Circle. Discontinuous range, separated by Greenland. Winter and summer ranges up to 2,000km apart. Vagrants have been recorded in Newfoundland, the UK, Germany, Belgium and the Netherlands, in the North Atlantic; and as far south as the Alaska Peninsula and the Commander Islands, in the North Pacific.

Winter distribution Wintering areas tend to be deep, offshore, ice-covered habitats along the continental slope. Few other cetaceans use areas with such dense sea-ice cover. Two-thirds of all narwhals winter in deep water offshore under dense pack ice in Baffin Bay and Davis Strait (between Baffin Island and Greenland), in two distinct 'grounds' (northern and southern); the east Greenland population winters offshore in deep waters of the Greenland Sea. On the wintering grounds, they spend six months in continuous darkness, in temperatures

as low as -40°C, where there is often less than 3 per cent open water (these offshore wintering grounds offer highly predictable food sources). In some areas they are vulnerable to ice entrapments, where hundreds can be trapped in small openings in the sea ice, and die.

Summer distribution Spends c. two months each summer in ice-free bays, fjords and island passages in the Canadian Arctic, western and eastern Greenland, Svalbard, and the northwestern Russian High Arctic. In some parts of the range, glacial fronts are an important summer habitat. It prefers deep water but will readily enter shallow water to hide from hunting killer whales.

MIGRATIONS

There are predictable migrations between the summering and wintering grounds, as the ice retreats in spring and refreezes in autumn, and in many areas narwhals pass certain promontories, bays and fjords at precisely the same time each year. Migrations last c. two months each way. In May and June, Baffin Bay and Davis Strait animals move north and east to west Greenland or north and west

---

FOOD AND FEEDING

Prey Fish (especially Greenland halibut, Arctic cod; also Arctic eelpout, polar cod, roughhead grenadier, capelin), squid (especially small deepwater *Gonatus* spp.), shrimp (especially deep-sea prawn); precise diet varies with region and season.

Feeding Most feeding in winter (November–March), very little or no feeding in summer (July–September), will feed under sea ice in spring and autumn; forages in deep water at or near seabed and higher in water column, depending on region and season; probably sucks prey into mouth and swallows it whole; no evidence of cooperative hunting.

Dive depth Summer 13–850m, though usually less than 50m; winter much deeper (typically spending over three hours per day at depths of at least 800m, during 18–25 dives – repeating this pattern every day for six months); over half winter dives reach 1,500m; maximum recorded 1,800m; believed to turn upside down soon after diving and remains upside down for much of dive (especially near seafloor).

Dive time Mostly 7–20 minutes, maximum documented 25 minutes.

Narwhal sub-populations: ranges and sizes.

Sub-population	Summer	Winter	Most recent estimated population
Northern Hudson Bay	Northwestern Hudson Bay (especially Repulse Bay and Southampton Island)	Eastern Hudson Strait	12,485 – stable
Somerset Island	Somerset Island region	Baffin Bay	49,768 – increasing
Admiralty Inlet	Admiralty Inlet region	Baffin Bay	35,043 – stable
Eclipse Sound	Eclipse Sound	Baffin Bay	10,489 – trend unknown
Eastern Baffin Island	Cumberland Sound and north along Baffin Island coast	Northern Davis Strait	17,555 – trend unknown
Jones Sound	Between Devon Island and Ellesmere Island, and in fjords of western Ellesmere Island	Unknown	12,694 – trend unknown
Smith Sound	Southeastern coast of Ellesmere Island	Unknown	16,360 – trend unknown
Inglefield Bredning	Inglefield Bredning	Unknown	8,368 – stable
Melville Bay	Melville Bay region	Southern Baffin Bay	3,091 – stable
East Greenland (excluding north-east)	Mainly 64°–72°N (reported up to 81°N)	Greenland Sea and Fram Strait	6,583 – trend unknown
Svalbard–Franz Josef Land	Mainly west and north Svalbard, and northwestern Russian High Arctic	Unknown	Minimum 837 in Svalbard – trend unknown

to Canada (where they crowd at the edges of the fast ice at the entrances to Eclipse Sound, Lancaster Sound, Jones Sound and others); from mid-September to mid-October, they move south (arriving back in central Baffin Bay around mid-November). Narwhals summering in Eclipse Sound, Canada, and Melville Bay, west Greenland, go to southern Baffin Bay and northern Davis Strait; those from Somerset Island, Canada, go to the more heavily populated northern Baffin Bay. There appears to be little exchange between these two areas.

BEHAVIOUR

Not given to spontaneous exuberance such as breaching or speed-swimming, but will occasionally spyhop and lunge. Frequently logs, with the top of its head and back visible, and it may roll around at the surface while socialising. Spends less time at the surface in choppy or rough seas. Male may wave its tusk in the air or rest it on the back of another individual. Before a deep dive, a narwhal often swims directly towards the ice edge, then flukes about 5–30m away. Navigates easily under ice (the lack of a

dorsal fin is probably an adaptation for this) and can travel several kilometres between breathing opportunities, or it will break through ice several centimetres thick (with its head or back); the only barrier to its movements is fast ice without cracks. Often associates with bowhead whales; rarely forms mixed herds with belugas. Often shy and wary of boats (especially where hunted), but in Canada, at least, can be less nervous of people standing on the floe edge or shore.

JOUSTING

Two tusks hitting one another sound like the 'clack' of drumsticks being hit together.

TEETH

Upper 2
Lower 0

Foetal narwhal have 16 tooth buds – 12 in the upper jaw, four in the lower – but 12 disappear, two remain vestigial and two are canines that become erupted or unerupted tusks.

GROUP SIZE AND STRUCTURE

Most narwhal pods or 'clusters' typically contain between two and 10 individuals (ranging from one to 50). Most of the time these are composed of a single sex: all males, or all females with young. There is no information on how long clusters last, or if there are enduring social bonds, but it is possible that their composition varies according to activity and resource distribution and accessibility. They often combine to form large dispersed herds, each with up to 600 clusters, containing hundreds or even thousands of individuals and a mix of sexes and ages.

PREDATORS

Killer whales and polar bears. Sea ice normally inhibits the movements of killer whales in the High Arctic, but with climate change they are already gaining more extensive access to sub-Arctic areas, for longer, and are likely to pose a greater threat to narwhals in the future. Summer sightings in the Hudson Bay region, for example, have increased exponentially in recent years. When killer whales are nearby, narwhals tend to slow down, gather in tighter groups and move into shallower water close to shore (where they are presumably less vulnerable). During an attack, they spread out and move far away from the attack site. Polar bears hunt narwhals along the floe edge, or when they become entrapped in small breathing holes in the ice. Young or injured animals may also be taken by Greenland sharks and walruses.

PHOTO-IDENTIFICATION

Nicks and notches on the dorsal ridge (which are found on 91 per cent of individuals and are relatively stable over time), combined with scars and pigmentation patterns (though these change from year to year so are more useful in short-term studies).

POPULATION

Total global abundance is *c.* 170,000, excluding north-east Greenland and the Russian Arctic (for which no estimates are available).

CONSERVATION

IUCN status: Least Concern (2017). Narwhals have been hunted by the Inuit in Canada and Greenland for thousands of years. The vitamin C-rich muktuk (spelt, variably, maqtaq, mattak or muktuq) – the skin and adhering blubber, eaten raw, cured or boiled – is highly valued (Arctic residents have little access to fresh fruit and vegetables); the meat is sometimes used as dog food. Narwhal tusks still command a high price, whole or carved, domestically and abroad, despite many limitations on international trade. During 2011–15, an average of 620 narwhals were officially landed in Canada every year (shot with rifles), *c.* 300 in west Greenland (mostly with kayaks and traditional harpoons) and *c.* 60+ in east Greenland (shot with rifles). During 1987–2009, trade in 4,923 narwhal tusks was reported; however, this figure is considered an underestimate. Despite harvest limits in most of the range (which may or may not be sustainable) compliance is questionable. A major concern is the

---

LIFE HISTORY

Sexual maturity Females 6–7 years, males 8–9 years.
Mating March–April in offshore pack ice of wintering grounds; polygynous (males mate with many females).
Gestation 13–16 (usually 14–15) months.
Calving Every 2–3 years, on average; single calf born late May–August, usually during northbound (or in some sub-populations inshore) migration, coinciding with receding sea ice; females carrying two foetuses have been reported.
Weaning After 12–20 months (but dependent longer – calf probably stays with mother until she's about to give birth again).
Lifespan At least 50 years (maximum known: female killed in west Greenland, aged 115).

Adults often (but not always) fluke when starting a deep dive (juveniles and immatures rarely fluke).

A male's tusk appears above the surface briefly before a deep dive.

After a deep dive, a narwhal will lie still at the surface for several minutes, breathing deeply, before diving again – note the distinctive indentation at the neck.

On surfacing, a distinctive line of water in front of the melon often gives away the presence of a tusk even when it is hidden beneath the surface.

A young narwhal with a small tusk.

significant (but unknown) number struck and killed, but lost (so not counted); many narwhals in Arctic Canada bear scars from bullet wounds. Other threats include overfishing of their prey species (especially Greenland halibut). They are also considered one of the three most sensitive marine mammals to climate change, which results in loss of crucial sea ice habitat and changes in the distribution of their predators and prey; global warming is also opening up the High Arctic to more commercial human activities, such as oil and gas development and commercial shipping, which are likely to degrade narwhal habitat.

TUSK BIOLOGY

The hollow tusk of the male (and on as many as one in 30 females) is unique among cetaceans. It is formed from the left upper canine (not incisor – as incorrectly stated in some references). It erupts when the animal is 2–3 years old, penetrates the upper lip, spirals out counterclockwise and grows continuously. Growth rate is variable according to age and between individuals; there is a burst of growth at sexual maturity, averaging 10cm per year. The tusk typically grows to *c.* 2m and weighs 10kg, though very old males may have tusks up to 3m

ong. It is surprisingly flexible, able to bend about 30cm n any direction without breaking.

The tusk's purpose has been widely debated. Unlikely past theories included spearing fish, stirring up the seabed n search of food, drilling through ice and sensing prey. Another unsubstantiated hypothesis is that it doubles up as a sensory organ, perhaps to detect changes in seawater salinity (to find air holes in the ice in the dark). It may, secondarily, be used for feeding – there is film footage of narwhals in Nunavut, Canada, stunning Arctic cod with quick, jagged movements of their tusks, then using their tusks to guide the fish into their mouths. But since most females do not have a tusk (and, indeed, live for longer) it is clearly not essential for day-to-day survival. Most evidence clearly points to its role as a secondary sexual characteristic, like the antlers of a stag, used by males to determine social rank and/or to impress females; females will typically mate with males with longer tusks (indeed, tusk length has been correlated with testes size). There is evidence that the tusk may be used aggressively, especially during the winter mating season, given the high incidence of broken tusks and significant head scarring on adult males.

The tusk may be the source of the unicorn myth. In the Middle Ages, 'unicorn horn' was thought to have magical cure-all properties and was worth many times its weight in gold (knowledge of the real-life narwhal was deliberately suppressed by crafty tusk traders to enhance its value).

VOCALISATIONS

Narwhals make two different types of sound: echolocation (click-trains and click-bursts – 19–48kHz) and social vocalisations (300Hz to 18kHz). They have the most directional echolocation beam reported for any cetacean, perhaps helping to reduce unwanted echoes off the sea ice. During social communication, especially when travelling, they make a riotous symphony of moos, whistles, trumpets, grunts, knocks (some like knocking on a door, others like running a stick along a picket fence), creaks, squeaks (like a squeaking door), pops and clicks. It is possible that each group has its own dialect and individuals even produce their own 'signature vocalisations'. Females also make low-frequency moans to communicate with their calves.

The tusk always spirals anticlockwise from the whale's-eye view.

BELUGA WHALE
Delphinapterus leucas

(Pallas, 1776)

Ancient mariners used to call the pale white beluga the 'sea canary', because of its great repertoire of groans, roars, whistles, squawks, moos, buzzes and trills. When seen from above the surface, its ghost-like glow is hard to mistake for any other species.

Classification Odontoceti, family Monodontidae.
Common name A derivation of the Russian word *beloye* or *belyi*, meaning 'white'.
Other names White whale; historically – sea canary.
Scientific name From the Latin *delphinus* for 'dolphin', *apterus* for 'without a fin' and *leucas* from *leukos* for 'white'.
Taxonomy No recognised forms or subspecies; 21 sub-populations currently recognised; some sub-populations may comprise distinct ecotypes.

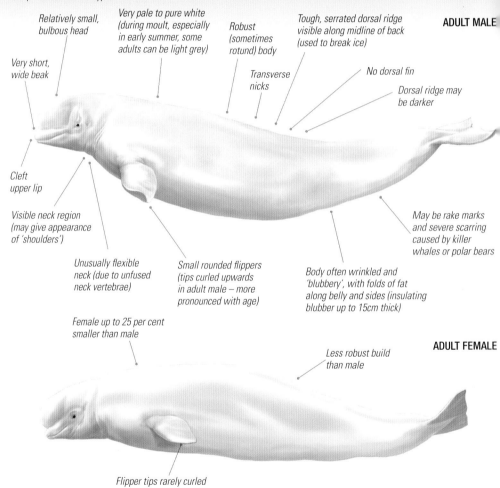

Relatively small, bulbous head

Very pale to pure white (during moult, especially in early summer, some adults can be light grey)

Robust (sometimes rotund) body

Tough, serrated dorsal ridge visible along midline of back (used to break ice)

ADULT MALE

Very short, wide beak

Transverse nicks

No dorsal fin

Dorsal ridge may be darker

Cleft upper lip

Visible neck region (may give appearance of 'shoulders')

May be rake marks and severe scarring caused by killer whales or polar bears

Unusually flexible neck (due to unfused neck vertebrae)

Small rounded flippers (tips curled upwards in adult male – more pronounced with age)

Body often wrinkled and 'blubbery', with folds of fat along belly and sides (insulating blubber up to 15cm thick)

Female up to 25 per cent smaller than male

Less robust build than male

ADULT FEMALE

Flipper tips rarely curled

AT A GLANCE
- Arctic and sub-Arctic
- Small to medium size
- Very pale to pure white, pale grey or yellowish with no mottling
- Robust body
- Small, bulbous head
- No dorsal fin
- Surfaces often with distinctive slow rolling motion

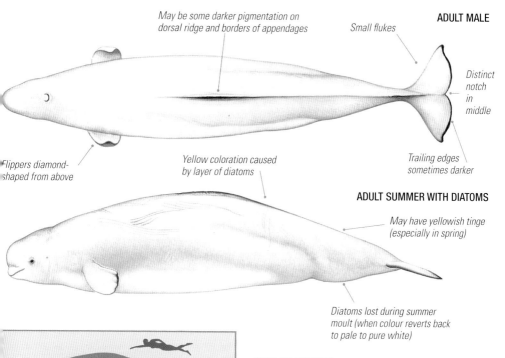

ADULT MALE

May be some darker pigmentation on dorsal ridge and borders of appendages

Small flukes

Distinct notch in middle

Flippers diamond-shaped from above

Yellow coloration caused by layer of diatoms

Trailing edges sometimes darker

ADULT SUMMER WITH DIATOMS

May have yellowish tinge (especially in spring)

Diatoms lost during summer moult (when colour reverts back to pale to pure white)

SIZE

L: ♂ 3.7–4.8m, ♀ 3.0–3.9m;
WT: 500–1,300kg; **MAX:** 5.5m, 1.9t
Calf – L: 1.5–1.6m; **WT:** 80–100kg.
Body size varies considerably between sub-populations: the largest occur in west Greenland and the Sea of Okhotsk, the smallest in northern Quebec and Hudson Bay; generally larger in the Arctic than the sub-Arctic.

SIMILAR SPECIES

The narwhal is the only similar-sized cetacean overlapping in range. Confusion is most likely with females (though the narwhal's mottling should help to separate the two), juveniles (young narwhals and belugas are both grey and look similar – but they are likely to be with adults) and older males (although they can appear fairly white at a distance, their tusks are distinctive). A skull found in West Greenland was a narwhal–beluga hybrid – dubbed a 'narluga'. Older Risso's dolphins can be almost white (due to scarring), but have a much more southerly range and a high dorsal fin.

DISTRIBUTION

Cold waters of the Arctic and sub-Arctic, ranging from 47°N to 82°N. Wide choice of habitat, including estuaries, coastal waters (as shallow as 1–3m), continental shelves and deep ocean basins, in open water and loose ice (it generally avoids dense pack ice, though commonly overwinters in polynyas). Will swim up rivers. Populations in Alaska, northern Canada and west Greenland make extensive migrations with the advancing ice edge, between summering and wintering grounds; populations

Beluga whale distribution

ADULT FACIAL EXPRESSIONS

Can alter shape of lips and melon (impressive array of facial expressions)

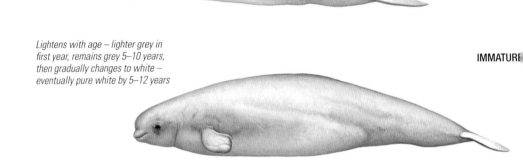

CALF

Uniform creamy pale grey when born but quickly turns darker grey (or pinkish brown)

May have slight beak

IMMATURE

Lightens with age – lighter grey in first year, remains grey 5–10 years, then gradually changes to white – eventually pure white by 5–12 years

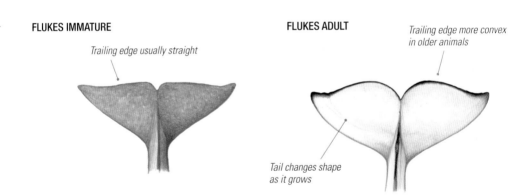

FLUKES IMMATURE

Trailing edge usually straight

FLUKES ADULT

Trailing edge more convex in older animals

Tail changes shape as it grows

DIVE SEQUENCE
- Swims in slow rolling motion (look for white arc that appears, grows, shrinks, then disappears).
- Low profile.
- White body often contrasts with dark sea (though can be difficult to pick out among whitecaps or floating ice).
- Flukes occasionally appear at low angle above water.
- Indistinct low, steamy blow (often not visible).

Hundreds of belugas gather to moult in shallow coastal waters in Northwest Territories, Canada.

in the White Sea (Russia), Svalbard (Norway) and Cook Inlet (Alaska) spend the summer in coastal areas and move offshore in winter (to avoid dense fast ice). There is an isolated population in the St Lawrence River estuary, Canada, which is resident year-round; and individuals are recorded as far south as Newfoundland almost annually. It is rare in east Greenland.

Dense concentrations are common in shallow coastal waters in summer, possibly to help with the annual moult (the warmer, low-salinity water may facilitate shedding of dead skin and epidermal regrowth), to avoid killer whale predation, and/or because warmer waters may be beneficial to calves. They tend to return, year after year, to the site where they were born. Many belugas summering in northern Canada spend the winter in the North Water Polynya (a large area of open water surrounded by sea ice in northern Baffin Bay), arriving in October and leaving in May or June, when the ice around the polynya breaks up. About one-third spend the winter in west Greenland (up to 100km offshore, in open water or moveable pack ice along the coast between Maniitsoq and Disko Bay). The Svalbard and Russian populations mostly winter in an area between Svalbard/Franz Josef Land and Novaya Zemlya.

BEHAVIOUR
Rarely given to aerial displays, though it can be more demonstrative (spyhopping, tail-waving and lobtailing) in nearshore concentrations. Able to turn its head sideways (the cervical vertebrae are unfused, making the neck

more flexible), which is unusual in cetaceans. Little fear of shallow water (if stranded, it is often able to wait and refloat on the next tide – assuming it is not found by a polar bear first). Sometimes shows curiosity towards boats and frequently towards snorkellers and divers. Some populations have regular feeding and resting bouts. Often associates with bowhead whales, though rarely forms mixed herds with narwhals. The annual moult, which involves rubbing along the seafloor to remove sloughed skin, is rare in cetaceans.

TEETH
Upper 16–20
Lower 16–20
Teeth are often heavily worn – even down to the gums in older animals.

GROUP SIZE AND STRUCTURE
Usually in groups of 5–20 (although large adults are occasionally seen alone). Many groups together may form herds of hundreds, or more than 1,000, which can be mixed or segregated by age and sex. Group structure tends to be fluid, with individuals coming and going and no stable associations (apart from cow–calf pairs). Beluga societies are complex and group members probably recognise one another.

PREDATORS
Killer whales and polar bears (especially when trapped in ice or stranded); young or injured animals may also be taken by Greenland sharks and walruses.

Belugas trapped in a hole in the ice (unable to reach the open sea), where they are highly susceptible to attacks by polar bears.

PHOTO-IDENTIFICATION
Distinctive natural markings and body scarring.

POPULATION
The total population could be more than 200,000 (though many parts of the range remain unsurveyed). The latest population estimates include Hudson Bay (including James Bay), Canada, *c.* 68,900 (excluding Ontario coast); Somerset Island, Canada, *c.* 21,200; Cumberland Sound, Canada, *c.* 1,150; St Lawrence River, Canada, *c.* 900; Bristol Bay, Alaska, *c.* 2,900; Cook Inlet, Alaska, *c.* 330. eastern Chukchi and eastern Beaufort Seas, *c.* 20,800; Sea of Okhotsk, Russia, *c.* 12,200; eastern Bering Sea, *c.* 7,000; White Sea, Russia, *c.* 5,600; Gulf of Anadyr *c.* 3,000. There are no survey figures for Svalbard, but pods ranging from a few to hundreds are seen regularly, and thousands irregularly.

CONSERVATION
IUCN status: Least Concern (2017); Cook Inlet sub-population Critically Endangered (2006). There is substantial uncertainty about numbers and trends in at least some of the 21 stocks or sub-populations currently recognised. There was intensive commercial hunting for the skin (to be tanned and used as leather), mainly by Russians and Europeans, in many parts of the range during the twentieth century, but this has now stopped. Hunting for human consumption is currently the biggest threat and there is concern about continuing harvests from small and depleted sub-populations, particularly in Canada and Greenland. Catch levels range from fewer than 10 to hundreds per year, depending on location. Other threats include entanglement in fishing gear, overfishing, habitat disturbance and modification (e.g. hydroelectric

FOOD AND FEEDING
Prey Wide variety from surface to seabed, depending on region and seasonal availability; mainly fish such as salmon, herring, Greenland halibut, smelt, Arctic and polar cod and capelin, but also squid, octopuses, shrimps, crabs, clams, mussels and even marine worms and large zooplankton.
Feeding Sucks prey into mouth with flexible lips; some evidence of cooperative hunting (e.g. in groups of 3–5 hunting smelt in the Sea of Okhotsk), but usually hunts alone (even within a group).
Dive depth Regularly 300–600m, sometimes beyond 800m and possibly deeper (maximum recorded 956m); it regularly dives to the seafloor.
Dive time 9–18 minutes (feeding dives typically 18–20 minutes); maximum documented 25 minutes; winter dives longer on average.

dams), oil and gas development, mining, global warming and chemical pollution; the St Lawrence River belugas are among the most contaminated marine mammals in the world. There is still a live-capture fishery in Russia, to provide animals for the worldwide oceanarium trade.

VOCALISATIONS

Belugas make two different types of sound: echolocation clicks and social vocalisations. They have one of most diverse vocal repertoires of any cetacean and their vocalisations can sometimes be heard above the water or through the hull of a boat. Around 50 call types are recognised, including groans, roars, whistles, squawks, moos, buzzes and trills. There is some geographical variation, though it is uncertain if different sub-populations use different dialects. Individuals can produce distinctive signature calls and are known to conduct exchanges with other individuals over long distances. Captive belugas are capable of mimicking human voices.

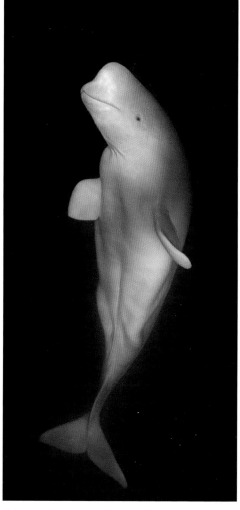

Belugas can be very inquisitive and will sometimes approach people in the water.

LIFE HISTORY

Sexual maturity Females 5–7 years, males 7–9 years (although some males do not become socially mature until several years later).

Mating Varies according to region but generally February–May, on wintering grounds or during spring migration.

Gestation 12–15 months.

Calving Every 2–4 years (usually three); single calf born April–May (but as late as September depending on population); twins rare; calf may 'ride' female's tailstock.

Weaning After six months to two years (takes solid food after one year); may remain with mother for 4–5 years.

Lifespan At least 30 years (oldest recorded 80 years).

Beluga surfacing in the Anadyr River, Russian Far East.

BAIRD'S BEAKED WHALE
Berardius bairdii

Stejneger, 188:

The largest of all the beaked whales, Baird's beaked whale is strikingly similar to Arnoux's beaked whale (though Baird's is slightly larger). Dividing the genus into two has been questioned in the past, but recent genetic studies seem to have settled the dispute in favour of two widely separated species. Baird's is one of few beaked whale species to be commercially hunted.

Classification Odontoceti, family Ziphiidae.
Common name After Spencer Fullerton Baird (1823–87), celebrated American naturalist and secretary of the Smithsonian Institution (colleague of Leonhard Hess Stejneger, who found the type specimen on Bering Island, in the Commander Islands, in 1882).
Other names Giant bottlenose whale, North Pacific bottlenose whale, four-toothed whale, northern fourtooth whale (and various combinations of these).
Scientific name *Berardius* from Auguste Bérard (1796–1852), captain of the French ship *Le Rhin*, which carried the type specimen of the genus (an Arnoux's beaked whale) from New Zealand to France in 1846); *bairdii* after Spencer Baird.
Taxonomy A dwarf form of Baird's beaked whale (p. 179) is likely to be named as a new species in the near future (although genetic evidence suggests that it may be more closely related to Arnoux's beaked whale); there may be no movement between east and west populations, but there is little information.

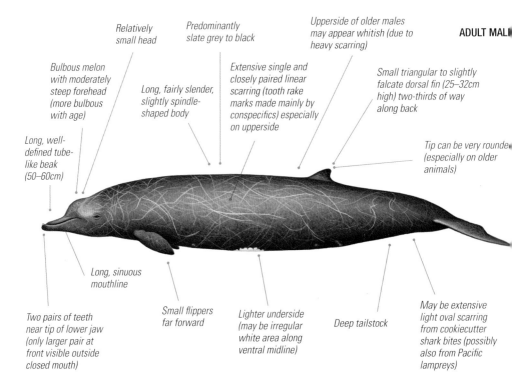

Relatively small head

Predominantly slate grey to black

Upperside of older males may appear whitish (due to heavy scarring)

ADULT MAL

Bulbous melon with moderately steep forehead (more bulbous with age)

Long, fairly slender, slightly spindle-shaped body

Extensive single and closely paired linear scarring (tooth rake marks made mainly by conspecifics) especially on upperside

Small triangular to slightly falcate dorsal fin (25–32cm high) two-thirds of way along back

Long, well-defined tube-like beak (50–60cm)

Tip can be very rounded (especially on older animals)

Long, sinuous mouthline

Two pairs of teeth near tip of lower jaw (only larger pair at front visible outside closed mouth)

Small flippers far forward

Lighter underside (may be irregular white area along ventral midline)

Deep tailstock

May be extensive light oval scarring from cookiecutter shark bites (possibly also from Pacific lampreys)

AT A GLANCE
- Cool offshore waters of northern North Pacific
- Predominantly dark with heavy scarring
- Medium to large size
- Bulbous melon
- Long, slender beak
- Two visible teeth at tip of lower jaw
- Small, rounded fin two-thirds of the way along back
- Tightly packed groups surface in unison

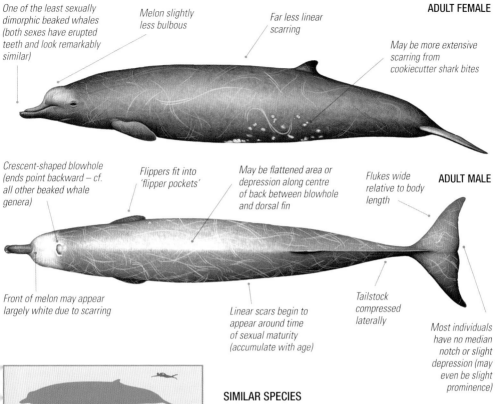

One of the least sexually dimorphic beaked whales (both sexes have erupted teeth and look remarkably similar)

Melon slightly less bulbous

Far less linear scarring

ADULT FEMALE

May be more extensive scarring from cookiecutter shark bites

Crescent-shaped blowhole (ends point backward – cf. all other beaked whale genera)

Flippers fit into 'flipper pockets'

May be flattened area or depression along centre of back between blowhole and dorsal fin

Flukes wide relative to body length

ADULT MALE

Front of melon may appear largely white due to scarring

Linear scars begin to appear around time of sexual maturity (accumulate with age)

Tailstock compressed laterally

Most individuals have no median notch or slight depression (may even be slight prominence)

SIZE
L: ♂ 9.1–10.7m, ♀ 9.8–11.1m;
WT: 8–12t; **MAX:** 13m, 12.8t
Calf – L: 4.5–4.9m; **WT:** unknown
Females slightly larger than males; individuals in Sea of Japan typically 60–70cm smaller.

SIMILAR SPECIES
One of the easiest beaked whales to identify in the North Pacific, with its unique head and dorsal fin shape, tooth position, conspicuous blow and densely packed schools. It is also much larger than any other member of the family in the region (Cuvier's, Hubbs', ginkgo-toothed, Blainville's, pygmy, Perrin's, Stejneger's and Longman's). A minke whale could be confused in some circumstances, from a distance, but there are significant differences in appearance and behaviour – Baird's beaked whale has a more visible blow, frequently floats at the surface and is rarely seen alone. Far away, a group lying at the surface may initially resemble a similar group of sperm whales; a travelling group can be confused with a pod of killer whales.

DISTRIBUTION
In summer, deep, offshore, cool temperate to sub-polar waters in the northern North Pacific and the adjacent Sea of Japan, Sea of Okhotsk and Bering Sea, at least between *c.* 30°N and 62°N. Winter distribution

Baird's beaked whale distribution

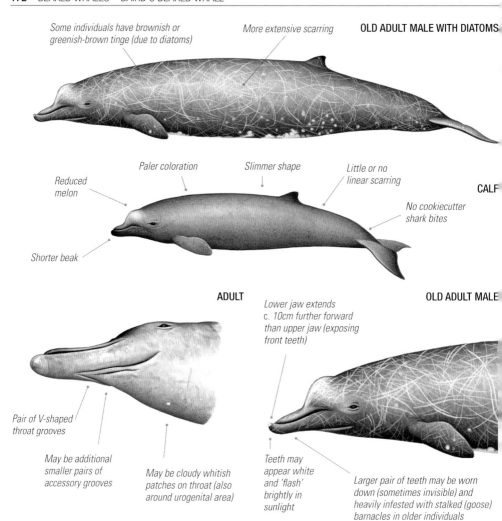

Some individuals have brownish or greenish-brown tinge (due to diatoms)

More extensive scarring

OLD ADULT MALE WITH DIATOMS

Reduced melon

Paler coloration

Slimmer shape

Little or no linear scarring

CALF

No cookiecutter shark bites

Shorter beak

ADULT

OLD ADULT MALE

Lower jaw extends c. 10cm further forward than upper jaw (exposing front teeth)

Pair of V-shaped throat grooves

May be additional smaller pairs of accessory grooves

May be cloudy whitish patches on throat (also around urogenital area)

Teeth may appear white and 'flash' brightly in sunlight

Larger pair of teeth may be worn down (sometimes invisible) and heavily infested with stalked (goose) barnacles in older individuals

DIVE SEQUENCE
- Typically in tight school, all surfacing in unison.
- Surfaces at shallow angle often showing beak and melon above surface.
- Body appears very long.
- Blows continuously while swimming slowly (easily identifiable from distance).
- Small domed head disappears just as dorsal fin appears.
- Shallow roll with little arching of back (more arching before deep dive).
- Rarely raises flukes before deep dive.

BLOW
- Strong, low, puffy or rather shapeless blow (up to c. 2m), quite conspicuous in calm weather (but tends to dissipate quickly).
- Sometimes angled slightly forward.

FOOD AND FEEDING

Prey Pelagic and benthic fish (including mackerel, sardines, pollock, sauries, codlings, grenadiers, rockfish, skate), squid (including boreoatlantic armhook squid), octopuses; diet varies regionally (fish 82 per cent of diet off Pacific coast of Japan, cephalopods 87 per cent of diet in southern Sea of Okhotsk); some crustaceans.

Feeding Often (but not exclusively) down to seafloor; pebbles in stomachs may reflect bottom-feeding; suction feeder.

Dive depth Deep dives routinely to 1,000m or more; maximum recorded 1,777m (Japan) but probably capable of deeper.

Dive time Maximum recorded 67 minutes (Pacific coast of Japan), unsubstantiated reports up to two hours. Bering Island animals usually surface for several minutes (up to 10) then dive for 20–40 minutes. Individual tracked for two days off the Pacific coast of Japan seems fairly typical: deep dive (average 45 minutes, to 1,400–1,700m, average 1,566m); followed by series of 5–7 intermediate, shallower dives (20–30 minutes, to 200–700m, average 379m) over 2–3 hours; followed by 80–200 minutes resting on or near surface (including shallow dives averaging 20m); followed by next deep dive. Deep dives may be to seafloor (scouting for distribution of prey in water column) and intermediate dives for foraging wherever found greatest prey densities.

s unknown. In the east, there are records as far south as La Paz (24°N) in the southern Gulf of California (although t is a rare visitor to the gulf); in the west, the southern limit is probably Kyushu, Japan (c. 33°N). Northern limit s probably determined by the relatively shallow waters of the Bering Sea, but the range extends north at least to the Aleutian Islands, Alaska (c. 55°N), and Cape Navarin, Chukchi Peninsula, Russia (62°N). Southern limit in the central Pacific Ocean is unclear. Appears to be migratory in most areas, with seasonal peaks in abundance (e.g. May–June off the Commander Islands, with a less pronounced peak in August–November; summer and autumn off the west coast of North America). In winter, it is believed to move into deeper waters away from the continental slope, with at least some time spent in the sub-tropics and tropics (extensive scarring from cookiecutter shark bites suggests long-range travels into warmer waters, but there is no detailed information). Occurs year-round in the Sea of Okhotsk (in waters as shallow as 500m, including in narrow cracks among drift ice) and throughout the Sea of Japan. Prefers continental slope waters, in 1,000–3,000m depths, and areas with complex topography such as submarine canyons, seamounts and ridges; it is sometimes on the shelf edge. May be seen close to shore where deep water approaches the coast (such as off the southwestern coast of Bering Island, in the Bering Sea).

BEHAVIOUR

Moderately aerially active. Will sometimes breach, landing on one side, leaping in a low arc or, especially in mixed groups, jumping on top of one another; may breach repeatedly. Will also spyhop, flipper-slap and lobtail. May swim belly up or sideways or roll at the surface, exposing one of the flukes (which can look like a killer whale dorsal fin from a distance). Reaction to vessels varies: it can be shy and difficult to approach, but sometimes unconcerned or even inquisitive. Japanese whalers regard it as one of the most dangerous of all whales to harpoon, because it

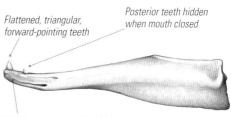

Flattened, triangular, forward-pointing teeth

Posterior teeth hidden when mouth closed

Anterior teeth up to 10cm high and 10cm at longest point (twice as large as peg-like posterior teeth)

ADULT LOWER JAW

can descend at incredible speed (one harpooned animal took 900m of line straight down).

TEETH

Upper 0

Lower 4

GROUP SIZE AND STRUCTURE

Typically 3–20, with some regional variation (average seven in Japan, eight in the Commander Islands); occasionally up to 50. There may be some sexual segregation. Studies in the Commander Islands found three main groupings: all male (average size eight), mixed male and female (average size 15), and nursery groups of females with calves and immatures (average

LIFE HISTORY

Sexual maturity Females 10–15 years, males 6–11 years; physically mature c. 20 years.

Mating Inter-male aggression seems to be common, judging by scarring.

Gestation c. 17 months (longest of all marine mammals).

Calving Every 2–4 years; single calf born in late winter to early spring.

Weaning Possibly less than six months.

Lifespan Females c. 50–55 years, males 80–85 years (oldest recorded female 54 years, male 84 years).

size six). Eleven animals that stranded near La Paz, Baja California, in 2006 were all male. There are stable associations between some individuals, lasting up to at least six years, but many show no apparent preferences for social partners; heavily scarred animals (probably older males) are more inclined to form stable associations. Larger, mixed-sex groups may be temporary aggregations of several smaller, more stable groups; these are often seen in the Commander Islands, for example, and social behaviour is common while they travel together for several hundred metres. Lone individuals are rare. Groups can be so tightly packed that individuals may be in physical contact with each other.

PREDATORS

Killer whales are likely to be the only predators. Scars from killer whale attacks are common on the flukes and flippers (in Japan, as many as 40 per cent of individuals examined at whaling stations bear tell-tale injuries from killer whale attacks).

PHOTO-IDENTIFICATION

Scarring (from intraspecific fighting, killer whale attacks and cookiecutter shark bites) and notches on the dorsal fin.

POPULATION

No overall abundance estimate. Approximate regional estimates include 5,029 for the Pacific coast of Japan, 1,260 for the eastern Sea of Japan, 660 for the southern Sea of Okhotsk, and 850 off California, Oregon and Washington State (extending to 550km from shore).

CONSERVATION

IUCN status: Data Deficient (2008). In the past, small numbers were hunted by the USSR, Canada and the US (fewer than 100 in the US in 1915–66). Japanese hunting of Baird's beaked whale began in the early 1600s and reached a peak after the Second World War, with a maximum reported annual catch of 322 in 1952; since 1987, more than 1,000 have been killed. The Japanese government currently permits a catch of 66 per year: 52 from the Pacific coast, 10 from the Sea of Japan and four from the Sea of Okhotsk; the meat is sold for human consumption. Other threats probably include incidental capture in fishing gear (especially driftnets), noise pollution (especially naval sonar and seismic surveys), vessel strikes and ingestion of plastic debris. The meat and blubber of whales killed in Japan contain high levels of mercury, PCBs and other pollutants.

A typical tight group of Baird's beaked whales, which often surface and blow in unison. Notice the heavily scarred bodies and bulbous heads.

ARNOUX'S BEAKED WHALE
Berardius arnuxii

Duvernoy, 1851

Despite closely resembling the relatively well-studied Baird's beaked whale, which lives far away in the North Pacific, Arnoux's beaked whale is very poorly known. Both species are unusual among beaked whales for several reasons: four teeth erupt in both males and females, there is little sexual dimorphism and the males seem to live much longer than the females.

Classification Odontoceti, family Ziphiidae.

Common name After French surgeon Louis Jules Arnoux (1814–67), who discovered the type specimen (on a beach near Akaroa, New Zealand) and presented its skull to the Museum of Natural History in Paris in 1846.

Other names Southern beaked whale, four-toothed whale, giant bottlenose whale, New Zealand beaked whale, southern porpoise whale (and various combinations of these).

Scientific name *Berardius* from Auguste Bérard (1796–1852), captain of the French corvette *Le Rhin*, which carried the type specimen from New Zealand to France in 1846; *arnuxii* from Louis Arnoux, who was chief surgeon on board (the 'o' from 'Arnoux' was accidentally omitted from the scientific name and, under the rules of zoological nomenclature, the original spelling has to be retained).

Taxonomy No recognised forms or subspecies. There are no known morphological differences between Arnoux's and Baird's beaked whales (although Arnoux's is slightly smaller and the apparent lack of differences may be more to do with a lack of specimens); however, while dividing the genus into two species has been questioned in the past, recent research shows that they are genetically distinct.

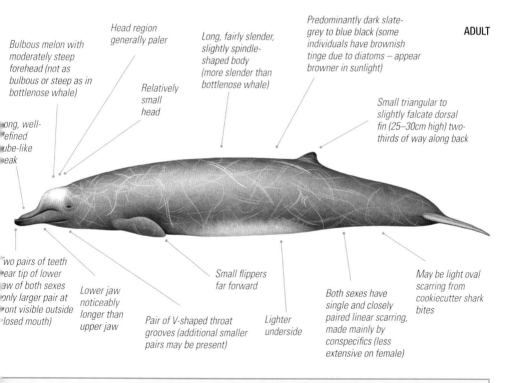

ADULT

Bulbous melon with moderately steep forehead (not as bulbous or steep as in bottlenose whale)

Head region generally paler

Relatively small head

Long, fairly slender, slightly spindle-shaped body (more slender than bottlenose whale)

Predominantly dark slate-grey to blue black (some individuals have brownish tinge due to diatoms – appear browner in sunlight)

Small triangular to slightly falcate dorsal fin (25–30cm high) two-thirds of way along back

Long, well-defined tube-like beak

Two pairs of teeth near tip of lower jaw of both sexes (only larger pair at front visible outside closed mouth)

Lower jaw noticeably longer than upper jaw

Pair of V-shaped throat grooves (additional smaller pairs may be present)

Small flippers far forward

Lighter underside

Both sexes have single and closely paired linear scarring, made mainly by conspecifics (less extensive on female)

May be light oval scarring from cookiecutter shark bites

AT A GLANCE
- Cool offshore waters, mainly in sub-Antarctic and Antarctic
- Slate grey to light brown with heavy scarring
- Medium size

- Bulbous melon
- Long, slender beak
- Two visible teeth at tip of lower jaw
- Small, rounded fin two-thirds of the way along back
- Tightly packed groups surface in unison

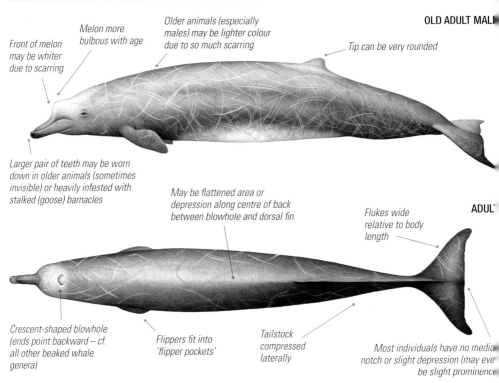

OLD ADULT MALE

Older animals (especially males) may be lighter colour due to so much scarring

Front of melon may be whiter due to scarring

Melon more bulbous with age

Tip can be very rounded

Larger pair of teeth may be worn down in older animals (sometimes invisible) or heavily infested with stalked (goose) barnacles

May be flattened area or depression along centre of back between blowhole and dorsal fin

Flukes wide relative to body length

ADULT

Crescent-shaped blowhole (ends point backward – cf. all other beaked whale genera)

Flippers fit into 'flipper pockets'

Tailstock compressed laterally

Most individuals have no median notch or slight depression (may even be slight prominence)

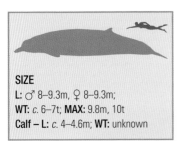

SIZE
L: ♂ 8–9.3m, ♀ 8–9.3m;
WT: c. 6–7t; MAX: 9.8m, 10t
Calf – L: c. 4–4.6m; WT: unknown

SIMILAR SPECIES

Easily confused with the southern bottlenose whale, which has a broadly similar body shape and overlaps in much of its range. If seen clearly, there are significant differences in coloration, amount of scarring, dorsal fin size, head shape and beak length; the teeth are more conspicuous in Arnoux's (if they are visible from any distance at all, it is probably Arnoux's). A minke whale could be confused in some circumstances, from a distance, but there are significant differences in appearance and Arnoux's beaked whale is rarely seen alone. Far away, a group lying at the surface may initially resemble a similar group of sperm whales.

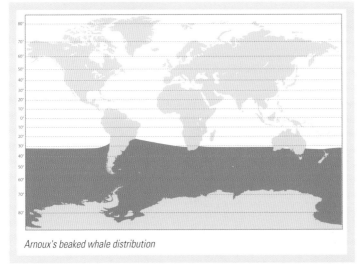

Arnoux's beaked whale distribution

DISTRIBUTION

Circumpolar in deep, offshore, cold temperate to polar waters, most abundant between 40°S and 77°S (though it is likely to reach 34°S in the South Pacific and there are records as far north as 24°S in the South Atlantic). The vast majority of strandings have been around New Zealand. Seen relatively frequently during the summer in the Tasman Sea, Cook Strait in New Zealand, and between Tierra del Fuego and the Antarctic Peninsula. May be adapted to sea ice conditions and often found close to the

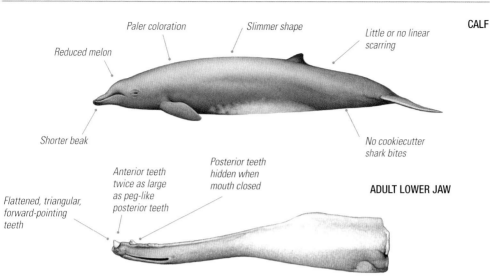

CALF

Paler coloration

Slimmer shape

Little or no linear scarring

Reduced melon

Shorter beak

No cookiecutter shark bites

Posterior teeth hidden when mouth closed

Anterior teeth twice as large as peg-like posterior teeth

ADULT LOWER JAW

Flattened, triangular, forward-pointing teeth

ce edge and in areas with extensive ice cover. Normally deeper waters over the continental slope and beyond, but it may be more coastal along the western side of the Antarctic Peninsula, where there are numerous intrusions of deepwater channels and canyons, and it has been seen in waters just 700–800m deep.

BEHAVIOUR

Breaches fairly frequently, normally exiting the water nearly vertically to about four-fifths of the body length. Will also spyhop, flipper-slap and lobtail. Reaction to vessels varies: it can be shy and difficult to approach, but sometimes unconcerned or even inquisitive; there have

been several close encounters with expedition cruise ships in Antarctica in recent years.

TEETH

Upper 0
Lower 4

GROUP SIZE AND STRUCTURE

Typically 6–15; several smaller groups may join together for periods. A group of about 80 was followed by researchers in the Antarctic for several hours; the whales eventually split into smaller groups of 8–15 and dispersed into the loose pack ice.

DIVE SEQUENCE
- Typically in tight school, all surfacing in unison.
- Surfaces at shallow angle, often showing beak and melon above surface.
- Body appears very long.
- Will cruise along surface some distance with top of melon and straight back visible.
- Small domed head typically disappears just as dorsal fin appears.
- Shallow roll with arching of back (more arching before deep dive).
- When logging or swimming slowly, may lift head and beak out of water and sink backwards under surface.
- Rarely raises flukes before deep dive.

BLOW
- Strong, low, puffy or rather shapeless blow (up to c. 2m), quite conspicuous in calm weather (but tends to dissipate quickly).
- Sometimes angled slightly forward.
- Blows continuously while swimming slowly (easily identifiable from distance).

FOOD AND FEEDING
Prey Deepwater squid, possibly some deepwater fish.
Feeding Probably often (but not exclusively) down to seafloor; suction feeder.
Dive depth Probably greater than 500m, possibly to 3,000m.
Dive time Typically 15–25 minutes (remaining at surface for *c.* 5–15 minutes in between deep dives); maximum recorded 70 minutes. One group followed by researchers in Antarctica travelled underwater for more than 6km and just over one hour.

PREDATORS
Killer whales are likely to be the only predators. Scars from killer whale attacks are common on the flukes and flippers.

PHOTO-IDENTIFICATION
May be possible using scarring (from intraspecific fighting, killer whale attacks and cookiecutter shark bites) and notches on the dorsal fin.

POPULATION
No overall abundance estimate. Appears to be less common than the overlapping southern bottlenose whale.

CONSERVATION
IUCN status: Data Deficient (2008). No significant hunting has been reported. Main threats probably include incidental capture in fishing gear (especially driftnets), noise pollution (especially naval sonar and seismic surveys), vessel strikes and ingestion of plastic debris.

LIFE HISTORY
Very little known, but probably similar to Baird's beaked whale.

Arnoux's beaked whales breach fairly frequently.

DWARF BAIRD'S BEAKED WHALE OR KARASU
Proposed: *Berardius* sp.

Whalers in Japan have traditionally recognised two different kinds of Baird's beaked whale: the relatively common 'slate-grey' form (p. 170) and a rarer, smaller 'black' form. It has long been suspected that the black form belongs to a new, unnamed species.

Classification Odontoceti, family Ziphiidae.

Common name Three possible common names proposed: dwarf Baird's beaked whale, black Baird's beaked whale, karasu.

Other names The Japanese call it the karasu (raven – after its dark colour) or kuro-tsuchi (black Baird's beaked whale).

Scientific name The new species is yet to be accepted by taxonomists and has not been named. Assuming it is, it will belong to the genus *Berardius* (the same as Baird's beaked whale), but the possible specific name is still under review; some researchers have suggested *B. beringiae*, after the sea where it has been found (although nearly half the known specimens are from outside the Bering Sea, so this may not be appropriate).

Taxonomy Limited genetic evidence suggests that this species may be more closely related to Arnoux's beaked whale than Baird's beaked whale (it indicates that there was an initial species divergence between the northern and southern hemispheres, resulting in the dwarf form in the north and the ancestor of Arnoux's and Baird's in the south; then there was a dispersal from the south to the north, resulting in Baird's); no information on forms or subspecies of the dwarf Baird's beaked whale.

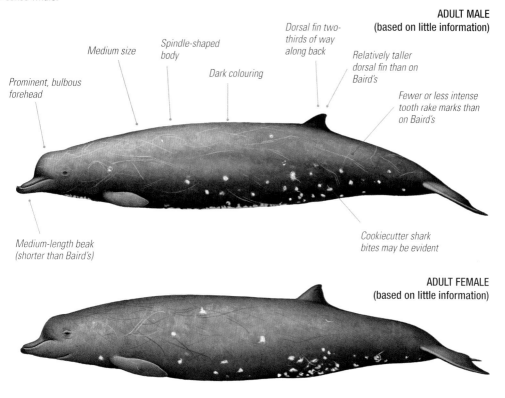

ADULT MALE
(based on little information)

Dorsal fin two-thirds of way along back

Medium size

Spindle-shaped body

Dark colouring

Relatively taller dorsal fin than on Baird's

Prominent, bulbous forehead

Fewer or less intense tooth rake marks than on Baird's

Medium-length beak (shorter than Baird's)

Cookiecutter shark bites may be evident

ADULT FEMALE
(based on little information)

AT A GLANCE
- Cool temperate and sub-Arctic waters of North Pacific
- Medium size (60–70 per cent of length of Baird's beaked whale)
- Predominantly black body colour
- Less scarring than Baird's beaked whale
- Dorsal fin relatively taller than Baird's beaked whale and two-thirds of the way along back

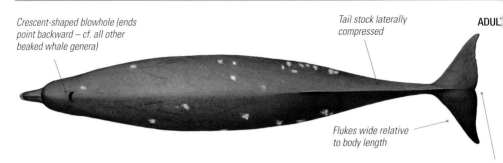

Crescent-shaped blowhole (ends point backward – cf. all other beaked whale genera)

Tail stock laterally compressed

ADUL

Flukes wide relative to body length

Most individuals have no median notch or a slight depression (may even be slight prominence)

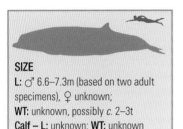

SIZE
L: ♂ 6.6–7.3m (based on two adult specimens), ♀ unknown;
WT: unknown, possibly *c.* 2–3t
Calf – L: unknown; **WT:** unknown

DORSAL FIN VARIATIONS

A POSSIBLE NEW SPECIES

The existence of a new species of Baird's beaked whale has been speculated for more than 70 years. In addition to incidental evidence from Japanese whalers, there are eight dead specimens: three from the Sea of Okhotsk near the northern tip of Hokkaido, Japan (with several more possible, but unconfirmed), and five from Alaska (three from the eastern Aleutian Islands, one from the Pribilof Islands and one from the southeastern Bering Sea). Amazingly, the skeleton of one was found hanging in the gymnasium of Unalaska High School in the Aleutians, while the skull of another

had been collected from the Aleutians in 1948 and held, unknowingly, in the Smithsonian Institution for many years. There are also five likely, but unconfirmed, reports from North Korea. Recent DNA studies on these specimens found a significant difference between them and Baird's beaked whale – indeed, a greater difference than between Baird's and Arnoux's beaked whales. This suggests that the black form is sufficiently different to be granted species status. A portion of a skull found on Bering Island, in Russia's Commander Islands (originally described in 1883 as a new species, *Berardius vegae*), has yet to be examined.

SIMILAR SPECIES

Confusion is most likely with Baird's beaked whale, but the proposed new species is two-thirds the size, much darker an with fewer tooth rake marks.

DISTRIBUTION

Cool temperate and sub-Arctic waters in the North Pacific, though the range may be very limited within this broad area. Currently known only from the far southern Sea of Okhotsk (northern Japan) and the Berinç Sea (primarily the eastern Aleutian Islands in Alaska), though the sample size is very small. Japanese whalers repeatedly see groups in the

Nemuro Strait

• locations where eight confirmed specimens were found

Dwarf Baird's beaked whale distribution

FOOD AND FEEDING
No information but it is probable that, like other beaked whales, it is a deep diver.

Nemuro Strait, near the northern tip of Hokkaido in the Sea of Okhotsk – the only location known to have regular sightings – from April to June. Bite scars from cookiecutter sharks suggest that at least some individuals migrate south to the tropics for at least part of the year (it is possible that the species spends considerable time in warmer, more southerly waters). Little is known about habitat preferences; it might be expected in waters with depths of more than 500m (mainly offshore but possibly also close to shore where the water is sufficiently deep) but has been reported in shallower coastal waters.

BEHAVIOUR
No scientist has ever identified one alive, due to the lack of information and difficulty in identifying this species. As with other beaked whales, it is likely to be found well offshore and probably spends little time at the surface. Japanese whalers in Abashiri, on the Sea of Okhotsk coast

LIFE HISTORY
No information.

of Hokkaido, say that it is difficult to approach within shooting distance.

TEETH
Upper 0
Lower 4
Teeth presumed to erupt in both male and female (as in Baird's beaked whale).

GROUP SIZE AND STRUCTURE
No information, though Japanese whalers have described 'small groups'.

PREDATORS
No information, but killer whales could be occasional predators.

POPULATION
No global estimate. Limited evidence suggests that it is relatively rare (or, at least, a less frequent visitor to continental slopes and canyons where it would be more readily observed).

CONSERVATION
IUCN status: not reviewed. It has the dubious honour of being one of only three kinds of beaked whale species ever targeted by commercial whalers – and may still be targeted by the Japanese whaling industry.

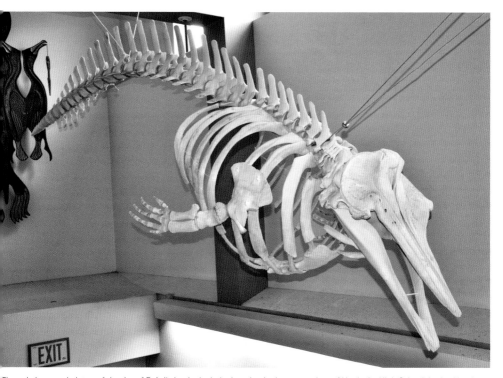

The only known skeleton of the dwarf Baird's beaked whale: hanging in the gymnasium of Unalaska High School, in the Aleutian Islands, Alaska.

CUVIER'S BEAKED WHALE
Ziphius cavirostris
G. Cuvier, 1823

Cuvier's beaked whale is one of the most frequently seen, easily recognisable and widely distributed species of beaked whale, though it is still poorly understood. It holds the records for the deepest and second-longest dives of any mammal.

Classification Odontoceti, family Ziphiidae.

Common name After the French anatomist Georges Cuvier (1769–1832), who first described the species from an imperfect skull found in Provence, France, in 1804; alternative name because the head profile is supposedly reminiscent of a goose's beak.

Other names Goose-beaked whale, goosebeak whale.

Scientific name *Ziphius* is an erroneous form of Latin *xiphias* for 'swordfish' or Greek *xiphos* for 'sword' (referring to the sharply pointed rostrum); *cavirostris* from Latin *cavum* for 'hollow' or 'concave' and rostrum for 'beak' (referring to the indentation on the skull in front of the blowhole).

Taxonomy No recognised forms or subspecies; there is a genetically distinct population in the Mediterranean Sea.

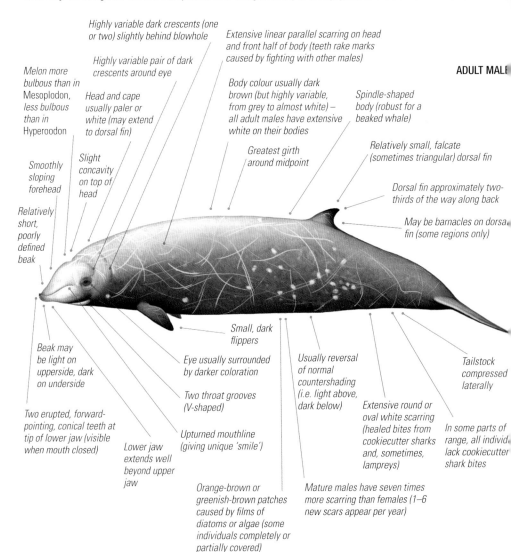

Highly variable dark crescents (one or two) slightly behind blowhole

Highly variable pair of dark crescents around eye

Extensive linear parallel scarring on head and front half of body (teeth rake marks caused by fighting with other males)

ADULT MALE

Melon more bulbous than in Mesoplodon, less bulbous than in Hyperoodon

Head and cape usually paler or white (may extend to dorsal fin)

Body colour usually dark brown (but highly variable, from grey to almost white) – all adult males have extensive white on their bodies

Spindle-shaped body (robust for a beaked whale)

Smoothly sloping forehead

Slight concavity on top of head

Greatest girth around midpoint

Relatively small, falcate (sometimes triangular) dorsal fin

Relatively short, poorly defined beak

Dorsal fin approximately two-thirds of the way along back

May be barnacles on dorsal fin (some regions only)

Beak may be light on upperside, dark on underside

Small, dark flippers

Eye usually surrounded by darker coloration

Usually reversal of normal countershading (i.e. light above, dark below)

Tailstock compressed laterally

Two erupted, forward-pointing, conical teeth at tip of lower jaw (visible when mouth closed)

Lower jaw extends well beyond upper jaw

Upturned mouthline (giving unique 'smile')

Two throat grooves (V-shaped)

Extensive round or oval white scarring (healed bites from cookiecutter sharks and, sometimes, lampreys)

In some parts of range, all individuals lack cookiecutter shark bites

Orange-brown or greenish-brown patches caused by films of diatoms or algae (some individuals completely or partially covered)

Mature males have seven times more scarring than females (1–6 new scars appear per year)

AT A GLANCE

- Worldwide except High Arctic and Antarctic
- Colour highly variable, from slate grey to brown to white
- May be covered in round or oval white scars from cookiecutter shark bites (some regions only – e.g. rare in north-west Atlantic)
- Numerous linear scars (especially on male)

- Medium size
- Smoothly sloping forehead with relatively short beak
- Upturned mouthline (giving unique 'smile')
- Two conical, forward-pointing teeth at tip of lower jaw of male (visible when mouth closed)
- Dorsal fin approximately two-thirds of the way along back

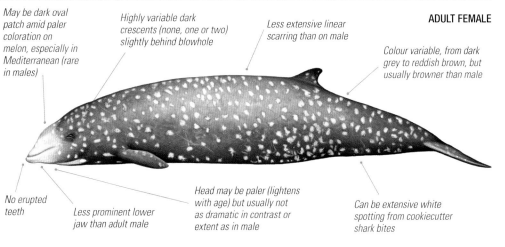

May be dark oval patch amid paler coloration on melon, especially in Mediterranean (rare in males)

Highly variable dark crescents (none, one or two) slightly behind blowhole

Less extensive linear scarring than on male

ADULT FEMALE

Colour variable, from dark grey to reddish brown, but usually browner than male

No erupted teeth

Less prominent lower jaw than adult male

Head may be paler (lightens with age) but usually not as dramatic in contrast or extent as in male

Can be extensive white spotting from cookiecutter shark bites

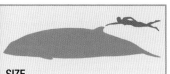

SIZE
L: ♂ 5.3–6m, ♀ 5.5–6m;
WT: 2.2–2.9t; **MAX:** 8.4m, 3t
Calf – L: 2.3–2.8m; **WT:** 250–300kg

SIMILAR SPECIES

Relatively easy to identify, but there could be confusion with other beaked whales. The unique head shape – and the lighter coloration around the head and on the back in front of the dorsal fin (especially in older males) – is distinctive at close range. When the head is not visible, look for the broad, domed back and the way it arches on surfacing (Blainville's beaked whale tends to surface and dive at a shallower angle). When the dorsal fin of Cuvier's is clear of the water, its head and blowhole are usually submerged (in Blainville's, both the dorsal fin and blowhole are usually clear of the water at the same time). In poor visibility, it could be confused with very light Risso's dolphins (look for the dolphin's large dorsal fin) and extremely white older animals with beluga whales (which lack a dorsal fin).

DISTRIBUTION

Widely distributed in cool polar to warm tropical waters worldwide, though generally absent from very high latitudes and water shallower than 200m. Present in many enclosed seas, including the Gulf of Mexico, Caribbean Sea, Sea of Okhotsk, Gulf

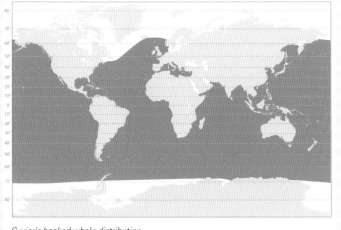

Cuvier's beaked whale distribution

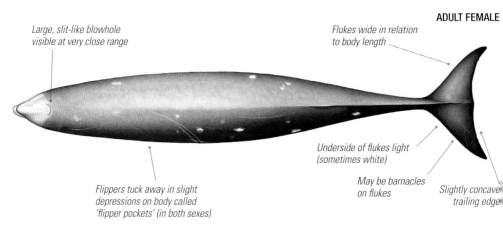

ADULT FEMALE

Large, slit-like blowhole visible at very close range

Flukes wide in relation to body length

Underside of flukes light (sometimes white)

May be barnacles on flukes

Slightly concave trailing edge

Flippers tuck away in slight depressions on body called 'flipper pockets' (in both sexes)

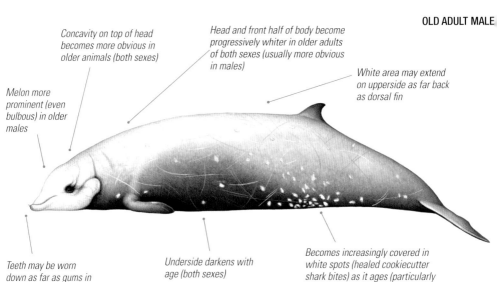

OLD ADULT MALE

Concavity on top of head becomes more obvious in older animals (both sexes)

Head and front half of body become progressively whiter in older adults of both sexes (usually more obvious in males)

White area may extend on upperside as far back as dorsal fin

Melon more prominent (even bulbous) in older males

Teeth may be worn down as far as gums in older animals (sharply pointed in younger males)

Underside darkens with age (both sexes)

Becomes increasingly covered in white spots (healed cookiecutter shark bites) as it ages (particularly in lower latitudes)

DIVE SEQUENCE
- Often exposes beak on surfacing.
- Entire head and part of body may be exposed when swimming fast or just before long dive (when often lunges out of water).
- When dorsal fin clear of water, head and blowhole usually submerged.
- Occasionally flukes before a deep dive in some regions (not north-west Atlantic).

BLOW
- Bushy blow usually about 1m high, projecting slightly forward and to left (but usually inconspicuous or invisible).

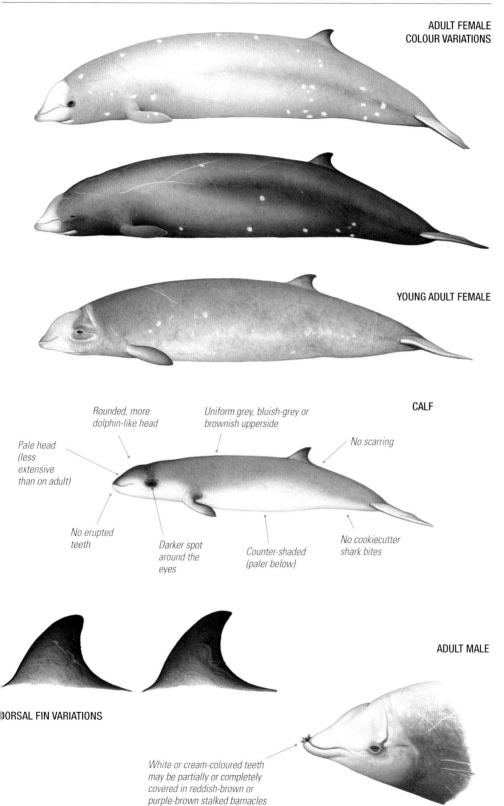

**ADULT FEMALE
COLOUR VARIATIONS**

YOUNG ADULT FEMALE

CALF

Rounded, more
dolphin-like head

Uniform grey, bluish-grey or
brownish upperside

No scarring

Pale head
(less
extensive
than on adult)

No erupted
teeth

Darker spot
around the
eyes

Counter-shaded
(paler below)

No cookiecutter
shark bites

DORSAL FIN VARIATIONS

ADULT MALE

White or cream-coloured teeth
may be partially or completely
covered in reddish-brown or
purple-brown stalked barnacles

FOOD AND FEEDING

Prey Primarily deepwater squid; may consume deepwater fish and crustaceans in some parts of range.

Feeding Most feeding occurs at or near seabed (though also sometimes in water column). Likely to be a suction feeder (has two throat grooves, enabling throat to stretch and expand to suck prey into mouth); individuals with missing jaws appear to be able to feed enough to survive.

Dive depth Holds mammalian record for dive depth (2,992m off southern California); the record was previously held by the southern elephant seal (2,388m). Believed to dive to more than 1,000m for 60 minutes or more day and night, non-stop, year-round (estimated to spend *c.* 67 per cent of life at depths greater than 1,000m); probably physiologically capable of diving much deeper (possibly to 5,000m); known to spend extended periods near seabed while foraging.

Dive time Feeding dives average *c.* 60 minutes, with *c.* 60-minute intervals, and non-feeding dives *c.* 12 minutes; in north-west Atlantic, makes *c.* four shorter 'bounce' dives (each 20–30 minutes long) between longer foraging dives; holds mammalian record (after sperm whale) for second-longest dive duration (137.5 minutes off southern California).

of California and the Mediterranean Sea. It is the only species of beaked whale commonly occurring in the Mediterranean, where research has identified key areas of high density: the Alboran Sea, Ligurian Sea, central Tyrrhenian Sea, southern Adriatic Sea and the Hellenic Trench. Seems to prefer deeper waters over and near the continental slope, or oceanic waters, with a complex seabed topography; most common in canyons along shelf margins or around oceanic islands or seamounts. Usually in water deeper than 1,000m; most sightings in Hawaiian waters (where it has been studied extensively) in depths of 1,500–3,500m. Evidence of seasonal movements in some parts of the range, but other populations appear to be resident. At least in some areas females show more long-term site fidelity.

REMARKS

Known in Japan as akabo-kujira, or baby-face whale, which is probably a reference to the small mouth and large, dark eyes.

BEHAVIOUR

Occasionally breaches. Lobtailing often observed in some regions, especially when there is more than one male in a group. Tends to be very sensitive to low levels of human-made noise, typically escaping quickly, and generally avoids boats; but it can be inquisitive in some areas. Strandings are relatively common in some parts of the range. Believed to headbutt during some aggressive encounters (though not in the north-west Atlantic).

Adult female Cuvier's beaked whale – a member of the resident population found off Kona, Hawaii.

ADULT MALE LOWER JAW

TEETH
Upper 0
Lower 2
Teeth erupt in male only; 8cm high (including portion buried in jawbone). Female's teeth are more slender and sharply pointed, but do not erupt. Rarely a second pair of erupted teeth appear behind main pair. Occasionally small vestigial teeth in gums.

GROUP SIZE AND STRUCTURE
Typically in small fluid groups of 1–4 (mean group size in the Southern California Bight is 2.4, in Hawaii it is 2.1, off the west coast of the United States it is 1.8); groups of up to 25 reported, but more than 10 is rare. Larger groups typically contain two adult males and two or three adult females and juveniles. Lone individuals are usually older males. Rarely interacts with other cetacean species.

PREDATORS
Tiger sharks, great whites and other large sharks. Killer whales are also likely to be occasional predators.

PHOTO-IDENTIFICATION
Pattern of white cookiecutter shark bites (Cuvier's beaked whale appears to be particularly susceptible to attacks by these sharks, perhaps because of their light colour underwater).

POPULATION
Cuvier's is the only beaked whale species for which a global abundance estimate has been attempted, with a tentative population figure in excess of 100,000. The most recent approximate regional estimates include 6,500 in the western North Atlantic, 5,800 in the Mediterranean Sea, 4,500 in California, 725 in Hawaiian waters and fewer than 100 in the northern Gulf of Mexico.

CONSERVATION
IUCN status: Least Concern (2008); Mediterranean sub-population Vulnerable (2018). Believed to be more sensitive to the impacts of naval sonar than any other species of cetacean; in the wake of high-intensity sonar, atypical mass strandings have occurred in Greece, the Canary Islands, Scotland and Ireland, off the coast of Africa, in the Bahamas and off Guam. It strands more than any other species of beaked whale. There is evidence of recent declines off the west coast of the United States, for unknown reasons. Small numbers have been taken by the Baird's beaked whale fishery in Japan and by fisheries in the Caribbean, Chile, Peru, Indonesia and Taiwan. Ingestion of marine debris is a major concern: plastic debris is commonly found in the stomachs of Cuvier's beaked whales (e.g. 40kg in the stomach of one individual stranded in the Philippines in 2019). Entanglement in deepwater driftnets and other fishing equipment is also likely to be a problem in some areas.

VOCALISATIONS
Echolocates mostly below 500m; it is believed to remain silent near the surface, perhaps in part to avoid alerting potential predators. The characteristic echolocation sounds during foraging are consistent across and between ocean basins.

LIFE HISTORY
Sexual maturity Both sexes 7–11 years.
Mating Little known; extensive scarring suggests males fight over females using their teeth; sperm competition may also be important.
Gestation *c.* 12 months.
Calving Single calf born year-round (peaking in spring – in temperate zones not tropics), possibly every 2–3 years.
Weaning After at least one year (calf may be reliant on mother for two years or more).
Lifespan Possibly up to 60 years.

NORTHERN BOTTLENOSE WHALE
Hyperoodon ampullatus

(Forster, 1770)

The northern bottlenose whale is the largest beaked whale in the North Atlantic, one of the best-known members of the family and one of the few to have been targeted by whalers on a large scale. The heads of males and females look so different that early anatomists believed them to be two separate species.

Classification Odontoceti, family Ziphiidae.

Common name 'Northern' because it lives in the northern hemisphere (it is endemic to the North Atlantic); 'bottlenose' for its stubby, bottle-shaped beak.

Other names Northern bottle-nosed whale, bottlehead, flathead, steephead, common bottlenose whale, North Atlantic bottlenose whale.

Scientific name *Hyperoodon* from the ancient Greek *hyperoon* for 'palate', and *odon* for 'tooth' (a misnomer, referring to the small bony rugosities on the palate originally mistaken for teeth); *ampullatus* from the Latin *ampulla* for 'flask', and *atus* a Latin suffix indicating 'possession' (referring to the rounded melon and narrow snout, purportedly resembling a Roman flask).

Taxonomy No recognised forms or subspecies.

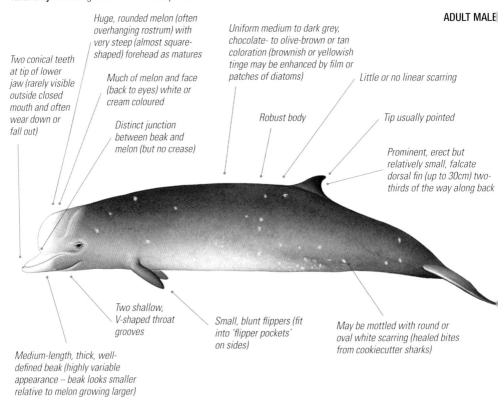

ADULT MALE

Huge, rounded melon (often overhanging rostrum) with very steep (almost square-shaped) forehead as matures

Two conical teeth at tip of lower jaw (rarely visible outside closed mouth and often wear down or fall out)

Much of melon and face (back to eyes) white or cream coloured

Distinct junction between beak and melon (but no crease)

Uniform medium to dark grey, chocolate- to olive-brown or tan coloration (brownish or yellowish tinge may be enhanced by film or patches of diatoms)

Little or no linear scarring

Robust body

Tip usually pointed

Prominent, erect but relatively small, falcate dorsal fin (up to 30cm) two-thirds of the way along back

Two shallow, V-shaped throat grooves

Small, blunt flippers (fit into 'flipper pockets' on sides)

May be mottled with round or oval white scarring (healed bites from cookiecutter sharks)

Medium-length, thick, well-defined beak (highly variable appearance – beak looks smaller relative to melon growing larger)

AT A GLANCE

- Cold, deep waters of North Atlantic
- Medium size (larger than other beaked whales in region)
- Grey, tan or brownish coloration
- Huge, squared-off, bulbous white or cream-coloured melon (especially in male)
- Medium-length, thick, well-defined beak
- Prominent falcate dorsal fin two-thirds of the way along back
- Little or no linear scarring
- Male's teeth not clearly visible
- Often inquisitive and may approach stationary vessels

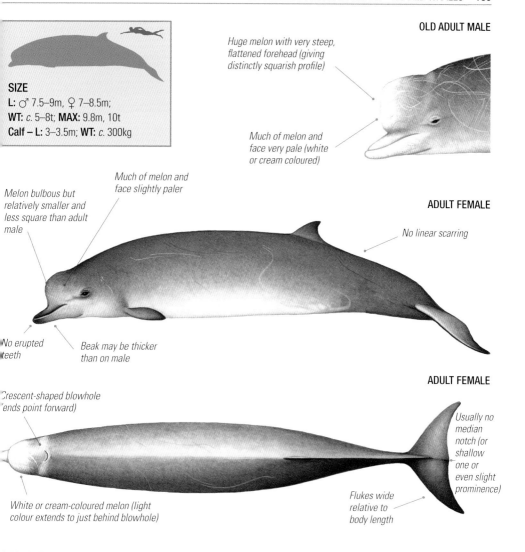

SIZE
L: ♂ 7.5–9m, ♀ 7–8.5m;
WT: *c.* 5–8t; **MAX:** 9.8m, 10t
Calf – L: 3–3.5m; **WT:** *c.* 300kg

OLD ADULT MALE

Huge melon with very steep, flattened forehead (giving distinctly squarish profile)

Much of melon and face very pale (white or cream coloured)

ADULT FEMALE

Much of melon and face slightly paler

Melon bulbous but relatively smaller and less square than adult male

No linear scarring

No erupted teeth

Beak may be thicker than on male

ADULT FEMALE

Crescent-shaped blowhole (ends point forward)

Usually no median notch (or shallow one or even slight prominence)

White or cream-coloured melon (light colour extends to just behind blowhole)

Flukes wide relative to body length

Northern bottlenose whale distribution (waters deeper than 500m)

SIMILAR SPECIES

Distinguishable from most other beaked whales that overlap in range – Blainville's, Sowerby's, Gervais', True's and Cuvier's – by its larger size and significant differences in head shape, beak and body colour. There could be confusion with long-finned pilot whales, but the colour, the beak, and the dorsal fin size, shape and position are all distinctive. From a distance, the shape and position of the dorsal fin is quite similar to that of a common minke whale, but the head shape is entirely different.

DISTRIBUTION

Cold temperate to Arctic waters in the North Atlantic. Ranges from the ice edge to *c.* 37°N. However, rarely seen south of *c.* 55°N – with one notable exception: a well-studied population in a submarine canyon called the Gully, 200km south-east of the Atlantic coast of Halifax, Nova Scotia. In the west, it ranges from southern

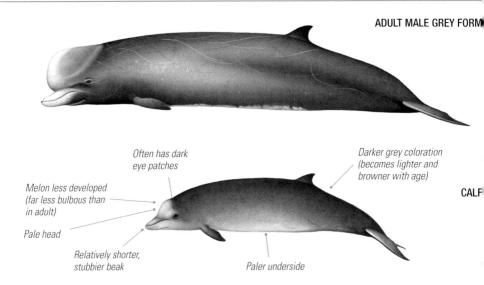

ADULT MALE GREY FORM

Often has dark eye patches

Darker grey coloration (becomes lighter and browner with age)

CALF

Melon less developed (far less bulbous than in adult)

Pale head

Relatively shorter, stubbier beak

Paler underside

Baffin Bay and southern Greenland to Nova Scotia, with occasional records as far south as North Carolina. In the east, it ranges from Svalbard to the Azores, with occasional records as far south as the Cape Verde Islands (although it is relatively rare south of the Bay of Biscay). There are no confirmed records from around Novaya Zemlya, but there have been sightings in the western Barents Sea. Generally not found in enclosed seas such as the Gulf of St Lawrence, Hudson Bay, the Barents Sea or the Mediterranean Sea (where there have been two known vagrants since 1880).

Based on whaling records, six possible distribution hotspots included: the eastern edge of the Scotian Shelf; northern Labrador to southern Baffin Bay; the region between the Faroe Islands, Iceland, east Greenland and Jan Mayen; south-west of Svalbard; off Andenes, northern Norway; and off Møre, western Norway. These days there are regular sightings along the eastern edge of the Scotian Shelf, between Iceland and Jan Mayen,

and north of the Faroe Islands; there are very few sightings off northern Norway.

It is unclear whether there are seasonal north–south or inshore–offshore migrations. However, in some regions with year-round sightings there are seasonal peaks (e.g. April–June in the Norwegian Sea, August–September in the Faroe Islands) and in others there appear to be year-round residents (e.g. the Gully and nearby canyons, where the whales inhabit in a core area of c. 200sq km).

Usually in waters deeper than 500m (with a preference for 800–1,800m) over the continental slope. Rarely strays over the continental shelf, except in submarine canyons, and prefers areas with complex seabed topography, such as the continental shelf edge, oceanic islands and seamounts. Occasionally enters broken ice fields, but generally in open water.

References to 'bottlenose whales' in the northern North Pacific refer to Baird's beaked whales.

DIVE SEQUENCE
- Melon appears first on surfacing, followed by upperside of beak.
- May lift head and body up slightly.
- Rolls forward, sometimes with head, back and dorsal fin visible simultaneously.
- Arches steeply before sounding dive.
- Rarely flukes.

BLOW
- Low, puffy blow (1–2m), often clearly visible and canted forward.

FOOD AND FEEDING

Prey Mainly deepwater squid (especially *Gonatus fabricii* in northern parts of range, *G. steenstrupi* off Scotian Shelf); sometimes fish (e.g. herring, redfish); rarely, in some regions, prawns, sea cucumbers, starfish.
Feeding Most feeding appears to be on or near seabed in deep water; probably suction-feeder.
Dive depth Routinely dives to 800m+ (average in one study 1,065m); maximum recorded 2,339m.
Dive time Routinely 30–40 minutes; maximum recorded 94 minutes; possibly capable of 2 hours; after long dive, typically surfaces for 10 minutes or more, blowing regularly, but may remain near surface for several hours.

BEHAVIOUR

Males may use their large, bulbous heads to headbutt each other (their foreheads are flattened as a result of large, dense maxillary crests on either side of the upper surface of the skull). When resting at the surface, both sexes and all ages may hang in the water at a 45° angle, with the entire melon and beak above the surface. Breaching and lobtailing are not uncommon. Occasionally strands, on both sides of the Atlantic. Known for 'standing by' injured companions – whalers took advantage of this to hunt entire groups. Can be very curious towards boats and even large ships, and will often approach closely and swim around stationary vessels for some time. Seems to be attracted by unfamiliar noises, such as those made by motors or generators.

ADULT MALE LOWER JAW

Two teeth erupt at tip of lower jaw (lean forward)

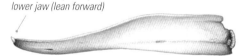

TEETH

Upper 0
Lower 2

Teeth erupt in male only (up to 5cm tall); second pair of teeth sometimes buried in gums (behind the first pair); there may also be 10–20 tiny vestigial teeth in the gums of the upper and/or lower jaws.

GROUP SIZE AND STRUCTURE

Typically 1–10, rarely more than 20. Group size varies according to region: 1–7 in the Faroes (average two), 1–14 in the Gully (average three). There is some segregation by age and sex, with all-male groups, mixed groups, and groups consisting of adult females and juveniles. Females appear to form loose, fluid associations, but pairs of males form long-term relationships that can last anything from days to 1–2 years (function unknown).

PREDATORS

Norwegian whalers reported attacks by killer whales, but the deep-diving capabilities of northern bottlenose whales may help them to avoid predation.

PHOTO-IDENTIFICATION

Mainly using nicks and notches on the trailing edge of the dorsal fin, combined with natural markings on the back (mottling, scarring or indentations); the melon shape is used mainly for gender determination.

POPULATION

There may have been *c.* 100,000 before intense whaling began in the 1880s, but this was reduced to a few tens of thousands after whaling ceased in the 1970s. There is a regional estimate of *c.* 20,000 in the north-east Atlantic; and there is a resident population of *c.* 140 in the Gully, Nova Scotia.

CONSERVATION

IUCN status: Data Deficient (2008). Heavily harvested throughout its range, mainly in 1880–1920 and 1937–73, with *c.* 65,000 killed (and many more struck and lost). Most hunting was by Norway, but also Canada, the UK and the Faroe Islands – for a form of spermaceti oil in the head, for blubber oil and for meat to be used as animal food. Some populations are probably still recovering. A drive fishery in the Faroe Islands has taken northern bottlenose whales opportunistically for centuries; 811 were killed in the period 1584–1993. This hunt was banned in 1986, but *c.* 1–2 have been taken annually since. Currently faces two main threats – entanglement in fishing gear and noise pollution from shipping, and seismic testing and military sonar – but ship strikes and pollution from contaminants may also a be a problem (particularly with increasing industrialisation of the Arctic as the ice melts).

LIFE HISTORY

Sexual maturity Females 8–13 years, males 7–11 years.
Mating Males headbutt rather than fight with teeth during aggressive encounters (cf. other beaked whales).
Gestation *c.* 12 months.
Calving Every 2–3 years; single calf born in the spring and summer, with regional peaks.
Weaning After at least 12 months.
Lifespan Possibly 25–40 years (oldest recorded 27 years for female, 37 years for male).

SOUTHERN BOTTLENOSE WHALE
Hyperoodon planifrons

Flower, 1882

Less well known than its slightly larger northern counterpart (with which it forms an antitropical species pair), the southern bottlenose whale has never been hunted commercially.

Classification Odontoceti, family Ziphiidae.
Common name 'Southern' because it lives in the southern hemisphere; 'bottlenose' for its stubby, bottle-shaped beak.
Other names Antarctic bottlenosed whale, Antarctic bottle-nosed whale, bottlehead, flathead, steephead, Pacific beaked whale, Flower's bottlenose whale.
Scientific name *Hyperoodon* from the ancient Greek *hyperoon* for 'palate', and *odon* for 'tooth (a misnomer, referring to the small bony rugosities on the palate originally mistaken for teeth); *planifrons* from the Latin *planus* for 'level' or 'flat', and *frons* for 'front' (referring to the unusual forehead).
Taxonomy No recognised forms or subspecies.

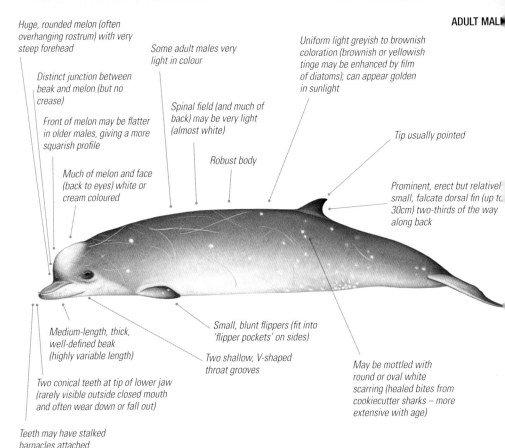

ADULT MALE

Huge, rounded melon (often overhanging rostrum) with very steep forehead

Some adult males very light in colour

Uniform light greyish to brownish coloration (brownish or yellowish tinge may be enhanced by film of diatoms); can appear golden in sunlight

Distinct junction between beak and melon (but no crease)

Front of melon may be flatter in older males, giving a more squarish profile

Spinal field (and much of back) may be very light (almost white)

Tip usually pointed

Much of melon and face (back to eyes) white or cream coloured

Robust body

Prominent, erect but relatively small, falcate dorsal fin (up to 30cm) two-thirds of the way along back

Medium-length, thick, well-defined beak (highly variable length)

Small, blunt flippers (fit into 'flipper pockets' on sides)

Two conical teeth at tip of lower jaw (rarely visible outside closed mouth and often wear down or fall out)

Two shallow, V-shaped throat grooves

May be mottled with round or oval white scarring (healed bites from cookiecutter sharks – more extensive with age)

Teeth may have stalked barnacles attached

AT A GLANCE
- Cool temperate to Antarctic waters of southern hemisphere
- Medium size
- Huge bulbous melon (especially in male), sometimes white or cream coloured
- Uniform light greyish to brownish coloration
- Medium-length, thick, well-defined beak
- Prominent falcate dorsal fin two-thirds of the way along back
- Extensive linear scarring
- No clearly visible teeth

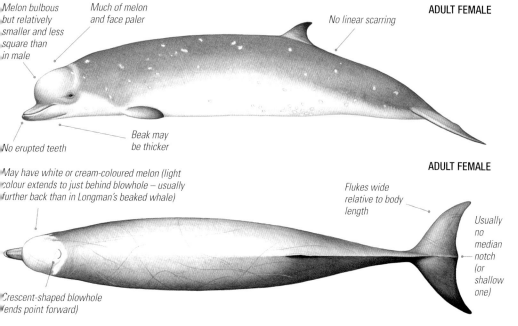

ADULT FEMALE

Melon bulbous but relatively smaller and less square than in male

Much of melon and face paler

No linear scarring

No erupted teeth

Beak may be thicker

ADULT FEMALE

May have white or cream-coloured melon (light colour extends to just behind blowhole – usually further back than in Longman's beaked whale)

Flukes wide relative to body length

Usually no median notch (or shallow one)

Crescent-shaped blowhole (ends point forward)

SIZE

L: ♂ 6–7m, ♀ 6.5–7.5m;
WT: 6–7.5t; **MAX:** 7.8m
Calf – L: 2–3m; **WT:** unknown

In contrast to the northern bottlenose whale, the female may be larger than the male (though the sample size is small).

SIMILAR SPECIES

Confusion is most likely with Arnoux's beaked whale, which has a broadly similar body shape and overlaps in much of the range. If seen clearly, there are significant differences: the southern bottlenose is lighter in colour and has less scarring, a more bulbous and paler melon, a shorter beak and a more erect, falcate dorsal fin; and the teeth are more conspicuous in Arnoux's (if they are visible from any distance at all, it is probably Arnoux's). Cuvier's beaked whale also overlaps, but the size, head shape and coloration are all distinctive. There is a remarkable similarity to Longman's beaked whale – which, in the past, was thought to be a species of tropical bottlenose whale – but there is little overlap in range; a good close view would be needed to tell them apart. From a distance, it could be confused with common minke or Antarctic minke whales, as the shape and position of the dorsal fin are quite similar, but the head shape is entirely different.

DISTRIBUTION

Distribution appears to be continuous in cold temperate to Antarctic waters in the southern hemisphere. Most sightings are from c. 57°S to 70°S, with areas of concentration between

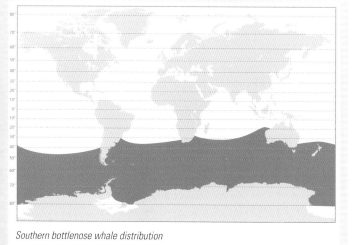

Southern bottlenose whale distribution

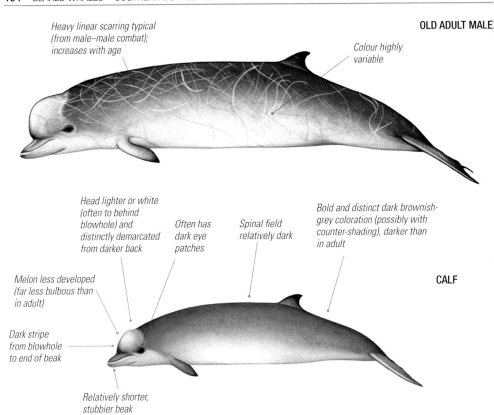

OLD ADULT MALE

Heavy linear scarring typical (from male–male combat); increases with age

Colour highly variable

CALF

Head lighter or white (often to behind blowhole) and distinctly demarcated from darker back

Often has dark eye patches

Spinal field relatively dark

Bold and distinct dark brownish-grey coloration (possibly with counter-shading), darker than in adult

Melon less developed (far less bulbous than in adult)

Dark stripe from blowhole to end of beak

Relatively shorter, stubbier beak

58°S and 62°S in the South Atlantic and eastern Indian Oceans. It sometimes ranges as far north as 30°S along the coasts of South America, Africa, Australia, and New Zealand. There seems to be a north–south migration in winter–summer, with movements of at least 1,000km known. During the summer, most frequently seen within 120km of the ice edge, where it appears to be quite common; it sometimes reaches the edge itself. Usually in waters deeper than 1,000m, preferring areas with complex seabed topography, such as submarine canyons, the continental shelf edge, oceanic islands and seamounts. There is an association with the southern boundary of the Antarctic Circumpolar Current front.

BEHAVIOUR

Breaching (often many times in rapid succession), lobtailing and other aerial behaviours are not uncommon. Unlike northern bottlenose whales, males of the southern species seem to fight with their teeth more than headbutt.

DIVE SEQUENCE
- Melon appears first on surfacing, followed by upperside of beak.
- May lift head and body up slightly.
- Rolls forward, sometimes with head, back and dorsal fin visible simultaneously.
- Arches steeply before sounding dive.
- Rarely flukes.

BLOW
- Low, puffy blow (1–2m), often clearly visible and canted forward.

FOOD AND FEEDING

Prey Mainly deepwater squid; occasionally fish (especially Patagonian toothfish); possibly crustaceans in some areas.
Feeding May compete with sperm whales for same prey species (bottlenose whales probably take smaller individuals).
Dive depth and time Unknown, but probably similar to northern bottlenose.

Two teeth erupt at tip of lower jaw (lean forward)

ADULT MALE LOWER JAW

TEETH

Upper 0
Lower 2

Teeth erupt in male only (up to 5cm tall); second pair of teeth sometimes buried in gums (behind the first pair); rarely, there may also be 10–20 tiny vestigial teeth in the gums of the upper and/or lower jaws.

GROUP SIZE AND STRUCTURE

Typically 1–5. Usually fewer than 10, with occasional sightings of up to 25. Nothing is known about group composition.

PREDATORS

Probably killer whales, but no information.

POPULATION

There is a crude estimate of *c.* 600,000 beaked whales south of the Antarctic Convergence during the southern

Southern bottlenose whales frequently breach.

summer (most of which were considered to be southern bottlenose); this figure is likely to be an underestimate. The most common beaked whale sighted in the Antarctic and apparently quite abundant.

CONSERVATION

IUCN status: Least Concern (2008). Never commercially hunted on a large scale. Some have been caught incidentally in driftnets and other fishing gear, but there are no figures. Other threats might include overfishing of prey species and noise pollution from shipping, seismic exploration and military sonar.

LIFE HISTORY

Very little known, but probably similar to northern bottlenose whale. In South Africa, calving peaks in spring and summer.

Heavy liner scarring is caused by male–male combat.

SHEPHERD'S BEAKED WHALE
Tasmacetus shepherdi
Oliver, 1937

One of the least known of all cetaceans – and yet among the most distinctive – with males, females and calves sharing the same contrasting colour pattern. This is also the only beaked whale to have a mouthful of functional teeth (present in both sexes).

Classification Odontoceti, family Ziphiidae.
Common name After George Shepherd (1872–1946), curator at the Alexander Museum (now Whanganui Regional Museum) in New Zealand, who obtained the type specimen.
Other names Tasman whale, Tasman beaked whale.
Scientific name *Tasma* refers to the Tasman Sea (after the sea in which the type specimen was found, on the west coast of the North Island, New Zealand), *cetus* from the Greek *ketos* or Latin *cetus* for 'whale'; *shepherdi* honours George Shepherd, who collected the type specimen.
Taxonomy No recognised forms or subspecies.

ADULT MALE

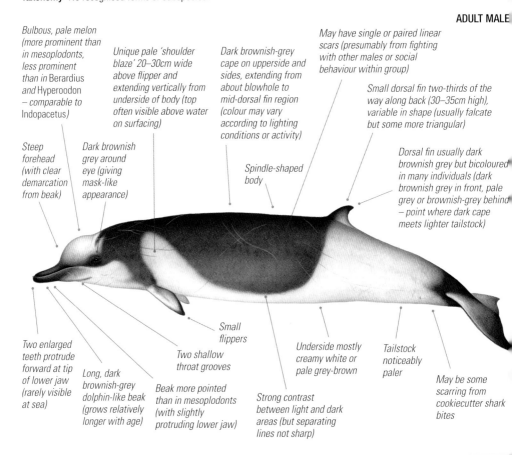

Bulbous, pale melon (more prominent than in mesoplodonts, less prominent than in Berardius and Hyperoodon – comparable to Indopacetus)

Unique pale 'shoulder blaze' 20–30cm wide above flipper and extending vertically from underside of body (top often visible above water on surfacing)

Dark brownish-grey cape on upperside and sides, extending from about blowhole to mid-dorsal fin region (colour may vary according to lighting conditions or activity)

May have single or paired linear scars (presumably from fighting with other males or social behaviour within group)

Small dorsal fin two-thirds of the way along back (30–35cm high), variable in shape (usually falcate but some more triangular)

Steep forehead (with clear demarcation from beak)

Dark brownish grey around eye (giving mask-like appearance)

Spindle-shaped body

Dorsal fin usually dark brownish grey but bicoloured in many individuals (dark brownish grey in front, pale grey or brownish-grey behind – point where dark cape meets lighter tailstock)

Small flippers

Two enlarged teeth protrude forward at tip of lower jaw (rarely visible at sea)

Long, dark brownish-grey dolphin-like beak (grows relatively longer with age)

Two shallow throat grooves

Beak more pointed than in mesoplodonts (with slightly protruding lower jaw)

Underside mostly creamy white or pale grey-brown

Strong contrast between light and dark areas (but separating lines not sharp)

Tailstock noticeably paler

May be some scarring from cookiecutter shark bites

AT A GLANCE
- Cool temperate deep waters of southern hemisphere
- Medium size (larger than mesoplodonts)
- Pale bulbous melon with steep forehead
- Contrasting dark brownish-grey cape and paler grey or brownish-grey tailstock
- Dark mask-like feature over eyes
- Top of pale 'shoulder blaze' often visible on surfacing
- Dorsal fin often bicoloured (darker in front, lighter behind)
- Mainly small, close-knit groups

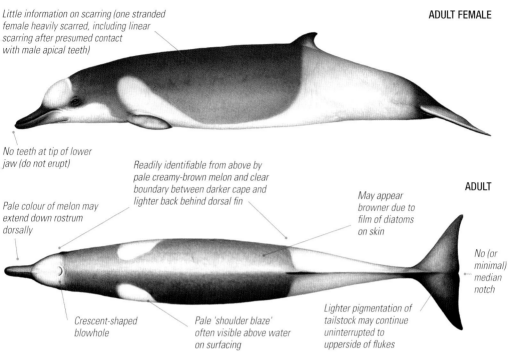

Little information on scarring (one stranded female heavily scarred, including linear scarring after presumed contact with male apical teeth)

ADULT FEMALE

No teeth at tip of lower jaw (do not erupt)

Readily identifiable from above by pale creamy-brown melon and clear boundary between darker cape and lighter back behind dorsal fin

May appear browner due to film of diatoms on skin

ADULT

Pale colour of melon may extend down rostrum dorsally

No (or minimal) median notch

Crescent-shaped blowhole

Pale 'shoulder blaze' often visible above water on surfacing

Lighter pigmentation of tailstock may continue uninterrupted to upperside of flukes

SIZE

L: ♂ up to 7m, ♀ up to 6.6m;
WT: *c.* 2.3–3.5t
Calf – L: *c.* 3–3.5m; **WT:** unknown
One 1940 record of a male 9.1m long is considered unlikely.

SIMILAR SPECIES

A relatively easy beaked whale to identify due to its unique colour pattern, though photographic evidence is required for verification. Appears larger than most mesoplodonts, with a steeper and more bulbous melon. The melon is less pronounced than in Arnoux's beaked whale or the southern bottlenose whale, and the clear vertical division in coloration between dark and light (roughly at the dorsal fin), as well as the visible top of the paler shoulder blaze, should be distinctive. The melon is similar in shape and colour to that of Longman's beaked whale, but there appears to be little or no overlap in range (and the body coloration is very different).

DISTRIBUTION

Presumed to have a circumpolar distribution in deep, cool temperate oceanic waters of the southern hemisphere. Known from fewer than 50 strandings and a couple of dozen sightings at sea, mostly between 30°S and 46°S. The northernmost record is of a stranded individual in Shark Bay, Western Australia, in 2008, at *c.* 26°S; however,

■ presumed range (from limited sightings and strandings)

Shepherd's beaked whale distribution

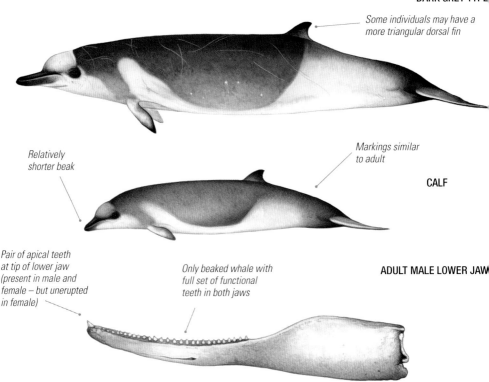

DARK GREY TYPE

Some individuals may have a more triangular dorsal fin

Markings similar to adult

CALF

Relatively shorter beak

Pair of apical teeth at tip of lower jaw (present in male and female – but unerupted in female)

Only beaked whale with full set of functional teeth in both jaws

ADULT MALE LOWER JAW

there have been no live sightings north of 33°38'S. Most reported strandings have been in New Zealand (including the Chatham Islands), but there are also records from Australia, Tristan da Cunha, Argentina and the Juan Fernandez Islands off Chile. Most validated sightings have been in New Zealand and southern Australia (including south of Tasmania), but there have been reported sightings from Shag Rocks near South Georgia and Tristan da Cunha. Purported strandings from South Africa and a widely reported sighting in the Seychelles are now believed to be incorrect. Dedicated marine mammal surveys and opportunistic field activities in southern Australia and New Zealand during 2008–17 had 13 vessel-based and five aerial sightings, greatly increasing knowledge of this species at sea; most were in mid- to upper continental slope waters, in depths greater than 310m (mostly much deeper) and in submarine canyons. Where there is a narrow continental shelf, it may sometimes occur in deep water close to shore. The mean depth of sightings in Australia and New

DIVE SEQUENCE
- Typically skims beak through surface (parallel to water) but may lift it entirely out of water (typically at angle of *c.* 30–40°).
- Tends to remain below surface between blows.
- Usually little arching of back on sounding dive.
- Does not show flukes.

BLOW
- Bushy blow 1–2m tall and canted forward (often visible from considerable distance).

FOOD AND FEEDING
Little known, but prey includes fish (especially eelpout), squid and crabs. Limited encounters suggest dive times last 5–15 minutes, with surface intervals of 4–17 minutes (blowing every 9–13 seconds).

Zealand was 1,208m; only one sighting (3,940m) was in water deeper than 2,000m.

BEHAVIOUR
Very little known. Some breaching, lobtailing and spyhopping observed. Individuals in a group typically surface and dive together; may swim in a moderately spaced 'chorus line' for several minutes at a time. Unless travelling, they often return to the surface within 100–150m of the original dive. No evidence of evasive behaviour in the presence of boats, and in some cases they have been known to approach closely.

TEETH
Upper 34–42
Lower 36–56
The only beaked whale to have full set of functional teeth in the upper and lower jaws (present in male and female).

GROUP SIZE AND STRUCTURE
Very little information, but the few reliable sightings suggest that group size ranges from two to 14 individuals with a mean of 5.4 (3–6 being most common). Individuals in a group tend to surface close together.

PREDATORS
Unknown, but may include killer whales and large sharks. However, there are records of killer whales apparently stealing prey from Shepherd's beaked whales – with no obvious signs of aggression.

PHOTO-IDENTIFICATION
May be possible using the variation in width of the pale 'shoulder blaze' (extending vertically from the underside, above the flipper, to about half to two-thirds of the way up the flank); there may be similarities to the variation in saddle patches observed in killer whales. The shape and colour of the dorsal fin (which is highly variable), combined with nicks on the trailing edge, and scars and other markings, may also be useful.

POPULATION
No overall global estimate. Like other beaked whales, it probably has a naturally low population.

CONSERVATION
IUCN status: Data Deficient (2018). Direct hunting has never been recorded. It is likely that some are caught as bycatch in driftnet (and possibly gillnet) fisheries, but there is no specific information. Like other beaked whales, it is probably threatened by the ingestion of plastic debris, and noise pollution from military sonar and seismic exploration.

LIFE HISTORY
Virtually nothing known. One adult male estimated to be 23 years old.

Shepherd's beaked whale photographed off Kaikoura, New Zealand – notice the unique pale 'shoulder blaze' and the pale, bulbous melon.

LONGMAN'S BEAKED WHALE
Indopacetus pacificus

(Longman, 1926)

Longman's beaked whale was one of cetology's great long-standing mysteries. Until 2003, the only evidence for its existence came from two weathered skulls: one found on an Australian beach, in 1882, and the other on the floor of a Somalian fertiliser factory, in 1955. However, live animals are now being seen with some regularity at scattered locations in the tropical Indo-Pacific and there have been at least two dozen strandings.

Classification Odontoceti, family Ziphiidae.

Common name After Herber Albert Longman (1880–1954), director of the Queensland Museum, who first described the proposed new species from a skull found on a beach in Mackay, Queensland, Australia.

Other names Indo-Pacific beaked whale, tropical bottlenose whale.

Scientific name *Indopacetus* from Latin *indicus* for 'Indian', *pacificus* for 'Pacific' and *cetus* for 'whale' (whale in two oceans); *pacificus* for the type locality.

Taxonomy Originally placed in the genus *Mesoplodon*, but morphological (later confirmed by genetic) studies proved that it should be in its own genus; no recognised forms or subspecies.

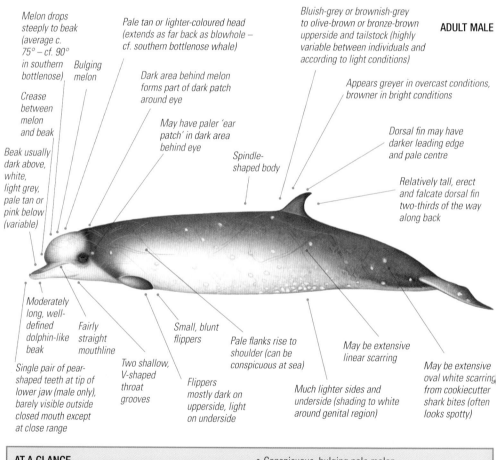

Melon drops steeply to beak (average c. 75° – cf. 90° in southern bottlenose)

Bulging melon

Crease between melon and beak

Pale tan or lighter-coloured head (extends as far back as blowhole – cf. southern bottlenose whale)

Dark area behind melon forms part of dark patch around eye

Bluish-grey or brownish-grey to olive-brown or bronze-brown upperside and tailstock (highly variable between individuals and according to light conditions)

ADULT MALE

May have paler 'ear patch' in dark area behind eye

Appears greyer in overcast conditions, browner in bright conditions

Beak usually dark above, white, light grey, pale tan or pink below (variable)

Spindle-shaped body

Dorsal fin may have darker leading edge and pale centre

Relatively tall, erect and falcate dorsal fin two-thirds of the way along back

Moderately long, well-defined dolphin-like beak

Fairly straight mouthline

Small, blunt flippers

Pale flanks rise to shoulder (can be conspicuous at sea)

May be extensive linear scarring

May be extensive oval white scarring from cookiecutter shark bites (often looks spotty)

Single pair of pear-shaped teeth at tip of lower jaw (male only), barely visible outside closed mouth except at close range

Two shallow, V-shaped throat grooves

Flippers mostly dark on upperside, light on underside

Much lighter sides and underside (shading to white around genital region)

AT A GLANCE
- Warm waters of the Indo-Pacific
- Medium size
- Spindle-shaped body
- Low bushy blow often angled forward

- Conspicuous, bulging pale melon
- Distinct, sharply demarcated beak
- Falcate, dolphin-like dorsal fin
- Fin two-thirds of the way along back
- Apparent colour varies according to weather conditions

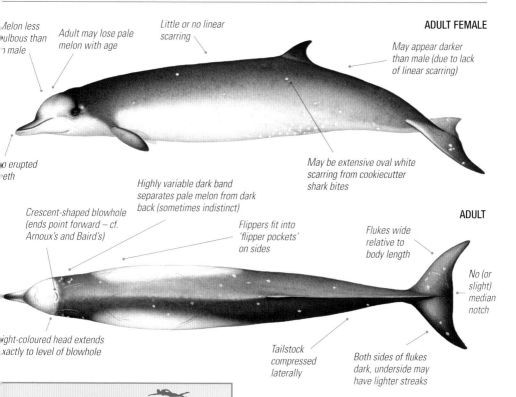

ADULT FEMALE

Melon less bulbous than in male

Adult may lose pale melon with age

Little or no linear scarring

May appear darker than male (due to lack of linear scarring)

No erupted teeth

May be extensive oval white scarring from cookiecutter shark bites

Highly variable dark band separates pale melon from dark back (sometimes indistinct)

ADULT

Crescent-shaped blowhole (ends point forward – cf. Arnoux's and Baird's)

Flippers fit into 'flipper pockets' on sides

Flukes wide relative to body length

No (or slight) median notch

Light-coloured head extends exactly to level of blowhole

Tailstock compressed laterally

Both sides of flukes dark, underside may have lighter streaks

SIZE

L: 5.7–6.5m (based on a handful of measured lengths); **WT:** *c.* 6–7.5t (guesstimate); **MAX:** *c.* 9m (estimated from sightings at sea and extrapolation from skull measurements)

Calf – L: *c.* 3m; **WT:** *c.* 230kg

SIMILAR SPECIES

The large size, bulging melon, distinct beak and tall, erect dorsal fin should distinguish Longman's beaked whale from most other beaked whales in the region. Confusion is most likely with southern bottlenose whales, though there is minimal overlap in range (historical sightings of what are now known to be Longman's beaked whales in tropical waters were often mistakenly identified as southern bottlenose whales); the angle of the forehead, extent of pale coloration and subtly different dorsal fin shapes are distinctive, and Longman's are usually in larger groups. Distant animals may be difficult to distinguish from Cuvier's beaked whales – but look for the head and beak shape and surfacing profile to tell apart.

DISTRIBUTION

Distribution is poorly known, but it appears to be widespread and fairly continuous in the tropical Indo-Pacific. Thought to be more abundant in the western part of its distribution,

Longman's beaked whale distribution

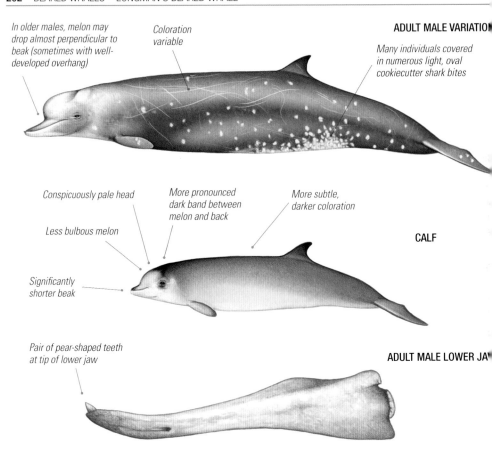

In older males, melon may drop almost perpendicular to beak (sometimes with well-developed overhang)

Coloration variable

ADULT MALE VARIATION

Many individuals covered in numerous light, oval cookiecutter shark bites

Conspicuously pale head

More pronounced dark band between melon and back

More subtle, darker coloration

Less bulbous melon

CALF

Significantly shorter beak

Pair of pear-shaped teeth at tip of lower jaw

ADULT MALE LOWER JAW

and appears to be especially common around the Maldives (with an average of one sighting per 21 days at sea – cf. one per 200 days in the Pacific). Has not been recorded in the Atlantic Ocean. Sightings tend to be in areas with surface water temperatures of 21–31°C and most are in water warmer than 26°C. May push further south or north with warm currents (such as the Agulhas Current, South Africa). Most sightings are oceanic, over or near areas with steep bottom topography, in depths of 250–2,500m or more. Collected specimens have come from Australia, Somalia, South Africa, Kenya, the Maldives, Sri Lanka, the Andaman Islands and mainland India, Myanmar, the Philippines, Taiwan, Japan, China, New Caledonia and Hawaii.

DIVE SEQUENCE

- Swims faster and more 'aggressively' than most other beaked whales.
- When surfacing quickly, head and beak appear quite high out of water as it throws up rooster-tail of spray.
- When surfacing slowly, head not raised right out of water and often hidden by bow wave.
- Long back visible.
- Dorsal fin usually appears before melon disappears.
- Little arching of back (cf. Cuvier's beaked whale) before long dive.

BLOW

- Low, bushy blow fairly conspicuous and angled slightly forwards.

FOOD AND FEEDING
Prey Presumed to feed mainly on deepwater squid, with some fish.
Feeding Unknown.
Dive depth Unknown, but probably a deep diver.
Dive time Average in western Indian Ocean 23 minutes (recorded range 11–33 minutes); one individual tracked underwater acoustically for 45 minutes (contact lost before it surfaced).

BEHAVIOUR
Known to associate with short-finned pilot whales, bottlenose dolphins and spinner dolphins. Breaching has been observed. Larger groups tend to be more active at the surface, and may ignore or approach boats; many spend less time underwater and often lift their heads above the surface.

TEETH (MALE)
Upper 0
Lower 2
Teeth do not erupt in female.

GROUP SIZE AND STRUCTURE
Tight groups of 1–110 recorded, with overall average of 8.5; regional averages include *c.* seven in the western

Indian Ocean, *c.* nine in the eastern tropical Pacific and *c.* 29 in the western tropical Pacific; group size in Hawaii ranges from 18 to 110. One of only three species of beaked whales that occur in large groups.

PREDATORS
Unknown, but probably killer whales and large sharks.

PHOTO-IDENTIFICATION
May be possible, using cookiecutter shark bite scars.

POPULATION
Unknown. Does not appear to be particularly common. Very rough estimate of *c.* 4,600 around Hawaii, *c.* 300 in the eastern North Pacific.

CONSERVATION
IUCN status: Data Deficient (2008). Little is known about threats. There is no known direct or regular exploitation. At least several have been entangled in fishing gear in Sri Lanka and Pakistan, and it is thought that gillnets, in particular, could be a problem. Other potential threats include noise pollution (especially naval sonar and seismic testing) and ingestion of plastic debris.

LIFE HISTORY
Virtually nothing known. Single calf born possibly in autumn and summer (September–December in southern Africa). Lifespan at least 20 years, based on limited samples (oldest recorded female 21–22 years, male 24–25 years).

Longman's beaked whale surfacing slowly in the Maldives.

PERRIN'S BEAKED WHALE
Mesoplodon perrini
Dalebout, Mead, Baker & van Helden, 200̶

Officially named in 2002, this is one of the least known beaked whales (all information is based on very few stranded specimens). Known only from southern California, it is most closely related to the Peruvian beaked whale.

Classification Odontoceti, family Ziphiidae.
Common name Named as a tribute to eminent American cetologist Dr W.F. Perrin, who retrieved two of the specimens.
Other names California beaked whale.
Scientific name *Mesoplodon* from the Greek *mesos* for 'middle', *hopla* for 'arms' or 'weapons', *odon* for 'tooth' (i.e. armed with a tooth in the middle of the jaw); *perrini* after Dr W.F. Perrin.
Taxonomy No recognised forms or subspecies.

ADULT MAL▸
(based on little informatio▸

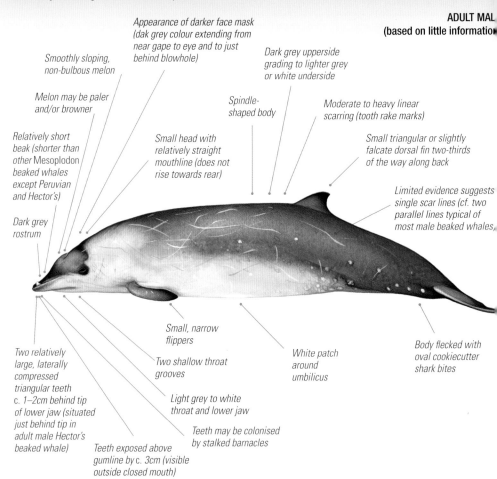

Appearance of darker face mask (dak grey colour extending from near gape to eye and to just behind blowhole)

Smoothly sloping, non-bulbous melon

Dark grey upperside grading to lighter grey or white underside

Melon may be paler and/or browner

Spindle-shaped body

Moderate to heavy linear scarring (tooth rake marks)

Relatively short beak (shorter than other Mesoplodon beaked whales except Peruvian and Hector's)

Small head with relatively straight mouthline (does not rise towards rear)

Small triangular or slightly falcate dorsal fin two-thirds of the way along back

Dark grey rostrum

Limited evidence suggests single scar lines (cf. two parallel lines typical of most male beaked whales)

Two relatively large, laterally compressed triangular teeth c. 1–2cm behind tip of lower jaw (situated just behind tip in adult male Hector's beaked whale)

Small, narrow flippers

White patch around umbilicus

Body flecked with oval cookiecutter shark bites

Two shallow throat grooves

Light grey to white throat and lower jaw

Teeth exposed above gumline by c. 3cm (visible outside closed mouth)

Teeth may be colonised by stalked barnacles

AT A GLANCE
- Eastern North Pacific
- Small to medium size
- Generally nondescript counter-shaded coloration
- Small triangular or slightly falcate dorsal fin two-thirds of the way along back

- Appearance of darker face mask
- Two large triangular teeth near tip of lower jaw may be visible at close range
- Looking for small beaked whales during the summer off southern California probably offers best odds of encountering this enigmatic species

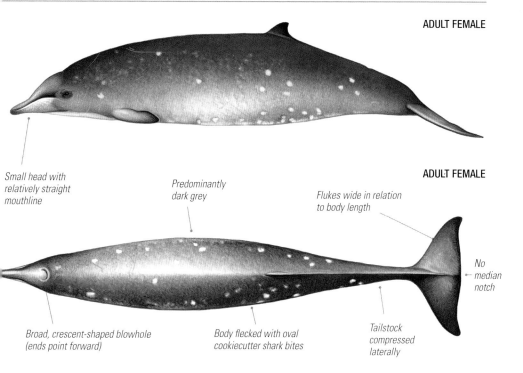

ADULT FEMALE

ADULT FEMALE

Small head with
relatively straight
mouthline

Predominantly
dark grey

Flukes wide in relation
to body length

No
median
notch

Broad, crescent-shaped blowhole
(ends point forward)

Body flecked with oval
cookiecutter shark bites

Tailstock
compressed
laterally

SIZE
L: ♂ 3.9m, ♀ 4.3–4.4m;
WT: *c.* 900kg; **MAX:** 4.53m
Calf – L: *c.* 2–2.1m; **WT:** unknown
(based on very few specimens).

SIMILAR SPECIES
With so little information, Perrin's beaked whale may be impossible to identify with absolute certainty at sea. However, its small size could help to distinguish it from all other beaked whales in the northern hemisphere, except Peruvian, while the absence of the male's white swathe, as well as the straight mouthline and teeth near the tip of the lower jaw (if visible at close range), could be distinctive. Females and immatures are likely to be almost impossible to distinguish from other *Mesoplodon* species if seen alone.

DISTRIBUTION
Currently known only from southern California. Strandings range from Torrey Pines State Reserve (32°55′N – just north of San Diego) north to Fisherman's Wharf, Monterey (36°37′N). It might be expected in waters with depths of more than 1,000m (mainly offshore but possibly also close to shore where the water is sufficiently deep). Researchers working off California in 2011–15 recorded signals from a beaked whale that are believed to have been Perrin's. Little is known about habitat preferences, but it might be expected in waters with depths of more than 500m.

BEHAVIOUR
This species has never been reliably identified at sea, so there is no information on behaviour (although two sightings of pairs of unidentified small beaked whales off southern California in July 1976 and September

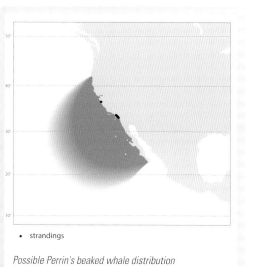

• strandings

Possible Perrin's beaked whale distribution

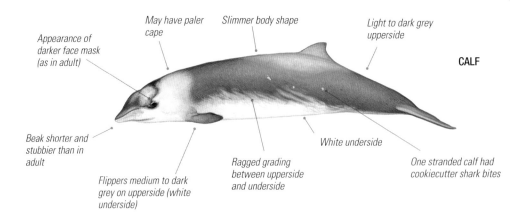

Appearance of darker face mask (as in adult)

May have paler cape

Slimmer body shape

Light to dark grey upperside

CALF

Beak shorter and stubbier than in adult

Flippers medium to dark grey on upperside (white underside)

Ragged grading between upperside and underside

White underside

One stranded calf had cookiecutter shark bites

FLUKES (underside)

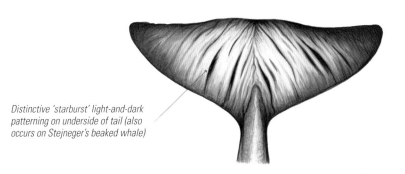

Distinctive 'starburst' light-and-dark patterning on underside of tail (also occurs on Stejneger's beaked whale)

1978, tentatively identified as Hector's beaked whales at the time, were likely to have been Perrin's). Probably unobtrusive and difficult to spot in anything but calm conditions. Linear scarring on the body of the only known adult male suggests that, as with most other beaked whales, there are aggressive encounters between males; however, instead of the parallel scarring normally caused by two beaked whale teeth, it had single scar lines.

TEETH

Upper 0
Lower 2

Laterally compressed teeth erupt in males only (females have similar teeth, but they do not erupt); the exposed portion is roughly the shape of an isosceles triangle; up to 64mm long.

DIVE SEQUENCE (speculative)
- May surface with shallow roll, showing top of head (perhaps also top of rostrum) and back.
- Slight arching of the back before diving.
- Does not show flukes.
- Probably spends little time at surface.

BLOW (speculative)
- Blow indistinct.

FOOD AND FEEDING
Virtually no information, but very limited evidence from stomach contents suggests primarily mid- and deepwater squid, but may also include deepwater fish and shrimps. Likely to forage at depths greater than 500m.

ADULT MALE LOWER JAW

ROUP SIZE AND STRUCTURE
o information.

NDING A NEW SPECIES
he first recorded specimen of Perrin's beaked whale as a dead male calf that washed up on a beach 50km orth of San Diego, in 1975; unfortunately, it had been un over by a vehicle and was in poor condition. The adly decomposed body of an adult female – probably its other and the only female known at the time – washed o on the same beach six days later. Then, in 1978, an dult male was found on a beach in nearby Carlsbad. A ourth specimen – this time a juvenile male – washed shore at Torrey Pines State Natural Reserve, within San ego city limits, in September 1979. A fifth animal, a ale, was found at Fisherman's Wharf, Monterey, in 1997. or many years, the animals were tentatively logged as e first northern hemisphere records of Hector's beaked hale, which at the time was itself known from only six pecimens. Then, in 1997, a new research technique using itochondrial DNA sequencing (to help identify species f beaked whales from small tissue samples) concluded at all the California animals actually belonged to a new pecies. It was officially named in 2002. The only record nce is of a 4.25m female that live-stranded on Venice each, southern California, in 2013 (the animal died before cientists arrived but was in good condition).

REDATORS
ossibly killer whales and large sharks.

POPULATION
No estimate of global abundance.

CONSERVATION
IUCN status: Data Deficient (2008). There is very little information on threats, but some can be deduced. Like other deep-diving beaked whales, it is likely to be vulnerable to noise pollution, especially from seismic surveys and naval sonar. Ingesting plastic debris could also be a problem (the Venice Beach female had a blue ball of monofilament in her stomach). Direct hunting of Perrin's beaked whale is not known and there is no evidence of it being caught regularly as bycatch in fisheries.

LIFE HISTORY
Unknown. The first calf found was a male 2.1m long and probably still suckling. One of the later strandings was a 2.45m immature animal, which was probably about one year old and had the remains of a squid in its stomach, suggesting that it had been (or was soon to be) weaned. Two of the adults found were both estimated to be nine years old when they died. It is unknown whether the marked concentration of sightings between May and September has any significance.

PERUVIAN BEAKED WHALE
Mesoplodon peruvianus

Reyes, Mead & Van Waerebeek, 199[?]

Formally described in 1991, the Peruvian or pygmy beaked whale is the smallest species of beaked whale. It is very poorly known: for many years the majority of records were curated specimens from Peru, but recently there have been more live sightings in the Gulf of California, Mexico, and elsewhere.

Classification Odontoceti, family Ziphiidae.
Common name Reflects its discovery in Peru, and that it is commonly found in Peruvian waters.
Other names Pygmy beaked whale, lesser beaked whale (reflecting the small size relative to other *Mesoplodon* beaked whales); there is strong evidence that this is the previously unnamed species formerly known as '*Mesoplodon* species A'.
Scientific name *Mesoplodon* from the Greek *mesos* for 'middle', *hopla* for 'arms' or 'weapons', *odon* for 'tooth' (i.e. armed with a tooth in the middle of the jaw); *peruvianus*, an abbreviation of the Latin for 'belonging to Peru' (where the type specimen was discovered, and the majority of curated specimens originated from).
Taxonomy No recognised forms or subspecies.

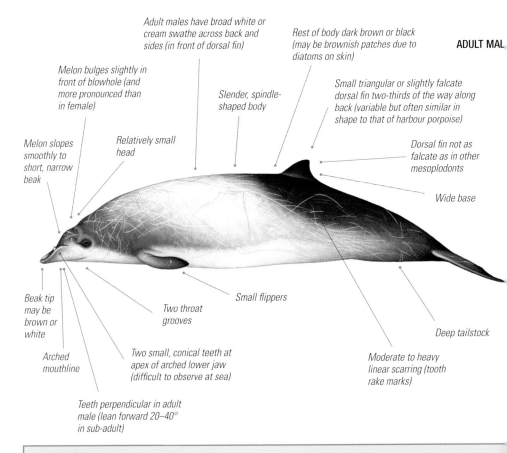

Adult males have broad white or cream swathe across back and sides (in front of dorsal fin)

Rest of body dark brown or black (may be brownish patches due to diatoms on skin)

ADULT MAL[E]

Melon bulges slightly in front of blowhole (and more pronounced than in female)

Slender, spindle-shaped body

Small triangular or slightly falcate dorsal fin two-thirds of the way along back (variable but often similar in shape to that of harbour porpoise)

Melon slopes smoothly to short, narrow beak

Relatively small head

Dorsal fin not as falcate as in other mesoplodonts

Wide base

Beak tip may be brown or white

Small flippers

Two throat grooves

Deep tailstock

Arched mouthline

Two small, conical teeth at apex of arched lower jaw (difficult to observe at sea)

Moderate to heavy linear scarring (tooth rake marks)

Teeth perpendicular in adult male (lean forward 20–40° in sub-adult)

AT A GLANCE
- Mainly warm waters of eastern Pacific Ocean
- Small size
- Adult male has broad white swathe across back and sides
- Small groups
- Dorsal fin variable but usually small, wide-based and roughly triangular
- Difficult to spot except in calm conditions
- Long dives between surfacings
- Male's teeth rarely visible at sea

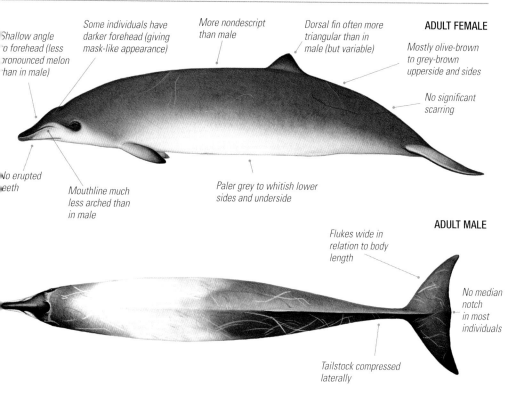

Shallow angle to forehead (less pronounced melon than in male)

Some individuals have darker forehead (giving mask-like appearance)

More nondescript than male

Dorsal fin often more triangular than in male (but variable)

ADULT FEMALE

Mostly olive-brown to grey-brown upperside and sides

No significant scarring

No erupted teeth

Mouthline much less arched than in male

Paler grey to whitish lower sides and underside

ADULT MALE

Flukes wide in relation to body length

No median notch in most individuals

Tailstock compressed laterally

SIZE
L: ♂ 3.4–3.9m, ♀ 3.4–3.6m;
WT: unknown; **MAX:** 4.1m
Calf – L: *c.* 1.6m; **WT:** unknown

SIMILAR SPECIES
The white swathe across the adult male's back and sides is unique to this species, making it easy to identify at sea. Females and immatures are almost impossible to distinguish from other *Mesoplodon* species if seen alone; however, their relatively small size, more triangular dorsal fin and limited distribution are good indicators.

DISTRIBUTION
Originally described primarily from freshly captured specimens landed in Peruvian fishing ports. However, in recent years it has become the most frequently sighted *Mesoplodon* in the sub-tropical and tropical eastern Pacific Ocean (although this is relative). Most sightings are concentrated in the warmest waters of this region – dubbed the 'Eastern Pacific Warm Pool' – an area with sea-surface temperatures greater than 27.5°C. Most live sightings are in the southern Gulf of California, Mexico. The northernmost record was of a female that stranded alive in Moss Landing, California (36°47'N), in January 2001; the southernmost record was another stranded specimen in north-central

(plus one stranding on South Island, New Zealand)

Peruvian beaked whale distribution

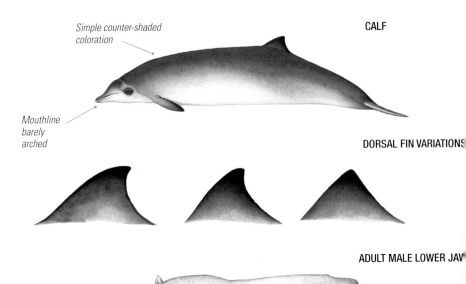

Simple counter-shaded coloration

CALF

Mouthline barely arched

DORSAL FIN VARIATIONS

ADULT MALE LOWER JAW

Chile (29°17'N) in May 1995. Occurs mainly in deep oceanic waters, but it can be seen close to shore if there is sufficient depth (500m or more). The only record away from the eastern Pacific was a single stranding of a male near Kaikoura, South Island, New Zealand (42°31'S), in 1991; this is currently considered by some to be a vagrant, but it could represent a significantly more extensive distribution. There are no known migrations or movements.

BEHAVIOUR
Generally unobtrusive and difficult to spot in anything but calm conditions. Groups typically dive for 15–30 minutes, surface again some distance away, breathe half a dozen times and then dive again. Has been known to approach small boats very closely (albeit briefly) but usually keeps its distance. Breaching, lobtailing and other surface behaviour have been recorded, but appear to be rare.

TEETH
Upper 0
Lower 2
Teeth erupt in male only; 31–65mm long.

GROUP SIZE AND STRUCTURE
Typically in groups of 2–5 (sometimes 1–8). Groups usually include mixed sex and age classes.

PREDATORS
Unknown, but probably large sharks and killer whales.

POPULATION
No global estimate, but believed to be reasonably common within its limited range.

CONSERVATION
IUCN status: Data Deficient (2008). There is very little information on threats, but a lot can be deduced. A large proportion of the specimen records for this species have

DIVE SEQUENCE
- Surfaces with shallow roll, showing top of head (sometimes also much of beak) and back.
- Slight arching of back before diving.

BLOW
- Blow indistinct and rarely visible.

FOOD AND FEEDING

Prey Limited evidence suggests primarily mid- and deepwater fish, but also probably deepwater squid and shrimps.
Feeding Unknown.
Dive depth Likely to forage at depths greater than 500m.
Dive time Typically 15–30 minutes (based on limited observations).

ⁿvolved animals that have died in gillnets set for sharks ⁿd other large fish off the coast of Peru, which is clearly problem; entanglement in deepwater gillnets set for illfish and tuna is also likely serious. Like other deep-iving beaked whales, it is likely to be vulnerable to noise ollution, especially from seismic surveys and naval sonar.

Peruvian beaked whales have been recorded ingesting plastic debris, which could ultimately kill them.

LIFE HISTORY
Unknown.

dult male Peruvian beaked whale showing the distinctive white swathe across its back and sides.

dult female showing the more nondescript colouring.

DERANIYAGALA'S BEAKED WHALE
Mesoplodon hotaula
Deraniyagala, 196?

Currently known from only 11 confirmed specimens and a handful of tentative sightings at sea. This poorly known beaked whale was originally described in 1963 from a specimen in Sri Lanka. For many years it was considered synonymous with the ginkgo-toothed beaked whale, but was formally accepted as a separate species in 2014.

Classification Odontoceti, family Ziphiidae.
Common name After the then director of National Museums of Ceylon, P.E.P. Deraniyagala, who collected, described and named the first specimen.
Other names Atoll beaked whale (though rarely used these days since specimens have been found in places other than atolls).
Scientific name *Mesoplodon* from the Greek *mesos* for 'middle', *hopla* for 'arms' or 'weapons', *odon* for 'tooth' (i.e. armed with a tooth in the middle of the jaw); *hotaula* from the local Sinhala words *hota*, for 'beak', and *ula*, for 'pointed'.
Taxonomy No recognised forms or subspecies.

ADULT MAL?
(Based on single adult mal?
from the Seychelles, 200?

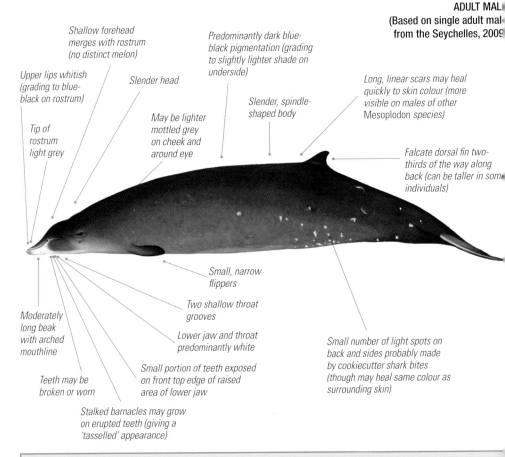

Shallow forehead merges with rostrum (no distinct melon)

Predominantly dark blue-black pigmentation (grading to slightly lighter shade on underside)

Upper lips whitish (grading to blue-black on rostrum)

Slender head

Long, linear scars may heal quickly to skin colour (more visible on males of other *Mesoplodon* species)

Slender, spindle-shaped body

Tip of rostrum light grey

May be lighter mottled grey on cheek and around eye

Falcate dorsal fin two-thirds of the way along back (can be taller in some individuals)

Small, narrow flippers

Two shallow throat grooves

Moderately long beak with arched mouthline

Lower jaw and throat predominantly white

Small number of light spots on back and sides probably made by cookiecutter shark bites (though may heal same colour as surrounding skin)

Teeth may be broken or worn

Small portion of teeth exposed on front top edge of raised area of lower jaw

Stalked barnacles may grow on erupted teeth (giving a 'tasselled' appearance)

AT A GLANCE
- Tropical Indian and west Pacific Oceans
- Small to medium size
- Predominantly dark with pale lower jaw and throat
- Possibly no long linear scarring
- Prominent falcate dorsal fin two-thirds of the way along back
- Visible teeth near apex of moderately arched mouthline
- Teeth may be covered in stalked barnacles

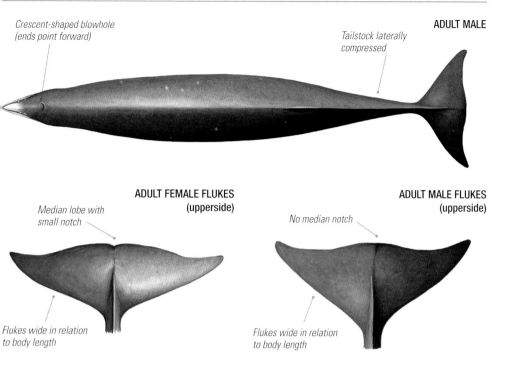

ADULT MALE

Crescent-shaped blowhole
(ends point forward)

Tailstock laterally
compressed

**ADULT FEMALE FLUKES
(upperside)**

Median lobe with
small notch

Flukes wide in relation
to body length

No median notch

**ADULT MALE FLUKES
(upperside)**

Flukes wide in relation
to body length

SIZE
L: ♂ 3.9–4.3m, ♀ 4.5–4.8m;
WT: unknown; **MAX:** unknown
Calf – L: unknown; **WT:** unknown.

SIMILAR SPECIES

DNA evidence is normally required for a positive identification. Differences in cranial and tooth morphology from the similar ginkgo-toothed beaked whale should be assessed by experts. Confusion is likely with the ginkgo-toothed beaked whale and dark forms of Cuvier's beaked whale (and potentially any mesoplodont in tropical waters). Deraniyagala's appears to have a grey tip to the lower jaw and a white chin and throat, while the ginkgo-toothed beaked whale appears to have a white tip to the lower jaw and a grey-brown chin and throat. It might also be distinguishable by healed cookiecutter shark bites, which seem to be white in ginkgo-toothed and the same colour as the surrounding skin in Deraniyagala's, though there is very little information.

DISTRIBUTION

Currently known only from a small number of widely scattered strandings and a few sightings in the Indo-Pacific. It appears to have a tropical range in the Indian Ocean and at least part of the Pacific Ocean. Little is known about habitat preferences, but it might be expected in waters with depths of more than 500m (mainly offshore but possibly also close to shore where the water is sufficiently

⧄ possible range   • stranding locations

Deraniyagala's beaked whale distribution

DORSAL FIN VARIATION

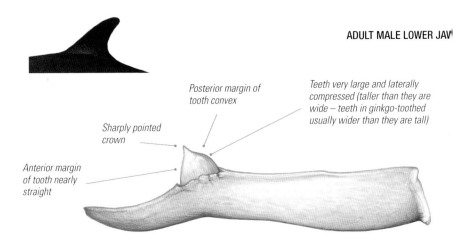

ADULT MALE LOWER JAW

Posterior margin of tooth convex

Teeth very large and laterally compressed (taller than they are wide – teeth in ginkgo-toothed usually wider than they are tall)

Sharply pointed crown

Anterior margin of tooth nearly straight

deep). Palmyra Atoll (southwest of Hawaii) or Tabiteuea Atoll (Republic of Kiribati), in the central Pacific, and the Maldives in the Indian Ocean probably offer the best odds of encountering this enigmatic species.

NAMING A NEW SPECIES

The first specimen was a dying female found washed ashore at Ratmalana, Sri Lanka, on 26 January 1963 (about 8km south of Colombo). Paulus Deraniyagala, then director of the National Museums of Ceylon, claimed its uniqueness and named it *Mesoplodon hotaula*. Its status as a new species was disputed for more than half a century, but recent DNA analysis of new specimens has proved Deraniyagala right.

A second specimen was collected 40 years after the first: a male found at Tabiteuea Atoll, Gilbert Islands, Kiribati, in 2003. Since then, a further nine specimens have been identified: a confirmed female, a possible female and a male at Palmyra Atoll, in the Line Islands, in 2005; a male at Hulhudhuffaru Atoll, in the Maldives, in 2007; a male on Desroches Island, in the Seychelles, in 2009; a female and her calf at Maco, Compostela Valley, in the Philippines, in 2012 (the calf was alive and was pushed back into the water); and at least one more specimen from the Gilbert Islands, Kiribati in 2013. An individual collected in Malaysia in 1954 (held in the British Museum of Natural History) is now also recognised as this species. Other tropical records may represent Deraniyagala's beaked whale, but DNA testing and further examination of cranial and tooth morphology will be required to confirm their identity.

The Tabiteuea Atoll specimen is particularly interesting: the tissue sample used to identify it (dried meat) was a gift from the islanders, left over from a feast. It was reportedly obtained from one of seven whales driven onto a beach

and killed in October 2002, when the whales came into the shallow lagoon. According to the islanders such events occurred several times a year. The whales were described as 'long ones' *c.* 4.6–6.1m in length.

The only scientific reports of possible live observations of this species have been from around Palmyra Atoll (05°50′N, 162°06′W). Also, beaked whale acoustic recordings from nearby Kingman Reef – made many times every day during four months of monitoring – are believed to be of this species.

BEHAVIOUR

Virtually nothing is known. There have been a number of possible sightings at Palmyra Atoll, in the central Pacific, and during two of these distant animals were observed leaping completely out of the water. The broken teeth of two male specimens may indicate that they use their teeth as weapons in male–male combat.

TEETH

Upper 0
Lower 2

Teeth erupt in male only; 10cm long, 9cm wide (in comparison, ginko-toothed beaked whale teeth are wider than they are long).

GROUP SIZE AND STRUCTURE

Most sightings of mesoplodonts likely to have been Deraniyagala's were of paired animals (including at least two mother–calf pairs), giving a mean group size of 2.2 individuals (ranging from two to three).

POPULATION

Unknown. The lack of records to date suggest that it may not be particularly common, although the number of

FOOD AND FEEDING
Prey Like other mesoplodonts, likely to feed primarily on squid; maybe also deepwater fish.
Feeding Unknown.
Dive depth Unknown.
Dive time Unknown.

acoustic recordings at Kingman Reef suggests a sizeable aggregation there at least.

CONSERVATION
IUCN status: Data Deficient (2018). Nothing is known about threats, but some can be deduced. The only known direct take is by local people on at least one of the 33 atolls in the Republic of Kiribati (the Gilbert Islands). No bycatch has been reported, although it is probably vulnerable to entanglement in nets and longlines. The stranded female in the Philippines apparently died after swallowing nylon rope and a piece of coal. As with all beaked whales, it is likely to be susceptible to noise pollution, especially from seismic surveys and naval sonar.

LIFE HISTORY
Unknown. The Philippines female stranded with a 2.4m calf.

A rare photograph: this small group of Deraniyagala's beaked whales was observed in the Maldives in November 2017.

GRAY'S BEAKED WHALE
Mesoplodon grayi

von Haast, 1876

Our knowledge of Gray's beaked whale has improved significantly in recent years, though it is still rarely seen at sea. However, strandings are fairly common and it is probably quite abundant. There was one extraordinary occasion, in June 2001, when a mother and calf spent almost five days in Mahurangi Harbour, North Island, New Zealand, giving researchers a rare opportunity to observe this species closely.

Classification Odontoceti, family Ziphiidae.

Common name After British zoologist John Edward Gray (1800–75), who had several other animals named in his honour and named several cetacean species himself.

Other names Scamperdown beaked whale, southern beaked whale, Haast's beaked whale, small-toothed beaked whale.

Scientific name *Mesoplodon* from the Greek *mesos* for 'middle', *hopla* for 'arms' or 'weapons', *odon* for 'tooth', meaning 'armed with a tooth in the middle of the jaw'; *grayi* after John Edward Gray.

Taxonomy No recognised forms or subspecies; an early proposal to put it in a new monotypic genus, *Oulodon*, was not widely supported.

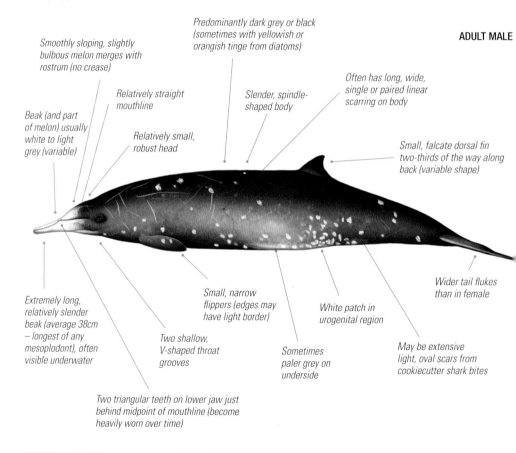

ADULT MALE

Predominantly dark grey or black (sometimes with yellowish or orangish tinge from diatoms)

Smoothly sloping, slightly bulbous melon merges with rostrum (no crease)

Relatively straight mouthline

Slender, spindle-shaped body

Often has long, wide, single or paired linear scarring on body

Beak (and part of melon) usually white to light grey (variable)

Relatively small, robust head

Small, falcate dorsal fin two-thirds of the way along back (variable shape)

Extremely long, relatively slender beak (average 38cm – longest of any mesoplodont), often visible underwater

Small, narrow flippers (edges may have light border)

Two shallow, V-shaped throat grooves

White patch in urogenital region

Wider tail flukes than in female

Sometimes paler grey on underside

May be extensive light, oval scars from cookiecutter shark bites

Two triangular teeth on lower jaw just behind midpoint of mouthline (become heavily worn over time)

AT A GLANCE
- Temperate waters of southern hemisphere
- Medium size
- Spindle-shaped body
- Relatively small head

- Long, slender white to light grey beak
- Beak appears at 45° angle above water on surfacing
- Small triangular teeth in middle of each side of lower jaw
- Possibly in small groups

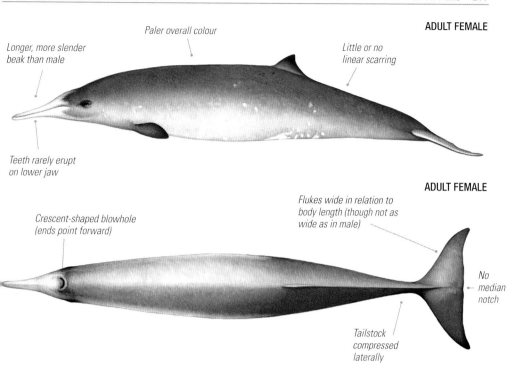

ADULT FEMALE

Paler overall colour

Longer, more slender beak than male

Little or no linear scarring

Teeth rarely erupt on lower jaw

ADULT FEMALE

Crescent-shaped blowhole (ends point forward)

Flukes wide in relation to body length (though not as wide as in male)

No median notch

Tailstock compressed laterally

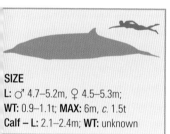

SIZE
L: ♂ 4.7–5.2m, ♀ 4.5–5.3m;
WT: 0.9–1.1t; **MAX:** 6m, *c.* 1.5t
Calf – L: 2.1–2.4m; **WT:** unknown

SIMILAR SPECIES

Confusion is most likely with other mesoplodonts of the region – including Andrews', Blainville's, True's, ginkgo-toothed, spade-toothed, strap-toothed and, in particular, the similarly white-beaked Hector's. To distinguish it from Hector's, look for the flattened teeth in the middle of the lower jaw (at the tip in Hector's) and the mostly single rake marks (mostly closely paired in Hector's). With a close look, adults can be distinguished from other members of the genus by their extremely long, slender white beaks and relatively straight mouthlines.

DISTRIBUTION

Circumpolar in temperate offshore waters of the southern hemisphere, with most records south of 30°S. Sometimes seen in Antarctic and sub-Antarctic waters; in summer months it appears near the Antarctic Peninsula and along the shores of the continent, even among sea ice. Commonly strands around the coasts of New Zealand (where it is the most commonly stranded beaked whale), but significant numbers have also stranded in South Australia and Victoria, South Africa, Argentina, Chile, Peru and the Falkland Islands. There appears to be a hotspot

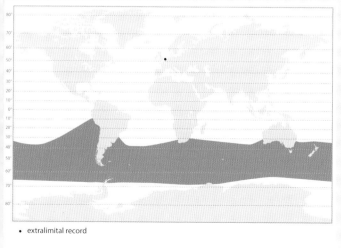

• extralimital record

Gray's beaked whale distribution

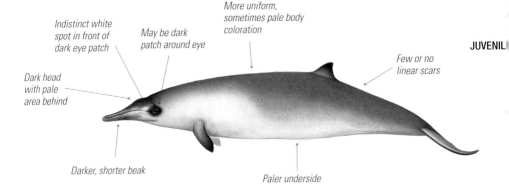

ADULT FEMALE VARIATION

May be more orangish or yellowish (exaggerated by film of diatoms)

Indistinct white spot in front of dark eye patch

May be dark patch around eye

More uniform, sometimes pale body coloration

JUVENILE

Few or no linear scars

Dark head with pale area behind

Darker, shorter beak

Paler underside

DORSAL FIN VARIATION

Some fins sweep further back

Can be quite hooked

Laterally flattened teeth can be quite wide (c. 6–10cm) and up to 10cm tall

Teeth remarkably similar (in size and shape) to those of ginkgo-toothed beaked whale

ADULT MALE LOWER JAW

Teeth tilt slightly forward (variable)

DIVE SEQUENCE
- Often surfaces at angle of 45° showing long white beak.
- Surfaces slowly.
- Rolls smoothly as dorsal fin comes into view.
- Typically does not raise flukes before sounding dive.

BLOW
- May be low, diffuse blow.

FOOD AND FEEDING

Very little known. Probably feeds on small deepwater squid and fish, and likely to forage at depths greater than 500m.

in the area between the North Island of New Zealand and the Chatham Islands. A single female stranded at Kijkduin in the Netherlands in 1927 – the only record from the northern hemisphere – which was undoubtedly extralimital. Usually in waters deeper than 200m along and beyond the continental shelf edge, but there have been sightings in shallow coastal areas (the summer–autumn seasonality of which suggests that inshore movements may be associated with calving or nursing). Likely to be more common in areas of complex seabed topography.

BEHAVIOUR

Breaching (usually at a shallow angle, sometimes entirely airborne), spyhopping, flipper-slapping and lobtailing have all been observed. May porpoise out of the water when swimming fast, making low, arc-shaped leaps.

TEETH

Upper 34–44
Lower 2

Unique among mesoplodonts in that adults of both sexes have very small teeth on each side of the upper jaw (17–22 pairs), less than 1cm tall, and protruding only a few millimetres above the gums or not at all; these are towards the back of the mouth, beginning at roughly the same position as the single pair of teeth in the lower jaw of the male. There are no teeth in front of the tusk teeth, in either sex. In females, it is rare for the lower teeth to erupt.

GROUP SIZE AND STRUCTURE

Most sightings have been of singles or pairs, with a few relatively small groups of up to five recorded. In a study of 113 Gray's beaked whales stranded in New Zealand over a 20-year period, 57 were alone and the remaining 56 were in 19 groups with a mean size of 3.4; none of the adults that stranded together was related. However, there have been several mass strandings (including one of 28 animals in the Chatham Islands, in 1874), which suggests that the species may be more gregarious than other mesoplodonts.

PREDATORS

Unknown. There is some evidence of shark bites. Killer whales are also likely to be predators, and certainly hunt beaked whales in Australia, but there are no confirmed records of hunting Gray's beaked whales.

POPULATION

Unknown. Possibly has a large population, based on genetic evidence and the number of records throughout the range.

CONSERVATION

IUCN status: Data Deficient (2008). Entanglement in fishing gear is probably the most significant threat, though there is little information. Like other beaked whales, it is likely to be affected by ingestion of plastic debris and noise pollution (especially military sonar and seismic testing). No significant exploitation is known.

LIFE HISTORY

Virtually nothing is known. Single calf may be born in the southern spring and summer (November–February).

An extensively scarred adult male Gray's beaked whale in the Drake Passage, Southern Ocean.

GINKGO-TOOTHED BEAKED WHALE
Mesoplodon ginkgodens
Nishiwaki and Kamiya, 1958

There are no confirmed sightings of a live ginkgo-toothed beaked whale at sea, although there have been several possible ones. It is known from fewer than 30 widely scattered strandings and captures, spread across the Pacific and Indian Oceans.

Classification Odontoceti, family Ziphiidae.
Common name From the Japanese *ginkyo*; in lateral view, the teeth resemble the fan-shaped leaves of the ginkgo tree (*Ginkgo biloba*) of Japan (where the type specimen, a mature male, was found in 1957).
Other names Japanese beaked whale, ginkgo-toothed whale.
Scientific name *Mesoplodon* from the Greek *mesos* for 'middle', *hopla* for 'arms' or 'weapons', *odon* for 'tooth', meaning 'armed with a tooth in the middle of the jaw'; *ginkgodens* from *ginkgo* (referring to the ginkgo tree), *dens* from the Latin for 'tooth' – i.e. 'ginkgo-toothed'.
Taxonomy No recognised forms or subspecies; for many years Deraniyagala's beaked whale was considered synonymous with ginko-toothed, but Deraniyagala's was formally accepted as a separate species in 2014.

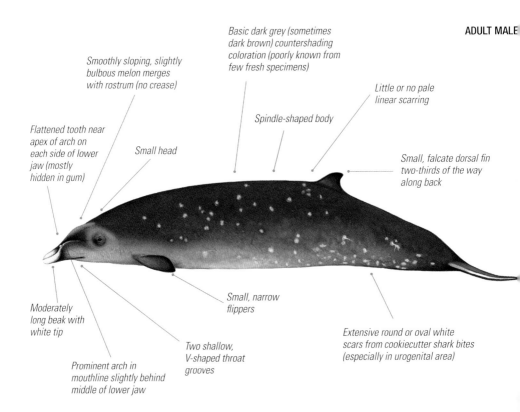

ADULT MALE

Basic dark grey (sometimes dark brown) countershading coloration (poorly known from few fresh specimens)

Smoothly sloping, slightly bulbous melon merges with rostrum (no crease)

Little or no pale linear scarring

Spindle-shaped body

Flattened tooth near apex of arch on each side of lower jaw (mostly hidden in gum)

Small head

Small, falcate dorsal fin two-thirds of the way along back

Moderately long beak with white tip

Small, narrow flippers

Prominent arch in mouthline slightly behind middle of lower jaw

Two shallow, V-shaped throat grooves

Extensive round or oval white scars from cookiecutter shark bites (especially in urogenital area)

AT A GLANCE
- Tropical to temperate waters of Pacific and Indian Oceans
- Medium size
- Little or no pale linear scarring
- Moderately long beak with white tip

- Smoothly sloping, slightly bulbous melon
- Prominent arch in mouthline slightly behind middle of lower jaw
- Wide tooth near apex of arch on each side of lower jaw
- Small, falcate dorsal fin two-thirds of the way along back

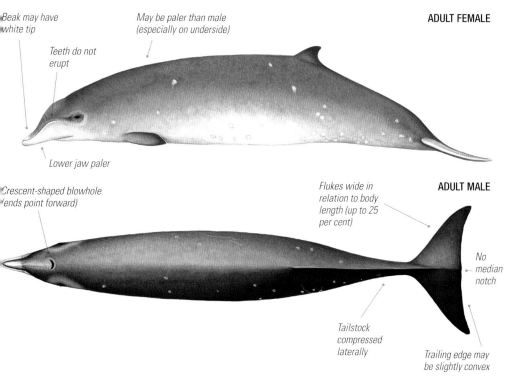

Beak may have white tip

Teeth do not erupt

Lower jaw paler

ADULT FEMALE

May be paler than male (especially on underside)

Crescent-shaped blowhole (ends point forward)

ADULT MALE

Flukes wide in relation to body length (up to 25 per cent)

No median notch

Tailstock compressed laterally

Trailing edge may be slightly convex

SIZE
L: ♂ 4.7–5.3m, ♀ 4.7–5.3m;
WT: *c*. 1–1.5t; MAX: 5.3m, 2t
Calf – L: 2–2.5m; WT: unknown

SIMILAR SPECIES

Confusion is most likely with other mesoplodonts overlapping in range – including Deraniyagala's, Hubbs' and Blainville's (or, if teeth only are examined, with Gray's beaked whale). Without further information, identification at sea will be difficult. The lack of obvious white linear scarring – characteristic of most other male beaked whales – could be a useful clue. Deraniyagala's appears to have a grey tip to the lower jaw and a white chin and throat, while the ginkgo-toothed beaked whale appears to have a white tip to the lower jaw and a grey-brown chin and throat. Hubbs' is distinguished by the adult male's diagnostic white 'cap' and beak. The adult male Blainville's has a higher arch in the lower jaw and a flatter head. Females and juveniles alone are probably indistinguishable from other mesoplodonts.

DISTRIBUTION

Exact distribution is unclear, due to the small number of records and, until recently, taxonomic confusion between the ginkgo-toothed beaked whale and Deraniyagala's beaked whale. Records are widely scattered across

■ possible range   • strandings

Ginkgo-toothed beaked whale distribution

ADULT MALE LOWER JAW

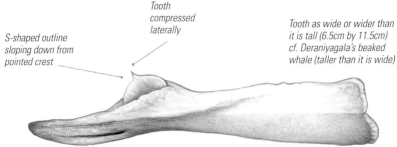

Tooth compressed laterally

S-shaped outline sloping down from pointed crest

Tooth as wide or wider than it is tall (6.5cm by 11.5cm) cf. Deraniyagala's beaked whale (taller than it is wide)

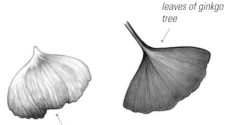

Teeth resemble leaves of ginkgo tree

Teeth similar (in size and shape) to those of Deraniyagala's beaked whale and wider-toothed variants of Gray's beaked whale

the Pacific and Indian Oceans (although Indian records are more likely to represent Deraniyagala's), with most concentrated in the west Pacific. Mainly deep tropical to temperate waters, and probably more common in areas of complex seabed topography.

A significant number of records are from around Japan (seven altogether – including the type specimen found near Tokyo in 1957), perhaps associated with the Kuroshio Current; a single record from Yamagata Prefecture suggests that it may also occur in the Sea of Japan. But there have also been strandings in Liaoning Province, China (one); Taiwan (four); Del Mar, southern California (one); the Galápagos Islands (one); Strait of Malacca, Indonesia (one); Pohnpei in Micronesia (one), which was previously mistakenly reported as Guam; Australia (one in Victoria, four in New South Wales); New Zealand (five); and the Maldives (one – a single tooth held in the National Museum, Malé). There was a reported stranding in the Philippines – but the identification is questionable.

Acoustic research has been picking up echolocation signals that are believed to be produced by ginkgo-toothed beaked whales extensively around Cross Seamount, about 300km south-west of Hawaii, and occasionally off Kona, Kaua'i, and Pearl and Hermes Atoll (in the Northwestern Hawaiian Islands).

BEHAVIOUR
There have been no confirmed sightings of live animals at sea, so there is no information on behaviour. The lack of linear scarring on males – in contrast to most other beaked whales – is likely due to the small amount of tooth exposed above the gum (they do not project above the upper jaw) rather than a lack of intraspecific fighting.

FOOD AND FEEDING
Very little known. Like other beaked whales, it is presumed to eat mainly deepwater squid, and some fish, and to forage at depths greater than 200m.

TEETH (MALE)
Upper 0
Lower 2

GROUP SIZE AND STRUCTURE
Nothing known.

PREDATORS
Unknown, but presumably killer whales and large sharks.

POPULATION
Unknown. Probably uncommon, given the small number of records.

CONSERVATION
IUCN status: Data Deficient (2008). Entanglement in gillnets and other fishing gear is probably the most significant threat; there are reports of some caught in deepwater drift gillnets and, in Taiwan, at least two hooked on longlines. Like other beaked whales, it is likely to be affected by ingestion of plastic debris and noise pollution (especially military sonar and seismic testing). Known to have been taken at least occasionally by Japanese and Taiwanese whalers.

LIFE HISTORY
Nothing known.

HECTOR'S BEAKED WHALE
Mesoplodon hectori

(Gray, 1871)

Known from only a few dozen strandings and just one confirmed sighting at sea, Hector's beaked whale is one of the least known of all cetaceans.

Classification Odontoceti, family Ziphiidae.

Common name After James Hector (1834–1907), founding curator of the Colonial Museum in Wellington, New Zealand where the type specimen originated).

Other names New Zealand beaked whale, skew-beaked whale (after the huge asymmetry of the skull).

Scientific name *Mesoplodon* from the Greek *mesos* for 'middle', *hopla* for 'arms' or 'weapons', *odon* for 'tooth' (i.e. armed with a tooth in the middle of the jaw); *hectori* after James Hector.

Taxonomy No recognised forms or subspecies.

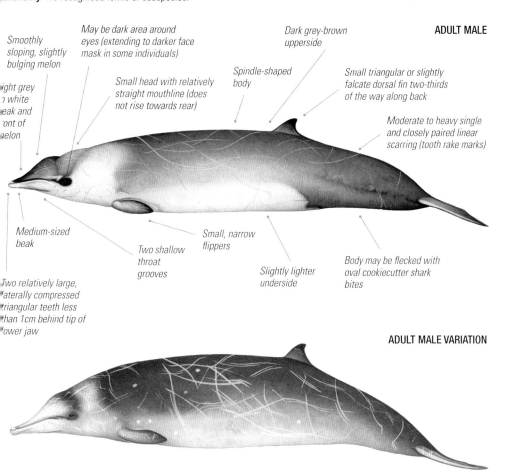

Smoothly sloping, slightly bulging melon

May be dark area around eyes (extending to darker face mask in some individuals)

Dark grey-brown upperside

ADULT MALE

Light grey to white beak and front of melon

Small head with relatively straight mouthline (does not rise towards rear)

Spindle-shaped body

Small triangular or slightly falcate dorsal fin two-thirds of the way along back

Moderate to heavy single and closely paired linear scarring (tooth rake marks)

Medium-sized beak

Two shallow throat grooves

Small, narrow flippers

Slightly lighter underside

Body may be flecked with oval cookiecutter shark bites

Two relatively large, laterally compressed triangular teeth less than 1cm behind tip of lower jaw

ADULT MALE VARIATION

AT A GLANCE
- Temperate waters of southern hemisphere
- Small to medium size
- Small triangular dorsal fin two-thirds of the way along back
- Light grey to white beak and front of melon
- Smoothly sloping melon
- Moderate to heavy scarring
- Two laterally compressed triangular teeth at tip of lower jaw

ADULT FEMAL

Dark grey
upper jaw

Relatively nondescript
colouring

Less linear
scarring

No erupted
teeth

Pale grey or whitish
blaze behind eyes

ADULT FEMAL

Broad flukes in
relation to body
length

N
m
nc

Crescent-shaped blowhole
(ends point forward)

Tailstock
compressed
laterally

Almost straigh
trailing edge

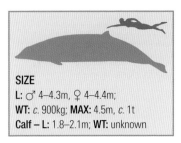

SIZE
L: ♂ 4–4.3m, ♀ 4–4.4m;
WT: *c.* 900kg; MAX: 4.5m, *c.* 1t
Calf – L: 1.8–2.1m; WT: unknown

SIMILAR SPECIES
Confusion is most likely with other mesoplodonts of the region – including Andrew's, Blainville's, ginkgo-toothed, True's, strap-toothed, spade-toothed and, in particular, the similarly white-beaked Gray's. Females and juveniles are probably indistinguishable at sea. To distinguish from Gray's, look for the flattened teeth at the tip of the lower jaw (in the middle in Gray's) and the mostly closely paired rake marks (mostly single in Gray's). Hector's beaked whale is virtually indistinguishable from Perrin's beaked whale (except by DNA testing), but the two species live in different hemispheres.

DISTRIBUTION
Cool temperate waters of the southern hemisphere, between 32°S and 55°S. Most records are from New Zealand southern Australia (including Tasmania), the Atlantic coast of southern South America (Brazil, Uruguay, Argentina and the Falkland Islands) and South Africa. There was also a stranding on Navarino Island, Tierra del Fuego, southern Chile. There are no records between New Zealand and the Pacific coast of South America – explained either by a break in distribution or simply a lack of data. It is presumed to occu in deep waters beyond the

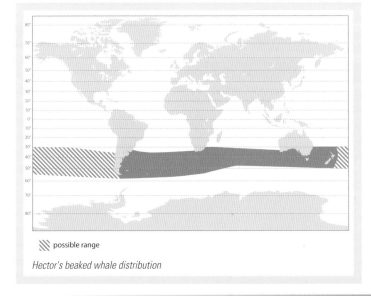

※ possible range

Hector's beaked whale distribution

FOOD AND FEEDING

Virtually unknown. It probably feeds in deep water on squid (possibly also fish and invertebrates). The only confirmed live sighting recorded dive times of up to four minutes, but the maximum is likely much longer.

ADULT MALE LOWER JAW

dge of the continental shelf (as other members of the genus). The seasonal nature of stranding records in New Zealand (December–April) suggests a possible inshore movement in summer. Four animals that stranded in southern California in 1975–79 were tentatively logged as Hector's beaked whales – believed to be the first northern hemisphere records for this species – but they are now known to be Perrin's beaked whales.

BEHAVIOUR

Known primarily from strandings. In the only confirmed sighting of this species alive at sea, a single 3m-long healthy-looking animal was observed in 1999 in shallow water about 50m from shore in southwestern Australia – almost certainly atypical habitat for the species – and it breached several times near a research vessel. It remained in the area for two weeks before disappearing.

TEETH

Upper 0
Lower 2

In 2016, the South Australian Museum conducted a necropsy on a juvenile female, which was found to have a pair of small erupted 'fangs' not seen before; underneath were the two triangular teeth typical of Hector's beaked whales (which do not erupt in females). The 'extra' teeth were possibly atavisms (evolutionary throwbacks) of some kind.

LIFE HISTORY

Virtually unknown. Single calf may be born in summer (based on very limited evidence).

GROUP SIZE AND STRUCTURE

No information, but likely to occur in small groups.

POPULATION

No estimate of global abundance. It may be naturally rare in most parts of its range – but the paucity of records may have as much to do with the lack of research and the challenge of identification at sea. Stranding records suggest that it may be relatively common around New Zealand.

CONSERVATION

IUCN status: Data Deficient (2008). There is very little information on threats, but some can be deduced. Like other deep-diving beaked whales, it is likely to be vulnerable to noise pollution, especially from seismic surveys and naval sonar. Ingesting plastic debris could also be a problem. Direct hunting of Hector's beaked whale is not known (apart from one individual taken in New Zealand in the 1800s) and there is no evidence of it being caught regularly as bycatch in fisheries.

An extremely rare photograph of a Hector's beaked whale at sea – a juvenile female near the coast off Western Australia.

HUBBS' BEAKED WHALE
Mesoplodon carlhubbsi

Moore, 1963

Known from fewer than 60 records in the North Pacific — mostly strandings with just a few reliable sightings at sea — Hubbs' beaked whale is very poorly understood. It is strikingly similar to Andrews' beaked whale, which lives far away in the cold waters of the Southern Ocean.

Classification Odontoceti, family Ziphiidae.
Common name Carl L. Hubbs (1894–1979) was an eminent marine biologist, who collected the type specimen in 1945 (later named in his honour by Joseph Curtis Moore); he and other faculty members at Scripps Institution of Oceanography, California, preserved its skeleton and then famously ate the whale (during Second World War meat rationing).
Other names Arch-beaked whale.
Scientific name *Mesoplodon* from the Greek *mesos* for 'middle', *hopla* for 'arms' or 'weapons', *odon* for 'tooth' (i.e. armed with a tooth in the middle of the jaw); *carlhubbsi* after Carl L. Hubbs.
Taxonomy Previously considered (by some) to be a subspecies of Andrew's beaked whale, but recent genetic studies confirm its specific distinctiveness; no recognised forms or subspecies.

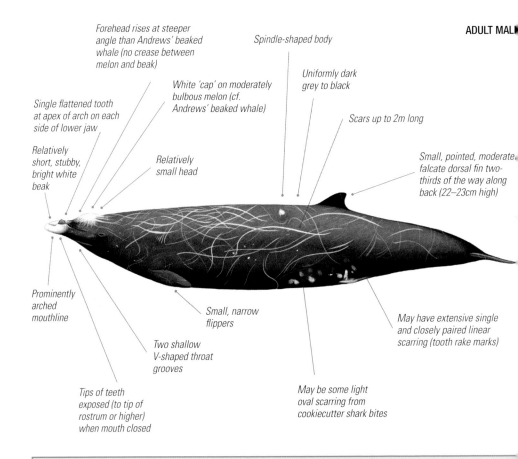

ADULT MALE

Forehead rises at steeper angle than Andrews' beaked whale (no crease between melon and beak)

Spindle-shaped body

White 'cap' on moderately bulbous melon (cf. Andrews' beaked whale)

Uniformly dark grey to black

Single flattened tooth at apex of arch on each side of lower jaw

Scars up to 2m long

Relatively short, stubby, bright white beak

Relatively small head

Small, pointed, moderate, falcate dorsal fin two-thirds of the way along back (22–23cm high)

Prominently arched mouthline

Small, narrow flippers

May have extensive single and closely paired linear scarring (tooth rake marks)

Two shallow V-shaped throat grooves

Tips of teeth exposed (to tip of rostrum or higher) when mouth closed

May be some light oval scarring from cookiecutter shark bites

---

AT A GLANCE
- Cool temperate North Pacific
- Medium size
- Uniformly dark
- Bright white 'cap' and beak
- Heavily scarred
- Small falcate dorsal fin two-thirds of way along back
- Two tusks on arched lower jaw

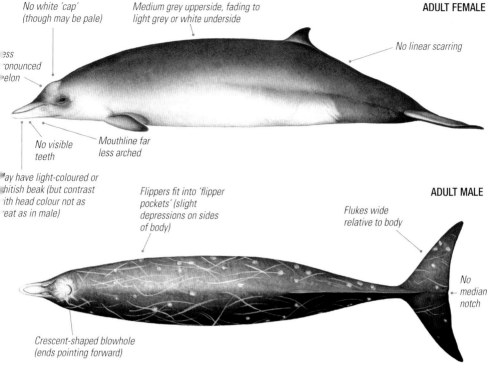

ADULT FEMALE

No white 'cap'
(though may be pale)

Medium grey upperside, fading to
light grey or white underside

No linear scarring

...ess
...onounced
...elon

No visible
teeth

Mouthline far
less arched

ADULT MALE

...ay have light-coloured or
...hitish beak (but contrast
...ith head colour not as
...eat as in male)

Flippers fit into 'flipper
pockets' (slight
depressions on sides
of body)

Flukes wide
relative to body

No
median
notch

Crescent-shaped blowhole
(ends pointing forward)

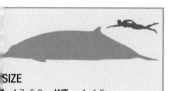

SIZE
L: 4.7–5.3m; **WT:** c. 1–1.5t
Calf – L: c. 1.7–2.3m; **WT:** unknown

SIMILAR SPECIES

Adult male is more readily identifiable than most other beaked whales. Baird's, Cuvier's, Stejneger's, ginkgo-toothed, Perrin's, Longman's and Blainville's beaked whales all overlap in range to varying degrees, but the combination of the white beak, white 'cap' on the melon and large tusks is diagnostic; the relative beak length, tooth position and mouthline can also help. Similar to Andrews' beaked whale (some previous records of Hubbs' were erroneously identified as Andrews') but they do not overlap in range. Females and young animals can be difficult to identify at sea, except possibly by experienced observers.

DISTRIBUTION

Distribution is known mainly from strandings. Endemic to deep offshore temperate waters of the North Pacific. The majority of records are from western North America, largely along the path of the south-flowing cold-water California Current, between 32°42'N (San Clemente Island, California) and 54°18'N (Prince Rupert, British Columbia). Also recorded on the Pacific coast of Japan, between 35°01'N

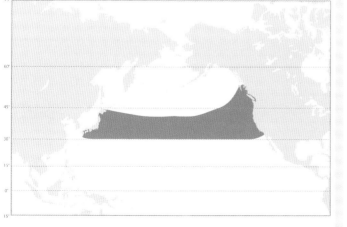

Hubbs' beaked whale distribution

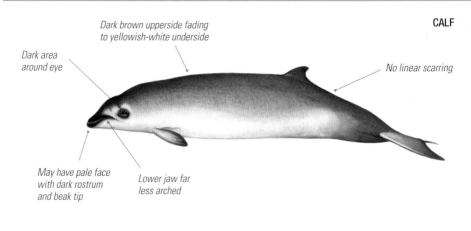

CALF

Dark brown upperside fading to yellowish-white underside

Dark area around eye

No linear scarring

May have pale face with dark rostrum and beak tip

Lower jaw far less arched

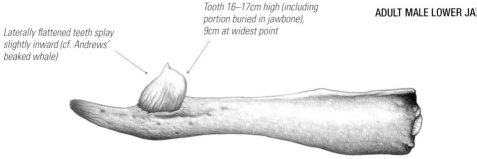

ADULT MALE LOWER JA[W]

Tooth 16–17cm high (including portion buried in jawbone), 9cm at widest point

Laterally flattened teeth splay slightly inward (cf. Andrews' beaked whale)

(Numazu, Suruga Bay, Honshu) and 43°19′N (Nemuro, Hokkaido), where it may be associated with the confluence of the north-flowing warm-water Kurishio Current and the south-flowing cold-water Oyashio Current. The lack of land masses where strandings could be recorded may account for the paucity of records in the central North Pacific, so it is possible that the distribution is continuous. However, given that there is only one record from the central Pacific (an individual caught in a high seas driftnet at 43°N 163°W) and there have been no records along the Aleutian Islands or in Hawaii, it is also possible that there are separate east and west populations. Believed to be restricted to water deeper than 200m.

BEHAVIOUR
There have been only a few confirmed sightings at sea. The only well-documented sighting was of two separate groups seen off Oregon, USA, on 26 July 1994, in excellent sea conditions, containing two and five animals respectively. A lone individual was seen briefly in Suruga Bay, Honshu, Japan, in 1997. And there was a probable sighting during a cetacean survey off Washington State, USA, in 2005. In 1989, two juveniles were found stranded alive on Ocean Beach, San Francisco; they were 'rescued' by an oceanarium, but died two weeks later.

DIVE SEQUENCE (speculative)
- Beak and white cap on head visible (one report of lifting head out of water on surfacing).
- Head disappears as low back and dorsal fin appear.
- Slight arching on dive.
- Probably does not show flukes.

BLOW
- Blow indistinct.

FOOD AND FEEDING

Prey Limited evidence suggests mainly deepwater squid, some deepwater fish; species taken including *Gonatus*, *Onychoteuthis*, *Octopateuthis*, *Histoteuthis* and *Mastigoteuthis* squid, lanternfish, Pacific viperfish.
Feeding Probably suction-feeder (sucks prey into mouth and swallows it whole).
Dive depth Possibly 500–3,000m.
Dive time Unknown, but likely up to one hour.

TEETH

Upper 0
Lower 2

Teeth erupt in male only.

GROUP SIZE AND STRUCTURE

Very little information suggests groups of one to five.

PREDATORS

Unknown, but probably killer whales and large sharks.

POPULATION

Unknown. Paucity of sightings suggests that it may be rare but, like all mesoplodonts, it is inconspicuous at sea and may simply be missed. The number of strandings on the North American coast appears to have decreased since the beginning of this century.

CONSERVATION

IUCN status: Data Deficient (2008). Occasionally taken by Japanese whalers in several small cetacean fisheries, and whale meat products from this species occasionally appear on the Japanese market. Probably susceptible to bycatch. Five individuals were caught between 1990 and 1995 in driftnets for swordfish and thresher sharks off the coast of California, but since acoustic warning devices (pingers) became mandatory in 1997, there have been no known entanglements. Like other species of beaked whales, it may be at risk from noise pollution (especially naval sonar and seismic surveys), ingestion of plastic debris and climate change (which has the potential for a proportionally large impact on all the cooler-water North Pacific beaked whales – because they cannot easily shift their ranges northwards).

LIFE HISTORY

Sexual maturity Unknown.
Mating Little known, but linear scarring suggests male–male combat, presumably to determine dominance for breeding (parallel scars probably made with mouth closed).
Gestation Unknown.
Calving Single calf probably born in summer (May–August).
Weaning Unknown.
Life Weaning Unknown.

BLAINVILLE'S BEAKED WHALE
Mesoplodon densirostris

(Blainville, 1817)

Blainville's beaked whale is the most commonly observed *Mesoplodon* in tropical waters worldwide (though this is relative) and is the most widely distributed member of the genus. It has a strongly arched lower jaw, with teeth that protrude like a pair of horns, and its rostrum is formed of the densest bone of any animal.

Classification Odontoceti, family Ziphiidae.
Common name After French zoologist and anatomist Henri Marie Ducrotay de Blainville (1770–1850), who described the species from an 18cm-long piece of upper jawbone.
Other names Dense-beaked whale, tropical beaked whale, cowfish, Atlantic beaked whale.
Scientific name *Mesoplodon* from the Greek *mesos* for 'middle', *hopla* for arms' or 'weapons', *odon* for 'tooth' (i.e. armed with a tooth in the middle of the jaw); *densirostris* from the Latin *densum* for 'dense' or 'thick' and rostrum for 'beak' (the upper jawbone of the type specimen had a higher density than elephant ivory).
Taxonomy No recognised forms or subspecies.

ADULT MALE

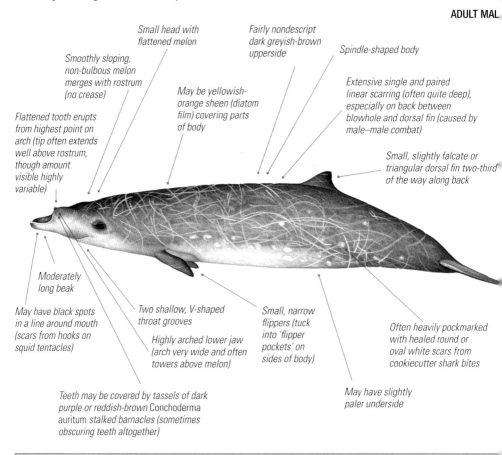

Small head with flattened melon

Fairly nondescript dark greyish-brown upperside

Spindle-shaped body

Smoothly sloping, non-bulbous melon merges with rostrum (no crease)

May be yellowish-orange sheen (diatom film) covering parts of body

Extensive single and paired linear scarring (often quite deep), especially on back between blowhole and dorsal fin (caused by male–male combat)

Flattened tooth erupts from highest point on arch (tip often extends well above rostrum, though amount visible highly variable)

Small, slightly falcate or triangular dorsal fin two-thirds of the way along back

Moderately long beak

May have black spots in a line around mouth (scars from hooks on squid tentacles)

Two shallow, V-shaped throat grooves

Small, narrow flippers (tuck into 'flipper pockets' on sides of body)

Often heavily pockmarked with healed round or oval white scars from cookiecutter shark bites

Highly arched lower jaw (arch very wide and often towers above melon)

Teeth may be covered by tassels of dark purple or reddish-brown Conchoderma auritum stalked barnacles (sometimes obscuring teeth altogether)

May have slightly paler underside

AT A GLANCE

- Tropical to warm temperate waters worldwide
- Medium size
- Mostly nondescript grey-brown colouring
- Pockmarked with healed cookiecutter shark bites
- Tangled web of mainly parallel linear scarring
- Very strongly arched lower jaw
- Flattened, forward-tilting teeth on jaw arches
- Stalked barnacles on teeth look like pompons
- Small head with flattened melon
- Small, slightly falcate or triangular dorsal fin two-thirds of the way along back

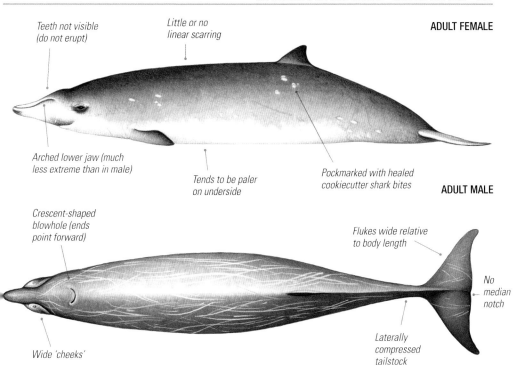

Teeth not visible
(do not erupt)

Little or no
linear scarring

ADULT FEMALE

Arched lower jaw (much
less extreme than in male)

Tends to be paler
on underside

Pockmarked with healed
cookiecutter shark bites

ADULT MALE

Crescent-shaped
blowhole (ends
point forward)

Flukes wide relative
to body length

No
median
notch

Laterally
compressed
tailstock

Wide 'cheeks'

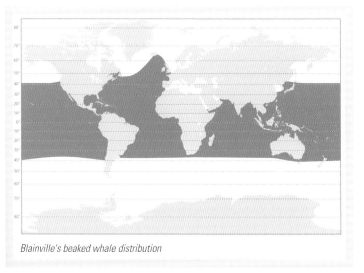

SIZE
L: ♂ 4.3–4.8m, ♀ 4.3–4.7m;
WT: 0.8–1t; **MAX:** 4.9m, 1.03t
Calf – L: 2–2.5m; **WT:** *c.* 60kg

SIMILAR SPECIES

At close range, adult male Blainville's beaked whales are among the easiest members of the genus to identify at sea (females and juveniles are more difficult to identify without an adult male present, although their arched jawlines are helpful). The only other mesoplodonts overlapping in range (to varying degrees) that have strongly arched lower jaws are Stejneger's (look for its dark 'hood' and the different tooth shape and position); ginkgo-toothed (which has no pale linear scarring); Hubbs' (which has a distinct white 'cap' on its head); Gervais' (look for the 'tiger stripes' on the dorsal ridge) and Andrews' (look for its white-tipped beak). The higher jaw arches and flattened melon of Blainville's are particularly distinctive. The strap-like teeth and straight mouthlines of strap-toothed beaked and spade-toothed whales are entirely different.

There is extensive overlap with Cuvier's beaked whale. Apart from the small size difference (Cuvier's are *c.* 20 per cent longer), and differences in head shape and colour, beak shape and tooth position, four more subtle features can be used to tell

Blainville's beaked whale distribution

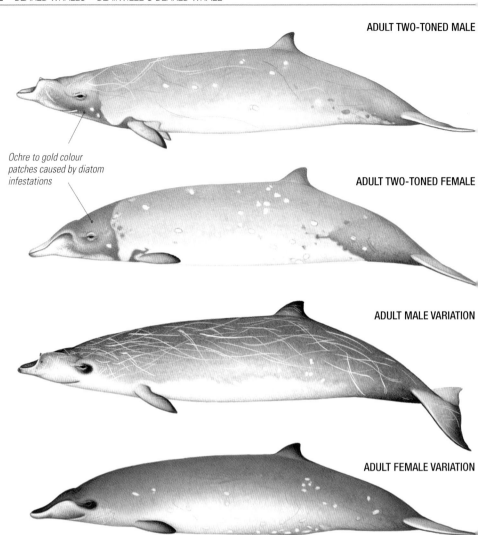

ADULT TWO-TONED MALE

ADULT TWO-TONED FEMALE

Ochre to gold colour patches caused by diatom infestations

ADULT MALE VARIATION

ADULT FEMALE VARIATION

DIVE SEQUENCE
- Briefly lifts beak out of water at angle of *c.* 45° on surfacing (entire head may clear surface).
- May be slight pause as levels and blows.
- Rolls forward at shallow angle, showing top of head and back to dorsal fin (blowholes and fin usually visible simultaneously).
- Tailstock appears as arches slightly and rolls forward to dive (arches higher on terminal dives).
- Rarely, if ever, shows flukes.
- Dive sequence typically consist of 3–10 shorter, shallower dives with 5–10 breaths between each, followed by longer surfacing with *c.* 40 breaths over 4–5 minutes immediately before deep, foraging dive.

BLOW
- Inconspicuous blow usually low and canted forward.

FOOD AND FEEDING
Prey Mainly deepwater squid and fish, with regional differences..
Feeding Foraging dives occur day and night; believed to forage along seabed, at least sometimes; suction-feeder.
Dive depth Tends to spend prolonged periods in upper 50m, but dives over 1,000m and lasting one hour not uncommon; one record in Hawaii of adult female diving to 800m accompanied all the way with calf; maximum recorded 1,599m.
Dive time Typically 20–45 minutes; maximum recorded 83.4 minutes.

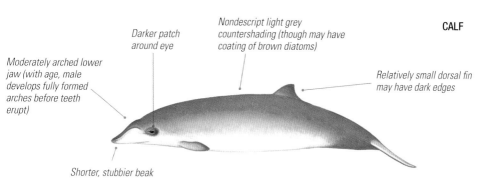

CALF

Darker patch around eye

Nondescript light grey countershading (though may have coating of brown diatoms)

Moderately arched lower jaw (with age, male develops fully formed arches before teeth erupt)

Relatively small dorsal fin may have dark edges

Shorter, stubbier beak

...em apart: Blainville's beaked whale tends to surface and ...ve at a shallower angle, with a lower profile above the ...ater; the dorsal fin and blowhole are usually clear of the ...ater at the same time in Blainville's (they are usually not ...Cuvier's); when viewed from behind or in front, Cuvier's ...as a relatively flat back, while Blainville's is more peaked; ...nd the dorsal fin of Blainville's appears to be larger, ...ompared to the amount of body visible above the surface.

There could be confusion with small baleen whales, ...specially minkes, but minkes are larger and, when diving, ...nd to arch their backs much higher than Blainville's.

...STRIBUTION
...opical to warm temperate waters in both hemispheres. ...ere have been 361 known strandings worldwide, ...volving 386 whales, and Blainville's beaked whale is ...en fairly frequently in a few key hotspots, including ...awaii, the Bahamas and the Canary Islands. It is one ...the most tropical of the mesoplodonts; higher-latitude

records are usually associated with warm-water currents. It occurs in many enclosed seas, including the Gulf of Mexico, the Caribbean Sea and the Sea of Japan, but is considered a vagrant in the Mediterranean.

Seems to prefer waters of intermediate depth (500–1,500m in Hawaii, and in the Bahamas) over continental shelf waters, deep submarine canyons and steeply sloping regions around seamounts. However, it is also known in much deeper waters (at least 5,000m) in the open ocean and has been reported in waters as shallow as 320m (the mean depth for seven sightings in the Canary Islands). In the few areas where it has been studied, it shows a high degree of site fidelity (known individuals have been seen repeatedly in the same area over one or two decades).

BEHAVIOUR
The behaviour of Blainville's beaked whale is better known than for any other species of *Mesoplodon*. It rarely breaches or performs other aerial behaviours. It is not known to occur in mixed aggregations with other cetaceans. Behaviour around boats varies enormously – in some areas, and on some occasions, it approaches and associates, but it may also take evasive action. Can be curious towards swimmers, but is generally evasive.

DENSE BEAK
The rostrum of Blainville's beaked whale becomes secondarily ossified as individuals mature, especially in males, forming the densest bone currently known. Three possible functions have been proposed. The heavy bones may act as ballast, reducing the energetic cost of deep

LIFE HISTORY
Sexual maturity Females and males probably *c.* 8–10 years (though females do not give birth to first calf until *c.* 9–15 years).
Mating Male–male competition likely intense.
Gestation *c.* 12 months.
Calving Single calf born every 3–4 years.
Weaning Probably after *c.* 12 months, but calf remains with mother for 2–3 years.
Lifespan Minimum 23 years, probably longer.

Breaching in Blainville's beaked whale is rare, but this adult male in Hawaii breached repeatedly.

diving (but that does not explain the energy needed to carry them back up to the surface); they could be an adaptation for transmitting sound, during echolocation; or they could be a sort of mechanical reinforcement to prevent impact damage to the skull during male–male combat. Preventing damage to the skull is the most likely explanation, but with one caveat. Despite being dense, the bones are extremely brittle and unbending, which, far from improving resistance to fracture, makes it more likely in head-on collisions; however, the longitudinal grain of the bone structure is believed to provide more protection against severe fractures if struck from other angles.

TEETH

Upper 0
Lower 2

Teeth erupt in male only.

GROUP SIZE AND STRUCTURE

Varies geographically, but typically in groups of 3–7; the largest groups observed in Hawaii and the Bahama each contained 11 individuals; can also be found in pairs or alone. Groups are usually harems, with a sing adult male accompanying several adult females with their calves and/or juveniles. Sub-adults appear to sta in separate groups, and tend to occur in less productiv

ADULT MALE LOWER JA

Out of socket, tooth measures c. 15–18cm tall, 8–9cm wide, 4.5cm deep (but typically less than 2cm extends above gums)

Flattened tooth erupts from top of bony arch (angled forward at c. 45°)

Stalked barnacles obscure the teeth on this Blainville's beaked whale.

waters. Occasional sightings of larger groups, including more than one adult male, are probably temporary aggregations of two or more groups.

PREDATORS

Tooth rake scars on the tail of one individual in Hawaii were probably from a killer whale attack, and a number of individuals have been seen with bite marks made by large sharks (probably including tiger, Galapagos and great white).

PHOTO-IDENTIFICATION

Using the long-term nicks, notches and scars on the dorsal fin, combined with unique scarring patterns on the body (caused by conspecifics and/or cookiecutter sharks).

POPULATION

No overall global estimate, but it appears to be relatively common in most tropical seas. There is an approximate estimate of just over 2,100 in Hawaiian waters.

CONSERVATION

IUCN status: Data Deficient (2008). Very little is known. Reports of hunting, such as around Pamilacan Island in the Philippines (by hand-held harpoons or harpoons fired from spearguns). Taken incidentally in driftnet fisheries, and by Japanese tuna boats off the Seychelles and western Australia. A major concern is noise pollution from seismic testing and military sonar, which is known to have caused strandings involving multiple individuals in the Bahamas and the Canaries (and, at the very least, to drive the whales away for days at a time); where there is frequent exposure to military sonar, the females may have fewer calves. Other threats probably include ingestion of plastic debris.

Blainville's beaked whale photographed in Tahiti, French Polynesia: note the gold patches caused by diatom infestations.

SOWERBY'S BEAKED WHALE
Mesoplodon bidens
(Sowerby, 1804)

Sowerby's beaked whale was the first *Mesoplodon* beaked whale to be described: a male stranded in 1800, in the Moray Firth, northeastern Scotland, and the skull was preserved. A few years later, James Sowerby, an English watercolour artist and naturalist, painted a picture of it and how he imagined the whole animal might have looked.

Classification Odontoceti, family Ziphiidae.
Common name After James Sowerby (1757–1822), who published the first description of the species.
Other names North Sea beaked whale, North Atlantic beaked whale.
Scientific name *Mesoplodon* from the Greek *mesos* for 'middle', *hopla* for 'arms' or 'weapons', *odon* for 'tooth', meaning 'armed with a tooth in the middle of the jaw'; *bidens* from the Latin *bis* for 'two' and *dens* for 'tooth'.
Taxonomy No recognised forms or subspecies; there appear to be lighter-coloured animals in the western North Atlantic.

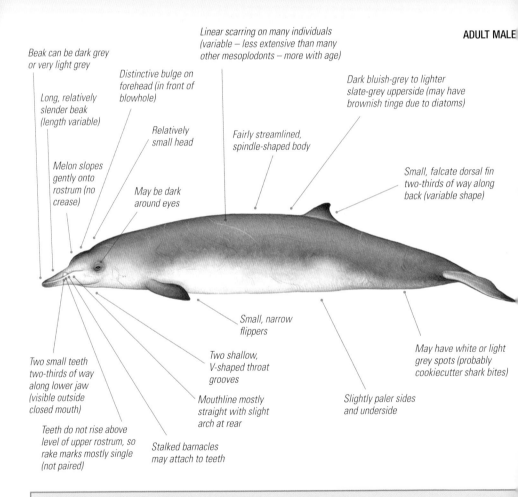

ADULT MALE

Linear scarring on many individuals (variable – less extensive than many other mesoplodonts – more with age)

Beak can be dark grey or very light grey

Distinctive bulge on forehead (in front of blowhole)

Dark bluish-grey to lighter slate-grey upperside (may have brownish tinge due to diatoms)

Long, relatively slender beak (length variable)

Relatively small head

Fairly streamlined, spindle-shaped body

Melon slopes gently onto rostrum (no crease)

May be dark around eyes

Small, falcate dorsal fin two-thirds of way along back (variable shape)

Small, narrow flippers

Two small teeth two-thirds of way along lower jaw (visible outside closed mouth)

Two shallow, V-shaped throat grooves

May have white or light grey spots (probably cookiecutter shark bites)

Teeth do not rise above level of upper rostrum, so rake marks mostly single (not paired)

Mouthline mostly straight with slight arch at rear

Slightly paler sides and underside

Stalked barnacles may attach to teeth

AT A GLANCE
- Cool waters of North Atlantic
- Nondescript light to dark grey above, lighter below
- White linear scars may be present
- Medium size
- Long, slender beak visible on surfacing
- Two teeth two-thirds of the way along beak
- Distinctive bulge on forehead
- Usually unobtrusive/elusive behaviour

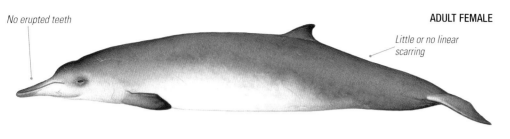

No erupted teeth

ADULT FEMALE

Little or no linear scarring

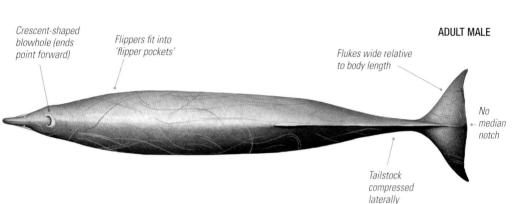

Crescent-shaped blowhole (ends point forward)

Flippers fit into 'flipper pockets'

ADULT MALE

Flukes wide relative to body length

No median notch

Tailstock compressed laterally

SIZE
L: ♂ 4.5–5.5m; ♀ 4.4–5.1m;
WT: 1–1.3t; **MAX:** 5.5m, 1.5t
Calf – L: 2.1–2.4m; **WT:** 170–185kg
Males slightly larger than females.

SIMILAR SPECIES
Can be difficult to distinguish from other mesoplodonts in the North Atlantic (True's, Gervais' and Blainville's) except at close range. The long, slender beak (which is often seen clearly as it surfaces at a steep angle), the straight and then slightly arched mouthline, and the teeth set further back are the most distinctive features for comparison. Females and young animals alone probably cannot be reliably identified at sea.

DISTRIBUTION
Deep, cold offshore waters of the northern North Atlantic (among the most northerly species of *Mesoplodon*). Appears to be considerably more common in the eastern North Atlantic and the centre of abundance appears to be northern Europe (where it is the most frequently stranded mesoplodont). Proportionately high number of strandings in the North Sea (with some in the English Channel), though this probably does not reflect part of the normal range, given that the waters are no deeper than 200m (strandings may relate to movements into unfamiliar territory following prey). There have been *c.* 50 strandings in Scotland alone (more than one-

• Mediterranean records   • extralimital record

Sowerby's beaked whale distribution

ADULT MALE BROWN VARIATION

DORSAL FIN VARIATIONS

Tip of dorsal fin can be falcate, rounded or hooked

third of all known). Extremely rare in the Mediterranean Sea – there have been strandings and/or sightings in the French Riviera, Corsica, Sardinia, Sicily, Greece and Turkey, although it is not clear whether these are extralimital or represent the easternmost part of the range. Occasionally reported in the Baltic Sea, but probably not resident.

There are fewer records in the western North Atlantic, where it has been recorded from Virginia to the Davis Strait. However, this may simply reflect a lack of research effort: abundance in the Gully submarine canyon, off Nova Scotia, increased by 21 per cent in 1988–2011; and Sowerby's beaked whales were heard quite regularly during a recent acoustic study in Norfolk Canyon, off Virginia. Known to aggregate near the Northeast Channel

and the eastern Scotian Shelf canyons (Gully, Shortland and Haldimand). There is an extralimital record from the Gulf Coast of Florida.

Most records are north of 30°N (the most southerly is 28°50'N in the Canary Islands) and it has been recorded in the Azores and Madeira. Ranges into high polar latitudes (the most northerly record is 71°30'N in the Norwegian Sea). The vast majority of strandings have been between 50°N and 60°N. Females with calves have been sighted twice (2015 and 2016) off the west coast of Ireland (55°N and 52°N, respectively). Occurs mainly in deep waters beyond the continental shelf edge – limited research effort suggests a preference for waters ranging from 450m to 2,000m – and often associated with areas of

DIVE SEQUENCE
- Usually surfaces at 30–45° angle, clearly showing beak.
- Melon and much of head may also be visible.
- Beak starts to dip back underwater as exhales.
- Dorsal fin appears as blowhole disappears.
- Rolls forward, barely arching back (higher arch before deep dive).
- Swimming behaviour often described as 'calm and unhurried'.

BLOW
- Invisible or inconspicuous (small and diffuse) blow angled slightly forward.

FOOD AND FEEDING
Prey Unusual among beaked whales in taking mainly small mid- and deepwater fish (including Atlantic cod, hake, lanternfish); some squid.
Feeding Unknown.
Dive depth Main prey typically 400–750m.
Dive time Typically 12–28 minutes, but probably capable *c.* one hour; may be 5–8 surfacings over a total of 20 seconds to two minutes between deep dives.

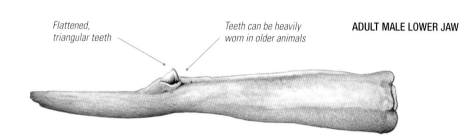

Flattened, triangular teeth

Teeth can be heavily worn in older animals

ADULT MALE LOWER JAW

omplex seabed topography. May be seen close to shore here deep water approaches the coast (such as near ceanic islands).

BEHAVIOUR
elatively few confirmed sightings at sea. Small groups pically surface within a couple of body lengths from each her. Breaching, spyhopping and tail-slapping have been observed. Not uncommonly seen with northern bottlenose hales, at least in the eastern Scotian Shelf area, and as been seen in mixed groups with Cuvier's beaked hales. Reaction to vessels varies: tends to be quite shy nd elusive, but there have been instances of approaching essels or indifference.

TEETH
Upper 0
Lower 2
eeth erupt in male only; both sexes also possess small estigial teeth, which do not normally erupt.

GROUP SIZE AND STRUCTURE
ery little information, but seems to be 3–10 (8–10 have een recorded on a number of occasions, on both sides of e Atlantic). At least some groups consist of females and alves or immatures and one or more males; small all-male roups have also been observed. Most strandings have volved lone animals or mother–calf pairs, but 'mass' randings of up to six have been recorded.

PREDATORS
obably killer whales and large sharks, but no direct vidence.

PHOTO-IDENTIFICATION
Possible, using distinctive nicks, notches and scars on the dorsal fin.

POPULATION
No overall abundance estimate.

CONSERVATION
IUCN status: Data Deficient (2008) (though listed under the Canadian Species at Risk Act as a species of Special Concern). In the past, small numbers have been killed by whalers in Newfoundland, Iceland and in the Barents Sea. Entanglements in fishing gear have been documented in several parts of the range, especially driftnets set at the continental shelf edge; 24 were killed in a small pelagic driftnet fishery along the continental shelf break off the eastern US from 1989 to 1998 (this fishery has now been closed). Other threats are likely to include noise pollution (especially naval sonar and seismic surveys), vessel strikes and ingestion of plastic debris.

LIFE HISTORY
Sexual maturity Possibly *c.* seven years.
Mating Little known, but linear scarring suggests male–male combat, presumably to determine dominance for breeding.
Gestation *c.* 12 months.
Calving Single calf born in late winter to spring.
Weaning Unknown.
Lifespan Unknown.

TRUE'S BEAKED WHALE
Mesoplodon mirus

True, 191:

True's beaked whale is very poorly known, with few confirmed sightings at sea and just a limited number of strandings providing the little information available. It is extremely difficult to identify with any certainty, especially in the North Atlantic.

Classification Odontoceti, family Ziphiidae.
Common name After Frederick W. True (1858–1914), a curator at the US National Museum (now the Smithsonian Institution), who described the type specimen (stranded in North Carolina in 1912).
Other names Wonderful beaked whale.
Scientific name *Mesoplodon* from the Greek *mesos* for 'middle', *hopla* for 'arms' or 'weapons', *odon* for 'tooth' (i.e. armed with a tooth in the middle of the jaw); *mirus* is Latin for 'wonderful'.
Taxonomy Two widely separated and morphologically distinct forms (North Atlantic and southern hemisphere) may warrant distinct subspecies or even species status.

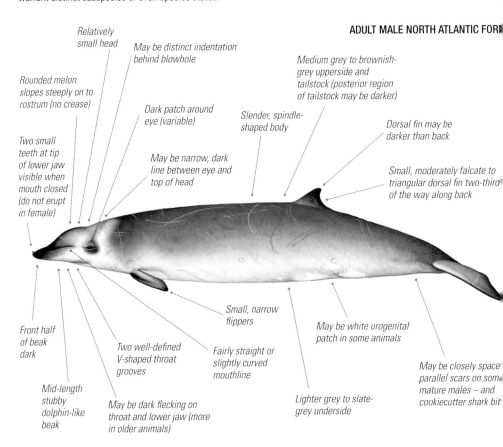

ADULT MALE NORTH ATLANTIC FOR

Relatively small head

May be distinct indentation behind blowhole

Medium grey to brownish-grey upperside and tailstock (posterior region of tailstock may be darker)

Rounded melon slopes steeply on to rostrum (no crease)

Dark patch around eye (variable)

Slender, spindle-shaped body

Dorsal fin may be darker than back

Two small teeth at tip of lower jaw visible when mouth closed (do not erupt in female)

May be narrow, dark line between eye and top of head

Small, moderately falcate to triangular dorsal fin two-third of the way along back

Small, narrow flippers

May be white urogenital patch in some animals

Front half of beak dark

Two well-defined V-shaped throat grooves

Fairly straight or slightly curved mouthline

May be closely space parallel scars on som mature males – and cookiecutter shark bit

Mid-length stubby dolphin-like beak

May be dark flecking on throat and lower jaw (more in older animals)

Lighter grey to slate-grey underside

AT A GLANCE
- North Atlantic and southern hemisphere
- Temperate offshore waters
- Medium size
- Rounded melon
- Mid-length beak with two small teeth at tip
- Closely spaced parallel scars
- Small dorsal fin two-thirds of way along back
- Groups of 1–5

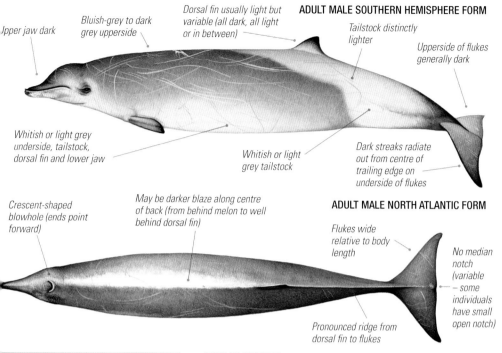

ADULT MALE SOUTHERN HEMISPHERE FORM

Upper jaw dark

Bluish-grey to dark grey upperside

Dorsal fin usually light but variable (all dark, all light or in between)

Tailstock distinctly lighter

Upperside of flukes generally dark

Whitish or light grey underside, tailstock, dorsal fin and lower jaw

Whitish or light grey tailstock

Dark streaks radiate out from centre of trailing edge on underside of flukes

ADULT MALE NORTH ATLANTIC FORM

Crescent-shaped blowhole (ends point forward)

May be darker blaze along centre of back (from behind melon to well behind dorsal fin)

Flukes wide relative to body length

No median notch (variable – some individuals have small open notch)

Pronounced ridge from dorsal fin to flukes

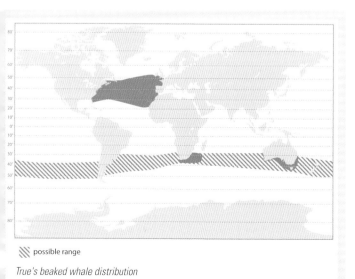

SIZE
L: ♂ 4.8–5.3m, **♀** 4.8–5.4m;
WT: 1–1.4t; **MAX:** 5.4m, 1.4t
Calf – L: 2–2.5m; **WT:** unknown
Females may be slightly larger than males.

SIMILAR SPECIES

Overlaps to varying degrees with Cuvier's, Blainville's, Sowerby's and Gervais' beaked whales in the North Atlantic. It is extremely difficult to distinguish from Gervais', in particular, but look for the more pronounced melon, straighter mouthline and closely spaced parallel scarring of True's and the (variable) pale/dark stripes on the upperside of some Gervais'. Southern hemisphere animals overlap with at least nine species of beaked whale, but True's should be easier to identify here, due to its unique colour pattern (whitish or light tailstock and dorsal fin).

DISTRIBUTION

Prefers deep, principally warm temperate offshore waters and, as with other mesoplodonts, may favour areas of complex seabed topography. Two populations, widely separated by the tropics (rarely occurs between 30°N and 30°S). In North America, it occurs from Cape Breton Island, Nova Scotia, to Flagler Beach, Florida, in the west (plus one stranding in the Bahamas); in the east, it occurs at least from the southern Bay of Biscay to the Canary Islands and the Azores (with records as far north as the Outer Hebrides, in

possible range

True's beaked whale distribution

ADULT MALE NORTH ATLANTIC FORM

May be a pale or whitish blaze covering melon from behind blowhole

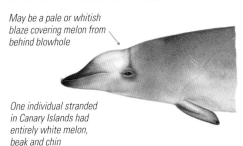

One individual stranded in Canary Islands had entirely white melon, beak and chin

FLIPPER POCKET

Small depression ('flipper pocket') on side (as in other mesoplodonts)

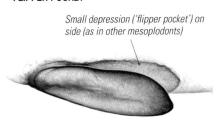

ADULT FEMALE NORTH ATLANTIC FORM

ADULT FEMALE SOUTHERN HEMISPHERE FORM

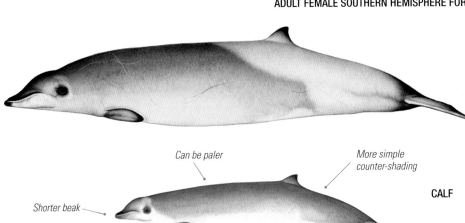

Can be paler

More simple counter-shading

CALF

Shorter beak

DIVE SEQUENCE
- Surfaces at angle, possibly showing entire beak and head (to just below eye level).
- Slowly rolls forward with slight arching.
- Flukes not visible.

BLOW
- Indistinct, low, columnar blow.

FOOD AND FEEDING

Prey Probably mostly deepwater squid (including *Loligo* and *Teuthowenia* spp.); some fish (including black scabbardfish, blue whiting, grenadiers, slender codling); in three Irish individuals, prey length mostly smaller than 12cm (range 1.1–110cm).
Feeding Unknown.
Dive depth Likely to forage deeper than 500m (one study suggests main prey found in waters 200–800m deep).
Dive time Unknown; a suction-cup digital acoustic recording tag was attached to an individual 320km off Cape Cod, Massachusetts, for the first time in 2018; the 12 hours of data are being analysed.

Acorn-shaped teeth angled slightly forward

Teeth relatively small (c. 5cm) and may become heavily worn with age

ADULT MALE LOWER JAW

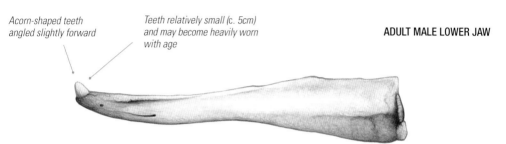

Scotland). Most strandings have been in the United States, but there have been others in Nova Scotia, Bermuda, Ireland, France, Spain (mainland), Portugal (mainland) and Morocco. In the southern hemisphere, it is known mainly from the Indian Ocean (South Africa, Mozambique and southern Australia); there is one record from the South Atlantic (a stranding in São Paolo State, Brazil) and one from the South Pacific (a stranding on the Tasman Sea side of the South Island, New Zealand).

BEHAVIOUR

Rarely identified in the wild, so little is known about its behaviour. Energetic breaching has been recorded on several occasions – including 24 times in a row (at intervals of 20–60 seconds) over a 12-minute period during a 2001 sighting from a ferry in the Bay of Biscay; the whale leapt vertically at an angle of 80° and fell back on its side, with the flukes remaining underwater.

LIFE HISTORY

Virtually nothing known. Gestation possibly *c.* 14–15 months, with a single calf born *c.* every two years. One record of a female simultaneously pregnant and lactating.

Another encounter in the Bay of Biscay, in 2018, involved four individuals that were also breaching (and tail-slapping). Reaction to vessels seems to vary: avoids boats off North Carolina, but reported milling around boats for up to 10 minutes in the Azores and Canary Islands.

TEETH

Upper 0
Lower 2
Teeth erupt in males only.

GROUP SIZE AND STRUCTURE

Typically 1–4 (based on a few rare sightings).

PREDATORS

Unknown.

POPULATION

No overall abundance estimate.

CONSERVATION

IUCN status: Data Deficient (2008). Very little information. Entanglement in fishing gear (especially driftnets for billfish and tuna) is probably the greatest threat, but probably also ingestion of plastic debris and noise pollution (military sonar and seismic testing). No records of hunting.

STEJNEGER'S BEAKED WHALE
Mesoplodon stejnegeri

True, 1885

Known mostly from strandings – predominantly along the west coast of Honsho, Japan, and in the Aleutian Islands, Alaska – Stejneger's beaked whale is rarely seen alive at sea. Sometimes called the sabre-toothed beaked whale, the male has two particularly large teeth, like tusks, that are used for fighting.

Classification Odontoceti, family Ziphiidae.
Common name After Norwegian-born zoologist Leonhard Hess Stejneger (1851–1943), former curator at the US National Museum (now the Smithsonian Institution), who collected the type specimen (a beach-worn skull on Bering Island, Kamchatka) in 1883; pronounced 'sty-ne-gers'.
Other names Bering Sea beaked whale, North Pacific beaked whale, sabre-toothed beaked whale.
Scientific name *Mesoplodon* from the Greek *mesos* for 'middle', *hopla* for 'arms' or 'weapons', *odon* for 'tooth' (i.e. armed with a tooth in the middle of the jaw); *stejnegeri* from Leonhard Stejneger.
Taxonomy No recognised forms or subspecies.

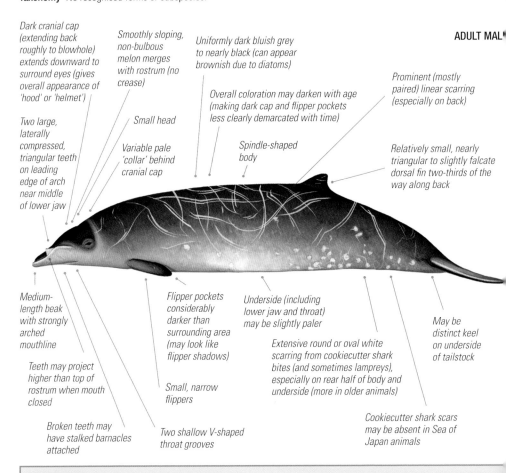

Dark cranial cap (extending back roughly to blowhole) extends downward to surround eyes (gives overall appearance of 'hood' or 'helmet')

Smoothly sloping, non-bulbous melon merges with rostrum (no crease)

Uniformly dark bluish grey to nearly black (can appear brownish due to diatoms)

ADULT MALE

Prominent (mostly paired) linear scarring (especially on back)

Overall coloration may darken with age (making dark cap and flipper pockets less clearly demarcated with time)

Two large, laterally compressed, triangular teeth on leading edge of arch near middle of lower jaw

Small head

Variable pale 'collar' behind cranial cap

Spindle-shaped body

Relatively small, nearly triangular to slightly falcate dorsal fin two-thirds of the way along back

Medium-length beak with strongly arched mouthline

Flipper pockets considerably darker than surrounding area (may look like flipper shadows)

Underside (including lower jaw and throat) may be slightly paler

May be distinct keel on underside of tailstock

Teeth may project higher than top of rostrum when mouth closed

Small, narrow flippers

Extensive round or oval white scarring from cookiecutter shark bites (and sometimes lampreys), especially on rear half of body and underside (more in older animals)

Broken teeth may have stalked barnacles attached

Two shallow V-shaped throat grooves

Cookiecutter shark scars may be absent in Sea of Japan animals

AT A GLANCE
- Cold offshore waters of northern North Pacific
- Medium size
- Spindle-shaped body
- Dark cranial 'cap'
- Gently-sloping forehead
- Strongly arched mouthline
- Two large, exposed, flattened teeth
- Small groups bunched together

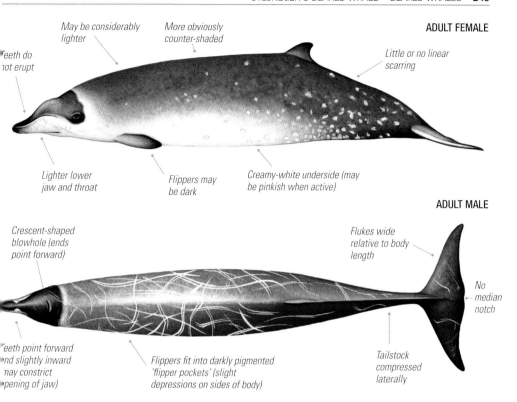

ADULT FEMALE

May be considerably lighter

More obviously counter-shaded

Teeth do not erupt

Little or no linear scarring

Lighter lower jaw and throat

Flippers may be dark

Creamy-white underside (may be pinkish when active)

ADULT MALE

Crescent-shaped blowhole (ends point forward)

Flukes wide relative to body length

No median notch

Teeth point forward and slightly inward may constrict opening of jaw

Flippers fit into darkly pigmented 'flipper pockets' (slight depressions on sides of body)

Tailstock compressed laterally

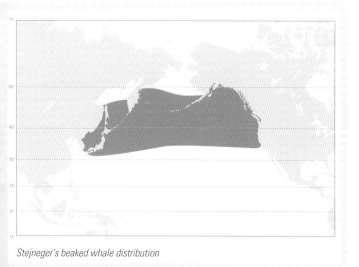

SIZE
L: ♂ 4.8–5.7m, ♀ 4.8–5.4m;
WT: 1–1.3t; **MAX:** 6m, 1.6t
Calf – L: 2.1–2.3m; **WT:** c. 80kg

SIMILAR SPECIES

Possible to identify an adult male with a good view. Confusion is most likely with Hubbs' and Blainville's beaked whales (although both species tend to range further south than most Stejneger's records). Look for the tooth shape and position, shape of the mouthline, smoothly sloping melon and dark 'hood'. Baird's and Cuvier's beaked whales overlap, but the larger size and longer beak of Baird's and the unique head shape and shorter beak of Cuvier's should be distinctive.

DISTRIBUTION

Primarily cold temperate and sub-Arctic waters of the North Pacific. Found from California north to at least the Commander and Pribilof Islands in the southern Bering Sea and south to the southern Sea of Japan; it also occurs in the southern Sea of Okhotsk. Probably the only mesoplodont common in Alaska and the Sea of Japan. The northernmost record was a stranding on Saint Lawrence Island in the Bering Strait (c. 64°N), the southernmost was another stranding at Cardiff, southern

Stejneger's beaked whale distribution

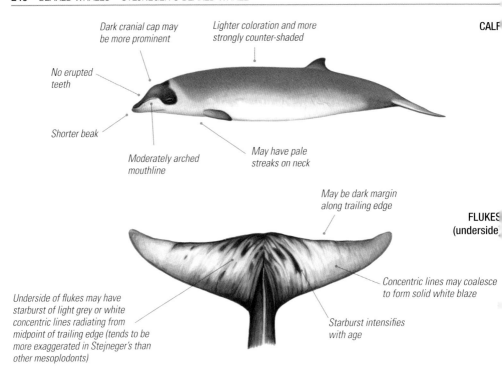

CALF

Dark cranial cap may be more prominent

Lighter coloration and more strongly counter-shaded

No erupted teeth

Shorter beak

Moderately arched mouthline

May have pale streaks on neck

May be dark margin along trailing edge

FLUKES (underside)

Underside of flukes may have starburst of light grey or white concentric lines radiating from midpoint of trailing edge (tends to be more exaggerated in Stejneger's than other mesoplodonts)

Concentric lines may coalesce to form solid white blaze

Starburst intensifies with age

California (c. 33°N). Seasonality of strandings suggests a north–south (summer–winter) migration in some areas, and cookiecutter shark bites on individuals in the east suggest a move to warmer waters for at least part of the year; there is some evidence of a resident population in the Sea of Japan and southern Sea of Okhotsk. Seems to prefer areas of complex seabed topography. Most live sightings have been in the Aleutian Trench, Alaska, and are closely associated with the steep slope of the continental shelf as it drops off into the Aleutian Basin in waters 730–1,560m deep.

BEHAVIOUR

Very little information. Known to breach. Appears to be shy and difficult to approach. Reports of roaring and groaning sounds made at the surface.

DIVE SEQUENCE
- Tip of beak breaks surface first.
- Blowhole and upperside of head appear briefly.
- Low profile as head quickly disappears and dorsal fin rolls forward.
- Slight arching of back.
- Flukes not visible.
- Typically 5–6 shallow dives, followed by longer dive of 10–15 minutes.

BLOW
- Blow indistinct.

FOOD AND FEEDING

Prey Mostly mesopelagic and bathypelagic squid (especially Gonatidae, Cranchiidae), some fish (e.g. pursues salmon in Japan).

Feeding Male's mouth can only open a few centimetres, which limits diet to small or soft-bodied prey and means suction is main feeding method.

Dive depth Preferred prey suggests at least 200m; presumably capable of diving much deeper (possibly to 1,500m).

Dive time At least 15 minutes, probably much longer.

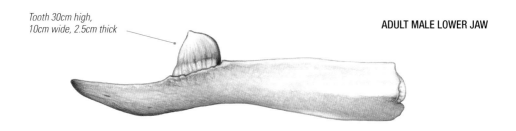

*Tooth 30cm high,
10cm wide, 2.5cm thick*

ADULT MALE LOWER JAW

TEETH

Upper 0
Lower 2

Teeth erupt in male only.

GROUP SIZE AND STRUCTURE

Typically 2–4 but ranges from one to 15. Groups may contain animals of mixed sexes and ages, or can be segregated; of 20 group strandings in Alaska (1975–94), one was all male, two were all female and the rest were a mix of both sexes. Groups may be tightly bunched together at the surface – sometimes touching or nearly touching – and typically swim and dive in unison.

LIFE HISTORY

Sexual maturity Unknown.

Mating Little known, but linear scarring suggests male–male combat, presumably to determine dominance for breeding (parallel scars probably made with mouth closed).

Gestation Unknown.

Calving Single calf born from spring to early autumn.

Weaning Unknown.

Lifespan Oldest recorded 36 years.

PREDATORS

Unknown, but presumably killer whales and sharks.

POPULATION

No overall abundance estimate, but given the infrequency of strandings and sightings it appears to be rare (at least outside the Aleutian Islands and Sea of Japan/Sea of Okhotsk). Estimated to be 7,100 in Japan (1998).

CONSERVATION

IUCN status: Data Deficient (2008). Entanglement in fishing gear is probably the most significant threat – it has certainly occurred in the driftnet and salmon gillnet fisheries in Japan, and in driftnets set for swordfish and sharks off the west coast of North America. It has also been hunted in Japan, along with other beaked whales. It is likely to be affected by ingestion of plastic debris and noise pollution (especially military sonar and seismic testing). Never observed in the Arctic, though warming seas could conceivably shift the range of this species northward.

GERVAIS' BEAKED WHALE
Mesoplodon europaeus
(Gervais, 1855)

Gervais' beaked whale is known from more than 300 records in the North Atlantic, and just six in the South Atlantic. Most of these are strandings – there have been few reliable sightings at sea – so information on its life and habits is sparse.

Classification Odontoceti, family Ziphiidae.

Common name After French zoologist and anatomist Paul François Louis Gervais (1816–79), who described the species.

Other names European beaked whale, Gulf Stream beaked whale, Antillean beaked whale.

Scientific name *Mesoplodon* from the Greek *mesos* for 'middle', *hopla* for 'arms' or 'weapons', *odon* for 'tooth', meaning 'armed with a tooth in the middle of the jaw' (the term was coined by Gervais in 1850); *europaeus* from the Latin *Europaeus* for 'of Europe' (the type specimen was found floating dead in the English Channel in 1840).

Taxonomy No recognised forms or subspecies; the teeth of individuals stranded on Ascension Island differ slightly from the teeth of those stranded in the North Atlantic and may represent a separate subspecies.

ADULT MALE

Single tooth on small arch c. one-third of the way along each side of lower jaw (7–10cm from tip), visible outside closed mouth

Medium to dark grey (sometimes brownish) upperside, paler underside (may become darker with age)

Smoothly sloping, slightly bulbous melon merges with rostrum (no crease)

Dark band down centre of back may be partially obscured by darker upperside (often more conspicuous in female and calf)

Relatively little pale linear scarring (usually single lines when present)

Dark patch around eye often more pronounced than in other mesoplodonts (variable)

Spindle-shaped body

Very small head

Small, wide-based, slightly falcate dorsal fin two-thirds of the way along back

Mid-length beak with relatively straight mouthline (slightly raised area around tusks)

Two shallow, V-shaped throat grooves

Small, narrow flippers (darker than underside of body)

AT A GLANCE
- Tropical to warm temperate waters of Atlantic Ocean
- Medium size
- Medium to dark grey above, paler below
- Little or no linear scarring
- Very small head with slightly bulbous melon
- Dark patch around eye
- Mid-length beak
- Two teeth on small arch one-third of the way along lower jaw
- Small dorsal fin two-thirds of the way along back
- Females and juveniles may have tiger-like stripes

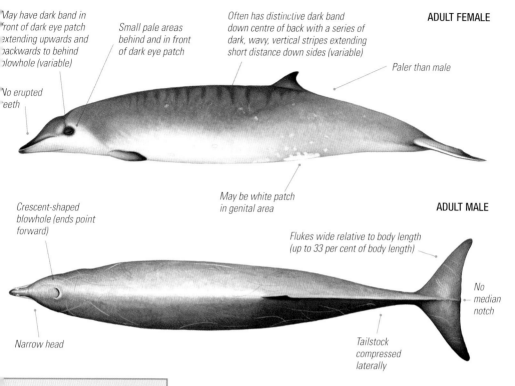

ADULT FEMALE

May have dark band in front of dark eye patch extending upwards and backwards to behind blowhole (variable)

Small pale areas behind and in front of dark eye patch

Often has distinctive dark band down centre of back with a series of dark, wavy, vertical stripes extending short distance down sides (variable)

Paler than male

No erupted teeth

May be white patch in genital area

ADULT MALE

Crescent-shaped blowhole (ends point forward)

Flukes wide relative to body length (up to 33 per cent of body length)

No median notch

Narrow head

Tailstock compressed laterally

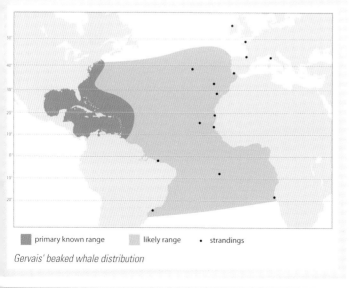

SIZE
L: ♂ 4.2–4.6m, **♀** 4.2–4.8m;
WT: 0.8–1t; **MAX:** 5.2m, 1.2t
Calf – L: c. 1.7–2.2m; **WT:** c. 80kg

SIMILAR SPECIES

The range overlaps with a number of other mesoplodonts – Blainville's, True's and Sowerby's – and telling these species apart at sea can be difficult. Sowerby's can be distinguished partly by range, but also look for its long, slender beak and the teeth set further back. Blainville's is best distinguished by the adult male's highly arched lower jaw, with the massive, flattened tooth (often covered in barnacles) sitting on the apex; its relatively flattened melon and the typical presence of large numbers of cookiecutter shark bites are also distinctive.

Separation between Gervais' and True's beaked whales is more tricky. The position of the male's teeth is the best clue (they are at the tip of the lower jaw in True's). However, there are three other key features to look for. First, the head profile: True's has a well-rounded melon that slopes steeply into the rostrum, with a straighter mouthline; Gervais' has a less bulbous melon that slopes more shallowly (almost diagonally) into the rostrum. Second, male True's often have parallel linear scarring (which can only be produced by an animal with two teeth protruding at the tip

■ primary known range ■ likely range • strandings

Gervais' beaked whale distribution

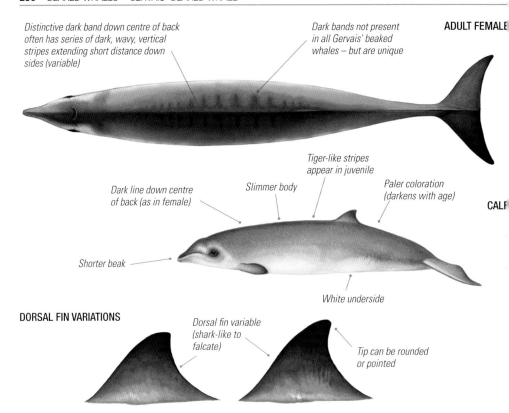

Distinctive dark band down centre of back often has series of dark, wavy, vertical stripes extending short distance down sides (variable)

Dark bands not present in all Gervais' beaked whales – but are unique

ADULT FEMALE

Tiger-like stripes appear in juvenile

Dark line down centre of back (as in female)

Slimmer body

Paler coloration (darkens with age)

CALF

Shorter beak

White underside

DORSAL FIN VARIATIONS

Dorsal fin variable (shark-like to falcate)

Tip can be rounded or pointed

of the lower jaw, or above the rostrum). Third, Gervais' often have a distinctive dark dorsal band with dark, wavy, vertical stripes (most visible in females and juveniles).

There is also overlap with Cuvier's beaked whales and northern bottlenose whales, but these two species are significantly larger and more robust.

DISTRIBUTION

Most records are from the western North Atlantic, from Massachusetts to Mexico – including the Gulf of Mexico, the Caribbean and the Bahamas. It is the most commonly

stranded beaked whale in the southeastern United States Florida and North Carolina account for more than 40 per cent of all worldwide records combined. For many years, the type specimen was the only record from the eastern North Atlantic, and most researchers considered it to be a vagrant carried out of its normal range by the Gulf Stream But more recent evidence (just over 50 records altogether) from the eastern North Atlantic offer a more complete picture. Approximately half of these (21 standings involving 24 individuals) are from the Canary Islands,

DIVE SEQUENCE
- May surface at angle of about 45°.
- Briefly shows beak and much of head (often at least to eye).
- Slight pause before rolls forward.
- Tends to sink below surface rather than arching back.
- Does not show flukes on sounding dive.

BLOW
- Inconspicuous blow.

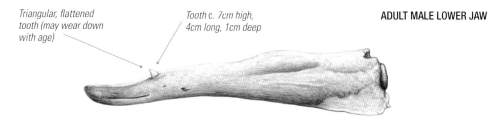

Triangular, flattened tooth (may wear down with age)

Tooth c. 7cm high, 4cm long, 1cm deep

ADULT MALE LOWER JAW

FOOD AND FEEDING
Little known. Feeds mainly on deepwater squid, possibly some deepwater fish; one record of mysid shrimp in stomach of stranded individual.

ut it has been recorded from Ireland, France, Spain, Madeira, Portugal, the Azores, the Cape Verde Islands, Mauritania and Guinea-Bissau. There is one record from the Mediterranean – an individual that stranded near Castiglioncello, Italy, in 2001.

South Atlantic records are from Ascension Island (three confirmed), Namibia (one) and Brazil (two). The most southerly record is a stranding at São Vicente, São Paulo State, Brazil (23°58′S) but, given the latitudinal range in the North Atlantic, its distribution could extend at least as far south as Uruguay in the west.

Seems to prefer deep waters in the tropics and sub-tropics, but there are records from warm temperate and even cold temperate waters. Likely to be more common in areas of complex seabed topography.

BEHAVIOUR
Virtually nothing known. Live-stranded individuals have been kept in captivity for short periods.

LIFE HISTORY
Little known. Single calf born after presumed 12-month gestation period. Lifespan estimated at least 27 years; oldest recorded 48 years.

TEETH (MALE)
Upper 0

Lower 2

Teeth erupt in male only.

GROUP SIZE AND STRUCTURE
Limited information suggests that Gervais' beaked whales are usually found alone or in small, close-knit groups of up to five individuals.

PREDATORS
Unknown, but presumably killer whales and sharks.

POPULATION
No overall global estimate. There is an estimate of 149 *Mesoplodon* whales in the northern Gulf of Mexico, but this is combined for three species (including Gervais'). Given the frequency of strandings, it is presumed to be relatively common (at least along the east coast of North America).

CONSERVATION
IUCN status: Data Deficient (2008). Entanglement in gillnets and other fishing gear is probably the most significant threat; there have been cases of entanglement in pound nets off New Jersey. Like other beaked whales, it is probably affected by ingestion of plastic debris and noise pollution (especially military sonar and seismic testing). Several atypical mass strandings of beaked whales, including Gervais', have been associated with naval activities in the Canary Islands. No exploitation is known.

The dark eye patch and dark vertical striping are clearly visible in this individual, photographed off Cape Hatteras, North Carolina.

ANDREWS' BEAKED WHALE
Mesoplodon bowdoini

Andrews, 1908

Andrews' beaked whale is one of the least known of all the world's cetaceans – there has never been a confirmed sighting at sea and our limited knowledge comes from just 48 strandings, all in the cooler waters of the southern hemisphere. It is strikingly similar to Hubbs' beaked whale, found in the North Pacific, but recent genetic and morphological studies confirm their specific distinctiveness.

Classification Odontoceti, family Ziphiidae.
Common name Roy Chapman Andrews (1884–1960) was assistant curator of mammals at the American Museum of Natural History in New York City (best known as the Gobi Desert dinosaur hunter); he was 24 years old when he concluded that the species was new to science.
Other names Splay-toothed (or splaytooth) beaked whale, deep-crested (or deepcrest) beaked whale, Bowdoin's beaked whale.
Scientific name *Mesoplodon* from the Greek *mesos* for 'middle', *hopla* for 'arms' or 'weapons', *odon* for 'tooth' (i.e. armed with a tooth in the middle of the jaw); *bowdoini* after George S. Bowdoin (1833–1913), a trustee and donor to the American Museum of Natural History, who helped to enlarge the museum's cetacean collection.
Taxonomy No recognised forms or subspecies.

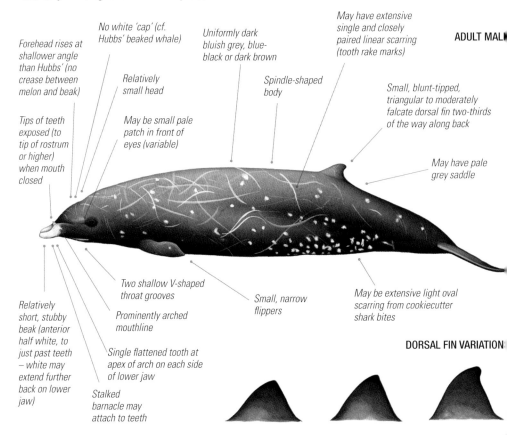

Forehead rises at shallower angle than Hubbs' (no crease between melon and beak)

No white 'cap' (cf. Hubbs' beaked whale)

Uniformly dark bluish grey, blue-black or dark brown

May have extensive single and closely paired linear scarring (tooth rake marks)

ADULT MALE

Relatively small head

Spindle-shaped body

Small, blunt-tipped, triangular to moderately falcate dorsal fin two-thirds of the way along back

Tips of teeth exposed (to tip of rostrum or higher) when mouth closed

May be small pale patch in front of eyes (variable)

May have pale grey saddle

Relatively short, stubby beak (anterior half white, to just past teeth – white may extend further back on lower jaw)

Two shallow V-shaped throat grooves

Prominently arched mouthline

Single flattened tooth at apex of arch on each side of lower jaw

Stalked barnacle may attach to teeth

Small, narrow flippers

May be extensive light oval scarring from cookiecutter shark bites

DORSAL FIN VARIATION

AT A GLANCE
- Cooler waters of southern hemisphere
- Small to medium size
- Uniformly dark
- Relatively short, heavy, white-tipped beak
- Heavily scarred
- Small, falcate fin two-thirds of way along back
- Two tusks on arched lower jaw

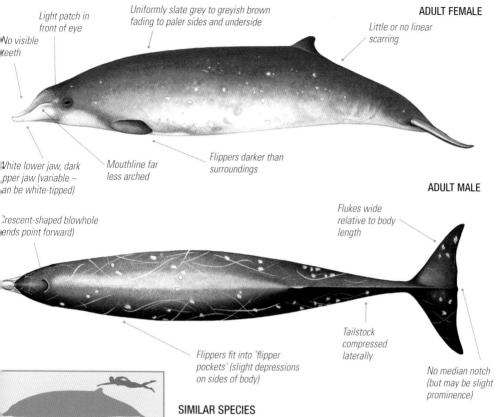

Light patch in front of eye

No visible teeth

Uniformly slate grey to greyish brown fading to paler sides and underside

ADULT FEMALE

Little or no linear scarring

White lower jaw, dark upper jaw (variable – can be white-tipped)

Mouthline far less arched

Flippers darker than surroundings

Crescent-shaped blowhole (ends point forward)

ADULT MALE

Flukes wide relative to body length

Tailstock compressed laterally

Flippers fit into 'flipper pockets' (slight depressions on sides of body)

No median notch (but may be slight prominence)

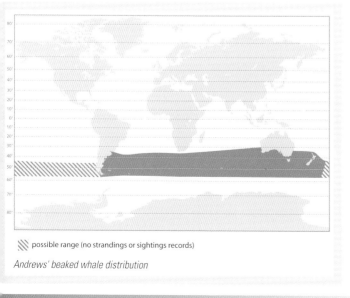

SIZE
L: 3.9–4.4m;
WT: possibly *c.* 1–1.5t
Calf – L: *c.* 2.2m; **WT:** unknown

SIMILAR SPECIES
Several other mesoplodonts overlap in range (Gray's, Hector's, True's, strap-toothed and, to a lesser extent, Blainville's, ginkgo-toothed and possibly spade-toothed). Blainville's, especially, may be difficult to distinguish. With a close look at the medium-sized beak, with its white tip and distinctive tusks, and the extent of the arched mouthline, it may be possible to identify males at sea. Females and juveniles are probably indistinguishable.

DISTRIBUTION
Known only from 48 strandings in cool temperate to sub-polar waters between 32°S and approximately the Antarctic Convergence. The northernmost authenticated record is from Bird Island, Western Australia, at 32°12'S; the southernmost is from Macquarie Island, about halfway between Australia and Antarctica, at 54°30'S. Most other stranding records have come from New Zealand and its surrounding islands (21 from South, Stewart, Chatham and Campbell Islands) and the southern coasts of Australia

possible range (no strandings or sightings records)

Andrews' beaked whale distribution

CALF

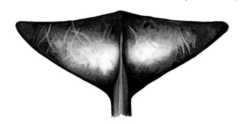

OLD ADULT MALE FLUKES (UNDERSIDE)

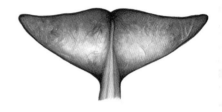

SUB-ADULT MALE FLUKES (UNDERSIDE

ADULT MALE LOWER JAW

Older animals may have deeply worn 'groove' or 'hollow' on anterior margin

Laterally flattened teeth splay slightly outward at up to 20° (cf. Hubbs' beaked whale)

Tooth up to 14cm high (including portion buried in jaw), 8cm at longest point

FOOD AND FEEDING
Prey Limited evidence suggests mainly deepwater squid, some deepwater fish.
Feeding Probably suction feeder (sucks prey into mouth and swallows it whole).
Dive depth Possibly 500–3,000m.
Dive time Unknown, but likely up to one hour.

(20 from Western Australia, South Australia, Victoria, New South Wales and Tasmania). There are also records from Tristan da Cunha (two), the Falkland Islands (three), Uruguay (one) and Tierra del Fuego in Argentina (one). These suggest that the overall range may be circumpolar in the southern hemisphere, although there is a large gap in the records between Chatham Island and the west coast of South America (which could represent a break in distribution or, more likely, reflect a general shortage of cetacean records from this part of the world). Presumably prefers deep offshore waters.

BEHAVIOUR
No information.

TEETH
Upper 0
Lower 2
Teeth erupt in male only.

GROUP SIZE AND STRUCTURE
Very little information but possibly groups of 1–5.

PREDATORS
Unknown, but probably killer whales and large sharks.

POPULATION
Unknown. The frequency of strandings around New Zealand and southern Australia, at least, suggests that it may not be all that rare. The complete lack of sightings in the wild may be because it is unobtrusive, difficult to detect and lives away from well-studied areas, rather than an indication of rarity.

CONSERVATION
IUCN status: Data Deficient (2008). No evidence of hunting or bycatch but, like other species of beaked whales, it may be at risk from driftnet and longline fisheries in particular, as well as noise pollution (especially naval sonar and seismic surveys) and ingestion of plastic debris.

LIFE HISTORY
Little known, but linear scarring suggests male–male combat, presumably to determine dominance for breeding (parallel scars probably made with mouth closed). Some evidence for a summer/autumn breeding season in New Zealand, at least.

STRAP-TOOTHED BEAKED WHALE
Mesoplodon layardii (Gray, 1865)

The largest of the *Mesoplodon* whales, the strap-toothed beaked whale is well known from strandings but rarely seen at sea. The adult male has two unique teeth on its lower jaw, which can arch over the upper jaw and form a muzzle; most likely used for fighting, rather than feeding, they prevent the whale from opening its mouth more than half as wide as the female.

Classification Odontoceti, family Ziphiidae.
Common name For the bizarre strap-like teeth of the adult male.
Other names Strap-toothed whale, straptooth beaked whale, Layard's beaked whale, long-toothed beaked whale.
Scientific name *Mesoplodon* from the Greek *mesos* for 'middle', *hopla* for 'arms' or 'weapons', *odon* for 'tooth', meaning 'armed with a tooth in the middle of the jaw'; *layardii* after Edgar Leopold Layard (1824–1900), curator of the South African Museum in Cape Town, who in 1865 sent drawings of a skull in the museum's collection to John Edward Gray (on which Gray based his description of the species).
Taxonomy No recognised forms or subspecies.

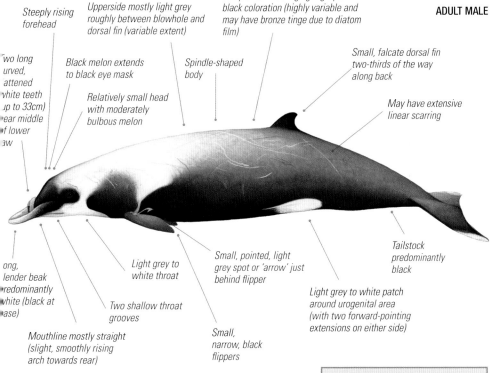

ADULT MALE

Steeply rising forehead

Upperside mostly light grey roughly between blowhole and dorsal fin (variable extent)

Complex contrasting light grey and black coloration (highly variable and may have bronze tinge due to diatom film)

Two long curved, flattened white teeth (up to 33cm) near middle of lower jaw

Black melon extends to black eye mask

Relatively small head with moderately bulbous melon

Spindle-shaped body

Small, falcate dorsal fin two-thirds of the way along back

May have extensive linear scarring

Long, slender beak predominantly white (black at base)

Light grey to white throat

Two shallow throat grooves

Small, pointed, light grey spot or 'arrow' just behind flipper

Small, narrow, black flippers

Light grey to white patch around urogenital area (with two forward-pointing extensions on either side)

Tailstock predominantly black

Mouthline mostly straight (slight, smoothly rising arch towards rear)

AT A GLANCE
• Cold temperate waters of southern hemisphere
• Medium size
• Complex contrasting light grey and black coloration
• Black melon and face 'mask'
• Predominantly white beak
• Strap-like teeth that can curve over upper jaw

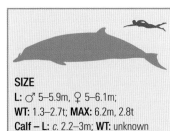

SIZE
L: ♂ 5–5.9m; ♀ 5–6.1m;
WT: 1.3–2.7t; MAX: 6.2m, 2.8t
Calf – L: *c.* 2.2–3m; WT: unknown
Female *c.* 5 per cent larger than male.

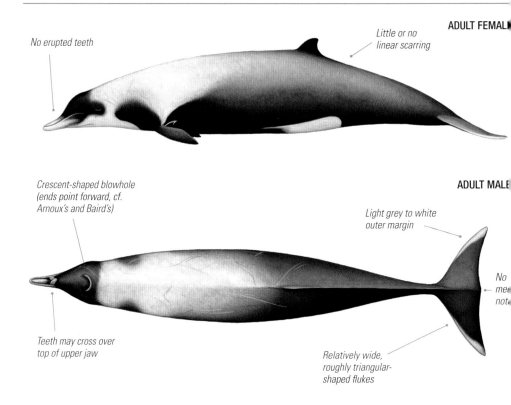

ADULT FEMALE

No erupted teeth

Little or no
linear scarring

Crescent-shaped blowhole
(ends point forward, cf.
Arnoux's and Baird's)

ADULT MALE

Light grey to white
outer margin

No
mee
notc

Teeth may cross over
top of upper jaw

Relatively wide,
roughly triangular-
shaped flukes

SIMILAR SPECIES

If the teeth are seen well, the adult male can be recognisable (though confusion is possible with the spade-toothed whale, which overlaps in range and has a broadly similar tooth morphology). The colour pattern is distinctive in both sexes and should help to distinguish them from other mesoplodonts in the region, such as Gray's, Hector's and Andrews' beaked whales (but bear in mind that, until the external appearance of the spade-toothed whale is better known, separating the two species for certainty will be difficult). Unless an adult male is present, calves and juveniles alone are virtually impossible to tell apart from other mesoplodonts; a genetic identification is often necessary to identify stranded and partially decomposed youngsters and females.

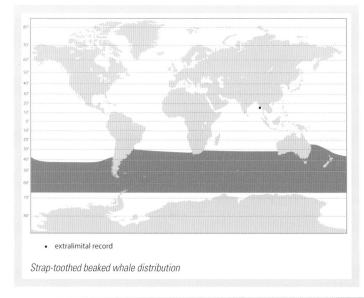

• extralimital record

Strap-toothed beaked whale distribution

DISTRIBUTION

Believed to have a continuous distribution in deep, cold temperate waters of the southern hemisphere, mostly between 35°S and 60°S. More than 190 strandings are known worldwide, with approximately half in Australia and New Zealand and the remainder in South Africa, Namibia, South Georgia, the Falkland Islands, Argentina, Uruguay, Brazil and Chile, as well as Macquarie, Heard, McDonald and the Kerguelen Islands. One record of a stranded adult male in Myanmar, in 2011, at 15°47'N was presumably extralimital;

May be patches of yellow-orange diatoms

ADULT FEMALE WITH DIATOMS

ADULT MALE

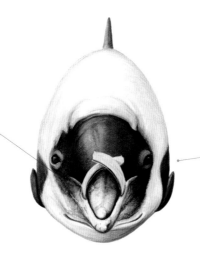

Tusks emerge from middle of lower jaw, curl backward around 45° and inward, crossing over top of upper jaw (often preventing it from opening more than 3–4cm)

Exposed portion of teeth may host large stalked barnacles and can be covered in greenish-brown diatoms

Similar pattern to adult but paler and pigmentation reversed

CALF

...ticeably pale melon (calves ...d juveniles generally lighter ...ey in front of blowhole, ...rker grey behind)

DIVE SEQUENCE
- Surfaces at angle of 45°.
- Head and beak often lifted right out of water (showing teeth of adult male).
- Dorsal fin appears as head begins to sink.
- Slowly rolls forward with little arching of back.
- Does not show flukes.

BLOW
- Indistinct blow.

FOOD AND FEEDING

Prey Mainly deepwater squid; may also take some fish and crustaceans; females/immatures eat longer squid than males, but no significant difference in prey weight.

Feeding Unknown how male eats with teeth that prevent mouth opening properly, though (like other beaked whales) presumably suction feeder; teeth may act as 'guard-rails' to keep food on direct path into mouth.

Dive depth As with other mesoplodonts, forages at depths greater than 500m; vampire squid (found in the stomachs of strap-toothed beaked whales) mainly found at depths of 700–1,500m.

Dive time Unknown.

it was more than 5,000km north of the known distribution of the species and 3,000km north of the previous record (a female, stranded in northeastern Brazil at 12°47'S, in 2002). Most sightings of live animals at sea have been in Australia and New Zealand, in water deeper than 2,000m and beyond the continental shelf. Believed to be more common in areas of complex seabed topography. There is reasonable evidence of seasonal migrations (there are more strandings in the northern part of the range in late summer and autumn, and stranded animals in South Africa have had sub-Antarctic squid in their stomachs).

BEHAVIOUR

Very little known. Several observations of breaching. There is a report of one basking at the surface on a calm, sunny day. Difficult to approach: in response to boats and ships, seen sinking slowly below the surface, or diving sideways (exposing a single flipper as it disappears).

ADULT MALE LOWER JAW

TEETH (MALE)

Upper 0
Lower 2
Teeth do not erupt in female.

Small, sharp denticle at tip of each tooth (probably for male–male fighting)

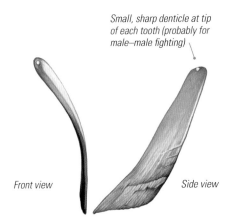

Front view   Side view

GROUP SIZE AND STRUCTURE

Few confirmed sightings, but in most cases it has been observed singly, in female–calf pairs, or in groups of up to four individuals. One group observed briefly off the south coast of Western Australia was estimated to contain 10 individuals of mixed age and both sexes. A group of four stranded on North Island, New Zealand, in 2002, and another group of four (two females and two juveniles) stranded on the north coast of South Island, in 2007.

PREDATORS

Killer whales are predators (on 16 February 2016, a pod of seven killer whales was observed attacking and killing a female strap-toothed beaked whale in Western Australia). Large sharks may also attack this species.

POPULATION

No overall global estimate. Like other beaked whales, it probably has a naturally low population; however, based on the number of strandings, it does not appear to be exceptionally rare.

CONSERVATION

IUCN status: Data Deficient (2008). Direct hunting has never been recorded. It is likely that some are caught as bycatch in driftnet (and possibly gillnet) fisheries, but there is no specific information. Like other beaked whales it is probably threatened by the ingestion of plastic debris, and by noise pollution from military sonar and seismic exploration.

LIFE HISTORY

Sexual maturity Unknown.
Mating Bizarre teeth of adult males likely used in male–male fighting for access to females (although never observed).
Gestation Probably *c.* 9–12 months.
Calving Single calf born in southern spring to summer.
Weaning Unknown.
Lifespan Unknown; one reproductively active female 44 years old.

SPADE-TOOTHED WHALE
Mesoplodon traversii

(Gray, 1874)

The spade-toothed whale is the least known of all the world's living cetaceans – and of all large mammals. The only proof of its existence is from two strandings (a mother and calf pair, and one adult male), two weathered skulls and a single jawbone with teeth. There has never been a confirmed sighting at sea.

Classification Odontoceti, family Ziphiidae.

Common name After the two teeth that erupt on the lower jaw of the male. The part of each tooth protruding from the gums is reminiscent of the oblong blade of the flensing knife (known as a 'spade') used by nineteenth-century whalers to strip the blubber from whales.

Other names Spade-toothed beaked whale, Bahamonde's beaked whale (after Chilean marine biologist Nibaldo Bahamonde, who founded the marine research station on Robinson Crusoe Island – the location of the only specimen discovered outside New Zealand), Travers' beaked whale.

Scientific name *Mesoplodon* from the Greek *mesos* for 'middle', *hopla* for 'arms' or 'weapons', *odon* for 'tooth', meaning 'armed with a tooth in the middle of the jaw'; *traversii* after lawyer and naturalist Henry Hammersley Travers (1844–1928), who brought back the type specimen from the Chatham Islands.

Taxonomy No recognised forms or subspecies; a 'new' species of beaked whale was named *M. bahamondi* in 1995, but further study showed it to be a spade-toothed whale (and *M. traversii* was deemed to be the valid scientific name).

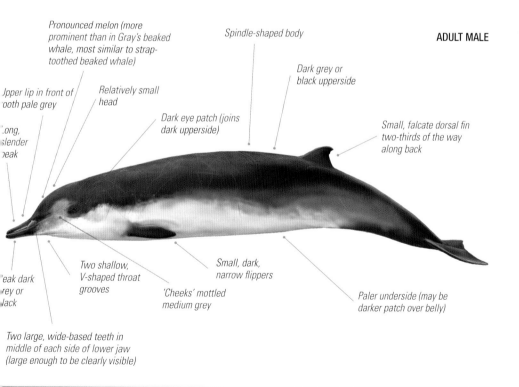

Pronounced melon (more prominent than in Gray's beaked whale, most similar to strap-toothed beaked whale)

Spindle-shaped body

ADULT MALE

Dark grey or black upperside

Upper lip in front of tooth pale grey

Relatively small head

Long, slender beak

Dark eye patch (joins dark upperside)

Small, falcate dorsal fin two-thirds of the way along back

Beak dark grey or black

Two shallow, V-shaped throat grooves

Small, dark, narrow flippers

'Cheeks' mottled medium grey

Paler underside (may be darker patch over belly)

Two large, wide-based teeth in middle of each side of lower jaw (large enough to be clearly visible)

AT A GLANCE
- Temperate (and possibly sub-tropical) waters of South Pacific (and possibly other oceans)
- Medium size
- Long, slender beak
- Pronounced melon
- Male has two large, backward-leaning teeth in middle of lower jaw
- Small, falcate dorsal fin two-thirds of the way along back

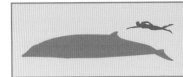

SIZE
L: ♂ 5.2m (based on single adult male), ♀ 5.3m (based on single adult female); **WT:** unknown
Calf – unknown; only known juvenile was 3.5m

ADULT FEMALE

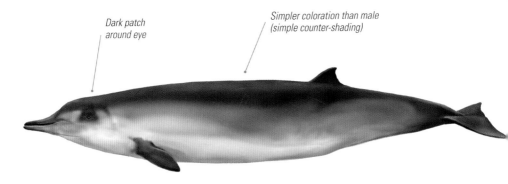

Dark patch around eye

Simpler coloration than male (simple counter-shading)

SIMILAR SPECIES

The appearance of this species is so poorly known that positive identification at sea is probably impossible until further information becomes available. It is likely to share at least some of its range with Gray's, strap-toothed and Hector's beaked whales, all of which have long, slender white beaks. The melon is less bulbous and only the tips of the teeth are exposed in Gray's; the coloration of strap-toothed is distinctive, and the teeth are longer and narrower; and the teeth in Hector's are located near the tip of the lower jaw.

DISTRIBUTION

Very little information, since there is only a handful of records – all to date have been in temperate waters between 33°S and 44°S in the South Pacific. However, it is possible that the spade-toothed whale has simply gone unnoticed elsewhere, and its distribution could include sub-tropical waters and other oceans.

On 31 December 2010, a female and juvenile male (a mother and calf) stranded on Opape Beach (38°S), North Island, New Zealand, and subsequently died. On 23 December 2017, an adult male was seen swimming in Waipiro Bay (38°S), North Island, New Zealand, before stranding and dying soon afterwards. These three animals have provided all the information available on the likely appearance of this species. Apart from them, there are just three specimens: a mandible with teeth from an adult male found on Pitt Island (44°S), in the Chatham Islands in 1872 (the type specimen – which i partially incomplete, but still in the good condition in whic it was collected); a skull without a mandible found on White Island (37°S), North Island, in the 1950s; and

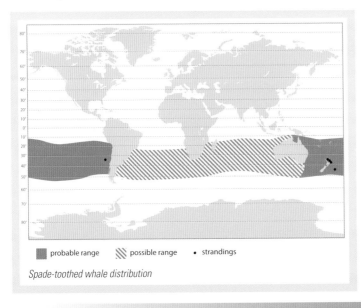

| probable range | possible range | • strandings |

Spade-toothed whale distribution

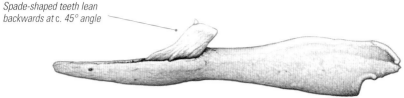

Spade-shaped teeth lean backwards at c. 45° angle

Large denticle at tip of tooth (may be worn down in older animals)

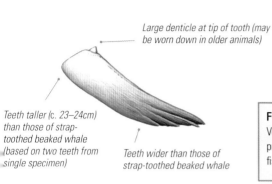

Teeth taller (c. 23–24cm) than those of strap-toothed beaked whale (based on two teeth from single specimen)

Teeth wider than those of strap-toothed beaked whale

another skull without a mandible found on Robinson Crusoe Island, in the Juan Fernández Islands, off Chile (33°S), in 1986.

BEHAVIOUR

With no confirmed sightings at sea, nothing is known about its behaviour.

TEETH (MALE)

Upper 0
Lower 2

GROUP SIZE AND STRUCTURE

Nothing known.

PREDATORS

Unknown, but presumably killer whales and sharks.

FOOD AND FEEDING

Very little known. Like other beaked whales, it is presumed to eat mainly deepwater squid, and some fish.

POPULATION

Unknown. Given the small number of records, it could be rare or it could simply have gone unnoticed (especially if it lives in deep offshore waters between New Zealand and South America).

CONSERVATION

IUCN status: Data Deficient (2008). There is no information on threats. Like other beaked whales, it is likely to be affected by ingestion of plastic debris, fishing gear interactions, and noise pollution (especially military sonar and seismic testing). No exploitation is known.

LIFE HISTORY

Nothing known.

KILLER WHALE OR ORCA
Orcinus orca   (Linnaeus, 1758)

Two thousand years ago, Roman scholar Pliny the Elder described the killer whale as 'an enormous mass of flesh armed with savage teeth'. Even as recently as the early 1970s, US Navy diving manuals described it as 'extremely ferocious', warning that it 'will attack human beings at every opportunity'. But the killer whale does not deserve its killer reputation any more than any other apex predator.

Classification Odontoceti, family Delphinidae.

Common name From 'whale killer' (name given by early Basque whalers, who witnessed its attacks on larger cetaceans), transposed over the years to killer whale; despite the vernacular name 'whale', it is an oceanic dolphin.

Other names Orca (used interchangeably with killer whale); blackfish (term normally used for non-taxonomic group of six dark-coloured members of Delphinidae); historically, grampus. See separate names for different ecotypes.

Scientific name *Orcinus* from ancient Roman mythology, meaning 'belonging to the kingdom of the dead'; *orca* from the Latin for 'shape of a barrel or cask' (reminiscent of the killer whale's body shape) or 'a kind of whale'.

Taxonomy Two subspecies provisionally recognised: Eastern North Pacific (ENP) resident and Eastern North Pacific (ENP) transient, or Bigg's, which split 700,000–750,000 years ago. Several possible contenders for separate species status include Bigg's, both Antarctic Type Bs and Antarctic Type C (possibly the same forms originally described in the early 1980s by Soviet researchers, who proposed putative species *O. nanus* and *O. glacialis*). In the meantime, the term 'ecotype' is used for ecologically distinct populations that do not interbreed (even if they inhabit the same waters) while recognising scientific uncertainty about killer whale taxonomy.

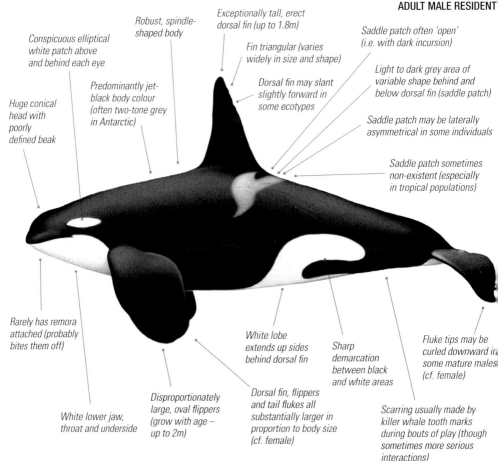

ADULT MALE RESIDENT

Conspicuous elliptical white patch above and behind each eye

Robust, spindle-shaped body

Exceptionally tall, erect dorsal fin (up to 1.8m)

Fin triangular (varies widely in size and shape)

Saddle patch often 'open' (i.e. with dark incursion)

Light to dark grey area of variable shape behind and below dorsal fin (saddle patch)

Dorsal fin may slant slightly forward in some ecotypes

Predominantly jet-black body colour (often two-tone grey in Antarctic)

Huge conical head with poorly defined beak

Saddle patch may be laterally asymmetrical in some individuals

Saddle patch sometimes non-existent (especially in tropical populations)

Rarely has remora attached (probably bites them off)

White lobe extends up sides behind dorsal fin

Sharp demarcation between black and white areas

Fluke tips may be curled downward in some mature males (cf. female)

White lower jaw, throat and underside

Disproportionately large, oval flippers (grow with age – up to 2m)

Dorsal fin, flippers and tail flukes all substantially larger in proportion to body size (cf. female)

Scarring usually made by killer whale tooth marks during bouts of play (though sometimes more serious interactions)

AT A GLANCE
- Worldwide distribution
- Medium size
- Two-tone colouring (predominantly jet black (or grey) and white)
- Exceptionally tall dorsal fin of male
- Pronounced sexual dimorphism
- White patch above and behind each eye
- Usually in family groups

ADULT MALE RESIDENT

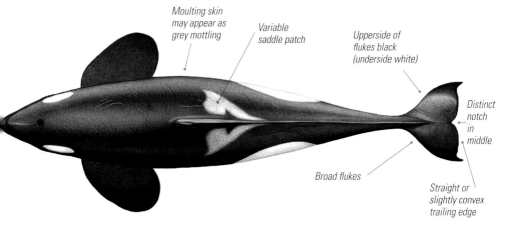

Moulting skin may appear as grey mottling

Variable saddle patch

Upperside of flukes black (underside white)

Distinct notch in middle

Broad flukes

Straight or slightly convex trailing edge

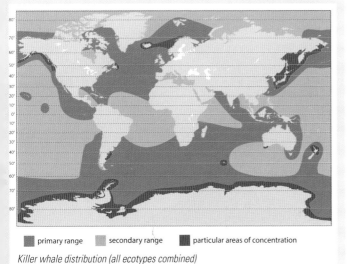

SIZE
L: ♂ 5.6–9m, **♀** 4.5–7.7m;
WT: 1.3–6.6t; **MAX:** 9.8m, 10t
Calf – L: 2–2.8m; **WT:** 160–200kg

Body size varies considerably among ecotypes. Highly sexually dimorphic – mature males up to 17 per cent longer and 40 per cent heavier than mature females.

SIMILAR SPECIES

Difficult to confuse with any other species but, at a distance, Risso's dolphins, pilot whales and false killer whales may look superficially similar to females and juveniles; Dall's porpoises are sometimes mistaken for 'baby' killer whales.

DISTRIBUTION

The most cosmopolitan cetacean, with worldwide (though patchy) distribution. Occurs in all oceans and many enclosed seas (including the White Sea, Mediterranean Sea, Red Sea, Persian Gulf, Sea of Okhotsk, Yellow Sea, Sea of Japan, Gulf of California, Gulf of Mexico and Gulf of St Lawrence); extralimital records from the Baltic Sea, but no records from the Black Sea; rare or absent from the East Siberian Sea and Laptev Sea. Found in all temperatures and depths, from tropical to polar waters and from the surf zone to the open sea, though the

primary range ▢ secondary range ▢ particular areas of concentration ▢

Killer whale distribution (all ecotypes combined)

ADULT MALE RESIDEN

ADULT FEMALE AN
CALF RESIDEN

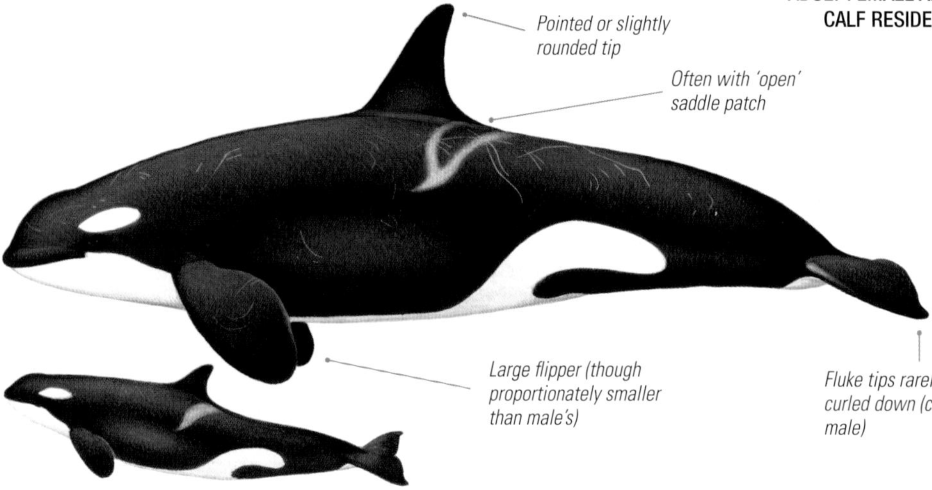

Smaller, falcate dorsal
fin (up to 90cm)

Pointed or slightly
rounded tip

Often with 'open'
saddle patch

Large flipper (though
proportionately smaller
than male's)

Fluke tips rarely
curled down (cf.
male)

JUVENILE RESIDEN

Falcate, female-like
dorsal fin in both sexes
(difficult to tell apart)

Dorsal fin starts to
grow quickly in male
when c. 15 years old

NEWBORN CALF RESIDENT

Falcate dorsal fin
in both sexes

May show
faint cape

Saddle patch indistinct or absent
(becomes consistently apparent at two
years – once formed, does not change)

More muted
colour pattern

Head slightly more
conical than adult

White areas typically have rusty
orange hue (until 6–12 months old)

MALE DORSAL FIN AND SADDLE PATCH COMPARISONS

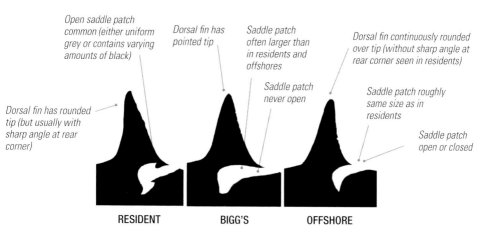

Open saddle patch common (either uniform grey or contains varying amounts of black)

Dorsal fin has pointed tip

Saddle patch often larger than in residents and offshores

Dorsal fin continuously rounded over tip (without sharp angle at rear corner seen in residents)

Saddle patch never open

Dorsal fin has rounded tip (but usually with sharp angle at rear corner)

Saddle patch roughly same size as in residents

Saddle patch open or closed

RESIDENT   BIGG'S   OFFSHORE

Dorsal fin collapse is rare in the wild (it is highly variable geographically but averages less than 1 per cent); however, it is fairly common in captivity (the loss of rigidity is caused by a lack of exercise, stress, traumatic injury or ill health).

highest densities are in cold temperate to polar coastal waters with high productivity. Most abundant in the Southern Ocean south of 60°S. Commonly enters heavy, consolidated ice in the Antarctic, but rarely does so in the Arctic (though it is becoming seasonally more abundant further north as pack-ice extent and duration decline with global warming); recorded to 80°N in Svalbard. Widespread but rare in tropical and offshore waters. At least some northern hemisphere populations move long distances following their prey. At least some Antarctic populations make short (6–7-week) trips to lower latitudes (e.g. from the Antarctic Peninsula 4,500km to subtropical waters off Brazil), presumably for skin regeneration in warmer water with minimal heat loss.

BEHAVIOUR

Can be very active at the surface, especially when socialising or after a successful hunt. Often breaches,

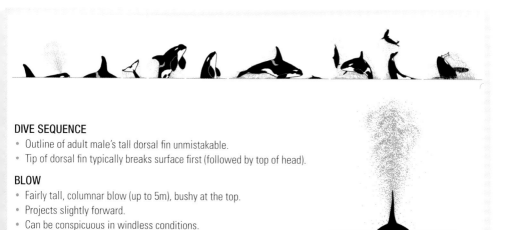

DIVE SEQUENCE
- Outline of adult male's tall dorsal fin unmistakable.
- Tip of dorsal fin typically breaks surface first (followed by top of head).

BLOW
- Fairly tall, columnar blow (up to 5m), bushy at the top.
- Projects slightly forward.
- Can be conspicuous in windless conditions.

FOOD AND FEEDING

Prey Apex predator with extremely diverse diet (*c.* 150 prey species known globally) but high level of specialisation depending on ecotype and location. Includes 31 species of cetaceans (including blue whale, subdued by repeated ramming), 19 species of pinnipeds, 44 species of bony fishes (including salmon, herring, ocean sunfish), 22 species of sharks and rays (including great white – records from California, Australia and South Africa), 20 species of seabirds (including penguins), five species of squid and octopus, two species of sea turtle and two species of terrestrial mammals (sitka black-tailed deer and moose, swimming between islands).

Feeding Huge range of feeding strategies, including 'beaching' in Punta Norte, Argentina, and Crozet Island, Indian Ocean, to catch seals on shore; 'wave-washing' in Antarctic, to wash Weddell seals from ice floes; 'endurance-exhaustion' in Strait of Gibraltar, to catch bluefin tuna; 'carousel feeding' in Iceland and Norway, to catch schooling herring. Often hunts cooperatively. Will take fish from longline fishing operations.

Dive depth Varies with prey and location; maximum recorded more than 1,000m (near South Georgia), but potentially even deeper (especially males); foraging residents usually dive less than 100m.

Dive time Varies with prey and location; foraging residents dive for 2–3 minutes, resting residents make 3–4 short, shallow dives followed by one 2–5-minute longer dive; transients typically dive for twice as long as residents (may exceed 10 minutes); maximum recorded 16 minutes.

flipper-slaps and lobtails. Frequently spyhops (slowly rising out of the water until the head and most of the flippers are above the surface, then gradually sinking out of sight); several animals may spyhop together. Occasionally bow-rides or (more frequently) wake-rides. Northern residents beach-rub on smooth pebbles in shallow water. When foraging (50–65 per cent of the time in residents, 80 per cent in transients), groups may spread over a wide area. When resting, they usually swim slowly in a tightly packed line abreast, diving and surfacing in synchrony and at regular intervals; or they may stop and rest motionless at the surface. Capable of speeds up to 55km/h. Behaviour around boats varies enormously, from avoidance behaviour or indifference to intense curiosity. They will often follow fishing vessels, sometimes for long periods (in the Bering Sea, one pod followed a fishing vessel for 1,600km over 31 days).

FLUKES

LIFE HISTORY

(Based on studies on residents in north-east Pacific.)

Sexual maturity Females 11–16 years (give birth to first viable calf at 12–14 years), males 15 years (reach full physical maturity at *c.* 21 years – do not breed successfully until 20s).

Mating Apparently takes place when two or more pods come together (to reduce chance of inbreeding since pod members normally all related); in some areas, may take place during gatherings of 'superpods' (100-plus whales from same community).

Gestation 15–18 months.

Calving Every 3–8 years (occasionally 2–14); in north-east Pacific, females can calve every three years, but because of relatively high calf mortality (37–50 per cent of all calves die in first year of life) intervals between viable calves averages *c.* five years; single calf born year-round, with peaks varying according to location (e.g. October–March in north-east Pacific); female produces 3–5 calves in her 25-year reproductive lifetime.

Weaning 1–2 years (occasionally up to three).

Lifespan Males average 29 years (maximum 60), females average 50 years (maximum 100-plus); regional variations include southern residents (male 22.1 years, female 39.4 years), northern residents (male 36.8 years, female 50.1 years), southern Alaska residents (male 41.2 years, female 49.5 years), Norway (male 34 years, female 43 years). Females stop reproducing at *c.* 40 years (act as repositories of information and leaders critical to survival of pod). Southern resident female dubbed Granny (J2 – matriarch leader of J-pod) oldest known killer whale: born 1911, died 2016 (aged 105). Age of growing males estimated using HWR coefficient (height of dorsal fin compared to width).

...ller whale skull: the teeth average 7–10cm long but can grow up to 13cm (though in some ecotypes they can be worn down to ...e gum line from eating abrasive prey such as sharks).

...EETH
...per 20–28
...wer 20–28
...hen the mouth closes, the teeth of the upper jaw fit ...to spaces between the teeth of the lower jaw, helping ...catch and bite prey. Teeth may be worn flat in some ...otypes.

...ROUP SIZE AND STRUCTURE
...groups of 2–150 or more, depending on the ecotype; ...wer than 20 typical for most. Reports of larger groups ...e probably temporary aggregations around seasonal ...ncentrations of prey, or for mating. Individuals seen ...one are almost always males.

...REDATORS
...obably only other killer whales. Infanticide has been ...cumented (an adult male killer whale and his post-...productive mother killed a newborn belonging to an ...related female from the same population in the North ...cific), and cannibalism has been reported in one ...stance.

...HOTO-IDENTIFICATION
...ze, shape and scarring of the dorsal fin, combined with ...e, shape, colour and scarring of the saddle patch. Some ...talogues also include eye patches, to help distinguish ...dividuals with nondescript fins and saddles. Most ...searchers photograph both the left and right sides (to ...oid confusion, since the grey saddle is asymmetrical).

POPULATION
There is no reliable global estimate, but the likely minimum is 50,000 (in reality, there are probably considerably more, especially given the lack of information from large oceanic areas and the Arctic, and likely underestimates in the Antarctic). Found in relatively large numbers mainly in cold, productive waters at high latitudes. The latest estimate for the Antarctic south of 60°S is *c.* 25,000–27,000 (some estimates are three times higher, on the basis that most animals are within the pack ice, where they are difficult to find). Other sizeable populations occur in the Bering Sea and Aleutian Islands, the Russian Far East, coastal waters of western North America, the Norwegian Sea, Japan and elsewhere.

VOCALISATIONS
Killer whales can be highly vocal, producing three main types of sound: echolocation clicks (for orientation and prey detection), whistles (high-frequency, single tones that can last for several seconds, probably used for communication over short distances), and so-called discrete or pulsed calls (unique patterns of sound, resembling squeaks, screams and squawks, which are lower frequency and probably for maintaining contact over longer distances of tens of kilometres).

Most vocalising in residents occurs when they are foraging (their fish prey cannot hear them coming); there is greatly reduced vocal activity when they are resting. Transients are generally silent when foraging (their mammalian prey can hear them coming) and, instead of echolocating, produce irregular 'cryptic clicks' that provide some additional information to help locate their prey; however, they can become quite vocal during and after a kill.

Each resident pod has its own unique dialect, consisting of vocalisations unique to its members as well as sounds shared by other pods; the degree of similarity between dialects reflects the degree of relatedness between them. Conversely, transients have more or less the same repertoire of only 4–6 call types (none of which is shared with residents); they do not have group-specific dialects because of their fluid social structure. Little is known about offshore killer whale dialects, and their calls are different from those of either residents or transients, but they do vocalise and echolocate frequently (they are fish-eaters, primarily feeding on sharks).

In Iceland, Norway and Scotland, killer whales feeding on herring make low-frequency, long-duration, high-intensity pulsed calls known as 'herding calls' (shortly before slapping the fish with their tails). These are below the most sensitive hearing range of killer whales, suggesting that they are not for communication between whales; however, they could scare the herring and cause them to cluster more densely – thus increasing the effectiveness of the underwater tail slaps.

CONSERVATION

IUCN status: Data Deficient (2017). The killer whale's medium size and low oil and meat yields meant that relatively small numbers were killed by commercial whalers (43 per year in 1946–81, by Japan; and 26 per year in 1935–79; plus 916 in 1979–80, by the Soviet Union in the Antarctic). Hunting was officially banned by the IWC in 1982. There are no records of a commercial take since then, but some poorly documented hunting continues in Greenland, some Caribbean Islands, Indonesia, Japan and elsewhere.

It is also persecuted because of a real or perceived threat to fisheries and because it is (erroneously) considered dangerous. Norway killed 56 per year in 1938–81, primarily to reduce competition with local fisheries; some fishermen (e.g. in Alaska) continue to shoot killer whales opportunistically. Killer whales removing fish from longlines is a growing problem in Alaska, the western Mediterranean, South Pacific, South Atlantic, Southern Ocean and elsewhere.

Since 1961, at least 148 have been captured for display in oceanaria worldwide (many more have been captured but only 'preferred' individuals – usually youngsters and males – are taken into captivity): at least 65 were taken alive from British Columbia and Washington State in 1962–77; 59 off Iceland in 1976–88; and small numbers off Japan (no figures available). Since 2012, at least 21 have

been captured in the Sea of Okhotsk, Russia (and a permit for 13 more was issued in 2018); they are destined for China. More have been bred in captivity in recent years, but periodic live captures continue. There are currently 56 killer whales in captivity (21 wild-captured and 35 captive born) in 15 marine parks in eight countries.

Other threats include: pollution (there are staggeringly high levels of PCBs and heavy metals in some populations and large oil spills can result in significant mortality), noise pollution and disturbance by vessel traffic (including whale-watching boats in some areas). Reduced prey availability can be a serious threat (e.g. recent declines of Chinook salmon stock in the north-east Pacific, due to overfishing and degradation of spawning grounds). Global warming is likely to affect ecotypes that depend on ice particularly badly.

KILLER WHALE ECOTYPES

Killer whales have a bewildering array of ecologically distinct forms, called ecotypes. Even if they inhabit the same waters, different ecotypes do not associate with each other and have different seasonal distribution patterns, social structures, behaviour, food and habitat preferences and vocal repertoires. They are reproductively isolated and genetically distinct. They differ in appearance too, and are identifiable by subtle differences in dorsal fin shape and saddle patch pigmentation, the size, shape and orientation of the eye patch, the presence or absence of a dorsal cape, and overall coloration.

In the northern hemisphere, resident, Bigg's (formerly known as transient) and offshore ecotypes are the best known, from extensive studies in the north-east Pacific, and reasonably well substantiated. It is possible that there was another ecotype in the eastern Pacific, too, called the LA pod, but it has not been seen since 1997. The situation is less clear in the North Atlantic, where there appear to be a number of distinct populations, but there is no agreement on specific ecotypes (if, indeed, they exist); it conceivable that at least some of these could be feeding on the same range of prey, but in different proportions. A further five are known in the Antarctic and adjacent waters: Type A, Large Type B (or Pack Ice), Small Type B (or Gerlache), Type C (or Ross Sea) and Type D (or Sub-Antarctic).

Limited evidence suggests that there could be further ecotypes (there are at least 40 distinct killer whale populations altogether). In New Zealand, one potentially new ecotype has approximately 200 identified individuals and feeds mainly on stingrays and sharks, but also on other fish and cetaceans. There is another one in the central tropical Pacific: a relatively small form, with less sexual dimorphism than other ecotypes, known to feed on a variety of prey, including cetaceans as large as humpback whales, sharks such as hammerhead and

geye thresher, and squid. South Africa probably has
everal different ecotypes, including some that are
recognisable visitors from Antarctica, but one in particular
unts opportunistically on everything from cetaceans and
inipeds to fish and seabirds. The killer whales around
eninsula Valdes, Argentina, are well known for beaching
emselves to hunt seals, but they have also been
oserved taking sevengill sharks, other fish and penguins.
Iarion Island, in the sub-Antarctic, has killer whales
iat feed on southern elephant seals, sub-Antarctic fur
eals and several species of penguin; they have also
een observed stealing Patagonian toothfish from the
cal longline fishery. There may be more ecotypes in the
orth Atlantic, too: one in Newfoundland and Labrador
ikes a wide variety of prey, but has a preference for
inke whales. There are likely to be others, as research
rogresses.

Recent DNA studies in the north-east Pacific confirm
iat residents and Bigg's began diverging some 700,000–
50,000 years ago, adding to mounting evidence for
eparate subspecies or even species status for at least
ome ecotypes. The northern hemisphere resident killer
hale is currently considered the nominate form.

However, there are likely to be generalists as well.
/hile killer whales in higher latitudes are able to
pecialise and become ecotypes (because prey is more
bundant), those in lower latitudes (where prey is scarcer)
end to take a wide variety of prey and feed on whatever
available. Consequently, they are less likely to become
stinctive ecotypes.

ILLER WHALE SOCIAL STRUCTURE

ong-term studies of resident killer whales in the north-
ast Pacific reveal one of the most stable societies known
mong non-human mammals. There are four levels:

- The basic social unit is a 'maternal group', 'matrilineal group' or 'matriline' (previously known as a 'sub-pod'), normally consisting of an older female, her sons and daughters, and her daughters' offspring; a matriline may consist of up to five generations, which spend all or most of their lives together; there may be as many as 17 members, but five or six is more usual. Both males and females remain in their natal group for life; no individual has ever been known to leave and join another maternal group on a long-term basis (apart from a few rare cases involving orphans). Members of a matriline travel together, rarely separated by more than a few kilometres or for more than a few hours at a time.
- The next level is a 'pod', normally consisting of three (1–11) closely related maternal groups (sharing a common maternal ancestor from the recent past) that associate with each other for at least 50 per cent of the time. A pod has a mean size of 18 whales (typically 10–25, but ranging from two to 49). Pods are less stable

than matrilines (members may travel apart for days or weeks at a time). Residents sometimes form large temporary aggregations, called 'superpods', which include multiple matrilines and pods.

3. Pods sharing similar vocal dialects (i.e. those descended from a common maternal heritage) belong to the same 'clan'; pods in the same clan rarely travel together and do not interbreed.

4. Pods that regularly associate with one another belong to the same 'community'. Communities are defined by association, rather than degree of maternal relatedness or acoustic similarity.

It is uncertain how much this social organisation is mirrored in other ecotypes elsewhere in the world (for instance, the basic social structure of Bigg's (or transient) killer whales is the maternal group, which typically consists of an adult female and her offspring; but, in this case, it is much more flexible and both male and female offspring may leave for extended periods or permanently).

HOW DANGEROUS ARE KILLER WHALES?

As far as is known, wild killer whales have never killed a person, though a surfer in California was bitten on the leg in 1972 (the whale immediately let go and the surfer's wound required 100 stitches). There were reports of attempted attacks on people during two early Antarctic expeditions (both, inexplicably, on photographers): Herbert Ponting (Scott's ill-fated second expedition in 1911) and Frank Hurley (Shackleton's 1915 *Endurance* expedition); on both occasions, whales tried to break through thin ice where they were standing. Killer whales have, on occasion, rammed and sunk small sailing boats; the people onboard were not injured, and the reasons for the attacks are not known. In captivity, they occasionally (and perhaps understandably) attack, and sometimes kill, trainers.

A killer whale's blow can be up to five metres high.

KNOWN KILLER WHALE ECOTYPES IN THE NORTH PACIFIC

RESIDENT (OR FISH-EATING) KILLER WHALE

- 'Typical' black-and-white killer whale
- Male dorsal fin tip usually more rounded than transient and ends in pointed trailing tip
- Typically a few nicks and scars on trailing edge of the dorsal fin
- Male dorsal fin may lean forward to varying degrees
- Fin tip tends to be positioned over front end of base
- Dorsal fin has wavy trailing edge (especially in older males)
- Leading edge of dorsal fin tends to be straight or slightly concave
- Saddle patch usually very open (considerable black incursion in otherwise pale grey) and rarely closed
- Middle of saddle patch rarely extends further forward than midpoint of dorsal fin base
- No obvious dorsal cape
- White eye patch a medium-sized oval (parallel to body axis)

L: M – 6.9m, F – 6m; MAX: 7.2m

Distribution Known mainly from the north-east Pacific, ranging from the Aleutian Islands, Alaska, through British Columbia and Washington State to Monterey Bay, California. May also occur elsewhere in the North Pacific: a large population of fish-eating killer whales in the Russian Far East, for example, corresponds in appearance, behaviour, acoustic activity and genetics with this ecotype (its range includes the central Sea of Okhotsk, southern and central Kamchatka Peninsula, the Commander and Kuril Islands, and the southern Bering Sea); it is known as Type R. Often inhabits sheltered coastal waterways and not known to venture far beyond the continental shelf. Maximum summer range is typically less than 200km.

Food and feeding Primarily a fish-eater. Takes mainly salmon in the east, with regional preferences (endangered Chinook in the Salish Sea; Chinook in spring, chum in early summer, coho in late summer and autumn in the Gulf of Alaska). Atka mackerel preferred in the Aleutian Islands and is an important prey in the Russian Far East. Also feeds on bottom-dwelling fishes such as Pacific halibut and Dover sole; and will take squid. Readily takes sablefish off longlines (a species normally beyond its diving range). Usually ignores marine mammals, which rarely show avoidance behaviour.

Group structure See p. 269. In the north-east Pacific there are three communities: Southern Residents, Northern Residents and Southern Alaska Residents.

Group size Pod typically composed of three matrilines (ranges from one to 11) with average total of 18 whales (typically 10–25, but ranging from two to 49).

Population Total in the north-east Pacific approximately 1,000 (75 Southern Residents, 290 Northern Residents, *c.* 700 Southern Alaska Residents); more than 1,600 individuals photo-identified in the Russian Far East (*c.* half in the Commander Islands).

Remarks The Society for Marine Mammalogy currently recognises the resident killer whale as a separate subspecies. The term 'resident' is rather misleading when describing the site-fidelity and movement patterns of these whales – so they are often referred to as fish-eating killer whales.

ADULT FEMALE AND CALF RESIDENT

BIGG'S (OR TRANSIENT) KILLER WHALE

- 'Typical' black-and-white killer whale
- Largest of three North Pacific ecotypes
- Male dorsal fin tip straighter and more pointed than resident
- Typically many nicks and scars on trailing edge of fin
- Fin tip tends to be positioned over centre of base
- Large saddle patch uniformly grey
- Saddle patch always closed (no black incursion into grey)
- Middle of saddle patch typically extends further forward (cf. residents) – often past midline of dorsal fin
- No obvious dorsal cape
- White eye patch medium-sized oval (slanted very slightly downwards towards rear)

L: M – 8m, F – 7m; MAX: 9.8m

Distribution Known mainly from the Bering Sea through British Columbia and Washington State to Baja California. May also occur elsewhere in the North Pacific: a very poorly known population of mammal-eating killer whales in the Russian Far East, for example, corresponds in appearance, behaviour and acoustic activity with this ecotype; known as Type T, it occurs mainly in coastal waters of the Sea of Okhotsk and Chukotka. Movement patterns coincide with preferred and seasonally available prey species. Coastal and offshore waters. Does not show marked seasonal shifts in distribution, but travels over a wider range than residents and movements tend to be erratic (rarely keeps to predictable routes or stays in the same place for long).

Food and feeding Primarily a mammal-hunter, especially taking cetaceans, pinnipeds and sea otters. The preference varies with location. Will kill swimming seabirds (though usually abandons the carcasses rather than eating them) and occasionally takes squid. Not known to take fish. This is the ecotype that hunts grey whale calves in Monterey Bay, California (mainly April–May), and the eastern Aleutian Islands (including Unimak Pass), Alaska (May–June).

ADULT MALE BIGG'S

ADULT FEMALE AND CALF BIGG'S

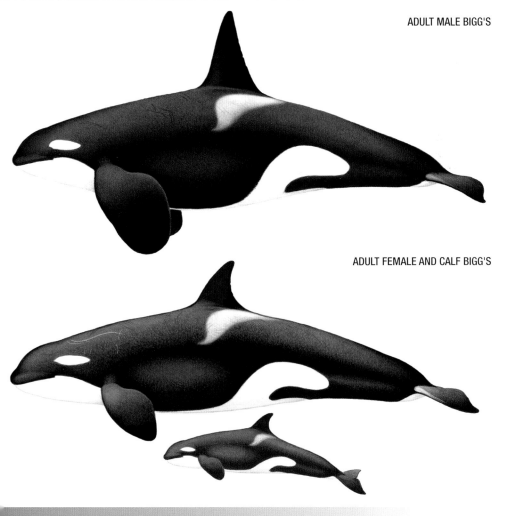

Group structure Transients live in smaller, less stable groups than residents (more appropriate for their foraging strategy – larger groups would increase the probability of being detected by mammalian prey). Offspring often leave their matrilines for extended periods, or permanently. Females typically leave their natal groups at sexual maturity and travel with other transient groups; they may rejoin their natal groups after they have had calves of their own, but usually only for short periods. Males disperse less frequently than females (only first-born males tend to maintain intense fidelity to their mothers). Bigg's populations do not seem to be acoustically subdivided into clans. In the north-east Pacific there are three communities: Gulf of Alaska, Aleutian Islands and Bering Sea; West Coast; and AT1 (or Chugach).

Group size Typically 2–6 animals, consisting of a mother and her offspring. In recent years, large temporary aggregations of 30 or more have been observed. Lone individuals (usually males) are sometimes seen.

Population Total in the north-east Pacific more than 1,000 (*c.* 590 Gulf of Alaska, seven AT1, *c.* 500 West Coast); unknown numbers in the Russian Far East (at least 100).

Remarks The consensus among researchers is that the ecotype formerly known as the 'transient killer whale' should be called 'Bigg's killer whale', in honour of the late Dr Michael Bigg (and because the term 'transient' is rather misleading when describing the site-fidelity and movement patterns of these whales). Bigg was a pioneering and visionary killer whale researcher in British Columbia from the early 1970s to the late 1980s; he was the first person to use the photographic identification of individuals based on natural markings. In the two decades of research since his death, the body of evidence that Bigg's killer whales should be declared a distinct species has become compelling (it is the most genetically divergent killer whale).

Bigg's (or transient) killer whale in south-east Alaska playing with a salmon (in its mouth).

OFFSHORE

- 'Typical' black-and-white killer whale
- Overall appearance very similar to resident
- Smallest of three known North Pacific ecotypes
- Relatively smaller dorsal fin
- Male dorsal fin tip continuously rounded over tip (more rounded than transient, without sharp corner of resident)
- Usually more nicks and scars on trailing edge of dorsal fin than resident
- May have oval scars from cookiecutter shark bites
- Grey saddle patch similar in size to that of resident
- Saddle patch usually quite faint (normally closed – i.e. no intrusion of black pigmentation into grey saddle – though open in some individuals)
- Regularly slaps tail when swimming
- Less sexual dimorphism than in residents or transients (tendency for male and female to be more similar in size)
- Extreme tooth wear normal even in sub-adults (often worn flat to gum line – likely from eating sharks that have abrasive skin); similar tooth wear unknown in residents or transients

: M – 6.5m, F – 5.5m; MAX: 7.2m

Distribution The least known of the three North Pacific ecotypes. Ranging between southern California and the eastern Aleuian Islands, Alaska, offshores travel extensively throughout their range. It is unclear whether they occur predominantly in the open ocean or over the continental shelf; they will sporadically visit coastal (and occasionally protected inshore) waters.

Food and feeding Bony and cartilaginous fish, especially sharks (including great white, blue, Pacific sleeper, Pacific spiny dogfish); also known to take Chinook salmon and Pacific halibut. There is no evidence of mammal-eating.

Group structure Poorly known, but believed to be a dynamic society with dispersal from the natal matriline, similar to that found in Bigg's, with occasional larger gatherings as in residents. Long-term associations are not known between reproductive females, though they have been observed between mothers and their sons.

Group size Normally large (50–100 animals is not unusual); occasionally 200-plus in temporary gatherings (possibly related to prey density).

Population *c.* 350–500 in the north-east Pacific.

Remarks When approached by boat, usually more evasive (erratic and prolonged dives) than residents or Bigg's.

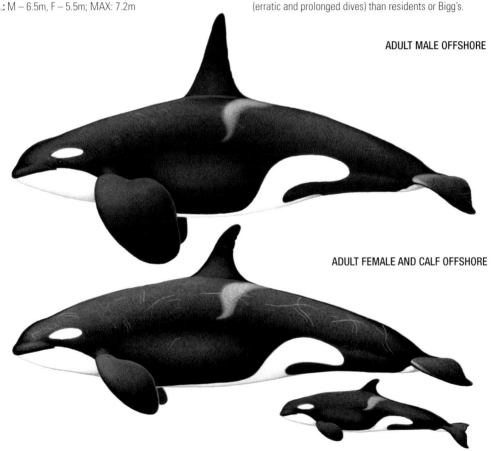

ADULT MALE OFFSHORE

ADULT FEMALE AND CALF OFFSHORE

LA POD (TENTATIVE)

An unofficial ecotype in the northern hemisphere, dubbed the 'LA Pod', was frequently seen during 1982–97 off Los Angeles (it ranged from the Farallon Islands, off San Francisco, south into the Sea of Cortez, Mexico). The group had 13–15 members. They were known to feed on sea lions, sharks (one female famously killed a great white shark at the Farallon Islands, 1997) and possibly other fish.

They were less vocal than either residents or offshores. It is possible that they have shifted their range south into Mexico, but they have not been seen for years.

- Small body size
- Dorsal fin with rounded tip
- Many trailing notches on the dorsal fin (often with stringy *Xenobalanus* barnacles dangling from their trailing edges)
- Closed, very narrow saddle

ADULT MALE LA POD

ADULT FEMALE LA POD

The main distinctive features of killer whale ecotypes: eye patch, dorsal fin and saddle patch.

RECOGNISED KILLER WHALE POPULATIONS IN THE NORTH ATLANTIC

Note: the generalist 'Type 1' and marine mammal specialist 'Type 2' classifications originally used for north-east Atlantic killer whales were adopted for museum and stranded specimens from northern European waters, and are no longer considered suitable for encapsulating the diversity of killer whales in the North Atlantic. Possible ecotype delineation is less clear in the North Atlantic than in some other parts of the world; also, there are still groups and populations in the North Atlantic that are understudied – their ecology and affinity to other known groups and populations remains unknown. The best known populations are described here.

ICELANDIC SUMMER-SPAWNING HERRING-FEEDERS

- 'Typical' black-and-white killer whale
- Smaller than those of West Coast Community
- More closely resembles north-east Pacific residents
- Medium- to large-sized oval eye patch (parallel to body axis)
- Front end of eye patch in front of blowhole
- Significant tooth wear (teeth often worn smooth to the gum line)
- Conspicuous saddle patch
- Worn teeth produce wide rake marks

L: M – 6.3m, F – 5.9m; MAX: 6.6m

ADULT MALE NORTH-EAST ATLANTIC
(ICELANDIC HERRING-FEEDERS,
NORWEGIAN HERRING-FEEDERS AND
NORTH-EAST ATLANTIC MACKEREL-FEEDERS)

ADULT FEMALE AND CALF NORTH-EAST ATLANTIC
(ICELANDIC HERRING-FEEDERS,
NORWEGIAN HERRING-FEEDERS AND
NORTH-EAST ATLANTIC MACKEREL-FEEDERS)

Distribution Iceland, but *c.* five per cent move to north-east Scotland in the spring and summer (especially Shetland, and, to a lesser extent, Caithness and Orkney). No contemporary movement has been detected between Iceland and Norway (though Icelandic summer-spawning herring and Norwegian spring-spawning herring used to overlap in range prior to the 1970s, and do again today). However, genetic analyses find that killer whales from these two herring grounds cluster as one population.

Food and feeding Primarily schooling herring, moving between the herring wintering, spawning and feeding grounds around Iceland. Carousel feeding frequently observed during winter and summer: the whales work in groups of 3–9 to round up herring; they split a group of fish from the larger school, swim in fast circles (blowing bubbles, flashing their undersides and lobtailing) to herd them into a tighter ball, whip their tails into the ball to stun or kill as many fish as possible, then pick them off one-by-one. Worn teeth suggest a feeding technique that involves 'sucking up' whole fish prey. Some Icelandic killer whales appear to specialise on herring and follow it year-round, while others feed on it only seasonally or opportunistically. At least 12 other prey species have been recorded in Icelandic waters, including minke whales, long-finned pilot whales, white-beaked dolphins (although these two species have been seen in non-predatory interactions, too, in both Scotland and Iceland), harbour porpoises, harbour and grey seals, eider ducks, fish (lumpfish, salmon, Atlantic halibut and Greenland halibut) and squid, but it is not yet clear if some or all of these are taken by the herring-feeding whales. In Scotland, killer whales feed on herring (offshore) and harbour and grey seals (inshore), and are known to take harbour porpoises, otters and seabirds such as auks, fulmars and eider ducks. Scottish individuals return to Iceland for the winter, where they feed on the same herring stocks as those that remain year-round. There are no clear differences in appearance between these two groups, but some slight genetic ones.

Group structure Wide range of short-term and long-term associations, including constant companionships (not unlike matrilineal groups in the north-east Pacific) and casual acquaintances.

Group size 4–6 when feeding on marine mammals; 6–30 when feeding on fish close to shore; up to 300 feeding on fish along the continental shelf edge.

Population 432 individuals (excluding calves) are currently identified in the Icelandic Orca Project photo-ID catalogue.

NORWEGIAN SPRING-SPAWNING HERRING-FEEDERS

- No discernible differences to Icelandic herring-feeding killer whales

L: M – 6.2m, F – 5.5m; MAX: 6.6m.

Distribution Most of Norway's killer whales follow the movements of its spring-spawning herring. These spawn off central Norway and around the Lofoten Islands in spring, spread out into the Norwegian Sea to feed in summer (April–September), and currently overwinter in an area north of the Lofoten Islands (some venturing to more than 80°N) and as far south as central Norway and around the Lofoten Islands themselves; since 1950, the herring (and therefore the killer whales) have used at least six overwintering locations for varying periods of time. No contemporary movement has been detected between Norway and Iceland.

Food and feeding Primarily schooling Atlantic herring; other prey items documented include mackerel, cod, salmon, squid and harbour porpoise. Some have been observed hunting harbour and grey seals, and these are most likely to be seen around haul-outs in coastal waters of Nordland, Troms and Finnmark during the pupping periods (June–July for harbour seals, September–October for grey seals, into November–December further north). It is possible that many killer whales in this population include seals in their diet on a regular basis (either as specialists or adapting seasonally to available prey).

Group structure Herring feeders probably similar to Icelandic killer whales; seal-feeders in small stable units that temporarily associate in larger groups (most likely for socialising and to teach hunting behaviours).

Group size Herring-feeding groups range in size from six to 30 individuals (median 15), while seal-feeding groups range from three to 11 (median five).

Population At least 1,000 in Norwegian coastal waters during times of high herring abundance; counts in the late 1980s estimated 7,000 during summer in the wider Norwegian Sea.

Remarks Non-predatory aggregations occur on the winter feeding grounds between killer whales and humpback whales (the humpbacks usually join after the killer whales have initiated feeding).

NORTH-EAST ATLANTIC MACKEREL-FEEDERS

- Subtly different features to Icelandic and Norwegian herring-feeding killer whales e.g. eye patch often smaller and male dorsal fin often more rounded at tip (butter knife shape)
- worn teeth (due to suction feeding)

L: M – 6.3m, F – 5.9m; MAX: 6.6m.

Distribution Ranges throughout the northern North Sea, the Irish Sea and the Norwegian Sea, and into the Arctic. Mostly offshore, but also coastal. Known mainly between Shetland, the Orkney Islands and southern Norway in mid to late autumn; west of the Hebrides in winter; and in the Norwegian Sea (including Iceland) up to 72°N during late summer. One killer whale aggregation targets mackerel moving from the North Sea into Irish waters in the late autumn/winter (October–January), but it is not yet known where they go for the rest of the year or if they are part of the mackerel-feeding population seen in the Norwegian Sea during summer.

Food and feeding Mackerel (for at least part of the year – whether it targets mackerel year-round or switches to other seasonally available prey is unknown). Frequently feeds around fishing trawlers (swimming in close to the fishing nets during hauling operations). In the Norwegian Sea, groups appear to use a similar carousel-feeding strategy to herring-eaters in Iceland and Norway.

Group structure Little known.

Group size Those feeding in the Norwegian Sea have been observed in groups ranging from one to 40 (mean eight); groups feeding around fishing trawlers range from one to 70 (mean 13). Maximum group size 200.

Population 271 individuals were observed during a two-year study period in the Norwegian Sea; however, the population is likely to be much larger given the low number of re-sightings between years.

WEST COAST COMMUNITY

- 'Typical' black-and-white killer whale
- Larger than Icelandic or Norwegian herring specialists
- More closely resembles north-east Pacific Bigg's and Antarctic Type A
- Medium- to large-sized oval eye patch (slanting down towards rear)
- Front end of eye patch behind blowhole
- Little or no tooth wear
- Faint saddle patch

L: M – unknown, F – 6.1m; MAX: unknown.

Distribution The UK and Ireland, patrolling a vast area from Pembrokeshire and the southern Irish Sea, along the entire west coast of Ireland, and north to the Outer Hebrides; however, they are known mainly from the west coast of Scotland, (which is where the community gets its name).

Food and feeding Little understood, but known to have taken harbour seals and harbour porpoises.

Group structure Most sightings of pairs or trios.

Group size Usually two to three, but too few animals to be certain.

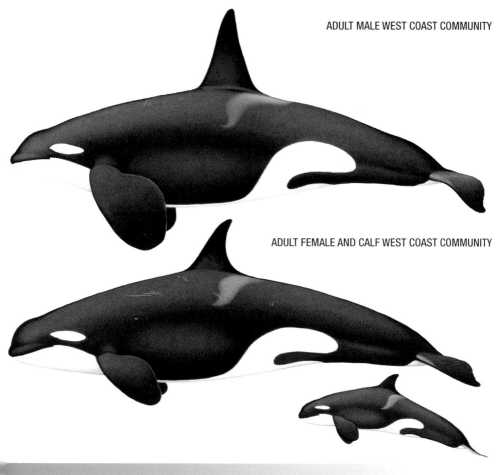

ADULT MALE WEST COAST COMMUNITY

ADULT FEMALE AND CALF WEST COAST COMMUNITY

Population Only eight members of the West Coast community were left in 2018 (with evidence of significant inbreeding, suggesting that they are isolated from neighbouring populations); no calves have been observed in over two decades.

Remarks It is possible that at least two other pods of killer whales – the 27s and 64s (forming the Northern Isles community) – may be resident in the UK; they appear year-round in Shetland and Orkney, and are not known in Iceland or Norway. There are likely to be other populations sharing at least some of the West Coast Community's characteristics (e.g. large, unworn teeth); such killer whales may occur in the Azores, the Faroe Islands and Svalbard. Many similarly-sized individuals were taken from across the North Atlantic by whalers during the last century, so these animals may represent a remnant of a more widespread ancestral population.

STRAIT OF GIBRALTAR BLUEFIN TUNA-FEEDERS

- 'Typical' black-and-white killer whale
- Medium- to large-sized oval eye patch (parallel to body axis)
- Male dorsal fin tip usually rounded and ends in pointed trailing tip (similar to north-east Pacific resident)
- Conspicuous saddle patch uniformly grey and closed

L: M – 6m, F – 5.3m; MAX: 7.3m.

Distribution Known from the Gulf of Cadiz, southern Spain (mainly during spring and summer) and central waters of the Strait of Gibraltar (mainly during summer). Little is known about their movements in autumn and winter, though it is possible that they follow bluefin tuna into the eastern Atlantic Ocean (after the tuna leave their spawning grounds in the Mediterranean Sea). They are not regularly present in the Mediterranean (though were sometimes observed there before 2000).

ADULT MALE STRAIT OF GIBRALTAR BLUEFIN TUNA-FEEDER

ADULT FEMALE STRAIT OF GIBRALTAR BLUEFIN TUNA-FEEDER

Bluefin tuna-feeders in the Strait of Gibraltar.

Food and feeding Atlantic bluefin tuna, which is chased at high speed and for up to 30 minutes at a time (known as an endurance-exhaustion technique) during spring. Approximately half the population (pods A1 and A2) frequently depredates tuna from baited hooks in a drop long-line fishery (since at least 1999) during summer. It is unknown whether they are dependent on tuna year-round; however, at least one pod (D) may opportunistically feed on coastal fish species.

Group structure No dispersion between pods has been observed; one pod (A) split into two (A1 and A2) in 2006, and strong associations remain.

Group size The small population is subdivided into five pods (A1, A2, B, C and D) comprising seven to 15 individuals.

Population 30–40.

Remarks Recent research suggests that there is no mixing between killer whales in the Strait of Gibraltar and the Canary Islands, and these two populations appear to be reproductively, socially and ecologically different. There has been a major decline in the Atlantic bluefin tuna population since the 1960s.

NORTH-WEST ATLANTIC

'Typical' black-and-white killer whale
Medium- to large-sized oval eye patch (parallel to body axis)
Dorsal fin tip usually rounded and ends in pointed trailing tip (similar to north-east Pacific resident)
Conspicuous saddle patch uniformly grey and mostly closed

M – 6.7m, F – 5.5-6.5m; MAX: unknown.

Distribution Known mainly from Greenland, northern Newfoundland and Labrador, especially in summer (though there is considerably less observer effort in winter, and the seasonal arrival of pack ice likely limits distribution in Labrador and along the northern coast of Newfoundland).

Fishermen are also reporting killer whales far offshore, on the Grand Banks of Newfoundland. There is currently no evidence of seasonal migratory movements in Atlantic Canada; however, an individual satellite-tagged off Baffin Island (one of a group of 20) spent the summer in Arctic Canada, then swam past the outer shelf of Labrador and Newfoundland waters, before crossing the Atlantic for warmer waters near the Azores. It appears to be less frequent on the Scotian Shelf, in the Gulf of St Lawrence, and in Nova Scotia and New Brunswick; and it is seldom seen in the eastern United States. Most sightings are relatively close to shore, in water less than 200m deep, though this may reflect observer effort (lone killer whales, and groups, have also been sighted more than 200km offshore, beyond the continental shelf and in water depths greater than 3,000m).

Food and feeding In Greenland, Newfoundland and Labrador, takes a variety of seals (including harp), other cetaceans (including common minke whale, Atlantic white-sided dolphin and white-beaked dolphin, and occasionally young humpback whale), fish (including herring, mackerel, salmon, cod and dogfish), and occasionally seabirds (including razorbill and eider duck). There appears to be some group-specific prey specialisation (e.g. fish and cephalopods in west Greenland, marine mammals in east Greenland).

Group structure Unknown.

Group size Typically two to six (average five); rarely more than 15, occasionally as many as 30; one-quarter of all sightings are lone individuals. Larger aggregations of 100 were reported in association with whaling operations in the 1970s (likely multiple smaller groups attracted to a prey source).

Population Little information (photo-identification catalogues are being developed); *c.* 150-200 in coastal waters of Newfoundland and Labrador.

Remarks Compared to many other parts of the world, relatively little is known about killer whales in the north-west Atlantic. It is not known whether they mix with killer whales from populations in adjacent areas.

Arctic Canada There has been a significant increase in the number of sightings in Arctic Canada, at least during the summer: as global temperatures rise, and the Arctic sea ice retreats, many former barriers are opening up and allowing killer whales to enter bays, fjords and inlets that were previously inaccessible. These particular killer whales are only known to feed on marine mammals (harp, ringed, bearded, hooded and harbour seals, narwhal, beluga and bowhead); however, fish predation cannot be ruled out.

KNOWN KILLER WHALE ECOTYPES IN THE ANTARCTIC AND ADJACENT WATERS

TYPE A (ANTARCTIC KILLER WHALE)

- 'Typical' black-and-white killer whale
- Possibly largest of Antarctic ecotypes (Large Type B may be equal in size)
- Medium-sized oval eye patch (oriented parallel to body axis)
- Usually no visible dorsal cape
- Saddle patch can be brownish
- Male saddle patch usually closed, female's can be slightly open
- White patches occasionally tinted slightly yellowish (with diatoms)
- Black body colour occasionally tinted slightly brownish (with diatoms)

L: M – 7.3m, F – 6.4m; MAX: 9.2m

Distribution During the southern summer, it is circumpolar in Antarctic waters, mostly in offshore, ice-free, open water; frequently seen around the Antarctic Peninsula. Seasonal movements are poorly understood, but it is known to migrate away from Antarctica to lower, warmer latitudes, at least for short periods. Killer whales that look like Type A have been observed in New Zealand, Australia, South Africa, West Africa and Chilean Patagonia, as well as the Crozet Archipelago, the Kerguelen Islands and Macquarie Island, but whether any of these other whales migrate to Antarctic waters is unknown. Currently, Type A is a 'catch-all' ecotype that includes anything that is not Type B, C or D – and, ultimately, it could include more than one ecotype.

Food and feeding In Antarctic waters, predominantly Antarctic minke whales and elephant seals, though it may take calves of other baleen whale species and other seals; it has also been observed chasing (though not catching) penguins. What this ecotype feeds on when it is away from Antarctic waters is unknown. Killer whales that look like Type A are known to take rays, sharks and pinnipeds in New Zealand; whales, seals, dugongs and pelagic fish in Australia and minke whales, southern elephant seals, penguins and fish at the Crozet Archipelago (where it frequently takes Patagonian toothfish from longline fishing boats).

Group structure Unknown.

Group size 10–15 (1–38).

Population Unknown; at least 372 have been photo-identified around the Antarctic Peninsula.

ADULT MALE TYPE A (ANTARCTIC)

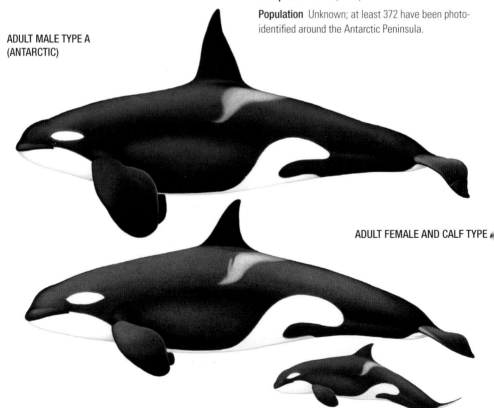

ADULT FEMALE AND CALF TYPE A

LARGE TYPE B (PACK ICE KILLER WHALE)

- Two-tone grey and white (not black and white)
- Larger and more robust body than Small Type B (Gerlache) killer whale
- Often covered in diatoms (turns white areas yellowish, grey areas brownish)
- Small oval scars from cookiecutter shark bites common
- Eye patch variable but always larger than any other killer whale (at least twice as large as in Antarctic Type A)
- Eye patch oriented parallel to body axis
- Saddle patch almost always closed
- Dark grey dorsal cape (often demarcated by narrow white border originating as an extension of lower saddle) stretching from forehead to just behind dorsal fin
- Very similar to Small Type B (Gerlache) killer whales but twice the size
- Often seen spyhopping around ice floes (looking for seals)

: M – unknown, F – unknown; MAX: 9m; estimated to be at least twice the bulk of the Gerlache killer whale.

Distribution Circumpolar in Antarctic waters during summer, mostly inshore around dense pack ice and, especially, floe ice. It is uncommon around the northern half of the Antarctic Peninsula and retreats south with the summer break-up of fast ice. Winter distribution is unknown but, while it apparently spends most of the year in Antarctic waters, it periodically undertakes rapid round-trip migrations to tropical and sub-tropical waters (30–37°S). These are known as 'maintenance migrations', believed to allow skin regeneration without the high cost of heat loss. The Antarctic Peninsula population migrates north, east of the Falkland Islands and Argentina, to Uruguay and Brazil. It is likely that 'clean' grey-and-white individuals have recently returned from the tropics (where they shed diatoms with their skin).

Food and feeding Feeds preferentially on Weddell seals (usually in coordinated groups, by 'wave-washing') and will often ignore crabeater and leopard seals. It occasionally takes Antarctic minke whales and elephant seals, and may also take humpback whale calves.

Group structure Unknown.

Group size Usually fewer than 10.

Population Unknown.

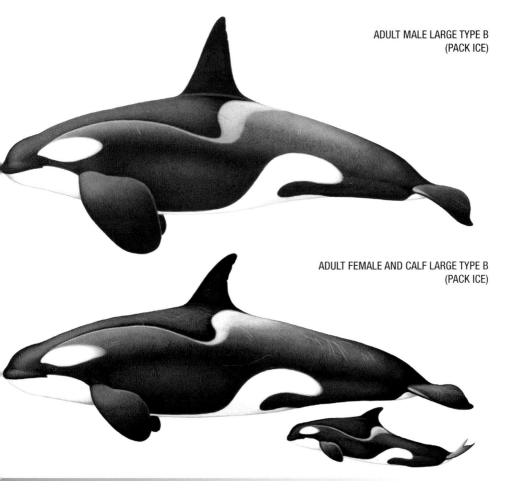

ADULT MALE LARGE TYPE B
(PACK ICE)

ADULT FEMALE AND CALF LARGE TYPE B
(PACK ICE)

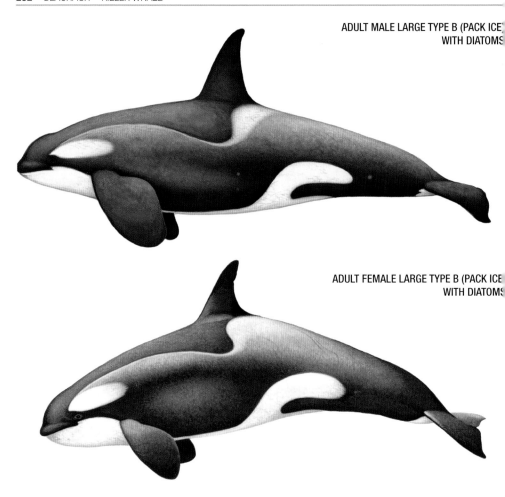

ADULT MALE LARGE TYPE B (PACK ICE)
WITH DIATOMS

ADULT FEMALE LARGE TYPE B (PACK ICE)
WITH DIATOMS

Antarctic Large Type B (Pack Ice) killer whales feed mainly on Weddell seals, but this individual is spyhopping to see if crabeater seals are potential prey.

SMALL TYPE B (GERLACHE KILLER WHALE)

- Two-toned grey and white (not black and white)
- Smaller and slimmer body than Large Type B (Pack Ice) killer whale
- Often covered in diatoms (turns white areas yellowish, grey areas brownish)
- Small oval cars from cookiecutter shark bites common
- Eye patch variable but always larger than in any other killer whale (except Pack Ice killer whale)
- Eye patch narrower than Pack Ice killer whale
- Eye patch may be oriented parallel to body axis or slightly slanted
- Saddle patch usually (but not always) closed
- Dark grey dorsal cape present (though can be indistinct), stretching from just in front of eye patch backward to just behind dorsal fin, and continuous with the lower leading edge of the saddle (often demarcated by narrow white border originating in saddle)
- Very similar to Large Type B (Pack Ice) killer whales but half the size

M – unknown, F – unknown; MAX: 7m; estimated to be roughly half the bulk of Pack Ice killer whales.

Distribution Known mainly from the Antarctic Peninsula (western side and the western Weddell Sea); the Gerlache Strait and Antarctic Sound are hotspots. Usually in more open water (it tends to avoid pack ice), often near penguin colonies. Spends much of the year in Antarctica, but periodically undertakes rapid (6–7-week) round-trip migrations to tropical and sub-tropical waters (30–37°S). These are known as 'maintenance migrations', believed to allow skin regeneration without the high cost of heat loss. It is likely that 'clean' grey-and-white individuals have recently returned from the tropics (where they shed diatoms with their skin).

Food and feeding Has only been observed feeding on penguins, especially gentoo and chinstrap (it eats only the breast muscles and discards the rest), but it probably feeds mainly on fish (and possibly squid) caught near the ocean floor (it is a deep diver).

Group structure Unknown.

Group size Often 50-plus.

Population Unknown.

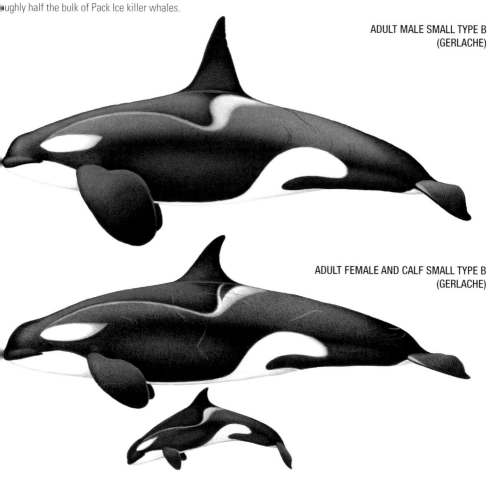

**ADULT MALE SMALL TYPE B
(GERLACHE)**

**ADULT FEMALE AND CALF SMALL TYPE B
(GERLACHE)**

ADULT MALE SMALL TYPE B (GERLACHE
WITH DIATOMS

TYPE C (ROSS SEA KILLER WHALE)

- Two-toned grey and white (not black and white)
- May be covered in diatoms (turns white areas yellow or orange, black and grey areas brown)
- Small oval scars from cookiecutter shark bites common
- Smallest killer whale ecotype known
- Dark grey dorsal cape usually visible (often demarcated by narrow white border originating in saddle)
- Small, narrow, wispy eye patch (slanted forwards at 45° angle to body axis)
- Saddle patch usually closed and very distinct

L: M – 5.6m, F – 5.2m; MAX: 6.1m; weighs several times less than Type A and Type B (Pack Ice) killer whales (which could conceivably prey on it).

Distribution Known only from East Antarctica, predominantly in the Ross Sea but also west along the Adélie Land to Wilkes Land coasts and with smaller numbers as far west as Prydz Bay. Commonly reported in McMurdo Sound. It lives in dense pack ice, polynyas and leads in the fast ice (often many kilometres from open water). Spends most of the year in Antarctica (and has been recorded in the sea ice during winter) but the presence of cookiecutter shark bites and sightings off New Zealand and Australia indicate that there are at least some migrations to tropical and sub-tropical waters. Has been observed in New Zealand during winter (as far north as the Bay of Islands) and in south-east Australia.

Food and feeding Only known to feed on fish; primarily large 2m-long Antarctic toothfish (but the population has been declining due to commercial fishing); also takes at

ADULT MALE TYPE
(ROSS SEA

east two other, much smaller, species of icefish) and may
ake super-abundant (but very small) Antarctic silverfish.
imited evidence of hunting penguins. It routinely dives to
00–400m, with a maximum of at least 700m.

Group structure   Unknown.

Group size   10–120 (up to 200); group size appears to
have been decreasing in recent years (current average
about 14).

Population   Unknown; average annual population in
McMurdo Sound estimated to be 470.

**ADULT FEMALE AND CALF TYPE C
(ROSS SEA)**

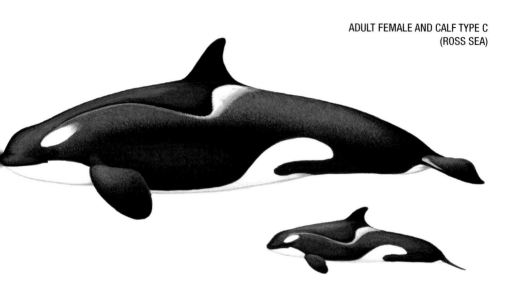

ntarctic Type C or Ross Sea killer whales: the smallest ecotype known.

TYPE D (SUB-ANTARCTIC KILLER WHALE)

- 'Typical' black-and-white killer whale
- Distinctive minuscule white eye patch (parallel to body axis) makes identification easy (sometimes absent)
- Noticeably bulbous melon, cf. other killer whales (more like pilot whale in some individuals)
- Male dorsal fin relatively short, narrow, noticeably swept back and with sharply pointed tip (more falcate and pointed than other Antarctic ecotypes)
- Marked sexual dimorphism in dorsal fin size and shape (as in other ecotypes)
- Moderately conspicuous saddle patch
- No conspicuous dorsal cape
- No yellowish or brownish colouring (caused in some ecotypes by diatoms)

L: M – unknown, F – unknown; MAX: 7.3m

Distribution Circumpolar in sub-Antarctic waters, ranging from 40°S to 60°S; sometimes associated with islands. The first record was of 17 individuals that stranded in Paraparaumu, New Zealand, in 1955. The first live whales were observed in 2004, in offshore waters near the Crozet Archipelago in the southwestern Indian Ocean. There have been 25 or so live sightings since, at the northern edge of the Southern Ocean (including at Crozet, South Georgia and New Zealand sub-Antarctic islands); and it is now being seen almost annually in the Drake Passage and between the Falkland Islands and South Georgia.

Food and feeding Little known, but certainly includes fish (it takes Patagonian toothfish from longline fisheries near the Crozet Archipelago and off Chile).

Group structure Unknown.

Group size Range 9–35, mean 18 (but based on little information).

Population Unknown.

Remarks This is the most distinctive-looking killer whale ecotype, immediately recognisable by its extremely small (or sometimes absent) white eye patch.

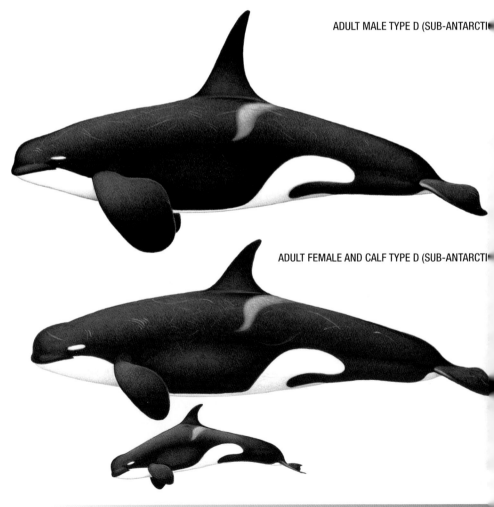

ADULT MALE TYPE D (SUB-ANTARCTIC)

ADULT FEMALE AND CALF TYPE D (SUB-ANTARCTIC)

he least known of the Antarctic killer whales: Type D.

immature Type D surfaces in the Drake Passage, between South America and Antarctica.

SHORT-FINNED PILOT WHALE
Globicephala macrorhynchus

Gray, 184●

The short-finned pilot whale is a distinctive-looking animal but, at sea, is virtually impossible to tell apart from its close relative, the long-finned pilot whale (the main distinguishing feature is a subtle difference in the length and shape of their flippers). Both species are highly sexually dimorphic in both size and appearance.

Classification Odontoceti, family Delphinidae.
Common name 'Short-finned' for the length of the flippers or pectoral fins (cf. long-finned), 'pilot' from an early theory that there is a leader, a cetacean navigator that pilots the group, and that the others continue to follow even if it means certain death.
Other names Shortfin pilot whale, Pacific pilot whale, pothead (after the bulbous melon), blackfish (refers to an informal grouping of six dark-coloured members of the dolphin family, all with 'whale' in their name).
Scientific name *Globicephala* from the Latin *globus* for 'sphere', 'globe' or 'round', and the Greek *kephale* for 'head' (a reference to the bulbous melon); *macrorhynchus* from the Greek *makros* for 'large', and *rhynchos* for 'snout' or 'beak'.
Taxonomy No recognised subspecies; there is genetic evidence of three types or forms of undetermined taxonomic status: one in the Atlantic and two in the Pacific/Indian Oceans. Two forms, exhibiting differences in body size, melon shape, brightness of the saddle patch, number of teeth, vocal repertoire, life history and genetics, were first noted in the colder Oyashio Current off northern Japan (called the shiho type) and in the warmer Kuroshio Current off southern Japan (the naisa type). It is now believed that these are more widespread: the shiho type occurs throughout the eastern Pacific, and the naisa type occurs throughout the remainder of the species' distribution; separated by the East Pacific Barrier, they are likely to be different subspecies. The naisa type may also be diverging, with one population in the Atlantic (the Atlan● type) and the other in the western and central Pacific and Indian oceans (separated by the Benguela Barrier off South Africa).

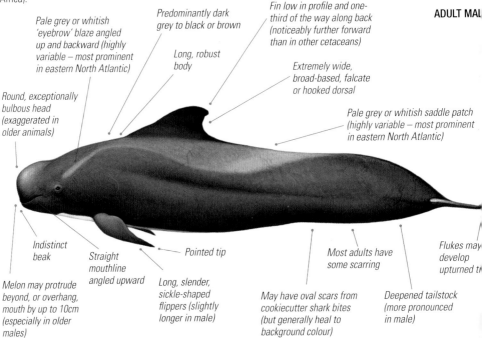

ADULT MAL●

Pale grey or whitish 'eyebrow' blaze angled up and backward (highly variable – most prominent in eastern North Atlantic)

Predominantly dark grey to black or brown

Long, robust body

Fin low in profile and one-third of the way along back (noticeably further forward than in other cetaceans)

Extremely wide, broad-based, falcate or hooked dorsal

Round, exceptionally bulbous head (exaggerated in older animals)

Pale grey or whitish saddle patch (highly variable – most prominent in eastern North Atlantic)

Indistinct beak

Straight mouthline angled upward

Pointed tip

Most adults have some scarring

Flukes may develop upturned t●

Melon may protrude beyond, or overhang, mouth by up to 10cm (especially in older males)

Long, slender, sickle-shaped flippers (slightly longer in male)

May have oval scars from cookiecutter shark bites (but generally heal to background colour)

Deepened tailstock (more pronounced in male)

AT A GLANCE
- Warm waters worldwide
- Medium size
- Black, blackish or brownish
- Rounded, bulbous melon
- Indistinct beak
- Broad-based, backswept dorsal fin far forward
- Small to large groups

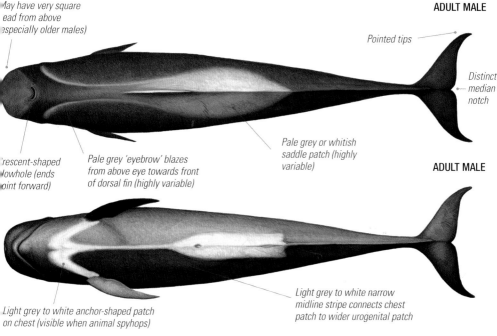

ADULT MALE

May have very square head from above (especially older males)

Pointed tips

Distinct median notch

Crescent-shaped blowhole (ends point forward)

Pale grey 'eyebrow' blazes from above eye towards front of dorsal fin (highly variable)

Pale grey or whitish saddle patch (highly variable)

ADULT MALE

Light grey to white anchor-shaped patch on chest (visible when animal spyhops)

Light grey to white narrow midline stripe connects chest patch to wider urogenital patch

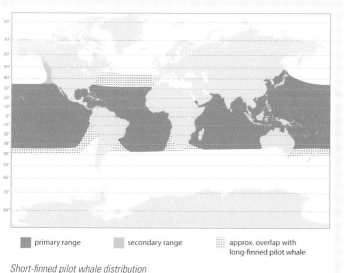

SIZE
L: ♂ 4.2–7.3m, ♀ 3.2–5.1m;
WT: 1–3.5t; **MAX:** 7.3m, 3.6t
Calf – L: 1.4–1.9m; **WT:** 40–85kg
Males up to 1.1m longer than females.

Short-finned pilot whale distribution

primary range   secondary range   approx. overlap with long-finned pilot whale

SIMILAR SPECIES

There is some range overlap with long-finned pilot whale. The morphological differences between the two species are subtle (relative length and shape of the flippers, differences in skull shape and tooth count) and it is difficult (if not impossible) to tell them apart at sea (except perhaps with a clear view of the flippers). Studies suggest that distinction between the two species in the north-west Atlantic is possible by experienced observers: in particular, the long-finned is generally darker and, if a saddle patch is present, it has a distinct boundary behind the dorsal fin (a saddle patch is always present on the short-finned and its boundary is not clearly defined). Otherwise, the flippers and the shape of the skull are the only definitive physical characteristics: the short-finned has a shorter and broader skull, while the long-finned skull is narrower. There is evidence of hybridisation between the two species in the Atlantic. Confusion with false killer whales is possible in the warmer parts of its range, but the false killer's head is more tapered, its pectoral fins are distinct, and the dorsal fin is more slender, more erect and further back on the body. Hybrids with common bottlenose dolphins have been reported in captivity.

DISTRIBUTION

Widely distributed in deep tropical, sub-tropical and warm temperate waters worldwide. Does not normally range north of 50°N or south of 40°S. Occurs in the southern Red Sea, but is absent from the Mediterranean Sea (where the long-finned pilot whale is resident) and unknown in the Persian Gulf. There are long-term residents in some areas (e.g. around the main Hawaiian Islands – some of which have been known by researchers since the late 1980s), but other populations may move long distances (individual whales have been recorded travelling up to 2,400km/month) before returning to preferred areas. Seasonal inshore–offshore (winter/early spring–summer/autumn) movements in some regions are related to the seasonal

ADULT MALE

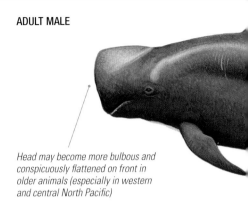

Head may become more bulbous and conspicuously flattened on front in older animals (especially in western and central North Pacific)

Less bulbous head

Significantly smaller dorsal fin

ADULT FEMAL

Less deepened tailstock

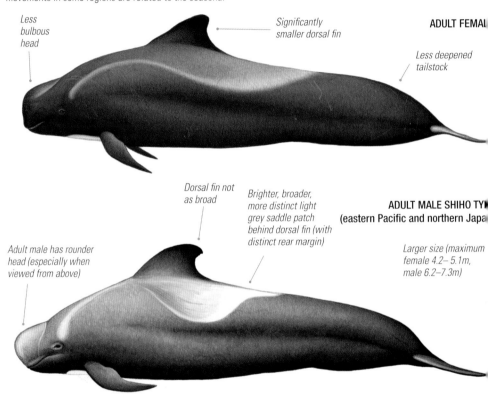

Dorsal fin not as broad

Brighter, broader, more distinct light grey saddle patch behind dorsal fin (with distinct rear margin)

ADULT MALE SHIHO TY
(eastern Pacific and northern Japa

Adult male has rounder head (especially when viewed from above)

Larger size (maximum female 4.2– 5.1m, male 6.2–7.3m)

Shiho form of short-finned pilot whale in the eastern North Pacific.

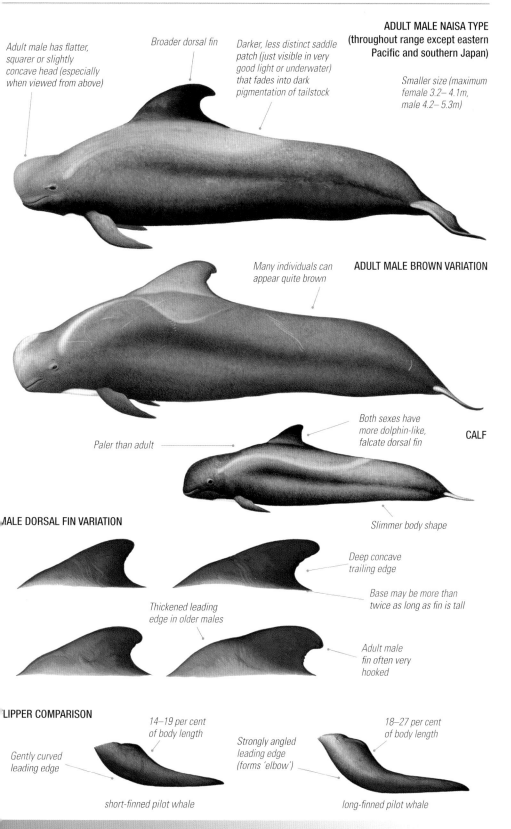

ADULT MALE NAISA TYPE
(throughout range except eastern Pacific and southern Japan)

Adult male has flatter, squarer or slightly concave head (especially when viewed from above)

Broader dorsal fin

Darker, less distinct saddle patch (just visible in very good light or underwater) that fades into dark pigmentation of tailstock

Smaller size (maximum female 3.2– 4.1m, male 4.2– 5.3m)

ADULT MALE BROWN VARIATION

Many individuals can appear quite brown

Paler than adult

Both sexes have more dolphin-like, falcate dorsal fin

CALF

Slimmer body shape

MALE DORSAL FIN VARIATION

Deep concave trailing edge

Base may be more than twice as long as fin is tall

Thickened leading edge in older males

Adult male fin often very hooked

FLIPPER COMPARISON

Gently curved leading edge

14–19 per cent of body length

Strongly angled leading edge (forms 'elbow')

18–27 per cent of body length

short-finned pilot whale

long-finned pilot whale

spawning migrations of squid. Prefers the continental shelf break, continental and island slope waters, and areas with complex topography such as seamounts and ridges. Abundance is lower in deep oceanic environments. Will approach nearshore areas where the water is sufficiently deep. In Hawaii, recorded in depths of 324–4,400m, but there is a clear peak in sightings rates at 500–3,000m.

BEHAVIOUR

Often observed in aggregations with many other species, including humpback whales, sperm whales, Cuvier's beaked whales, melon-headed whales, pygmy killer whales, false killer whales, and pantropical spotted, rough-toothed and common bottlenose dolphins. There are accounts of pilot whales behaving aggressively toward other cetaceans and they tend to harass larger whales, but the role is sometimes reversed with smaller species, such as melon-headed whales, when the pilot whales are the victims. Oceanic whitetip sharks often follow pilot whales, to scavenge on lost or discarded prey (or they rely on the whales to find prey at depth). More aerially active than the long-finned pilot whale, breaching occasionally (though not as often as many smaller delphinids) and spyhopping and lobtailing. Spends much of the day logging (resting) at the surface.

The male's larger size and enlarged features may be for display or for increased mate access, or may aid in defence of their schools from attacks by killer whales and sharks. More prone to mass strandings than almost any other cetacean (apart from the long-finned pilot whale), probably in part because of its strong social bonds. Will grieve for dead members of the group and will carry a dead calf around for hours or days.

Reaction to boats varies according to location, but may approach slow-moving boats or behave indifferently (if the boat does not approach too quickly). Rarely bow-rides. Usually ignores swimmers, or dives to avoid them (despite two incidents in Hawaii: in 1992, an adult male grabbed a swimmer and took her down to 10–12m before bringing her back up to the surface; and, in 2003, a juvenile harassed and bit three free divers).

TEETH

Upper 14–18
Lower 14–18

GROUP SIZE AND STRUCTURE

Highly social, living in matrilineal groups (consisting of a matriarch with her immediate kin) similar in structure to killer whale groups (though not quite as stable). Typical group size is 15–50 (average 18 around the main Hawaiian islands, 15 in Madeira), including all ages and sexes (though there tend to be more adult females). They remain in the family group for life. Males will mate during temporary aggregations of separate family groups. Several family groups may join together to form a pod or school, typically with 30–90 members (up to several hundred). Rarely seen alone (very occasionally, lone adult males are reported).

PREDATORS

No evidence, though killer whales and large sharks are potential predators. There is little scarring, which suggests that attacks are either rare or only on small individuals and usually fatal.

PHOTO-IDENTIFICATION

Nicks, scars and other distinctive marks on the dorsal fin and back, combined with the height and shape of the fin, and skin lesions. The shape of the saddle patch, if present can also be useful.

DIVE SEQUENCE

- Quite leisurely dive sequence.
- Head raised relatively high above surface (eyes often visible).
- Creates distinctive bow wave in calm seas.
- Dorsal fin and large portion of back clearly visible.
- Tailstock strongly arches.
- Flukes sometimes raised above surface before deep dive.
- Several whales typically surface close together.
- May porpoise while travelling.
- Occasionally breaches and spyhops.

BLOW

- Strong, low, shapeless blow (up to *c*. 1m), quite conspicuous in calm weather (but tends to dissipate quickly).

FOOD AND FEEDING

Prey Mainly squid (especially market squid, European flying squid, glass squid, common arm squid, colossal squid, possibly giant squid in some areas); some octopus, and mid- and deepwater fish.

Feeding While foraging may spread out in 'chorus line' up to 3km long; in the Canaries uses energetic sprints to chase down prey, then ram-and-suction technique.

Dive depth Foraging dives can exceed 1,000m, but depth varies greatly with region and time of day; limited evidence in some regions of shallow foraging at night, tracking rise of deep scattering layer, with deeper dives during day (e.g. in Hawaii, where typically to 700–1,000m during day, 300–500m at night); in Canary Islands performs deep dives day and night; maximum recorded 1,552m.

Dive time Typically 12–15 (occasionally 20) minutes (varies with sex, size and behaviour); maximum recorded 27 minutes (Hawaii).

POPULATION

No overall abundance estimate. Approximate regional estimates include 589,000 in the eastern tropical Pacific, nearly 60,000 off Japan (including 53,609 of the naisa form and 4,321 of the shiho form), 21,500 in the western North Atlantic, 19,000–20,000 in Hawaiian waters, 7,700 in the Sulu Sea of the Philippines, at least 2,400 in the Gulf of Mexico, 836 off the west coast of the USA and 150 in the Strait of Gibraltar.

CONSERVATION

IUCN status: Least Concern (2018). Hunted in many parts of the world for centuries and there are still harpoon and drive fisheries for short-finned pilot whales in Japan, the Lesser Antilles in the Caribbean, the Philippines, Indonesia and Sri Lanka. Japan and the Caribbean have the largest hunts, each taking 100-plus annually. Particularly susceptible to entanglement in driftnets, such as for swordfish and sharks in the North Pacific; the overall numbers involved are unknown but annual take may be in the low thousands. Tries to remove bait or catch from pelagic long lines in many areas and gets hooked

as a result (or shot in retaliation). Has been captured for public display and research in the US and Japan. As a top predator, it is a repository of heavy metals and organochlorines, which accumulate through the marine food chain. Sometimes hit by vessels, due to its tendency to rest motionless on the surface. Noise pollution from commercial shipping, marine construction, seismic testing and military sonar may also be a threat in some areas. May also be threatened by the overfishing of prey species.

VOCALISATIONS

Complex repertoire of sounds is used in foraging and social communication. As well as echolocating for navigation and finding prey, it produces specific tonal and pulsed calls for social communication and foraging (essentially to maintain contact). Calls are generally more complex with active behaviour, and simpler with less active behaviour. They are of a higher frequency (mean 7.9kHz) and a wider frequency range than those of long-finned pilot whales. Matrilines may have distinct call repertoires (similar in nature to the pod-specific dialects of killer whales) and there may even be individual signatures.

LIFE HISTORY

Sexual maturity Females 8–9 years, males 13–17 years (though male does not mate successfully until several years later); females continue to grow until c. 22 years, males until c. 27 years.

Mating Presumed polygynandrous (both males and females have multiple mating partners); males may move between family groups to mate.

Gestation 14–16 months.

Calving Every 3–5 years, up to eight years in older females (average female has 4–5 calves in her lifetime); single calf born year-round, with peaks in spring and autumn in southern hemisphere, autumn and winter in most northern hemisphere populations (though in Hawaii and southern Japan, July–November, peaking in July).

Weaning After 2–3 years or longer (but post-reproductive female may continue to suckle last calf for up to seven years (females) or 15 years (males), perhaps to give reproductive edge); calves can eat solid food from c. six months.

Lifespan Females at least 60 years, males 35–45 years (oldest recorded male 46 years, female 63 years); females go through menopause (like killer whales) when c. 35–40 years; older, non-breeding females may provide babysitting services and/or be keepers of ecological wisdom.

LONG-FINNED PILOT WHALE
Globicephala melas

(Traill, 1809)

With experience, it is possible to tell the sex and approximate age of long-finned and short-finned pilot whales by looking at their dorsal fins: they change shape as they grow older and are quite different on females and males. The adult male pilot whale's fin is like no other: low in profile and exceptionally broad-based (the base can be more than twice as long as the fin is tall).

Classification Odontoceti, family Delphinidae.
Common name 'Long-finned' for the length of the flippers or pectoral fins (cf. short-finned), 'pilot' from an early theory that there is a leader, a cetacean navigator that pilots the group, and that the others continue to follow even if it means certain death.
Other names Longfin pilot whale, Atlantic pilot whale, northern pilot whale, caaing whale, pothead (after the bulbous melon), blackfish (refers to an informal grouping of six dark-coloured members of the dolphin family, all with 'whale' in their name).
Scientific name *Globicephala* from the Latin *globus* for 'sphere', 'globe' or 'round', and the Greek *kephale* for 'head' (a reference to the bulbous melon); *melas* is Greek for 'black'.
Taxonomy Three subspecies recognised: North Atlantic long-finned pilot whale (*G. melas melas*), southern long-finned pilot whale (*G. m. edwardii*), and an unnamed subspecies in Japanese waters (now extinct) known as the North Pacific long-finned pilot whale; species status has been argued for the two extant taxa. There is also some morphological evidence, as well as different ecological markers such as fatty acids, suggesting that the northern subspecies may consist of two ecotypes, in the north-east Atlantic and north-west Atlantic (possibly separated geographically by the gyre currents).

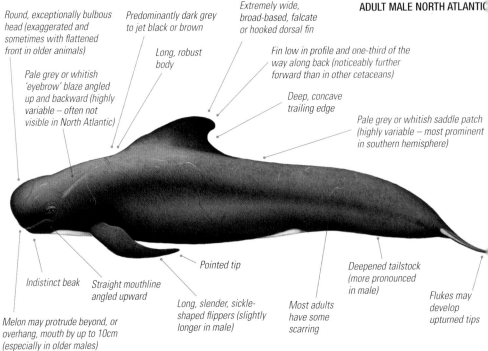

ADULT MALE NORTH ATLANTIC

Round, exceptionally bulbous head (exaggerated and sometimes with flattened front in older animals)

Pale grey or whitish 'eyebrow' blaze angled up and backward (highly variable – often not visible in North Atlantic)

Predominantly dark grey to jet black or brown

Long, robust body

Extremely wide, broad-based, falcate or hooked dorsal fin

Fin low in profile and one-third of the way along back (noticeably further forward than in other cetaceans)

Deep, concave trailing edge

Pale grey or whitish saddle patch (highly variable – most prominent in southern hemisphere)

Indistinct beak

Straight mouthline angled upward

Melon may protrude beyond, or overhang, mouth by up to 10cm (especially in older males)

Pointed tip

Long, slender, sickle-shaped flippers (slightly longer in male)

Most adults have some scarring

Deepened tailstock (more pronounced in male)

Flukes may develop upturned tips

AT A GLANCE
- Cold waters of North Atlantic and southern hemisphere
- Medium size
- Black, blackish or brownish
- Rounded, bulbous melon
- Indistinct beak
- Broad-based, backswept dorsal fin far forward
- Small to large groups

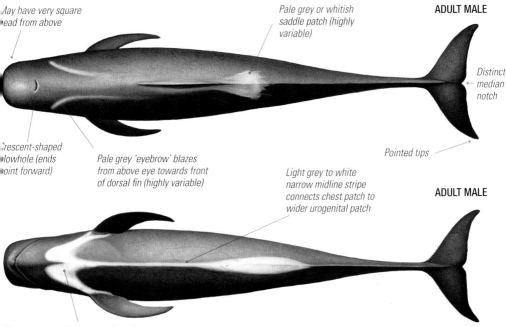

ADULT MALE

May have very square head from above

Pale grey or whitish saddle patch (highly variable)

Distinct median notch

Crescent-shaped blowhole (ends point forward)

Pale grey 'eyebrow' blazes from above eye towards front of dorsal fin (highly variable)

Pointed tips

Light grey to white narrow midline stripe connects chest patch to wider urogenital patch

ADULT MALE

Light grey to white anchor-shaped patch on chest (visible when animal spyhops)

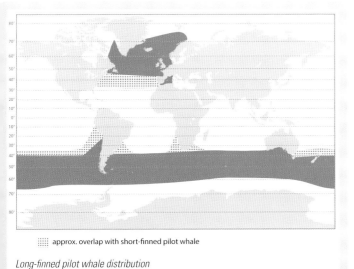

SIZE

L: ♂ 4–6.7m, ♀ 3.8–5.7m; **WT:** 1.3–2.3t;
MAX: 6.7m, 2.3t
Calf – L: 1.7–1.8m; **WT:** c. 75–80kg
Males up to c. 1m longer than females.

SIMILAR SPECIES

There is some range overlap with short-finned pilot whales. The morphological differences between the two species are subtle (relative length and shape of the flippers, differences in skull shape, and tooth count) and it is difficult (if not impossible) to tell them apart at sea (except perhaps with a clear view of the flippers). The flippers and shape of the skull are the only definitive physical characteristics: the long-finned has a narrower skull, while the short-finned skull is shorter and broader. There is some evidence of hybridisation between the two species in the north-east Atlantic. Confusion with false killer whales is possible in the warmer parts of its range, but the false killer's head is more tapered and the dorsal fin is more slender, more erect and farther back on the body.

DISTRIBUTION

The two extant subspecies are widely distributed in deep cold temperate to sub-polar waters of the North Atlantic and southern hemisphere, and are separated by a wide tropical belt. In the North Atlantic it ranges no further south than approximately the Tropic of Cancer, as far north as 65°N in the west and 75°N in the east, and occurs in the Gulf

:::: approx. overlap with short-finned pilot whale

Long-finned pilot whale distribution

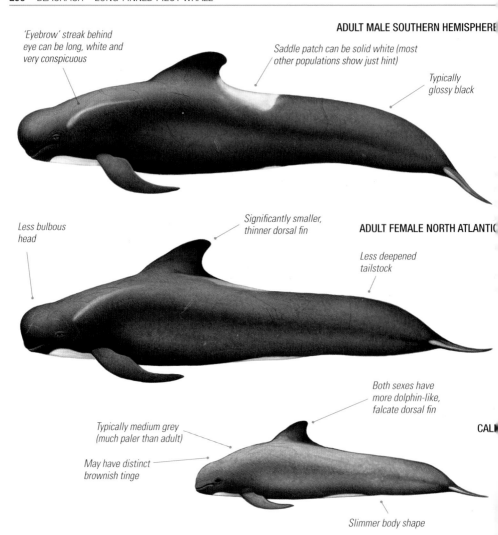

ADULT MALE SOUTHERN HEMISPHERE

'Eyebrow' streak behind eye can be long, white and very conspicuous

Saddle patch can be solid white (most other populations show just hint)

Typically glossy black

ADULT FEMALE NORTH ATLANTIC

Less bulbous head

Significantly smaller, thinner dorsal fin

Less deepened tailstock

Both sexes have more dolphin-like, falcate dorsal fin

CALF

Typically medium grey (much paler than adult)

May have distinct brownish tinge

Slimmer body shape

DIVE SEQUENCE
- Quite leisurely dive sequence.
- Head raised relatively high above surface (eyes often visible).
- Creates distinctive bow wave in calm seas.
- Dorsal fin and large portion of back clearly visible.
- Tailstock strongly arches.
- Flukes sometimes lifted above surface before deep dive.
- Several whales typically surface close together.
- May porpoise while travelling.
- Occasionally spyhops.

BLOW
- Strong, low, bushy blow (up to c. 1m), quite conspicuous in calm weather (but tends to dissipate quickly).

FLIPPER COMPARISON

*Gently curved
leading edge*

*14–19 per cent
of body length*

short-finned pilot whale

*Strongly angled
leading edge
(forms 'elbow')*

*18–27 per cent of body
length (occasionally
14–30 per cent)*

long-finned pilot whale

...f St Lawrence, North Sea, western Mediterranean Sea ...especially the Alboran Sea) and as far north as the Barents ...ea. In the southern hemisphere, it occurs mostly from ...bout 30°S (14°S off the west coast of South America) ...o beyond the Antarctic Convergence (at least 68°S in ...he central South Pacific). Prefers the continental shelf ...reak, continental and island slope waters, and areas with ...omplex topography such as seamounts and ridges. In the ...vestern North Atlantic, it is found in highest densities over ...he continental slope in winter and spring, and over the ...helf in summer and autumn. Most sightings are recorded ...n waters deeper than 2,000m. Will approach nearshore ...reas where the water is sufficiently deep. Generally ...omadic, but may be some north–south (summer–winter) ...novements, such as in the north-east Atlantic. Seasonal ...nshore–offshore (winter/early spring–summer/autumn) ...novements are related to the seasonal spawning ...nigrations of squid and mackerel. Previously in the western ...Jorth Pacific (skulls dating back to the twelfth century have ...een found in Japan) but it now appears to be extinct there ...erhaps exterminated by early drive fisheries).

BEHAVIOUR

Often observed in mixed species aggregations, particularly with common minke whales, Atlantic white-sided dolphins and common bottlenose dolphins, but with other species as well. Regularly chases away fish-eating killer whales in the Strait of Gibraltar. Less aerially active than the short-finned pilot whale, often spyhopping and lobtailing but only occasionally breaching. Spends much of the day logging (resting) at the surface (especially at sunrise, after a night of foraging).

Male's larger size and enlarged features may be for display or for increased mate access, or may aid in defence from attacks by killer whales and sharks. More prone to mass strandings than almost any other cetacean (apart from the short-finned pilot whale), probably in part because of its strong social bonds. Will grieve for dead members of the group and will carry a dead calf around for hours or days.

Reaction to boats varies according to location, but may approach slow-moving boats or behave indifferently (if the boat does not approach too quickly). Rarely bow-rides.

...e distinctive light anchor-shaped patch on the chest is clearly visible when long-finned pilot whales spyhop.

FOOD AND FEEDING

Prey Mainly squid (including northern short-finned squid, European flying squid, armhook squid, greater hooked squid) and other cephalopods; some small to medium-sized fish (including mackerel, Atlantic cod, Greenland turbot, herring, hake, dogfish) especially in North Atlantic; occasionally shrimps; however, great variation according to location (e.g. in Iberia takes much more octopus than squid).

Feeding Deep foraging tends to be at night in most regions.

Dive depth Most feeding 30–500m; maximum recorded 828m (Faroe Islands) but likely capable of deeper.

Dive time Typically 2–12 minutes, depending on region and prey; maximum recorded 18 minutes.

TEETH

Upper 16–26

Lower 16–26

GROUP SIZE AND STRUCTURE

Highly social, living in matrilineal groups (consisting of a matriarch with her immediate kin) similar in structure to killer whale groups (though not quite as stable). Typical family group size is 8–20 (average 11–14 in the North Atlantic and Mediterranean), with considerable geographical variation, including all ages and sexes (though there tend to be more adult females). They remain in the family group for life. Males will mate during temporary aggregations of separate family groups. Several family groups may join together to form a pod or school, frequently with as many as 50 members, sometimes more than 100 (the average in Atlantic Canada is 110); occasionally as many as 1,200 have been recorded.

PREDATORS

No evidence, though killer whales and large sharks are potential predators. There is little scarring, which suggests that attacks are either rare or only on small individuals and usually fatal.

PHOTO-IDENTIFICATION

Nicks, scars and other distinctive marks on the dorsal fin and back, combined with the height and shape of the fin, and skin lesions. The shape of the saddle patch, if present, can also be useful.

POPULATION

No overall abundance estimate, although a very rough guesstimate of *c.* 1 million has been suggested. Approximate regional estimates include 590,000 for Iceland and the Faroe Islands, 200,000 south of the Antarctic Convergence (though this figure is old – for the summer 1976–78), at least 16,000 in Canadian Atlantic waters, 9,200 in west Greenland, 258 in east Greenland, and just over 200 in the Strait of Gibraltar. Some of these figures may include short-finned pilot whales, because of identification problems where they overlap.

CONSERVATION

IUCN status: Least Concern (2018). Hunted in many parts of the North Atlantic for centuries, including Scotland (Orkney Islands and the Hebrides), Ireland, the Faroe Islands, Norway, Iceland, Greenland, Cape Cod and Newfoundland. The Newfoundland fishery was the most extreme, with more than 54,000 pilot whales taken (1947–71) and a peak of 10,000 in 1956; the hunt stopped after it had substantially reduced the local population. As many as 350 are still hunted every year in Greenland. The highly controversial drive fishery in the Faroes continues today, with hunting statistics dating back to 1584 (and unbroken records from 1709 to the present day); during the past three centuries, more than a quarter of a million long-finned pilot whales have been killed in some 1,900 drives (an average of 544 per year during 2007–16). A drive fishery in the Falkland Islands took whales from the

LIFE HISTORY

Sexual maturity Females *c.* eight years, males *c.* 12 years (though male does not mate successfully until several years later).

Mating Polygynous; males move between natal groups to mate during temporary aggregations.

Gestation 12–16 months.

Calving Every 3–5 years; single calf born mainly during spring and summer (April–September North Atlantic, October–April southern hemisphere).

Weaning After 2–3 years or longer.

Lifespan Females at least 60 years, males 35–45 years; females go through menopause (like killer whales) when *c.* 35–40 years (though one case of pregnancy at 55 years); older females may provide babysitting services and/or be keepers of ecological wisdom.

outhern population. The tight social structure makes
ne species particularly vulnerable to drive fisheries.
usceptible to entanglement in driftnets, as well as
rawls and longlines, though the overall numbers involved
re unknown. Regular incidental catches are known off
Jewfoundland, over the continental shelf break in the
ortheastern USA, southwestern UK, the Mediterranean,
ne Atlantic coast of France, southern Brazil and
lsewhere. As a top predator, it is a repository of heavy
netals and organochlorines, and North Atlantic animals
re particularly heavily contaminated. Sometimes hit by
essels, due to its tendency to rest motionless on the
urface. Noise pollution from commercial shipping, marine
onstruction, seismic testing and military sonar may
lso be a threat in some areas. In 2006–07 there was an
utbreak of morbillivirus among long-finned pilot whales

in the Mediterranean, responsible for at least 60 deaths.
May also be threatened by the overfishing of prey species,
and it has been captured for public display and research.

VOCALISATIONS
Complex repertoire of sounds is used in foraging and
social communication. As well as echolocating for
navigation and finding prey, it produces specific tonal
and pulsed calls for social communication and foraging
(essentially to maintain contact). Calls are generally more
complex with active behaviour and simpler with less active
behaviour. They are of a lower frequency (mean 4.4kHz)
and a narrower frequency range than those of short-finned
pilot whales. Matrilines may have distinct call repertoires
(similar in nature to the pod-specific dialects of killer
whales) though, as yet, this has only been found in short-
finned pilot whales.

family group of long-finned pilot whales off the coast of Vesteralen, Norway.

FALSE KILLER WHALE
Pseudorca crassidens

(Owen, 1846)

Despite its name, the false killer whale belongs taxonomically to the dolphin family, Delphinidae, and it often behaves more like one of its energetic and sprightly smaller relatives.

Classification Odontoceti, family Delphinidae.

Common name From the similarity in skull morphology (rather than external appearance or behaviour) to that of the killer whale.

Other names Pseudorca (pronounced 'soo-dawr-ka' or 'syoo-dawr-ka'), false pilot whale, thicktooth grampus, lesser killer whale, blackfish ('blackfish' refers to an informal grouping of six dark-coloured members of the dolphin family, all with 'whale' in their name).

Scientific name *Pseudorca* from the Greek *pseudos* for 'false', and Latin *orca* for 'a kind of whale' (but specifically from the scientific name for killer whale); *crassidens* from the Latin *crassus* for 'thick', and the Greek *dens* for 'tooth'.

Taxonomy No recognised forms or subspecies; however, recent genetic, photo-ID and satellite-tagging studies in Hawaii have confirmed the highly significant ecological and genetic uniqueness of the two resident populations (around the main Hawaiian Islands and the Northwestern Hawaiian Islands) and of offshore animals from the central and eastern North Pacific.

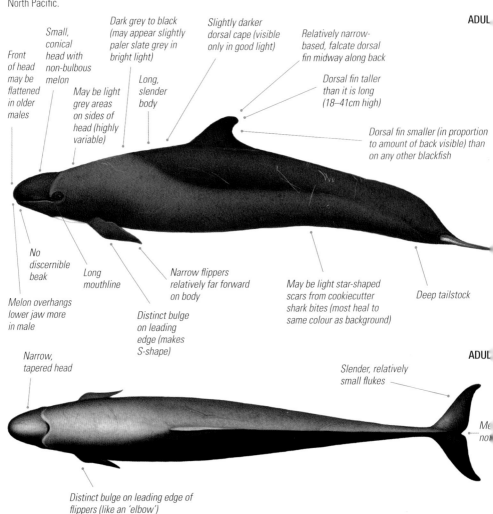

ADULT

Small, conical head with non-bulbous melon

Front of head may be flattened in older males

Dark grey to black (may appear slightly paler slate grey in bright light)

Slightly darker dorsal cape (visible only in good light)

Relatively narrow-based, falcate dorsal fin midway along back

May be light grey areas on sides of head (highly variable)

Long, slender body

Dorsal fin taller than it is long (18–41cm high)

Dorsal fin smaller (in proportion to amount of back visible) than on any other blackfish

No discernible beak

Long mouthline

Narrow flippers relatively far forward on body

May be light star-shaped scars from cookiecutter shark bites (most heal to same colour as background)

Deep tailstock

Melon overhangs lower jaw more in male

Distinct bulge on leading edge (makes S-shape)

Narrow, tapered head

Slender, relatively small flukes

ADULT

Me no

Distinct bulge on leading edge of flippers (like an 'elbow')

AT A GLANCE

- Warm (mainly offshore) waters worldwide
- Medium size
- Dark grey to black
- Long, slender body

- Relatively narrow-based, falcate dorsal fin
- Small, conical head with no beak
- Distinct bulge on leading edge of flippers
- Small, often exuberant groups

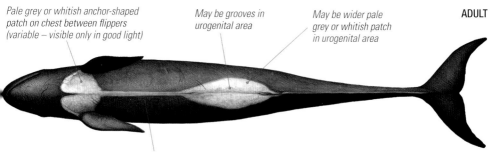

Pale grey or whitish anchor-shaped patch on chest between flippers (variable – visible only in good light)

May be grooves in urogenital area

May be wider pale grey or whitish patch in urogenital area

ADULT

Pale grey or whitish stripe down middle of underside

SIZE

L: ♂ 4–6m, ♀ 4–5.1m; **WT:** 1.1–2t;
MAX: 6.1m, 2.2t
Calf – L: 1.5–2.1m; **WT:** *c.* 80kg
Males larger than females; regional size differences (e.g. 10–20 per cent larger in Japan than South Africa).

SIMILAR SPECIES

Confusion is most likely with other 'blackfish'. False killer whales are twice as long as melon-headed and pygmy killer whales; in juvenile false killers look for the more elongated head, the relatively smaller (in relation to the amount of visible back) and more rounded dorsal fin, and the diagnostic S-shaped flippers. Pilot whales are similar in size, but their more bulbous head and larger, wider-based dorsal fin located further forward on the back should be distinctive. Confusion is also possible with some dolphins at a distance – the dorsal fin shapes may appear similar but the animals are quite different at close range. Hybrids with common bottlenose dolphins have been reported in captivity.

DISTRIBUTION

Tropical to warm temperate waters worldwide, mainly between *c.* 50°N and *c.* 50°S. Density is much higher in lower latitudes; in the North Pacific, density drops dramatically north of *c.* 15°N and it is rarely seen north of Mexico in the eastern North Pacific. Found in many semi-enclosed seas, including the Gulf of Mexico, Gulf of California, Sea of Japan, Yellow Sea, Timor Sea and Arafura Sea; it occasionally visits the Mediterranean Sea, Red Sea and Persian Gulf. Sightings in cooler temperate waters (such as the Baltic Sea, the UK and British Columbia) are generally considered extralimital.

There is little information on movements. In Hawaii, it shows strong site fidelity to the archipelago as a whole, although individuals move up

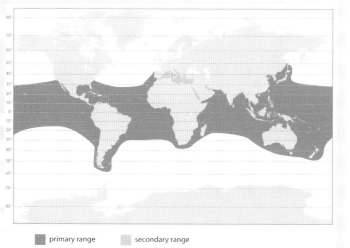

■ primary range   ■ secondary range

False killer distribution

DORSAL FIN VARIATIONS

*Fin shape
highly variable*

*Usually
rounded tip*

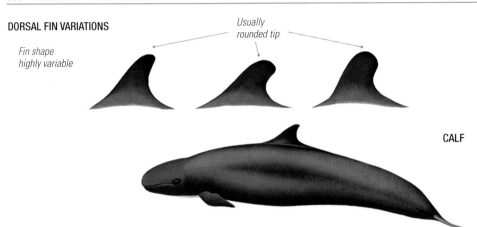

CALF

to 283km between islands. In Northern Territory, Australia, one tagged individual travelled 7,577km over 104 days (backwards and forwards – not in a straight line).

Primarily deep oceanic waters, from the continental slope and beyond, particularly in depths greater than 1,500m; it also occurs where deep water approaches the coast, especially around oceanic islands. However, it is known over the continental shelf in some areas and certain populations appear to be more coastal and occur in shallower water: notably off Costa Rica, the main Hawaiian islands, the North Island of New Zealand and western Africa (Gabon and Côte d'Ivoire); four tagged individuals in the Timor Sea off northern Australia spent nearly five months in water with a median depth of 36m (never deeper than 118m).

BEHAVIOUR

An exuberant and fast-swimming cetacean. Often leaps clear of the water, especially when attacking prey (sometimes leaving the water upside down, while striking the fish with the underside of its flukes); will often breach with prey in the mouth, and may throw it quite high into the air. Mass strandings are fairly common (likely due to strong social bonds). Resting during the day by floating motionless at the surface (which is common in melon-headed whales, pygmy whales and short-finned pilot whales) is extremely rare in the false killer whale. Regularly associates with other cetaceans – particularly rough-toothed dolphins and common bottlenose dolphins, but occasionally spinners and other species – and long-term associations with bottlenose dolphins have been documented (lasting more than five years, in New Zealand). However, it occasionally behaves aggressively towards other cetaceans. Not shy of boats and will readily bow-ride and wake-ride. May be energetic and playful around whale-watching vessels. Often inquisitive toward snorkellers and divers, and has been documented offering fish to people in the water and even boaters (like prey-sharing with other false killer whales). A lone individual originally dubbed 'Rufus' (later called 'Willy the Whale') live-stranded on the west coast of Vancouver Island, in 1987, was successfully refloated and then spent the next 17 years associating closely with boats and people along the British Columbia coast.

DIVE SEQUENCE

Slow swimming
- Head and melon break surface (eyes may be visible).
- Rolls forward and dorsal fin disappears – may strongly arch tailstock.
- Flukes rarely visible.
- Short, bushy blow, sometimes visible.

Fast swimming
- May porpoise just clear of water in low, flat arcs but often shows little more than splash and dorsal fin.
- Flukes may be visible when diving quickly.

FOOD AND FEEDING

Prey Varies by region, but mainly large fish (including salmon, mahi-mahi, yellowfin tuna, albacore tuna, skipjack tuna, broadbill swordfish, Indo-Pacific sailfish, Japanese seabass); also takes squid; will attack and eat other cetaceans (mainly injured pantropical spotted and spinner dolphins released from tuna purse-seine nets in eastern tropical Pacific – with one dubious report of killing a humpback whale calf in Hawaii).

Feeding Cooperative feeder and will share prey (even some observations of cooperatively feeding with common bottlenose dolphins); documented harassing sperm whales in the Galapagos Islands (likely form of kleptoparasitism – forcing them to regurgitate squid for false killers to eat); hunts day and night.

Dive depth Most feeding near surface, but will forage along seafloor; capable of more than 1,000m.

Dive time Long dives typically 4–6 minutes; maximum recorded 18 minutes.

TEETH

Upper 14–22
Lower 16–24

GROUP SIZE AND STRUCTURE

Highly variable depending on location, typically ranging from 10 to 60 (less commonly 2–100); exceptionally up to 300–400, and even larger groups have been reported (the largest mass stranding involved at least 835 animals). Where there is one small group, there are often other small groups scattered over a wider area. Smaller groups known as 'clusters' by researchers in Hawaii) consist primarily of closely related individuals and are of mixed age and sex; they are similar to 'pods' in killer whales, and females (and possibly males) seem to remain within the social group in which they were born. Highly social with strong bonds: long-term associations lasting up to 15 years are common. Larger groups (often spread over many kilometres – up to 20km in some cases) are likely temporary associations of smaller, more stable groups.

PREDATORS

One documented attack by killer whales (in New Zealand), and occasionally attacked by large sharks such as tiger and great white.

LIFE HISTORY

Sexual maturity Females 8–11 years, males 11–19 years.

Mating Unknown.

Gestation 14–16 months.

Calving Every 6–7 years; single calf born year-round, with possible peaks according to region (late winter in Hawaii and other areas, spring to early autumn in Japan).

Weaning After 18–24 months; stops growing at 25–30 years.

Lifespan Probably 60, possibly 70 or even 80 years (oldest recorded male 58 years, female 63 years); females go through menopause (like killer whales and pilot whales) when c. 40–45 years.

PHOTO-IDENTIFICATION

Mainly using distinctive nicks, notches and scars on the dorsal fin.

POPULATION

No overall abundance estimate, but naturally rare as a top predator. The only recent abundance estimates are for Hawaii: 150–200 around the main islands, 550–600 in the Northwestern Hawaiian Islands and 1,550 in the pelagic population.

CONSERVATION

IUCN status: Near Threatened (2018). The greatest threat is probably bycatch, which is known to occur in northern Australia, the Andaman Islands, the Arabian Sea, China, the southern coasts of Brazil, the eastern tropical Pacific and probably elsewhere. Where figures are known, bycatch rates are considered unsustainable (several hundred are taken every year in the coastal Chinese gillnet and trawl fisheries alone). It is particularly vulnerable to longline fisheries, which are common throughout all tropical and subtropical oceans; the whales become hooked when they try to take commercially valuable catch or bait from the lines (the resulting injuries can be lethal), and fishermen sometimes retaliate by shooting or harpooning them. Recent research in Hawaii shows that females may be more likely to be injured in hook and line fisheries. Some 2,643 were killed in Japan, in 1972–2008, as bycatch to reduce competition with the yellowtail amberjack fishery. Taken opportunistically as direct catch in Japan, Taiwan, Indonesia and the Lesser Antilles in the Caribbean; in the past, it was targeted by a drive fishery in the Penghu Islands, Taiwan. False killer whale meat is frequently for sale in local markets in South Korea. Some individuals caught alive (mostly in Hawaii in the 1960s and 1970s, and later in Japan and Taiwan) were sold for captive display in oceanaria. Other threats include reduced prey availability due to overfishing, ingestion of plastic debris, chemical pollution (especially from persistent organic pollutants such as DDT and PCBs) and noise pollution (particularly from military sonar and seismic testing).

PYGMY KILLER WHALE
Feresa attenuata

Gray, 1874

Despite its name, the pygmy killer whale belongs taxonomically to the dolphin family, Delphinidae. Until 1952 it was known from only two skulls, collected in 1827 and 1874. It is still poorly known, but our knowledge has improved dramatically in recent years.

Classification Odontoceti, family Delphinidae.
Common name From shared characteristics with the much larger killer whale.
Other names Slender pilot whale, lesser killer whale, slender blackfish ('blackfish' refers to an informal grouping of six dark-coloured members of the dolphin family, all with 'whale' in their name).
Scientific name *Feresa* from *féres* (French vernacular name for dolphin); *attenuata* from the Latin *attenuatus* for 'thin, reduced or diminished' (referring to the tapering of the rostrum on the skull).
Taxonomy No recognised forms or subspecies.

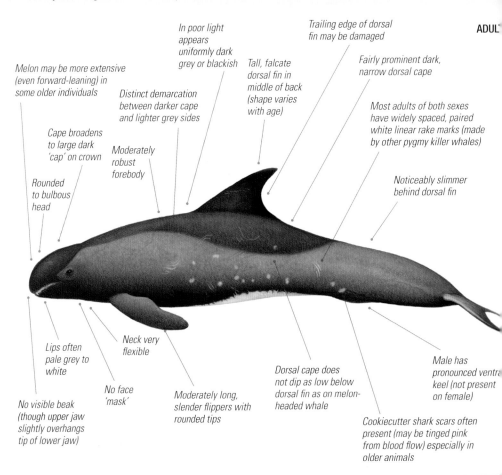

In poor light appears uniformly dark grey or blackish

Trailing edge of dorsal fin may be damaged

ADULT

Melon may be more extensive (even forward-leaning) in some older individuals

Fairly prominent dark, narrow dorsal cape

Tall, falcate dorsal fin in middle of back (shape varies with age)

Distinct demarcation between darker cape and lighter grey sides

Most adults of both sexes have widely spaced, paired white linear rake marks (made by other pygmy killer whales)

Cape broadens to large dark 'cap' on crown

Moderately robust forebody

Noticeably slimmer behind dorsal fin

Rounded to bulbous head

Lips often pale grey to white

Neck very flexible

Male has pronounced ventral keel (not present on female)

No visible beak (though upper jaw slightly overhangs tip of lower jaw)

No face 'mask'

Moderately long, slender flippers with rounded tips

Dorsal cape does not dip as low below dorsal fin as on melon-headed whale

Cookiecutter shark scars often present (may be tinged pink from blood flow) especially in older animals

AT A GLANCE
- Tropical and subtropical waters worldwide
- Small size
- Appears uniformly dark in poor light
- Distinct dark dorsal cape and no face 'mask'
- Relatively large, broad dorsal fin in middle of back
- Rounded to bulbous head
- Generally slow and lethargic
- Typically in small herds of fewer than 50

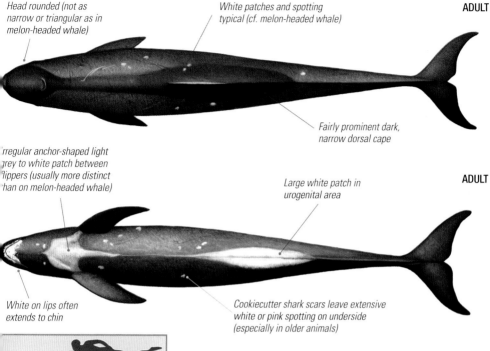

Head rounded (not as narrow or triangular as in melon-headed whale)

White patches and spotting typical (cf. melon-headed whale)

ADULT

Fairly prominent dark, narrow dorsal cape

Irregular anchor-shaped light grey to white patch between flippers (usually more distinct than on melon-headed whale)

Large white patch in urogenital area

ADULT

White on lips often extends to chin

Cookiecutter shark scars leave extensive white or pink spotting on underside (especially in older animals)

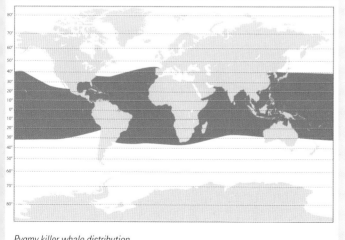

SIZE
L: ♂ 2–2.6m, ♀ 2–2.4m; **WT:** 110–170kg; **MAX:** 2.7m, 228kg
Calf – L: c. 80cm **WT:** c. 15kg
The smallest cetacean that has 'whale' in its common name

SIMILAR SPECIES
Difficult to tell apart from the melon-headed whale at sea. The pygmy killer whale has a more rounded head, a relatively distinct and straight dorsal cape that does not extend as far below the dorsal fin, linear rake marks, rounded tips to the flippers, a dark cap on the crown and no dark face 'mask'. In good light, the cape and head shape are usually the best features for telling the two species apart. Behavioural differences can separate them at a distance: the pygmy killer whale tends to be a slow swimmer and does not porpoise. Group size is another indicator: if there are fewer than 50 they are more likely to be pygmy killers.

DISTRIBUTION
Tropical and sub-tropical waters worldwide, between 40°N and 35°S, overlapping almost exactly with the melon-headed whale. Rare records from higher latitudes are usually associated with incursions of warm-water currents. Most sightings are in deep waters offshore from the continental shelf seaward, and around oceanic islands where deep, clear waters are found near the coast; Hawaii appears to be an exception, where they are resident on the island slopes. There are no known migrations or regular movement patterns, and the

Pygmy killer whale distribution

HEAD VARIATIONS

FLIPPER COMPARISON

Melon-headed whale   *Pygmy killer whale*   *False killer whale*

  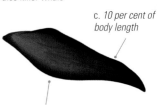

c. *20 per cent of body length*

c. *18–23 per cent of body length*

c. *10 per cent of body length*

Slightly convex leading edge, straight trailing edge

Accutely pointed tip

Convex leading edge, concave trailing edge

Rounded tip

Characteristic 'elbow' on leading edge gives S-shaped appearance

species appears to be a year-round resident at least in some parts of its range. There are historical records from the Mediterranean Sea, Red Sea and Persian Gulf, but these have never been authenticated.

BEHAVIOUR

One of the least-known members of the dolphin family (although it has been studied in Hawaii since the 1980s).

Pygmy killer whales can be quite difficult to spot and, while high breaches have been observed, rarely engage in aerial behaviour. Their reaction to boats is extremely variable: from avoidance behaviour (when they usually move away slowly and calmly) to curiosity. It is worth stopping and putting the boat in neutral 50–100m away to see if they will spyhop or approach; they can be curious about boats

DIVE SEQUENCE
- Usually slow, sluggish swimmer.
- Surfaces quietly and discreetly, and rarely porpoises.
- Keeps low profile as it surfaces with top of head, back and dorsal fin visible.
- Gentle rolls as it dives.
- Tail flukes rarely visible.
- Herd often swims shoulder to shoulder in coordinated 'chorus line'.

BLOW
- Blow rarely visible.

FOOD AND FEEDING
Prey Mostly squid and fish; known to attack and possibly eat other dolphins in eastern tropical Pacific; believed to take bait or fish off fishermen's hooks in Hawaii.
Feeding Most feeding seems to occur at night.
Dive depth Believed to feed at depth; in Hawaii, most commonly seen in water 500–3,500m deep.
Dive time Unknown.

nat are motionless and will occasionally bow-ride slow-moving vessels. In captivity, they can be very aggressive towards keepers and other cetaceans – charging, biting, jaw-snapping and even growling – and will kill other animals in the tank. Mass strandings have been recorded, especially in Taiwan and off the coasts of Florida and Georgia in the United States. They spend most of the day travelling slowly, socialising or resting motionless at the surface (frequently lying with just the back visible and the dorsal fin mostly underwater, or rolling onto one side with the head partially or fully out of the water). Occasionally seen in mixed groups with short-finned pilot whales and known to bow-ride alongside rough-toothed dolphins.

EETH
pper 16–22
ower 22–26

ROUP SIZE AND STRUCTURE
sually 12–50, although they have been encountered in airs and herds of up to several hundred; the average group size in Hawaii is nine. Bonds within a herd appear to be strong and enduring (but it is not known whether they are closely related or just long-term companions).

PREDATORS
Large sharks and, probably, killer whales. The location of bite wounds on their backs suggests that they roll over as a defence mechanism if they detect a shark about to bite (to protect the more vulnerable belly).

POPULATION
No overall abundance estimate. It could be a naturally rare species and/or its cryptic behaviour could explain why it is rarely seen. Approximate regional estimates include 39,000 in the eastern tropical Pacific (1993); 400 in the northern Gulf of Mexico (2006); and as many as 3,500 in the Hawaiian archipelago (2017).

CONSERVATION
IUCN status: Least Concern (2017). No regular large hunts are known, but pygmy killer whales are taken in small numbers in harpoon and drive fisheries in St Vincent in the Caribbean, Japan, Taiwan, Sri Lanka, the Philippines and Indonesia, either as food or to be used as bait in other fisheries. Relatively small numbers are also caught as bycatch in fisheries. They are believed to be vulnerable to chemical and noise pollution (including military sonar and seismic surveying), and overfishing of prey stocks.

LIFE HISTORY
Virtually nothing known. Calf born in August–October (based on very limited evidence).

ygmy killer whale in Hawaii: notice the rounded flipper tips.

MELON-HEADED WHALE
Peponocephala electra

(Gray, 1846)

Despite its name, the melon-headed whale belongs taxonomically to the dolphin family, Delphinidae. It was known only from skeletons until the 1960s, but nowadays is seen regularly in several parts of the world.

Classification Odontoceti, family Delphinidae.
Common name After the shape of the head.
Other names Electra dolphin, little killer whale, many-toothed blackfish, little blackfish, Hawaiian blackfish ('blackfish' refers to an informal grouping of six dark-coloured members of the dolphin family, all with 'whale' in their name); sometimes affectionately called a 'pep', after the scientific name.
Scientific name *Peponocephala* from the Greek *pepon* for 'melon' or Latin *pepo* for 'pumpkin', and the Greek *kephale* for 'head'; *electra* either from the sea nymph *Electra* in Greek mythology, or from the Greek *elektra* for 'amber' (the colour of the bones).
Taxonomy No recognised forms or subspecies.

ADULT MALE

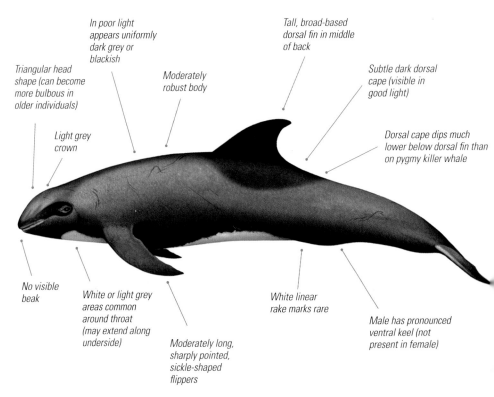

In poor light appears uniformly dark grey or blackish

Tall, broad-based dorsal fin in middle of back

Triangular head shape (can become more bulbous in older individuals)

Moderately robust body

Subtle dark dorsal cape (visible in good light)

Light grey crown

Dorsal cape dips much lower below dorsal fin than on pygmy killer whale

No visible beak

White or light grey areas common around throat (may extend along underside)

Moderately long, sharply pointed, sickle-shaped flippers

White linear rake marks rare

Male has pronounced ventral keel (not present in female)

AT A GLANCE
- Tropical and subtropical waters worldwide
- Small size
- Indistinct dark dorsal cape and face 'mask' visible in good light
- Appears uniformly dark in poor light
- Tall, broad-based dorsal fin in middle of back
- Triangular, pointed head
- May swim at high speed
- Typically in large herds of 100+

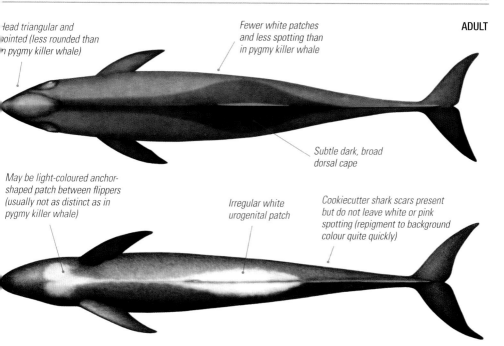

Head triangular and pointed (less rounded than in pygmy killer whale)

Fewer white patches and less spotting than in pygmy killer whale

ADULT

Subtle dark, broad dorsal cape

May be light-coloured anchor-shaped patch between flippers (usually not as distinct as in pygmy killer whale)

Irregular white urogenital patch

Cookiecutter shark scars present but do not leave white or pink spotting (repigment to background colour quite quickly)

SIZE

L: ♂ 2.4–2.7m, ♀ 2.3–2.6m;
WT: 160–210kg; **MAX** 2.8m, 275kg
Calf – L: 1–1.2m; **WT:** *c.* 15kg

SIMILAR SPECIES

Difficult to tell apart from the pygmy killer whale at sea. The melon-headed has a more pointed and triangular head, a relatively indistinct dorsal cape that dips well below the dorsal fin, no linear rake marks, sharply pointed flippers, a light (instead of dark) crown, and a dark face 'mask'. In good light, the cape and head shape are usually the best features for telling the two species apart. Group size is another indicator: if there are more than 100, they are more likely to be melon-headed.

DISTRIBUTION

Tropical and sub-tropical waters worldwide, overlapping almost exactly with the pygmy killer whale. Most records are between 20°N and 20°S, and it is rarely seen north of 40°N or south of 35°S (rare records from higher latitudes are usually associated with incursions of warm-water currents). Most sightings are in deep waters offshore from the continental shelf edge seaward, and around oceanic islands where deep, clear waters are found near the coast. It seems to be drawn to areas of equatorial upwelling. There no known migrations or regular movement patterns, and it appears to be a year-round resident in at least some parts of its range; there is some evidence of inshore movements during the day (for resting and socialising) and offshore movements to feed at night.

Melon-headed whale distribution

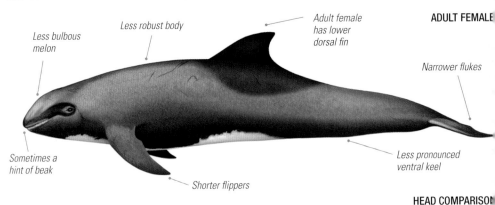

ADULT FEMALE

Less bulbous melon

Less robust body

Adult female has lower dorsal fin

Narrower flukes

Sometimes a hint of beak

Shorter flippers

Less pronounced ventral keel

HEAD COMPARISON

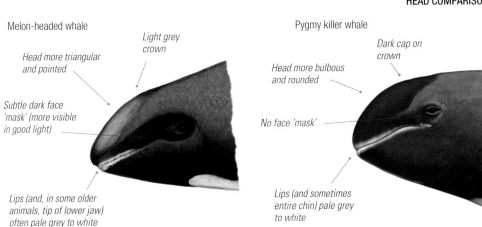

Melon-headed whale

Head more triangular and pointed

Light grey crown

Subtle dark face 'mask' (more visible in good light)

Lips (and, in some older animals, tip of lower jaw) often pale grey to white

Pygmy killer whale

Dark cap on crown

Head more bulbous and rounded

No face 'mask'

Lips (and sometimes entire chin) pale grey to white

DORSAL FIN VARIATION

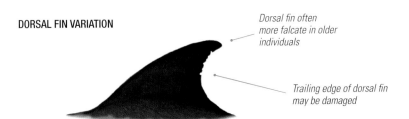

Dorsal fin often more falcate in older individuals

Trailing edge of dorsal fin may be damaged

DIVE SEQUENCE
Slow swimming
- Blow rarely visible.
- Head and melon break surface briefly before dorsal fin appears.
- Tail flukes rarely visible.

Fast swimming
- Blow rarely visible.
- Porpoises clear of water or skims the surface, producing much spray.

BEHAVIOUR

Melon-headed whales are usually encountered in large, dense, fast-swimming herds, which are notorious for suddenly changing direction. They are often in mixed aggregations with Fraser's dolphins, and have been observed with spinner, Atlantic spotted, pantropical spotted, common bottlenose and rough-toothed dolphins, short-finned pilot whales and humpback whales. They are also seen in association with Parkinson's and other petrels. They tend to flee from approaching vessels in the eastern tropical Pacific, but will enthusiastically bow-ride elsewhere in their range (often displacing other species from the bow). Breaching and spyhopping are fairly common, especially during periods of social activity. During the day in calm seas, large groups often rest by logging or milling about at the surface, with the tops of their heads, backs and part of their dorsal fins visible, and their tails hanging down in the water. Mass strandings are relatively common. In captivity, they have been aggressive towards keepers and other cetaceans; in the wild, they are usually mildly evasive to curious towards people in the water.

TEETH

Upper 40-52
Lower 40-52

GROUP SIZE AND STRUCTURE

Usually in large, tight-knit groups of 100–500, with exceptional sightings of up to 2,000 individuals; average group size in Hawaii is 250 individuals. Larger herds comprise smaller sub-groups (with some segregation by sex and age) that may be seen separately; they coalesce into larger groups, especially during the day.

PREDATORS

Large sharks and, probably, killer whales. The location of bite wounds on their backs suggests that they roll over as a defence mechanism if they detect a shark about to bite (to protect the more vulnerable belly).

POPULATION

Global abundance is estimated to be at least 60,000, and the species appears to be relatively common in some parts of its range. Approximate regional estimates include 45,000 in the eastern tropical Pacific (1993), 2,250 in the northern Gulf of Mexico (2009), 900 in the eastern Sulu Sea (2006) and 1,400 in Tañon Strait (between Cebu and Negros), in the Philippines. There are two known populations in Hawaii: a small resident population of 400–500 off the Big Island, and a larger, wider-ranging population of more than 8,000 (2010).

CONSERVATION

IUCN status: Least Concern (2008). No regular large hunts are known, but melon-headed whales are taken in small numbers in harpoon and drive fisheries in St Vincent in the Caribbean, Japan, Taiwan, Sri Lanka, the Philippines and Indonesia, either as food or to be used as bait in other fisheries. Relatively small numbers are also caught as bycatch in fisheries. They are believed to be vulnerable to chemical and noise pollution (including military sonar and seismic surveying), and overfishing of prey stocks.

FOOD AND FEEDING

Prey Mainly squid, but also small fish and crustaceans; may also prey opportunistically on dolphins in some areas.
Feeding Most feeding seems to occur at night.
Dive depth Typically (but not exclusively) prefers depths greater than 1,000m, feeding deep in water column; maximum recorded 472m.
Dive time Maximum recorded 12 minutes.

LIFE HISTORY

Sexual maturity Based on limited evidence, females *c.* 11.5 years, males *c.* 15–16.5 years.
Mating Unknown.
Gestation *c.* 12–13 months.
Calving Every 3–4 years; single calf born year-round, with different peaks at different latitudes.
Weaning Possibly after 1–2 years.
Lifespan At least 22 years for males, 30 years for females (oldest recorded 36 years).

Melon-headed whale clearly showing the dark dorsal cape, white lips and pointed flippers.

RISSO'S DOLPHIN
Grampus griseus

(G. Cuvier, 1812)

Risso's dolphin is the most heavily scarred of all the dolphins and the largest species called 'dolphin'. There is huge variation in colour – between individuals, age classes and regions – and this is one of the most distinctive characteristics of the species.

Classification Odontoceti, family Delphinidae.
Common name After the Italian-French naturalist Antoine Risso (1777–1845), whose account of the type specimen formed the basis of Georges Cuvier's formal description of the species.
Other names Grampus; grey, mottled or white-headed grampus; grey dolphin; historically – bosom-headed whale (for the apparent 'cleavage' in the melon); in older literature, the killer whale was also called grampus.
Scientific name *Grampus* probably originated from the medieval Latin *crassus piscis*, meaning 'fat fish' or 'great fish', then adapted to Middle French *graundepose* and Middle English *grampoys* (historically applied by whalers to all medium-sized toothed whales); *griseus* from the medieval Latin *griseus* for 'grey' or, more specifically, 'grizzled' or 'mottled with grey'.
Taxonomy No recognised forms or subspecies; Risso's dolphins in the Mediterranean are genetically differentiated from those in the eastern Atlantic. Most closely related to the blackfish.

ADULT MALE HIGHER LATITUDES

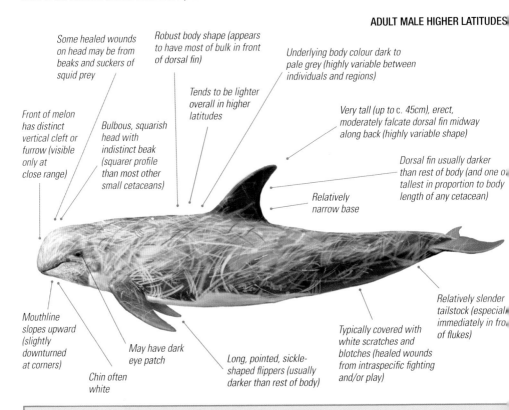

Some healed wounds on head may be from beaks and suckers of squid prey

Robust body shape (appears to have most of bulk in front of dorsal fin)

Underlying body colour dark to pale grey (highly variable between individuals and regions)

Tends to be lighter overall in higher latitudes

Front of melon has distinct vertical cleft or furrow (visible only at close range)

Bulbous, squarish head with indistinct beak (squarer profile than most other small cetaceans)

Very tall (up to c. 45cm), erect, moderately falcate dorsal fin midway along back (highly variable shape)

Dorsal fin usually darker than rest of body (and one o. tallest in proportion to body length of any cetacean)

Relatively narrow base

Mouthline slopes upward (slightly downturned at corners)

May have dark eye patch

Chin often white

Long, pointed, sickle-shaped flippers (usually darker than rest of body)

Typically covered with white scratches and blotches (healed wounds from intraspecific fighting and/or play)

Relatively slender tailstock (especial. immediately in fro. of flukes)

AT A GLANCE
- Worldwide from tropics to cool temperate waters
- Small size
- Robust body
- Squarish head (side view) with indistinct beak
- Cleft melon

- Extensive linear scarring
- Highly variable coloration within single group
- Older animals almost white
- Appendages usually darker than rest of body
- Very tall, erect dorsal fin

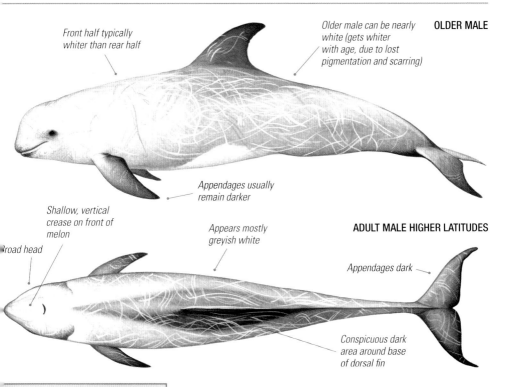

Front half typically whiter than rear half

Older male can be nearly white (gets whiter with age, due to lost pigmentation and scarring) **OLDER MALE**

Appendages usually remain darker

Shallow, vertical crease on front of melon

Broad head

Appears mostly greyish white

ADULT MALE HIGHER LATITUDES

Appendages dark

Conspicuous dark area around base of dorsal fin

SIZE

L: ♂ 2.9–3.8m, ♀ 2.8–3.8m;
WT: 300–400kg; **MAX:** 4.1m, *c.* 500kg
Calf – L: 1–1.5m; **WT:** 20–30kg

SIMILAR SPECIES

Quite easy to identify at close range – the only smallish, blunt-headed cetacean that is typically light in colour. From a distance, confusion may be possible with bottlenose dolphins, melon-headed whales, and even female and immature male killer whales (due to the exceptionally tall dorsal fin), but the extensive light scarring and squarish head should be distinctive. Hybrids with common bottlenose dolphins have been reported, in captivity and in the wild. The extensive scarring is shared by some male beaked whales, but the head and beak shape should eliminate confusion. Young, darker, almost unscarred animals could be confused with pygmy or melon-headed whales, but they are rarely seen alone. Belugas occasionally stray south of their normal range, but they lack a dorsal fin and are more evenly grey or white. The vertical crease on the melon is unique to Risso's dolphin.

DISTRIBUTION

Widely distributed in both hemispheres, from the tropics to cool temperate waters, between at least *c.* 64°N and 46°S, occurring in all habitats from coastal to oceanic. However, it shows a strong

Risso's dolphin distribution

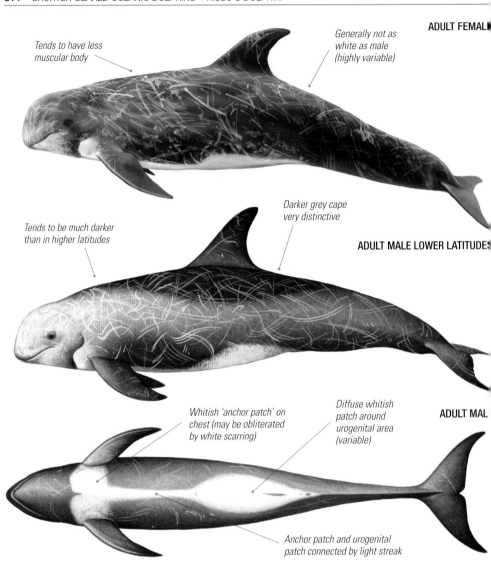

ADULT FEMALE

Generally not as white as male (highly variable)

Tends to have less muscular body

Darker grey cape very distinctive

ADULT MALE LOWER LATITUDES

Tends to be much darker than in higher latitudes

ADULT MALE

Whitish 'anchor patch' on chest (may be obliterated by white scarring)

Diffuse whitish patch around urogenital area (variable)

Anchor patch and urogenital patch connected by light streak

DIVE SEQUENCE
- Usually surfaces slowly at 45° angle.
- Eye usually appears above surface.
- Tall dorsal fin conspicuous as back arches slightly.
- Shows little of tailstock as rolls forward and disappears (shows more of tailstock and sometimes flukes before deep dive).
- Members of cluster often travel and surface in synchrony.

BLOW
- Indistinct blow (more distinct after long dive).

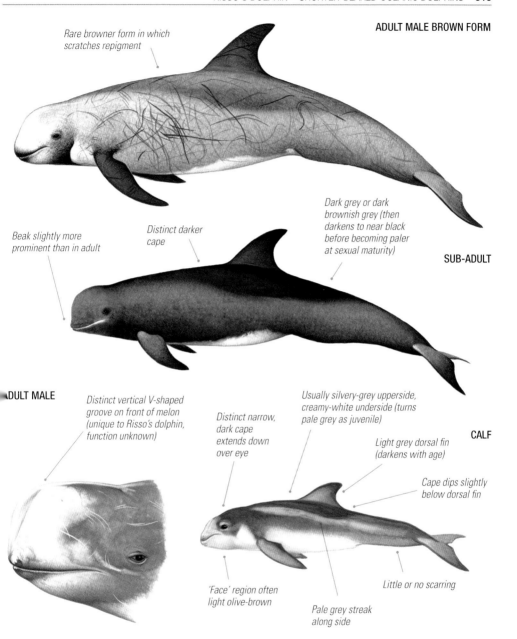

ADULT MALE BROWN FORM

Rare browner form in which scratches repigment

Beak slightly more prominent than in adult

Distinct darker cape

Dark grey or dark brownish grey (then darkens to near black before becoming paler at sexual maturity)

SUB-ADULT

ADULT MALE

Distinct vertical V-shaped groove on front of melon (unique to Risso's dolphin, function unknown)

Distinct narrow, dark cape extends down over eye

Usually silvery-grey upperside, creamy-white underside (turns pale grey as juvenile)

Light grey dorsal fin (darkens with age)

CALF

Cape dips slightly below dorsal fin

'Face' region often light olive-brown

Pale grey streak along side

Little or no scarring

ange-wide preference for mid-temperate waters of the ontinental shelf and slope, between *c.* 30° and 45° atitude. Does not occur in high-latitude polar regions. ange includes many semi-enclosed seas, such as the Gulf f Mexico, Red Sea, North Sea, Mediterranean Sea, Gulf f California and Sea of Japan, but it is absent from very hallow seas such as the Persian Gulf (though is relatively ommon in the western portion of the English Channel).

Prefers water warmer than 12°C (it is rarely found n water less than 10°C). This results in seasonal ovements in some regions, such as between summer

feeding grounds off northern Scotland and winter breeding grounds in the Mediterranean; and it could account for *c.* 10 times as many appearing off California during winter compared with summer. Found at higher densities where the temperature is more stable. Long-term changes in distribution in some areas are linked to oceanographic conditions and movements of spawning squid (it went from rare to common off southern California after the El Niño of 1982–83).

Prefers deep waters of the continental shelf break, upper slopes and submarine canyons, especially in areas

FOOD AND FEEDING
Prey Mainly deepwater squid and octopuses, but also some cuttlefish and, rarely, krill.
Feeding Most feeding appears to be during late afternoon and at night (taking advantage of nocturnal migrations to surface by oceanic squid); evidence of cooperative feeding; probably feeds by suction.
Dive depth Often less than 50m, typically up to 300m; maximum recorded 460m.
Dive time Typically 1–10 minutes, then surfaces for 1–4 minutes (typically taking up to 12 exhalations at 15–20-second intervals); research in California revealed foraging bouts of 7–11 dives; likely capable of more than 10 minutes (one report – unverified – of 30 minutes).

with steep seafloor topography (generally 400–1,000m deep). It also occurs in some oceanic areas beyond the continental slope (such as in the eastern tropical Pacific) and will enter shallow coastal waters (such as in the south-west English Channel) to feed seasonally on cuttlefish. Appears to have a patchy distribution that loosely outlines continents and oceanic islands. There is evidence that habitat use is coordinated to avoid spatial and temporal overlap with other deep-diving odontocetes, including Cuvier's beaked whales and sperm whales.

BEHAVIOUR
During daytime, it is usually socialising, resting or travelling. When socialising it can be aerially active and will breach, spyhop (often revealing the entire head and body down to the flippers), head-slap, lobtail and flipper-slap. Reported in the Maldives, off the coast of Tanzania and in other areas in the Indian Ocean to hold its flukes high out of the water, while maintaining a head-down position (significance unknown). Sometimes porpoises when travelling fast (usually when being pursued by predators or stressed). Commonly associates with other delphinids, including northern right whale, Pacific white-sided, Atlantic white-sided, common, striped and Fraser's dolphins, as well as pilot whales, and sometimes grey whales and other large mysticetes. There have been reports of aggressive behaviour towards other species that also feed on cephalopods (especially sperm, pilot and false killer whales). Readily bow-rides, wake-rides and associates with boats in some areas, but elsewhere it does not approach boats; it is not particularly shy or nervous, but typically maintains a 'personal space' and slowly turns away. A famous exception was Pelorus Jack, which escorted boats across Cook Strait, New Zealand, for 24 years from 1888 to 1912.

Highly variable coloration within a single group is characteristic of Risso's dolphins.

Risso's Dolphins often breach, especially when socialising.

TEETH

Upper 0–4 (vestigial – usually unerupted)
Lower 4–14

Teeth present in both sexes near the front of the lower jaw (usually 6–8); may be worn down in older adults (or missing).

GROUP SIZE AND STRUCTURE

Typically 5–30, but often up to 100; there are reports of as many as 4,000 together, especially off California. There appears to be a 'stratified' group structure, with a mean of 3–12 individuals in stable clusters grouped by age and sex classes. Males cluster in highly stable social units and females form stable nurseries during the calving season. Young animals appear to remain in the vicinity of their natal group for some years after being weaned, then form bachelor pods of sub-adults at the age of 6–8 years.

PREDATORS

Wounds indicate attacks by sharks and killer whales.

PHOTO-IDENTIFICATION

Using the dorsal fin – its shape and long-term nicks, notches and scarring – combined with unique scarring on the body.

POPULATION

No overall global estimate (though the sum of existing estimates is 350,000 – which would be a fraction of the actual total). Surveys off California in 1991–92 found abundance to be almost an order of magnitude higher in winter (32,376, cf. 3,980 in summer). The most recent available regional estimates include 175,800 in the eastern tropical Pacific; 11,069 on the European continental shelf (with highest densities off eastern Ireland and northwest Scotland); 18,250 off the eastern United States; 7,256 in Hawaiian waters; 6,336 off California, Oregon and Washington; 1,589 in the northern Gulf of Mexico; 1,250 in the Azores; and 70–100 in the western Ligurian Sea.

CONSERVATION

IUCN status: Least Concern (2018); Mediterranean Sea population Data Deficient (2010). Hunted in several countries, for food, fish bait and fertiliser. Risso's dolphins are caught in drive hunts in Japan (250–500 annually) and the Faroe Islands; and they are killed with harpoons or nets in Sri Lanka (up to 1,300 taken annually), St Vincent and the Grenadines in the Caribbean, Taiwan, the Philippines and Indonesia. However, mercury levels in Risso's dolphin meat (as in the meat of most small cetaceans) are high enough to be considered unsafe for human consumption. Caught incidentally in fisheries worldwide and it seems especially vulnerable to longline gear (it is the species reported most often hooked in the Hawaii-based swordfish longline fishery); occasionally killed in retaliation for stealing bait and squid from longlines. As a deep diver, it is likely to be vulnerable to noise pollution, especially from military sonar and seismic testing. Other threats include pollution, ingestion of plastic and recreational disturbance (Risso's dolphins seem to spend significantly less time resting and socialising when whale-watching activities are greatest). In the past, it has been captured for live display.

LIFE HISTORY
Sexual maturity Females 8–10 years, males 10–12 years.
Mating Extensive scarring may have evolved at least partly as way to gauge 'quality' of other group members; probably promiscuous mating system, with sperm competition.
Gestation 13–14 months.
Calving Every 2–3 years (up to four years in some regions); single calf born year-round, probably with regional peaks (e.g. summer in North Atlantic and South Africa, summer/autumn in western Pacific, autumn/winter in eastern Pacific).
Weaning Male after *c.* 12 months, female after *c.* 20–24 months.
Lifespan Possibly 40–50 years, based on skin appearance studies (oldest estimated using dental growth layers was 38-year-old reproductive female).

FRASER'S DOLPHIN
Lagenodelphis hosei

Fraser, 1956

For many years, Fraser's dolphin was known only from a partial skeleton found on a beach in Sarawak, Borneo, some time before 1895. It was sold to the British Museum (Natural History) in London (now the Natural History Museum), but languished in the museum's collection for more than 50 years before it was recognised as unique. The first official record in the wild was in 1971, but nowadays it is a fairly familiar sight in several parts of the world.

Classification Odontoceti, family Delphinidae.
Common name After Francis Charles Fraser (1903–78), a renowned cetologist at the British Museum (Natural History), who described the species from the Bornean skull.
Other names Sarawak dolphin, Bornean dolphin, white-bellied dolphin, shortsnout dolphin, shortsnouted whitebelly dolphin, Hose's dolphin, Fraser's porpoise, white porpoise.
Scientific name New genus created by merging *Lagenorhynchus* with *Delphinus*, recognising that Fraser's dolphin displays morphological features of both groups; *hosei* after Charles E. Hose (1863–1929), a British-born physician and naturalist living in Borneo, who (with his brother, Ernest) found the type specimen at the mouth of the Lutong River in Sarawak.
Taxonomy No recognised forms or subspecies; Atlantic animals may be larger, and have weaker face-to-anus stripes.

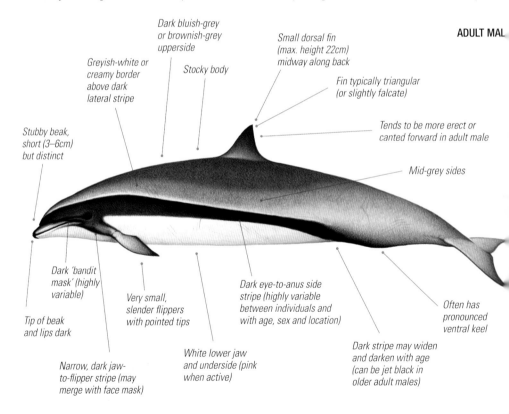

Dark bluish-grey or brownish-grey upperside

Greyish-white or creamy border above dark lateral stripe

Stocky body

Small dorsal fin (max. height 22cm) midway along back

ADULT MALE

Fin typically triangular (or slightly falcate)

Stubby beak, short (3–6cm) but distinct

Tends to be more erect or canted forward in adult male

Mid-grey sides

Dark 'bandit mask' (highly variable)

Very small, slender flippers with pointed tips

Dark eye-to-anus side stripe (highly variable between individuals and with age, sex and location)

Often has pronounced ventral keel

Tip of beak and lips dark

Narrow, dark jaw-to-flipper stripe (may merge with face mask)

White lower jaw and underside (pink when active)

Dark stripe may widen and darken with age (can be jet black in older adult males)

AT A GLANCE
- Deep tropical and sub-tropical waters worldwide
- Small size
- Stocky body
- Short but distinct beak
- Male often has dark 'bandit mask' and lateral stripe
- Small, triangular dorsal fin, flippers and flukes
- Much individual variation within herds
- Splashy, tight-knit herds leave distinct wake

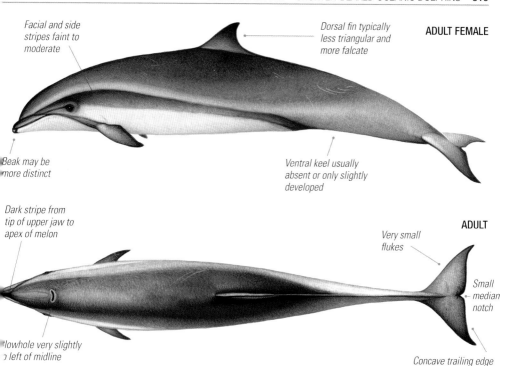

ADULT FEMALE

Facial and side stripes faint to moderate

Dorsal fin typically less triangular and more falcate

Beak may be more distinct

Ventral keel usually absent or only slightly developed

Dark stripe from tip of upper jaw to apex of melon

ADULT

Very small flukes

Small median notch

Blowhole very slightly to left of midline

Concave trailing edge

SIZE
L: ♂ 2.2–2.7m, **♀** 2.1–2.6m; **WT:** 130–200kg; **MAX:** 2.7m, 209kg
Calf – L: 1–1.1m; **WT:** 15–20kg
Males larger than females.

SIMILAR SPECIES

Unlikely to be confused with any other species (although it can be difficult to pick out a small number of Fraser's dolphins in a large mixed school of other species). At a distance, the appearance of a school of Fraser's (tight-knit with an obvious wake) is characteristic. In a school of sufficient size, at least some individuals will have the distinctive 'bandit mask' and black stripe along the side. The light-coloured V-shaped shoulder blaze of the striped dolphin is characteristic (and absent on Fraser's dolphin).

DISTRIBUTION

Tropical, sub-tropical and occasionally warm temperate waters in the Atlantic, Pacific and Indian Oceans, mainly between 30°N and 30°S. Sometimes to c. 34°S (associated with southward warm-water extensions of the Agulhas Current off South Africa). Recent sightings in the Azores (c. 38°N) and Madeira (c. 33°N) reveal the species as a potential bio-indicator of climate change. Strandings in southeastern Australia, France, Scotland and Uruguay are considered extralimital (probably influenced by temporary warm-water incursions during oceanographic events).

Fraser's dolphin distribution

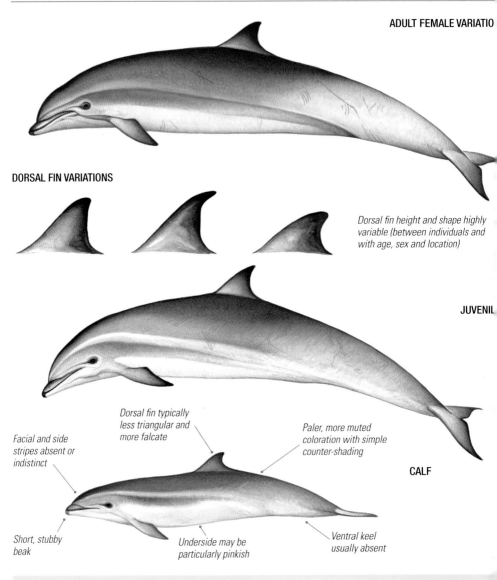

ADULT FEMALE VARIATIO

DORSAL FIN VARIATIONS

*Dorsal fin height and shape highly
variable (between individuals and
with age, sex and location)*

JUVENIL

CALF

*Dorsal fin typically
less triangular and
more falcate*

*Facial and side
stripes absent or
indistinct*

*Paler, more muted
coloration with simple
counter-shading*

*Short, stubby
beak*

*Underside may be
particularly pinkish*

*Ventral keel
usually absent*

DIVE SEQUENCE

Slow swimming
- Indistinct blow.
- Only blowhole, part of back and dorsal fin exposed.
- Rolls forward with slight arching of back.
- Tip of dorsal fin disappears last.
- Does not fluke.

Fast swimming
- Porpoises in long, low-angled, splashy leaps (large herds create much white water).

FOOD AND FEEDING

Prey Mesopelagic fish (especially lanternfish, hatchetfish), cephalopods (especially enoploteuthid squid, some cuttlefish), crustaceans; compared with other pelagic dolphins, tends to feed selectively on larger prey inhabiting deeper waters.
Feeding Unknown.
Dive depth Near surface to c. 600m; physiological studies indicate capable of deep diving.
Dive time Unknown.

Mainly oceanic, preferring offshore waters beyond the continental shelf in water deeper than 1,000m; sometimes as close as 100m from shore where deep water approaches the coast (such as in the Philippines, the Indo-Malay archipelago, Taiwan, the Maldives, and the Lesser Antilles in the Caribbean). Often associated with areas of upwelling. Commonest in the Pacific. Most North Atlantic sightings are from the Gulf of Mexico and Caribbean Sea (particularly Guadeloupe), but sightings at sea are scattered throughout the region.

BEHAVIOUR

Active and energetic swimmers, usually in tight, fast-moving schools that whip the sea surface into a froth. Frequently found in association or mixed groups with other species, especially melon-headed whales, short-finned pilot whales and common bottlenose dolphins, but also (depending on the region) Risso's, spinner and pantropical spotted dolphins, and sometimes sperm whales. Occasionally performs low, relatively undemonstrative breaches. Response to boats varies from avoidance to quite approachable. In the eastern tropical Pacific, schools often tighten as a vessel approaches, then within 0–100m suddenly explode into high-speed swimming and rapidly change direction, slowing down only when some distance away. Will bow-ride in some areas, such as the Gulf of Mexico and the Maldives, but often only briefly. Bow-riders may be displaced by other species. Occasionally strands en masse.

TEETH

Upper 72–88
Lower 68–88

GROUP SIZE AND STRUCTURE

Herds tend to be large, typically with 40–1,000 animals, but groups as small as 4–15 and as large as 2,500 are occasionally seen; mean group sizes include 283 in Hawaii, 215 in the Maldives, 50–80 in the Caribbean and 15–30 in the Gulf of Mexico.

PREDATORS

Killer whale predation has been reported in the Bahamas and likely occurs elsewhere. False killer whales are occasional predators and predation by large sharks is likely.

POPULATION

No overall abundance estimate, but at least 350,000. Approximately 289,000 in the eastern tropical Pacific, 51,500 in Hawaii, 13,500 in the eastern Sulu Sea, 700 in the northern Gulf of Mexico. Sighting rates are relatively high in the Lesser Antilles, in the Caribbean and in the Philippines (elsewhere it is noticeably less abundant).

CONSERVATION

IUCN status: Least Concern (2018). Hunting with hand-held harpoons or drive nets has been documented in Indonesia, the Philippines, Sri Lanka, Japan, Taiwan, the Lesser Antilles in the Caribbean and likely elsewhere. Caught incidentally in purse seine nets in the eastern tropical Pacific and the Philippines; trap nets in Japan; gillnets and driftnets in South Africa, Ghana, Sri Lanka, the Arabian Sea, Taiwan, the Philippines and Japan; and in anti-shark nets in South Africa. There are few figures, but in the 1990s fisheries operating in northern Mindanao and Palawan, in the Philippines, killed hundreds per year for bait and human consumption.

LIFE HISTORY

Sexual maturity Females 5–8 years, males 7–10 years.
Mating Believed to be promiscuous.
Gestation 12–13 months.
Calving Every two years; single calf born year-round, with seasonal peaks varying regionally: e.g. summer in South Africa, spring and autumn in Japan.
Weaning Unknown.
Lifespan Possibly 15 years or more (oldest recorded 19 years).

ATLANTIC WHITE-SIDED DOLPHIN
Lagenorhynchus acutus

(Gray, 1828)

Calling the Atlantic white-sided dolphin 'white-sided' is a bit of misnomer – its markings are complex, bold and more colourful than those of most other dolphins – though the brilliant white patch on either side is one of the most striking features of this gregarious dolphin.

Classification Odontoceti, family Delphinidae.
Common name 'Atlantic' because this species is endemic to the North Atlantic; 'white-sided' because of the elongated white patch on either side.
Other names Atlantic whiteside dolphin, white-side, springer, jumper (for its frequent breaching), skunk porpoise; as with all *Lagenorhynchus* dolphins, affectionately called a 'lag' by researchers (from the generic name).
Scientific name *Lagenorhynchus* from the Latin *lagena* for 'bottle' or 'flask', and *rhynchus* for 'beak' or 'snout' (referring to the shape of the beak); *acutus* from the Latin *acutus* for 'sharp' or 'pointed' (referring to the dorsal fin).
Taxonomy *Lagenorhynchus* genus is under revision: Atlantic white-sided dolphin is likely to be put into its own genus, *Leucopleurus*, in the near future. No recognised forms or subspecies.

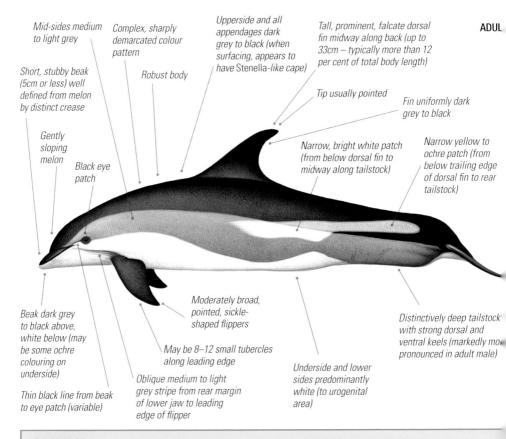

Mid-sides medium to light grey

Complex, sharply demarcated colour pattern

Upperside and all appendages dark grey to black (when surfacing, appears to have Stenella-like cape)

Tall, prominent, falcate dorsal fin midway along back (up to 33cm – typically more than 12 per cent of total body length)

ADUL

Short, stubby beak (5cm or less) well defined from melon by distinct crease

Robust body

Tip usually pointed

Fin uniformly dark grey to black

Gently sloping melon

Black eye patch

Narrow, bright white patch (from below dorsal fin to midway along tailstock)

Narrow yellow to ochre patch (from below trailing edge of dorsal fin to rear tailstock)

Beak dark grey to black above, white below (may be some ochre colouring on underside)

Moderately broad, pointed, sickle-shaped flippers

Distinctively deep tailstock with strong dorsal and ventral keels (markedly more pronounced in adult male)

May be 8–12 small tubercles along leading edge

Underside and lower sides predominantly white (to urogenital area)

Thin black line from beak to eye patch (variable)

Oblique medium to light grey stripe from rear margin of lower jaw to leading edge of flipper

AT A GLANCE
- Cold temperate to sub-Arctic waters of the North Atlantic
- Small size
- Complex, sharply demarcated colour pattern
- Yellow to ochre patch on tailstock
- Bold, bright white patch on side
- Very tall, pointed, falcate dorsal fin midway along back
- Short, stubby beak
- Distinctive dorsal and ventral keels on tailstock
- Often lively and acrobatic

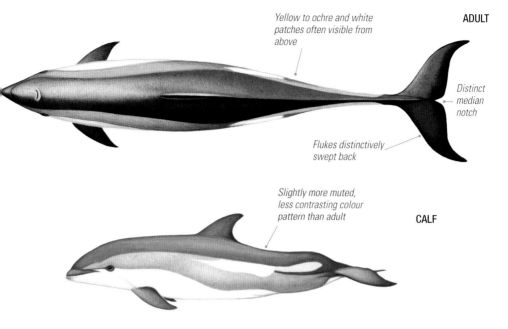

ADULT

Yellow to ochre and white patches often visible from above

Distinct median notch

Flukes distinctively swept back

Slightly more muted, less contrasting colour pattern than adult

CALF

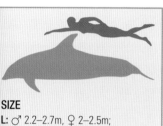

SIZE
L: ♂ 2.2–2.7m, ♀ 2–2.5m;
WT: 170–230kg; **MAX:** 2.8m, 235kg
Calf – L: 1–1.2m; **WT:** c. 24–30kg

SIMILAR SPECIES
The white-beaked dolphin shares a nearly identical range (although it extends into colder waters further north) and is most likely to cause confusion, but the Atlantic white-sided's smaller size, more slender shape, sharply demarcated markings with clear yellow to ochre and white patches on the sides and tailstock, lack of a white or light grey 'saddle' behind the dorsal fin, and dark upperside of the beak are distinctive. There can be some confusion with the common dolphin, but this species has a much longer, more slender beak, a slighter overall build and a unique criss-cross or hourglass pattern on the sides; its yellowish-tan patch is wider and much further forward. There are reports of aberrant individuals with more white or with the white and yellow to ochre patches missing from the flanks.

DISTRIBUTION
Cold temperate to sub-Arctic waters of the North Atlantic, typically within a temperature range of 1–16°C (preferring 5–11°C). In the western North Atlantic, it ranges from c. 35°N off North Carolina (mostly north of Georges Bank, southern Gulf of Maine) north to southern Greenland (possibly to c. 70°N in west Greenland) and perhaps as far east as 29°W at the mid-Atlantic Ridge. In the eastern North Atlantic, it ranges from 48°N off Brittany

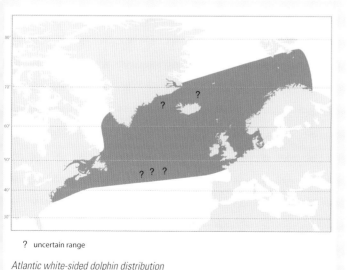

? uncertain range

Atlantic white-sided dolphin distribution

Bubbles often appear before an Atlantic white-sided dophin's head breaks the surface.

(although there are records as far south as the Strait of Gibraltar and possibly the Azores) north to at least 75°N off southern Svalbard. The extreme northerly limits are poorly known. Sometimes travels far up the St Lawrence River, Canada. It occurs in the North Sea, but there are no records from the inner Baltic Sea (there are some from the Skagerrak and Kattegat straits).

Prefers fairly deep waters with high seabed relief of the outer continental shelf and slope – primarily in 100–500m depths – but also occurs in oceanic waters and will enter fjords and inlets less than 50m deep. There are large-scale seasonal shifts in abundance in some regions: typically to northern latitudes and/or closer to shore during warmer months.

BEHAVIOUR

Lively and acrobatic, especially in larger groups and in social contexts. Will often leap and, less often, lobtail. Two categories of leaping: simple (no spinning or twisting – clearing and re-entering the water with a smooth arc), and complex (higher, and involving twists and turns in th air). Will associate and feed with large baleen whales – especially fin and humpback – and sometimes forms mixed groups with long-finned pilot whales, bottlenose dolphins, white-beaked dolphins and other delphinids. Often strands in large groups of 100 or more. Keen bow-rider and wake-rider, and will ride the bow waves of mysticetes.

TEETH

Upper 58–80
Lower 62–76
Small, conical teeth.

GROUP SIZE AND STRUCTURE

Small, possibly stable, sub-groups of 2–10, aggregation of 30–100 typical, and large aggregations of up to 500 not uncommon; groups of 1,000+ have been observed

DIVE SEQUENCE
* Briefly shows much of beak and head (including eyes).
* Yellow and white patches often visible simultaneously.
* Strongly arches back.
* Flukes occasionally break surface.

BLOW
* Indistinct blow (bubbles often appear before head breaks surface).

FOOD AND FEEDING

Prey Mainly small schooling fish (especially herring, cod, mackerel, silvery pout, blue whiting, American sand lance, rainbow smelt, silver hake), squid (especially northern shortfin), shrimps.
Feeding Known to feed cooperatively on sand lance off New England, by herding prey into tight ball against surface.
Dive depth Unknown, but likely fairly shallow.
Dive time Usually less than one minute; maximum recorded four minutes.

ff the Faroes; exceptional records of up to 4,000. Varies with location and behaviour (group sizes tend to be larger during travel and social interaction). The average group size is fewer than 10 off the United Kingdom and Iceland, 52 off New England (ranging from a mean of 35 April–June, to 72 August–October), 50–60 off Newfoundland and 60 around the Faroe Islands (ranging from one to 544). There may be some segregation by age and sex (older juveniles generally live in separate schools, at least part of the time, and some males may form bachelor groups). Both sexes disperse from their natal groups.

PREDATORS

Probably killer whales and large sharks, but there is little information.

PHOTO-IDENTIFICATION

Using notches, nicks and scars on the dorsal fin, combined with body colour and anomalous pigmentation.

POPULATION

No overall global estimate, but it appears to be quite abundant and 150,000–300,000 may be a reasonable guesstimate. Regional estimates include 48,819 in the western North Atlantic, 15,510 in European Atlantic waters (excluding Iceland, Greenland or Svalbard) and 11,740 in the Gulf of St Lawrence, Canada.

CONSERVATION

IUCN status: Least Concern (2008). Large numbers have been killed in drive fisheries historically, especially in Newfoundland and Norway; in the Faroe Islands during 1872–2009, 9,435 Atlantic white-sided dolphins were taken in 158 drives, and drive hunts continue. Still hunted opportunistically in Greenland and eastern Canada. Incidental catches in fisheries are a threat across much of the range, especially in pelagic trawls targeting mackerel, such as off southwestern Ireland (the dolphins feed behind trawl nets, making them more vulnerable to incidental catch), but also in gillnets and other gear. Also appears to be susceptible to contamination from heavy metals and organochlorine pollutants.

LIFE HISTORY

Sexual maturity Females 6–12 years, males 7–11 years.
Mating Unknown.
Gestation *c.* 11 months.
Calving Every 1–2 years; single calf born mainly in summer, with peak June–July in western Atlantic, extending into autumn in eastern Atlantic.
Weaning After 18 months.
Lifespan Possibly 20–30 years (oldest recorded 22 years for male, 27 years for female).

Atlantic white-sided dolphins can be lively and acrobatic.

PACIFIC WHITE-SIDED DOLPHIN
Lagenorhynchus obliquidens

Gill, 1865

The Pacific white-sided dolphin is remarkably lively and energetic, repeatedly leaping high out of the water and doing a variety of somersaults, backflips, spins and cartwheels. A large school of these gregarious dolphins often throws up so much spray that their splashes can be seen long before the dolphins themselves.

Classification Odontoceti, family Delphinidae.

Common name 'Pacific' because this species is endemic to the North Pacific; 'white-sided' because of the large, pale grey thoracic patch.

Other names Pacific whiteside dolphin, Pacific white-striped dolphin, Pacific striped porpoise, white-striped porpoise, hook-finned porpoise (and various combinations of these); as with all *Lagenorhynchus* dolphins, affectionately called a 'lag' by researchers (from the generic name).

Scientific name *Lagenorhynchus* from the Latin *lagena* for 'bottle' or 'flask', and *rhynchus* for 'beak' or 'snout' (referring to the shape of the beak); *obliquidens* from the Latin *obliquus* for 'slanting' or 'oblique', and *dens* for 'tooth' (the teeth are slightly curved).

Taxonomy *Lagenorhynchus* genus is under revision, and this species may be moved to a separate genus (probably *Sagmatias*) in the near future, perhaps with its sister species the dusky dolphin (it was once claimed – erroneously – to be a subspecies of the dusky). No recognised subspecies, but there may be as many as six geographical forms (three in the eastern North Pacific, two in the western North Pacific, and one in offshore waters) differing slightly in length and skull characteristics; these are not distinguishable in the field. There are a number of uncommon anomalous colour patterns or 'morphs', including all-black and largely all-white (though not albinistic) individuals; the commonest is the 'Brownell type', named after zoologist Robert L. Brownell Jr, who first described it.

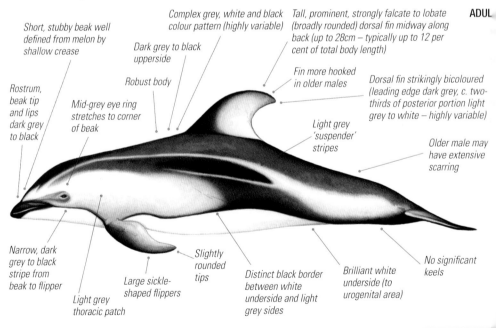

ADUL

Short, stubby beak well defined from melon by shallow crease

Complex grey, white and black colour pattern (highly variable)

Tall, prominent, strongly falcate to lobate (broadly rounded) dorsal fin midway along back (up to 28cm – typically up to 12 per cent of total body length)

Dark grey to black upperside

Fin more hooked in older males

Dorsal fin strikingly bicoloured (leading edge dark grey, c. two-thirds of posterior portion light grey to white – highly variable)

Rostrum, beak tip and lips dark grey to black

Robust body

Mid-grey eye ring stretches to corner of beak

Light grey 'suspender' stripes

Older male may have extensive scarring

Narrow, dark grey to black stripe from beak to flipper

Large sickle-shaped flippers

Light grey thoracic patch

Slightly rounded tips

Distinct black border between white underside and light grey sides

Brilliant white underside (to urogenital area)

No significant keels

AT A GLANCE

- Cool temperate waters of the North Pacific
- Small size
- Tall, prominent, strikingly bicoloured dorsal fin
- Complex grey, white and black coloration
- Brilliant white underside
- Pale grey thoracic patch
- Light grey 'suspender' stripes along back
- Short, stubby beak
- Acrobatic and demonstrative
- Tends to approach boats

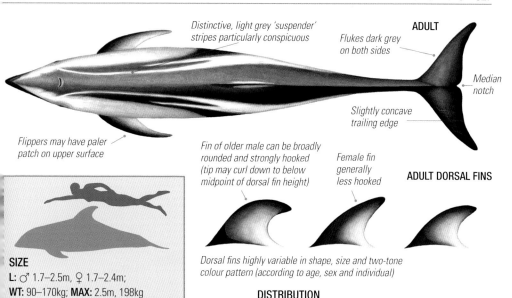

Distinctive, light grey 'suspender' stripes particularly conspicuous

ADULT

Flukes dark grey on both sides

Median notch

Slightly concave trailing edge

Flippers may have paler patch on upper surface

Fin of older male can be broadly rounded and strongly hooked (tip may curl down to below midpoint of dorsal fin height)

Female fin generally less hooked

ADULT DORSAL FINS

Dorsal fins highly variable in shape, size and two-tone colour pattern (according to age, sex and individual)

SIZE
L: ♂ 1.7–2.5m, ♀ 1.7–2.4m;
WT: 90–170kg; **MAX:** 2.5m, 198kg
Calf – L: 90–110cm; **WT:** c. 15kg
Average 10cm shorter in western North Pacific than eastern North Pacific.

SIMILAR SPECIES
There may be confusion with common dolphins at a distance, but the beak length of Pacific white-sided is much shorter, and the dorsal fins and colour patterns are quite different. Fast-moving animals may resemble slightly smaller Dall's porpoises – and can produce a similar rooster tail of spray – but the coloration, dorsal fin size and shape, head shape and behaviour are all distinctive (Dall's porpoises do not leap clear of the water and are generally in small groups of fewer than 10). It looks remarkably similar to the dusky dolphin, but there is no overlap in range.

DISTRIBUTION
Found in a continuous band across cool temperate waters of the North Pacific and some adjacent seas (including the Yellow Sea, Sea of Japan, Sea of Okhotsk, southern Bering Sea and southern Gulf of California). In the western North Pacific, it ranges from c. 27°N in the East China Sea off southern China (records further south, around Taiwan, are considered to be misidentifications), north to c. 55°N off the Commander Islands. In the eastern North Pacific, it ranges from c. 22°N just south of Baja California, north to 61°N in the Gulf of Alaska and west to Amchitka, in the Aleutian Islands. Most common at about 35–47°N.

Widely distributed in deep oceanic waters, but also in shelf and slope waters of continental margins. It is usually within 200km of the coast. Also occurs in very nearshore waters where deeper water approaches closer to shore (such as inside coastal passages of British Columbia and Washington State, and in submarine canyons in Monterey Bay, California). There appear to be some seasonal inshore–offshore and north–south movements (especially in the southern and northern parts of the range). In the eastern Pacific, increasing water temperature caused by global warming is believed to have caused a poleward shift in the range over the past 30 years (it has become more abundant in Canada and south-east Alaska, and less abundant, with smaller group sizes, in the southern Gulf of California).

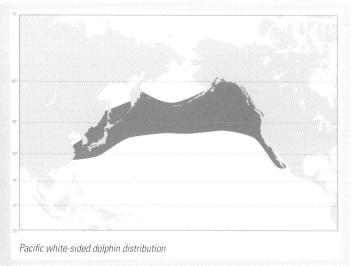

Pacific white-sided dolphin distribution

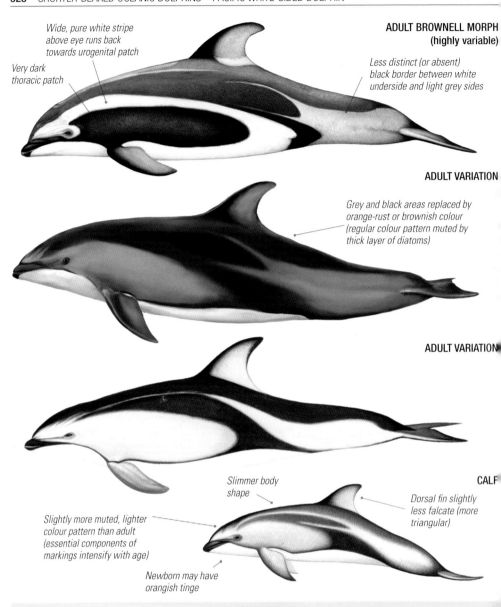

ADULT BROWNELL MORPH
(highly variable)

Wide, pure white stripe above eye runs back towards urogenital patch

Very dark thoracic patch

Less distinct (or absent) black border between white underside and light grey sides

ADULT VARIATION

Grey and black areas replaced by orange-rust or brownish colour (regular colour pattern muted by thick layer of diatoms)

ADULT VARIATION

CALF

Slimmer body shape

Dorsal fin slightly less falcate (more triangular)

Slightly more muted, lighter colour pattern than adult (essential components of markings intensify with age)

Newborn may have orangish tinge

DIVE SEQUENCE
- Typically surfaces quite fast.
- May produce Dall's porpoise-like rooster tail of spray.
- Upperside of head and back appear at shallow angle almost simultaneously (eyes visible if travelling faster).
- Strongly arches back and drops below surface.
- May porpoise with body mostly or completely clearing water.
- May cut through water with just dorsal fin showing (shark-like).

FOOD AND FEEDING

Prey Opportunistically feeds on small schooling fish (60 species, including lanternfish, Pacific whiting, northern anchovy, capelin, horse mackerel, sauries, hake, salmon, sardine) and cephalopods (20 species, including California market squid); occasionally shrimps in some regions.

Feeding Large herds cooperatively corral schools of fish into bait balls close to surface; in pursuit of prey, capable of burst speed of 28km/h.

Dive depth Offshore populations pursue fish found at depths of 500–1,000m; coastal populations mostly eat surface-schooling prey.

Dive time Average 24 seconds, with longer dives rarely more than three minutes; maximum 6.2 minutes.

BEHAVIOUR

Highly acrobatic, especially while travelling, with single leaps more common while feeding or socialising. Breaches may include side-slaps and belly-flops, and it will also flipper-slap and lobtail. Often seen in association with a wide variety of other marine mammals, especially Risso's dolphins and northern right whale dolphins (there may be consistent associations with certain groups of northern right whale dolphins); and it occasionally feeds with humpback whales, California sea lions and seabirds in mixed-species aggregations. Extremely inquisitive – it may even approach stationary boats, divers and snorkellers – and an avid bow-rider and wake-rider. It rarely misses an opportunity to ride on the waves of all sizes of vessels, from small speedboats to cruise ships, or in ocean waves.

TEETH

Upper 46–72
Lower 46–72

GROUP SIZE AND STRUCTURE

Highly gregarious, typically in herds of up to 100, but sometimes up to several thousand. Large herds are often segregated into sub-groups, according to age and sex; small, tight bachelor groups of adult males are common. Cohesiveness differs according to behaviour: they tend to travel in large, compact groups (with all members moving in the same direction and at the same speed), then split into smaller, more dispersed sub-groups for foraging and socialising. Herds can disperse over several miles (in small groups) and still remain in acoustic contact.

PREDATORS

Killer whales are significant predators. Pacific white-sided dolphins are quick to flee Bigg's killer whales, but they are regularly seen near or even associating with groups of resident killer whales (they can tell the difference between the two ecotypes). In inland waterways of British Columbia, killer whales used to corral and chase dolphins onto beaches (but the dolphins appear to have learned to avoid this trap). Great white sharks are known predators and they may be taken by other large sharks.

PHOTO-IDENTIFICATION

Scars and nicks on the trailing edge of the dorsal fin, as well as its shape and variation in the two-toned pigmentation. Researchers also use unusually coloured dolphins, such as leucistic animals and Brownell morphs, as 'herd markers'.

POPULATION

No overall global estimate, but possibly in excess of one million. The most recent estimate for California, Oregon and Washington State combined is 26,814, with numbers fluctuating greatly by season and year (in response to oceanographic changes). There is a 2005 estimate of 25,900 in coastal British Columbia waters. One of the most abundant pelagic dolphins in the region.

CONSERVATION

IUCN status: Least Concern (2018). Historically, the greatest threat was large-scale Japanese, Taiwanese and Korean high-seas driftnet fisheries for squid and salmon throughout the central and western North Pacific: during the 1970s and 1980s, *c.* 100,000 were killed altogether, before it was banned in 1993. There have been relatively low levels of mortality in a wide variety of other fisheries, such as the swordfish and thresher shark fisheries in the eastern Pacific. In 2007, Japan placed the Pacific white-sided dolphin on a list of species allowed to hunt and set an annual quota of 360; it is occasionally caught in the Taiji drive hunt. In British Columbia, there have been declines correlated with the use of underwater acoustic deterrent devices by the salmon farming industry (though these deterrents are now banned).

LIFE HISTORY

Sexual maturity Females 8–11 years, males 9–12 years (varies by region).

Mating Probably promiscuous, with sperm competition.

Gestation 11–12 months.

Calving Every 4–5 years; single calf born mainly May–September, with some regional variation.

Weaning After 8–10 months.

Lifespan Probably 35–45 years (oldest recorded 44 years in male, 46 years in female).

DUSKY DOLPHIN
Lagenorhynchus obscurus

(Gray, 1828)

'Duskies' are so acrobatic that at least some animals in a large school are likely to be in mid-air at any one time – performing the extraordinary high leaps and somersaults for which they are so well known. This is the best studied 'lag' – an affectionate term used by researchers for the six dolphins in the *Lagenorhynchus* genus.

Classification Odontoceti, family Delphinidae.
Common name 'Dusky' probably refers to the dark-coloured beak.
Other names Dusky, beakless dolphin, Gray's dusky dolphin; as with all *Lagenorhynchus* dolphins, called a 'lag' by researchers (from the generic name); see taxonony for subspecies common names.
Scientific name *Lagenorhynchus* from the Latin *lagena* for 'bottle' or 'flask', and *rhynchus* for 'beak' or 'snout' (referring to the shape of the beak); *obscurus* from the Latin *obscurus* for 'dark' or 'indistinct' (referring to the colour and/or size of the beak).
Taxonomy *Lagenorhynchus* genus is under revision, and this species may be moved to a separate genus (probably *Sagmatias*) in the near future. Its sister species, the Pacific white-sided dolphin, was once claimed – erroneously – to be a subspecies of the dusky. Four subspecies are currently recognised (but probably indistinguishable in the field): Argentinian dusky dolphin or Fitzroy's dolphin (*L. o. fitzroy*), named after Captain Robert Fitzroy of HMS *Beagle*, who illustrated an early specimen (collected by Charles Darwin off Patagonia); African dusky dolphin (*L. o. obscurus*); Chilean/Peruvian dusky dolphin (*L. o. posidonia*); and New Zealand dusky dolphin (unnamed subspecies, but possibly *L. o. superciliosis*).

ADUL

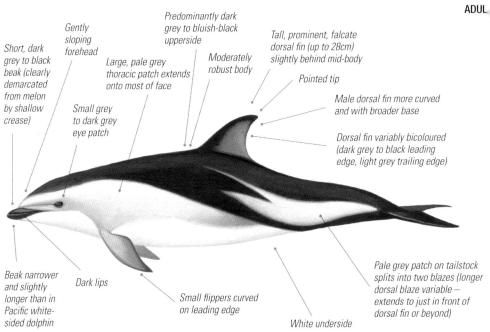

Short, dark grey to black beak (clearly demarcated from melon by shallow crease)

Gently sloping forehead

Large, pale grey thoracic patch extends onto most of face

Small grey to dark grey eye patch

Predominantly dark grey to bluish-black upperside

Moderately robust body

Tall, prominent, falcate dorsal fin (up to 28cm) slightly behind mid-body

Pointed tip

Male dorsal fin more curved and with broader base

Dorsal fin variably bicoloured (dark grey to black leading edge, light grey trailing edge)

Beak narrower and slightly longer than in Pacific white-sided dolphin

Dark lips

Small flippers curved on leading edge

White underside

Pale grey patch on tailstock splits into two blazes (longer dorsal blaze variable – extends to just in front of dorsal fin or beyond)

AT A GLANCE
- Cool temperate waters of southern hemisphere
- Small size
- Complex black, white and grey coloration
- Pale grey face and thoracic patch
- Two forward-pointing, pale grey side blazes
- White underside
- Tall, prominent, bicoloured dorsal fin
- Gently sloping forehead
- Short, dark beak
- Gregarious and highly acrobatic

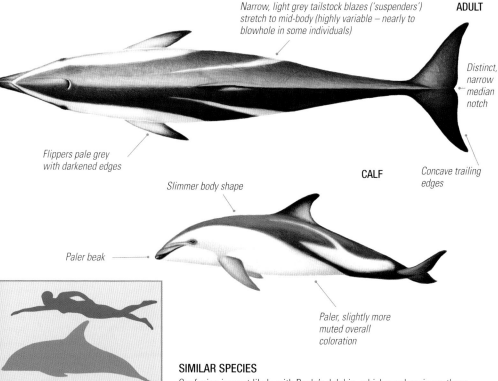

Narrow, light grey tailstock blazes ('suspenders') stretch to mid-body (highly variable – nearly to blowhole in some individuals)

ADULT

Distinct, narrow median notch

Flippers pale grey with darkened edges

Concave trailing edges

CALF

Slimmer body shape

Paler beak

Paler, slightly more muted overall coloration

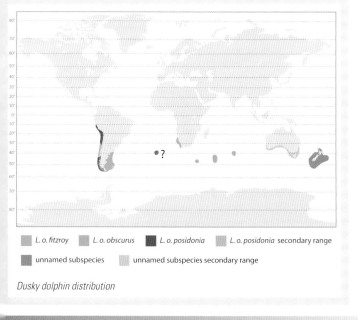

SIZE
L: ♂ 1.7–2m, ♀ 1.7–2m;
WT: 70–85kg; **MAX:** 2.1m, 100kg
Calf – L: 80–100cm; **WT:** *c.* 9–10kg
Some regional size variations.

SIMILAR SPECIES

Confusion is most likely with Peale's dolphin, which overlaps in southern South America and has a broadly similar body shape and coloration. Dusky dolphin appears lighter overall, and has a lighter face and beak and a brighter thoracic patch (without a dark border line at the bottom); it also tends to occur in larger, generally more energetic groups than Peale's dolphin. Duskies look remarkably similar to Pacific white-sided dolphins, but there is no overlap in range. Hybrids with common dolphins and southern right whale dolphins have been reported.

DISTRIBUTION

Discontinuous range in cool temperate waters of the southern hemisphere. There are seven apparently disjunct populations:
1. New Zealand (including the Chatham and Campbell Islands). Associated with the cool Southland and Canterbury Currents.
2. Southern and central South America. From *c.* 8°S in northern Peru to Cape Horn in the Pacific, and to *c.* 36°S in the Atlantic (including the Falkland Islands). There may be a low-density hiatus along

Legend:
- L. o. fitzroy
- L. o. obscurus
- L. o. posidonia
- L. o. posidonia secondary range
- unnamed subspecies
- unnamed subspecies secondary range

Dusky dolphin distribution

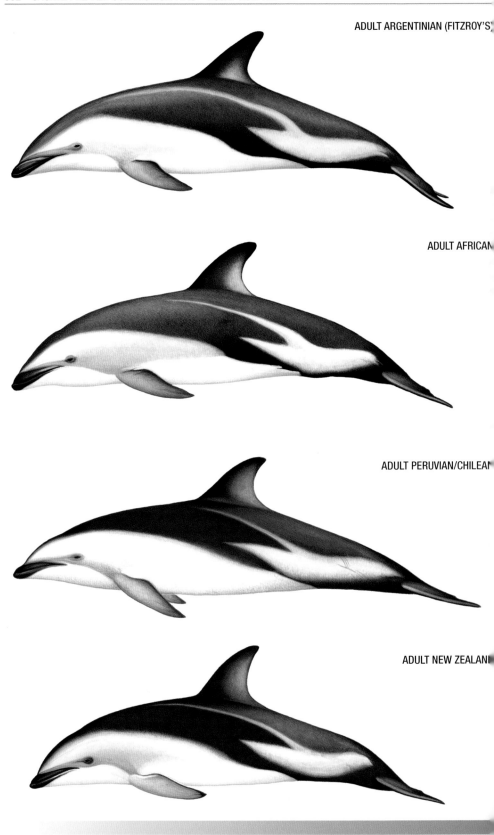

ADULT ARGENTINIAN (FITZROY'S)

ADULT AFRICAN

ADULT PERUVIAN/CHILEAN

ADULT NEW ZEALAND

HYBRID WITH SOUTHERN RIGHT WHALE DOLPHIN

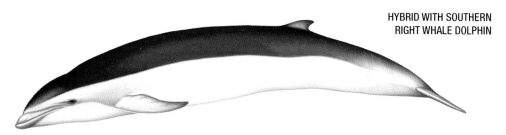

1,000km of the Chilean coast between *c.* 36°S and 46°S (although there have been more records in recent years). Associated with the cool Humboldt Current on the west coast and the Falklands (Malvinas) Current on the east coast. There is evidence that the range extends far south into the Southern Ocean, to at least 60°S (south of the Antarctic Convergence) but it is not known from any islands south of the convergence.

3. Southwestern Africa. From False Bay, South Africa, to Lobito Bay, Angola. There may be a low-density hiatus around the Orange River mouth, on the South Africa/Namibia border between 27°S and 30°S. Associated with the cold Benguela Current: the northern limit in Angola (at about 12°S) is likely determined by the position of the front between the warm Angola and cold Benguela Currents.

4. Amsterdam and St Paul Islands, in the Indian Ocean.

5. Prince Edward, Marion and Crozet Islands, in the Indian Ocean. There are no confirmed records from Kerguelen/Heard Islands.

6. Tristan da Cunha and Gough Islands (primarily Gough), in the South Atlantic. There is a resident population of 300-plus around Gough; most records from Tristan waters are 100–200km offshore.

7. Southern Australia (including Tasmania). There are occasional sightings and strandings in Australian waters,

where it appears to be a transient (probably from New Zealand).

Associated with cool upwelling areas and cold currents. Mainly coastal, it prefers shallow waters (less than 500m, typically less than 200m) and is found predominantly over the continental shelf. Sometimes in deeper slope waters, but rarely deeper than 2,000m. Prefers sea surface temperatures of 10–18°C, but will venture into colder waters.

There are various diurnal and seasonal inshore– offshore shifts in abundance, according to region. Groups with calves tend to be more common in shallow nearshore waters – often less than 20m – probably for protection from killer whales and sharks. There may be some north– south movements in summer–winter (with movements up to 780km recorded) but other populations appear to be largely resident.

BEHAVIOUR
Highly acrobatic and frequently leaps high out of the water multiple times (as many as 36 times in one bout). Breaches can be neat arc-shaped leaps (returning to the water head first); side, belly or back slaps that slam the body against the surface to make maximum splash; or tumbling somersaults. Associates with common dolphins, southern right whale dolphins, pilot whales and a wide variety

DIVE SEQUENCE
- When swimming slowly, tip of beak breaks surface first.
- Most of head and eyes briefly visible as it blows.
- Head dips below surface as back and dorsal fin appear.
- Tailstock often barely visible.
- Porpoises with neat re-entry when swimming fast.
- May cut through water with just dorsal fin showing (shark-like).

FOOD AND FEEDING
Prey Wide variety of schooling fish (including southern anchovy, Peruvian anchoveta, pilchard, hake, sculpin, lanternfish) and squid (including Patagonian squid, jumbo flying squid); feeds from surface to seabed, with huge variation in prey and foraging strategies according to time of day, season and locality.
Feeding Large groups cooperate to feed on schooling fish; forages mainly at night in some regions (on prey associated with deep scattering layer), day and night in others.
Dive depth Maximum recorded 156m.
Dive time Non-foraging dives average *c.* 21 seconds, foraging dives more than 90 seconds.

of other cetaceans. In Peru, often part of large feeding aggregations with common dolphins and seabirds. In New Zealand, near the Kaikoura Canyon, typically forages at night on lanternfish and squid associated with the deep scattering layer, socialises in the morning and afternoon, and rests during the middle of the day. In shallow bays, it reverses this trend to feed on schooling fish (such as pilchards) in the daytime. Generally approachable and curious around boats; frequently bow-rides.

TEETH
Upper 52–78
Lower 52–78

GROUP SIZE AND STRUCTURE
Ranging from two to 1,000 or more (occasionally 2,000), with group size and structure varying greatly according to season, activity, prey and location. Fission-fusion dynamics is the norm, in which groups frequently fluctuate in size and composition, as the dolphins move between large mixed groups of all ages and both sexes, and sub-groups for mating, nursing and foraging. Off Kaikoura, New Zealand, groups are larger when offshore in winter (more than 1,000) and smaller when inshore in summer (fewer than 1,000). In some regions, groups are generally smaller (3–20) in winter and larger (20–500+) in summer. There is evidence of long-term preferred – and avoided – companions and associates.

PREDATORS
Killer whales are significant predators in some regions (e.g. Argentina and New Zealand) and duskies will move into very shallow water to avoid them. Also likely to be taken by large sharks, including great white, blue and shortfin mako; dusky dolphin body parts have been found in the stomachs of broadnose sevengill sharks off Patagonia

Dusky dolphins are highly acrobatic and make frequent high leaps, as here in Kaikoura, New Zealand.

he tall, bicoloured dorsal fin is typical of dusky dolphins.

HOTO-IDENTIFICATION

imarily nicks and notches on the trailing edge of the dorsal , combined with the overall shape of the fin, and any dditional rake marks, scars or disfigurements on the body.

OPULATION

o overall global estimate, though it appears to be bundant in most parts of its range. Approximate regional stimates include: 12,000–20,000 off New Zealand ncluding *c.* 2,000 present in Kaikoura at any one time); d at least 6,600 off Patagonia, Argentina.

ONSERVATION

JCN status: Data Deficient (2008). The biggest threat is robably illegal hunting with driftnets and harpoons off eru, which began in the early 1970s. Some 5,000–15,000 e killed annually for shark bait and a further 3,000 for uman consumption, despite a 1996 ban. One estimate ggests 700 still being killed every year in a single port alaverry). Relatively small numbers are probably also ken in Chile and South Africa. Incidental capture in shing nets is a concern in most countries within its range, ough there are no recent figures. Mussel farms in New ealand may affect foraging behaviour and limit available abitat. Overfishing of prey species may also be a problem some areas.

LIFE HISTORY

Sexual maturity Females 4–6 years, males 4–5 years (varies according to location – in New Zealand, age of first reproduction is 7–8 years).

Mating Probably promiscuous mating system (both males and females mate with multiple partners), with sperm competition; no male–male aggression (males may form alliances to pursue females in high-speed chases).

Gestation 11–13 months (varies with region).

Calving Every 2–3 years; single calf born with regional peaks (August–October in Peru, November–January in New Zealand, November–February in Argentina, January–March in South Africa).

Weaning After 12–18 months (varies according to region – *c.* 12 months off Peru, at least 18 months off New Zealand).

Lifespan Possibly *c.* 25–35 years (oldest recorded 36 years).

HOURGLASS DOLPHIN
Lagenorhynchus cruciger

(Quoy and Gaimard, 1824)

Uniquely, the hourglass dolphin was formally described – and accepted as a valid species – solely on the basis of rough drawings made at sea in 1820. It is often seen, particularly in the Drake Passage, but there have been few specimens to study and it remains one of the least known of all the dolphins.

Classification Odontoceti, family Delphinidae.
Common name Wide white lateral streaks taper into a fine white line just below the dorsal fin in many animals, creating the characteristic hourglass pattern.
Other names Rarely – springer, southern white-sided dolphin, sea skunk, Wilson's dolphin, cruciger dolphin; as with all *Lagenorhynchus* dolphins, affectionately called a 'lag' by researchers (from the generic name).
Scientific name *Lagenorhynchus* from the Latin *lagena* for 'bottle' or 'flask', and *rhynchus* for 'beak' or 'snout' (referring to the shape of the beak); *cruciger* from the Latin *crucis* for 'cross', and *gero* for 'to carry' (literally 'cross-carrier', after the black markings (which, from above, vaguely resemble a Maltese cross)).
Taxonomy *Lagenorhynchus* genus is under revision and the hourglass dolphin is likely to be reassigned to another genus, *Sagmatias*, in the near future; no recognised forms or subspecies.

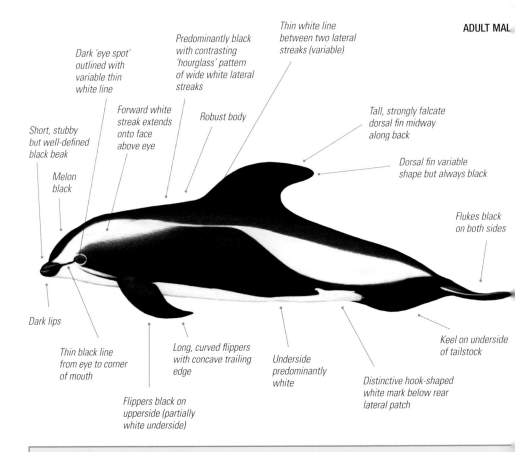

ADULT MALE

Dark 'eye spot' outlined with variable thin white line

Predominantly black with contrasting 'hourglass' pattern of wide white lateral streaks

Thin white line between two lateral streaks (variable)

Forward white streak extends onto face above eye

Robust body

Tall, strongly falcate dorsal fin midway along back

Short, stubby but well-defined black beak

Dorsal fin variable shape but always black

Melon black

Flukes black on both sides

Dark lips

Keel on underside of tailstock

Thin black line from eye to corner of mouth

Long, curved flippers with concave trailing edge

Underside predominantly white

Distinctive hook-shaped white mark below rear lateral patch

Flippers black on upperside (partially white underside)

AT A GLANCE
- Oceanic waters in sub-Antarctic and Antarctic
- Small size
- Sharply demarcated black-and-white coloration
- Tall, falcate black dorsal fin
- Porpoises like a penguin when swimming fast
- Eager bow-rider

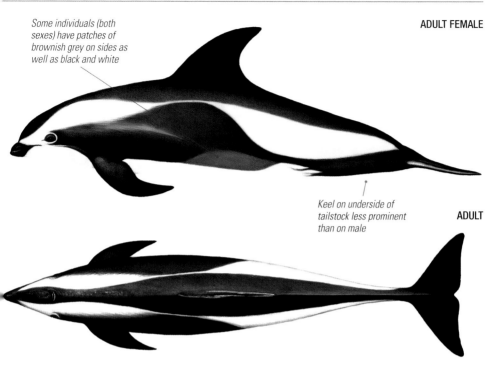

Some individuals (both sexes) have patches of brownish grey on sides as well as black and white

ADULT FEMALE

Keel on underside of tailstock less prominent than on male

ADULT

SIZE
L: ♂ 1.6–1.9m, ♀ 1.4–1.8m;
WT: 70–90kg; **MAX:** 1.9m, 94kg
Calf – L: c. 0.9–1.2m; **WT:** unknown

SIMILAR SPECIES
The only small oceanic dolphin with a pointed dorsal fin regularly found south of the Antarctic Convergence. Above the convergence, it could be confused with dusky dolphins or Peale's dolphins, but they lack the striking black-and-white body pattern. The southern right whale dolphin is black and white, and overlaps, but has no dorsal fin. The black-and-white Commerson's dolphin is mainly coastal.

DISTRIBUTION
Circumpolar in both Antarctic and sub-Antarctic waters. Most sightings are between 45°S and 65°S, with exceptional records as far north as 33°40'S in the South Pacific (off Valparaiso, Chile) and 36°14'S in the South Atlantic, and as far south as 67°38'S in the South Pacific. Found near the ice edge in some areas. Occurs on both sides of the Antarctic Convergence. Closely associated with the Antarctic Circumpolar Current, it is most often seen in areas with turbulent seas. Most sightings are in water colder than 7°C, but recorded in sea surface temperatures ranging from -0.3°C to 13.4°C. Mainly deep offshore waters but

Hourglass dolphin distribution

Bold black-and-white pattern can vary greatly in size and shape

ADULT MALE VARIATIO

Occasional individuals leucistic (showing partial loss of pigmentation)

ADULT MALE VARIATIO

DIVE SEQUENCE

Three main types of surfacing:

Slow travelling

- Blow rarely visible.
- Top of head appears first.
- Back and dorsal fin appear while head still visible.
- Head drops below surface.
- Gentle roll to dive.
- Flukes may appear (or sometimes slapped onto surface).

High, fast travelling

- Leaps at long, low angles and then swims rapidly just below surface (similar to porpoising penguins).

Low, fast travelling

- Travels very close to surface with only top of head and dorsal fin visible.
- Produces distinctive 'rooster tail' of spray (similar to that made by Dall's porpoise).

FOOD AND FEEDING
Prey Small fish, squid and crustaceans; preferred prey includes rhombic lanternfish, juvenile Argentinian hake, hooked squid, lesser shining bobtail squid, Patagonian squid (based on limited samples).
Feeding Often forages in association with great shearwaters, black-browed albatrosses and other seabirds; sometimes feeds in plankton swarms.
Dive depth Prey choice suggests feeds mainly in surface waters.
Dive time Unknown.

DORSAL FINS

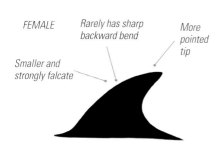

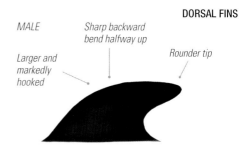

ometimes in depths less than 200m near islands and anks (especially off South America – even in the Beagle hannel – and the Antarctic Peninsula). No long-distance novements are known, but it may move north into subntarctic waters, or nearer shore, in winter.

EHAVIOUR
ourglass dolphins often associate with fin whales (to uch a degree that whalers used them to find whales) nd, less often, with sei and minke whales, southern ottlenose whales, Arnoux's beaked whales, killer hales, long-finned pilot whales and southern right rhale dolphins; there is one record of them travelling ith southern right whales. Will even bow-ride in front f large whales. Seem to be attracted to ships and will ten change course and approach from a considerable stance to bow-ride enthusiastically, or surf in the rake, remaining for as long as 30 minutes or more; they ppear so quickly that they are easily overlooked as ey slip onto the bow. Active, generally fast swimmers, specially enjoying wave-surfing in high seas, they often each and have been known to spin on their longitudinal xes. Calves are rarely seen, perhaps because they ave escaped notice in rough seas or mother–calf pairs /oid ships.

TEETH
Upper 52–68
Lower 54–70

GROUP SIZE AND STRUCTURE
Typically 1–12; groups of up to 100 have been reported.

PREDATORS
No predators are known, but killer whales and leopard seals are possibilities. One animal had wounds that may have been made by a shark.

PHOTO-IDENTIFICATION
Might be feasible using the individually recognisable variations in the black-and-white colour pattern.

POPULATION
The only abundance estimate is 144,300 south of the Antarctic Convergence, during summer, based on combined data from two old surveys (1976–77 and 1987–88).

CONSERVATION
IUCN status: Least Concern (2018). No known major threats – its remote oceanic habitat keeps it away from people most of the time. A few isolated reports of incidental catches in fishing nets, but no systematic exploitation.

LIFE HISTORY
Sexual maturity Unknown.
Mating Believed to have a promiscuous mating system, with sperm competition.
Gestation Possibly *c.* 13 months.

Calving Believed to be every 2–3 years; single calf born in southern summer (possibly January–February).
Weaning Unknown.
Lifespan Unknown, but likely to be 25 years or more.

WHITE-BEAKED DOLPHIN
Lagenorhynchus albirostris

(Gray, 1846)

Despite their name, not all white-beaked dolphins have white beaks – many are actually quite dark or flecked. Their Greenlandic name (*aarluarsuk*) means 'killer whale look-alike'.

Classification Odontoceti, family Delphinidae.
Common name After the beak colour of many individuals.
Other names White-beaked porpoise, white-nosed dolphin, squidhound, jumper, springer; as with all *Lagenorhynchus* dolphins, affectionately called a 'lag' by researchers (from the generic name).
Scientific name *Lagenorhynchus* from the Latin *lagena* for 'bottle' or 'flask', and *rhynchus* for 'beak' or 'snout' (referring to the shape of the beak); *albirostris* from the Latin *albus* for 'white', and rostrum for 'beak'.
Taxonomy *Lagenorhynchus* genus is under revision; the white-beaked dolphin is the type species and could ultimately be the only remaining member (that said, recent research suggests it is more similar to the Atlantic white-sided dolphin than other members of its own genus); no recognised forms or subspecies, but populations on either side of the Atlantic are morphologically distinct and probably do not often mix.

ADUL

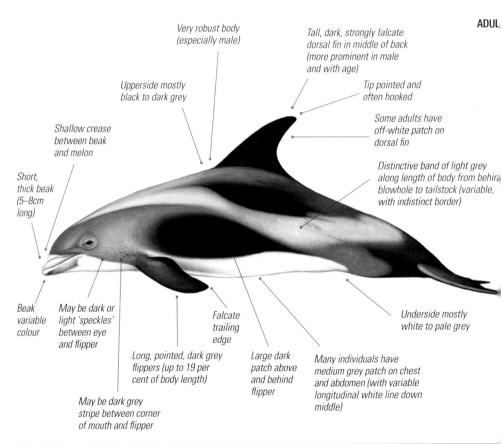

Very robust body (especially male)

Tall, dark, strongly falcate dorsal fin in middle of back (more prominent in male and with age)

Upperside mostly black to dark grey

Tip pointed and often hooked

Shallow crease between beak and melon

Some adults have off-white patch on dorsal fin

Short, thick beak (5–8cm long)

Distinctive band of light grey along length of body from behin blowhole to tailstock (variable, with indistinct border)

Beak variable colour

May be dark or light 'speckles' between eye and flipper

Falcate trailing edge

Underside mostly white to pale grey

Long, pointed, dark grey flippers (up to 19 per cent of body length)

Large dark patch above and behind flipper

Many individuals have medium grey patch on chest and abdomen (with variable longitudinal white line down middle)

May be dark grey stripe between corner of mouth and flipper

AT A GLANCE
- Cool waters of the North Atlantic
- Small size
- Complex, diffuse (and variable) grey, black and white coloration

- Distinctive band of light grey along side
- Very robust body
- Greyish-white 'saddle' behind dorsal fin
- Short, thick beak (often white)
- Tall, dark, falcate dorsal fin

ADULT

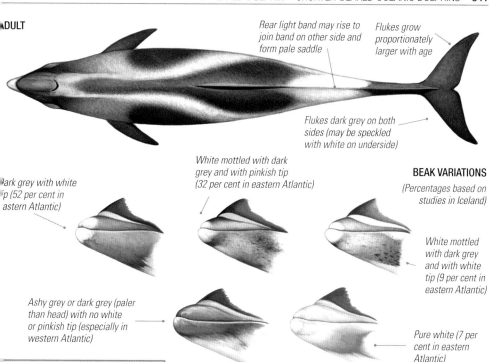

Rear light band may rise to join band on other side and form pale saddle

Flukes grow proportionately larger with age

Flukes dark grey on both sides (may be speckled with white on underside)

Dark grey with white tip (52 per cent in eastern Atlantic)

White mottled with dark grey and with pinkish tip (32 per cent in eastern Atlantic)

BEAK VARIATIONS

(Percentages based on studies in Iceland)

White mottled with dark grey and with white tip (9 per cent in eastern Atlantic)

Ashy grey or dark grey (paler than head) with no white or pinkish tip (especially in western Atlantic)

Pure white (7 per cent in eastern Atlantic)

SIZE
L: 2.4–3.1m; **WT:** 180–275kg;
MAX: 3.2m, 354kg
Calf – L: 1.1–1.3m; **WT:** *c.* 40kg
Male slightly larger than female.

SIMILAR SPECIES

Most likely to be confused with the Atlantic white-sided dolphin, which has an almost identical range. The white-beak's more robust shape, the lack of a yellow streak, the white or light grey 'saddle' behind the dorsal fin and the (usually) white or whitish beak are distinctive.

DISTRIBUTION

Cold temperate to ice-free polar waters of the North Atlantic. Range includes the southern Davis Strait, Gulf of St Lawrence, Barents Sea and North Sea. There have been occasional sightings in the Baltic Sea and Bay of Biscay, and along the Iberian Peninsula, and there are a few questionable records from the western Mediterranean. Four areas of high density have been identified: the Labrador Shelf (including south-west Greenland), Iceland, Scotland (including the northern Irish Sea and the northern North Sea) and the small shelf stretch along the northern coast of Norway (extending north into the White Sea). More common in European waters than North American. A frequent visitor to Svalbard in summer (at least as far north as *c.* 80°) and sometimes

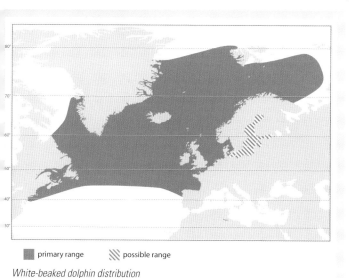

■ primary range   ░ possible range

White-beaked dolphin distribution

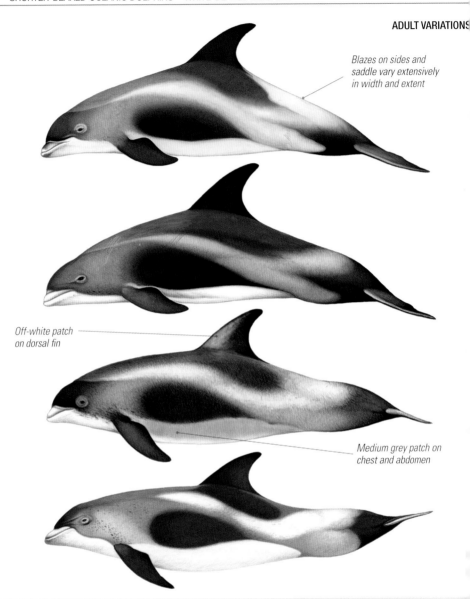

ADULT VARIATIONS

Blazes on sides and saddle vary extensively in width and extent

Off-white patch on dorsal fin

Medium grey patch on chest and abdomen

DIVE SEQUENCE

Fast swimming
- When travelling fast, tends not to porpoise cleanly out of water – skims over surface, producing distinctive 'rooster-tail' spray.

Slow swimming
- When travelling slowly, indistinct blow (small fine spray).
- Head, back and top of beak appear above surface.
- Tall dorsal fin appears.
- Gently rolls to dive.

FOOD AND FEEDING

Prey Pelagic schooling and benthic fish, including Atlantic cod, haddock, capelin, whiting, European hake; may also take squid, octopus and benthic crustaceans.
Feeding Feeds alone deep underwater and cooperatively to herd fish against sea surface.
Dive depth Unknown; one Icelandic individual reached 45m.
Dive time Very little information; average in Iceland 24–28 seconds; maximum recorded 78 seconds.

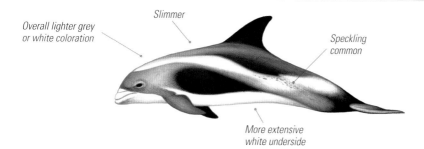

Overall lighter grey or white coloration

Slimmer

Speckling common

CALF

More extensive white underside

ccurs up to the edge of the pack ice. Prefers sea surface emperatures of 5–15°C. Mainly coastal, in water less han 200m, but also occurs over the continental shelf and eyond in offshore waters. Present year-round in some reas, but in others (especially in the far north) there is a eneral north–south (summer–winter) movement.

EHAVIOUR

crobatic, frequently leaping out of the water and erforming a range of aerial behaviours. Associates with her cetaceans while feeding, including fin, sei and umpback whales (scavenging on escaping fish), and occurs mixed groups with long-finned pilot whales, killer whales, ottlenose dolphins, common dolphins, Risso's dolphins nd Atlantic white-sided dolphins. Can be quite elusive in ome areas, but in others frequently approaches boats from distance to bow-ride and jump in the wake. Can reach peeds of 30km/h (though mean speed is 3.5–5km/h).

EETH

pper 46–56
ower 44–56
rst three teeth in each row often concealed within the um.

ROUP SIZE AND STRUCTURE

sually 5–30; average nine in Iceland, six in Svalbard, –6 in Denmark. Rarely seen alone. Some indication that roups are segregated by age and sex. Groups of several undred known, especially offshore, and occasionally ore than 1,500 (probably consisting of many smaller ub-groups).

REDATORS

nknown, but probably killer whales and large sharks specially great white). There is one record of polar bears eying on white-beaked dolphins that were trapped in ice Svalbard.

PHOTO-IDENTIFICATION

Using scarring and nicks on the trailing edge of the dorsal fin, combined with the shape and extent of lateral and dorsal fin patches and skin lesions.

POPULATION

No overall abundance estimate, but likely many tens of thousands and possibly low hundreds of thousands. Rough estimates include: *c.* 22,700 on the European Atlantic continental shelf, *c.* 31,653 in Icelandic coastal waters, *c.* 27,000 in Greenland, *c.* 7,856 in the North Sea and *c.* 2,000 in nearshore eastern Canada.

CONSERVATION

IUCN status: Least Concern (2018). Historically, has been hunted opportunistically in Norway, Iceland, the Faroe Islands and Canada (Labrador and Newfoundland), mostly for human consumption. Direct catches still occur in southwestern Greenland (40–250 annually) and opportunistically in Canada, but these are not thought to be a major threat. Incidentally caught in gillnets, cod traps and trawl fisheries throughout the range, though in relatively small numbers. Known to carry high loads of organochlorines and heavy metals. The white-beaked dolphin is particularly sensitive to noise disturbance, such as from seismic exploration.

LIFE HISTORY

Sexual maturity Females 8–9 years, males 9–10 years.
Mating Unknown.
Gestation *c.* 11–12 months.
Calving Single calf born in May–September (peak June–July).
Weaning Unknown.
Lifespan Oldest recorded 39 years.

PEALE'S DOLPHIN
Lagenorhynchus australis

(Peale, 1849)

With complex markings broadly similar to those of dusky and Pacific white-sided dolphins, the poorly known Peale's dolphin is best identified by its distinctive dark face.

Classification Odontoceti, family Delphinidae.

Common name After Titian Ramsay Peale (1799–1885), an American naturalist and artist who observed and illustrated this species for the first time in 1839 and formally described it six years later.

Other names Rarely – black-chinned dolphin, black-faced dolphin, southern white-sided dolphin, plough-share dolphin; as with all *Lagenorhynchus* dolphins, affectionately called a 'lag' by researchers (from the generic name).

Scientific name *Lagenorhynchus* from the Latin *lagena* for 'bottle' or 'flask', and *rhynchus* for 'beak' or 'snout' (referring to the shape of the beak); *australis* from the Latin *australis* for 'southern'.

Taxonomy *Lagenorhynchus* genus is under revision and Peale's dolphin is likely to be reassigned to a resurrected genus, *Sagmatias* (it would become the type species for the genus); no recognised forms or subspecies.

ADULT

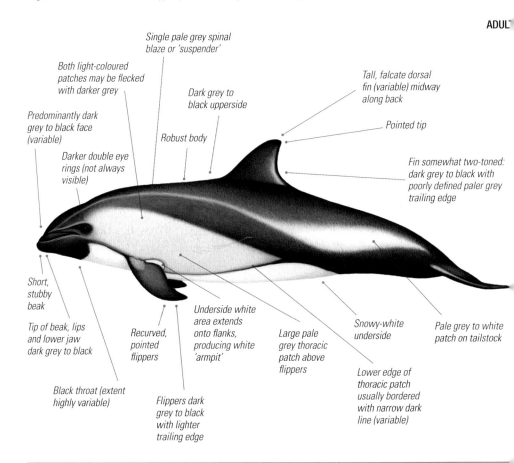

Single pale grey spinal blaze or 'suspender'

Both light-coloured patches may be flecked with darker grey

Dark grey to black upperside

Tall, falcate dorsal fin (variable) midway along back

Predominantly dark grey to black face (variable)

Robust body

Pointed tip

Darker double eye rings (not always visible)

Fin somewhat two-toned: dark grey to black with poorly defined paler grey trailing edge

Short, stubby beak

Tip of beak, lips and lower jaw dark grey to black

Recurved, pointed flippers

Underside white area extends onto flanks, producing white 'armpit'

Large pale grey thoracic patch above flippers

Snowy-white underside

Pale grey to white patch on tailstock

Lower edge of thoracic patch usually bordered with narrow dark line (variable)

Black throat (extent highly variable)

Flippers dark grey to black with lighter trailing edge

AT A GLANCE
- Shallow waters of southern South America
- Often associated with kelp
- Small size
- Stocky body
- Indistinct beak
- Complex grey, black and white coloration
- Dark mask-like face
- Tall, falcate dorsal fin

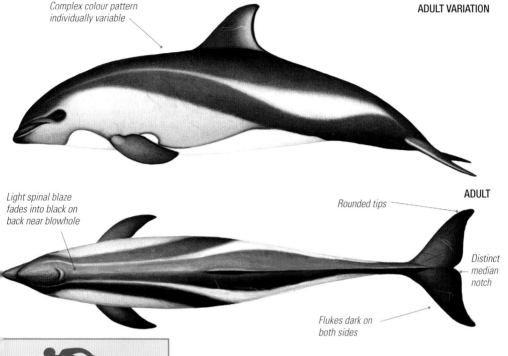

ADULT VARIATION

Complex colour pattern individually variable

ADULT

Rounded tips

Light spinal blaze fades into black on back near blowhole

Distinct median notch

Flukes dark on both sides

SIZE
L: ♂ 1.4–2.2m, ♀ 1.3–2.1m;
MAX: 115kg
Calf – L: 1–1.3m; **WT:** unknown

SIMILAR SPECIES
Confusion is most likely with dusky dolphins, which overlap in range and have a broadly similar body shape and coloration. Peale's dolphins appear more robust and darker overall. Their dark faces and beaks, and greyer thoracic patches (terminating at the eyes and with a dark line border at the bottom), are distinctive at close range; they also tend to occur in smaller, generally less energetic groups than dusky dolphins.

DISTRIBUTION
Cold temperate and subpolar waters along both coasts of southern South America. Ranges from 33°S (near Santiago, Chile) on the Pacific side, well into the Drake Passage south of Cape Horn (59°S), and up to 38°S (about 300km south of Buenos Aires, Argentina) on the Atlantic side. Found in Tierra del Fuego, Magellan Strait, the Falkland Islands and over Namuncúra (Burdwood) Bank (200km south of the Falklands). Occurs in two different habitats: protected bays, channels and fjord entrances in southern Chile; and open, wave-washed coasts over shallow continental shelves in northern Chile (north of Chiloé) and throughout most of its range in Argentina. Movements are poorly known: while some populations appear to be resident, there is evidence of inshore–offshore (summer–winter) movement in others.

Frequently seen close to shore – within sight of land and often in less than 20m of water – but sometimes as far as 300km offshore in some areas. Prefers shallow water and abundance decreases with greater depth; rarely in

░░ possible range

Peale's dolphin distribution

DORSAL FIN VARIATIONS

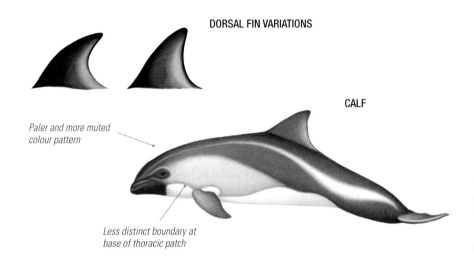

CALF

Paler and more muted colour pattern

Less distinct boundary at base of thoracic patch

water deeper than 200m. Often seen swimming in and around kelp forests (considered a critical habitat), in the rip-tides at entrances to fjords and channels, and around islands. Occurs mainly where the sea surface temperature is *c.* 5–15°C.

BEHAVIOUR

Ponderous and slow-moving much of the time, swimming quite inconspicuously, but prone to bursts of activity. Typical dive pattern consists of three short dives over a minute or so, followed by one longer dive. Often observed in mixed-species groups with other dolphins, especially Commerson's and, to a lesser degree, dusky and Risso's. Frequently plays in coastal surf and may breach repeatedly. Often slaps its head, flukes or flippers onto the surface, and sometimes spyhops. Commonly

and energetically bow-rides, often speeding ahead and leaping high into the air. Will also wake-ride.

TEETH

Upper 54–74
Lower 54–72

GROUP SIZE AND STRUCTURE

Usually 2–5 (the average in a recent study in southern Patagonia was 3.4); sometimes up to 30; aggregations of up to 100 rarely observed. Group size varies according to behaviour (larger groups while socialising, smaller groups while travelling).

PREDATORS

Unknown, but likely to fall prey to killer whales and sharks (including sevengill, great white, Pacific sleeper

DIVE SEQUENCE

Two main types of surfacing:
Slow swimming
* Indistinct blow.
* Only blowhole, small part of back and dorsal fin exposed.
Fast swimming
* Mostly hidden behind wall of spray as water splashes up high around face (thus nickname 'plough-share dolphin').
* Groups tend to surface together in rhythm – may also make long, low leaps – frequently breaches.

FOOD AND FEEDING

Prey Variety of fish, cephalopods and crustaceans, including hagfish, pink cusk-eel, Patagonian cod, Patagonian grenadier, southern red octopus, Patagonian squid, Argentinian red shrimp.
Feeding Forages in kelp beds (where it picks small octopuses off fronds) and open waters; cooperative herding using 'sunburst' formation (encircling prey).
Dive depth Unknown, but feeds mostly near bottom in shallow water.
Dive time Average 28 seconds (ranges from three seconds to two minutes 37 seconds).

and shortfin mako), though none of these is particularly common within the range; in the extreme south, leopard seals could potentially prey on calves.

PHOTO-IDENTIFICATION

Possible, using dorsal fin shape combined with notches, nicks and scars on the fin and upper body.

POPULATION

No overall abundance estimate. A survey of the Patagonian shelf (roughly 1,300km along southern Argentina) estimated *c.* 20,000. There are estimates of *c.* 2,400 in the Magellan region, *c.* 1,900 in inshore waters of the Falkland Islands and *c.* 200 in a local population off Chiloé Island.

CONSERVATION

IUCN status: Least Concern (2018). Hunted in both Argentina and Chile from the 1970s until at least the early 1990s, for human consumption and bait (especially for the lucrative king crab fisheries). Hunting is now illegal

(although enforcement in remote areas is practically impossible), and the crab fishery has declined and new forms of bait have become available, but killing inevitably continues to some extent. Perhaps a bigger concern is the recent expansion of industrialised salmon and mussel farms: the dolphins are displaced from important habitats, disturbed by boat traffic and drown in nets set to keep predatory sea lions away. Bycatch mortality in gillnets is also a problem.

LIFE HISTORY

Sexual maturity Unknown.
Mating Unknown.
Gestation Probably 10–12 months.
Calving Single calf born with peak in October–April.
Weaning Unknown.
Lifespan Oldest recorded 13 years, but maximum age probably much higher.

The dark face of the Peale's dolphin is quite distinctive; this individual is bow-riding in front of a ship in the Drake Passage.

CHILEAN DOLPHIN
Cephalorhynchus eutropia

(Gray, 1846)

Found in shallow waters along the southwestern coast of South America, the porpoise-like Chilean dolphin is poorly known and seems to be uncommon.

Classification Odontoceti, family Delphinidae.
Common name Endemic to Chile (although recent research has revealed small numbers in Argentina); 'black' dolphin (an alternative name) is a misnomer, though it darkens quickly to black after death.
Other names Black dolphin, Chilean black dolphin; rarely – white-bellied dolphin, piebald dolphin, southern dolphin, eutropia dolphin.
Scientific name *Cephalorhynchus* from the Greek *kephale* for 'head', and *rhynchos* for 'beak' or 'snout' (referring to the gradual slope from the head to the beak); *eutropia*, either from the Greek *eutropos* for 'versatile', or *eu* for 'true' and *tropidos* for 'keel' (referring to the strongly keeled skull).
Taxonomy No recognised forms or subspecies.

ADULT MALE

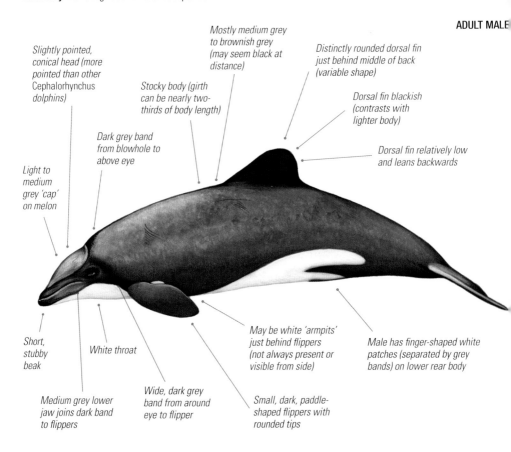

Slightly pointed, conical head (more pointed than other Cephalorhynchus dolphins)

Mostly medium grey to brownish grey (may seem black at distance)

Distinctly rounded dorsal fin just behind middle of back (variable shape)

Stocky body (girth can be nearly two-thirds of body length)

Dorsal fin blackish (contrasts with lighter body)

Dark grey band from blowhole to above eye

Dorsal fin relatively low and leans backwards

Light to medium grey 'cap' on melon

Short, stubby beak

White throat

May be white 'armpits' just behind flippers (not always present or visible from side)

Male has finger-shaped white patches (separated by grey bands) on lower rear body

Medium grey lower jaw joins dark band to flippers

Wide, dark grey band from around eye to flipper

Small, dark, paddle-shaped flippers with rounded tips

AT A GLANCE
- Mainly central and southern Chile
- Shallow coastal waters
- Small size
- Prominent, dark, distinctly rounded dorsal fin
- Complex shades of grey and white
- Finger-shaped white band on lower rear body
- Indistinct beak
- Small groups

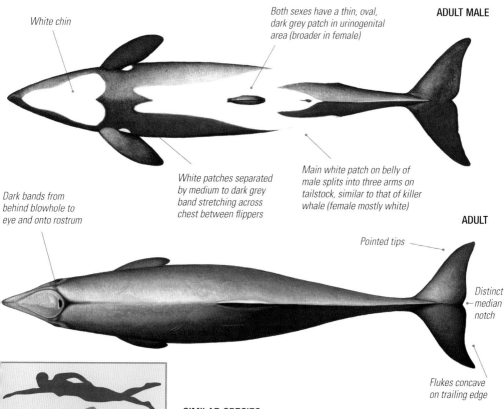

ADULT MALE

White chin

Both sexes have a thin, oval, dark grey patch in urinogenital area (broader in female)

Dark bands from behind blowhole to eye and onto rostrum

White patches separated by medium to dark grey band stretching across chest between flippers

Main white patch on belly of male splits into three arms on tailstock, similar to that of killer whale (female mostly white)

ADULT

Pointed tips

Distinct median notch

Flukes concave on trailing edge

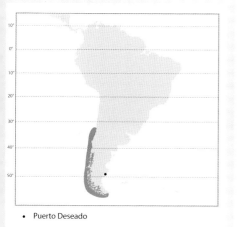

SIZE
L: ♂ 1.2–1.7m, ♀ 1.2–1.7m;
WT: 30–60kg; **MAX:** 1.7m, 63kg
Calf – L: c. 0.9–1m; **WT:** c. 8–10kg

SIMILAR SPECIES
Commerson's dolphins overlap partially in the Strait of Magellan and Tierra del Fuego, but they are strikingly black (or dark grey) and white; possible Chilean/ Commerson's crosses – intermediate in coloration – have been observed at Puerto Deseado in Argentina, and in the Chilean fjords. Peale's dolphins and Burmeister's porpoises are sympatric, but they can be distinguished even at a distance by dorsal fin shape.

DISTRIBUTION
Occurs along 2,600km of the central and southern Chilean coast; there have also been a small number of vagrants in Argentina. Known to range from Valparaiso (33°06'S) to near Cape Horn (55°15'S), including the eastern side of the Strait of Magellan and (to a lesser extent) the west coast of Tierra del Fuego, with occasional northerly records as far as 30°S. Unevenly distributed, it tends to aggregate in distinct hotspots such as Arauco Gulf near Concepción, channels around the Greater Island of Chiloé, and in some bays in the Chilean fjords. Most sightings are within 500m of the coast, and the species is not seen more than 1km offshore (though there has been little survey effort in adjacent offshore waters). Found in cold, dark, shallow waters along the coast and in the intricate network of fjords, channels and sheltered bays, as well as estuaries and rivers (as far as 12km upstream). Prefers shallow water of 3–15m (rarely deeper than 30m), particularly in areas with a high tidal range and rapid tidal flow, near rivers or over shallow banks

• Puerto Deseado

Chilean dolphin distribution

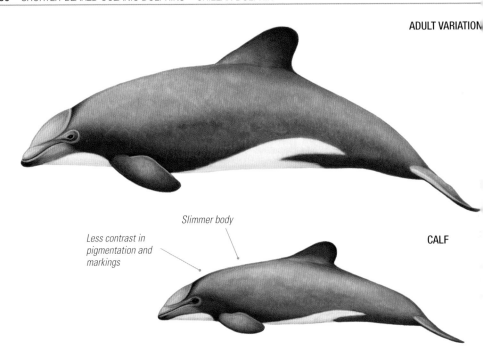

ADULT VARIATION

Slimmer body

Less contrast in pigmentation and markings

CALF

at fjord entrances. Often seen in the surf zone. Movements appear to be quite limited – they spend a large proportion of their time in areas as small as 1km radius – and groups often concentrate their activities in discrete bays and channels. There are small numbers in the Beagle Channel (shared between Argentina and Chile) and, since 2009, three males have been observed around Puerto Deseado (47º45'S), Argentina, more than 600km north of the nearest normal range.

BEHAVIOUR
Can be quite active, porpoising and occasionally breaching. Tends to be shy and elusive around boats in the southern parts of the range – perhaps a learned response to hunting – but some groups approach boats in the north and bow-ride or surf in the wake. Mixed-species aggregations with Peale's dolphins are sometimes observed foraging and socialising in some areas (such as in the Guaitecas Archipelago), but elsewhere there is a clear pattern of spatial and temporal partitioning between the two species. Sometimes seen around feeding seabirds.

DIVE SEQUENCE
- Indistinct blow (sometimes visible).
- Tip of rostrum appears first, closely followed by melon.
- Body rolls relatively high in water as rounded dorsal fin appears.
- Head submerges and dorsal fin disappears.
- Flukes rarely visible.
- Vertical leaps usually with headfirst re-entry (little splash).

FOOD AND FEEDING
Prey Small benthic and pelagic schooling fishes (including sardines, anchovy, rock cod), as well as squid, octopuses and crustaceans (including squat lobster); green algae found in stomachs (but may have been ingested accidentally).
Feeding Some evidence of cooperative feeding.
Dive depth Probably less than 30m.
Dive time Usually less than three minutes.

TEETH
Upper 58–68
Lower 58–68

GROUP SIZE AND STRUCTURE
Usually 2–3, often 4–10, sometimes up to 15; occasionally as many as 50 (probably the merging of several small groups) especially in the north. Exceptionally large aggregations of *c.* 400 have been reported along the open coast north of Valdivia. Group size varies according to location and habitat, and appears to increase during the breeding season.

LIFE HISTORY
Sexual maturity Females and males 5–9 years.
Mating Unknown.
Gestation 10–11 months.
Calving Every two years (occasionally 3–4); single calf born in southern spring to late summer (October–April).
Weaning Unknown.
Lifespan Unknown, but probably at least 20 years (oldest recorded 19 years).

PREDATORS
Unknown, but likely to fall prey to killer whales and sharks (including sevengill, great white and shortfin mako), though none of these is particularly common within the range; in the extreme south, leopard seals could potentially prey on calves.

PHOTO-IDENTIFICATION
Shape of the dorsal fin, combined with scars.

POPULATION
No overall abundance estimate. The population appears to be small (low thousands at most), but the perceived rarity may be due to a lack of search effort and to its shyness and evasive behaviour. The population is believed to be decreasing.

CONSERVATION
IUCN status: Near Threatened (2017). Much of the range is largely uninhabited by humans, but there are threats. It was hunted for many years, for human consumption and bait (for the lucrative king crab fisheries, as well as for swordfish and rock cod). Hundreds, or even low thousands, were probably being killed annually during the 1970s and 1980s. Hunting is now illegal (although enforcement in such remote areas is practically impossible), the crab fishery has declined and new forms of bait have become available, but killing inevitably continues to some extent. Perhaps a bigger concern is the recent expansion of industrialised salmon and mussel farms: the dolphins are displaced from important habitats, disturbed by boat traffic and drown in nets set to keep predatory sea lions away. Bycatch mortality in coastal gillnets and other fishing gear dates back to at least 1962; there are few statistics, but it is clearly still a problem throughout the species' range.

Three Chilean dolphins surface together.

COMMERSON'S DOLPHIN
Cephalorhynchus commersonii

(Lacépède, 1804)

Commerson's dolphin is one of the world's smallest dolphins. It has the strangest distribution: the main stronghold is in southern South America and around the Falkland Islands, but there is also an isolated population in the Kerguelen Islands, 8,500km away in the Indian Ocean.

Classification Odontoceti, family Delphinidae.
Common name After Philibert Commerson (1727–73), a French physician and botanist, who first described the species after observing it in the Strait of Magellan in 1767.
Other names Black-and-white dolphin, piebald dolphin, skunk dolphin, Jacobite; Kerguelen Islands Commerson's dolphin.
Scientific name *Cephalorhynchus* from the Greek *kephale* for 'head', and *rhynchos* for 'beak' or 'snout' (referring to the gradual slope from the head to the beak); *commersonii* from Philibert Commerson.
Taxonomy Two subspecies recognised: South American Commerson's dolphin (*C. c. commersonii*) in southern South America, and Kerguelen Islands Commerson's dolphin (*C. c. kerguelenensis*) in the French Southern and Antarctic Territory of Kerguelen; the Kerguelen subspecies was founded by only a few individuals *c.* 10,000 years ago; there is growing evidence that Falkland Islands animals may be another subspecies and there appear to be multiple genetically distinct stocks along the South American coast.

ADULT COMMERSON'S

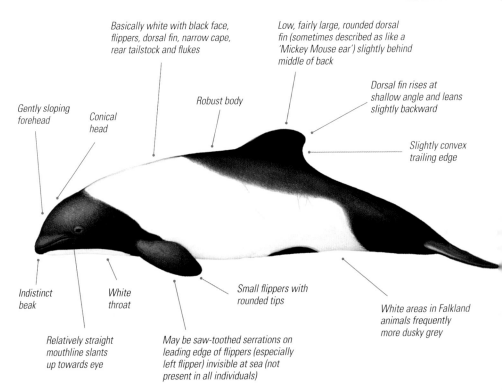

Basically white with black face, flippers, dorsal fin, narrow cape, rear tailstock and flukes

Low, fairly large, rounded dorsal fin (sometimes described as like a 'Mickey Mouse ear') slightly behind middle of back

Dorsal fin rises at shallow angle and leans slightly backward

Robust body

Gently sloping forehead

Conical head

Slightly convex trailing edge

Indistinct beak

White throat

Small flippers with rounded tips

White areas in Falkland animals frequently more dusky grey

Relatively straight mouthline slants up towards eye

May be saw-toothed serrations on leading edge of flippers (especially left flipper) invisible at sea (not present in all individuals)

AT A GLANCE
- Southern South America and Falkland Islands
- Small population in Kerguelen Islands
- Shallow, coastal waters
- Small size

- Porpoise-like appearance
- Low, rounded dorsal fin
- Sharply demarcated black and white
- Fast and active
- Likely to approach boats

SIZE – SOUTH AMERICAN	SIZE – KERGUELEN
L: ♂ 1.2–1.4m, ♀ 1.3–1.5m;	**L:** ♂ 1.4–1.7m, ♀ 1.5–1.7m;
WT: 25–45kg; **MAX:** 1.5m, 66kg	**WT:** 30–50kg; **MAX:** 1.74m, 86kg
Calf – L: 65–75cm; **WT:** 4.5–8kg	**Calf – L:** 65–75cm; **WT:** 4.5–7kg
	Female slightly larger than male.

ADULT KERGUELEN

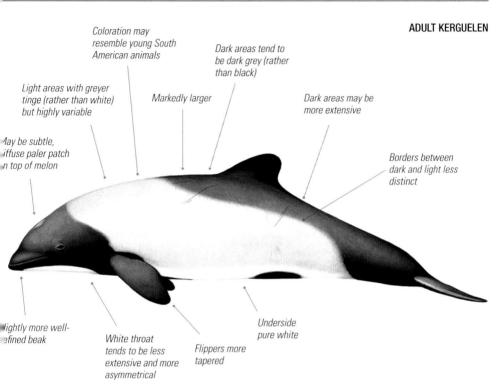

Coloration may resemble young South American animals

Dark areas tend to be dark grey (rather than black)

Light areas with greyer tinge (rather than white) but highly variable

Markedly larger

Dark areas may be more extensive

May be subtle, diffuse paler patch on top of melon

Borders between dark and light less distinct

Slightly more well-defined beak

White throat tends to be less extensive and more asymmetrical

Flippers more tapered

Underside pure white

SIMILAR SPECIES

Confusion is possible at a distance with Chilean dolphin, Burmeister's porpoise and spectacled porpoise, which all overlap in range to varying degrees, but the combination of sharply demarcated coloration, conspicuous white swathe along the sides and back, and low, rounded dorsal fin is distinctive. Possible Chilean/ Commerson's crosses – intermediate in coloration – have been observed at Puerto Deseado, in Argentina, and in the Chilean fjords.

DISTRIBUTION – SOUTH AMERICAN

Two subspecies widely separated, with lack of suitable habitat in between, so interchange between them seems unlikely. South American Commerson's dolphin is endemic to the cold, shallow, nearshore waters of Argentina, southernmost Chile and the Falkland Islands. Northern limits are c. 41°30'S on the

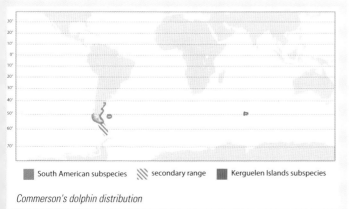

■ South American subspecies   ⊠ secondary range   ▥ Kerguelen Islands subspecies

Commerson's dolphin distribution

ADULT

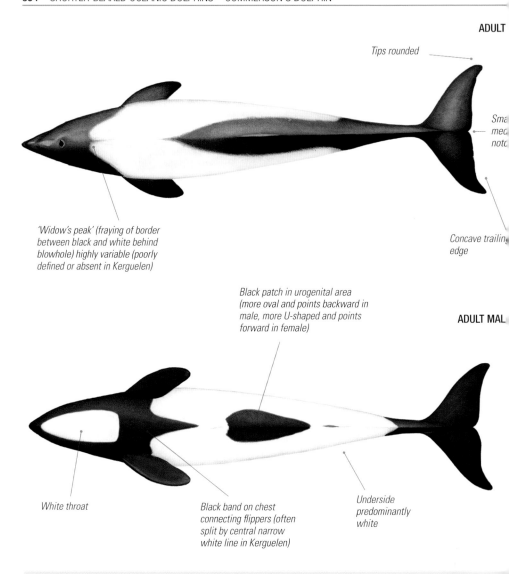

Tips rounded

Sma
mea
notc

'Widow's peak' (fraying of border between black and white behind blowhole) highly variable (poorly defined or absent in Kerguelen)

Concave trailin edge

Black patch in urogenital area (more oval and points backward in male, more U-shaped and points forward in female)

ADULT MAL

White throat

Black band on chest connecting flippers (often split by central narrow white line in Kerguelen)

Underside predominantly white

DIVE SEQUENCE

Slow swimming

- Small, diffuse blow sometimes visible in very cold conditions.
- Rolls forward slowly as dorsal fin appears.
- Head submerges, then fin disappears.

Fast swimming

- Will porpoise out of water with low, horizontal leaps.

'WIDOW'S PEAK' VARIATIONS

'WIDOW'S PEAK' VARIATIONS

DORSAL FIN VARIATIONS

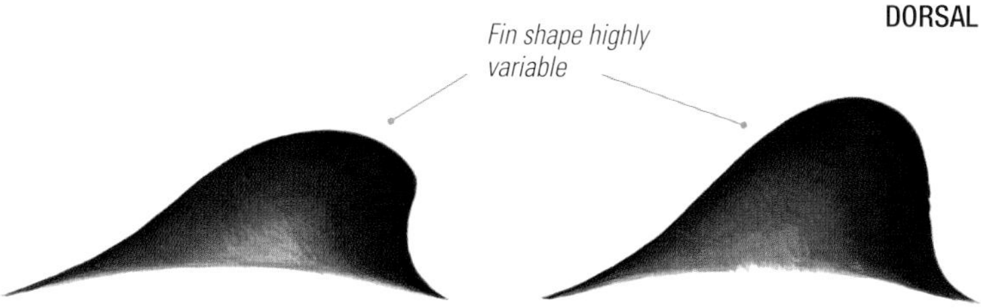

Fin shape highly variable

CALF

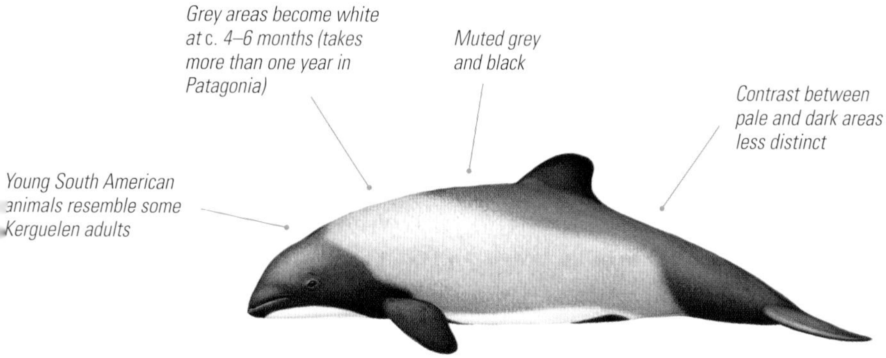

Grey areas become white at c. 4–6 months (takes more than one year in Patagonia)

Muted grey and black

Contrast between pale and dark areas less distinct

Young South American animals resemble some Kerguelen adults

lantic coast (occasionally to 31°S off Brazil), 52°91'S on the Pacific coast (with one recent sighting the Chilean fjords, some 1,200km north of the Magellan ait). Southern limit is beyond Cape Horn (55°15'S) and metimes well into the Drake Passage to just north of e South Shetland Islands (61°50'S). Overall numbers crease towards the southern parts of the range, but it is re at the extremities. Particularly abundant in Argentina tween Peninsula Valdes and Tierra del Fuego; in Chile, is found mostly in the Strait of Magellan and nearby aterways such as Seno Almirantazgo, Seno Otway and zroy Channel. There are unsubstantiated reports from uth Georgia. Prefers sheltered habitats such as fjords, rrow passages, bays, harbours and river estuaries, d where there are strong currents and/or a great tidal nge. Nearly always seen in green water within sight of d, typically in depths less than 200m (sometimes inside astal breakers, as shallow as 1m). May move towards

shore with the tide. Often seen in the surf zone, especially in summer, and at home in turbulent water close to shore. Attracted to kelp beds. Seen as far as 24km upriver in Patagonia. Prefers sea surface temperature of 4–16°C.

No known long-distance migrations (the longest recorded was *c.* 300km). Both subspecies show seasonal shifts in distribution – offshore during colder winter months, inshore during summer – perhaps following prey species or avoiding higher summer sea surface temperatures.

DISTRIBUTION – KERGUELEN

At Kerguelen, it is restricted to the immediate vicinity of the islands, inhabiting open waters, kelp-lined coastlines and protected areas between islets, and ranging from 48°30'S to 49°45'S. Prefers sea surface temperatures of 1–8°C. Most abundant in the semi-enclosed Morbihan Gulf (east coast of Grande Terre) during summer, but moves out of the gulf during winter. Sightings have

FOOD AND FEEDING

Prey Opportunistic: wide variety of fish (including Argentinian hake, silverside, anchovy), squid, octopuses, small crustaceans, marine worms, other benthic invertebrates; Kerguelen subspecies has a more restricted diet – mostly fish (especially mackerel icefish).

Feeding Single animals forage on seabed, in kelp forests and in tidal areas; large groups coordinate to herd schooling fish against surface or shore (or use any other suitable barrier, e.g. moored boats, rocky shores, jetties); terns often follow feeding groups (good indication of their presence).

Dive depth Unknown.

Dive time Typically 20–30 seconds (surfacing 2–3 times between dives).

also been reported in other bays and fjords along the northeastern and southern coasts. A recent sighting south of Cape Town, South Africa, was extralimital.

BEHAVIOUR

Commerson's dolphin may resemble a porpoise in appearance, but it is all dolphin in behaviour. Quick, active and playful, it seems to delight in surfing and darting through breakers, and it often swims upside down or spins on its longitudinal axis underwater. It has been seen surfacing under seabirds and nudging them. Strongly attracted to boats, it readily bow-rides and wake-rides, often swims figures of eight under the vessel and leaps out of the water (sometimes repeatedly, though perhaps not as acrobatically as some dolphins). Known to associate with Peale's dolphins, in particular, but also Chilean dolphins, Burmeister's porpoises and South American sea lions. Stationary 'floating' or 'bobbing' behaviour has been observed in some areas, and is very common on calm days.

TEETH

Upper 56–70
Lower 56–70

GROUP SIZE AND STRUCTURE

Usually 1–10; sometimes up to 15; aggregations of 100-plus have been reported, but these tend to be short-lived (10–30 minutes). Solitary individuals and small groups of 2–4 are more common in the north, larger groups more common in the south.

PREDATORS

Killer whales are likely the principal predator (Commerson's dolphins show clear avoidance behaviour i their presence); possibly also large sharks; in the extreme south, leopard seals could potentially prey on calves.

PHOTO-IDENTIFICATION

Possible, at least in South American animals, using notche on the dorsal fin, scarring on the fin and back, the black

Commerson's dolphins surfing the waves in the Falkland Islands.

ommerson's dolphins often swim upside down and spin longitudinally underwater.

vidow's peak' and differences in pigmentation patterns.
Vidow's peak is poorly defined in Kerguelen animals.

OPULATION

o overall figures, but probably the most abundant
ephalorhynchus species. Estimated *c.* 40,000 in Argentina
om the coastline to the 100m isobath, and between
⅜°S and 55°S). There is another estimate of c. 22,000
r the Patagonian shelf. No estimates for Kerguelen,
though the population is thought to be small; in 2013,
e population in the Morbihan Gulf was estimated to be
⅜ ± 13.

ONSERVATION

CN status: Least Concern (2017); subspecies
rguelensis has not been assessed separately. Hunted
both Argentina and Chile from the 1970s until at
ast the early 1990s, for human consumption and bait
specially for the lucrative king crab fisheries). Hunting is
w illegal (though enforcement in such remote areas is
actically impossible), and the crab fishery has declined
d new forms of bait have become available, but killing
evitably continues to some extent. Commerson's dolphin
the cetacean most frequently caught in fishing nets off

southern South America, and is especially vulnerable to
coastal gillnets, as well as trammel nets, pelagic trawls
and purse-seine nets. Overfishing of prey species is
another concern. Occasionally killed for sport, and it has
been captured for display in oceanaria.

*The distinctive black-and-white coloration and rounded dorsal
fin make Commerson's dolphin unmistakable.*

LIFE HISTORY

Sexual maturity Females 6–9 years, males 5–9 years.
Mating Unknown.
Gestation 11–12 months.
Calving Every two years (occasionally every 3–4 years); single calf born from late spring to summer (September–
March) with peak in mid-January.
Weaning After 10–12 months.
Lifespan Probably *c.* 10–20 years; oldest in wild is female from San Julián, which has been observed by researchers
since 1996; one individual in captivity was 26 years old.

HEAVISIDE'S DOLPHIN
Cephalorhynchus heavisidii

(Gray, 1828)

Endemic to the Benguela ecosystem along the southwestern coast of Africa, this beautiful small dolphin is fond of surfing and can often be seen playing in the waves close to shore.

Classification Odontoceti, family Delphinidae.

Common name The common name should have been Haviside's dolphin (after a captain of the British East India Company, who carried the type specimen from South Africa to England in 1827); however, the species was accidentally named after Captain Heaviside, an eminent naval surgeon who happened to sell some non-cetacean anatomical specimens at about the same time; the incorrect name persists because it is conventional to use a common name with the same spelling as the scientific name (which, under the rules of nomenclature, cannot be changed).

Other names Haviside's dolphin, Benguela dolphin.

Scientific name *Cephalorhynchus* from the Greek *kephale* for 'head', and *rhynchos* for 'beak' or 'snout' (referring to the gradual slope from the head to the beak); *heavisidii* see above.

Taxonomy No recognised forms or subspecies.

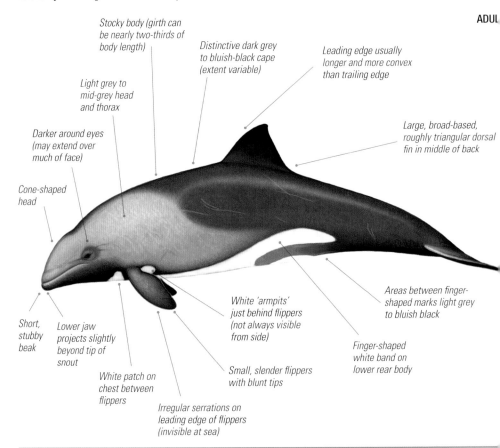

ADULT

Stocky body (girth can be nearly two-thirds of body length)

Distinctive dark grey to bluish-black cape (extent variable)

Leading edge usually longer and more convex than trailing edge

Light grey to mid-grey head and thorax

Darker around eyes (may extend over much of face)

Large, broad-based, roughly triangular dorsal fin in middle of back

Cone-shaped head

Short, stubby beak

Lower jaw projects slightly beyond tip of snout

White patch on chest between flippers

Irregular serrations on leading edge of flippers (invisible at sea)

Small, slender flippers with blunt tips

White 'armpits' just behind flippers (not always visible from side)

Areas between finger-shaped marks light grey to bluish black

Finger-shaped white band on lower rear body

AT A GLANCE
- Atlantic coast of southern Africa
- Small size
- Complex, sharply demarcated black, grey and white body pattern
- Finger-shaped white marks on lower rear body
- Large, wide-based triangular dorsal fin in middle of back
- Indistinct beak
- Small group size
- Very energetic

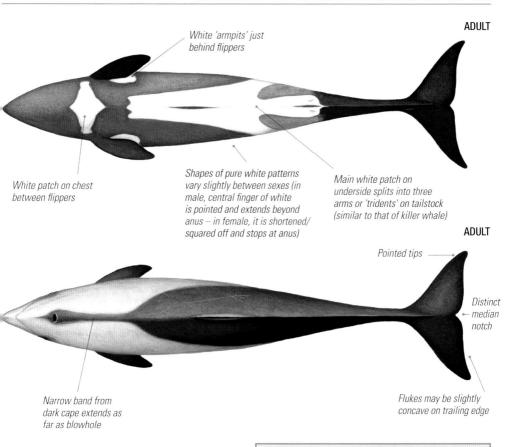

ADULT

White 'armpits' just behind flippers

White patch on chest between flippers

Shapes of pure white patterns vary slightly between sexes (in male, central finger of white is pointed and extends beyond anus – in female, it is shortened/squared off and stops at anus)

Main white patch on underside splits into three arms or 'tridents' on tailstock (similar to that of killer whale)

ADULT

Pointed tips

Distinct median notch

Narrow band from dark cape extends as far as blowhole

Flukes may be slightly concave on trailing edge

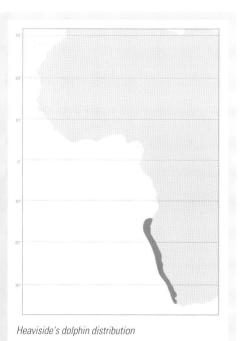

Heaviside's dolphin distribution

SIZE
L: 1.2–1.7–m;
WT: 50–75kg; **MAX:** 1.8m, 75kg
Calf – L: 80–85cm; **WT:** unknown, but possibly *c.* 10kg

SIMILAR SPECIES

There is overlap with several other small cetaceans within the range, including the slightly larger, sympatric dusky, but Heaviside's dolphin's triangular dorsal fin (compared to the dusky's falcate fin) and striking markings are distinctive. Group size is another distinctive feature: Heaviside's typically occurs in smaller groups of fewer than 10, dusky generally in much larger groups.

DISTRIBUTION

Restricted to cool waters of the Benguela ecosystem along 2,500km of coastline in southern Angola, Namibia and South Africa. It ranges from at least 16°30'S at Baia dos Tigres, southern Angola (possibly further north – but there is little information), to 34°20'S at Cape Point, South

CALF

Africa; sightings of animals in the warmer waters to the east of Cape Point are considered vagrants. It occurs continuously within this range, though there are areas of higher and lower density linked with prey abundance (particularly hake). Associated with the cool waters of the Benguela Current, it prefers sea surface temperatures of 9–15°C. There is evidence of site fidelity to small home ranges stretching along 50–90km of coast. It tends to stay in water less than 100m deep, but regularly ranges up to 30km from shore (with records up to 85km from shore, and in water up to 200m deep). In most parts of the range, it moves inshore in the mornings (to rest, socialise and probably avoid sharks) and several kilometres offshore in the afternoons (to feed – its prey migrates closer to the surface at night). It is generally closest to shore between sunrise and midday – preferring areas with sandy shores and big swells, such as at the exposed ends of bays (especially in the breakers). It is furthest offshore between mid-afternoon and sunrise. Often seen from major population centres such as Cape Town and Walvis Bay.

BEHAVIOUR
Energetic and sometimes boisterous. Fond of surfing and can often be seen playing and jumping in the waves. Performs a variety of leaps (in competitive pairs or small groups). Occasionally seen doing somersaults or back flips, up to 2m high, ending with the dolphin slapping the surface with its belly and tail. Readily approaches boats (especially inshore and in larger groups – less so when dispersed and feeding offshore), frequently bow-rides and will sometimes play in the wake. Occasionally in mixed groups with dusky dolphins.

TEETH
Upper 44–56
Lower 44–56

GROUP SIZE AND STRUCTURE
Usually 2–3, but ranges from one to 10; larger aggregations of multiple groups numbering 100 individuals can occur in some high-density areas, such as Table Bay, South Africa, and Diaz Point and Pelican Point, Namibia. There is a high turnover of group membership.

PREDATORS
Killer whales are rare within the range, but have been observed taking Heaviside's dolphins. Several individuals have been seen bearing scars from shark bites.

PHOTO-IDENTIFICATION
Possible but difficult, using dorsal fin nicks, since only 15–30 per cent of individuals have the natural dorsal fin

DIVE SEQUENCE
- Blow invisible.
- Head appears first, closely followed by tip of dorsal fin.
- Body rolls relatively high in water.
- Head submerges and dorsal fin disappears.
- Flukes rarely visible.
- When swimming at high speed, often clears surface at low angle.
- Vertical leaps usually with headfirst re-entry (little splash).

FOOD AND FEEDING

Prey Mainly demersal (some pelagic) fish, especially juvenile shallow-water hake, but also kingklip, bearded goby, horse mackerel and others; will take squid and octopus.
Feeding Most feeding at night.
Dive depth Forages mostly on or near seabed in relatively shallow water (less than 100m).
Dive time Unknown.

markings required for individual identification. Scarring on the fin is more common, but usually restricts identification to single sides and short time periods.

POPULATION

A population estimate for the southern end of the range (390km of coastline, from Table Bay to Lambert's Bay) was 6,345. It would not be unreasonable to assume twice this number for South Africa as a whole. Estimates for Namibia include about 500 animals each for Walvis Bay and Lüdertiz.

CONSERVATION

IUCN status: Near Threatened (2017). There are concerns simply because of its limited range and vulnerable coastal habitat, although human population densities in the region are mostly low. Direct mortality from bycatch is small but probably the greatest threat: unknown numbers are taken incidentally in gillnets, purse seines, beach seines, trawls and other fishing gear. A potential emerging concern is the experimental midwater trawl

fishery for horse mackerel. Long-term climate change and its possible impact on the Benguela Ecosystem is another worry. Little is known about the potential effects of increasing boat traffic in the region.

VOCALISATIONS

High-frequency narrow-band echolocation clicks. *Cephalorhynchus* dolphins do not whistle, as do many other dolphins.

LIFE HISTORY

Sexual maturity Females 5–9 years, males 6–9 years.
Mating Year-round.
Gestation 10–11 months.
Calving Every 2–4 years (occasionally every year); single calf believed to be born with peak in southern summer (October–January).
Weaning Unknown.
Lifespan Oldest recorded 26 years.

Heaviside's dolphin's triangular dorsal fin and striking markings are distinctive.

HECTOR'S DOLPHIN
Cephalorhynchus hectori

(Van Bénéden, 1881)

One of the smallest dolphins in the world, Hector's dolphin is found only in New Zealand and has one of the most restricted distributions of any cetacean. Its numbers and range have declined dramatically in the past 30 years, and now one of the two subspecies – Maui dolphin – is on the brink of extinction.

Classification Odontoceti, family Delphinidae.
Common name After Scotland-born scientist James Hector (1834–1907), Curator of the Colonial Museum (now Te Papa) in Wellington, who described the type specimen (a dolphin shot in Cook Strait in 1873); Maui from Te-Ika -a-Māui (the Maori word for North Island).
Other names New Zealand dolphin, New Zealand white-front dolphin, white-headed dolphin, little pied dolphin; see taxonomy for subspecies common names.
Scientific name *Cephalorhynchus* from the Greek *kephale* for 'head', and *rhynchos* for 'beak' or 'snout' (referring to the gradual slope from the head to the beak); *hectori* after James Hector.
Taxonomy Two subspecies are recognised: South Island Hector's dolphin (*C. hectori hectori*) and Maui dolphin or North Island Hector's dolphin (*C. h. maui*); they look identical (Maui is marginally larger) but they are genetically distinct and there is no evidence of interbreeding. South Island dolphins are further fragmented into at least four genetically and geographically distinct sub-populations (west coast, east coast, north coast, south coast); these sub-populations are further fragmented into small, local populations – several of which number fewer than 100 individuals.

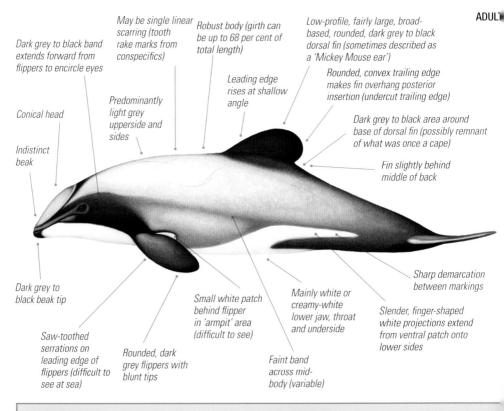

ADULT

Dark grey to black band extends forward from flippers to encircle eyes

May be single linear scarring (tooth rake marks from conspecifics)

Robust body (girth can be up to 68 per cent of total length)

Low-profile, fairly large, broad-based, rounded, dark grey to black dorsal fin (sometimes described as a 'Mickey Mouse ear')

Conical head

Predominantly light grey upperside and sides

Leading edge rises at shallow angle

Rounded, convex trailing edge makes fin overhang posterior insertion (undercut trailing edge)

Indistinct beak

Dark grey to black area around base of dorsal fin (possibly remnant of what was once a cape)

Fin slightly behind middle of back

Dark grey to black beak tip

Sharp demarcation between markings

Saw-toothed serrations on leading edge of flippers (difficult to see at sea)

Rounded, dark grey flippers with blunt tips

Small white patch behind flipper in 'armpit' area (difficult to see)

Mainly white or creamy-white lower jaw, throat and underside

Faint band across mid-body (variable)

Slender, finger-shaped white projections extend from ventral patch onto lower sides

AT A GLANCE
- Shallow coastal waters of New Zealand
- Small size
- Mainly light grey with dark appendages
- White on belly
- Mostly dark face
- Rounded dorsal fin leans backward
- Small groups

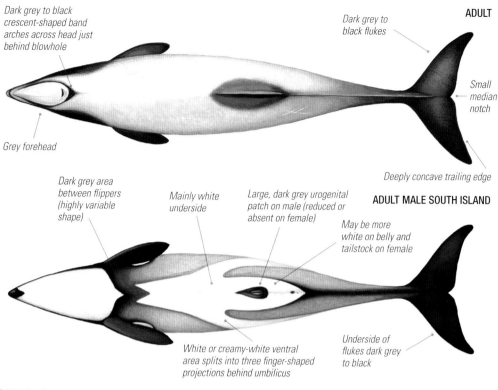

Dark grey to black crescent-shaped band arches across head just behind blowhole

Dark grey to black flukes

ADULT

Small median notch

Grey forehead

Deeply concave trailing edge

Dark grey area between flippers (highly variable shape)

Mainly white underside

Large, dark grey urogenital patch on male (reduced or absent on female)

ADULT MALE SOUTH ISLAND

May be more white on belly and tailstock on female

White or creamy-white ventral area splits into three finger-shaped projections behind umbilicus

Underside of flukes dark grey to black

SIMILAR SPECIES

Easy to distinguish from other dolphins in the region (mainly bottlenose, dusky and common). No other species in New Zealand has a rounded dorsal fin, and the significantly smaller size, 'chunky' body shape, indistinct beak (shared only with dusky dolphin) and coloration of Hector's dolphin are also distinctive.

DISTRIBUTION – HECTOR'S

Hector's dolphin is most common along the middle sections of the east and west coasts of the South Island, mainly between 41°30'S and 44°30'S. The highest abundance occurs at Banks Peninsula in the east, and between Greymouth and Westport in the west. Absent from Fiordland. Preferred sea surface temperature ranges from 6° to 22°C (most abundant where it is greater than 14°C). Individuals usually range over about 50km of shoreline (the record is 106km) and some have been resighted in the same general area year-round for more

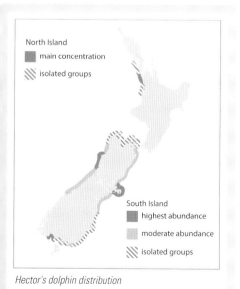

North Island
■ main concentration
▨ isolated groups

South Island
■ highest abundance
■ moderate abundance
▨ isolated groups

Hector's dolphin distribution

SIZE – SOUTH ISLAND
L: ♂ 1.2–1.4m, ♀ 1.3–1.5m; **WT:** 35–50kg;
MAX: 1.5m, 50kg;
Calf – L: 60–70cm; **WT:** 8–10kg

SIZE – NORTH ISLAND
L: ♂ 1.3–1.5m, ♀ 1.3–1.6m; **WT:** 40–60kg;
MAX: 1.6m, 65kg
Calf – L: 60–75cm; **WT:** 8–10kg
Females slightly larger than males.

ADULT VARIATION

Same basic coloration as adult but with dark grey hue (fades to adult's light grey over about six months)

CALF

than 20 years. There is no evidence of long-distance migrations.

Typical habitat is in depths of less than 100m, and within 40km of shore (the distribution of both subspecies is related to water depth, rather than distance from shore). This varies according to location – it ranges to about 12km in the relatively deep waters off the west coast, and to 37km in the much shallower waters off the east coast. It is often seen just beyond the surf line, or inside harbours. In most areas, densities are highest close to shore in

mid-summer (December–February); there is much more variation in range depth and distance from shore during the rest of the year.

DISTRIBUTION – MAUI

Maui dolphin was once found along most of the west coast of the North Island, from Cook Strait to Ninety Mile Beach, but today is found along only *c.* 200km in the north-west, between 36°30'S and 38°20'S. Relatively higher densities can be found along a 40km stretch of

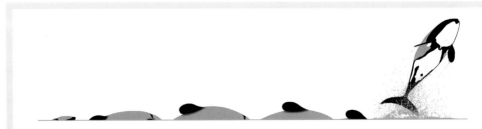

DIVE SEQUENCE
- Typically surfaces slowly and leisurely.
- Indistinct blow.
- Little or no splash.
- Rolls slowly forward.
- Dorsal fin disappears below surface.
- When feeding, typical dive sequence consists of *c.* six surfacings over *c.* 54 seconds, followed by a long dive of *c.* 90 seconds.
- During social behaviour, typical dive sequence consists of surfacings every 25–30 seconds and no long dives.
- Fast travel occasionally observed with active surfacing and splash.

FOOD AND FEEDING

Prey Opportunistic, taking a wide variety of small fish (usually less than 10cm long) such as yelloweyed mullet, ahuru, red cod, sprat, sole, New Zealand sand stargazer, Hector's lanternfish; also squid (especially arrow squid) and octopus; diet more varied on east coast of South Island (eight species make up 80 per cent of diet) than west coast (four species make up 80 per cent).

Feeding Feeds throughout water column, from surface to seafloor; strongly attracted to inshore trawlers (groups of up to 50 may follow trawlers for several hours, with different individuals joining and leaving, to feed on fish stirred up by net).

Dive depth Probably to 50m or more.

Dive time Longest dives typically *c.* 90 seconds or less.

coast between Manukau Harbour and Port Waikato (however, almost all the recent research effort has been in this area). Recent research reveals some movement of South Island individuals into the Maui range, but the current genetic isolation of the two subspecies is largely maintained by the relatively substantial geographic distance between them and their typically small home ranges. New Zealand dolphins are also occasionally sighted off the east coast of the North Island, but it is still unclear whether these belong to the Hector's or Maui subspecies.

BEHAVIOUR

Quite aerially active. Large groups are particularly boisterous, with lots of chasing, leaping, bubble-blowing and vigorous tail slapping (while swimming normal way up or upside down). The amount of social behaviour increases dramatically when small groups of 2–7 individuals join to form temporary larger groups of 20–50 individuals. Three different leaps are recognised: 'horizontal' leaps are long and low, usually while swimming fast; 'vertical' leaps are high and clean, re-entering the water head first and with minimal splash (they are usually associated with social activity or courtship and are often performed by a male and a female, one leaping just a fraction of a second later than the other); and 'noisy' leaps, which are designed to make as much splash and underwater noise as possible by falling back into the water on the back, front or side (this is the least common leap, but is usually repeated many times). Will also spyhop. Frequently surfs, especially in rough weather, and in some places in very shallow water, coming right into the beach with the waves (often in water less than 1m deep). Readily plays with pieces of seaweed and other objects. Strongly attracted to small boats, especially those travelling less than 10 knots, and

Hector's dolphins can be aerially active, especially in large groups.

LIFE HISTORY

Sexual maturity Females 6–9 years, males 5–9 years.
Mating Promiscuous (both males and females have multiple mates).
Gestation 10–11 months.
Calving Every 2–3 years (sometimes four); single calf born in spring to late summer (mainly early November–mid-February).
Weaning At least six months; calf stays with mother for 2–3 years.
Lifespan At least 18–20 years, probably 25 years.

readily bow-rides (though it frequently turns back after a few hundred metres). Will often hang around a drifting boat.

TEETH

Upper 48–62
Lower 48–62

GROUP SIZE AND STRUCTURE

Typically 2–10. Frequently several small groups in close range – coming together to form large, temporary groups of *c.* 25 (up to 50 or more), mingling and separating again within 10–30 minutes – often swapping members in the process. Groups are not families, and long-term associations among adults are rare. Segregation by age or sex is common: groups with fewer than six members are often all male, all female or all juvenile; nursery groups of mothers and young calves frequently stay away from (often high-spirited) males. Tends to spread out and form smaller groups in winter.

PREDATORS

Large sharks and probably killer whales.

PHOTO-IDENTIFICATION

Mainly using nicks and other damage along the trailing edge of the dorsal fin, combined with body scars and sometimes blotches and 'tattoos' caused by a viral skin disease (though these change slowly over time).

POPULATION

The latest estimate for South Island Hector's dolphin is 14,849 (11,923–18,492): *c.* 8,969 on the east coast, *c.* 5,642 on the west coast and *c.* 238 on the south coast. Numbers have decreased substantially on the west and south coasts since the previous estimate in the late 1990s, but have increased five-fold on the east coast (it is still unclear if this is due to differences in the survey methods used). The total population was previously estimated to be *c.* 7,300. There are currently 63 Maui dolphins left, including just *c.* 10 breeding females (down from 111 in 2004).

The beautiful markings and distinctive rounded, backward-leaning dorsal fin, with an undercut trailing edge, make Hector's dolphin unmistakable.

The distinctive crescent-shaped band behind the blowhole.

Hector's dolphins typically surface slowly and leisurely.

The typical group size is two to 10.

In the early 1970s there were roughly 50,000 Hector's dolphins altogether (including *c.* 2,000 Maui dolphins).

CONSERVATION

IUCN status: Endangered (2008); Maui subspecies Critically Endangered (2008). A slow population growth (no more than 2 per cent per year in the absence of human impacts, compared with the average for larger, longer-lived dolphins of 2–4 per cent per year) and a preference for inshore waters (where human activity is highest) make both subspecies especially vulnerable. The main threat is entanglement in gillnets (set by recreational and commercial fishermen), accounting for 60 per cent of all deaths. Gillnet fishing has expanded dramatically since the early 1970s, following the invention of monofilament plastic. Trawl fisheries also cause mortality and are potentially as much

of a threat as gillnet fisheries (the catch rate per day fishing is lower, but there is much more trawling than gillnetting in New Zealand waters). Protection has slowly improved – through legislation and the creation of sanctuaries such as the 4,130sq km Banks Peninsula Marine Mammal Sanctuary – helping to reduce mortality in recent years. But much of the range falls outside protected areas, and more needs to be done in terms of enforcement and making the transition back to dolphin-friendly fishing methods. Current levels of mortality are unsustainable and there is no doubt that bycatch mortality needs to be reduced to near zero if Hector's dolphin is to survive. Additional threats include pollution, disease, vessel traffic, and habitat modification and disturbance (including recent seismic testing for oil and gas in the ranges of both subspecies).

NORTHERN RIGHT WHALE DOLPHIN

Lissodelphis borealis

(Peale, 1848)

The two species of right whale dolphins may look superficially similar, but they do differ strikingly in coloration and are widely separated geographically.

Classification Odontoceti, family Delphinidae.
Common name For the absence of a dorsal fin (a trait shared with right whales).
Other names Pacific right whale porpoise, white-bellied right whale dolphin, snake porpoise; affectionately called a 'lisso' by researchers (from the generic name).
Scientific name From the Greek *lissos* for 'smooth' (referring to the lack of a dorsal fin or ridge), and *delphis* for 'dolphin'; *borealis* from the Latin *borealis* for 'of the north'.
Taxonomy No recognised forms or subspecies; some populations are characterised by a 'swirled' colour morph (which may resemble the southern right whale dolphin), sometimes mistakenly claimed to be a subspecies (*L. b. albiventris*).

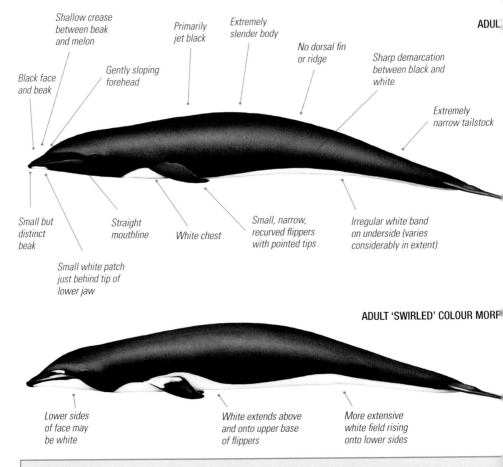

ADULT

Shallow crease between beak and melon

Primarily jet black

Extremely slender body

No dorsal fin or ridge

Sharp demarcation between black and white

Gently sloping forehead

Black face and beak

Extremely narrow tailstock

Small but distinct beak

Straight mouthline

White chest

Small, narrow, recurved flippers with pointed tips

Irregular white band on underside (varies considerably in extent)

Small white patch just behind tip of lower jaw

ADULT 'SWIRLED' COLOUR MORPH

Lower sides of face may be white

White extends above and onto upper base of flippers

More extensive white field rising onto lower sides

AT A GLANCE

- Deep temperate waters of the North Pacific
- Small size (appears even smaller at sea)
- No dorsal fin
- Mainly black with white band on underside
- Extremely slender body
- Small but distinct beak
- Low-angled leaps
- Usually in sizeable groups

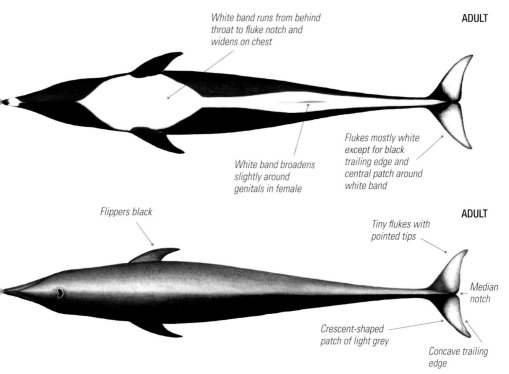

ADULT

White band runs from behind throat to fluke notch and widens on chest

White band broadens slightly around genitals in female

Flukes mostly white except for black trailing edge and central patch around white band

Flippers black

ADULT

Tiny flukes with pointed tips

Median notch

Crescent-shaped patch of light grey

Concave trailing edge

SIZE

L: ♂ 2.2–2.6m, ♀ 2.1–2.3m;
WT: 60–100kg; **MAX:** 3.1m, 113kg
Calf – L: *c.* 0.8–1m; **WT:** unknown
Male larger than female.

SIMILAR SPECIES

Unmistakable – the only small cetacean in its range without a dorsal fin. Confusion may be possible with porpoising sea lions at a distance. There are records of all-black and all-white individuals.

DISTRIBUTION

Cool to warm temperate waters in the North Pacific. Range is mainly from 31°N to 50°N in the east and 35°N to 51°N in the west. Rarely enters the Bering Sea (there are extralimital records from the Aleutian Islands and Gulf of Alaska) and not believed to enter the Sea of Japan, Okhotsk Sea or Gulf of California. Mainly deep oceanic waters from the outer continental shelf and beyond, but also where deep waters approach the coast (such as in submarine canyons); seems to prefer coastal waters in the California Current system. Occasional movements further south (such as to 29°N off Baja California, Mexico) are associated with anomalous incursions of cold water. Most abundant where sea surface temperatures are within 8–19°C. Movements are poorly known, but at least in some areas there appears to be an inshore and

Northern right whale dolphin distribution

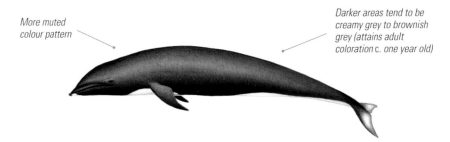

More muted colour pattern

Darker areas tend to be creamy grey to brownish grey (attains adult coloration c. one year old)

CALF

southward movement in winter, offshore and northward in summer (possibly to stay in waters within the preferred temperature range).

BEHAVIOUR
Fast swimmer, capable of bursts of speed up to 34km/h. Frequently associates with at least 14 other cetacean species, especially Pacific white-sided dolphins, but also short-finned pilot whales and Risso's dolphins. May erupt into bouts of high excitement, with much aerial activity such as breaching, spyhopping, belly-flopping and side- and fluke-slapping, and bursts of energetic swimming. Response to boats varies enormously, from vigorous avoidance to enthusiastic interaction, but it will bow-ride (especially in the presence of Pacific white-sided dolphins or other species that readily approach vessels). Can be skittish and easily startled.

TEETH
Upper 74–104
Lower 84–108

GROUP SIZE AND STRUCTURE
Highly gregarious: 100–200 common, but sometimes up to 2,000–3,000; average in the eastern North Pacific is 110, in the western North Pacific 200. Rarely seen alone. Herds usually travel in a V-shape or a 'chorus line' – either very tightly packed with no obvious sub-groups or more dispersed with sub-groups within the main group.

PREDATORS
Probably killer whales and large sharks.

PHOTO-IDENTIFICATION
Currently not possible.

POPULATION
Believed to be low hundreds of thousands. Estimates made in 1993 ranged from 68,000 to 535,000, with huge levels of uncertainty. Surveys during 2008–2014 estimated 26,556 along the California, Oregon and Washington State coasts.

CONSERVATION
IUCN status: Least Concern (2018). Huge numbers have died in large-scale high-seas driftnet fisheries, between about 38°N and 46°N. There are no overall figures, but total numbers killed by the squid driftnet fleets of Japan, South Korea and Taiwan in the late 1980s were estimated at about 15,000–24,000 per year. The UN moratorium on these driftnets, which came into force in 1993, has relieved some pressure – but large high-seas driftnets are still being used illegally and inside exclusive economic zones. Incidental catches still occur in Japanese and

DIVE SEQUENCE
Fast swimming
- Graceful, 'bouncing', low-angled leaps (up to 7m) or splashy belly flops, creating much surface disturbance.
- Almost eel-like.

Slow swimming
- Low-profile roll, barely breaking surface to breathe (exposing just top of head and blowhole).
- Easy to miss.

Swirled colour morph: notice the white extending onto the upper base of the flippers.

FOOD AND FEEDING

Prey Mainly fish (especially lanternfish – makes up 89 per cent of fish diet in central North Pacific – but also Pacific hake, saury and others), but some squid (especially market squid in southern California).
Feeding Unknown.
Dive depth Probably capable of 200m+.
Dive time 10–75 seconds; maximum recorded 6.2 minutes.

Russian purse seines, Japanese salmon driftnets, and US driftnets set for thresher sharks and broadbill swordfish. There has never been an extensive direct hunt, but relatively low numbers have been taken in Japan's small cetacean fisheries since the 1940s (especially in the Dall's porpoise harpoon fishery). Yankee whalers occasionally took this species for food in the mid-nineteenth century.

LIFE HISTORY

Sexual maturity Females and males 10 years.
Mating Unknown.
Gestation *c.* 12 months.
Calving Every two years (occasionally 1–3); single calf born in summer (peak July–August).
Weaning Unknown.
Lifespan Probably 25 years or more (oldest recorded 42 years).

The northern right whale dolphin is the only small cetacean in its range that lacks a dorsal fin.

SOUTHERN RIGHT WHALE DOLPHIN
Lissodelphis peronii

(Lacépède, 1804)

Dolphins living in high latitudes tend to be just black and white, and the southern right whale dolphin is no exception. With its striking black-and-white markings, slender body and complete lack of a dorsal fin, it is easy to recognise.

Classification Odontoceti, family Delphinidae.
Common name For the absence of a dorsal fin (a trait shared with right whales).
Other names Southern right whale porpoise, mealy mouthed porpoise, Peron's dolphin.
Scientific name From the Greek *lissos* for 'smooth' (referring to the lack of a dorsal fin or ridge), and *delphis* for 'dolphin'; *peronii* for François Péron (1775–1810), a French naturalist aboard the vessel *Géographe*, who in 1802 observed these dolphins south of Tasmania.
Taxonomy No recognised forms or subspecies.

ADULT

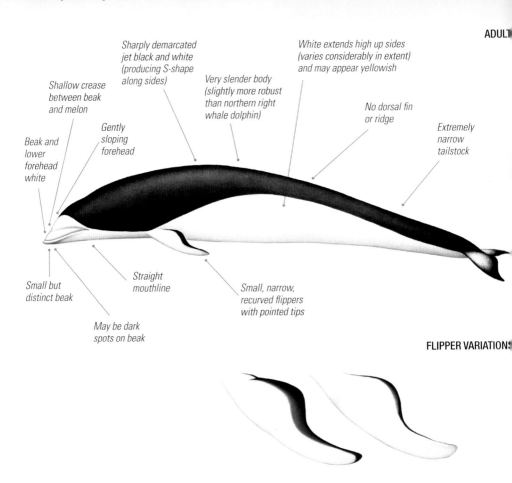

Shallow crease between beak and melon

Sharply demarcated jet black and white (producing S-shape along sides)

Very slender body (slightly more robust than northern right whale dolphin)

White extends high up sides (varies considerably in extent) and may appear yellowish

No dorsal fin or ridge

Extremely narrow tailstock

Gently sloping forehead

Beak and lower forehead white

Small but distinct beak

Straight mouthline

Small, narrow, recurved flippers with pointed tips

May be dark spots on beak

FLIPPER VARIATIONS

AT A GLANCE
- Deep cold waters of the southern hemisphere
- Small size
- No dorsal fin
- Strikingly black-and-white coloration
- Slender body
- Small but distinct beak
- Mostly white face and beak
- Low-angled leaps
- Usually in sizeable groups

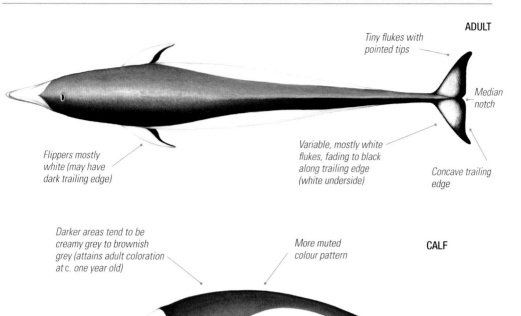

ADULT

Tiny flukes with pointed tips

Median notch

Flippers mostly white (may have dark trailing edge)

Variable, mostly white flukes, fading to black along trailing edge (white underside)

Concave trailing edge

Darker areas tend to be creamy grey to brownish grey (attains adult coloration at c. one year old)

More muted colour pattern

CALF

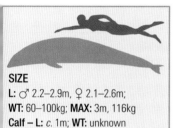

SIZE
L: ♂ 2.2–2.9m, ♀ 2.1–2.6m;
WT: 60–100kg; **MAX:** 3m, 116kg
Calf – L: *c.* 1m; **WT:** unknown
Male larger than female.

SIMILAR SPECIES

Unmistakable – the only small cetacean in its range with no dorsal fin. Spectacled porpoise is jet black above and white below, but has a distinctive dorsal fin and is chunkier. Confusion may be possible with porpoising sea lions, fur seals or even penguins at a distance. There are records of all-black individuals. There is a report from Argentina of a hybrid with a dusky dolphin.

DISTRIBUTION

Cool temperate to sub-Antarctic waters in the southern hemisphere. Circumpolar, mainly between about 25°S and 61°S. The range extends furthest north along the west coasts of continents (due to the cold counterclockwise currents of the southern hemisphere) – to 23°S in the Benguela Current (Walvis Bay, Namibia) and 12°S in the Humboldt Current (Lima, Peru) – taking it into lower sub-tropical zones. The southern limit appears to be the Antarctic Convergence, which ranges from about 48°S to 61°S (its exact position varies with time and longitude, and it is usually further north in the Atlantic than in

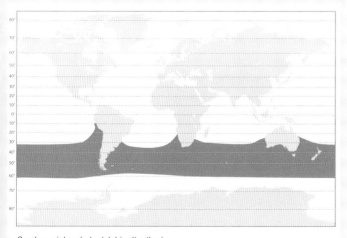

Southern right whale dolphin distribution

HYBRID WITH DUSKY DOLPHIN

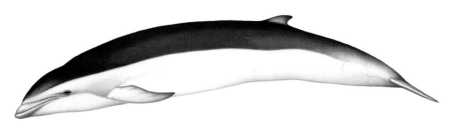

the Pacific). Most abundant off Chile, in the Falklands Current (between Patagonia and the Falkland Islands), and along the West Wind Drift in the Indian Ocean. Range includes the Great Australian Bight, Tasman Sea and Chatham Islands. Mainly in deep oceanic waters from the outer continental shelf and beyond, but also where water deeper than 200m approaches the coast, such as off Chile, Namibia and New Zealand. One group remained in the shallow waters of the Magellan Strait, Chile, for at least 17 days in 2018. Mostly where sea surface temperatures are within 1–20°C. Movements are poorly known but, in some areas such as western South America, there is evidence of an inshore and northward movement in spring and summer, offshore and southward in winter; other populations, such as off Namibia, appear to be resident year-round.

BEHAVIOUR
Relatively fast swimmer, capable of bursts of speed up to 25km/h. May erupt into bouts of high excitement, with much aerial activity such as breaching, spyhopping, belly-flopping and side- and fluke-slapping, and bursts of energetic swimming. Frequently in mixed groups with other cetaceans, especially long-finned pilot whales, dusky dolphins and hourglass dolphins. Response to boats varies, but it does not appear to be particularly attracted and only rarely bow-rides (though it does bow-ride more often in the company of other species that readily approach vessels).

TEETH
Upper 78–98
Lower 78–98

GROUP SIZE AND STRUCTURE
Highly gregarious. Often in hundreds, sometimes up to 1,000; average 210 in Chile. Herds usually travel in a V-shape or a 'chorus line' – either very tightly packed with no obvious sub-groups, or more dispersed with obvious sub-groups within the main group.

FOOD AND FEEDING
Prey Mainly fish (especially lanternfish, bigeye tuna) and squid; possibly some krill.
Feeding Unknown.
Dive depth Probably capable of 200m-plus (main prey at 200–1,000m).
Dive time 10–75 seconds; maximum recorded 6.4 minutes.

DIVE SEQUENCE
Fast swimming
- Graceful, 'bouncing', low-angled leaps or splashy belly flops, creating much surface disturbance.
- Rather penguin-like.

Slow swimming
- Low-profile roll, barely breaking surface to breathe (exposing just top of head and blowhole).
- Easy to miss.

The striking black-and-white markings of southern right whale dolphins.

PREDATORS
Probably killer whales and large sharks. A 1.7m Patagonian toothfish taken off Chile in 1983 had a southern right whale calf in its stomach.

LIFE HISTORY
Sexual maturity Females and males probably *c.* 10 years.
Mating Unknown.
Gestation *c.* 12 months.
Calving Every two years; single calf believed to be born in winter or early spring.
Weaning Unknown.
Lifespan Unknown, but probably similar to northern right whale dolphin (oldest recorded 42 years).

PHOTO-IDENTIFICATION
Currently not possible.

POPULATION
Unknown, though considered fairly common throughout its range.

CONSERVATION
IUCN status: Least Concern (2018). Poorly known. There is no evidence of large-scale hunting (although unknown numbers are killed illegally for human consumption and used as crab bait in Chile and Peru). Bycatch in gillnet fisheries is probably the main concern, including off northern Chile (particularly for swordfish), Peru, southern Africa and South Australia, though there is very little information.

A group of southern right whale dolphins can look remarkably like penguins from a distance.

AUSTRALIAN SNUBFIN DOLPHIN
Orcaella heinsohni

Beasley, Robertson and Arnold, 2005

Until recently, the Australian snubfin dolphin was regarded as a form of Irrawaddy dolphin, but the two were separated in 2005 (largely by skull morphology and genetics, but also external characters such as coloration, height of the dorsal fin, and presence or absence of a dorsal groove). Their closest relative is the killer whale.

Classification Odontoceti, family Delphinidae.
Common name 'Australian' because it is best known and most studied in Australia; 'snubfin' after the characteristically 'snubby' (short and wide) dorsal fin.
Other names None.
Scientific name *Orcaella* from the Latin *orca* for 'a kind of whale', and *ella* for 'little'; *heinsohni* after pioneering Australian cetologist George Heinsohn, who conducted some of the first research on this species in Australian waters.
Taxonomy No recognised forms or subspecies (although there is apparent genetic differentiation between widely separated populations).

ADULT

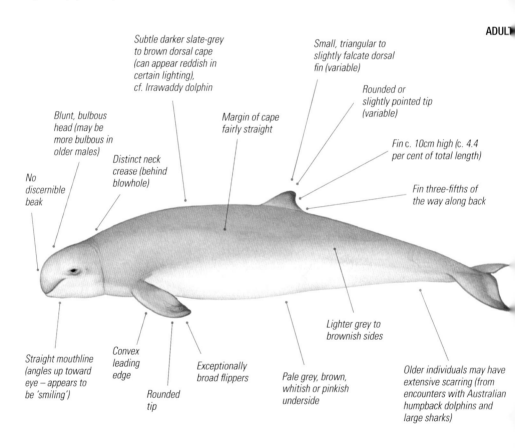

Subtle darker slate-grey to brown dorsal cape (can appear reddish in certain lighting), cf. Irrawaddy dolphin

Small, triangular to slightly falcate dorsal fin (variable)

Rounded or slightly pointed tip (variable)

Blunt, bulbous head (may be more bulbous in older males)

Margin of cape fairly straight

Fin c. 10cm high (c. 4.4 per cent of total length)

Distinct neck crease (behind blowhole)

No discernible beak

Fin three-fifths of the way along back

Straight mouthline (angles up toward eye – appears to be 'smiling')

Convex leading edge

Rounded tip

Exceptionally broad flippers

Pale grey, brown, whitish or pinkish underside

Lighter grey to brownish sides

Older individuals may have extensive scarring (from encounters with Australian humpback dolphins and large sharks)

AT A GLANCE
- Coastal northern Australia and southern Papua New Guinea
- Small size
- Subtle three-toned grey to brown coloration
- Bulbous head with no beak
- Small dorsal fin behind midpoint of back
- No dorsal groove
- Cryptic, low surfacing
- Usually in small groups

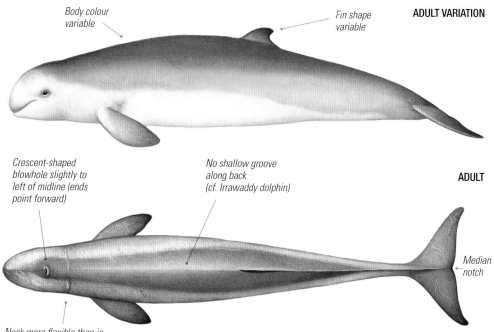

Body colour variable

Fin shape variable

ADULT VARIATION

Crescent-shaped blowhole slightly to left of midline (ends point forward)

No shallow groove along back (cf. Irrawaddy dolphin)

ADULT

Median notch

Neck more flexible than in most other dolphins (first two neck vertebrae unfused)

Generally greyer, more subdued coloration

CALF

SIZE
L: ♂ 2.1–2.7m, ♀ 1.9–2.3m;
WT: 114–130kg; **MAX:** 2.7m, 133kg
Calf – L: *c.* 1m; **WT:** *c.* 10–12kg
Males larger than females.

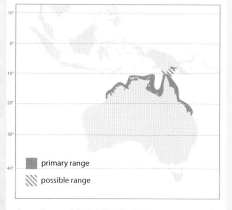

☐ primary range
▨ possible range

Australian snubfin dolphin distribution

SIMILAR SPECIES

The only small cetacean in the region without a distinct beak. Confusion is possible with dugongs, though the snubfin dolphin has a dorsal fin (dugongs do not). The Australian snubfin and Irrawaddy dolphins are not thought to be sympatric but they can be distinguished by coloration (three-toned in snubfin, two-toned in Irrawaddy); the snubfin also lacks a dorsal groove and has a more distinct neck crease. A hybrid with an Australian humpback dolphin has been confirmed in Australia.

DISTRIBUTION

Poorly documented range in a narrow strip of shallow, protected coastal and estuarine tropical and sub-tropical waters of the Sahul Shelf (part of the continental shelf extending from the northern coast of Australia to New Guinea). Occurs throughout northern Australia – although the distribution is fragmented – and in the Kikori Delta in the Gulf of Papua, southern Papua New Guinea. In Australia, it ranges from Roebuck Bay, Western Australia, north-east through the Northern Territory and south along the Queensland coast to Keppel Bay, central Queensland. Records from as far south as the North West Cape in Western Australia and the Brisbane River in Queensland are considered extralimital. In Papua New Guinea, it is known to range from Morigio Island east to Baimuru and is likely to occur as far as the headwaters of the Purari River. There are anecdotal records from the Solomon Islands, though identification is uncertain. There is strong evidence of high site fidelity (though there may be some seasonal movements along the northern coast of Australia) and there appears to be little movement between sites.

Most sightings are within 6km of shore, though up to 20km where the water is shallow (e.g. the Gulf of Carpentaria, Northern Territory, where it is still only c. 10m). Rarely more than 20km from the nearest river mouth. Typically in water less than 18m deep, but some populations regularly enter water as shallow as 2m. Highest abundance around tidal creek mouths and in sheltered, mangrove-lined bays, but also around seagrass beds; reported to use dredged channels in some locations. Unlike the Irrawaddy dolphin, it does not regularly inhabit freshwater, but has been recorded up to 50km upstream in some larger tidal rivers.

BEHAVIOUR

Not particularly acrobatic and usually makes only low leaps when disturbed, socialising or swimming against a strong current. Spyhopping, body rubbing, rolling sideways and tail-slapping are sometimes observed. Groups may suddenly become energetic, performing playful, splashy leaps. Can spit a narrow, well-directed jet of water 1–2m into the air, usually in association with feeding (perhaps to herd small fish). Sometimes occurs with Australian humpback dolphins and Indo-Pacific bottlenose dolphins, and interactions vary – the humpback dolphins can be aggressive, or show sexual behaviour, but the two species

Australian snubfin dolphins can spit a well-directed jet of water up to 2m into the air.

may forage and travel together. Usually shy of vessels and not known to bow-ride.

TEETH

Upper 27–42
Lower 29–37

GROUP SIZE AND STRUCTURE

Typically 2–6, but sometimes alone or in aggregations of up to 25. Average group size in north-east Queensland is 5.3, in the Kimberley region of Western Australia is 2–4 (depending on precise locality). Groups can be fluid, but there can be strong, long-lasting bonds.

PREDATORS

Shark predation is probably high. In a recent study, 72 per cent of snubfin dolphins showed evidence of shark bites – more than half attributable to tiger sharks – which is among the highest reported for any dolphin.

PHOTO-IDENTIFICATION

Nicks, scars and other distinctive marks on the dorsal fin and back, as well as the flukes for secondary identification features.

DIVE SEQUENCE

- Indistinct blow (can be heard).
- Surfaces inconspicuously with little splash.
- Blowhole and only uppermost part of body visible.
- Rolls forward into dive, showing little or nothing of tailstock.
- May arch back slightly or glide beneath surface.
- Occasionally lifts flukes out of water before steep dive.
- Rarely porpoises with low, horizontal, splashy leaps.

FOOD AND FEEDING

Prey Opportunistic feeder taking a wide variety of fish (including cardinalfish, toothpony, sardines, anchovies, grunters), squid (*Uroteuthis* spp., *Loliolus* spp., *Sepioteuthis lessoniana*), octopus, cuttlefish and crustaceans (prawns).
Feeding Feeds throughout water column to seafloor; known to hunt cooperatively; may spit water to assist in capturing fish (see Behaviour).
Dive depth Unknown.
Dive time Typically 30 seconds to three minutes; maximum recorded 12 minutes (when disturbed).

POPULATION

No overall abundance estimate, though probably fewer than *c.* 10,000 mature individuals. Typically found in small local populations of fewer than 150. Regional estimates include: Northern Territory – *c.* 1,000 along the western Gulf of Carpentaria, 136–222 in Port Essington, 19–70 in the Darwin region; Western Australia – 133 in Roebuck Bay, 48–54 in Cygnet Bay; Queensland – 64–76 in Cleveland Bay, 71–80 in the Keppel Bay region.

CONSERVATION

IUCN status: Vulnerable (2017) (likely to be moved to Endangered). Nearshore habitat and slow reproductive rate make it particularly vulnerable to threats from human activities. Habitat loss, degradation and disturbance – caused by the development of port and marina facilities, aquaculture, modifications for mining and agricultural activities, residential development and increased vessel activity – are major threats in many areas. Inshore gillnets, particularly those set across creeks, rivers and shallow estuaries to catch barramundi and threadfin salmon, routinely trap snubfin dolphins. There are few figures, but alarming levels of bycatch are known in Papua New Guinea. Gillnetting is banned or strictly regulated in some regions of Australia, but enforcement is difficult. A major threat from the early 1960s was accidental capture in nets used across many Queensland beaches to reduce the perceived risk of shark attack on bathers; following a gradual change from nets to baited hook drum-lines, starting in 1992, the number of mortalities has declined (though it is still an issue in some areas). No direct takes are known, although historically it may have been hunted by some indigenous communities in Australia and there are anecdotal reports of deliberate catches in southern Papua New Guinea. Other threats include prey depletion, noise pollution, chemical pollution and ingestion of marine debris.

LIFE HISTORY

Sexual maturity Females and males 8–10 years.
Mating Unknown.
Gestation *c.* 14 months.
Calving Every 2–3 years (occasionally up to five years); single calf (season unknown).
Weaning Unknown.
Lifespan Probably 28–30 years.

The blunt, bulbous head and distinct neck crease are characteristic of Australian snubfin dolphins.

IRRAWADDY DOLPHIN
Orcaella brevirostris

(Owen in Gray, 1866)

Superficially like a finless porpoise with a dorsal fin, or the equatorial equivalent of a beluga, the Irrawaddy dolphin is not classified as a 'river dolphin' yet is found in rivers, estuaries and lagoons. With a reduction in both range and abundance in recent years, it is now endangered.

Classification Odontoceti, family Delphinidae.

Common name After the Irrawaddy River (also known as the Ayeyarwady) in Myanmar; one of the earliest specimens was found 1,450km upstream.

Other names Mahakam River dolphin, pesut.

Scientific name *Orcaella* from the Latin *orca* for 'a kind of whale', and *ella* for 'little'; *brevirostris* from the Latin *brevis* for 'short', and *rostrum* for 'beak'.

Taxonomy No recognised forms or subspecies (although freshwater sub-populations are clearly distinct and new subspecies designations may be warranted); *Orcaella* was recently (2005) split into two species (Irrawaddy and Australian snubfin dolphins) based largely on skull morphology and genetics, but also external characteristics such as coloration, height of the dorsal fin, and presence or absence of a dorsal groove.

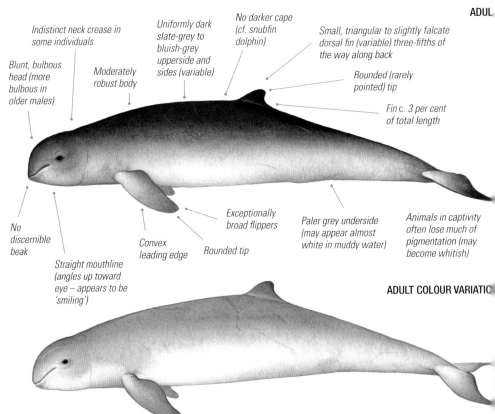

ADUL

Indistinct neck crease in some individuals

Uniformly dark slate-grey to bluish-grey upperside and sides (variable)

No darker cape (cf. snubfin dolphin)

Small, triangular to slightly falcate dorsal fin (variable) three-fifths of the way along back

Blunt, bulbous head (more bulbous in older males)

Moderately robust body

Rounded (rarely pointed) tip

Fin c. 3 per cent of total length

No discernible beak

Straight mouthline (angles up toward eye – appears to be 'smiling')

Convex leading edge

Exceptionally broad flippers

Rounded tip

Paler grey underside (may appear almost white in muddy water)

Animals in captivity often lose much of pigmentation (may become whitish)

ADULT COLOUR VARIATIO

AT A GLANCE
- Tropical and sub-tropical Indo-Pacific
- Coastal, brackish and fresh waters
- Small size
- Two-toned grey coloration

- Bulbous head with no beak
- Small dorsal fin behind midpoint of back
- Shallow dorsal groove
- Cryptic, low surfacing
- Usually in small groups

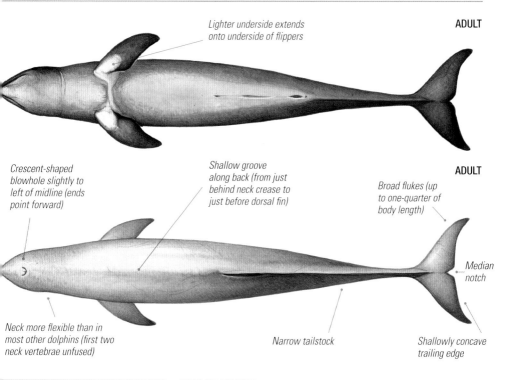

Lighter underside extends onto underside of flippers

ADULT

Crescent-shaped blowhole slightly to left of midline (ends point forward)

Shallow groove along back (from just behind neck crease to just before dorsal fin)

ADULT

Broad flukes (up to one-quarter of body length)

Median notch

Neck more flexible than in most other dolphins (first two neck vertebrae unfused)

Narrow tailstock

Shallowly concave trailing edge

SIZE

L: ♂ 1.7–2.7m, ♀ 1.7–2.2m;
WT: 115–130kg; **MAX:** 2.8m, 130kg
Calf – L: *c.* 1m; **WT:** *c.* 10–12kg

SIMILAR SPECIES

Confusion is possible with the Indo-Pacific finless porpoise and even dugong, but the Irrawaddy dolphin has a dorsal fin (the other two species do not). It overlaps with the South Asian river dolphin in the Sundarbans, but the river dolphin has a long beak. The Irrawaddy and Australian snubfin dolphins are not thought to be sympatric (they are separated by deep oceanic waters, and probably have been since before the Pleistocene ice ages) but they can be distinguished by coloration (two-toned in Irrawaddy, three-toned in snubfin); the Irrawaddy also has a dorsal groove and a less distinct neck crease.

DISTRIBUTION

Poorly documented range in shallow, protected coastal, estuarine and fresh waters of the Sunda Shelf (part of the Southeast Asian continental shelf). Found throughout tropical and sub-tropical South and Southeast Asia, with an affinity for low-salinity waters. Fragmented into relatively small populations, and absent from long stretches of coastline within the overall range (due to lack of freshwater inputs or local extinctions). Also occurs in three brackish water bodies (Songkhla Lake in Thailand, Chilika Lake in India

Irrawaddy dolphin distribution

CAL

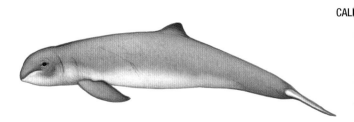

and Malampaya Sound in the Philippines) and three large river systems (the Irrawaddy or Ayeyarwady in Myanmar, up to 1,450km upstream, though now confined during the dry season to a 370km stretch of river in the far upstream reaches above Mandalay; the Mahakam in Borneo, Indonesia, up to 560km upstream, though now mainly a 195km stretch of the main stream; and the Mekong in Lao PDR and Cambodia, up to 690km upstream, though now mainly a 190km river segment to Khone Falls just upstream from the Lao PDR–Cambodia border). May enter the lower reaches (up to *c.* 86km) of other rivers.

Coastal populations are typically within a few kilometres of shore and of river estuaries; also in large lagoons and mangrove forests. Preferred water depth varies according to region: typically in 0.6–2.5m in Chilika Lake, 2–5.4m in Sarawak, shallower than 6m in Malampaya Sound, 7.5m in coastal waters of Bangladesh, and 14.6m in Balikpapan Bay, Indonesia. Riverine populations are concentrated in relatively deep pools (10–50m) at confluences or above and below rapids.

The distribution of some populations shifts inshore (or downstream) during high tide, offshore (or upstream) during low tide. Seasonal movements in response to changes in freshwater input in some areas. Otherwise, home ranges are relatively small (low tens of kilometres).

BEHAVIOUR
Not particularly acrobatic and usually makes only low leaps when disturbed, socialising or swimming against a strong current. Spyhopping, body rubbing and tail-slapping are sometimes observed. Can spit a narrow, well-directed jet of water 1–2m into the air, usually in association with feeding (perhaps to herd small fish). Remarkable habit in the Irrawaddy (Ayeyarwady) River is fishing cooperatively with cast-net fishermen. Usually shy of vessels and not known to bow-ride.

TEETH
Upper 16–38
Lower 22–36
Teeth may not erupt in some populations (e.g. Mahakam River).

GROUP SIZE AND STRUCTURE
Typically 2–6, but varies with location; up to 20 when two or more groups come together, and as many as 30 in some deepwater riverine pools during the dry season.

PREDATORS
No confirmed natural predators, but probably large sharks

PHOTO-IDENTIFICATION
Possible, using nicks, scars and other distinctive marks or the dorsal fin and back.

POPULATION
No overall abundance estimate. Typically found in small local populations of 10s to low 100s, with the primary exception of open estuarine waters of Bangladesh, which had an estimated population of *c.* 5,400 in 2007. Approximate regional estimates include 451 in the Sunderbans mangrove forest in Bangladesh; 423 along the Trat coast in the Gulf of Thailand; 233 in Kuching Bay, Sarawak, Malaysia; 111 in Chilika Lake, India;

DIVE SEQUENCE
- Indistinct blow (can sometimes be heard).
- Surfaces inconspicuously with little splash.
- Blowhole and only uppermost part of body (including dorsal fin) visible.
- Arches back as rolls forward into dive.
- May lift flukes out of water before steep dive or flip to one side, showing single fluke.
- Rarely porpoises (low, horizontal, splashy leaps).

FOOD AND FEEDING
Prey Wide variety of fish (including catfish), squid, octopus, cuttlefish and crustaceans.
Feeding Primarily a diurnal feeder; known to hunt cooperatively; may spit water to assist in capturing fish (see Behaviour).
Dive depth Unknown.
Dive time Typically 30 seconds to three minutes; maximum recorded 12 minutes (when disturbed).

30 in the Mekong River, Cambodia and Lao PDR; 77 in the Mahakam River, Indonesia; 58–72 in the Irrawaddy or Ayeyarwady River in Myanmar; 69 in Koh Kong, Cambodia; 50 in Balikpapan Bay, Kalimantan, Indonesia; and 35 in Malampaya Sound, Philippines.

CONSERVATION
IUCN status: Endangered (2017); Mahakan River, Indonesia, sub-population Critically Endangered (2008). Four other geographically isolated sub-populations (each with fewer than 80 mature individuals): Irrawaddy or Ayeyarwady River, Myanmar; Mekong River, Lao PDR and Cambodia; Songkhla Lake, Thailand; Malampaya Sound, Philippines. Nearshore and freshwater habitats and slow reproductive rate make the species particularly vulnerable to threats from human activities.

The main threat is bycatch in small-scale fisheries, especially gillnets; annual mortality rates of up to 9.3 per cent in some areas are not sustainable (the maximum annual increase without human-induced threats is estimated to be 3.8 per cent). Illegal electrofishing in the Irrawaddy River may pose another severe threat. Habitat loss, degradation and disturbance – caused by planned and proposed dams (especially in the Irrawaddy and Mekong Rivers), modifications for gold, sand and gravel mining and agricultural activities, fish farms and barrier fish traps – are major threats. It was hunted during the 1970s by the Khmer Rouge in Cambodia (and extirpated from Tonlé Sap Lake) and is sometimes shot for target practice, but is also revered by local people in parts of its range. It has been captured in Thailand, Indonesia and Myanmar for live display in oceanaria, though this is no longer common. Other threats include prey depletion, pollution (oil, pesticides, industrial waste, coal dust) and vessel strikes.

LIFE HISTORY
Sexual maturity Females and males 8–10 years.
Mating High-energy, synchronised surfacing, aggressive swimming, and 'piling up' on each other, then swimming abreast while maintaining body contact.
Gestation *c.* 14 months.
Calving Every 2–5 years; single calf born year-round, with peak varying according to location (often April–June, in pre-monsoon season).
Weaning After *c.* 24 months; takes solid food after six months.
Lifespan Probably 28–30 years.

s nearshore habitat makes the Irrawaddy dolphin particularly vulnerable to threats from human activities.

ROUGH-TOOTHED DOLPHIN
Steno bredanensis

(G. Cuvier in Lesson, 1828)

Unmistakable at close range, with its smoothly sloping forehead, the rough-toothed dolphin has been described as looking more like an extinct ichthyosaur (a marine reptile from the age of the dinosaurs) than a cetacean.

Classification Odontoceti, family Delphinidae.
Common name After the fine longitudinal wrinkles or ridges on the teeth, which feel rough to the touch.
Other names Roughtooth dolphin, slopehead, steno; rarely – black porpoise.
Scientific name *Steno* either after Danish scientist Nicolaus Steno (1638–86) or from the Greek *stenos* for 'narrow' (referring to the beak); *bredanensis* after the Dutch artist J.G.S. van Breda (1788–1867), who painted and described the type specimen, and *ensis* from the Latin for 'belonging to'.
Taxonomy No recognised forms or subspecies.

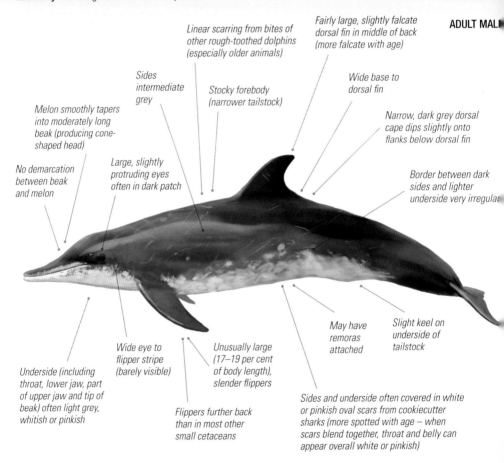

Linear scarring from bites of other rough-toothed dolphins (especially older animals)

Fairly large, slightly falcate dorsal fin in middle of back (more falcate with age)

ADULT MALE

Sides intermediate grey

Stocky forebody (narrower tailstock)

Wide base to dorsal fin

Melon smoothly tapers into moderately long beak (producing cone-shaped head)

Narrow, dark grey dorsal cape dips slightly onto flanks below dorsal fin

No demarcation between beak and melon

Large, slightly protruding eyes often in dark patch

Border between dark sides and lighter underside very irregular

May have remoras attached

Slight keel on underside of tailstock

Underside (including throat, lower jaw, part of upper jaw and tip of beak) often light grey, whitish or pinkish

Wide eye to flipper stripe (barely visible)

Unusually large (17–19 per cent of body length), slender flippers

Flippers further back than in most other small cetaceans

Sides and underside often covered in white or pinkish oval scars from cookiecutter sharks (more spotted with age – when scars blend together, throat and belly can appear overall white or pinkish)

AT A GLANCE
- Offshore waters in tropics and sub-tropics
- Small size (but chunky)
- Complex three-toned coloration
- Prominent, slightly falcate dorsal fin
- Cone-shaped head
- Melon slopes smoothly into moderately long beak
- Unusually large flippers
- May be covered in pink or white blotches
- Almost reptilian in appearance
- Often 'skims' along surface

SIZE
L: ♂ 2.2–2.7m, ♀ 2.1–2.6m;
WT: 90–155kg; **MAX:** 2.8m
Calf – L: *c.* 1–1.2m; **WT:** *c.* 15kg
Male slightly larger than female.

ADULT FEMALE

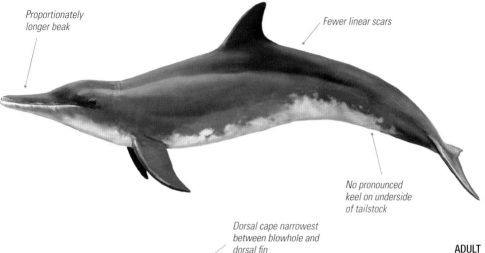

Proportionately longer beak

Fewer linear scars

No pronounced keel on underside of tailstock

Dorsal cape narrowest between blowhole and dorsal fin

ADULT

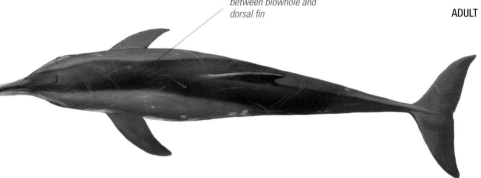

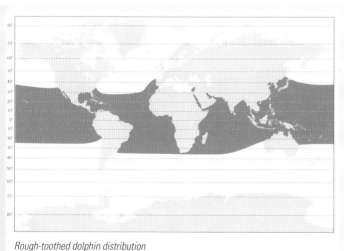

Rough-toothed dolphin distribution

SIMILAR SPECIES

At a distance, confusion is most likely with bottlenose dolphins. But the smoothly sloping forehead with no beak demarcation makes identification quite easy; the light-coloured lips and lower jaw (if light-coloured), and the blotchiness caused by cookiecutter shark bites, are also distinctive (the bites quickly repigment close to the original background grey colour in bottlenose dolphins). Hybrids with bottlenose dolphins have been reported in captivity.

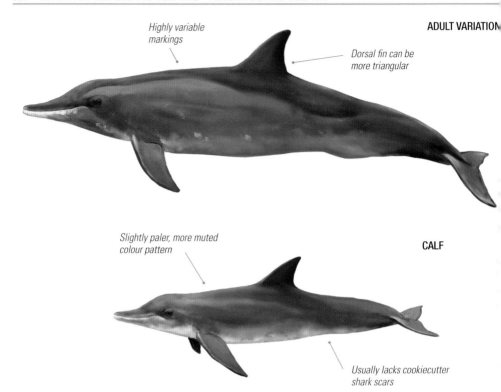

Highly variable markings

ADULT VARIATION

Dorsal fin can be more triangular

Slightly paler, more muted colour pattern

CALF

Usually lacks cookiecutter shark scars

DISTRIBUTION

Tropical to sub-tropical (and some warm temperate) waters in the Atlantic, Pacific and Indian Oceans. Mainly from *c.* 40°N to *c.* 35°S. Also in many semi-enclosed seas, including the Red Sea, Gulf of California, Gulf of Mexico and Caribbean Sea. Formerly considered a vagrant in the Mediterranean, but a small, relict population is present in the far eastern corner (east of the Sicilian Channel, mostly within the Levant Basin). Prefers deep offshore waters beyond the continental shelf – usually deeper than *c.* 1,000m – and rarely close to land except around islands with steep drop-offs. In some parts of the range, sighting rates increase with depth. However, also found in shallow coastal waters in the eastern Mediterranean, Brazil, West

DIVE SEQUENCE

Two main types of surfacing:

Slower speed

- Surfaces quite subtly and unobtrusively (though dorsal fin striking).
- Indistinct blow.
- Top of head and rostrum appear.
- Body rises out of water showing part of back and dorsal fin.
- Slight arching of back as it dives.
- In between, may swim just under surface with tip of dorsal fin visible.

Moderate speed

- Skims along with head and chin just above surface, forming distinctive walls of spray (looks rather like surfing).

FOOD AND FEEDING
Prey Fish, squid and octopus, including needlefish, flying fish; may specialise on mahi-mahi over 1m long; algae found in some stomachs may have been ingested accidentally.
Feeding Sometimes hunts cooperatively; thought to feed primarily on near-surface species, so seabirds often associated with foraging groups.
Dive depth Not a particularly deep diver; deepest recorded 399m (though morphologically capable of deeper); deeper dives at night.
Dive time Varies with location; average 4–7 minutes in Hawaii; maximum recorded 15 minutes.

frica and possibly elsewhere. Shows fidelity to at least ome oceanic islands and no long-distance migrations are nown.

BEHAVIOUR
an appear quite lethargic and inactive, and it is not ildly acrobatic, but it does breach fairly regularly and ften multiple times in a row (although not particularly igh). Spyhopping, surface-slapping and low-angled arced eaping are quite common. Well known for swimming houlder to shoulder in a synchronised 'chorus line'. egularly observed with other cetaceans, including umpback whales, short-finned pilot whales, false killer hales, melon-headed whales, bottlenose dolphins, ootted dolphins, spinner dolphins and Fraser's dolphins. here have been several observations of care-giving to sick adividuals, and support to dead ones, for hours or even everal days. Often attracted to logs and other flotsam r fish-aggregating devices) to feed on the associated sh. Known to scavenge fish from false killer whales and, Hawaii at least, regularly steals bait and catch from shermen's hooks. Reaction to boats varies from evasive ehaviour to extreme interest. In most places, it is quite asy to approach as long as it is not actively foraging. ften bow-rides and wake-rides, and will sometimes even :ay with slow-moving vessels.

TEETH
pper 38–52
ower 38–56

GROUP SIZE AND STRUCTURE
lost common group size is 10–20, though occasionally maller groups or alone; up to 50 not uncommon in the

eastern tropical Pacific and central Atlantic; some reports of more than 300 (probably aggregations of sub-groups). Some evidence of more group stability – in terms of a few preferred companions – than in most dolphin species.

PREDATORS
Unknown, but probably killer whales and large sharks (the lack of healed wounds suggests that most attacks are fatal).

PHOTO-IDENTIFICATION
Individuals are identified by the notches on the trailing edge of the dorsal fin and the blotching pigmentation patterns.

POPULATION
Total abundance possibly more than 250,000. There are estimated to be *c.* 146,000 in the eastern tropical Pacific, more than 72,000 around Hawaii and 2,750 in the northern Gulf of Mexico.

CONSERVATION
IUCN status: Least Concern (2008). No known major threats. Taken in relatively small numbers in directed dolphin fisheries in Sri Lanka, Taiwan, Japan, Indonesia, the Solomon Islands, Papua New Guinea, St Vincent and the Grenadines, West Africa and (historically) St Helena in the South Atlantic. There is more concern about incidental capture in fishing gear in Brazil, Sri Lanka, Taiwan, American Samoa, the Arabian Sea, offshore in the North Pacific and inevitably elsewhere. Has been captured for display in oceanaria. Other potential threats include chemical and noise pollution, dynamite fishing in some areas, and reprisals for stealing bait and catch from fishing hooks.

LIFE HISTORY
Sexual maturity Females 8–10 years, males 5–14 years.
Mating Unknown.
Gestation Possibly *c.* 12 months.

Calving Single calf probably born in summer.
Weaning Unknown.
Lifespan At least 32–36 years (oldest recorded 48 years).

ATLANTIC HUMPBACK DOLPHIN
Sousa teuszii
(Kükenthal, 1892

The Atlantic humpback dolphin lives up to its name: its dorsal fin sits on top of an extraordinary elongated hump. It is a very rare dolphin, with a fragmented distribution along the west coast of Africa, and immediate action is required to save it from extinction.

Classification Odontoceti, family Delphinidae.

Common name 'Atlantic' because this species is endemic to the eastern Atlantic; 'humpback' after the fleshy raised 'hump' on which the dorsal fin sits (the dolphin version of the humpback whale's fin/hump arrangement).

Other names Humpbacked dolphin, Atlantic hump-backed dolphin, West African hump-backed dolphin, Cameroon dolphin, Cameroon river dolphin, Teusz's dolphin (after Eduard Tëusz).

Scientific name The meaning of *Sousa* is unclear, but it may be based on an Indian vernacular name for river dolphin (created by Gray in 1866); *teuszii* after German naturalist Eduard Tëusz, who recovered the first known specimen in 1892 (a skull found in the Bay of Warships, Douala, Cameroon; famously, the skull was somehow mixed up with the shark-mauled carcass of a West African manatee, causing much confusion at the time).

Taxonomy The taxonomy of humpback dolphins has been debated for more than two centuries, although the existence of the Atlantic humpback dolphin has been widely accepted since 2004; recent work describes four valid species. There is a possible fifth species in the Bay of Bengal. No recognised forms or subspecies of Atlantic humpback dolphin (though there have been no targeted genetic or morphological studies, and field observations suggest visible differences between some populations).

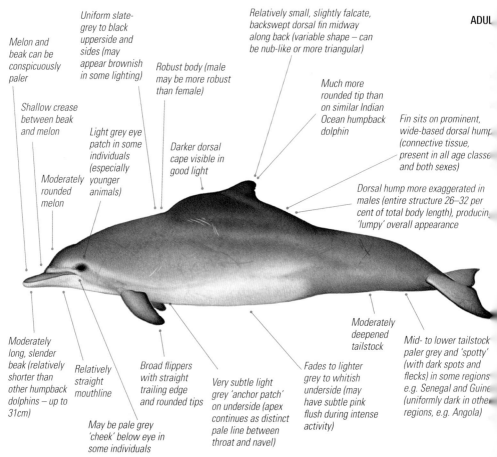

Uniform slate-grey to black upperside and sides (may appear brownish in some lighting)

Melon and beak can be conspicuously paler

Relatively small, slightly falcate, backswept dorsal fin midway along back (variable shape – can be nub-like or more triangular)

ADUL

Shallow crease between beak and melon

Robust body (male may be more robust than female)

Much more rounded tip than on similar Indian Ocean humpback dolphin

Fin sits on prominent, wide-based dorsal hump (connective tissue, present in all age classe and both sexes)

Light grey eye patch in some individuals (especially younger animals)

Darker dorsal cape visible in good light

Moderately rounded melon

Dorsal hump more exaggerated in males (entire structure 26–32 per cent of total body length), producin 'lumpy' overall appearance

Moderately long, slender beak (relatively shorter than other humpback dolphins – up to 31cm)

Relatively straight mouthline

Broad flippers with straight trailing edge and rounded tips

May be pale grey 'cheek' below eye in some individuals

Very subtle light grey 'anchor patch' on underside (apex continues as distinct pale line between throat and navel)

Fades to lighter grey to whitish underside (may have subtle pink flush during intense activity)

Moderately deepened tailstock

Mid- to lower tailstock paler grey and 'spotty' (with dark spots and flecks) in some regions e.g. Senegal and Guine (uniformly dark in other regions, e.g. Angola)

AT A GLANCE

- Tropical and sub-tropical West Africa
- Nearshore waters
- Small size
- Dorsal fin sits on distinctive elongated hump
- Dorsal profile often appears uniform brown, grey or black (depending on light)
- Robust body with deepened tailstock
- Moderately long, slender beak exposed on surfacing
- Often indifferent or shy towards boats

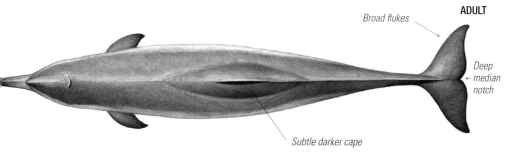

ADULT

Broad flukes

Deep median notch

Subtle darker cape

SIZE

L: 2.3–2.8m; **WT:** 140–280kg (based on assumptions using Indian Ocean humpback dolphin as a guideline); **MAX:** recorded for Atlantic humpback dolphin: 2.85m, 166kg **Calf – L:** *c.* 1m; **WT:** *c.* 10kg Males may be slightly larger than females, but little information.

SIMILAR SPECIES

Confusion is most likely with the common bottlenose dolphin, which overlaps in range (the two sometimes form mixed-species groups). Look for the beak length, dorsal fin size and shape, and the presence of a pronounced dorsal hump in Atlantic humpback. Bottlenose dolphins tend to form larger, more active groups. Very similar in appearance to the Indian Ocean humpback dolphin (although the dorsal fin tends to be more rounded in the Atlantic) but the two species are separated geographically by cold water associated with the Benguela Current, and are presumed not to mix.

DISTRIBUTION

Mainly shallow, nearshore tropical and sub-tropical waters along the west coast of mainland Africa in the eastern Atlantic. Ranges from Dakhla Bay, Western Sahara (23°54'N), south to southern Angola (15°38'S). It has been confirmed in 13 African range states, but is not yet documented in a further six within the likely range (Sierra Leone, Liberia, Côte d'Ivoire, Ghana, Equatorial Guinea or the tiny coastline of the Democratic Republic of Congo); however, there has been relatively little survey effort in these areas. It does not occur around offshore islands such as Cape Verde or São Tomé and Principe. Distribution may not be continuous – there are long stretches of coastline without any reported sightings – but it is hard to know if this represents a lack of abundance or merely a lack of information. The main areas where sightings have been reported are Banc D'Arguin, Mauritania; the Saloum Delta, Senegal; the Bijagós Archipelago and adjacent mainland coast,

Atlantic humpback dolphin distribution

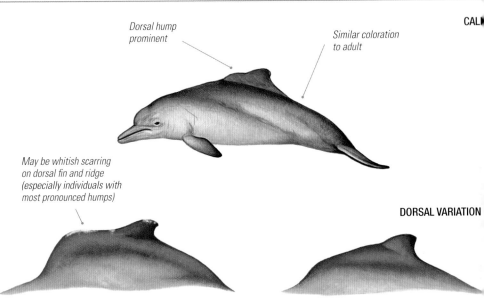

Dorsal hump prominent

Similar coloration to adult

CAL

May be whitish scarring on dorsal fin and ridge (especially individuals with most pronounced humps)

DORSAL VARIATION

Guinea-Bissau; the coastal waters of Guinea; the coastal waters of southern Gabon and the Republic of the Congo; and southern Angola.

Prefers soft-sediment bottoms and habitats strongly influenced by tidal and wave motion, such as surf zones, estuaries, channels, mudflats and sandbars, including mangroves and exposed open coasts; often 'patrols' beaches just beyond the breaking waves. Typically in less than 20m of water (frequently as shallow as 3m) with a mean sighting depth of 5m. Usually within 1–2km of shore and frequently within 100m; recorded as far as 13km from shore, where the water is sufficiently shallow. There are no records seaward of the continental shelf. Preferred water temperature is approximately 16–32°C. Occasionally occupies rivers where there is tidal influence (exceptionally to 53km upstream at Foundiougne in the Saloum River); there is no evidence of separate freshwater populations. No known long-distance migrations; limited evidence suggests high site fidelity in some regions, and local movements in others.

BEHAVIOUR

Generally inconspicuous and most often seen quietly travelling or foraging. Not as aerially active as most other dolphins, but it does occasionally leap (usually simple forward leaps or falling back onto one side). Will sometimes hang vertically in the water, with the head out (spyhopping) during social behaviour. Known to form mixed-species groups with common bottlenose dolphins. Reaction to boats varies, but if it is approache cautiously there is usually just a subtle avoidance response (it typically continues its activities while maintaining a 'personal space' of 15–20m from the boat). It may approach closer if the engine is switched off. Without care, however, groups may split up, dive, change direction underwater and reappear unpredictab some distance away. Does not bow-ride. There are old reports from Mauritania of it fishing cooperatively with common bottlenose dolphins and fishermen, by herding mullet.

DIVE SEQUENCE
- Tends to be slow, deliberate swimmer.
- Beak (and often much of head, including eyes) lifted clear of water on surfacing (often rises at angle of more than 45°).
- Small, indistinct blow.
- Body arched (showing much of back, hump and dorsal fin) in a high, tight roll.
- Flukes often lifted above surface before deep foraging dive (most frequently in relatively deeper water).

FOOD AND FEEDING

Prey Nearshore coastal, estuarine and reef fish (including mullet, grunts, bongo shad, snapper, Atlantic emperor, West African spadefish, sardines, croakers, Atlantic bonito).

Feeding Sometimes forages cooperatively to herd mullet, but may also spread out over area and forage individually (foraging independently for a few minutes, then regrouping for a few minutes); tail-up dives suggest hunting for non-schooling benthic and reef fish; may sometimes use shoreline to trap prey.

Dive depth Details unknown, but usually shallow (probably less than 20m).

Dive time Typically 40–60 seconds.

TEETH

Upper 54–64
Lower 52–62

GROUP SIZE AND STRUCTURE

Group size varies according to geographical location, habitat, season (for example, in Angola average group size is significantly smaller in summer) and structure. The typical group size is 1–10 (accounting for 65 per cent of sightings), but as many as 20 have been seen off Mauritania and Guinea-Bissau, 37 off Senegal, 40 off Gabon, and 45 in the Gulf of Guinea. There appear to be long-lasting and stable affiliations between individuals in a small sub-population in southern Angola, but elsewhere the stability of groups is unknown.

PREDATORS

No direct evidence, but large sharks are the most likely predators.

PHOTO-IDENTIFICATION

Possible, using nicks, notches and other damage on the trailing edge of the dorsal fin, as well as scarring and other temporary markings on the fin.

POPULATION

No overall abundance estimate, but there are probably fewer than 3,000 (and numbers are suspected to be declining). Most sub-populations appear to have considerably fewer than 100 individuals. There are few recent accurate regional estimates: a minimum of 103 in the Saloum Delta, Senegal; a minimum of 47 in a 375sq km area of the Río Nuñez region of northern Guinea; and 10 along a 35km stretch of coast in southern Angola.

CONSERVATION

IUCN status: Critically Endangered (2017). Suspected to be declining throughout its range. Its inshore distribution and susceptibility to disturbance make it particularly vulnerable to human activities. The greatest immediate threat is incidental capture in fishing nets, which has been documented or strongly inferred in most range states. Entanglement in nearshore artisanal gillnets appears to be the main problem – they are deployed regularly within 1km of the coast and inside bays used by dolphins – but it is also caught on octopus lines and in beach seines and fish traps. There is at least some local hunting for human consumption (the 'marine bushmeat' trade) and shark bait. Other potential threats include habitat loss and degradation (especially from harbour construction and coastal development), vessel strikes, overfishing of prey species, chemical pollution and noise pollution.

LIFE HISTORY

Virtually nothing is known. Possibly similar to Indian Ocean humpback dolphin.

Male with a highly exaggerated dorsal hump.

The throat and lower jaw are lighter grey and there may be pale grey on the 'cheeks', such as on this individual.

INDO-PACIFIC HUMPBACK DOLPHIN

Sousa chinensis (Osbeck, 1765)

Previously, all humpback dolphins from South Africa to China and Australia were classified as the Indo-Pacific humpback dolphin (*Sousa chinensis*). But in 2014 this was split into three distinct species: Indo-Pacific, Indian Ocean and Australian humpback dolphins. There is still great uncertainty about the taxonomic status of several Indo-Pacific populations and much of the extensive geographical variation in appearance is yet to be properly documented.

Classification Odontoceti, family Delphinidae.

Common name 'Indo-Pacific' because this species is endemic to the eastern Indian Ocean and western Pacific Ocean; 'humpback' because it belongs to the same genus as species that have a distinctive elongated hump on the back.

Other names Indo-Pacific hump-backed dolphin, Pacific humpback dolphin, Chinese humpback dolphin, Taiwanese humpback dolphin, Chinese white dolphin, Borneo white dolphin, Taiwanese white dolphin, speckled dolphin.

Scientific name The meaning of *Sousa* is unclear, but it may be based on a Hindi vernacular name for river dolphin (originally erected as a sub-genus of *Steno* by Gray in 1866); *chinensis* from China and the Latin *ensis*, meaning 'belonging to'.

Taxonomy The taxonomy of humpback dolphins has been debated for more than two centuries. Recent work currently recognises four valid species but, given the genetic distinctiveness of humpback dolphins in Bangladesh, and the anomalous appearance of other individuals in the Bay of Bengal, there may ultimately be a fifth species (tentatively *S. lentiginosa*, but provisionally included as *S. chinensis* until the taxonomic status is clarified). There is also uncertainty about the exact taxonomic status of the *borneensis*-type in mainland Malaysia and Borneo. A unique and recently accepted subspecies, called the Taiwanese humpback dolphin (*S. c. taiwanensis*), exists in Taiwan; all other Indo-Pacific humpback dolphins become *S. c. chinensis*.

ADULT CHINA, TAIWAN AND HONG KONG MALE

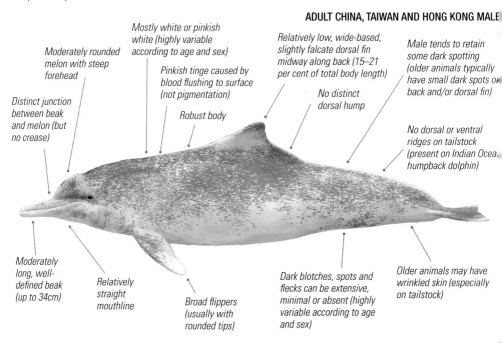

Moderately rounded melon with steep forehead

Mostly white or pinkish white (highly variable according to age and sex)

Pinkish tinge caused by blood flushing to surface (not pigmentation)

Distinct junction between beak and melon (but no crease)

Robust body

Relatively low, wide-based, slightly falcate dorsal fin midway along back (15–21 per cent of total body length)

No distinct dorsal hump

Male tends to retain some dark spotting (older animals typically have small dark spots on back and/or dorsal fin)

No dorsal or ventral ridges on tailstock (present on Indian Ocean humpback dolphin)

Moderately long, well-defined beak (up to 34cm)

Relatively straight mouthline

Broad flippers (usually with rounded tips)

Dark blotches, spots and flecks can be extensive, minimal or absent (highly variable according to age and sex)

Older animals may have wrinkled skin (especially on tailstock)

AT A GLANCE

- Tropical to warm temperate waters in South Asia and Southeast Asia
- Small size
- Nearshore waters, usually near freshwater inputs
- Mostly white coloration (often with pinkish tinge)
- Often with dark blotches, spots and flecks
- No distinct dorsal hump
- Low, wide-based, slightly falcate to triangular dorsal fin midway along back
- Moderately long, well-defined beak

SIZE
L: ♂ 2–2.6m, ♀ 2–2.6m;
WT: 200–240kg; **MAX:** 2.7m, 240kg
Calf – L: *c.* 1m; **WT:** *c.* 10–12kg

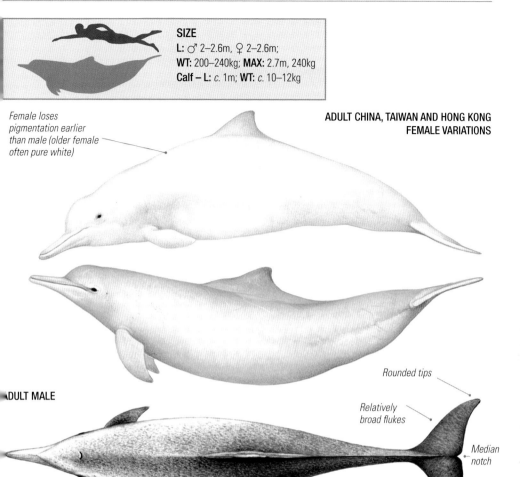

*Female loses
pigmentation earlier
than male (older female
often pure white)*

**ADULT CHINA, TAIWAN AND HONG KONG
FEMALE VARIATIONS**

ADULT MALE

Rounded tips

*Relatively
broad flukes*

*Median
notch*

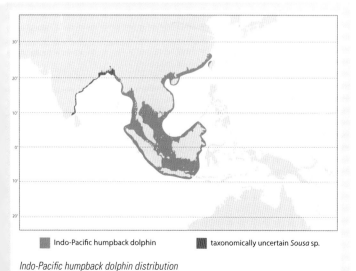

Indo-Pacific humpback dolphin distribution

■ Indo-Pacific humpback dolphin   ▨ taxonomically uncertain *Sousa* sp.

SIMILAR SPECIES

There may be some overlap with the Indian Ocean humpback dolphin in the Bay of Bengal (depending on ultimate decisions about taxonomy), but the lack of a prominent dorsal hump, the wider-based dorsal fin with a more rounded tip, and the much lighter colour of adult Indo-Pacific humpback dolphins can be distinctive. Indo-Pacific and common bottlenose dolphins differ in colour (especially when Indo-Pacific individuals are pink) and dorsal fin and head shape.

DISTRIBUTION

Precise distribution will be

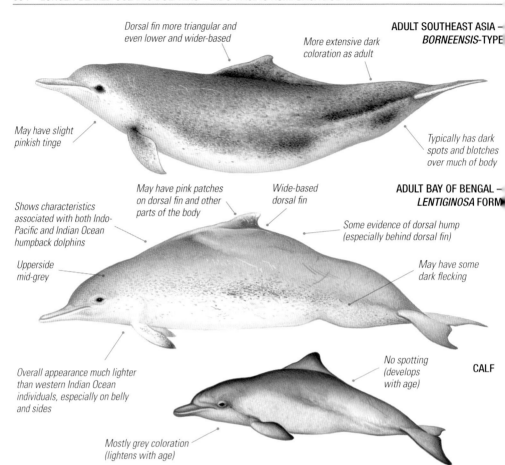

ADULT SOUTHEAST ASIA – *BORNEENSIS*-TYPE

Dorsal fin more triangular and even lower and wider-based

More extensive dark coloration as adult

May have slight pinkish tinge

Typically has dark spots and blotches over much of body

ADULT BAY OF BENGAL – *LENTIGINOSA* FORM

Shows characteristics associated with both Indo-Pacific and Indian Ocean humpback dolphins

May have pink patches on dorsal fin and other parts of the body

Wide-based dorsal fin

Some evidence of dorsal hump (especially behind dorsal fin)

Upperside mid-grey

May have some dark flecking

No spotting (develops with age)

CALF

Overall appearance much lighter than western Indian Ocean individuals, especially on belly and sides

Mostly grey coloration (lightens with age)

uncertain until the taxonomy of humpback dolphins in the Bay of Bengal is determined. For this review, it is assumed that the Indo-Pacific humpback dolphin occurs in tropical to warm temperate waters from central China (the northernmost records are from near the mouth of the Yangtze River) in the east, through the Indo-Malay archipelago at least as far south as Indonesia, and west around the coastal rim of Myanmar, Bangladesh, and eastern India. However, the confirmed range extends only as far west as the Myanmar/Bangladesh border,

and the taxonomic status of populations from there through Bangladesh and eastern India remains unknown.

Therefore the species certainly occurs in Taiwan (only in a small stretch of coastal waters off western Taiwan, in the eastern Taiwan Strait), China (including Hong Kong and Macau), Vietnam, Cambodia, Thailand, Malaysia, Singapore, Indonesia and Brunei. There is one extralimital record from the southern Philippines, probably carried there by currents from Borneo.

DIVE SEQUENCE

- Tends to be a slow, deliberate swimmer.
- Beak (and often much of head, including eyes) lifted clear of water on surfacing.
- Small, indistinct blow.
- Body arched (showing much of back, hump, dorsal fin and tailstock) in a high, tight roll.
- Flukes often lifted above surface before deep foraging dive.

FOOD AND FEEDING

Prey Opportunistically preys on a wide variety of nearshore, estuarine and reef fish; occasionally cephalopods and crustaceans in some regions; takes 24 species of fish and one species of cephalopod in Hong Kong.
Feeding In Hong Kong sometimes seen with mud on bodies, suggesting bottom feeding; in Bay of Bengal, frequently seen feeding on fish that fall out of nets being pulled to surface.
Dive depth Shallow diver, typically to maximum 30m.
Dive time Typically 40–60 seconds; maximum *c.* five minutes.

Found in shallow coastal waters – typically less than 20–30m deep – and rarely more than a few kilometres from shore. Will range further offshore where the water is sufficiently shallow. Highest densities occur in and around estuaries, but it also occurs along open coasts, over rocky reefs, in bays, coastal lagoons and mangrove swamps, and in areas with sandbanks and mudbanks. It will sometimes enter rivers and inland waterways, but rarely travels more than a few kilometres upstream (remaining within the range of tidal influence). The distribution is discontinuous, with long stretches of coastline between river mouths often having low or zero densities. Ranging patterns vary, depending on the type of coastline, and some seasonal shifts in abundance have been identified.

BEHAVIOUR
Moderately acrobatic – breaches, acrobatic leaps and spyhops are not uncommon (especially when reproductive activity is at its peak). Groups in Hong Kong used to feed behind fishing trawlers (trawling there is now illegal, but continues to occur). Reaction to boats varies with region: in Hong Kong the species is very used to heavy vessel traffic, but in other areas it can be shy and wary. Rarely bow-rides or wake-rides.

TEETH
Upper 64–76
Lower 58–76

GROUP SIZE AND STRUCTURE
Typically in small groups of 2–6, sometimes up to 10, but with larger groups in some regions. The average in Bangladesh is considerably higher (median 19, with one record of a single group of *c.* 330 individuals) and

aggregations of as many as 30–40 have been seen in Hong Kong (usually following fishing boats). Group structure appears to vary according to region, with fluidity normal in Hong Kong, and more stability in Mozambique and Taiwan (though this could be more a reflection of research effort).

PREDATORS
Unknown, but possibly large sharks and killer whales (though both are uncommon in the dolphin's favoured estuarine waters and evidence of bites are very rarely seen).

PHOTO-IDENTIFICATION
Using nicks, notches and other damage on the trailing edge of the dorsal fin and spotting/flecking patterns of coloration, as well as scarring and other temporary markings on the fin and back.

POPULATION
No overall global estimate, but the total population is unlikely to be much greater than 16,000. The sum total of all available abundance estimates is 5,056 (or 5,692 including Bangladesh); this includes 4,730 in the main Chinese sites. By far the largest population – in the Pearl River Estuary, southern China – was estimated to contain 2,637 animals (2007), plus an additional 82 or so in Hong Kong (2013). Most studied populations appear to be declining (including the small population of *c.* 74 dolphins off Taiwan's west coast in 2010).

CONSERVATION
IUCN status: Vulnerable (2015); Taiwanese subspecies Critically Endangered (2017). Its nearshore habitat puts the Indo-Pacific humpback dolphin in direct contact with people and, especially, with a huge number of artisanal fishermen. The primary threat is incidental entanglement in fishing gear – especially coastal gillnets, trawl nets and shore seines; more than 30 per cent of the dolphins in the Eastern Taiwan Strait exhibit injuries caused by fishing gear. No significant direct hunting is known (although any take of the Taiwanese subspecies would be significant). It has been captured for the aquarium industry in the past. Other threats include habitat loss and disturbance (including coastal development, dredging, aquaculture and land reclamation), noise pollution, severe reduction of river flow to estuaries, trace metals, organochlorines and other forms of pollution, and vessel strikes.

LIFE HISTORY

Sexual maturity Females 9–10 years, males 12–14 years.
Mating Unknown.
Gestation 11–12 months.
Calving Every 3–5 years; single calf born year-round, with a spring/summer seasonal peak in most areas.
Weaning After 2–5 years.
Lifespan Possibly well into 40s (oldest recorded 38 years).

INDIAN OCEAN HUMPBACK DOLPHIN
Sousa plumbea
(G. Cuvier, 1829)

There is considerable uncertainty regarding the taxonomy of humpback dolphins in the Indian Ocean. Those in the west are considered to be Indian Ocean humpback dolphins, but those in the east (the Bay of Bengal) could be a different form of either Indian Ocean or Indo-Pacific humpback dolphin, an entirely new species of *Sousa* (tentatively *S. lentiginosa*), or a combination of all three.

Classification Odontoceti, family Delphinidae.

Common name 'Indian Ocean' because this species is endemic to the Indian Ocean; 'humpback' after the fleshy raised 'hump' on which the dorsal fin sits (the dolphin version of the humpback whale's fin/hump arrangement).

Other names Indian humpback dolphin, plumbeous dolphin.

Scientific name The meaning of *Sousa* is unclear, but it may be based on a Hindi vernacular name for river dolphin (originally erected as a sub-genus of *Steno* by Gray in 1866); *plumbea* from the Latin *plumbea* for 'lead-coloured' or 'heavy' (perhaps in reference to the hump).

Taxonomy The taxonomy of humpback dolphins has been debated for more than two centuries, but recent work currently describes four valid species, and there may be a fifth. The Indian Ocean humpback dolphin was recognised as a distinct species in 2014 (previously, all humpback dolphins from South Africa to Australia were classified as Indo-Pacific (*Sousa chinensis*)). No recognised subspecies, but there may be a dwarf form in the Persian Gulf.

ADULT

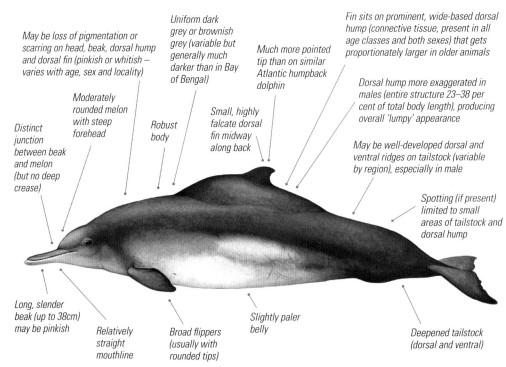

May be loss of pigmentation or scarring on head, beak, dorsal hump and dorsal fin (pinkish or whitish – varies with age, sex and locality)

Uniform dark grey or brownish grey (variable but generally much darker than in Bay of Bengal)

Much more pointed tip than on similar Atlantic humpback dolphin

Fin sits on prominent, wide-based dorsal hump (connective tissue, present in all age classes and both sexes) that gets proportionally larger in older animals

Moderately rounded melon with steep forehead

Robust body

Small, highly falcate dorsal fin midway along back

Dorsal hump more exaggerated in males (entire structure 23–38 per cent of total body length), producing overall 'lumpy' appearance

Distinct junction between beak and melon (but no deep crease)

May be well-developed dorsal and ventral ridges on tailstock (variable by region), especially in male

Spotting (if present) limited to small areas of tailstock and dorsal hump

Long, slender beak (up to 38cm) may be pinkish

Relatively straight mouthline

Broad flippers (usually with rounded tips)

Slightly paler belly

Deepened tailstock (dorsal and ventral)

AT A GLANCE
- Tropical to warm temperate waters of western Indian Ocean
- Small size
- Robust body
- Uniform dark grey or brownish-grey coloration
- May be some loss of pigmentation
- Small, pointed dorsal fin sits on exceptionally large hump
- Long, slender beak
- Moderately rounded melon with steep forehead

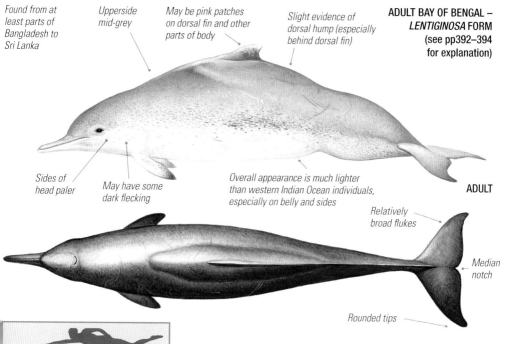

Found from at least parts of Bangladesh to Sri Lanka

Upperside mid-grey

May be pink patches on dorsal fin and other parts of body

Slight evidence of dorsal hump (especially behind dorsal fin)

ADULT BAY OF BENGAL – *LENTIGINOSA* FORM (see pp392–394 for explanation)

Sides of head paler

May have some dark flecking

Overall appearance is much lighter than western Indian Ocean individuals, especially on belly and sides

ADULT

Relatively broad flukes

Median notch

Rounded tips

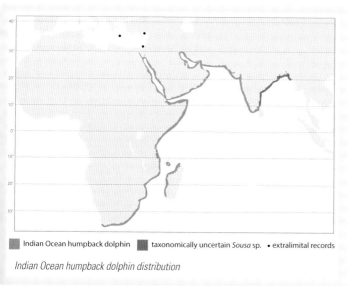

SIZE

L: ♂ 1.8–2.7m, ♀ 1.7–2.5m;
WT: 200–250kg; **MAX:** 2.8m, 260kg
Calf – L: *c.* 1–1.1m; **WT:** 14kg
Reported lengths of 3m or greater are considered unlikely.

SIMILAR SPECIES

The tiny dorsal fin on the exceptionally large hump on the back is unmistakable, unlike any other cetacean in the region. There may some overlap with the Indo-Pacific humpback dolphin in the Bay of Bengal (depending on ultimate decisions about taxonomy), but the more prominent dorsal hump, smaller and more pointed dorsal fin, and much darker colour of adult Indian Ocean humpback dolphins should be distinctive. Indo-Pacific and common bottlenose dolphins lack the dorsal hump and have a significantly larger dorsal fin, a different head shape and a more distinct crease between the beak and the melon.

DISTRIBUTION

Precise distribution will be uncertain until the taxonomy of humpback dolphins in the Bay of Bengal is properly understood. For this review, it is assumed that the Indian Ocean humpback dolphin occurs from False Bay, South Africa, to the southern tip of India and northern Sri Lanka. Humpback dolphins east of there – from the eastern coast of India, Bangladesh and Myanmar – are included under the Indo-Pacific humpback dolphin (but may be another species).

Found exclusively in tropical to warm temperate waters

■ Indian Ocean humpback dolphin   ■ taxonomically uncertain *Sousa* sp.   • extralimital records

Indian Ocean humpback dolphin distribution

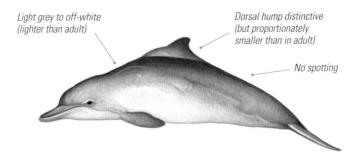

Light grey to off-white (lighter than adult)

Dorsal hump distinctive (but proportionately smaller than in adult)

CALF

No spotting

in the Indian Ocean, along a narrow, shallow, coastal strip. It occurs in 23 different countries and territories, including semi-enclosed seas such as the Gulf of Aden, Red Sea and Persian Gulf, and around several offshore islands, including the Andamans, Mayotte, the Bazaruto Archipelago and Zanzibar. Large portions of the range have not been surveyed, but its distribution appears to be discontinuous: it is likely to be absent along exposed and deep coastlines, and in areas of high human impact.

Three individuals have found their way into the Mediterranean (presumably from the Red Sea via the Suez Canal): recorded in Israel in 2001, Turkey in 2016 and Crete, Greece, in 2017; they are considered to be extralimital. The apparently healthy individual that reached the north coast of Crete must have travelled a minimum distance of 1,000km from the exit of the Suez Canal at Port Said, across deep offshore waters, or up to 2,330km if it hugged shallow coastal waters (the longest distances recorded for this species).

There is evidence of some long-term site fidelity, but there are also seasonal changes in distribution and abundance in some regions. In South Africa, the median ranging distance along the shore is 120km (varying from 30km to 500km). Strong preference for protected areas, such as sandy bays, coastal lagoons, rocky reefs, river estuaries and mangroves. Rarely occurs more than 3km from shore (often only a few hundred metres) or in waters deeper than 25m (sometimes as shallow as 2m).

BEHAVIOUR

Occasionally breaches and performs other aerial manoeuvres. Often patrols parallel to the shore. Tends to be quite shy of boats and very rarely bow-rides. When approached, a group will typically split up and change course underwater, reappearing unexpectedly some distance away.

TEETH

Upper 66–78

Lower 62–74

GROUP SIZE AND STRUCTURE

Typically fewer than 10 individuals, though larger groups in some regions (30–100 is not unusual in Arabian waters). Most groups consist of both sexes and all age classes. There are signs of long-term group stability in Mozambique, but this is considered unusual (elsewhere, a fission-fusion society is more common).

PREDATORS

Tiger, great white and bull sharks are likely predators, and possibly killer whales.

PHOTO-IDENTIFICATION

Using natural marks present on the dorsal fin and hump.

POPULATION

No overall global estimate, but possibly no greater than 10,000 and certainly no more than low tens of thousands.

DIVE SEQUENCE

- Tends to be a slow, deliberate swimmer.
- Beak (and often much of head, including eyes) lifted clear of water on surfacing.
- Small, indistinct blow.
- Body arched (showing much of back, hump, dorsal fin and tailstock) in a high, tight roll.
- Flukes often lifted above surface before deep foraging dive.

Indian Ocean humpback dolphins tend to occur in shallow, coastal waters.

FOOD AND FEEDING
Prey Wide variety of nearshore, estuarine and reef fish; occasionally squid, octopuses and crustaceans in some regions.
Feeding Typically forages near seabed in shallow, murky water; in the Arabian Gulf and Mozambique's Bazaruto Archipelago, has been observed deliberately and temporarily stranding on exposed sandbanks in pursuit of fish.
Dive depth Shallow diver, typically to maximum 25m.
Dive time Typically 40–60 seconds; maximum *c.* 5 minutes.

does not appear to be particularly abundant anywhere nd numbers are believed to be declining. All populations at have been assessed are small (always fewer than 500 dividuals, often fewer than 200 and many fewer than 00). There are recent estimates of *c.* 500 in South Africa own from fewer than 1,000 in the late 1990s) and *c.* 700 Abu Dhabi waters (the largest known population).

ONSERVATION
CN status: Endangered (2015). Its nearshore habitat puts e Indian Ocean humpback dolphin in direct contact with eople and, especially, with a huge number of artisanal shermen. The primary threat is incidental entanglement fishing gear – especially coastal gillnets, but also in

trawl nets, and anti-shark nets off South Africa. High, and clearly unsustainable, mortality rates have been reported from several study areas, and many animals (e.g. 41 per cent in Pemba, Tanzania) show signs of injury from encounters with fishing gear. There are some retaliatory killings in India, where the dolphins cause damage to fishing gear and take fish catch. There are believed to be some direct hunts, including a drive hunt in south-west Madagascar for human consumption; humpback dolphin meat has been reported for sale in western India. Other threats include habitat loss and disturbance (including dredging, land reclamation, and port and harbour construction), oil spills, organochlorines and other forms of pollution, and vessel strikes.

LIFE HISTORY
Sexual maturity Females *c.* 10 years, males *c.* 12–13 years.
Mating Characterised by high levels of physical interaction (including touching, biting and rubbing).
Gestation 10–12 months.
Calving Typically every three years; single calf born year-round, with seasonal peaks (austral spring or summer in South Africa).
Weaning After two years; mother–calf bond remains strong for at least 3–4 years.
Lifespan Probably 40–50 years.

AUSTRALIAN HUMPBACK DOLPHIN
Sousa sahulensis

Jefferson and Rosenbaum, 2014

Split from the Indo-Pacific humpback dolphin (*Sousa chinensis*) in 2014, the Australian humpback dolphin is now recognised as a distinct species and differs from other members of the genus in genetics, morphology, coloration and range.

Classification Odontoceti, family Delphinidae.

Common name 'Australian' refers to the main area of its known range and the source of most information available on this species to date; 'humpback' because it belongs to the same genus as the species that have a distinctive elongated hump on the back.

Other names Hump-backed dolphin, Sahul dolphin.

Scientific name The meaning of *Sousa* is unclear, but it may be based on a Hindi vernacular name for river dolphin (originally erected as a sub-genus of *Steno* by Gray in 1866); *sahulensis* is based on the known range of the species over the shallow Sahul Shelf (part of the continental shelf extending from the northern coast of Australia to New Guinea).

Taxonomy The taxonomy of humpback dolphins has been debated for more than two centuries, but recent work describes four valid species. There is a possible fifth species in the Bay of Bengal. No recognised forms or subspecies of Australian humpback dolphin.

ADULT MALE

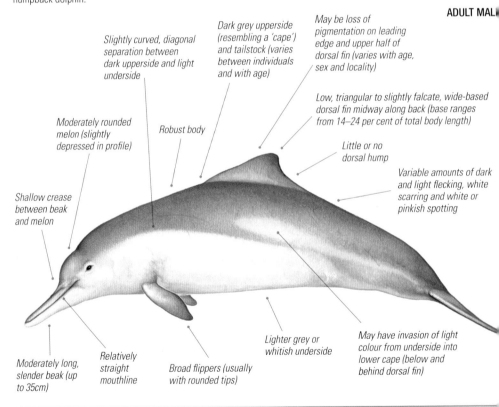

Slightly curved, diagonal separation between dark upperside and light underside

Dark grey upperside (resembling a 'cape') and tailstock (varies between individuals and with age)

May be loss of pigmentation on leading edge and upper half of dorsal fin (varies with age, sex and locality)

Moderately rounded melon (slightly depressed in profile)

Robust body

Low, triangular to slightly falcate, wide-based dorsal fin midway along back (base ranges from 14–24 per cent of total body length)

Little or no dorsal hump

Shallow crease between beak and melon

Variable amounts of dark and light flecking, white scarring and white or pinkish spotting

Moderately long, slender beak (up to 35cm)

Relatively straight mouthline

Broad flippers (usually with rounded tips)

Lighter grey or whitish underside

May have invasion of light colour from underside into lower cape (below and behind dorsal fin)

AT A GLANCE

- Coastal tropical and sub-tropical Australia and southern New Guinea
- Small size
- Robust body
- Broadly two-toned grey coloration

- Diagonal dorsal cape
- Little or no dorsal hump
- Low, very wide-based dorsal fin
- Moderately long, slender beak
- Usually shy and difficult to approach

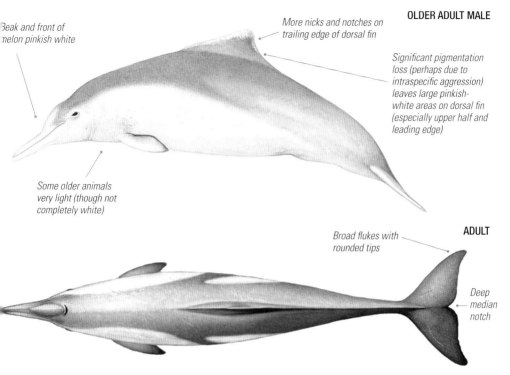

OLDER ADULT MALE

Beak and front of melon pinkish white

More nicks and notches on trailing edge of dorsal fin

Significant pigmentation loss (perhaps due to intraspecific aggression) leaves large pinkish-white areas on dorsal fin (especially upper half and leading edge)

Some older animals very light (though not completely white)

ADULT

Broad flukes with rounded tips

Deep median notch

SIZE
L: ♂ 2.1–2.6m, ♀ 2–2.6m; **WT:** *c.* 240kg; **MAX:** 2.7m
Calf – L: *c.* 1m; **WT:** *c.* 10–12kg
Males may be slightly larger than females.

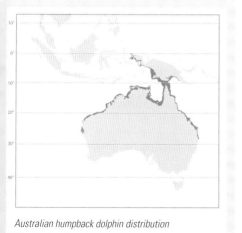

Australian humpback dolphin distribution

SIMILAR SPECIES
Confusion is most likely with common and Indo-Pacific bottlenose dolphins, which overlap in range. Look for the beak length, head shape, dorsal fin shape and coloration. The surfacing behaviour is also different (though experience with all three species is necessary for this to be useful). Australian snubfin dolphins and common dolphins overlap, but should be easy to distinguish by size, general colour pattern, head shape and dorsal fin shape. A hybrid between a male humpback dolphin and a female Australian snubfin dolphin has been documented in northwestern Australia.

DISTRIBUTION
Shallow coastal tropical and sub-tropical Australia and southern New Guinea. Ranges from Shark Bay, Western Australia (25°51'S) in the west, and the Queensland–New South Wales border (31°27'S) in the east, to southern New Guinea in the north. The few surveys conducted in New Guinea reported sightings primarily around Bird's Head Seascape, West Papua (4°70'S), and the Kikori Delta, in the Gulf of Papua, Papua New Guinea (7°41'S). It is uncertain to what extent the species occurs further north. The North West Cape, Western Australia, appears to be a particular centre of abundance (with a density of *c.* one dolphin per square kilometre – the highest recorded anywhere), but distribution throughout the range is mostly sparse. Generally within *c.* 10km of shore and often much closer; little survey work has been done further offshore,

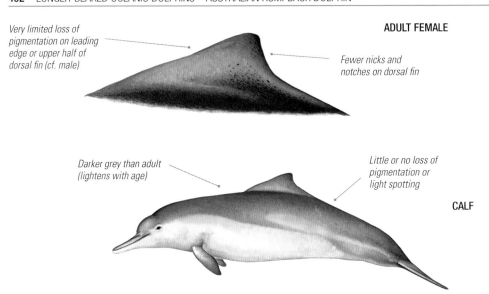

Very limited loss of pigmentation on leading edge or upper half of dorsal fin (cf. male)

ADULT FEMALE

Fewer nicks and notches on dorsal fin

Darker grey than adult (lightens with age)

Little or no loss of pigmentation or light spotting

CALF

but it has been recorded up to 56km from land (especially in sheltered and protected waters such as around the Great Barrier Reef). Sometimes found in water as shallow as 1–2m, most frequently less than 10m and less commonly deeper than 20m; depth preference varies with location. It is uncertain if the species occurs in the deep waters (up to 90m) over the continental shelf between Australia and New Guinea. Found in shallow and protected coastal habitats such as inlets, shallow bays, sandy-bottomed estuaries, major tidal rivers (up to 50km upstream), reefs, coastal archipelagos, seagrass meadows, mangroves and occasionally in dredged channels; rarely in open stretches of coastline. Varying degrees of site fidelity: in Queensland, some animals appear to be permanent residents, others are more transitory. The boundary between the Australian humpback dolphin and the Indo-Pacific humpback dolphin is roughly the Wallace Line (an important biogeographic boundary for many plants and animals, between Asia

and Australia, proposed by the nineteenth-century British naturalist Alfred Russel Wallace).

BEHAVIOUR

Poorly known. Moderately acrobatic, capable of making high leaps and somersaults. In Moreton Bay, at least, ofte feeds behind fishing trawlers, sometimes in association with Indo-Pacific bottlenose dolphins. Social interactions with Australian snubfin dolphins have been observed. Males are regularly observed carrying marine sponges – which they appear to use for posturing in sexual displays (the use of objects in sexual displays by mammals, other than humans, is rare); some bottlenose dolphins use sponges to protect their beaks from stingray barbs and other dangers while probing for food in the seabed. Tends to be relatively shy of boats but will feed behind trawlers; bow-riding has not been observed, but can be unconcerne or even inquisitive in some areas.

DIVE SEQUENCE
- Tends to be a slow, deliberate swimmer.
- Beak (and often much of head, including eyes) lifted clear of water on surfacing.
- Small, indistinct blow.
- Body arched (showing much of back, hump and dorsal fin) in a high, tight roll.
- Flukes often lifted above surface before deep foraging dive (most frequently in relatively deeper water).
- Sometimes performs high leaps and somersaults.

FOOD AND FEEDING

Prey Opportunistic; mostly nearshore, estuarine and reef fish (including grunts, tooth ponyfishes, croakers, flatheads, whitings, anchovies, false trevally, barracudas); rarely cephalopods or crustaceans.

Feeding Solitary feeding mainly near seafloor, during long dives; large groups usually feed close to surface; will feed in extremely shallow water and strand while pursuing prey, before wriggling back into water.

Dive depth Details unknown, but mainly shallow (usually less than 20m).

Dive time Typically 40–60 seconds; maximum *c.* five minutes.

TEETH

Upper 62–70
Lower 62–68

GROUP SIZE AND STRUCTURE

Typically 1–5 (up to 10); as many as 30–35 have been observed in feeding aggregations, especially while following trawlers. Fluid group structure appears to be the norm, with groups often changing in size and composition.

PREDATORS

Large sharks are the most likely predators and there is evidence of scarring from shark attack.

PHOTO-IDENTIFICATION

Possible, using nicks, notches and other damage on the trailing edge of the dorsal fin, as well as scarring and other temporary markings on the fin.

LIFE HISTORY

Sexual maturity Possibly females 9–10 years, males 12–14 years.

Mating Characterised by high levels of physical interaction (including touching, biting and rubbing) and frequent aerial behaviour; pairs of adult males form temporary coalitions during sexual displays.

Gestation 10–12 months.

Calving Single calf every three years.

Weaning After *c.* two years.

Lifespan Possibly more than 40 years; oldest recorded estimated 52 years in 2018 (captive in Sea World, Australia).

POPULATION

No overall abundance estimate, but a recent assessment of available data suggests that there are probably fewer than 10,000 mature individuals. The very few recent regional estimates range from 14 to 207 individuals, but most sub-populations appear to have fewer than 50. Numbers are believed to be declining.

CONSERVATION

IUCN status: Vulnerable (2015). Its inshore distribution and susceptibility to disturbance make this species particularly vulnerable to human activities. The main threat appears to be incidental capture in fishing nets, especially inshore gillnets set across creeks, rivers and shallow estuaries for barramundi and threadfin salmon. Gillnetting is banned or strictly regulated in some regions of Australia, but enforcement is difficult. A major threat since the early 1960s has been accidental capture in nets used across many New South Wales and Queensland beaches, to reduce the perceived risk of shark attack on bathers; following a gradual change from nets to baited hook drum-lines in Queensland since 1992, the number of mortalities there has declined, but the problem continues in New South Wales. No significant hunting is known, though there are anecdotal reports of direct catch for use as shark bait in New Guinea. Habitat loss, degradation and disturbance – caused by the development of port and marina facilities, aquaculture, modifications for mining and agricultural activities, residential development and increased vessel activity – are major threats in many areas. Other threats include overfishing of prey species, vessel strikes, noise pollution and chemical pollution. At least eight individuals were caught in the 1960s and 1970s for live display, but this is no longer permitted under Australian law.

COMMON BOTTLENOSE DOLPHIN
Tursiops truncatus
(Montagu, 1821)

The bottlenose dolphin is the quintessential dolphin and, thanks to its coastal habits, prevalence in captivity and frequent appearances on television, one of the best-known cetaceans. But its taxonomy is still in dispute – due to huge geographical variation in size, shape, skull morphology and coloration. Over the years, more than 20 nominal species have been proposed, but only two are currently recognised (common bottlenose and Indo-Pacific bottlenose). Others could be accepted in the future.

Classification Odontoceti, family Delphinidae.
Common name 'Common' to distinguish it from 'Indo-Pacific bottlenose dolphin'; 'bottlenose' for the shape of the beak.
Other names Bottlenose dolphin, bottle-nosed dolphin, grey porpoise, black porpoise; see taxonomy for subspecies common names.
Scientific name *Tursiops* from the Latin *tursio* for 'fish like a dolphin' in Pliny the Elder's *Natural History IX*, and the Greek suffix *ops* for 'appearance' (i.e. 'looking like a dolphin'); *truncatus* from the Latin *trunco* or *truncare* for 'truncated' or 'cut off' (either referring to the relatively short beak, or to the worn, flattened teeth on the type specimen, which were considered by George Montagu to be the key identifying characteristic).
Taxonomy Currently three accepted subspecies: common bottlenose dolphin (*T. t. truncatus*), found in tropical to temperate waters worldwide; Lahille's bottlenose dolphin (*T. t. gephyreus*), a larger, coastal form found in the western South Atlantic; and Black Sea bottlenose dolphin (*T. t. ponticus*), known only from the Black Sea, Kerch Strait (and connecting part of the Azov Sea), and the Turkish Straits system. There is a strong argument for giving Lahille's bottlenose dolphin species status.

The Burrunan bottlenose dolphin (*Tursiops australis*) was described as a new species in 2011 and does appear to be a distinct form with some unique coloration, but it has not been accepted by the Society for Marine Mammalogy (more rigorous re-evaluation of the relevant data and arguments is needed). Found off southern and southeastern Australia (including Tasmania), its name is an Aboriginal Australian word meaning 'large sea fish of the porpoise kind'; it is also referred to as the *australis*-type bottlenose dolphin. In the North Atlantic, there appear to be two 'ecotypes' – a smaller, coastal form and a larger, more robust offshore form – that may be separated in the future (but differences are subtle and vary according to location).

ADUL

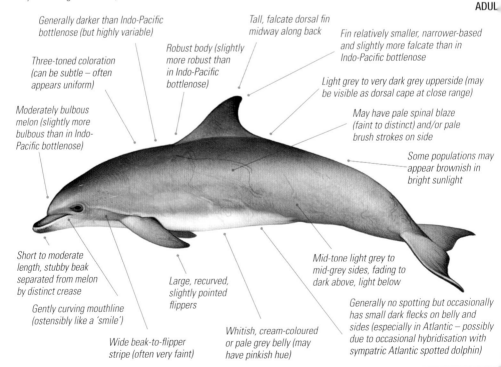

Generally darker than Indo-Pacific bottlenose (but highly variable)

Three-toned coloration (can be subtle – often appears uniform)

Moderately bulbous melon (slightly more bulbous than in Indo-Pacific bottlenose)

Short to moderate length, stubby beak separated from melon by distinct crease

Gently curving mouthline (ostensibly like a 'smile')

Wide beak-to-flipper stripe (often very faint)

Large, recurved, slightly pointed flippers

Robust body (slightly more robust than in Indo-Pacific bottlenose)

Tall, falcate dorsal fin midway along back

Fin relatively smaller, narrower-based and slightly more falcate than in Indo-Pacific bottlenose

Light grey to very dark grey upperside (may be visible as dorsal cape at close range)

May have pale spinal blaze (faint to distinct) and/or pale brush strokes on side

Some populations may appear brownish in bright sunlight

Mid-tone light grey to mid-grey sides, fading to dark above, light below

Whitish, cream-coloured or pale grey belly (may have pinkish hue)

Generally no spotting but occasionally has small dark flecks on belly and sides (especially in Atlantic – possibly due to occasional hybridisation with sympatric Atlantic spotted dolphin)

AT A GLANCE

- Tropical to temperate waters worldwide
- Small size
- Robust body
- Short, stubby beak
- Archetypal dolphin
- Ostensibly 'smiling' mouthline
- Three-toned coloration (subtle to distinct)
- Rarely has small dark flecks on underside
- In coastal waters usually in small groups
- Often bow-rides

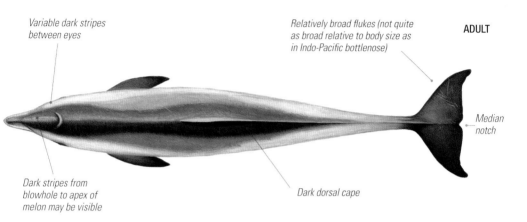

Variable dark stripes between eyes

Relatively broad flukes (not quite as broad relative to body size as in Indo-Pacific bottlenose)

ADULT

Median notch

Dark stripes from blowhole to apex of melon may be visible

Dark dorsal cape

SIZE

L: ♂ 1.9–3.8m, ♀ 1.8–3.5m;
WT: 136–600g; **MAX:** 3.9m, 635kg
Calf – L: 1–1.5m; **WT:** *c.* 15–25kg

Wide variation in size between populations (body size appears to be inversely related to water temperature in many regions); largest and most robust individuals live at the extremes of their range (such as along the north-east coast of Scotland, in the eastern North Atlantic); male generally slightly bigger than female.

SIMILAR SPECIES

Confusion is possible with a number of other dolphin species, depending on the region, and identification is best done through a process of elimination. Atlantic spotted dolphins can look very similar: differences in size and robustness can help, but they are subtle and tricky to distinguish. Heavily spotted animals are likely to be Atlantic spotted dolphins, but beware that some are nearly unspotted and some bottlenose dolphins have limited spotting. The common bottlenose can be particularly difficult to distinguish from the very similar Indo-Pacific bottlenose dolphin, which overlaps in range. Differences can be subtle, but the common bottlenose is generally larger and more robust, is darker in colour, and has a less distinct cape; it also tends to have a less prominent spinal blaze, a less rounded melon, little or no ventral spotting, a subtly shorter

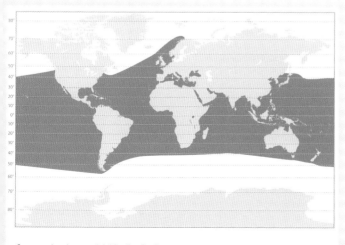

Common bottlenose dolphin distribution

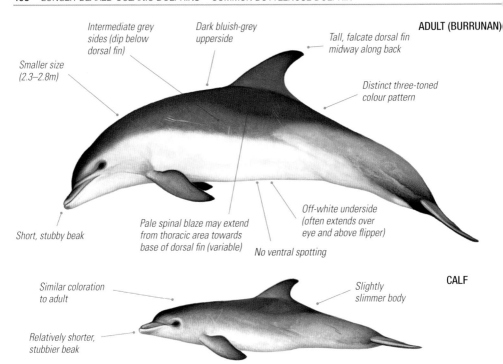

ADULT (BURRUNAN)

Intermediate grey sides (dip below dorsal fin)

Dark bluish-grey upperside

Tall, falcate dorsal fin midway along back

Distinct three-toned colour pattern

Smaller size (2.3–2.8m)

Short, stubby beak

Pale spinal blaze may extend from thoracic area towards base of dorsal fin (variable)

No ventral spotting

Off-white underside (often extends over eye and above flipper)

CALF

Similar coloration to adult

Slightly slimmer body

Relatively shorter, stubbier beak

and stubbier beak, and a more falcate, narrower-based dorsal fin. Hybridisation is known with species from at least six delphinid genera, including Indo-Pacific bottlenose, common, Risso's and rough-toothed dolphins, and short-finned pilot whales and false killer whales.

DISTRIBUTION

Widespread in tropical to temperate waters worldwide. Most abundant between 45°N and 45°S, except in northern Europe (with significant numbers around the United Kingdom and as far north as the Faroe Islands at 62°N). Smaller numbers pushing to the southern Sea of Okhotsk, southern New Zealand and Tierra del Fuego. Occurs in most semi-enclosed seas, including the Black Sea,

Mediterranean Sea, North Sea, Gulf of Mexico, Caribbean Sea, Red Sea, Persian Gulf, Sea of Japan and Gulf of California. It is considered extralimital in the Baltic Sea.

Most often seen in shallow coastal waters and around oceanic islands, but also out to the continental shelf edge and most abundant in deep offshore waters. Frequently in bays, lagoons, channels and around harbours, and ventures into rivers for brief periods. Frequently near population centres. In the Indian Ocean, where Indo-Pacific bottlenose dolphins can be prevalent along the coast, common bottlenose dolphins tend to live mainly offshore.

Coastal populations are generally non-migratory and maintain long-term, multi-generational home ranges in

DIVE SEQUENCE
- When swimming slowly, tip of beak breaks surface first.
- Upperside of melon (sometimes eyes) briefly visible as it blows.
- Head dips below surface.
- Back and dorsal fin appear briefly.
- Tailstock often barely visible.
- Porpoises with neat re-entry when swimming fast.

ADULT VARIATIONS

FOOD AND FEEDING

Prey Generalist feeder as a species, with specialisation within populations and among individuals; wide variety of fish (especially croaker, mackerel, mullet), cephalopods and crustaceans; noise-producing fish make up large part of diet (presumably easier to locate); mainly benthic prey, but some pelagic; will attempt to swallow absurdly large prey (can take 15 minutes to gulp down fully grown Atlantic salmon).

Feeding Wide variety of techniques, depending on prey and location, including high-speed chasing, bubble-blowing to herd prey towards surface, 'fish-whacking' (knocking fish out of water with flukes – sometimes catching them in mid-air), 'strand-feeding' (sending wave of water that pushes fish onto mudbanks, then temporarily beaching themselves to grab the fish), 'kerplunking' (scaring fish out from seagrass beds and other vegetative cover with bubble-forming tail slaps), and 'mud-ringing' (one dolphin creates ring-shaped mud plume, then others catch fish in mid-air as they leap out of ring); will feed behind shrimp trawlers (to eat discarded fish) and steal fish from fishing gear; in Mauritania and Brazil, regularly drive mullet towards fishermen holding nets in shallow water; different age and sex classes may eat in different areas (e.g. mothers with calves inshore, immatures offshore, non-breeding adults even further offshore).

Dive depth Highly variable depending on location and prey; typically up to 70m, but offshore often several hundred metres; maximum *c.* 1,000m.

Dive time Offshore average *c.* 1–5 minutes (maximum recorded 13 minutes); inshore typically 30 seconds to two minutes (maximum recorded eight minutes).

particular areas; resident dolphin communities along Florida's west coast, for example, have been observed for nearly half a century and over at least five generations. There can be seasonal changes in habitat use within these home ranges. Some coastal populations living in cold-water extremes of the distribution may make seasonal migrations, with a general southerly movement in winter (e.g. along the Atlantic coast of the US). Less is known about the movements of offshore populations, but they appear to travel longer distances, with one study showing average daily movements of 33–89km.

BEHAVIOUR

Tends to be active much of the time and will leap, lobtail, porpoise, body surf and perform other aerial behaviours. Keen bow-rider and wake-rider, in both inshore and offshore waters, often leaping out of the water while riding. It will bow-ride any vessel, from a small motor boat to a large oceanic cargo vessel or cruise ship, and will even ride the bow-waves in front of large whales ('snout-riding').

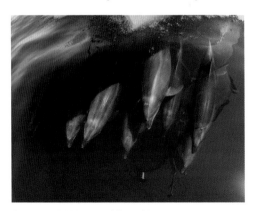

Bottlenose dolphins are avid bow-riders.

Frequently in mixed schools with Atlantic spotted dolphins, Atlantic humpback dolphins, Indo-Pacific humpback dolphins, false killer whales, and a variety of other large whales and dolphins (including Indo-Pacific bottlenose dolphins in some areas). Some observations of playful interactions with humpback whales. Other associations can be more aggressive, such as towards Atlantic spotted dolphins in the Bahamas and Guiana dolphins in southeastern Brazil.

Known to attack and kill harbour porpoises in Scotland, Wales and California. This is not simply the aberrant behaviour of one or two individuals, but more widespread. The reason is unclear: it could be due to prey competition, feeding interference, heightened aggression in male bottlenose dolphins due to high levels of testosterone, for fighting practice, object-oriented play, or somehow be related to the infanticidal behaviour that has been observed among bottlenose dolphins.

Some wild common bottlenose dolphins have become 'friendly' – solitary individuals, not part of a social group, which hang around harbours and befriend people, apparently preferring to associate with boats, divers and swimmers rather than with other dolphins. Some stay for weeks or months, others for years. The UK and New Zealand are particular hotspots for friendlies.

TEETH

Upper 36–54
Lower 36–54
Teeth often worn down or missing in older animals.

GROUP SIZE AND STRUCTURE

Typically 2–15, but offshore sometimes in large herds of several hundred (especially in the eastern tropical Pacific and the western Indian Oceans); groups of more than 1,000 have been reported. Generally, groups are smaller close to shore (but growth in group size is not linear with increasing distance from shore). Group structure varies greatly, but tends to be relatively fluid. Research on coastal populations in the tropics reveals that basic social units (which can be stable over time) commonly consist of nursery groups, juveniles of both sexes, strongly bonded adult male pairs and individual adult males; however, there is no evidence of strong male–male pairs or nursery groups in Scottish waters, for example.

PREDATORS

Mainly sharks – especially great white, tiger, bull and dusky. When encountering sharks, mutual tolerance is probably typical, but there are reports of dolphins attacking sharks by butting them with their beaks. This might explain an apparently high survival rate (as many as half of all bottlenose dolphins in some regions bear shark-bite scars). Most scars are on the rear half of the body and the underside – an indication of the sharks attacking from behind and below. Killer whales are probably occasional predators. Unknown numbers of coastal common bottlenose dolphins are killed by stingrays (either wounded by the sting or, after ingestion, by the barb penetrating vital organs).

PHOTO-IDENTIFICATION

Nicks and notches on the trailing edge of the dorsal fin, combined with the size and shape of the fin, and any other distinctive marks and scars.

POPULATION

There is a rough worldwide guesstimate of at least 600,000. Approximate regional estimates include 243,500 in the eastern tropical Pacific; 168,000 in the western North Pacific (including 37,000 in Japanese coastal waters); 100,000 in the northern Gulf of Mexico; 126,000 off the eastern coast of North America; low 10,000s in the Mediterranean; 19,000 in the eastern North Atlantic; 3,215 in Hawaiian waters; and 2,000 in offshore waters off the western coast of North America.

CONSERVATION

IUCN status: Least Concern (2008); Fiordland, New Zealand, population Critically Endangered (2010); Mediterranean population Vulnerable (2009); Black Sea subspecies Endangered (2008).

Hunted in many parts of its range. The largest takes have been in the Black Sea, where at least 24,000–28,000 were killed in the period 1946–83, for human consumption, manufacturing oil and leather. Commercial hunting of Black Sea cetaceans was banned in 1966 by the former USSR, Bulgaria and Romania, and in 1983 by Turkey. However, hunting continues to varying degrees – for human consumption, to reduce perceived competition with commercial fisheries and for shark bait – in Peru, the Faroe Islands, the Caribbean, West Africa, Japan, Sri Lanka, Taiwan, Indonesia and inevitably elsewhere.

The common bottlenose dolphin was the first species of cetacean to be held in captivity and, since it is so highly adaptable and easily trained, is still the most commonly held species. Currently, c. 800–1,000 are being held in at least 17 countries for public display, research and military use. More than 1,000 (not including accidental deaths during capture) have been caught in the Black Sea since the 1960s; live captures are now prohibited in all Black Sea countries and there have been no official records of captures in recent years. They continue to be live-captured in other parts of the world, including Cuba, the Solomon Islands, Japan, China and Russia.

Entanglement in fishing gear is a serious threat throughout the range, in gillnets, driftnets, purse seines and trawls, and on hook-and-line gear. Ingestion of recreational fishing gear is another concern. Other threats include habitat degradation, destruction and disturbance (especially for coastal populations), vessel strikes, environmental contaminants and other forms of pollution. There are also concerns about irresponsible, unregulated and high-volume dolphin watching and swimming in some areas.

LIFE HISTORY

Sexual maturity Females 5–13 years, males 9–14 years.
Mating Research on coastal populations in tropical regions suggests male alliances and coalitions traverse home range seeking oestrous females (once female separated from her group, males compete and fight to mate with her); herding of females can last up to several weeks; however, no evidence of this behaviour elsewhere (mating systems likely to vary according to habitat and location). Like some other dolphins, copulates frequently (even when no possibility of impregnating female), probably to strengthen social bonds.

Gestation 12–12.5 months.
Calving Every 3–6 years (occasionally every year); single calf born year-round, with seasonal peak according to region (usually spring and summer or spring and autumn).
Weaning After 1.5–2 years (longer for last-born calf); calf remains with female for 3–6 years (may separate when next calf born, but in some populations remains associated with mother long afterwards).
Lifespan Female c. 50 years, male 40–50 years (oldest recorded 67 years for female, 52 years for male); females up to 48 years have successfully given birth and raised calves.

INDO-PACIFIC BOTTLENOSE DOLPHIN
Tursiops aduncus

(Ehrenburg, 1833)

Split from the common bottlenose dolphin in 2000, the slightly smaller Indo-Pacific bottlenose dolphin is the only cetacean known to use tools. In Shark Bay, Western Australia, more than 70 individuals have learned to 'wear' marine sponges on their beaks as protective 'gloves' or shields when foraging for prey along the seafloor.

Classification Odontoceti, family Delphinidae.
Common name 'Indo-Pacific' because this species is endemic to the Indian Ocean and western Pacific Ocean; 'bottlenose' for the shape of the beak.
Other names Indian Ocean bottlenose dolphin.
Scientific name *Tursiops* from the Latin *tursio* for 'fish like a dolphin' in Pliny the Elder's *Natural History IX*, and the Greek suffix *ops* for 'appearance' (i.e. 'looking like a dolphin'); *aduncus* is from the Latin *aduncus*, meaning 'hooked' (this word was originally used in 1832 and the meaning is unclear; it could refer to the hooked dorsal fin or to the slightly upturned lower jaw).
Taxonomy No recognised forms or subspecies. Recent genetic research suggests that bottlenose dolphins off southern Africa – currently recognised as *T. aduncus* – might be a third species in the *Tursiops* genus (currently thought unlikely). The well-known bottlenose dolphins in Shark Bay, Western Australia, might also represent a separate lineage.

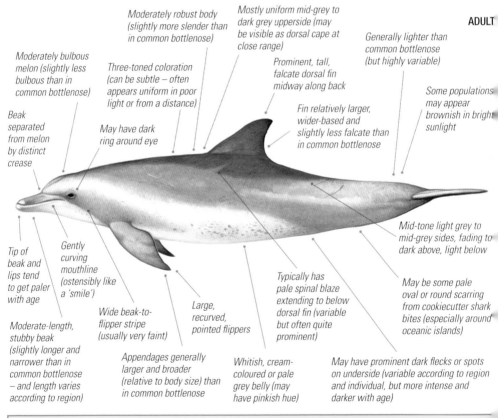

Moderately robust body (slightly more slender than in common bottlenose)

Mostly uniform mid-grey to dark grey upperside (may be visible as dorsal cape at close range)

ADULT

Generally lighter than common bottlenose (but highly variable)

Moderately bulbous melon (slightly less bulbous than in common bottlenose)

Three-toned coloration (can be subtle – often appears uniform in poor light or from a distance)

Prominent, tall, falcate dorsal fin midway along back

Some populations may appear brownish in bright sunlight

Beak separated from melon by distinct crease

May have dark ring around eye

Fin relatively larger, wider-based and slightly less falcate than in common bottlenose

Tip of beak and lips tend to get paler with age

Gently curving mouthline (ostensibly like a 'smile')

Mid-tone light grey to mid-grey sides, fading to dark above, light below

Moderate-length, stubby beak (slightly longer and narrower than in common bottlenose – and length varies according to region)

Wide beak-to-flipper stripe (usually very faint)

Large, recurved, pointed flippers

Typically has pale spinal blaze extending to below dorsal fin (variable but often quite prominent)

May be some pale oval or round scarring from cookiecutter shark bites (especially around oceanic islands)

Appendages generally larger and broader (relative to body size) than in common bottlenose

Whitish, cream-coloured or pale grey belly (may have pinkish hue)

May have prominent dark flecks or spots on underside (variable according to region and individual, but more intense and darker with age)

AT A GLANCE
- Tropical to temperate waters of Indo-Pacific
- Small size
- Moderately robust body
- Moderate-length, stubby beak

- Ostensibly 'smiling' mouthline
- Three-toned coloration (subtle to distinct)
- May have dark flecking or spotting on underside
- Usually in small to medium-sized groups
- Occasionally bow-rides

SIZE
L: ♂ 1.8–2.6m, ♀ 1.8–2.6m;
WT: 120–200kg; **MAX:** 2.7m, 230kg
Calf – L: 0.8–1.2m; **WT:** 9–21kg
Wide variation in size between populations.

ADULT

Dark stripes from blowhole to apex of melon may be visible

Dark dorsal cape

Relatively broad flukes

Median notch

SIMILAR SPECIES

Confusion is possible with a number of other dolphin species, depending on the region, and identification is best done through a process of elimination. It can be particularly difficult to distinguish from the very similar common bottlenose dolphin, which overlaps in range. Differences can be subtle, but the Indo-Pacific bottlenose is generally smaller and less robust, is lighter in colour and has a more distinct cape; it also tends to have a more prominent spinal blaze, a more rounded melon, considerably dark ventral spotting and flecking, a subtly longer and less stubby beak, and a less falcate, wider-based dorsal fin. In captivity, hybridisation between the two bottlenose dolphin species has produced fertile offspring.

DISTRIBUTION

Widespread but discontinuous distribution throughout coastal tropical to temperate waters in the Indian and western Pacific Oceans. Ranges from the southern tip of South Africa in the west to southern and eastern Australia and New Caledonia in the east. Found throughout the islands and peninsulas of the Indo-Malay archipelago, and around some oceanic islands (such as the Maldives, the Seychelles, Réunion and Madagascar). Also in some cool temperate waters (such as the northern coast of central Honsho in Japan, northern China, southern Australia and South Africa). Occurs in some semi-enclosed seas, including the Gulf of Thailand, Red Sea and Persian Gulf. Preferred sea surface temperature is generally 18–30°C, but this varies greatly between regions and seasons.

Almost exclusively over the continental shelf, especially in shallow coastal waters (less than 100m deep) in areas with sandy or rocky bottoms, as well as reefs and seagrass beds. Frequently around oceanic islands, and will concentrate in and around estuaries.

Generally non-migratory, exhibiting year-round residency and maintaining long-term, multi-generational home ranges within limited coastal waters. Typical home range probably 20–200sq km. There is some evidence of seasonal movements, especially in temperate regions, and occasional records of long-distance travel across hundreds of kilometres of deep oceanic waters, with males tending to range more widely than females.

BEHAVIOUR

Generally less acrobatic than the common bottlenose dolphin, but still capable of some high leaps. Tail walking – in which the dolphin rises vertically out of the water and

Indo-Pacific bottlenose dolphin distribution

ADULT VARIATIONS

Relatively shorter,
stubbier beak

Slightly
slimmer body

Similar coloration
to adult

CALF

No dark flecks or spots
(may develop around sexual maturity)

maintains this position by vigorously kicking its tail – was observed for a number of years in a small community of Indo-Pacific bottlenose dolphins in the Port River Estuary, southern Australia (following the rehabilitation of a temporarily captive animal that had been with other dolphins trained to tail walk). Sometimes in mixed groups with Indo-Pacific humpback dolphins, spinner dolphins, common dolphins, false killer whales and other delphinids (including common bottlenose dolphins). Can be a keen bow-rider and wake-rider. In Australia, there are several locations where Indo-Pacific bottlenose dolphins come into shallow water to be fed by people.

TEETH
Upper 46–58
Lower 46–58

GROUP SIZE AND STRUCTURE
Typically 6–60, but sometimes in large groups of several hundred. Groups of more than 100 are quite common around Japan and up to 600 have been reported in South Africa. Groups tend to be larger when calves are present. Most are relatively fluid, and individuals are often seen with a variety of different conspecifics on a daily basis. Males may form alliances (2–3 individuals) to challenge other groups of males for access to reproductive females; females (sometimes related) may also form cooperative groups to avoid such male coercion, as well as to help raise calves and reduce shark predation.

DIVE SEQUENCE
- When swimming slowly, tip of beak breaks surface first.
- Upperside of melon (sometimes eyes) briefly visible as it blows.
- Head dips below surface – back and dorsal fin appear briefly – tailstock often barely visible.
- Porpoises with neat re-entry when swimming fast.

FOOD AND FEEDING

Prey Wide variety of prey; predominantly benthic and reef-dwelling fish, and cephalopods; will occasionally eat small benthic sharks; some pelagic species; most prey less than 30cm long; little overlap with preferred prey of common bottlenose dolphin.

Feeding Wide variety of techniques, depending on prey and location, including 'bottom-grubbing' (sticking rostrum into seagrass beds or seabed to flush out prey), 'sponging' (carrying marine sponges on beak, probably as protection from rubbing against ocean floor while foraging), 'shelling' (lifting large shells out of water to dislodge fish hiding inside), 'strand-feeding' (sending wave of water that pushes fish onto mudbanks, then temporarily beaching itself to grab the fish), 'snacking' (chasing fish 'belly up' near surface); 'octopus tossing' (throwing octopuses in the air before consumption, to avoid risk of suffocation); and 'kerplunking' (scaring fish out from seagrass beds and other vegetative cover with bubble-forming tail slaps); feeds behind shrimp trawlers off eastern Australia to eat discarded fish (often in association with Australian humpback dolphins).

Dive depth Highly variable depending on location and prey, but usually quite shallow; maximum 200m.

Dive time Typically 30 seconds to two minutes (maximum recorded 10 minutes).

PREDATORS

Great white, bull, tiger and dusky sharks are significant predators, at least in some parts of the range (e.g. South Africa and Western Australia). In Shark Bay, Western Australia, more than 74 per cent of non-calf dolphins bear scars from shark attacks. There is no record of predation by killer whales, but it is likely in parts of the range.

PHOTO-IDENTIFICATION

Nicks and notches on the trailing and leading edges of the dorsal fin, combined with the size and shape of the fin, and any other distinctive marks and scars.

POPULATION

No overall global estimate. Local populations tend to be small and relatively isolated, typically containing a few tens to several hundred animals. Approximate regional estimates include 520–530 off KwaZulu-Natal, South Africa; more than 1,600 in the eastern gulf of Shark Bay, Western Australia; 700–1,000 off Point Lookout, Australia; 334 in Moreton Bay, Australia; 380 off Japan; 185 in Bunbury, Western Australia; and 136–179 in Zanzibar.

CONSERVATION

IUCN status: Data Deficient (2008). The Indo-Pacific bottlenose dolphin was one of several species hunted in a large-scale drive fishery in the Penghu Islands, Taiwan, until it was banned in 1993. Unknown numbers are still being hunted – for human consumption and shark bait – in Sri Lanka, the Solomon Islands, the Philippines, Australia, Taiwan, East Africa and possibly Indonesia.

Entanglement in fishing gear, including in gillnets, driftnets, purse seines and trawls, and on hook-and-line gear, is the greatest concern throughout the range. In the 1980s, as many as 2,000 were caught every year by a Taiwanese shark driftnet fishery; this was banned in Australia, but the fishery moved into Indonesian waters, where it has continued largely unmonitored. Bycatch in China is not monitored either, but there are more than 3.5 million gillnets in Chinese and Taiwanese coastal waters, so the potential threat is huge. Significant numbers are also killed in anti-shark gillnets in South Africa and Australia that are used to protect bathers.

The Indo-Pacific bottlenose dolphin is a preferred species for captive display in oceanaria and tourist resorts, particularly in Asia. Live captures have taken place in Taiwan, Indonesia, Japan and the Solomon Islands in recent years.

The species' nearshore distribution makes it particularly vulnerable to a range of other threats, including habitat degradation, vessel strikes, environmental contaminants and other forms of pollution, and overfishing of prey species. There are also concerns about irresponsible, unregulated and high-volume dolphin watching and swimming in some areas.

LIFE HISTORY

Sexual maturity Females 12–15 years, males 10–15 years.

Mating Male alliances and coalitions traverse home range seeking oestrous females (once female separated from her group, males compete and fight to mate with her); herding of females can last up to several weeks. Like some other dolphins, copulates frequently (even when no possibility of impregnating female), probably to strengthen social bonds.

Gestation 12 months.

Calving Every 3–6 years (occasionally 1–2 years); single calf born year-round, with peaks in months with highest water temperatures.

Weaning After 3–5 years (occasionally as short as 18–20 months); mother–calf bond extremely strong (females observed to protect dead offspring for extended periods).

Lifespan At least 50 years for female, 40 years for male (oldest recorded 50 years).

PANTROPICAL SPOTTED DOLPHIN
Stenella attenuata

(Gray, 1846)

The pantropical spotted dolphin is highly variable in appearance, between ages, individuals and regions, from virtually unspotted to very heavily spotted. Even though it has been severely depleted by tuna purse-seine fishing in the eastern tropical Pacific, it is still one of the most abundant cetaceans on the planet.

Classification Odontoceti, family Delphinidae.

Common name 'Pantropical' because this species is endemic to tropical waters worldwide; 'spotted' for the extensive dark and light spotting on many individuals.

Other names Spotter, spotted porpoise, spotted dolphin, bridled dolphin, narrow-snouted dolphin, slender-beaked dolphin, sharp-beaked dolphin, white-spotted dolphin, Graffman's dolphin.

Scientific name *Stenella* from the Greek *stenos* for 'narrow', and *ella* for 'little' (referring to the beak); *attenuata* from the Latin *attenuatus* for 'thin, reduced or diminished' (it is believed that John E. Gray (1800–75), who named the species, may have mistakenly believed this to mean 'sharp', because he referred to it as the 'sharp-beaked dolphin').

Taxonomy Taxonomy of the spotted dolphins was revised in 1987, resulting in two accepted species. Two subspecies of pantropical spotted dolphin are currently recognised (based on cranial measurements and genetic data): offshore (*S. a. attenuata*), which is slightly smaller, more slender and lightly spotted, and is found in oceanic tropical waters worldwide; and coastal (*S. a. graffmani*), which is slightly larger, stockier and heavily spotted, and is found in coastal waters of the eastern tropical Pacific (along the west coasts of Mexico, Central America, and South America to northern Peru). Taxonomy of the *Stenella* genus is currently in dispute and is likely to be revised in the near future.

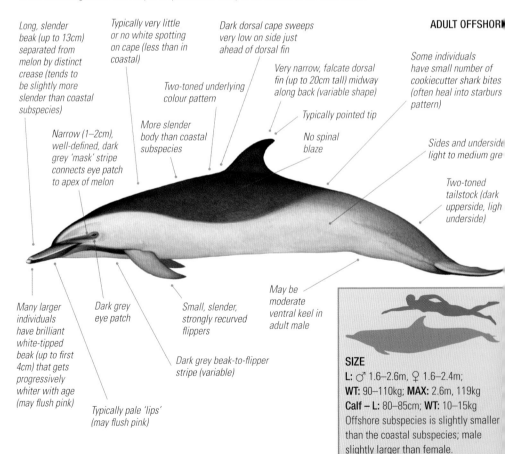

ADULT OFFSHORE

Long, slender beak (up to 13cm) separated from melon by distinct crease (tends to be slightly more slender than coastal subspecies)

Typically very little or no white spotting on cape (less than in coastal)

Dark dorsal cape sweeps very low on side just ahead of dorsal fin

Very narrow, falcate dorsal fin (up to 20cm tall) midway along back (variable shape)

Some individuals have small number of cookiecutter shark bites (often heal into starburst pattern)

Two-toned underlying colour pattern

Typically pointed tip

Narrow (1–2cm), well-defined, dark grey 'mask' stripe connects eye patch to apex of melon

More slender body than coastal subspecies

No spinal blaze

Sides and underside light to medium grey

Two-toned tailstock (dark upperside, light underside)

Many larger individuals have brilliant white-tipped beak (up to first 4cm) that gets progressively whiter with age (may flush pink)

Dark grey eye patch

Small, slender, strongly recurved flippers

May be moderate ventral keel in adult male

Dark grey beak-to-flipper stripe (variable)

Typically pale 'lips' (may flush pink)

SIZE
L: ♂ 1.6–2.6m, ♀ 1.6–2.4m;
WT: 90–110kg; **MAX:** 2.6m, 119kg
Calf – L: 80–85cm; **WT:** 10–15kg
Offshore subspecies is slightly smaller than the coastal subspecies; male slightly larger than female.

AT A GLANCE
- Tropical to sub-tropical waters worldwide
- Small size
- Two-toned tailstock
- Dark dorsal cape dips lowest just ahead of dorsal fin
- Highly variable dark and light spotting
- Long, slender beak with white tip
- White or pale grey 'lips'
- Two-toned underlying colour pattern
- No spinal blaze
- Tall, falcate dorsal fin midway along back
- Highly variable appearance within group

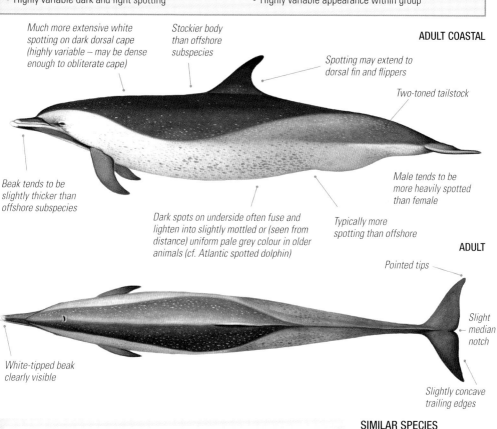

ADULT COASTAL

Much more extensive white spotting on dark dorsal cape (highly variable – may be dense enough to obliterate cape)

Stockier body than offshore subspecies

Spotting may extend to dorsal fin and flippers

Two-toned tailstock

Beak tends to be slightly thicker than offshore subspecies

Dark spots on underside often fuse and lighten into slightly mottled or (seen from distance) uniform pale grey colour in older animals (cf. Atlantic spotted dolphin)

Typically more spotting than offshore

Male tends to be more heavily spotted than female

ADULT

Pointed tips

Slight median notch

White-tipped beak clearly visible

Slightly concave trailing edges

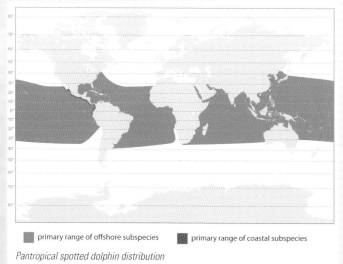

primary range of offshore subspecies   primary range of coastal subspecies

Pantropical spotted dolphin distribution

SIMILAR SPECIES

Given such wide variation in spotting (see overleaf), the best features for identification of adult pantropical spotted dolphins is the shape and intensity of the dark dorsal cape (which always dips very low just ahead of the dorsal fin) and the lack of a white underside. Confusion is likely with some spinner dolphins, but they can be distinguished by differences in colour pattern, beak length and thickness, and dorsal fin shape. In the Atlantic, there is overlap with Atlantic spotted dolphins, but they are stockier,

Note: the pantropical spotted dolphin is usually classified into four different colour phases, according to age: 'two-tone' calf (from birth to average *c.* three years old), 'speckled' juvenile (average *c.* 3–8 years old), 'mottled' young adult (average *c.* 8–10 years old) and 'fused' adult (older than *c.* 10 years).

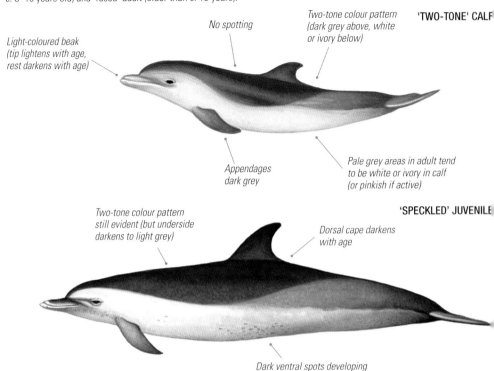

'TWO-TONE' CALF

No spotting

Two-tone colour pattern (dark grey above, white or ivory below)

Light-coloured beak (tip lightens with age, rest darkens with age)

Appendages dark grey

Pale grey areas in adult tend to be white or ivory in calf (or pinkish if active)

'SPECKLED' JUVENILE

Two-tone colour pattern still evident (but underside darkens to light grey)

Dorsal cape darkens with age

Dark ventral spots developing (especially on belly and lower sides of head)

have a light-coloured spinal blaze, a broadly three-toned underlying colour pattern, and a tailstock that is not divided into dark upper and light lower portions. Common and Indo-Pacific bottlenose dolphins can also be spotted to varying degrees (usually on the belly), but there are significant differences in size and body shape, beak and dorsal fin shape, and in the shape and intensity of the

dorsal cape; they also have a variable light spinal blaze. Possible hybrids with spinner dolphins have been observed off the Fernando de Noronha archipelago, Brazil.

DISTRIBUTION

Tropical and some sub-tropical waters in the Pacific, Atlantic and Indian Oceans, between *c.* 40°N and 40°S, with occasional records in colder waters. Most abundant in lower

DIVE SEQUENCE
- When swimming slowly, tip of beak breaks surface first.
- Upperside of melon briefly visible as it blows.
- Head dips below surface.
- Back and dorsal fin appear briefly.
- Tailstock often barely visible.
- Porpoises with neat re-entry when swimming fast.

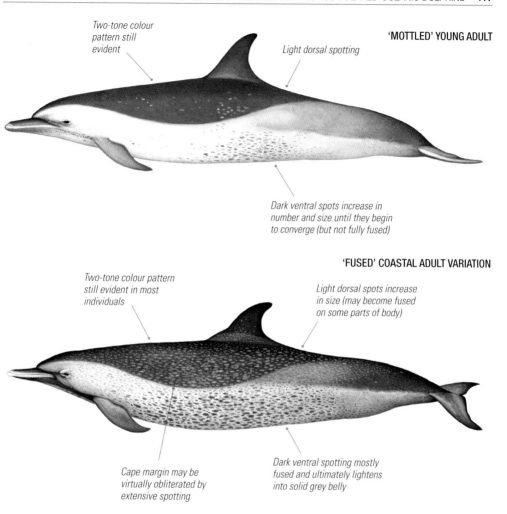

'MOTTLED' YOUNG ADULT

Two-tone colour pattern still evident

Light dorsal spotting

Dark ventral spots increase in number and size until they begin to converge (but not fully fused)

'FUSED' COASTAL ADULT VARIATION

Two-tone colour pattern still evident in most individuals

Light dorsal spots increase in size (may become fused on some parts of body)

Cape margin may be virtually obliterated by extensive spotting

Dark ventral spotting mostly fused and ultimately lightens into solid grey belly

atitudes within this range. Present in the Red Sea, Persian Gulf and Arabian Sea, but absent from the Mediterranean Sea and the Gulf of California. There is a single (2009) record of 16 individuals in the Yellow Sea, China. The North Pacific range is well documented, but details of the species' occurrence elsewhere is less well known.

The offshore subspecies is found mainly in oceanic waters, beyond the continental shelf edge, and around some oceanic islands such as in Hawaii, the Caribbean, the Philippines and Indian Ocean, but it does occur nearshore where sufficiently deep water approaches the coast. Primarily inhabits waters with surface water temperatures of over 25°C and with a sharp, shallow (less than 50m) thermocline. The coastal subspecies is usually within 130km of shore (rarely more than 200km), along the west coasts of Latin America from southern Mexico to northern Peru, often in water shallower than 50m.

Little is known about seasonal movements, but there is evidence of north–south, east–west and inshore–offshore movements in different regions. Some individuals have been known to range as far as 2,400km over 9–10 months, others appear to be more resident.

FOOD AND FEEDING

Prey Offshore subspecies – mainly small epipelagic and mesopelagic fish (especially lanternfish, flying fish), squid (especially flying squid) and crustaceans; coastal subspecies – possibly mainly larger, bottom-living species.

Feeding Forages mainly at night; offshore subspecies exploits deep scattering layer.

Dive depth Typically shallower (5–50m) during day, deeper (25–250m) at night (varies according to region); maximum recorded 342m.

Dive time Typically 30 seconds to two minutes; maximum 5.4 minutes.

LIFE HISTORY

Sexual maturity Females 9–11 years, males 12–15 years.
Mating Unknown.
Gestation 11–11.5 months.
Calving Every 2–3 years (4–6 years in the western Pacific); single calf born year-round, with regional peaks (e.g. July–October in Hawaii; one in spring, one in autumn in eastern tropical Pacific).
Weaning After average nine months (at least two years in some individuals); takes solid food at *c*. six months.
Lifespan Probably at least 40 years (oldest recorded 46 years).

BEHAVIOUR

Fast swimmer (in short bursts it may exceed 22km/h). Can be highly acrobatic (though it does not spin) and frequently performs breaches and side-slaps. Juveniles make especially high leaps (often up to three times the body length); at least some of the leaping appears to be to dislodge remoras. In the eastern tropical Pacific and western Indian Oceans, it frequently associates with yellowfin tuna and skipjack tuna (perhaps for foraging efficiency or protection from predators). It is also seen in mixed groups with spinner dolphins, bottlenose dolphins, rough-toothed dolphins and other cetaceans. Readily approaches boats and bow-rides (except on tuna fishing grounds in the eastern tropical Pacific, where it generally avoids boats); females and juveniles are more likely to bow-ride than males.

TEETH

Upper 68–96
Lower 68–94

GROUP SIZE AND STRUCTURE

Coastal subspecies generally in groups of 10–20 (ranging from one to *c*. 100). Offshore herds can number in the hundreds or thousands, sometimes spread out over several kilometres. There may be some segregation within a large group by age and sex: mother–calf pairs, juveniles and sub-adults, and adult males, which tend to remain within their own subgroups. Groups frequently fluctuate in size and composition.

PREDATORS

Mainly killer whales and even large sharks; probably also false killer whales and pygmy killer whales. Successful

A pantropical spotted dolphin (the offshore subspecies) in the Gulf of Mexico: notice the lack of spotting and the dark cape dipping very low below the dorsal fin.

A more heavily spotted coastal pantropical spotted dolphin in the eastern Pacific.

attacks have been observed – by a tiger shark in Hawaii, and a smooth hammerhead shark off south-east Brazil.

PHOTO-IDENTIFICATION

Unique spotting (if present) – with age estimates based on spot development – combined with nicks and notches in the trailing edge of the dorsal fin and any other long-term marks.

POPULATION

Possibly one of the most abundant dolphins in the world, numbering at least 2.5 million (not including populations yet to be assessed). Approximate regional estimates include 278,000 coastal spotters and 1.3 million offshore spotters in the eastern tropical Pacific; 440,000 off Japan; 6,000 in open-ocean Hawaiian waters; 51,000 in the northern Gulf of Mexico; and 15,000 in the eastern Sulu Sea, in the Philippines.

CONSERVATION

IUCN status: Least Concern (2018). There was very heavy mortality in the northeastern tropical Pacific purse-seine fishery west of Mexico and Central America, where large yellowfin tuna swim together with pantropical spotted, spinner and (to a lesser extent) common dolphins. Commercial fishing fleets were capturing the tuna and dolphins together – and, in total, more than 6 million dolphins have been killed. As many as 4 million of these were pantropical spotted dolphins, and the northeastern tropical Pacific population was reduced by *c.* 76 per cent.

Changes in legislation, as well as major modifications to fishing gear and practices (including the release of captured dolphins) – and public support for 'dolphin-safe tuna' – have reduced mortality greatly (to fewer than 1,000 annually). However, despite three decades of protection, the stock is showing minimal signs of recovery. There are several possible reasons: the stress of repeatedly being captured and released, separations of calves from their mothers, possible changes in the carrying capacity of the ecosystem for this species, or even under-reporting of current catch.

There is still incidental capture in a number of other purse-seine, gillnet and trawl fisheries throughout the range. Significant numbers are killed in the Japanese and Solomon Islands drive and harpoon hunts (just over 27,000 between 1972 and 2008 in Japan alone), and smaller numbers for human consumption and bait in dolphin hunts in the Caribbean, Sri Lanka, India, Taiwan, Indonesia and the Philippines; there are no precise figures. Other threats may include noise pollution from seismic surveys and disturbance from boat traffic (especially during daytime rest periods).

ATLANTIC SPOTTED DOLPHIN
Stenella frontalis

(G. Cuvier, 1829)

In many ways, the Atlantic spotted dolphin more closely resembles the Indo-Pacific bottlenose dolphin than it does the pantropical spotted dolphin. It is highly variable in appearance, between ages, individuals and regions, from virtually unspotted to very heavily spotted.

Classification Odontoceti, family Delphinidae.

Common name 'Atlantic' because this species is endemic to the Atlantic Ocean; 'spotted' for the extensive dark and light spotting on many individuals.

Other names Spotted dolphin, Gulf Stream spotted dolphin, spotter, spotted porpoise, bridled dolphin, Cuvier's porpoise, long-snouted dolphin (or various combinations of these).

Scientific name *Stenella* from the Greek *stenos* for 'narrow', and *ella* for 'little' (referring to the beak); *frontalis* from the Latin *frons* for 'forehead' or 'brow', and *alis* for 'pertaining to' (evidently referring to the melon).

Taxonomy Taxonomy of the spotted dolphins was revised in 1987, resulting in two accepted species. Currently no recognised subspecies of the Atlantic spotted dolphin. However, there appear to be two forms (which may prove to be subspecies): a larger, heavy-bodied, heavily spotted form occurring mainly over the continental shelf in warmer waters of the western North Atlantic (previously known as *S. plagiodon*); and a smaller, slimmer, lightly spotted or unspotted form in more oceanic areas over the continental slope in the Gulf Stream and the central North Atlantic (and around offshore islands, such as the Azores). Taxonomy of *Stenella* is currently in dispute and is likely to be revised in the near future; this species might be moved to a different genus.

'FUSED' ADULT HEAVILY SPOTTED FORM

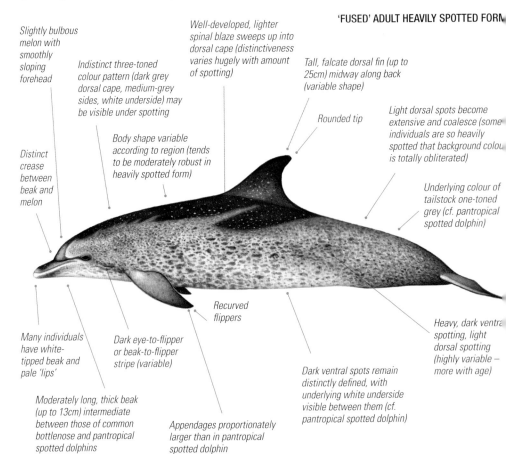

Slightly bulbous melon with smoothly sloping forehead

Well-developed, lighter spinal blaze sweeps up into dorsal cape (distinctiveness varies hugely with amount of spotting)

Indistinct three-toned colour pattern (dark grey dorsal cape, medium-grey sides, white underside) may be visible under spotting

Tall, falcate dorsal fin (up to 25cm) midway along back (variable shape)

Rounded tip

Light dorsal spots become extensive and coalesce (some individuals are so heavily spotted that background colour is totally obliterated)

Body shape variable according to region (tends to be moderately robust in heavily spotted form)

Distinct crease between beak and melon

Underlying colour of tailstock one-toned grey (cf. pantropical spotted dolphin)

Recurved flippers

Many individuals have white-tipped beak and pale 'lips'

Dark eye-to-flipper or beak-to-flipper stripe (variable)

Heavy, dark ventral spotting, light dorsal spotting (highly variable – more with age)

Dark ventral spots remain distinctly defined, with underlying white underside visible between them (cf. pantropical spotted dolphin)

Moderately long, thick beak (up to 13cm) intermediate between those of common bottlenose and pantropical spotted dolphins

Appendages proportionately larger than in pantropical spotted dolphin

AT A GLANCE

- Tropical to warm temperate waters of the Atlantic
- Small size
- Generally chunkier than pantropical spotted dolphin
- Many populations heavily spotted
- Highly variable appearance within group
- Light diagonal spinal blaze
- Three-toned underlying colour pattern
- Tall, falcate dorsal fin midway along back
- Moderately long, white-tipped beak

ADULT HEAVILY SPOTTED FORM

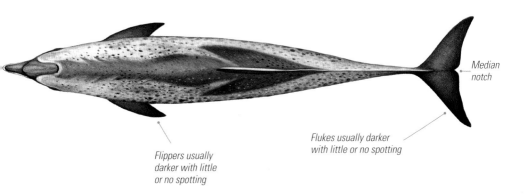

Median notch

Flukes usually darker with little or no spotting

Flippers usually darker with little or no spotting

SIZE
L: ♂ 1.7–2.3m, ♀ 1.7–2.3m;
WT: 110–140kg; **MAX:** 2.3m, 143kg
Calf – L: 0.8–1.2m; **WT:** *c.* 10–15kg

SIMILAR SPECIES
Easy to misidentify because of huge variation in the amount of spotting. Confusion is most likely with common bottlenose dolphins (there is no overlap in range with Indo-Pacific bottlenose dolphins); differences in size and robustness can help, but they are subtle and tricky to distinguish. Heavily spotted animals are likely to be Atlantic spotted dolphins, but be aware that some are nearly unspotted and some bottlenose dolphins have spotting. Pantropical spotted dolphins in the Atlantic are best distinguished by their generally more slender body, the lack of a light-coloured spinal blaze, the broadly two-toned underlying colour pattern, and the tailstock divided into dark upper and light lower portions. Hybrids with both pantropical spotted and common bottlenose dolphins are known.

DISTRIBUTION
Tropical to warm temperate waters in the Atlantic Ocean, in both hemispheres, between *c.* 50°N and 33°S. In the west, it ranges from at least southern Brazil north to New England (although distribution is discontinuous in the western South Atlantic). In the east, it ranges from at least Gabon north to at least Mauritania (the exact limits are poorly known). Occurs around some oceanic

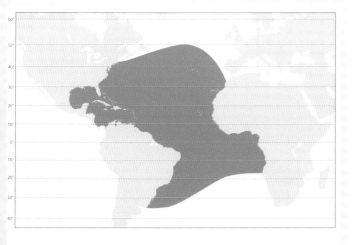

Atlantic spotted dolphin distribution

Note: the Atlantic spotted dolphin is usually classified into four different colour phases, according to age: 'two-tone' calf (from birth to average *c.* 3 years old), 'speckled' juvenile (average *c.* 4–8 years old), 'mottled' young adult (average *c.* 9–15 years old), and 'fused' adult (older than *c.* 15 years).

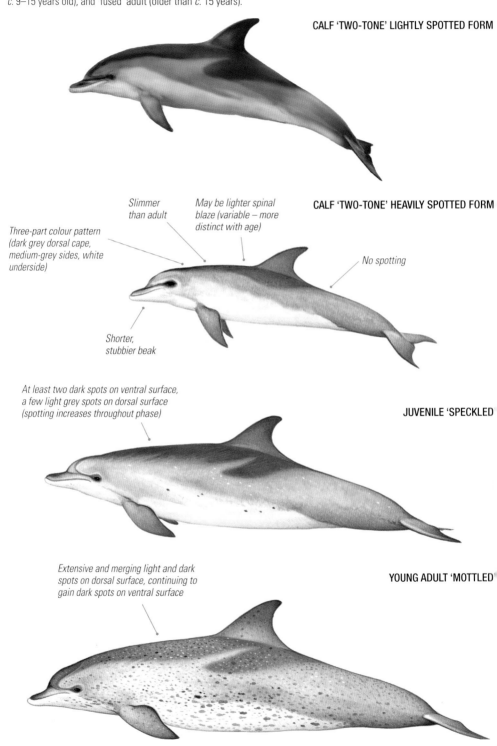

CALF 'TWO-TONE' LIGHTLY SPOTTED FORM

CALF 'TWO-TONE' HEAVILY SPOTTED FORM

Slimmer than adult

May be lighter spinal blaze (variable – more distinct with age)

Three-part colour pattern (dark grey dorsal cape, medium-grey sides, white underside)

No spotting

Shorter, stubbier beak

At least two dark spots on ventral surface, a few light grey spots on dorsal surface (spotting increases throughout phase)

JUVENILE 'SPECKLED'

Extensive and merging light and dark spots on dorsal surface, continuing to gain dark spots on ventral surface

YOUNG ADULT 'MOTTLED'

ADULT LIGHTLY SPOTTED FORM

Body shape variable according to region (tends to be moderately slender in lightly spotted form)

Well-developed, lighter spinal blaze sweeps up into dorsal cape

Distinct three-toned colour pattern (dark grey dorsal cape, medium-grey sides, white underside)

Little or no spotting

DORSAL FIN VARIATIONS

islands, such as the Azores and the Bahamas. Present in the Gulf of Mexico, but absent from the Mediterranean Sea.

The heavily spotted form prefers shallow continental shelf waters, usually within the 200m isobath and up to 250–350km from shore (typically at least 8–20km offshore). The lightly spotted form occurs over the outer continental shelf, the upper continental slope and in deep oceanic waters. Less common in nearshore waters, although there are exceptions (e.g. Ilha Grande Bay, southeastern Brazil) and it may prefer shallower waters around oceanic islands (e.g. over shallow (6–12m) sand banks in the Bahamas). There may be some seasonal inshore–offshore movements.

BEHAVIOUR

Highly acrobatic and capable of some exceptionally high leaps. Often plays with kelp and other objects. Regularly in uneven groups with common bottlenose dolphins (typically 2–3 times as many Atlantic spotted as common); the bottlenose dolphins are almost twice as large and can be aggressive towards the Atlantic spotted dolphins. In the Azores, it will join temporary mixed-species feeding aggregations with tuna, seabirds, common dolphins, common bottlenose dolphins and sometimes other cetaceans. An avid bow-rider in most of its range, and it may swim far to join a fast-moving vessel. Residents in the Bahamas have become

DIVE SEQUENCE

- When swimming slowly, tip of beak breaks surface first.
- Upperside of melon briefly visible as it blows.
- Head dips below surface.
- Back and dorsal fin appear briefly.
- Tailstock often barely visible.
- Porpoises with neat re-entry when swimming fast.

FOOD AND FEEDING

Prey Wide variety of small to large fish (including herring, anchovy, flounder) and squid; feeds nocturnally on flying fish; occasionally benthic invertebrates; some regional differences in diet.

Feeding Offshore form cooperates in herding balls of fish against surface; in Bahamas, catches fish hiding in soft, sandy seabed (by sticking beaks into sand); known to follow trawlers to eat discarded fish in some regions.

Dive depth Most dives are less than 10m; maximum recorded 60m.

Dive time Mostly 2–4 minutes; maximum recorded six minutes.

accustomed to divers and snorkellers. Well known for its signature whistles – stereotyped whistles that are unique to each individual and used to broadcast the identity of the whistler, or by conspecifics to address particular individuals.

TEETH

Upper 64–84
Lower 60–80

GROUP SIZE AND STRUCTURE

Generally in small to medium-sized groups of up to 50 animals (occasionally up to 200). Group sizes tend to be smaller (5–15) nearer shore and larger offshore. Groups are often segregated by age and sex, and frequently fluctuate in size and composition. There is evidence of close male alliances involving two or three individuals.

PREDATORS

Sharks (such as tiger and bull) and killer whales are known predators. It may also be preyed on by other blackfish.

PHOTO-IDENTIFICATION

Unique spotting pattern, combined with nicks and notches on the trailing edge of the dorsal fin and any other long-term marks. Age estimates are based on spot pattern development.

POPULATION

No overall abundance estimate. Approximate regional estimates include 45,000 in the western North Atlantic (lower Bay of Fundy to central Florida); and 38,000 in the northern Gulf of Mexico (considered an underestimate).

CONSERVATION

IUCN status: Least Concern (2018). Incidental catches in fishing gear are known in the Caribbean, the western North Atlantic, Venezuela, Brazil, Mauritania, Ghana and probably elsewhere, but there are no figures; at least some of the animals are used for human consumption or as shark bait. No direct hunting is known, although there are occasional catches in the Lesser Antilles in the Caribbean, and possibly off West Africa. Other threats are unknown, but are likely to include organochlorine pollutants.

A largely unspotted group of Atlantic spotted dolphins in the Azores.

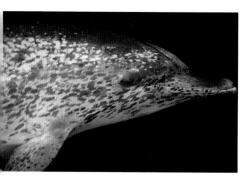

Limited evidence suggests that Atlantic spotted dolphins have a more offshore distribution in the east than in the west: this individual is in the Gulf of Mexico.

LIFE HISTORY

Sexual maturity Females 8–15 years, males 18 years.
Mating Polygynous mating system (single male mates with multiple females)
Gestation *c.* 11–12 months.
Calving Every 3–4 years (ranges from one to five); single calf born year-round in tropical regions, with seasonal peaks elsewhere.
Weaning After 3–5 years.
Lifespan Probably at least 50 years; maximum known: 55 years.

Atlantic spotted dolphins are avid bow-riders in most of their range.

SPINNER DOLPHIN
Stenella longirostris

(Gray, 1828)

Named for its spectacular habit of leaping out of the water and spinning up to seven times longitudinally, before falling back with a great splash, the spinner dolphin is a familiar sight in many parts of the tropics. There is more geographical variation in form and colour pattern in this species than in almost any other cetacean.

Classification Odontoceti, family Delphinidae.
Common name 'Spinner' for its distinctive aerial spinning.
Other names Long-snouted spinner dolphin, long-snouted dolphin, long-beaked dolphin, pantropical spinner dolphin, longsnout, spinner, rollover; see taxonomy for subspecies common names.
Scientific name *Stenella* from the Greek *stenos* for 'narrow', and *ella* for 'little' (referring to the beak); *longirostris* from the Latin *longus* for 'long' and *rostrum* for 'beak' (literally 'narrow little long beak').
Taxonomy Four subspecies currently recognised: Gray's spinner (sometimes 'Hawaiian') dolphin (*S. l. longirostris*), the 'typical' spinner dolphin found in most tropical oceanic waters worldwide; Central American (previously 'Costa Rican') spinner dolphin (*S. l. centroamericana*), along the Pacific coast of Central America; eastern spinner dolphin (*S. l. orientalis*), in offshore waters of the eastern tropical Pacific; and dwarf spinner dolphin (*S. l. roseiventris*), in Southeast Asia and northern Australia. There is also a hybrid – called the whitebelly or white-bellied spinner – that is intermediate between Gray's and eastern spinner dolphins, found in the eastern tropical Pacific where these two 'parent' subspecies meet. Taxonomy of *Stenella* is currently in dispute and is likely to be revised in the near future.

GRAY'S ADUL

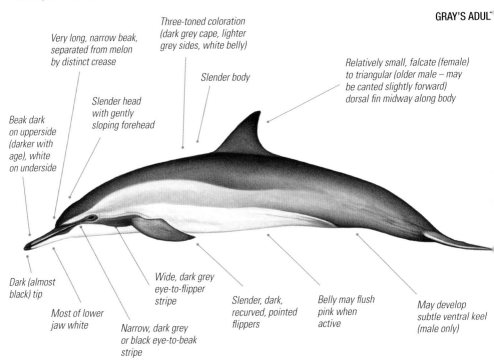

Very long, narrow beak, separated from melon by distinct crease

Three-toned coloration (dark grey cape, lighter grey sides, white belly)

Slender body

Relatively small, falcate (female) to triangular (older male – may be canted slightly forward) dorsal fin midway along body

Slender head with gently sloping forehead

Beak dark on upperside (darker with age), white on underside

Dark (almost black) tip

Most of lower jaw white

Wide, dark grey eye-to-flipper stripe

Narrow, dark grey or black eye-to-beak stripe

Slender, dark, recurved, pointed flippers

Belly may flush pink when active

May develop subtle ventral keel (male only)

AT A GLANCE
- Tropical and sub-tropical waters worldwide
- Small size
- Usually slender body
- Erect dorsal fin (sometimes canted forward) midway along back
- Huge variation in appearance according to region
- Long, slender beak
- Gently sloping melon
- Performs high spinning leaps
- Usually quite gregarious

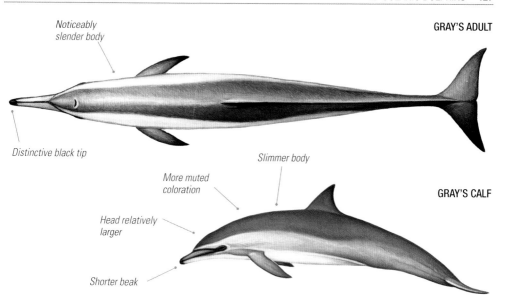

Noticeably slender body

GRAY'S ADULT

Distinctive black tip

Slimmer body

GRAY'S CALF

More muted coloration

Head relatively larger

Shorter beak

SIMILAR SPECIES

Other dolphins occasionally spin with a couple of revolutions, but the spinner is instantly identifiable by its unique and multiple aerial spinning. Confusion is possible with other long-beaked oceanic dolphins with a similar body shape, especially at a distance, but there are significant differences in relative beak length, dorsal fin shape and colour patterns. Gray's spinner dolphin is particularly similar to the Clymene dolphin, which overlaps in the Atlantic, but is slimmer, with a longer and more slender beak, less rounded melon, and a typically less falcate dorsal fin (though this is highly variable and there is overlap); the colour pattern is different, too – look for the two dips in the Clymene's cape and the dark 'moustache' on the top of the beak. Pantropical spotted dolphins have a very similar range and often are only lightly spotted; the two species are best distinguished by differences in beak length and thickness, dorsal fin shape (less falcate in spinner) and colour pattern (the pantropical spotted dolphin's dark dorsal cape always dips very low just ahead of the dorsal fin). Possible hybrids between spinner dolphins and pantropical spotted and Clymene dolphins have been observed off the Fernando do Noronha archipelago, Brazil. Central American and eastern spinner dolphins are virtually identical; females and young, in particular, may not be distinguishable.

DISTRIBUTION

Found in all tropical and most sub-tropical waters in the Pacific, Atlantic and Indian Oceans, roughly between 30–40°N and 20–40°S. Best known in coastal waters, around

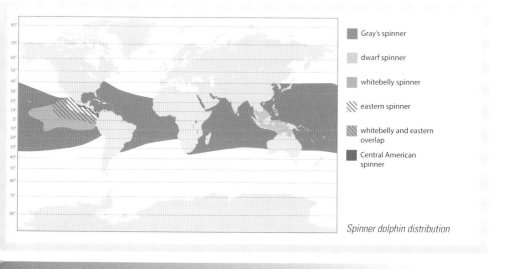

Gray's spinner

dwarf spinner

whitebelly spinner

eastern spinner

whitebelly and eastern overlap

Central American spinner

Spinner dolphin distribution

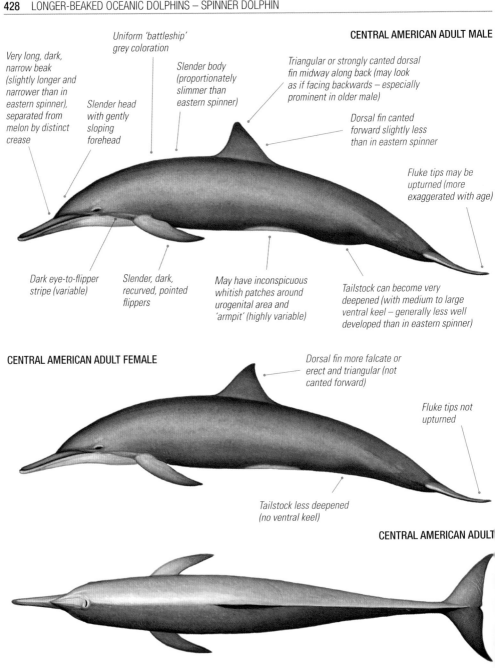

CENTRAL AMERICAN ADULT MALE

Uniform 'battleship' grey coloration

Very long, dark, narrow beak (slightly longer and narrower than in eastern spinner), separated from melon by distinct crease

Slender body (proportionately slimmer than eastern spinner)

Slender head with gently sloping forehead

Triangular or strongly canted dorsal fin midway along back (may look as if facing backwards – especially prominent in older male)

Dorsal fin canted forward slightly less than in eastern spinner

Fluke tips may be upturned (more exaggerated with age)

Dark eye-to-flipper stripe (variable)

Slender, dark, recurved, pointed flippers

May have inconspicuous whitish patches around urogenital area and 'armpit' (highly variable)

Tailstock can become very deepened (with medium to large ventral keel – generally less well developed than in eastern spinner)

CENTRAL AMERICAN ADULT FEMALE

Dorsal fin more falcate or erect and triangular (not canted forward)

Fluke tips not upturned

Tailstock less deepened (no ventral keel)

CENTRAL AMERICAN ADULT

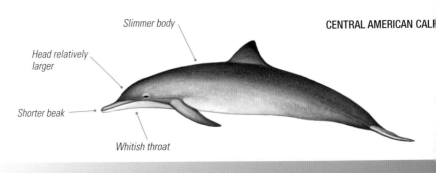

Slimmer body

Head relatively larger

Shorter beak

Whitish throat

CENTRAL AMERICAN CALF

DWARF ADULT

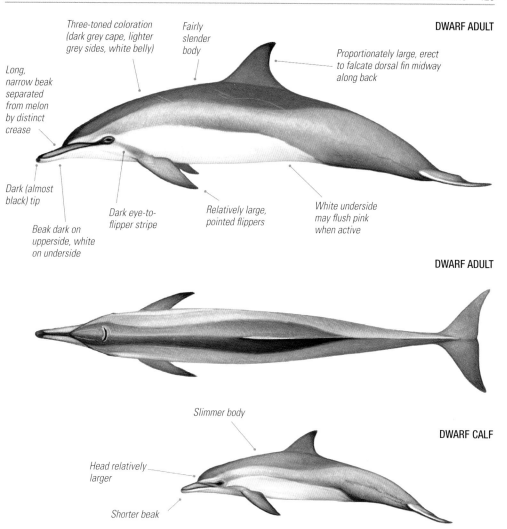

Three-toned coloration (dark grey cape, lighter grey sides, white belly)

Fairly slender body

Proportionately large, erect to falcate dorsal fin midway along back

Long, narrow beak separated from melon by distinct crease

Dark (almost black) tip

Beak dark on upperside, white on underside

Dark eye-to-flipper stripe

Relatively large, pointed flippers

White underside may flush pink when active

DWARF ADULT

DWARF CALF

Slimmer body

Head relatively larger

Shorter beak

SIZE – CENTRAL AMERICAN
L: ♂ 1.9–2.2m, ♀ 1.8–2.1m;
WT: 55–75kg; **MAX:** 2.2m, 82kg
Calf – L: 75–80cm; **WT:** *c.* 10kg

SIZE – WHITEBELLY
L: ♂ 1.6–2.4m, ♀ 1.6–2m;
WT: 55–75kg; **MAX:** 2.4m, 75kg
Calf – L: 75–80cm; **WT:** *c.* 10kg

SIZE – GRAY'S
L: ♂ 1.6–2.1m, ♀ 1.4–2m;
WT: 55–70kg; **MAX:** 2.2m, 80kg
Calf – L: 75–80cm; **WT:** *c.* 10kg

SIZE – EASTERN
L: ♂ 1.6–2m, ♀ 1.5–1.9m;
WT: 55–70kg; **MAX:** 2m, 75kg
Calf – L: 75–80cm; **WT:** *c.* 10kg

SIZE – DWARF
L: ♂ 1.4–1.6m, ♀ 1.3–1.5m;
WT: 23–35kg; **MAX:** 1.6m, 36kg
Calf – L: 50–70cm; **WT:** 5–7kg

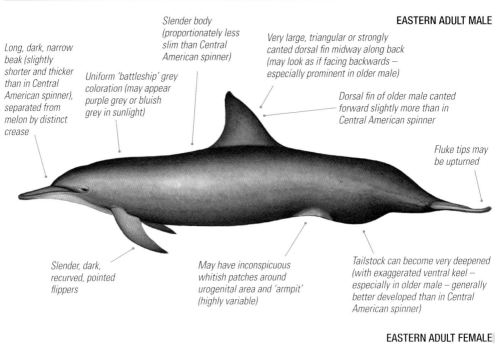

EASTERN ADULT MALE

Long, dark, narrow beak (slightly shorter and thicker than in Central American spinner), separated from melon by distinct crease

Slender body (proportionately less slim than Central American spinner)

Uniform 'battleship' grey coloration (may appear purple grey or bluish grey in sunlight)

Very large, triangular or strongly canted dorsal fin midway along back (may look as if facing backwards – especially prominent in older male)

Dorsal fin of older male canted forward slightly more than in Central American spinner

Fluke tips may be upturned

Slender, dark, recurved, pointed flippers

May have inconspicuous whitish patches around urogenital area and 'armpit' (highly variable)

Tailstock can become very deepened (with exaggerated ventral keel – especially in older male – generally better developed than in Central American spinner)

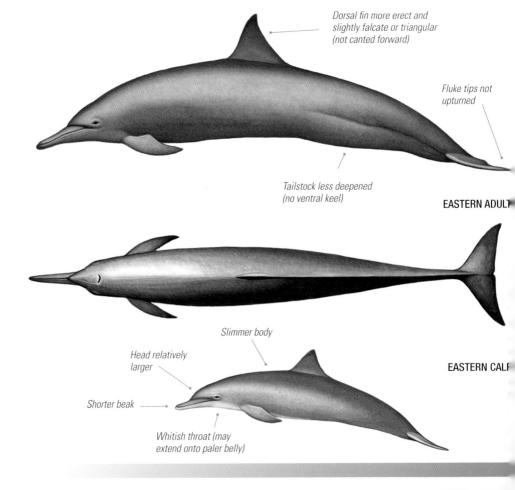

EASTERN ADULT FEMALE

Dorsal fin more erect and slightly falcate or triangular (not canted forward)

Fluke tips not upturned

Tailstock less deepened (no ventral keel)

EASTERN ADULT

Slimmer body

Head relatively larger

EASTERN CALF

Shorter beak

Whitish throat (may extend onto paler belly)

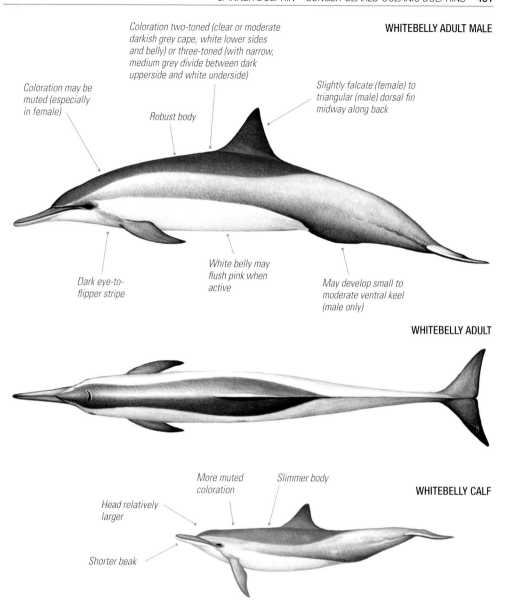

WHITEBELLY ADULT MALE

Coloration two-toned (clear or moderate darkish grey cape, white lower sides and belly) or three-toned (with narrow, medium grey divide between dark upperside and white underside)

Coloration may be muted (especially in female)

Robust body

Slightly falcate (female) to triangular (male) dorsal fin midway along back

Dark eye-to-flipper stripe

White belly may flush pink when active

May develop small to moderate ventral keel (male only)

WHITEBELLY ADULT

WHITEBELLY CALF

More muted coloration

Slimmer body

Head relatively larger

Shorter beak

oceanic islands and over shallow banks, but it also occurs in very large numbers on the high seas and ranges over vast distances of open water. Coastal spinners – especially around oceanic islands – frequently move into shallow sandy bays in the morning and rest until late afternoon or early evening; the light-coloured sand may help them to detect approaching sharks (their requirements for good daytime resting habitat seem to be fairly strict); they venture out to deeper water at night to feed. In some places, they rest actually inside the lagoons of coral atolls. Site fidelity is high in some regions.

Central American

Endemic to a narrow 150km band of shallow coastal waters in the eastern tropical Pacific. Ranges from the Gulf of Tehuantepec, Mexico, to Costa Rica.

Gray's

Found worldwide in most parts of the spinner dolphin range, except in limited parts of tropical Asia and the eastern tropical Pacific. Mainly around oceanic islands, but does occur in the open ocean.

Eastern

Eastern tropical Pacific, east of 145°W and from Baja California, Mexico, south to northern Ecuador (roughly at the equator). Typically in offshore waters in the Eastern Pacific Warm Pool.

Dwarf
Almost exclusively in shallow coastal waters of Southeast Asia and northern Australia, in the tropical Indo-Pacific. Mainly over coral reefs in less than 50m of water. It is replaced in deeper, offshore waters in this region by Gray's spinner dolphin.

Whitebelly
Offshore waters of the eastern tropical Pacific. Occurs roughly where eastern spinners meet Gray's spinners, with extensive overlap in range with eastern.

BEHAVIOUR
One of the most aerial of all dolphins. As well as spinning, it will perform more traditional breaches, as well as arc-shaped leaps, tail-over-head leaps, side-slaps, fluke-slaps and flipper-slaps. Particularly acrobatic during the change from rest to foraging: in Hawaii, spinner dolphins spending the daytime resting in shallow sandy bays often engage in 'zigzag' swimming, with a lot of stereotyped aerial behaviour, thought to test the readiness of the school to move offshore. Frequently associates with pantropical spotted dolphins in the eastern tropical Pacific and Indian Oceans and occasionally with other marine mammal species. In many parts of the range it readily approaches boats and bow-rides (except on tuna fishing grounds in the eastern tropical Pacific, where it generally avoids boats).

SPINNING
Best known for leaping up to 3m into the air, spinning on its longitudinal axis up to seven times and then falling back into the water – often up to 14 times in a descending series (each less vigorous than the previous one). It starts spinning underwater, just before emerging from the surface.

Individuals of all ages spin and, once one dolphin starts, others typically join in. Some other dolphin species spin, but not as many times or with the same frequency.

There are a number of possible explanations: spinning may be to generate enough force on water re-entry to dislodge attached remoras (although remoras are not always present); it may be a social display related to courtship; it could be a way of flexing muscles or preparing for night-time foraging; or the large underwater bubble plume created by the spinning and re-entry may serve as a distinct acoustic target for communication across a widely dispersed school.

TEETH
Upper 80–124
Lower 80–124
There are small differences in tooth count between subspecies.

GROUP SIZE AND STRUCTURE
Highly variable according to activity and location, ranging from 10–50 up to several thousand. The largest schools tend to occur offshore, the smallest in coastal waters. Social structure varies greatly between regions: there is a fission-fusion system around the main Hawaiian islands (with individuals periodically joining up and then

DIVE SEQUENCE
- When swimming slowly, tip of beak often breaks surface first.
- Upperside of melon briefly visible as it blows.
- Head dips below surface.
- Back and prominent dorsal fin appear briefly – some individuals look back-to-front.
- Tailstock quickly arches (usually high).
- Normally does not show flukes.
- When swimming fast, may porpoise with clean re-entry.
- Large, travelling schools often churn water into foam.

FOOD AND FEEDING

Prey Wide variety of small (less than 20cm) midwater fish, squid, sergestid shrimps; dwarf spinner feeds on benthic reef fish and invertebrates.

Feeding Most feeding at night, resting during day (except dwarf spinners – feed during day); some populations feed cooperatively (off Hawaii herd schooling fish into bait balls against sea surface).

Dive depth Varies with subspecies; offshore, frequently to 200–300m, but capable of 600m or deeper

Dive time When resting, 1–2 minutes (spends most of time at surface); when foraging, 3–4 minutes (spends c. 30 seconds at surface between deep dives).

separating on a daily basis), for example, but in the Northwestern Hawaiian Islands there are stable groups of long-term associates. There is some evidence of segregation by age and sex.

PREDATORS

Large sharks are probably the most significant predators; judging by lack of observations of spinner dolphins with healed wounds from shark attacks, it is assumed that most are fatal. Given their small size, even cookiecutter shark bites can be fatal. Probably also killer whales, and possibly false killer whales and even pygmy killer whales.

PHOTO-IDENTIFICATION

Nicks and notches on the trailing edge of the dorsal fin (though only c. 15 per cent are sufficiently distinctive to be individually identifiable).

POPULATION

No overall global estimate, but probably one of the most abundant dolphins in the world. Many regions have not been assessed, but known abundances add up to more than 1 million. Approximate regional estimates include 801,000 whitebelly spinners and 613,000 eastern spinners in the eastern tropical Pacific; 31,000 in the southeastern Sulu Sea; 12,000 in the northern Gulf of Mexico; and 1,800–2,000 around Hawaii.

CONSERVATION

IUCN status: Least Concern (2018); eastern spinner subspecies Vulnerable (2008). There was very heavy mortality in the northeastern tropical Pacific purse-seine fishery west of Mexico and Central America, where large yellowfin tuna swim together with spinner, pantropical spotted and (to a lesser extent) common dolphins.

Commercial fishing fleets were capturing the tuna and dolphins together – and, in total, more than 6 million dolphins have been killed. As many as 2 million of these were spinner dolphins and the northeastern tropical Pacific population was reduced by c. 65 per cent.

Changes in legislation, as well as major modifications to fishing gear and practices (including the release of captured dolphins) – and public support for 'dolphin-safe tuna' – have reduced mortality greatly (to fewer than 1,000 annually). However, despite three decades of protection, the spinner stock is not showing significant signs of recovery. There are several possible reasons: the stress of repeatedly being captured and released, separations of calves from their mothers, possible changes in the carrying capacity of the ecosystem for this species, or even under-reporting of current catch.

There is still incidental capture in a number of other purse-seine, driftnet and trawl fisheries throughout the range, some of which are likely unsustainable; dwarf spinner dolphins are caught incidentally in shrimp trawls in the Gulf of Thailand. In some cases, human use of by-caught spinners has led to active hunting. Direct kills for human consumption and shark bait take place in the Solomon Islands, the Caribbean, Sri Lanka, India, Taiwan, Indonesia and the Philippines, and occasionally Japan and possibly West Africa. There are no precise figures, but annual takes in the order of thousands have been reported from some countries in the Indian Ocean.

Other threats may include disturbance (especially harassment by dolphin-watching boats and swimmers in some shallow coastal waters where the dolphins are trying to rest), ingestion of (and entanglement in) marine debris, chemical pollution and noise pollution.

LIFE HISTORY

Sexual maturity Females 8–9 years, males 7–10 years.

Mating System ranges from polygynous (single male mates with multiple females) in eastern and Central American spinners, to polygynandrous (both males and females have multiple mating partners) in Gray's, dwarf and whitebelly spinners; varying degrees of male–male competition for females (depending on subspecies), from overt competition to sperm competition.

Gestation 10 months.

Calving Every three years; single calf born year-round, with seasonal peaks from late spring to autumn according to region.

Weaning After 1–2 years.

Lifespan Possibly 25–30 years (oldest recorded 26 years).

CLYMENE DOLPHIN
Stenella clymene

(Gray, 1850)

Molecular studies reveal that the Clymene dolphin may have evolved through extensive hybridisation between spinner and striped dolphins and, in many ways, it appears almost intermediate between the two species. Initially believed to be a variant of the spinner dolphin, it was not fully accepted as a distinct species until 1981.

Classification Odontoceti, family Delphinidae.

Common name After Clymene, the sea nymph and Titan goddess in Greek mythology; the 'C' in 'Clymene' should always be capitalised; it is normally pronounced 'Cly-me-nee'.

Other names Short-snouted spinner dolphin, Atlantic spinner dolphin, Senegal dolphin, helmet dolphin (after the distinctive line from the tip of the beak to the melon, which supposedly looks like the visor on a tenth-century Norman helmet).

Scientific name *Stenella* from the Greek *stenos* for 'narrow', and *ella* for 'little' (referring to the beak); Clymene after the mythological sea nymph (although some argue it is from the Greek *klymenos* for 'notorious' or 'infamous').

Taxonomy There is some evidence that the Clymene dolphin evolved through hybrid speciation (its outward appearance and behaviour are similar to the spinner dolphin, its skull to the striped dolphin) and, if so, it would be the first marine mammal known to have arisen in this way; no recognised forms or subspecies; taxonomy of *Stenella* is currently in dispute and the genus is likely to be revised in the near future.

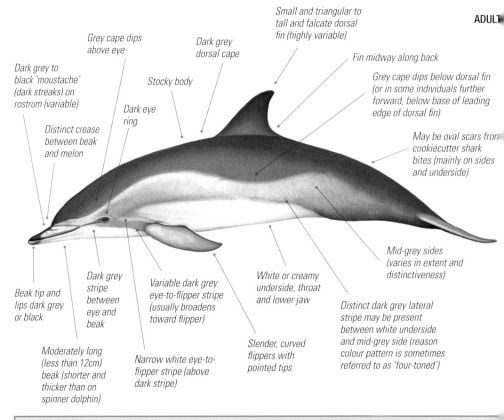

Small and triangular to tall and falcate dorsal fin (highly variable)

ADULT

Grey cape dips above eye

Dark grey dorsal cape

Fin midway along back

Dark grey to black 'moustache' (dark streaks) on rostrum (variable)

Stocky body

Grey cape dips below dorsal fin (or in some individuals further forward, below base of leading edge of dorsal fin)

Dark eye ring

Distinct crease between beak and melon

May be oval scars from cookiecutter shark bites (mainly on sides and underside)

Mid-grey sides (varies in extent and distinctiveness)

Dark grey stripe between eye and beak

Variable dark grey eye-to-flipper stripe (usually broadens toward flipper)

White or creamy underside, throat and lower jaw

Beak tip and lips dark grey or black

Distinct dark grey lateral stripe may be present between white underside and mid-grey side (reason colour pattern is sometimes referred to as 'four-toned')

Moderately long (less than 12cm) beak (shorter and thicker than on spinner dolphin)

Narrow white eye-to-flipper stripe (above dark stripe)

Slender, curved flippers with pointed tips

AT A GLANCE
- Warm waters of Atlantic Ocean
- Small size
- Stocky body
- Three-toned colour pattern (highly variable)

- Two distinctive dips in the dark cape (giving wavy appearance)
- Nearly triangular or slightly falcate dorsal fin
- Medium-length, robust beak
- Dark 'moustache' on surface of beak

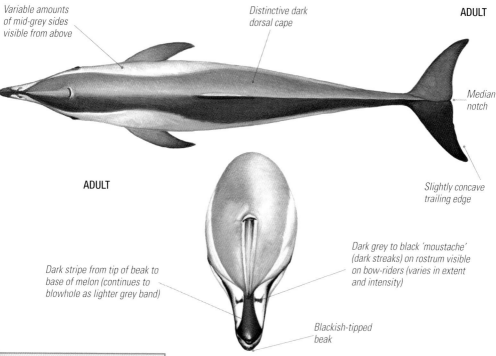

Variable amounts of mid-grey sides visible from above

Distinctive dark dorsal cape

ADULT

Median notch

ADULT

Slightly concave trailing edge

Dark grey to black 'moustache' (dark streaks) on rostrum visible on bow-riders (varies in extent and intensity)

Dark stripe from tip of beak to base of melon (continues to blowhole as lighter grey band)

Blackish-tipped beak

SIZE
L: ♂ 1.8–2m, ♀ 1.7–1.9m;
WT: 50–80kg; **MAX:** 2m, 80kg
Calf – L: 0.9–1.2m; **WT:** *c.* 10kg

SIMILAR SPECIES
Similar in appearance to Gray's spinner dolphin, but smaller and more robust, with a shorter and stockier beak, more rounded melon and a typically more falcate dorsal fin (though this is highly variable and there is overlap); the colour pattern is different, too – look for the two dips in the Clymene's cape and the dark 'moustache' on the top of the beak. The 'clean' throat is useful for separating Clymene from some other dolphins but, unfortunately, not from spinner (Gray's spinner has a similar throat). There may be some confusion from a distance with similarly shaped common dolphins, but their dorsal cape dips into a sharp V-shape below the dorsal fin, whereas Clymene's dips into a smooth curve; the Clymene's 'clean' throat, white lower jaw (also present on Gray's spinner dolphins) and the 'moustache' on the beak are also good ways to separate it from common. There are superficial similarities with the striped dolphin, but on close inspection the colour pattern is very different. A hybrid between Clymene and spinner dolphins has been observed off the Fernando de Noronha archipelago, Brazil.

DISTRIBUTION
Tropical, sub-tropical and occasionally warm temperate waters in the Atlantic Ocean,

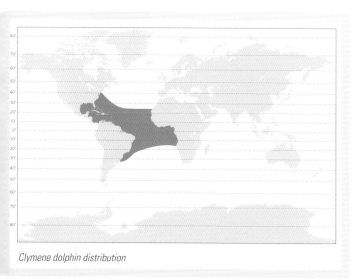

Clymene dolphin distribution

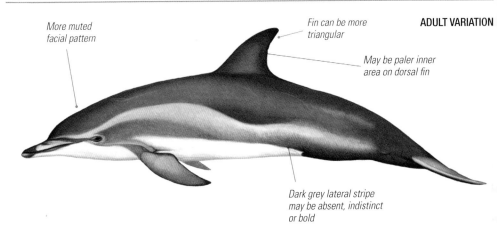

More muted facial pattern

Fin can be more triangular

ADULT VARIATION

May be paler inner area on dorsal fin

Dark grey lateral stripe may be absent, indistinct or bold

including the Caribbean Sea and the Gulf of Mexico; it is not known to enter the Mediterranean Sea. In the east, it extends from at least southern Angola (c. 14°S) north to central Mauritania (c. 19°N); its southerly limit along the western seaboard of Africa is likely to be limited by the cold-water Benguela Current (although it probably occurs further south in offshore waters in the mid-Atlantic, where sea temperatures are warmer). In the west, it has been recorded from Rio Grande do Sul, Brazil (c. 30°S), north to New Jersey (c. 39°N). There are two mid-Atlantic records. Restricted to warm waters, within a sea surface temperature range of 19.6°C to 31.1°C (preferring higher than 25°C in most regions). Strongly influenced by warm currents such as the Gulf Stream, the North Equatorial Current and the Brazil Current. An oceanic species, occurring mainly seaward of the continental shelf (preferring the slope and beyond) and rarely seen near shore (except where deep water approaches the coast). Recorded in depths of 400–5,000m. Found in tropical areas year-round, with no known long-distance migrations.

BEHAVIOUR
Quick, agile and often aerially active. Breaches and spins longitudinally; may spin up to four times before falling back into the water on its side or back (though the leaps are lower and less frequent, and the spins less elaborate and acrobatic than those of the spinner dolphin – the only other species that routinely exhibits longitudinal rotations). As with all pelagic dolphins, it is not uncommon to see 'quiet' schools that are relatively inactive at the surface as well. Reported occasionally to associate with common dolphins off West Africa, and with spinner dolphins in the Caribbean and elsewhere. Response to boats varies from avoidance to quite inquisitive. Avid bow-rider in some areas and will often approach vessels from a distance.

TEETH
Upper 78–104
Lower 76–96

GROUP SIZE AND STRUCTURE
Ranges from one to 1,000, with an overall average of c. 70–80 (though roughly half as many in the Gulf of Mexico)

DIVE SEQUENCE
- Only blowhole, part of back and dorsal fin exposed.
- Rolls forward with slight arching of back.
- Tailstock disappears below surface.
- Does not fluke.
- Porpoises when swimming fast.

BLOW
- Indistinct blow.

FOOD AND FEEDING
Prey Small mesopelagic fish (including lanternfish, herring smelt, codlets) and squid.
Feeding Most feeding at night; cooperative foraging has been observed in Gulf of Mexico during the day.
Dive depth Unknown.
Dive time Unknown.

PREDATORS
No predation events have been documented, but predators probably include killer whales and large sharks.

POPULATION
No overall abundance estimate. There are dated abundance estimates for the northern Gulf of Mexico (6,575 in 2003–04) and the US east coast (6,086 in 1998). The scarcity of records is considered to be due to a paucity of survey effort and identification difficulties rather than low numbers.

CONSERVATION
IUCN status: Least Concern (2018). Known to be taken by handheld harpoons in dolphin fisheries in the Lesser Antilles in the Caribbean. Likely significant incidental captures in fishing nets are known to occur in Venezuela (where the meat is utilised for shark bait and human consumption), the Gulf of Guinea and probably throughout much of the range; it is the most common cetacean landed in Ghanaian fishing ports. Bycatch and directed takes are known in West Africa, but the extent of the problem remains unclear. No other major conservation problems are known, although routine activites and accidental spills associated with oil and gas exploration and extraction are potential threats.

LIFE HISTORY
Virtually no information, though probably similar to the spinner dolphin. Believed to become sexually mature at *c.* 1.7m. Oldest recorded 16 years.

Porpoising Clymene dolphins in the Gulf of Mexico – note the variations in the dark grey lateral stripes.

STRIPED DOLPHIN
Stenella coeruleoalba
(Meyen, 1833)

Ancient Greeks marvelled at the beautiful brushstrokes and colours of striped dolphins, and depicted them in their frescoes several thousand years ago. Widely distributed in warm waters in both hemispheres, and with an estimated population of more than 2 million, the species is a familiar sight in many parts of the world.

Classification Odontoceti, family Delphinidae.
Common name For the distinctive long, dark stripe that runs from the beak, along the side of the body to the anus.
Other names Streaker (for its habit of dashing away from boats in some areas), streaker porpoise, blue-white dolphin, euphrosyne dolphin, Gray's dolphin, Meyen's dolphin, Greek dolphin, whitebelly.
Scientific name *Stenella* from the Greek *stenos* for 'narrow', and *ella* for 'little' (referring to the beak); *coeruleoalba* from the Latin *coeruleus* for 'dark blue' or 'sky blue' and *albus* for 'white' (referring to the diagnostic pattern of dark and light streaks, blazes and stripes).

Taxonomy Currently no recognised forms or subspecies, but there is significant geographic variation in skull morphology and body size; Mediterranean and eastern North Atlantic sub-populations are genetically differentiated. Taxonomy of *Stenella* is currently in dispute and the genus is likely to be revised in the near future.

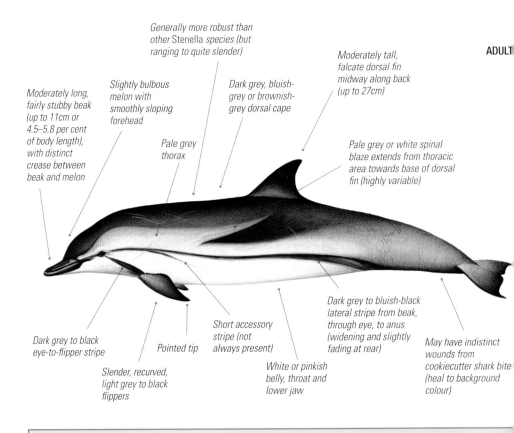

Generally more robust than other *Stenella* species (but ranging to quite slender)

Moderately tall, falcate dorsal fin midway along back (up to 27cm)

ADULT

Moderately long, fairly stubby beak (up to 11cm or 4.5–5.8 per cent of body length), with distinct crease between beak and melon

Slightly bulbous melon with smoothly sloping forehead

Dark grey, bluish-grey or brownish-grey dorsal cape

Pale grey thorax

Pale grey or white spinal blaze extends from thoracic area towards base of dorsal fin (highly variable)

Dark grey to black eye-to-flipper stripe

Pointed tip

Short accessory stripe (not always present)

Dark grey to bluish-black lateral stripe from beak, through eye, to anus (widening and slightly fading at rear)

May have indistinct wounds from cookiecutter shark bite (heal to background colour)

Slender, recurved, light grey to black flippers

White or pinkish belly, throat and lower jaw

AT A GLANCE
- Deep tropical to warm temperate waters worldwide
- Small size
- Complex three-toned colour pattern
- Long, dark lateral stripe

- Underside bright white or pinkish
- Light grey spinal blaze sweeps back and up towards dorsal fin
- Moderately tall, falcate dorsal fin midway along back
- Active, energetic and fast swimmer

ADULT

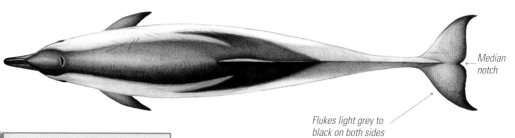

Median notch

Flukes light grey to black on both sides

SIZE
L: ♂ 2.2–2.6m, ♀ 2.1–2.4m;
WT: 100–150kg; **MAX:** 2.6m, 156kg;
Calf – L: 90–100cm; **WT:** 10–15kg

SIMILAR SPECIES
Confusion is possible with several delphinids but, while there is considerable geographical and individual variation in the appearance of striped dolphins, the dark lateral stripe and light spinal blaze should rule out all other species. Spotted and bottlenose dolphins may also have a light spinal blaze, but spotted dolphins are generally heavily spotted and the bottlenose dolphin blaze tends to be muted. Common dolphins are broadly similar in size and shape, but the colour pattern is quite different. Fraser's dolphins also have a dark (albeit wider) eye-to-anus stripe, but they are much more robust, with a shorter beak and a disproportionately small dorsal fin.

DISTRIBUTION
Widely distributed in the Atlantic, Pacific and Indian Oceans and many adjacent seas, in both hemispheres. Approximately between 50°N and 40°S; in the North Pacific, most records are below 43°N. Primarily found in tropical to warm temperate waters, it extends into higher latitudes than other *Stenella* dolphins (it is the only member of the genus that routinely reaches northern Europe). The most abundant dolphin in the Mediterranean. Its full range in the Indian Ocean is poorly known. Uncommon in the Sea of Japan and East China Sea. There are extralimital records from Kamchatka, the western Aleutian Islands, southern Greenland, Iceland, the Faroe Islands and the Prince Edward Islands (in the sub-Antarctic Indian Ocean), and it is considered a vagrant in the Red Sea and Persian Gulf.

Typically in water deeper than 1,000m (in many areas sighting rates increase dramatically with greater depth). Generally outside the continental shelf (over the continental slope out to oceanic waters) but occurs close to shore where it is sufficiently deep. In the Mediterranean, it is sometimes in shallower water relatively close to shore. Prefers sea surface temperatures of 18–22°C, but it is reported within a range of 10–26°C. Depending on the population, there may be diurnal inshore–offshore movements, seasonal movements with ocean currents, or seasonal movements according to changes in sea surface temperature.

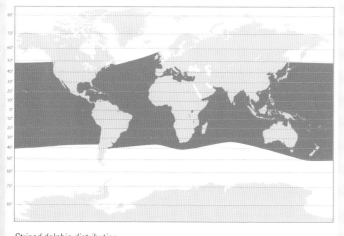

Striped dolphin distribution

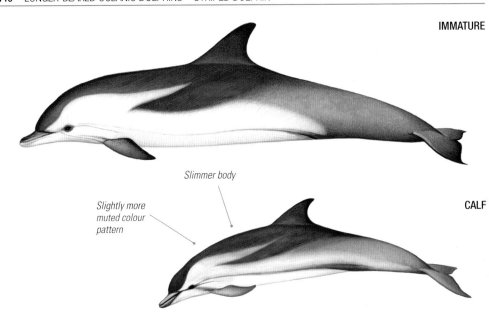

IMMATURE

Slimmer body

Slightly more
muted colour
pattern

CALF

BEHAVIOUR

Very acrobatic, frequently breaching up to 5–7m high, porpoising upside down and chin-slapping. Performs a unique behaviour called 'roto-tailing', in which it makes a high arcing leap while vigorously whipping its tail in a circle. Infrequently associates with other cetaceans or seabirds (adults occasionally associate with common dolphins and, rarely, with Risso's dolphins; juvenile schools sometimes associate with tuna schools); occasionally seen 'bow-riding' fin whales in the Mediterranean. Especially nervous of vessels in the eastern tropical Pacific; elsewhere, it will bow-ride and wake-ride, but can be more easily 'spooked' than other tropical dolphins and often dashes away (with low, splashy leaps) for no apparent reason.

TEETH

Upper 78–110
Lower 78–110

GROUP SIZE AND STRUCTURE

Typically 10–100 in a dense school, sometimes to 500, with several thousand reported occasionally. Great variation between regions: average *c.* 10–30 in the eastern North Atlantic, 26 in the western Mediterranean Sea, 53 in offshore Hawaiian waters, 100 off Japan. Group size tends to increase the further offshore and deeper the water. There may be segregation according to age and sex, with individuals moving between groups. Three main groups: juveniles, adults and mixed (consisting of females with their calves). Adult groups are either breeding (females and males) or non-breeding (pregnant and lactating females, or males living separately). Calves leave mixed groups to join juvenile groups 1–2 years after weaning, then join adult groups after reaching sexual maturity.

PREDATORS

Killer whales and sharks. Possibly also false killer whales and pygmy killer whales.

DIVE SEQUENCE

- Usually seen swimming fast, in long, low arcing leaps.
- Surfaces at shallow angle and re-enters tip of beak first.
- May throw tail high in air mid-leap.
- When not clearing surface, typically throws up Dall's porpoise-like rooster tail of spray.

FOOD AND FEEDING
Prey Variety of small fish (generally less than 17cm), especially lanternfish; squid (especially in the Mediterranean and north-east Atlantic); some crustaceans.
Feeding Probably mostly nocturnal.
Dive depth May be capable of 700m, but limited information.
Dive time Unknown.

PHOTO-IDENTIFICATION
Possible, but very difficult because the natural markings are not as obvious in striped dolphins and large populations make it difficult to spot a previously sighted individual. It can be done using a combination of dorsal fin notches and scarring on the dorsal surface, together with variations in colour pattern.

POPULATION
More than 2.4 million worldwide. Approximate regional estimates include *c.* 1.5 million in the eastern tropical Pacific; 570,000 in the western North Pacific; 118,000 in the western Mediterranean (excluding the Tyrrhenian Sea) and possibly twice that many in the entire Mediterranean; 74,000 in the Bay of Biscay; 29,000 off California, Oregon and Washington; and 20,000 in the southern Adriatic Sea.

CONSERVATION
IUCN status: Least Concern (2018). Mediterranean sub-population Vulnerable (2010). The main delphinid species caught in Japanese small cetacean hand-harpoon fisheries and drive hunts. Catch levels vary widely, but as many as 21,000 have been killed in some years since 1978 (when proper records began); the annual take in recent years has averaged 500–750 animals. Other hunts take place in smaller numbers in Taiwan, Sri Lanka, the Solomon Islands, and St Vincent and the Grenadines in the Caribbean, for human consumption, protection of fisheries and as bait for shrimp traps. Tens of thousands were killed in high-seas driftnets in the 1970s and 1980s, before a European-wide ban came into effect in 2002 (although they are still used illegally in the Mediterranean, for tuna and swordfish). Incidental capture in other fishing gear – especially purse seines, pelagic trawls and driftnets – is a threat in many regions, with hundreds to thousands being killed annually in certain fisheries. Organochlorine pollutants are believed to have been the root cause of a massive die-off of many thousands of striped dolphins in the Mediterranean in 1990–92 (due to lowered immunity to disease); there have been similar, smaller-scale, incidents since. Overfishing (reducing availability of prey species) may be another threat. Captive animals usually die within 1–2 weeks.

Close-up showing the distinctive spinal blaze.

Striped dolphin porpoising in the Canary Islands.

LIFE HISTORY
Sexual maturity Females 5–13 years, males 7–15 years.
Mating Likely to be polygynous mating system (single male mates with multiple females).
Gestation 12–13 months.
Calving Every 3–4 years (occasionally two years); single calf born year-round, with seasonal peaks (in Japan, two peaks: one in summer, one in winter).
Weaning After 12–18 months.
Lifespan Probably at least 50 years (oldest recorded 58 years; oldest pregnant female 48 years).

COMMON DOLPHIN
Delphinus delphis

Linnaeus, 1758

Aristotle and Pliny the Elder described the common dolphin in great detail – and it was the first dolphin species to be scientifically described – yet there has been ongoing debate about whether it should be classified as one, two or more species ever since. Large, boisterous groups of common dolphins, whipping the ocean's surface into a froth, are a common sight in many parts of the world.

Classification Odontoceti, family Delphinidae.
Common name Reflecting the wide distribution and abundance of this species.
Other names Crisscross dolphin, hourglass dolphin, common porpoise; Atlantic – Atlantic dolphin, saddleback dolphin, saddleback porpoise, cape dolphin; Pacific – Pacific dolphin, white-bellied (or whitebelly) dolphin, Baird's dolphin, Indo-Pacific common dolphin, neritic common dolphin; (and various combinations).
Scientific name *Delphinus* from the Latin *delphinus* for 'dolphin-like'; *delphis* from the Greek *delphis* for 'dolphin'; probably related to *delphys*, which is Greek for 'womb' (i.e. bearing live young).
Taxonomy Much confusion over taxonomy, with more than 20 species described since 1758. Most experts considered it to be a single species (*Delphinus delphis*) until 1994, when it was split into two – the short-beaked common dolphin (*D. delphis*) and the long-beaked common dolphin (*D. capensis*). Recent research questioned this split and, since 2016, it has once again been considered a single species. However, this is still under review. There are currently four recognised subspecies: common dolphin (*D. delphis delphis*), Eastern North Pacific long-beaked common dolphin (*D. d. bairdii*), Indo-Pacific common dolphin (*D. d. tropicalis*), and Black Sea common dolphin (*D. d. ponticus*). It is likely that the Eastern North Pacific long-beaked common dolphin, off California, may yet constitute a unique species.

ADULT *DELPHIS*
(Atlantic (including Mediterranean) and Pacific)

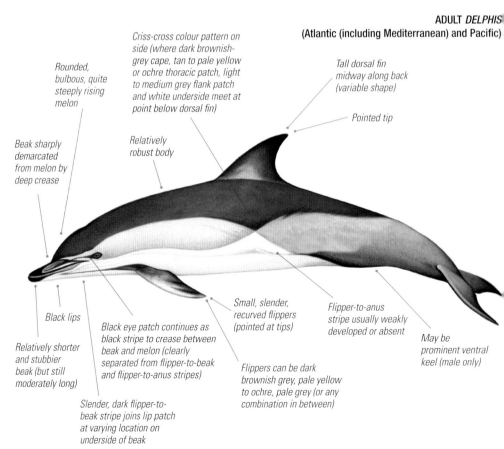

Rounded, bulbous, quite steeply rising melon

Criss-cross colour pattern on side (where dark brownish-grey cape, tan to pale yellow or ochre thoracic patch, light to medium grey flank patch and white underside meet at point below dorsal fin)

Tall dorsal fin midway along back (variable shape)

Pointed tip

Beak sharply demarcated from melon by deep crease

Relatively robust body

Black lips

Relatively shorter and stubbier beak (but still moderately long)

Black eye patch continues as black stripe to crease between beak and melon (clearly separated from flipper-to-beak and flipper-to-anus stripes)

Small, slender, recurved flippers (pointed at tips)

Flipper-to-anus stripe usually weakly developed or absent

May be prominent ventral keel (male only)

Flippers can be dark brownish grey, pale yellow to ochre, pale grey (or any combination in between)

Slender, dark flipper-to-beak stripe joins lip patch at varying location on underside of beak

AT A GLANCE

- Tropical to temperate waters worldwide
- Small size
- Criss-cross or 'hourglass' colour pattern on sides
- Dark brownish-grey cape dips to 'V' under dorsal fin
- Tan to pale yellow or ochre thoracic patch
- Light to medium grey flank patch
- White underside
- Details of colour pattern highly variable
- Tall, moderately falcate dorsal fin midway along back
- Often in fast-moving, splashy groups

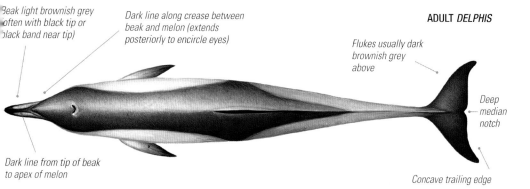

Beak light brownish grey often with black tip or black band near tip)

Dark line along crease between beak and melon (extends posteriorly to encircle eyes)

ADULT *DELPHIS*

Flukes usually dark brownish grey above

Deep median notch

Dark line from tip of beak to apex of melon

Concave trailing edge

SIZE – *delphis*
L: ♂ 1.7–2.5m, ♀ 1.6–2.4m;
WT: 150–200kg; **MAX:** 2.7m, 235kg
Larger in the North Atlantic than the North Pacific.

SIZE – *ponticus*
L: ♂ 1.5–1.8m, ♀ 1.5–1.7m;
WT: *c.* 150kg; **MAX:** 2.2m

SIZE – *bairdii*
L: ♂ 2–2.6m, ♀ 1.9–2.2m;
WT: 150–235kg; **MAX:** 2.6m

SIZE – *tropicalis*
L: ♂ 2–2.6m, ♀ 1.9–2.2m;
WT: 150–235kg; **MAX:** 2.6m
Calf – L: 80–93cm; **WT:** *c.* 7–10kg

SIMILAR SPECIES

The unique criss-cross or hourglass colour pattern on the sides of common dolphins should distinguish them from most other dolphins, including spinner and striped dolphins (which have a similar body shape), and Atlantic white-sided dolphins (which have a narrow ochre patch on the tailstock instead of the similarly coloured thoracic patch). In the Atlantic, there may be some confusion from a distance with the similarly shaped Clymene dolphin, but its dorsal cape dips into a smooth curve below the dorsal fin (rather than a sharp 'V'); the Clymene's 'clean' throat, white lower jaw and the 'moustache' on the beak are also good ways to separate it from common dolphins. Hybrids with common bottlenose dolphins in captivity and dusky dolphins in the wild have been reported.

DISTRIBUTION

Tropical to temperate waters worldwide, roughly from 40°N (North Pacific) and 60°N

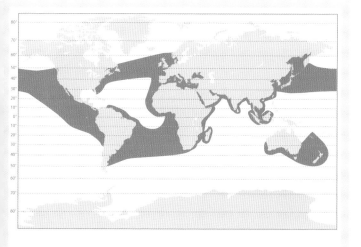

Common dolphin distribution

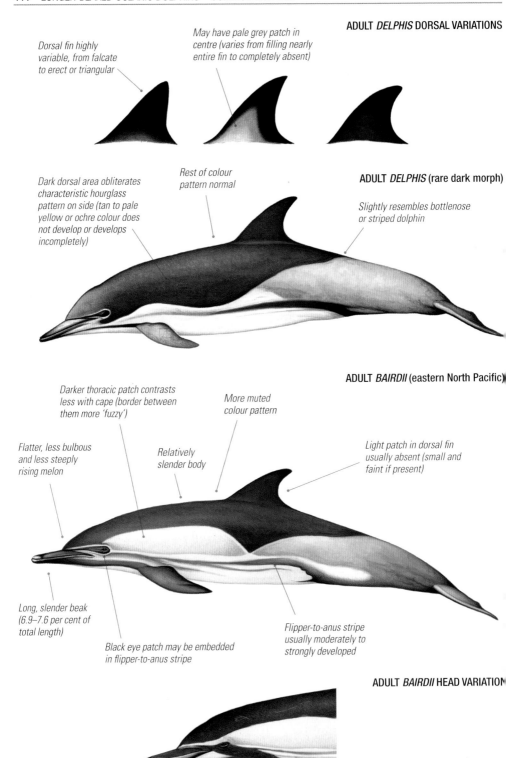

ADULT *DELPHIS* DORSAL VARIATIONS

Dorsal fin highly variable, from falcate to erect or triangular

May have pale grey patch in centre (varies from filling nearly entire fin to completely absent)

ADULT *DELPHIS* (rare dark morph)

Dark dorsal area obliterates characteristic hourglass pattern on side (tan to pale yellow or ochre colour does not develop or develops incompletely)

Rest of colour pattern normal

Slightly resembles bottlenose or striped dolphin

ADULT *BAIRDII* (eastern North Pacific)

Darker thoracic patch contrasts less with cape (border between them more 'fuzzy')

More muted colour pattern

Flatter, less bulbous and less steeply rising melon

Relatively slender body

Light patch in dorsal fin usually absent (small and faint if present)

Long, slender beak (6.9–7.6 per cent of total length)

Black eye patch may be embedded in flipper-to-anus stripe

Flipper-to-anus stripe usually moderately to strongly developed

ADULT *BAIRDII* HEAD VARIATION

Eye-to-flipper stripe can be dark and wide (may form 'bandit mask')

ADULT *TROPICALIS* (Indian Ocean (including Red Sea, Persian Gulf, Gulf of Thailand) and far western Pacific Ocean)

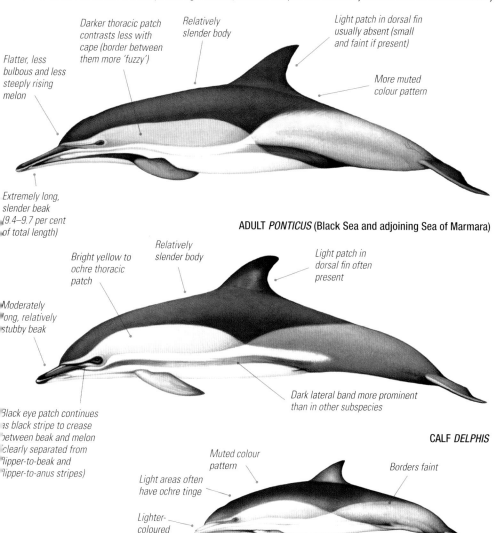

Darker thoracic patch contrasts less with cape (border between them more 'fuzzy')

Relatively slender body

Light patch in dorsal fin usually absent (small and faint if present)

Flatter, less bulbous and less steeply rising melon

More muted colour pattern

Extremely long, slender beak (9.4–9.7 per cent of total length)

ADULT *PONTICUS* (Black Sea and adjoining Sea of Marmara)

Bright yellow to ochre thoracic patch

Relatively slender body

Light patch in dorsal fin often present

Moderately long, relatively stubby beak

Black eye patch continues as black stripe to crease between beak and melon (clearly separated from flipper-to-beak and flipper-to-anus stripes)

Dark lateral band more prominent than in other subspecies

CALF *DELPHIS*

Muted colour pattern

Borders faint

Light areas often have ochre tinge

Lighter-coloured beak

North Atlantic) to about 50°S. May occasionally follow warm-water currents outside the normal latitudinal distribution. Separate populations occur in some semi-enclosed seas, such as the Mediterranean and Black Seas. Absent from the Gulf of Mexico and most parts of the Caribbean. From nearshore waters to thousands of kilometres offshore. Some forms (e.g. the Eastern North Pacific long-beaked common dolphin) will enter shallow water just a few metres deep, very near shore. Abundance varies seasonally and with fluctuations in sea surface temperature (or with migrating temperature-dependent prey species). Preferred sea surface temperature is 10–28°C. In most areas, it has a strong preference for areas of strong upwelling, and with a steeply sloping seabed (e.g. seamounts and escarpments).

BEHAVIOUR

Aerially active – frequently performing a variety of acrobatic leaps and somersaults (sometimes to 6–7m high), as well as flipper-slapping and lobtailing. Will also 'pitch-pole', a distinctive aerial display in which the dolphin leaps straight out of the water and slams back lengthwise to create maximum splash. Can also make clean entries, with no splash. Typically porpoises out of the water when travelling at high speed (burst speeds of up to 40km/h have been recorded). Frequently associates with pilot whales; striped, spinner and Risso's dolphins; various *Lagenorhynchus* dolphins; and other cetaceans. Often in mixed feeding associations with frenzies of seabirds. Will aid injured companions, sometimes supporting them near the surface to breathe. An enthusiastic and energetic bow-rider and wake-rider – even riding the 'snout waves' of large mysticete whales – and will often approach boats and ships from a distance especially to bow-ride (except in parts of the eastern tropical Pacific, where there is tuna fishing); however, not all individuals in a herd bow-ride.

TEETH
Upper 82–134
Lower 82–128

GROUP SIZE AND STRUCTURE
Highly gregarious, in groups of 10–10,000 or more. Group composition is poorly known, but large herds are believed to be composed of smaller social units of 20–30 individuals that are not necessarily genetically related. Individuals may swim with preferred associates, but group membership appears to be fluid. There may be some segregation in the form of 'nursery groups' (mature females – unrelated but usually at the same reproductive stage – accompanied by their calves) and 'bachelor groups' (mature males). However, mixed groups of males and females with sub-adults and calves appear to be the most common grouping. School size and composition may change seasonally. In the north-east Pacific, the largest groups are usually encountered during the day, when they are mostly socialising and resting, but these separate into smaller groups in the late afternoon and at night, to feed in the deep scattering layer; the small feeding groups then coalesce back into large groups in the morning.

PREDATORS
Killer whales and sharks are significant predators of small dolphins, and this includes common dolphins. Predation by false killer whales has been observed in the eastern tropical Pacific. May occasionally be attacked by pygmy killer whales and pilot whales.

PHOTO-IDENTIFICATION
Possible using dorsal fin pigmentation (which is stable over time). Also, to a lesser degree, nicks and notches on the trailing and leading edges of the dorsal fin (though these are not particularly frequent on common dolphins) and any other distinctive scarring or marking.

POPULATION
Abundant. At least 4–5 million (based on relatively dated regional estimates). No recent figures, but (bearing in mind that some of these regions overlap) approximate numbers include 2,963,000 in the eastern tropical Pacific; *c.* 1.1 million along the US west coast; 70,000 along the US east coast; 165,000 in Baja California, Mexico; 273,000 in European offshore waters (between 53°N and 57°N); 63,000 in European continental shelf waters; 15,000–20,000 in South Africa; 19,000 in the western Mediterranean; and at least several tens of thousands in the Black Sea.

LONG-BEAKED OR SHORT-BEAKED?
Taxonomic uncertainties arise because of the extraordinary amount of variability in size, shape and coloration between common dolphins around the world. Morphological and genetic studies, published in 1994, provided evidence that there were two different species living in sympatry in the north-east Pacific (they often occur in the same general area at the same time, though do not form mixed schools and appear to be reproductively isolated). They were classified as the long-beaked common dolphin (*D. capensis*) and the short-beaked common dolphin (*D. delphis*). The latest evidence suggests that, while there may be a separate species of long-beaked common dolphin in the north-east Pacific, it was incorrect to assume that this distinction holds true worldwide (in some regions long-beaked common dolphins are genetically more closely related to short-beaked common dolphins than to long-beaked elsewhere). The conclusion is that *D. capensis* is not, after all, a valid species. However, there is probably a unique species of long-beaked common dolphin in the north-east Pacific (tentatively named *D. bairdii*).

DIVE SEQUENCE
- Surfaces at shallow angle (often begins to blow underwater).
- Most of head (including eye) and entire beak briefly visible.
- Underside of beak skims along surface.
- May be faint walls of water on either side of head.
- Slides forward (rather than rolls) with little arching of back.
- Rarely shows flukes.

FOOD AND FEEDING

Prey Wide variety of small (less than 20cm) schooling fish and squid (including pilchards, sardines, herring, mackerel, anchovies, hake, bonito, smelt, lanternfish, flying fish, market squid); some crustaceans (including pelagic red crabs, krill); diet varies with season, region and time.

Feeding In some areas, feeds mostly at night on prey associated with deep scattering layer (migrates towards surface in dark); in other areas, feeds mostly on epipelagic schooling fish; cooperative feeding techniques often used to herd fish schools.

Dive depth Most foraging shallower than 50m, but dives to 280m recorded.

Dive time Typically *c.* 10 seconds to three minutes; maximum *c.* eight minutes.

CONSERVATION

IUCN status: currently still listed as two species – *D. delphis* Least Concern (2008) (Mediterranean sub-population Endangered (2003), Black Sea sub-population Vulnerable (2008)); and *D. capensis* Data Deficient (2008). The main threat is high incidental mortality in fisheries throughout the range, especially in pelagic driftnets (which are responsible for tens of thousands of deaths every year – including 12,000–15,000 in the Mediterranean broadbill swordfish fishery around the Strait of Gibraltar alone). Also killed incidentally in small-scale gillnet, trawl and purse-seine fisheries. Large numbers were caught in the eastern tropical Pacific, where common dolphins (as well as spotted and spinner dolphins) associate with yellowfin tuna and are captured by fishermen using purse-seine nets; however, since 1986 (when the annual incidental take of common dolphins was 24,307) better regulations have resulted in a 98 per cent reduction in mortality.

Hunted historically – at least until the 1990s – by more than a dozen countries. During 1931–66, an estimated 1.57 million were taken in the Black Sea, by the USSR, Romania and Bulgaria, before commercial hunting of small cetaceans was banned by all three countries in 1966. Turkey killed an estimated 159,000–161,000 in the Black Sea in 1962–83, before banning small cetacean hunting in 1983. Direct take for human consumption and shark bait is still a threat in some areas, including Japan (where they are sometimes taken in drive fisheries), Taiwan, Venezuela (where they are killed with harpoons), Peru and Mexico.

Other threats include overfishing of prey species, heavy metal and organochlorine contamination, and noise pollution from oil and gas exploration and military sonar (which was probably the cause of a mass stranding of common dolphins in the UK in 2008). Some have been live-captured for display.

There has been a major decline of at least 50 per cent in the Mediterranean during the past 30–40 years due to variety of factors, including historical culling campaigns, prey depletion due to overfishing, poor habitat quality and incidental capture in fishing nets.

VOCALISATIONS

Highly vocal, with an extensive repertoire, including clicks, whistles and burst pulse calls. Clicks are short-duration sounds (ranging from 23kHz to more than 100kHz) that occur in rapid succession at regular intervals and are used mainly in echolocation. Whistles (usually simple upsweeps and downsweeps, from 3kHz to 24kHz) are used mainly for communication, and are unique to individuals; each dolphin produces a distinctive and stereotyped whistle (typically lasting less than 1–4 seconds) that others recognise (called a 'signature whistle'). Burst pulse calls are a series of rapidly produced clicks – up to 10 times faster than the clicking used for echolocation – used in communication; they are often used when the dolphins are interacting socially – perhaps to convey information about emotional state (e.g. 'angry', 'aggressive', 'excited' or 'let's play'). Common dolphins also produce 'buzzes' (otherwise known as 'barks', 'yelps' or 'squeals'), especially during aggressive encounters; these are click trains so fast that to the human ear they appear to be continuous sounds.

LIFE HISTORY

Sexual maturity Females 2–10 years (2–4 years in Black Sea, 6–9 years in eastern Pacific and western Atlantic, 9–10 years in north-east Atlantic); males 3–12 years (three years in Black Sea, 7–12 years in eastern Pacific and western Atlantic).

Mating Modest sexual dimorphism suggests promiscuous mating system (dependent on sperm competition).

Gestation 10–11.5 months.

Calving Every 1–4 years (varies with region, e.g. one year in Black Sea, 2–3 years in North Pacific, four years in eastern North Atlantic); single calf born year-round in some (especially more tropical) regions, with regional peaks elsewhere; parental care augmented by 'aunts' that assist with young calves.

Weaning After 10–19 months; solid food eaten after 2–3 months.

Lifespan Possibly 25–35 years (both sexes).

TUCUXI
Sotalia fluviatilis

(Gervais and Deville in Gervais, 1853)

The tucuxi (pronounced 'too-koo-shee') is the only member of the dolphin family Delphinidae to be found exclusively in freshwater – and one of two dolphins found in the Amazon River basin (the other is the Amazon river dolphin). It was recently separated from the very similar and closely related Guiana dolphin.

Classification Odontoceti, family Delphinidae.

Common name From tucuchi-una in the (now extinct) Tupi language, once spoken by indigenous Tupi Indians in the Brazilian Amazon.

Other names Brazilian dolphin, Guianian river dolphin, grey dolphin, grey river dolphin.

Scientific name The origin of *Sotalia* is unknown, though it was reputedly coined arbitrarily; *fluviatilis* from the Latin *fluviatilis* for 'of a river'.

Taxonomy No recognised forms or subspecies. The taxonomy of the genus *Sotalia* has been a matter of debate for over 140 years. Five species (three riverine, two coastal) were described in the late 1800s, then this was reduced to two, and then to just a single species, *S. fluviatilis* (with riverine and marine subspecies or ecotypes). In 2007, these were formally separated into two distinct species – the tucuxi (*S. fluviatilis*) in the Amazon River basin, and the Guiana dolphin (*S. guianensis*) in coastal waters of Central and South America and the Orinoco River system; in addition to ecological differences, the distinction is based primarily on genetic differences and skull shape.

ADUL

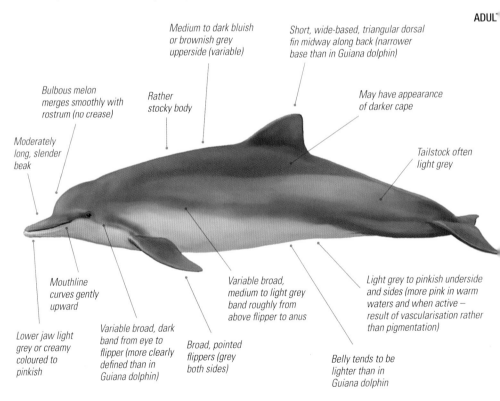

Medium to dark bluish or brownish grey upperside (variable)

Short, wide-based, triangular dorsal fin midway along back (narrower base than in Guiana dolphin)

Bulbous melon merges smoothly with rostrum (no crease)

Rather stocky body

May have appearance of darker cape

Moderately long, slender beak

Tailstock often light grey

Mouthline curves gently upward

Variable broad, medium to light grey band roughly from above flipper to anus

Light grey to pinkish underside and sides (more pink in warm waters and when active – result of vascularisation rather than pigmentation)

Lower jaw light grey or creamy coloured to pinkish

Variable broad, dark band from eye to flipper (more clearly defined than in Guiana dolphin)

Broad, pointed flippers (grey both sides)

Belly tends to be lighter than in Guiana dolphin

AT A GLANCE
- Amazon River basin
- Small size (smaller than Guiana dolphin)
- Dark grey above, pinkish white below
- Bulbous melon merges smoothly with rostrum (no crease)
- Moderately long, slender beak
- Wide-based, triangular dorsal fin midway along back
- Can be aerially active

ADULT MALE

Flukes grey on both sides

DORSAL FIN COMPARISON

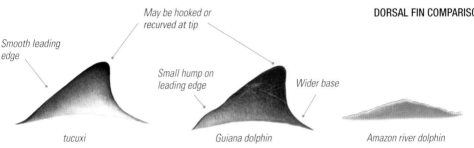

May be hooked or recurved at tip

Smooth leading edge

Small hump on leading edge

Wider base

tucuxi

Guiana dolphin

Amazon river dolphin

SIZE
L: ♂ 1.4–1.5m, ♀ 1.3–1.5m;
WT: *c.* 35–45kg; **MAX:** 1.5m, 53kg
Calf – L: 71–83cm; **WT:** *c.* 8kg

SIMILAR SPECIES

A very distinctive small, dumpy appearance. The only other cetacean overlapping significantly in range is the Amazon river dolphin, which is quite different in size, colour, dorsal fin shape and head shape. There may be some overlap with the Guiana dolphin near the mouth of the Amazon; it is nearly impossible to tell the two species apart in the field, but the tucuxi is somewhat smaller, its belly tends to be lighter and there are subtle differences in dorsal fin shape.

DISTRIBUTION

Throughout the Amazon River basin. It appears to be continuous along the Amazon River and is found in most of its tributaries, including the Putumayo and Caquetá Rivers, in Colombia; the Ucayali and Marañón Rivers, in Peru; the Napo and Cuyabeno Rivers, in Ecuador; and the Negro, Madeira, Purus and Tapajos Rivers, in Brazil. Absent from the Beni/Mamoré River basin in Bolivia, and it is not known in the upper Rio Negro above the city of Barcelos. The population is segmented by impassable shallow areas, rapids and waterfalls. There is possible overlap between the two *Sotalia* species in the mouth of the Amazon River.

Frequently inhabits lakes and oxbows connected to the main system. Recorded in all three types of river water in this region (sediment-rich whitewater, acidic blackwater

Amazon basin

Tucuxi distribution

Age class can be identified by strength of pink coloration (newborn have a strong pinkish colour over whole body; on older calves only small portion of dorsal fin remains pink on upperside)

CALF

and clearwater); hotspots are often where a whitewater channel meets a blackwater channel. Distribution is influenced by seasonal river level fluctuations; during the flood season it may move into smaller tributaries and lakes but, unlike the sympatric Amazon river dolphin, it does not enter the flooded forests to feed. At least in some regions rarely in rivers less than 3m deep, or in lakes less than 1.8m deep. Strongly prefers areas with reduced current: waterway junctions, within 50m of riverbanks (rather than in mid-stream), and in lakes.

Despite earlier theories, recent genetic research confirms that the *Sotalia* species living in the lower reaches of the Orinoco River system is the Guiana dolphin, not the tucuxi.

BEHAVIOUR
Can be quite aerially active and performs a variety of leaps and somersaults (especially during low-water periods). Frequently spyhops, rolls at the surface, lobtails, and flipper-slaps. Largely sympatric with the Amazon river dolphin, but the two species rarely interact (when they do, the tucuxi appears to be dominant). Generally shy and more difficult to approach than the Guiana dolphin, and not known to bow-ride.

TEETH
Upper 56–70
Lower 52–66

GROUP SIZE AND STRUCTURE
Typically up to four (occasionally six) in mixed groups of adults and calves. Mean group size in one recent wide-ranging study was 3.37. As many as 30 have been reported on occasion. Groups are fluid, and long-term individual associations are rare.

PREDATORS
No known predators, but possibly bull sharks.

PHOTO-IDENTIFICATION
Using permanent distinctive marks on the dorsal fin (especially nicks and notches on the trailing edge), combined with any distinctive marking on the sides and depigmentation.

POPULATION
No overall global estimate. Regional estimates include 1,545 in an area of 592sq km of the Amazon, Loretoyacu and Javari Rivers, in Colombia; and 1,319 in an area of 554sq km of the Marañón and Samiria Rivers of Peru. Studies in Mamirauá Reserve, Brazil, show that over a 22-year period – even in this protected area – the population is in steep decline, halving every nine years.

CONSERVATION
IUCN status: Data Deficient (2010). A large proportion of the range is close to human habitation, making it particularly vulnerable. Incidental capture in fishing gear, especially gillnets, seine nets and shrimp and fish traps, is

DIVE SEQUENCE
* Head and beak appear at angle of *c.* 45° (eye often visible).
* Surfaces quickly (typically spends less than 1 second at surface).
* Noisy exhalation but invisible blow.
* Back arched.
* Flukes rarely visible.
* May porpoise rapidly when travelling at high speed.

FOOD AND FEEDING

Prey At least 27 species of fish, 5–37cm long, in 13 families; preference for toothless characins, croakers, catfish.
Feeding Feeds individually and in groups, sometimes appearing to use cooperative feeding techniques.
Dive depth Unknown.
Dive time Typically 20 seconds to two minutes, with shorter dives of 5–10 seconds in between.

ommon in many parts of the range. In recent years, there as been increasing demand for dolphin meat (mainly mazon river dolphin, but also tucuxi) to be used as bait in legal piracatinga fisheries (fuelled by the ever-increasing emand for fish in big cities in Brazil, Colombia, Peru, olivia and elsewhere). The genital organs, teeth and eyes ay have a small local market as amulets or love charms, while teeth and bones are sometimes used for arts and rafts. There may be some protection from myths and gends that discourage killing. Dams and hydroelectric power facilities interrupt fish migrations, reduce fish prey abundance, and limit dolphin movements (disrupting gene flow); up to 200 dams are proposed for the Amazon's major tributaries. Other threats include overfishing of prey species, dynamite fishing, habitat loss and destruction, pollution (from mercury used to refine fluvial gold, pesticides, sewage, industrial waste, and contaminants) and increasing vessel traffic. In the past, there have also been live captures for display in aquaria (illegal since 2005).

LIFE HISTORY

Sexual maturity Females 5–8 years, males *c.* seven years.
Mating Believed to have a promiscuous mating system, based on sperm competition, with little or no fighting between males.
Gestation *c.* 10–11 months.

Calving Every two years (occasionally three or four years); single calf born during low-water season in September–November.
Weaning Possibly after 7–9 months.
Lifespan Probably 30–35 years (oldest recorded 43 years).

e tucuxi's lower jaw is typically light grey or creamy coloured to pinkish.

GUIANA DOLPHIN
Sotalia guianensis
(Van Bénéden, 1864)

Recently separated from the closely related and very similar freshwater tucuxi, the Guiana dolphin lives mainly in warm coastal waters (although its presence has recently been confirmed in the Orinoco River). At first glance, it resembles a small bottlenose dolphin.

Classification Odontoceti, family Delphinidae.
Common name There is still controversy over a definitive international common name for this species and it may yet change to 'costero' (Spanish for 'coastal') or 'boto-cinza' (Portuguese for 'grey dolphin'); 'Guiana dolphin' is from the scientific name.
Other names Costero, estuarine dolphin, marine tucuxi, grey dolphin.
Scientific name The origin of *Sotalia* is unknown, though it was reputedly coined arbitrarily; *guianensis* because Van Bénéden's original description was based on three specimens collected from the mouth of the Marowijne River, on the border between Suriname and French Guiana.
Taxonomy No recognised forms or subspecies. The taxonomy of the genus *Sotalia* has been a matter of debate for over 140 years. Five species (three riverine, two coastal) were described in the late 1800s, then this was reduced to two and then to just a single species, *S. fluviatilis* (with riverine and marine subspecies or ecotypes). In 2007, these were formally separated into two distinct species – the tucuxi (*S. fluviatilis*) in the Amazon River basin, and the Guiana dolphin (*S. guianensis*) in coastal waters of Central and South America and the Orinoco River system; in addition to ecological differences, the distinction is based primarily on genetic differences and skull shape.

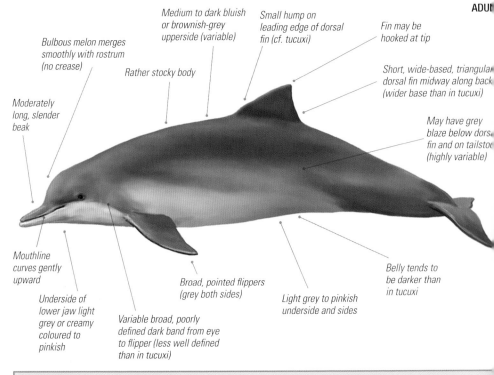

ADUL

Medium to dark bluish or brownish-grey upperside (variable)

Small hump on leading edge of dorsal fin (cf. tucuxi)

Fin may be hooked at tip

Bulbous melon merges smoothly with rostrum (no crease)

Rather stocky body

Short, wide-based, triangular dorsal fin midway along back (wider base than in tucuxi)

Moderately long, slender beak

May have grey blaze below dorsal fin and on tailstock (highly variable)

Mouthline curves gently upward

Belly tends to be darker than in tucuxi

Underside of lower jaw light grey or creamy coloured to pinkish

Broad, pointed flippers (grey both sides)

Light grey to pinkish underside and sides

Variable broad, poorly defined dark band from eye to flipper (less well defined than in tucuxi)

AT A GLANCE
- Atlantic coasts of Central and northern South America (and Orinoco River)
- Small size (larger than tucuxi)
- Dark grey above, pinkish white below
- Bulbous melon merges smoothly with rostrum (no crease)
- Moderately long, slender beak
- Wide-based, triangular dorsal fin midway along back
- Can be aerially active

ADULT VARIATION

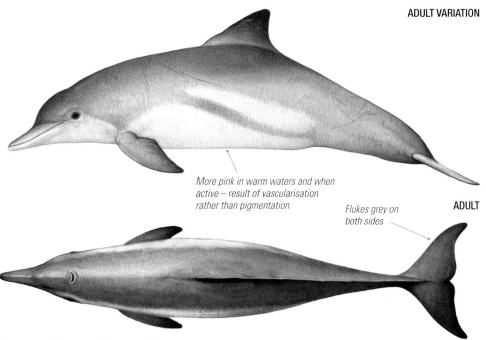

More pink in warm waters and when
active – result of vascularisation
rather than pigmentation

Flukes grey on
both sides

ADULT

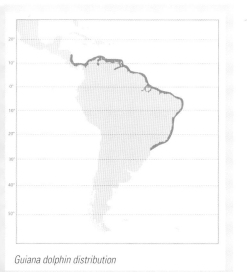

SIZE
L: ♂ 1.6–1.9m, ♀ 1.6–2m;
WT: *c.* 50–80kg; **MAX:** 2.2m, 121kg
Calf – L: 90–106cm; **WT:** 12–15kg

Guiana dolphin distribution

SIMILAR SPECIES
The head profile is distinctive, since the rounded melon is not separated from the beak by a crease (unlike in most other delphinids). The dorsal fin is shorter, more triangular, and more wide-based than in the much larger bottlenose dolphin; some hybridisation may occur between these two species. There could be confusion with the franciscana, if not seen well, but look for the franciscana's smaller body, much longer beak, squarer flippers and shorter, more rounded dorsal fin. There may be some overlap with tucuxi near the mouth of the Amazon; it is nearly impossible to tell the two species apart in the field, but the Guiana dolphin is somewhat larger, its belly tends to be darker, and there are subtle differences in dorsal fin shape.

DISTRIBUTION
Range appears to be discontinuous along the tropical and sub-tropical Caribbean and Atlantic coasts of Central and northern South America. It occurs from the mouth of the Layasiksa River, in northern Nicaragua (14°N), to Florianópolis, in southern Brazil (27°S). There is an unconfirmed report from further north in Honduras (15°N). The southernmost limit may be determined by the convergence of the warm, south-flowing Brazil Current and the cold, north-flowing waters of the Falkland (Malvinas) Current. A population has also been described in Maracaibo Lake, a large semi-enclosed estuarine system in northwestern Venezuela. There is possible overlap between the two *Sotalia* species in the mouth of the Amazon River. Displays high site fidelity, with little

Age class can be identified by strength of pink coloration (newborn has a strong pinkish colour over whole body; on older calves only small portion of dorsal fin remains pink on upperside)

CALF

dispersal from the region of birth, and some individuals have been observed in the same area for up to 10 years at a time.

Mostly in shallow nearshore marine waters, especially in estuaries, bays, large gulfs and other protected, shallow coastal waters. Found in a wide range of water depths, temperatures, salinity and turbidity, but mostly in shallower habitats less than 5m deep (deeper on the Rio de Janeiro coast, Brazil). Rarely, if ever, sighted in pelagic waters, and most sightings are within 100m of shore; however, there are reports from some Caribbean islands, including Trinidad and Tobago, and from the Abrolhos Archipelago of Brazil (70km off the coast of Bahia State).

Genetic research confirms that the Guiana dolphin also lives in the Orinoco River system. A *Sotalia* species has been known at least as far as 300km upriver, near Cuidad Bolívar, Venezuela – where it is effectively isolated from the Amazon River basin by rapids and falls – and the identity of the species has, until recently, been unclear. It is believed to be isolated from coastal populations.

BEHAVIOUR

Can be quite aerially active and performs a variety of leap and somersaults. Frequently spyhops, rolls at the surface, lobtails and flipper-slaps. Known to associate in mixed groups with bottlenose dolphins off Costa Rica. Typically indifferent to quiet boats, and easier to approach than the tucuxi, but often avoids approaches by boats with running engines. Not known to bow-ride, but it may surf in the waves and wakes produced by passing boats.

TEETH

Upper 60–72
Lower 56–64

GROUP SIZE AND STRUCTURE

Typically up to 10 (4–6 most common) in mixed groups of adults and calves, with up to 50–60 not uncommon. Groups are fluid and long-term individual associations are rare, though family groups of a mother and calf with an assisting adult may last for months. Larger, cooperative feeding aggregations are most common in southern Brazil – especially along the Rio de Janeiro coast – with up

Fast swimming

DIVE SEQUENCE

- Head and beak appear at angle of *c.* 45 degrees (eye often visible).
- Surfaces quickly (typically spends less than one second at surface).
- Noisy exhalation but invisible blow.
- Back arched.
- Flukes rarely visible.
- May porpoise rapidly when travelling at high speed.

Slow swimming

FOOD AND FEEDING

Prey At least 70 species of fish from 25 families (1–115cm long, but prefers younger age classes 3–16cm long); sometimes cephalopods; occasionally crustaceans (shrimps and crabs).

Feeding Feeds individually and in groups, using wide variety of feeding techniques, sometimes cooperatively; feeding often associated with seabirds; in Cananéia Estuary, Brazil, groups almost strand while herding fish onto sloping beaches and cooperate with local fishermen using artisanal fishing traps; sometimes uses bubbles as barrier; hairless vibrissal pits on beak serve as electroreceptors, likely useful in prey detection (unique among mammals, apart from monotremes).

Dive depth Unknown.

Dive time Typically 20 seconds to two minutes, with shorter dives of 5–10 seconds in between.

o 200 (Baía de Sepetiba) and 400 (Baía da Ilha Grande) observed together.

PREDATORS

Little known, but likely sharks and killer whales. Bites from sharks have been reported and there was one observation of a predation attempt by a bull shark. Encounters with bottlenose dolphins in southern Brazil have resulted in aggression by the bottlenose dolphins or escape behaviour by the Guiana dolphins.

PHOTO-IDENTIFICATION

Using permanent distinctive marks on the dorsal fin especially nicks and notches on the trailing edge), combined with any other marks on the sides.

POPULATION

No overall global estimate. It appears to be abundant in few parts of its range, but numbers in some areas have declined substantially in the past three decades. Regional estimates for Brazil include c. 420 in Guanabara Bay, 7–124 in Caravelas River estuary, 389–430 in Cananéia stuary, 182-plus in Paranaguá estuary, and 245 in

Babitonga Bay; and 2,205 in an area of 1,684sq km in the Orinoco River, Venezuela.

CONSERVATION

IUCN status: Near Threatened (2017). A large proportion of the range is close to human habitation, making it particularly vulnerable. Incidental capture in fishing gear, especially gillnets, seine nets and shrimp and fish traps, is believed to be a serious problem in many parts of the range; there is a record of more than 80 individuals caught in a single net. Despite legal protection, there has been some direct killing for human consumption and shark and shrimp bait (especially in northern Brazil). The genital organs, teeth and eyes may have a small local market as amulets or love charms. There may be some protection from myths and legends that discourage killing. Other threats include habitat loss and destruction (especially due to shrimp farming), overfishing of prey species, pollution (including pesticides, sewage, industrial waste and contaminants), increasing vessel traffic and hand-feeding from tourist boats. In the past, there have also been live captures for display in aquaria (illegal since 2005).

LIFE HISTORY

Sexual maturity Females 5–8 years, males 6–7 years.
Mating Believed to have a promiscuous mating system, based on sperm competition, with little or no fighting between males.
Gestation 11.5–12 months.

Calving Every two years (occasionally three or four years); single calf born year-round, with some evidence of seasonal regional peaks.
Weaning Possibly after 8–10 months.
Lifespan Probably 30–35 years (oldest recorded 29 years for male, 33 years for female).

SOUTH ASIAN RIVER DOLPHIN
Platanista gangetica

(Roxburgh, 1801)

Living in the muddy waters of its riverine home, the endangered South Asian river dolphin is functionally blind (at most, it can probably detect changes in light intensity and direction) and relies almost entirely on echolocation to navigate and find food.

Classification Odontoceti, family Platanistidae.

Common name After the region in which it lives; 'blind' river dolphin because its tiny, pinhole eyes are poorly developed and lack crystalline lenses; susu (and some other vernacular names) is onomatopoeic, imitating the sound as it breathes at the surface.

Other names Ganges river dolphin: susu, Ganga river dolphin, Gangetic dolphin, Indian river dolphin, shushuk, swongsu, and many other vernacular names. Indus river dolphin: bhulan; blind river dolphin.

Scientific name *Platanista* from the Greek *platanistes* for 'flat' or 'broad' – referring to the relatively flattened beak (though popularly referenced by Pliny as a 'fish'), and *gangetica* from the Latin for 'of the Ganges'.

Taxonomy Originally classified as two subspecies; then (1971–98) classified as two species: Ganges river dolphin *Platanista gangetica* (Roxburgh, 1801) and Indus river dolphin *P. minor* Owen, 1853; currently recognised as two subspecies, *P. g. gangetica* and *P. g. minor*; however, recent studies reveal sufficient differences in DNA and skull morphology for separate species status (they are estimated to have diverged *c.* 550,000 years ago, although have been connected temporarily as recently as 5,000 years ago); splitting would have a significant impact on conservation efforts. Indus river dolphins may be slightly smaller on average, otherwise there are no obvious external differences.

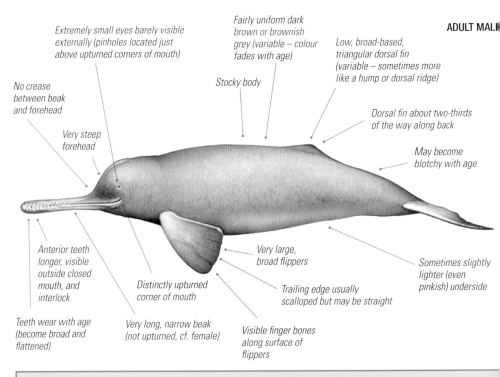

ADULT MALE

Extremely small eyes barely visible externally (pinholes located just above upturned corners of mouth)

Fairly uniform dark brown or brownish grey (variable – colour fades with age)

Low, broad-based, triangular dorsal fin (variable – sometimes more like a hump or dorsal ridge)

Stocky body

No crease between beak and forehead

Very steep forehead

Dorsal fin about two-thirds of the way along back

May become blotchy with age

Anterior teeth longer, visible outside closed mouth, and interlock

Very large, broad flippers

Sometimes slightly lighter (even pinkish) underside

Distinctly upturned corner of mouth

Trailing edge usually scalloped but may be straight

Teeth wear with age (become broad and flattened)

Very long, narrow beak (not upturned, cf. female)

Visible finger bones along surface of flippers

AT A GLANCE
- River systems in India, Bangladesh, Nepal, Pakistan and, rarely, Bhutan
- Fairly uniform dark brown or brownish-grey colour (variable)
- Small size
- Very long, narrow (vaguely gharial-like) beak
- Long teeth visible at front end of beak when mouth closed
- Low, broad-based triangular dorsal fin
- Surfaces quietly, cryptically, unpredictably and very rapidly

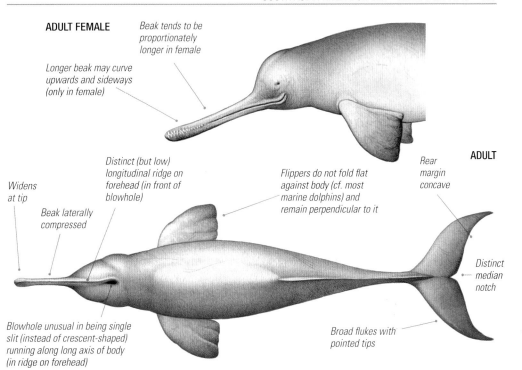

ADULT FEMALE

Beak tends to be proportionately longer in female

Longer beak may curve upwards and sideways (only in female)

Distinct (but low) longitudinal ridge on forehead (in front of blowhole)

Flippers do not fold flat against body (cf. most marine dolphins) and remain perpendicular to it

Rear margin concave

ADULT

Widens at tip

Beak laterally compressed

Distinct median notch

Blowhole unusual in being single slit (instead of crescent-shaped) running along long axis of body (in ridge on forehead)

Broad flukes with pointed tips

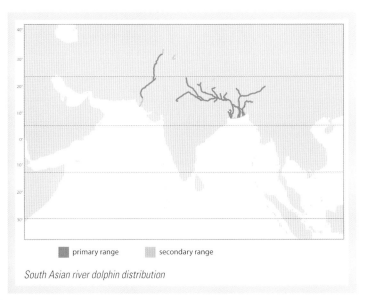

SIZE
L: ♂ 1.7–2.2m, ♀ 1.8–2.5m;
WT: 70–85kg; **MAX:** 2.6m, 114kg
Calf – L: 70–90cm; **WT:** 4–7.5kg

SIMILAR SPECIES

Confusion is possible between Ganges river dolphins and Irrawaddy, bottlenose and Indo-Pacific humpback dolphins or finless porpoises (mainly in the Sundarbans and near the mouths of the Hooghly, Karnaphuli and Sangu Rivers). The low dorsal fin should be distinctive (cf. the prominent fins of the much larger bottlenose and Indo-Pacific humpback dolphins, and the complete lack of a fin in finless porpoises). The absence of a beak should make the Irrawaddy dolphin distinguishable. Indus river dolphins do not overlap in range with any other cetacean species.

DISTRIBUTION

Usually in turbid, relatively shallow (often less than 3m) waters in river systems in India, Bangladesh, Nepal, Pakistan and, rarely, Bhutan. Able to tolerate a wide range in water temperature (from *c.* 5°C in winter to 35°C in summer), they occur from river deltas in the south where the salinity level is below 10 parts per thousand, upstream to the Himalayan and Karakoram foothills or where they are blocked by rocky barriers, shallow water, fast currents or, more recently, dams and barrages (low, gated, diversion dams). They are most common in areas that create

South Asian river dolphin distribution

▨ primary range   ▨ secondary range

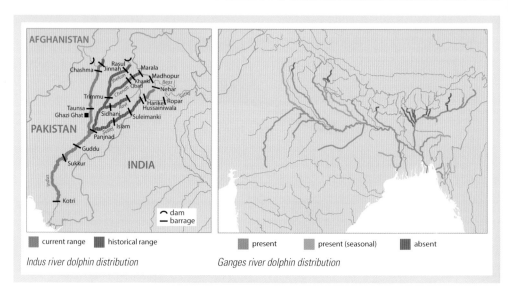

Indus river dolphin distribution

current range ■ historical range

Ganges river dolphin distribution

■ present ■ present (seasonal) ■ absent

⌒ dam
— barrage

ADULT COLOUR VARIATION

ADULT

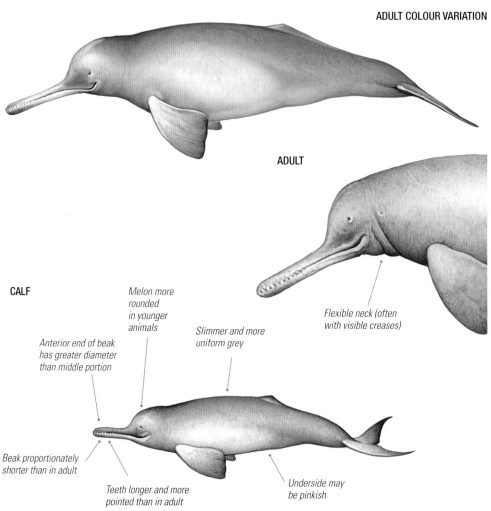

CALF

Melon more
rounded
in younger
animals

Slimmer and more
uniform grey

Flexible neck (often
with visible creases)

Anterior end of beak
has greater diameter
than middle portion

Beak proportionately
shorter than in adult

Teeth longer and more
pointed than in adult

Underside may
be pinkish

FOOD AND FEEDING

Prey Wide variety of fish (including catfish, carp and swamp eels) and invertebrates (including freshwater prawns, snails and clams); diet varies according to location and season.

Feeding Feeds from surface to riverbed, using long beak to probe mud; some evidence that feeding declines during summer monsoon; as many as 8–10 observed hunting cooperatively in Ganges.

Dive depth Unknown, but usually in water shallower than 30m; in Sundarbans, consistent preference for water *c.* 12m deep.

Dive time Average dive time 30 seconds to 2.5 minutes (maximum eight minutes 24 seconds).

eddy countercurrents, such as small islands, sand bars, river bends or meanderings, and at the confluences of rivers and tributaries, where they find refuge in slower water and prey is abundant. Distribution tends to be quite patchy and is highly variable according to season – they are concentrated downstream in the main river channels during the dry winter season and spread upstream and into smaller tributaries and some lakes during monsoon-driven summer floods. However, in many places, dams and irrigation barrages now block these seasonal movements.

GANGES RIVER DOLPHIN

Historically, the Ganges river dolphin occurred throughout the Ganges–Brahmaputra–Megna and Karnaphuli–Sangu river systems, in the main rivers and both small and large tributaries. It still has a relatively broad range in north-east India and Bangladesh, with a small, isolated sub-population in the Karnali River and tributaries (southwestern Nepal) and occasional reported sightings during the monsoon season in Bhutan. But it has disappeared from many upstream areas, in particular. It no longer occurs regularly in the upper reaches of the Ganges and is extinct or scarce in at least a dozen large tributaries. The greatest densities occur in the middle and lower reaches of the Ganges River in India (although many rivers are yet to be surveyed); the

500km stretch in the state of Bihar, between Buxar and Maniharighat, supports the maximum density. Ganges river dolphins have been reported moving along the coast of the Bay of Bengal when monsoons flush freshwater out along the east coast of India.

INDUS RIVER DOLPHIN

In the 1870s, the Indus river dolphin was widely distributed throughout 3,400km of the Indus River and its five large tributaries (Jhelum, Chenab, Ravi, Sutlej and Beas) in Pakistan and northwestern India. However, this historical range has declined by 80 per cent in the past century – it has been extirpated from the upper and lower reaches of the Indus and from all but one of the large tributaries. Development of the vast Indus Basin Irrigation System has severely fragmented the population within a network of irrigation barrages (the Indus is one of the most fragmented and modified rivers in the world). The current range is only a 690km stretch of the Indus River and active connecting channels in Pakistan, between the Jinnah and Kotri barrages, plus a very small surviving sub-population in the Beas River, north-west India. There were 17 fragmented sub-populations, but just six survive (five in Pakistan, one in India). Only three of these are likely to be viable: between the Chashma and Taunsa, Taunsa and

DIVE SEQUENCE

- Usually surfaces quietly, cryptically, unpredictably and very rapidly (spending *c.* one second at surface).
- Virtually never flukes.
- Each individual surfaces alone (except females with very young calves).
- Three main types of surfacing:
    1. Only top of head or beak appears above surface.
    2. Most of head, upper rostrum, back and tailstock visible above surface.
    3. Beak breaks surface at 45° angle and surfaces energetically with most or all of body visible (though rarely the flukes) – body bends sharply – beak re-enters water first (as above).
- May make lobtail movement with distinct splash in distress.
- Calves and sub-adults may briefly leap out of water.

ADULT SIDE-SWIMMING

Guddu, and Guddu and Sukkur barrages. The largest sub-population is in Sindh Province, Pakistan, between Guddu and Sukkur barrages – a legally protected stretch of river designated the 'Indus Dolphin Reserve' in 1974.

BEHAVIOUR
Generally cryptic and difficult to observe well in the wild, especially if there is any water disturbance. Frequently lives near humans, but it does not bow-ride. The Ganges river dolphin will follow oar-driven fishing boats for several kilometres, probably to catch fish as they are disturbed. It has been known to spyhop, but rarely breaches (though it sometimes surfaces energetically, showing most of the head and body). In captivity, it often swims on its side (usually the right side) and probably does this in the wild, too (the water is too turbid for direct observations); while side-swimming, it trails one flipper along the bottom and moves its heads continuously from side to side.

TEETH
Upper 26–39
Lower 26–35
Teeth more sharply pointed in younger animals (more peg-like, from wear, in older animals).

GROUP SIZE AND STRUCTURE
Usually solitary, in mother–calf pairs or in fluid groups of up to 10 animals; loose aggregations of as many as 30 have been reported.

LIFE HISTORY
Sexual maturity Females and males 10 years.
Mating Little known; one observation of 4–5 males chasing lone female, with one ultimately mating.
Gestation *c.* 9–10 months.
Calving Every 2–3 years; single calf born year-round, with possible peaks for Ganges river dolphins in December–January and March–May, and Indus river dolphins in April–May.
Weaning After *c.* 10–12 months (though possibly starts feeding on soft insect larvae and small fish *c.* 5–6 months).
Lifespan Estimated *c.* 33–35 years (though oldest recorded was 28 years).

PHOTO-IDENTIFICATION
Most individuals do not have identifying marks, making photo-ID almost impossible.

PREDATORS
None known.

POPULATION
There are no rigorous assessments of overall abundance. The Ganges river dolphin population was tentatively estimated at 4,000–5,000 in the early 1980s and approximately 3,500 in 2014, although substantial portions of its range have not yet been surveyed; approximately 70 per cent of these are in the main Ganges River and tributaries, with 20 per cent in the Brahmaputra and tributaries, and less than 10 per cent in the Sundarbans; there is a 2015 estimate of about 50 animals in Nepal. There are some minimum population estimates for the Indus river dolphin in Pakistan: 1,200 in 2001, 1,550–1,750 in 2006, and 1,452 in 2011; the latest tentative estimate is 1,300, with some 75 per cent living along a 126km stretch of river between the Guddu and Sukkur barrages (this sub-population may have increased by 5.65 per cent annually from 1974 to 2008). There are believed to be fewer than 10 surviving Indus river dolphins in India (between Beas city and Harike barrage).

CONSERVATION
IUCN status: Endangered (2017); *gangetica* subspecies Endangered (2004); *minor* subspecies Endangered (2004). South Asian river dolphins are among the most endangered cetaceans in the world. Water development projects have dramatically affected their habitat, abundance and population structure throughout the range. In particular, dams and irrigation barrages have severely fragmented their populations (dams are an absolute barrier to their movements, though it is possible that some individuals are able to move downstream through irrigation barrages) and have reduced the amount and quality of suitable habitat downstream. India's National Waterways Act 2016 – which identifies 106 rivers that will be engineered into cargo-carrying waterways and will involve the construction of more dams and barrages, as well as heavy dredging – will adversely affect 90 per cent of the Ganges river dolphin's range; there are fears

A Ganges river dolphin surfaces, showing its extraordinarily elongated beak and long teeth visible outside the closed mouth.

that this could be the final nail in the coffin. Meanwhile, the dolphins are especially vulnerable to entanglement in fishing nets, because they hunt in key fishing grounds. Deliberate killing has declined in many areas but still occurs, at least occasionally (e.g. in the upper Brahmaputra and the middle reaches of the Ganges); the meat is not popular and consumed only by very poor people or (at least in Bangladesh) used to feed livestock; the oil is used as a liniment and as a fish attractant. Direct

hunting was banned in Pakistan and India in 1972 (and the Ganges river dolphin was given the status of National Aquatic Animal of India in 2010). Other threats include chemical pollution, noise pollution, overfishing of prey species and vessel strikes.

VOCALISATIONS
Produces echolocation clicks almost continuously. No other sounds have been recorded.

A clear view of an Indus river dolphin surfacing energetically.

AMAZON RIVER DOLPHIN
Inia geoffrensis

(Blainville, 1817)

The Amazon river dolphin can be brilliant pink in colour. It is feared and revered by some river-dwelling communities, and is reputed to turn into a man under cover of darkness and seduce women (thereby explaining unexpected human pregnancies). Currently, there is one species, but it may be split into two or more in future.

Classification Odontoceti, family Iniidae.
Common name After the main range; boto is the Brazilian Portuguese name, but has been adopted as a common English name.
Other names Boto, boutu (incorrect phonetic spelling), pink river dolphin, bufeo, tonina.
Scientific name *Inia* is the native name given to this dolphin by Guarayo Indians in Bolivia; *geoffrensis* after a French professor of natural history, Étienne Geoffroy St Hilaire (1772–1844), who in 1810 was sent by Napoleon Bonaparte to plunder Portuguese museums (after the French invasion) and who procured the type specimen for this species (which had come from the lower Amazon).
Taxonomy Subject of many contradictory studies in recent decades. Currently, two subspecies are recognised: Amazon river dolphin or common boto (*I. g. geoffrensis*) in the Amazon and Orinoco drainage systems of Brazil, Peru, Ecuador, Colombia and Venezuela; and Bolivian river dolphin or Bolivian bufeo (*I. g. boliviensis*) in the upper Madeira River drainage of Bolivia and along the Bolivia–Brazil border; some claim a third, the Orinoco river dolphin (*I. g. humboldtiana*) in the Orinoco basin of Venezuela and Colombia. There have been proposals for three separate species – Amazon river dolphin (*I. geoffrensis*), Bolivian river dolphin (*I. boliviensis*) and Araguaian river dolphin (*I. araguaiaensis*) – but current morphological and genetics evidence suggests that they may not be valid.

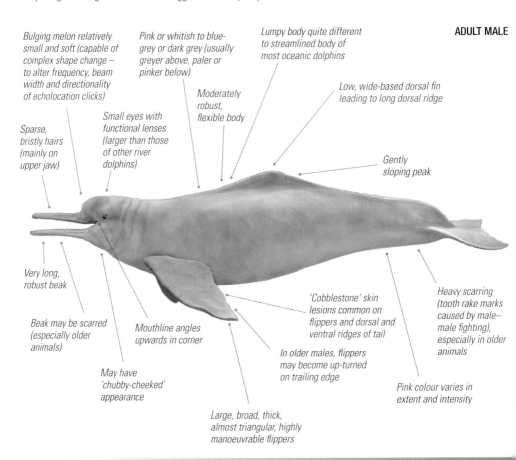

ADULT MALE

Bulging melon relatively small and soft (capable of complex shape change – to alter frequency, beam width and directionality of echolocation clicks)

Pink or whitish to blue-grey or dark grey (usually greyer above, paler or pinker below)

Lumpy body quite different to streamlined body of most oceanic dolphins

Moderately robust, flexible body

Low, wide-based dorsal fin leading to long dorsal ridge

Sparse, bristly hairs (mainly on upper jaw)

Small eyes with functional lenses (larger than those of other river dolphins)

Gently sloping peak

Very long, robust beak

Beak may be scarred (especially older animals)

Mouthline angles upwards in corner

May have 'chubby-cheeked' appearance

'Cobblestone' skin lesions common on flippers and dorsal and ventral ridges of tail

In older males, flippers may become up-turned on trailing edge

Heavy scarring (tooth rake marks caused by male-male fighting), especially in older animals

Pink colour varies in extent and intensity

Large, broad, thick, almost triangular, highly manoeuvrable flippers

AT A GLANCE
- Rivers and lakes in northern South America
- Exclusively freshwater
- Small size
- Mid-grey to brilliant pink colour
- Very long, slender beak
- Low, wide-based dorsal fin leading to dorsal ridge
- Large flippers
- Bulbous forehead
- Alone or in small groups

ADULT MALE COLOUR VARIATION

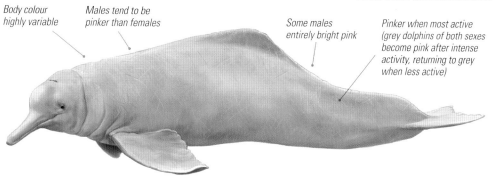

Body colour highly variable

Males tend to be pinker than females

Some males entirely bright pink

Pinker when most active (grey dolphins of both sexes become pink after intense activity, returning to grey when less active)

SIZE
L: ♂ 2.2–2.5m, ♀ 1.8–2.3m;
WT: 70–185kg; **MAX:** 2.7m, 207kg
Calf – L: 75–90cm; **WT:** 10–13kg
Male averages 16 per cent longer, 55 per cent heavier than female; one of the most sexually dimorphic cetaceans.

SIMILAR SPECIES
The tucuxi is the only other dolphin that overlaps in range. It is smaller, with a comparatively shorter beak and a tall, falcate dorsal fin; it also tends to be more energetic and prefers deeper water in the centre of rivers.

ONE, TWO OR THREE SPECIES?
Are there significant morphological and genetic differences to justify separate species or subspecies status for different populations of *Inia* dolphins? Have they been geographically separated for long enough? These are questions with no firm answers. The main morphological differences are suggested to be body size, the relative lengths of their beaks, the number of teeth and the width of their skulls, but differentiation by these characteristics has been disputed because they are highly variable and the sample sizes are relatively small. It is also very difficult to confirm that there is no overlap in their distribution.

Bolivian river dolphin In 2012, the Society for Marine Mammalogy initially accepted this as a new species, but it was not supported by further genetic sampling and was returned to subspecies status. It is claimed to be geographically isolated from Amazon river dolphins by *c.* 400km of waterfalls and rapids (between Guayaramerin, Boliva, and Porto Velho, Brazil), and DNA studies suggest that there has been no interbreeding for many tens (possibly hundreds) of thousands of years. However, since dolphins have been observed between and below the rapids, these do not form a total

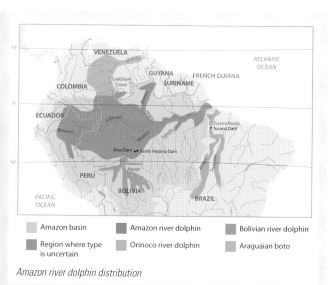

Amazon basin
Region where type is uncertain
Amazon river dolphin
Orinoco river dolphin
Bolivian river dolphin
Araguaian boto

Amazon river dolphin distribution

BOLIVIAN RIVER DOLPHIN

ARAGUAIAN RIVER DOLPHIN

barrier. This has since changed with the construction of the Jirau and Santo Antônio hydroelectric dams on the Madeira River in Brazil in 2013 – which have completely blocked all passage of dolphins in either direction. Currently found only in the upper reaches of the Madeira River, upstream from the Teotônio rapids, and in the Beni and Mamoré river systems. If accepted, it would be the only cetacean species present in a landlocked country.

TEETH
Upper 62–70
Lower 62–70
(Including 36–44 molar-type teeth).

Araguaian river dolphin Proposed as a new species in 2014, on the (disputed) basis that it has been geographically separated from Amazon river dolphins for *c.* 2 million years. However, samples were taken from locations at distant extremes of *Inia*'s distribution and diagnostic differences were based on very few specimens, so the Society for Marine Mammalogy is not convinced. Endemic to Brazil, ranging along *c.* 1,500km of the Araguaia River, with additional habitat (fragmented by seven hydroelectric dams, with two more planned) in the Tocantins River basin. There is a rough population estimate of 975–1,525.

TEETH
Upper 48–56
Lower 48–56
(Including 24–32 molar-type teeth).

Orinoco river dolphin Claimed as a separate subspecies. It exhibits behavioural differences (e.g. it is more aerially active than other Amazon river dolphins) and its dorsal fin is higher. However, movement between the Orinoco and Amazon basins is likely to occur through the Casiquiare Canal (which connects the Orinoco with the Negro, a tributary of the Amazon), so its validity as a subspecies is questionable.

WHY PINK?
Many Amazon river dolphins – especially older males – are bright pink in colour, but this is not caused by pigmentation. Instead, a progressive loss of the natural grey colour, and the build-up of heavy scar tissue from fighting, makes the blood underneath the skin more visible. The degree of pinkness varies greatly, according to age, water temperature and clarity, geographic location and, in particular, the level of activity. It is believed to advertise maturity and could have the same display function as the tusk in narwhals. There is some overlap, but males are generally much pinker than females, and older males are the pinkest.

DISTRIBUTION
Endemic to the Amazon and Orinoco drainage basins in northern South America – a vast area of about 7 million sq km in Brazil, Bolivia, Colombia, Venezuela, Peru and Ecuador (and possibly some southern rivers in Guyana). In the Amazon Basin, it is found along the entire Amazon River and its principal tributaries, smaller rivers and lakes. In the Orinoco Basin, it occurs in the main Orinoco River and its principal tributaries (except the Caroni and upper Caura Rivers above Para falls in Venezuela) and lakes.

Occurs almost everywhere it can physically reach, without venturing into brackish or marine waters.

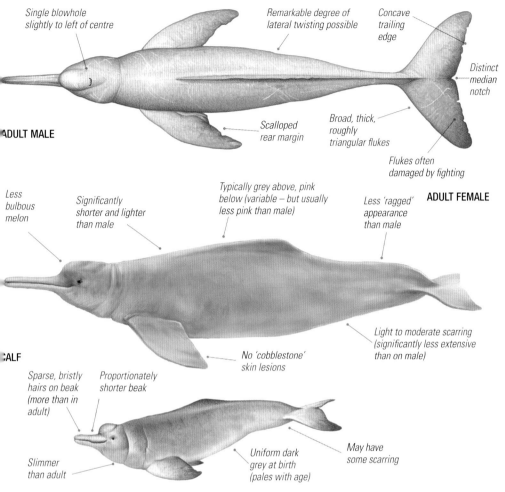

Single blowhole slightly to left of centre

Remarkable degree of lateral twisting possible

Concave trailing edge

Distinct median notch

ADULT MALE

Scalloped rear margin

Broad, thick, roughly triangular flukes

Flukes often damaged by fighting

Less bulbous melon

Significantly shorter and lighter than male

Typically grey above, pink below (variable – but usually less pink than male)

Less 'ragged' appearance than male

ADULT FEMALE

Light to moderate scarring (significantly less extensive than on male)

No 'cobblestone' skin lesions

CALF

Sparse, bristly hairs on beak (more than in adult)

Proportionately shorter beak

Slimmer than adult

Uniform dark grey at birth (pales with age)

May have some scarring

oncentrated in the main river channels during the dry eason (*c.* July–November, depending on the region), but isperses into the complex mosaic of flooded forests, kes, channels and floodplains during the wet season *. December–June). Yearly seasonal fluctuations in water evels may be as great as 15m. During low water, all vailable habitats are used equally by both sexes. During igh water, the sexes are segregated: adult females and eir offspring prefer the complex floodplain habitats /here currents are reduced and small fish are abundant, vhile adult and sub-adult males tend to remain along the argins of large rivers (where they typically outnumber emales by five to one). Seasonal movements can be undreds of kilometres; daily movements of tens of lometres are not unusual, though the species tends to ave great site fidelity.

 Prefers highly productive turbid water the colour of vhite coffee; however, it also occurs in water the colour of ack coffee (even though it is less productive). The most referred (but least common) habitats are where black-

water and white-water rivers meet and fish densities are greatest; however, any confluences, in particular, as well as river bends or lakes, are favoured. Generally, densities tend to be higher at river margins, where most fish prey tends to live, declining with distance towards the centre of the river; the dolphin is capable of swimming in water shallower than 2m and frequently comes very close to shore.

BEHAVIOUR

Truly a dolphin of the flooded forest, able to twist and bend to navigate between partially submerged trees and roots, moving its large flippers independently for great manoeuvrability (it can even swim backwards). Typically slow-moving – though capable of short bursts of speed – it will wave a flipper above the surface, spyhop, lobtail and occasionally breach (young tend to breach more than adults). The 'chubby' cheeks are believed to obstruct downward vision, which may be why it is often observed swimming upside down.

 Adult males (and occasionally sub-adult males) have a socio-sexual object-carrying display in which they carry

FOOD AND FEEDING

Prey Mainly fish (43 species known, ranging from 5cm to 80cm long, especially catfish); some crabs and molluscs, occasionally turtles.

Feeding Usually a solitary feeder, but may work cooperatively to herd and trap fish in shallow water; larger fish torn to pieces rather than swallowed whole; most feeding early morning and mid- to late afternoon.

Dive depth Unknown, but probably shallow.

Dive time Usually less than one minute (30–40 seconds typical); maximum one minute 50 seconds.

non-edible inanimate objects around in their beaks. This behaviour is unknown in any other mammal apart from humans. The objects are usually branches, large seeds or weeds – though sometimes snakes and turtles – and are often repeatedly thrashed against the surface of the water or thrown with a violent movement of the head. Alternatively, lumps of hard clay from the river bottom are gripped in the beak while the male slowly rises above the surface, sometimes spinning longitudinally, and then sinks back down. Carrying behaviour occurs throughout the year (with peaks in March and June–August) but increases with the number of females in the group, and may be a form of lekking behaviour (with males competing to gain the attention of mate-seeking females). Aggression – mostly between adult males – is 40 times more likely in groups

that display object-carrying behaviour than those that do not. There is also some aggressive behaviour (a form of sexual harassment) by males towards females.

Responses to people range from shy to curious and playful. The species does not bow-ride but will often approach boats (as well as floating houses and people standing on riverbanks) and sometimes grabs fishermen's paddles or rubs against wooden canoes. May form loose aggregations with tucuxis to hunt fish cooperatively.

TEETH

Upper 46–70

Lower 48–70

Uniquely among cetaceans, it has two types of dentition: 66–104 conical grasping front teeth and 24–44 molar-like rear teeth (for crushing hard-bodied prey).

DIVE SEQUENCE

- Typically surfaces for less than one second.
- Flukes rarely visible (except in Orinoco – where often visible).
- Blow can be explosively loud (like a snort or sneeze) and visible (up to 2m), or quiet and indistinct.
- Occasionally breaches (rarely leaves water entirely).

Two main types of surfacing:

'Sneak' sequence (above)

- Most common.
- Surfaces slowly at shallow angle.
- Shows upper part of melon, blowhole, tip of rostrum and sometimes dorsal ridge simultaneously (with body relatively horizontal).
- Back arches slightly to dive.

'Arch and roll' sequence (above)

- Head breaks water first.
- Entire beak often exposed.
- Back appears clearly, showing full length of dorsal ridge before a high-arching roll to dive.

GROUP SIZE AND STRUCTURE

Mostly solitary, though frequently 2–3; most pairs are mothers and calves. Loose aggregations of up to 19 occur where there is a rich food supply. Long-term relationships (apart from females with dependent offspring) are unknown.

PREDATORS

None known, but potential predators include black caimans, jaguars, anacondas and bull sharks.

PHOTO-IDENTIFICATION

Difficult, but possible, using notches and scars on the dorsal fin, combined with distinctive pigmentation patterns on the back.

POPULATION

Unknown. One guesstimate is 15,000, but possibly tens of thousands. A 2006/07 study estimated 3,201 and 1,369 in areas of 1,113.5sq km and 389sq km respectively, in Bolivia; 917 in an area of 554.4sq km, in Peru; 147 in an area of 144sq km, in Ecuador; 1,115 and 1,016 in areas of 592.6sq km and 1,231.1sq km, respectively, in Colombia; 1,779 in an area of 1,684sq km in Venezuela. This totals 9,544. In some areas, it occurs in the highest densities known for any species of cetacean – as many as 5.9 individuals per sq km. However, there are clear signs of population declines (at least 10 per cent per year in parts of the range).

CONSERVATION

IUCN status: Endangered (2018). Still widespread and relatively numerous in many parts of its range, but as human communities expand in the region and extract more resources from the river ecosystem, the dolphins are under increasing pressure. Threats include incidental entanglement in fishing gear, prey depletion, damming of rivers, deforestation, and chemical pollution from organochlorine and heavy metals. Thousands die in gillnets and other nets every year; these were first

The pinkish colour, long beak, small eyes, bulbous forehead and bendy neck are all distinctive characteristics of Amazon river dolphins.

introduced to the region in the 1960s and are now used by almost every riverside household. At least as many are harpooned or shot (illegally) – especially in Brazil and Peru – to use as bait to catch piracatinga (a type of catfish), to reduce perceived competition for fish, and because they damage fishing nets; this may now be the primary threat affecting the survival of the species. Fishing with explosives is illegal but common in some areas. Mercury is often used to separate gold from soil and rock in illegal mining operations along the Amazon – the high levels in the river give cause for concern. Another major and growing threat is habitat loss and fragmentation as a result of hydroelectric dams: 13 dams already affect the distribution of Amazon river dolphins, while three more are under construction and seven are planned. Local people in Brazil have regularly fed Amazon river dolphins since the late 1990s, and this has become a tourist attraction; although now licensed, the activity is insufficiently regulated and aggressive interactions between dolphins (and sometimes between dolphins and tourists) are common as they jostle for food. The Amazon river dolphin was once highly sought after by oceanaria – more than 100 were exported to the United States and Europe alone from 1956 until the early 1970s – but this trade has now stopped.

LIFE HISTORY

Sexual maturity Both sexes five years.
Mating Females likely to select males that have asserted dominance through fighting and display; very aggressive sexual behaviour in males.
Gestation *c.* 10–11 months.
Calving Every 2–3 years, occasionally every year; single calf born year-round, with peaks varying according to location (during falling water in Peru and Bolivia, rising water in Venezuela and high water in Brazil).
Weaning After *c.* 12 months; females sometimes simultaneously lactating and pregnant.
Lifespan 10–30 years (oldest recorded 45 years).

FRANCISCANA
Pontoporia blainvillei

(Gervais and d'Orbigny, 1844)

Despite being classified as a river dolphin, the franciscana is primarily a marine species. One of the smallest dolphins in the world, it is known to fishermen as the 'white ghost', because it is often light in colour and tends to disappear when it sees humans.

Classification Odontoceti, family Pontoporiidae.

Common name Franciscana because the skin colour is reminiscent of the habits of Franciscan monks; the mouth of the La Plata River is where the type specimen was collected in 1842.

Other names La Plata river dolphin, La Plata dolphin, toninha.

Scientific name *Pontoporia* from the Greek *pontos*, meaning 'open sea' or 'high sea', and *poros* for 'passage' or 'crossing' (in the belief that the species moved between fresh and marine waters); *blainvillei* after the French naturalist Henri Marie Ducrotay de Blainville (1777–1850).

Taxonomy No recognised subspecies; at least two geographical (and genetically distinct) forms – a smaller one in central and northern Brazil north of 27°S, and a larger one in southern Brazil, Uruguay and Argentina south of 32°S; those in the far north are intermediate in size.

ADULT MALE

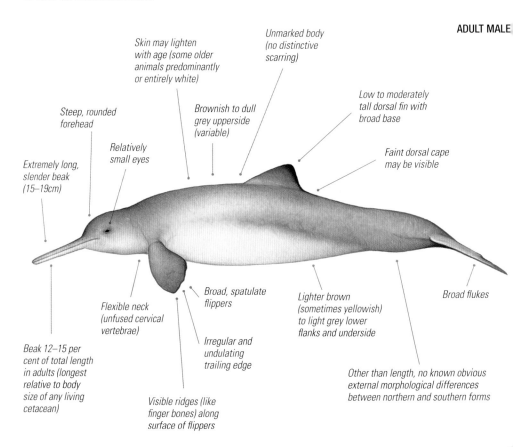

Skin may lighten with age (some older animals predominantly or entirely white)

Unmarked body (no distinctive scarring)

Steep, rounded forehead

Brownish to dull grey upperside (variable)

Low to moderately tall dorsal fin with broad base

Relatively small eyes

Faint dorsal cape may be visible

Extremely long, slender beak (15–19cm)

Broad, spatulate flippers

Lighter brown (sometimes yellowish) to light grey lower flanks and underside

Broad flukes

Flexible neck (unfused cervical vertebrae)

Irregular and undulating trailing edge

Beak 12–15 per cent of total length in adults (longest relative to body size of any living cetacean)

Visible ridges (like finger bones) along surface of flippers

Other than length, no known obvious external morphological differences between northern and southern forms

AT A GLANCE

- Shallow tropical and temperate waters along east coast of South America
- Simple pale counter-shaded colour pattern
- Small size
- Very long beak, often lifted into air on surfacing
- Broad-based, rounded dorsal fin
- Surfaces quietly and cryptically with little or no splash

ADULT

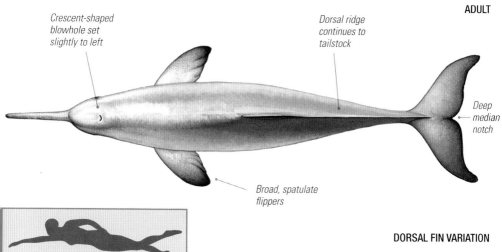

Crescent-shaped
blowhole set
slightly to left

Dorsal ridge
continues to
tailstock

Deep
median
notch

Broad, spatulate
flippers

DORSAL FIN VARIATION

SIZE
L: ♂ 1.2–1.4m, ♀ 1.5–1.6m;
WT: 20–40kg; **MAX:** 1.8m, 53kg
Calf – L: 70–80cm; **WT:** 6–8.5kg

Dorsal fin highly variable (triangular to slightly
falcate) but often appears backswept and
always has bluntly rounded tip

Some fins can
resemble those
of small sharks.

SIMILAR SPECIES

Several other small cetaceans overlap in range, but the
very long beak, small eyes and broad-based, rounded
dorsal fin should be distinctive. The 'fingered' flippers
are unlike those of any other dolphin in the region, but
are difficult to observe at sea. Young franciscanas, with
relatively short beaks, could be confused with Guiana
dolphins, but they are bigger, their beaks are shorter and
stubbier, and their dorsal fin shape is different.

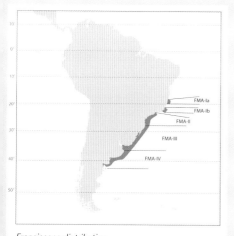

Franciscana distribution
(see Population for explanation)

DISTRIBUTION

Endemic to tropical and temperate waters along the east
coast of South America (Brazil, Uruguay and Argentina),
the franciscana prefers shallow, turbid water in a narrow
strip beyond the surf to about the 30m depth. It tends
to avoid deep, clear and cold waters, although there
have been sightings in water deeper than 50m and as
far as 55km offshore (especially in the northern part
of the range); however, beyond 30m, density declines
dramatically with distance from shore. It ranges from
Itaúnas, Espirito Santo State, southeastern Brazil
(18°25′S), to Golfo San Matías, central Argentina
(41°10′S), though it is not distributed continuously. Major
gaps occur in two areas of the northern part of its range,
where it is extremely rare or absent: Piraquê-Açu River
mouth, Santa Cruz (19°57′S), in the state of Espírito
Santo, to Barra de Itabapoana (21°18′S) in the state of
Rio de Janeiro; and from Armação dos Búzios (22°44′S)
to Piraquara de Dentro (22°59′S) in Rio de Janerio. It
sporadically enters the La Plata River estuary and other
estuaries. No migrations are known, although seasonal
inshore – offshore movements have been documented in
some areas. It probably does not leave the area in which
it was born and has a small home range of a few tens
of kilometres.

BEHAVIOUR

Generally cryptic and difficult to observe well in the wild,
so little is known about its behaviour. Usually shy, it avoids

The franciscana has the longest beak (relative to body size) of any living cetacean.

ADULT FEMALE

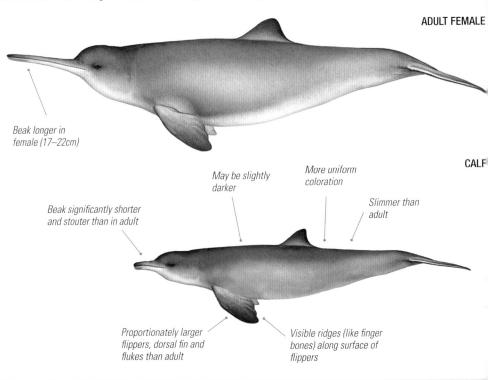

Beak longer in female (17–22cm)

CALF

May be slightly darker

More uniform coloration

Slimmer than adult

Beak significantly shorter and stouter than in adult

Proportionately larger flippers, dorsal fin and flukes than adult

Visible ridges (like finger bones) along surface of flippers

DIVE SEQUENCE
- Beak and head break surface first (beak often lifted into air and clearly visible).
- Back and dorsal fin appear briefly with low surfacing profile.
- Surfaces quietly and cryptically, with little or no splash.
- Individuals in same group often surface and breathe in synchrony.
- When travelling, dives average 15–21 seconds (3–4 short dives followed by one longer one).

FOOD AND FEEDING

Prey Wide variety of small marine fish (especially Sciaenidae), with at least 63 species known; will also take squid and octopuses (seven species) and crustaceans (six species); prey typically smaller than 10cm; diet changes according to seasonal prey fluctuations; juveniles commonly eat shrimps, then switch to fish after one year.
Feeding Feeds mostly near seabed, but will also take some pelagic prey; cooperative feeding behaviour has been observed in Argentina.
Dive depth Unknown, but less common in water deeper than 30m.
Dive time Foraging dives average 22 seconds (range 3–83 seconds); in Argentina, spends up to 75 per cent time diving and foraging.

essels and does not bow-ride. It does not appear to be erially active and interactions with other cetacean species re rare or non-existent. Foraging seems to increase, and avelling decrease, during incoming and high tides.

EETH

pper 53–58
ower 51–56

ROUP SIZE AND STRUCTURE

sually solitary or in small groups of 2–5, but herd sizes up 30 recorded.

REDATORS

iller whales and several species of sharks (including roadnose sevengill, hammerhead, sand tiger and tiger).

OPULATION

or conservation purposes, the franciscana's range as been divided into four 'Franciscana Management reas', or FMAs (see map). The latest (very approximate) opulation figures available are: FMA-I, fewer than 2,000 1 2011; FMA-II, *c.* 8,500 in 2008–09; FMA-III, *c.* 42,000 in 996; and FMA-IV, *c.* 14,000 in 2003–04. There is strong vidence that the population is declining.

ONSERVATION

JCN status: Vulnerable (2017). The franciscana's reference for shallow coastal waters makes it highly ulnerable to human-induced threats. Incidental catches in

gillnets are the main threat and have been a problem since at least the early 1940s. There are few recent figures, but it is likely that at least several thousand drown in gillnets every year – a level of mortality that probably exceeds the birth rate and therefore is unsustainable.

Other threats include habitat degradation and disturbance, chemical pollution, noise pollution and diminished fish stocks due to overfishing. Stomach contents have included many kinds of debris, including discarded fishing gear, cellophane and plastic. There is no indication of direct exploitation.

LIFE HISTORY

Sexual maturity Females 2–5 years, males 3–4 years.
Mating Males appear to be monogamous and do not have fighting scars; they may guard female and calf – possibly for mating purposes or even paternal care (which would be unique).
Gestation 10.5–11.2 months.
Calving Every 1–2 years; single calf born throughout the year in northern range, but in southern range peaks October–February; one of shortest reproduction cycles of any cetacean.
Weaning After 6–9 months.
Lifespan Usually less than 12 years (oldest recorded 23 years for female, 16 years for male).

he franciscana's beak is often clearly visible as it surfaces.

YANGTZE RIVER DOLPHIN
Lipotes vexillifer

Miller, 1918

The Yangtze river dolphin has the unfortunate distinction of being the first cetacean to have been driven to extinction by human activity. Occasional sightings are reported, but their validity is highly suspect.

Classification Odontoceti, family Lipotidae.

Common name After the recent historical range, in China; alternative name baiji from *bai* meaning 'white', and *ji* for 'river dolphin' or 'freshwater dolphin' (specifically in the Yangtze River). The similarly named Chinese white dolphin, from Hong Kong, is a subspecies of the Indo-Pacific humpback dolphin.

Other names Baiji (pronounced 'by-gee' and used interchangeably with Yangtze river dolphin), Chinese river dolphin; rarely – Changjiang dolphin, whitefin dolphin, whiteflag dolphin, ji, peh ch'i (merely an older way of transliterating the Chinese – i.e. the same as baiji).

Scientific name *Lipotes* from the Greek *lipos*, meaning 'fat'; *vexillifer* from Latin *vexillum* for 'flag', and *fer* for 'to carry or bear' (a reference to the dorsal fin).

Taxonomy No recognised forms or subspecies.

ADULT

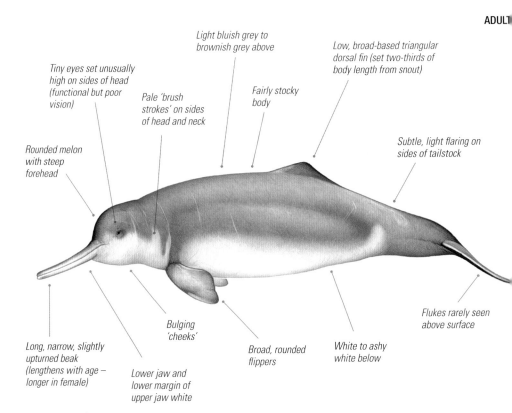

Light bluish grey to brownish grey above

Tiny eyes set unusually high on sides of head (functional but poor vision)

Pale 'brush strokes' on sides of head and neck

Fairly stocky body

Low, broad-based triangular dorsal fin (set two-thirds of body length from snout)

Subtle, light flaring on sides of tailstock

Rounded melon with steep forehead

Long, narrow, slightly upturned beak (lengthens with age – longer in female)

Bulging 'cheeks'

Lower jaw and lower margin of upper jaw white

Broad, rounded flippers

White to ashy white below

Flukes rarely seen above surface

AT A GLANCE
- Probably extinct
- Historical range in lower and middle reaches of Yangtze River, China
- Small size

- Light bluish grey to brownish grey above
- Long, narrow, slightly upturned beak
- Low, triangular dorsal fin
- Yangtze finless porpoise only other species within range

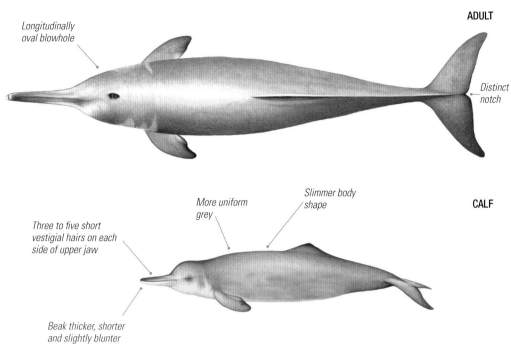

ADULT

Longitudinally oval blowhole

Distinct notch

Slimmer body shape

More uniform grey

CALF

Three to five short vestigial hairs on each side of upper jaw

Beak thicker, shorter and slightly blunter

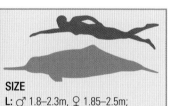

SIZE
L: ♂ 1.8–2.3m, ♀ 1.85–2.5m;
WT: 40–170kg; **MAX:** 2.6m, 240kg
Calf – L: 80–95cm; **WT:** 2.5–4.8kg

SIMILAR SPECIES

The Yangtze finless porpoise is the only other cetacean resident in the Yangtze River (although Indo-Pacific humpback dolphins have been recorded in the lower reaches). Molecular studies suggest that the Yangtze river dolphin was more closely related to the Amazon river dolphin and franciscana than to the South Asian river dolphin.

DISTRIBUTION

The species' recent historical range was a 1,700km stretch of the middle and lower reaches of the Yangtze River, China, and smaller connecting rivers, from the Three Gorges area to the river mouth near Shanghai. It also occurred in the Qiantang (Fuchun) River, south of the Yangtze River mouth, until construction of a hydroelectric power station began in 1958; and it occurred in two large lakes connected to the Yangtze (Dongting and Poyang). Previously also in the Yangtze estuary. There were no known migrations, although it was wide-ranging (one individual travelled at least 200km) and there is anecdotal evidence of an upstream movement in spring and a downstream movement in winter. The preferred habitat

Yangtze river dolphin historical distribution

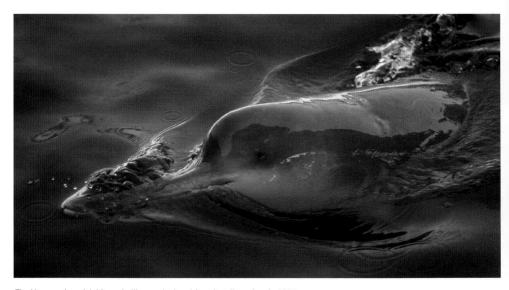

The Yangtze river dolphin, or baiji, was declared functionally extinct in 2007.

was anywhere near interrupted water flow (such as below bends in the river, mud banks and sand bars) providing high biodiversity and refuge from the strong current.

BEHAVIOUR

Elusive and difficult to approach, typically making a long dive and changing direction underwater. Most active during the day, resting at night in areas where the current is slow. No evidence of aerial behaviour such as breaching. Used to associate with Yangtze finless porpoises (the two species were together in 63 per cent of official sightings).

TEETH

Upper 62–68
Lower 64–72

GROUP SIZE AND STRUCTURE

There were typically 3–4 animals in a group (ranging from two to six); the largest number recorded together was 16 (no more than 10 after 1980).

PHOTO-IDENTIFICATION

Facial pattern, combined with scars and nicks on the dorsal fin.

POPULATION

Probably extinct. The Yangtze River was once described as 'teeming' with dolphins by Guo Pu (AD276–324), a scholar of the Jin dynasty. Genetic analysis estimated an effective population size of more than 100,000 *c.* 1,000 years ago. The population shrank to possibly low thousands in the 1950s, then to *c.* 400 by 1980, fewer than 100 by 1990 and as few as 13 (including one calf) by 1997. The last authenticated sightings were of a stranded pregnant female in 2001 and a live animal photographed in 2002. There was an intensive visual and acoustic survey – a final search for survivors – from 6 November to 13 December 2006, using two vessels operating independently and covering the entire historical range; they failed to find any evidence of dolphins. Another range-wide survey took place in November to December

DIVE SEQUENCE

- Surfaces slowly and smoothly, without causing white water.
- Typically only top of head, dorsal fin and small part of back visible (though sometimes entire head and beak visible).
- Frequent, short dives (10–30-second intervals), followed by longer dive (up to three minutes 20 seconds).
- Blow barely visible (but audible at close range – like high-pitched sneeze).

FOOD AND FEEDING
Prey Freshwater fish.
Feeding Unknown.
Dive depth Unknown.
Dive time Typically 10–30 seconds, maximum recorded three minutes 20 seconds.

2017, but that also failed to find any evidence. There are none in captivity. The species was declared functionally extinct in 2007 (in other words, even if a few individuals survive, there is no hope of recovery).

CONSERVATION
IUCN status: Critically Endangered (Possibly Extinct) (2017); IUCN is taking a precautionary approach, given occasional unconfirmed reports of sightings. Fishing was probably the main cause of the species' decline: in the 1970s and 1980s, at least half of all known deaths were due to snagging on rolling hook longlines or accidental capture and drowning in nets; in the 1990s, electrofishing accounted for 40 per cent of all deaths. Before the twentieth century, the species was hunted for its oil (reportedly used for caulking boats and lighting, and in traditional medicine). Hunting for the skin, for commercial production of leather, may have taken place on a small scale; and dolphins were occasionally eaten during periods of limited food availability or famine in the 1950s–70s.

Other threats included depletion of prey through overfishing, collisions with vessels, noise pollution, agricultural run-off, industrial and domestic pollution, riverbank development and riverbed dredging. Dam construction may have fragmented dolphin populations and made important feeding and breeding areas inaccessible; construction of the Three Gorges Dam in the 1990s dramatically changed water levels, stratification, currents and sandbanks, although the Yangtze river dolphin was already almost extinct by this point. The Chinese government gave the species official protection in 1975 and declared it a 'national treasure'. But its fate was sealed by an outrageous lack of funds, ineffective project management, and a lack of coordination and agreement between conservation groups, western scientists and Chinese authorities. The result was too little, too late.

LIFE HISTORY
Sexual maturity Males four years, females six years.
Mating January–June.
Gestation 10–11 months.
Calving Every two years; single calf born mainly February–April.
Weaning Estimates range from eight to 20 months.
Lifespan Probably more than 20 years; oldest recorded *c.* 24 years.

After being injured by fishing hooks in 1980, Qi Qi (pronounced 'chee-chee') spent 22 years at the Institute of Hydrobiology, in Wuhan, China; he was a crucial source of information about the species until his death in 2002.

DALL'S PORPOISE
Phocoenoides dalli

(True, 1885)

Dall's porpoise is probably the fastest small cetacean, typically seen as a splashy blur when it breaks the surface at high speed. Unlike other porpoises, it often approaches boats and readily bow-rides and wake-rides.

Classification Odontoceti, family Phocoenidae.
Common name After the American naturalist William H. Dall (1845–1927), who collected the first specimen in Alaska in 1873.
Other names Dall porpoise, True's porpoise, True porpoise.
Scientific name *Phocoenoides* from the Greek *phokaina* or Latin *phocaena* for 'porpoise', and *oides* from the Greek *eides* for 'like'; *dalli* after William H. Dall.
Taxonomy Two subspecies recognised (based on body colour pattern): *P. d. dalli* (*dalli*-type) and *P. d. truei* (*truei*-type); the *dalli*-type is the nominate form. There are also two minor colour morphs of the *dalli*-type, distinguished by differences in white patch size (larger in North Pacific–Bering Sea populations and smaller in Sea of Japan–Okhotsk Sea populations).

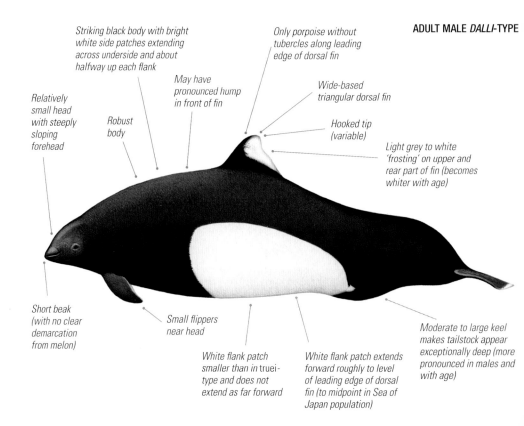

ADULT MALE *DALLI*-TYPE

Striking black body with bright white side patches extending across underside and about halfway up each flank

Only porpoise without tubercles along leading edge of dorsal fin

May have pronounced hump in front of fin

Wide-based triangular dorsal fin

Relatively small head with steeply sloping forehead

Robust body

Hooked tip (variable)

Light grey to white 'frosting' on upper and rear part of fin (becomes whiter with age)

Short beak (with no clear demarcation from melon)

Small flippers near head

White flank patch smaller than in truei-type and does not extend as far forward

White flank patch extends forward roughly to level of leading edge of dorsal fin (to midpoint in Sea of Japan population)

Moderate to large keel makes tailstock appear exceptionally deep (more pronounced in males and with age)

AT A GLANCE
- Cool, deep waters of the North Pacific and adjacent seas
- Striking black body with prominent white side patch
- Highly distinctive 'rooster tail' of spray common on surfacing
- Can be energetic and almost hyperactive (behaviour more dolphin-like)
- Wide-based, triangular two-toned dorsal fin
- Small size
- Exceptionally deep tailstock

ADULT MALE *DALLI*-TYPE

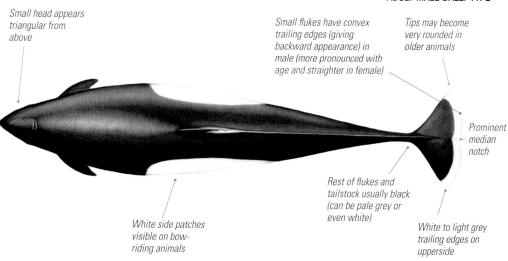

Small head appears triangular from above

Small flukes have convex trailing edges (giving backward appearance) in male (more pronounced with age and straighter in female)

Tips may become very rounded in older animals

Prominent median notch

Rest of flukes and tailstock usually black (can be pale grey or even white)

White side patches visible on bow-riding animals

White to light grey trailing edges on upperside

SIZE

L: ♂ 1.8–2.4m, **♀** 1.7–2.2m;
WT: 135–200kg; **MAX:** 2.4m, 218kg
Calf – L: 0.9–1.2m; **WT:** *c.* 11kg
Body length appears to increase from east to west; Sea of Japan individuals largest.

SIMILAR SPECIES

The Pacific white-sided dolphin can produce a similar 'rooster tail', but its dorsal fin is distinctive. Dall's porpoises are sometimes mistaken for 'baby killer whales' by inexperienced observers. The harbour porpoise may look superficially similar to a slow-rolling Dall's when backlit at a distance (but the white frosting on the dorsal fin of most Dall's should be distinctive and harbour porpoises generally inhabit shallower water). Female Dall's and male harbour porpoise hybrids are known, especially in British Columbia; they are reproductively viable, usually seen with Dall's porpoises, and typically behave like Dall's porpoises. Hybrids between *dalli*- and *truei*-types occur rarely.

DISTRIBUTION

Deep cool temperate to sub-Arctic waters of the northern North Pacific and adjacent seas, including the Sea of Japan, the southern Bering Sea and the Okhotsk Sea. Prefers water colder than 17°C, with peak abundance below 13°C. Mainly offshore, but also in coastal areas where the water is deeper than 100m. Seasonal movements vary with locality and even within populations (north–south, inshore–offshore or resident). Particularly abundant in areas of strong tidal mixing and over continental shelf and slope waters.

Dalli-type Occurs throughout the species' range, from 63°N in the central Bering Sea to 35°N in southern Japan and

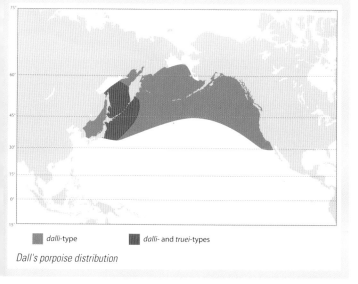

■ *dalli*-type   ■ *dalli*- and *truei*-types

Dall's porpoise distribution

ADULT MALE *DALLI*-TYPE VARIATION

Some individuals may have
flecks of black on white
patch (can be extensive)

Fin often canted
forward (mostly in
large, older males)

OLD ADULT MALE *DALLI*-TYPE

Exaggerated dorsal
and ventral keels

Dorsal fin
not canted
forward

Less robust
body

ADULT FEMALE *DALLI*-TYPE

Less deep
tailstock

Slate grey
instead of
black

No 'frosting' on
dorsal fin or flukes

CAL

Flukes have
concave
trailing edge

Flank patch light grey
instead of white (often
with orange tinge)

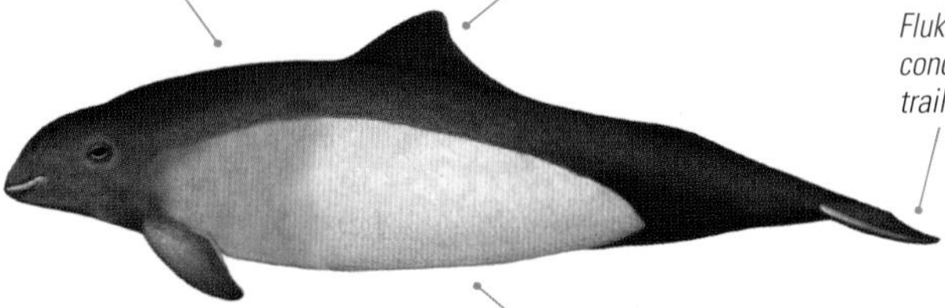

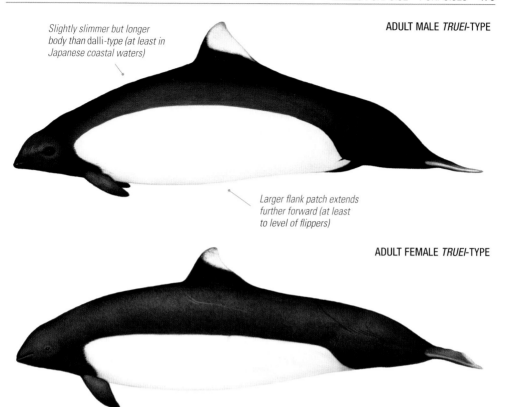

ADULT MALE *TRUEI*-TYPE

Slightly slimmer but longer body than dalli-type (at least in Japanese coastal waters)

Larger flank patch extends further forward (at least to level of flippers)

ADULT FEMALE *TRUEI*-TYPE

30°N in southern California (occasionally to 28°N off Baja California, Mexico, during influxes of exceptionally cold water). Rarer where it overlaps with the *truei*-type (accounting for 4–20 per cent of individuals, according to location). Sea of Japan population migrates through Tsugaru Strait and Soya Strait to summer breeding grounds along the Pacific coast of Hokkaido and in the southern Okhotsk Sea.

***Truei*-type** Occurs mainly in the western North Pacific and Okhotsk Sea, from 35°N to 54°N; absent from the Sea of Japan. Winters along the Pacific coast of central and northern Japan, and migrates through the Kuril Islands to summer breeding grounds in the southern and central Okhotsk Sea. Occurrence decreases from west to east and it is mostly absent east of 170°E; very occasionally seen as far east as the Aleutian Islands, with one 1989 record in California.

BEHAVIOUR

An energetic porpoise that can be almost hyperactive, darting jerkily and zigzagging around at high speed (up to 55km/h). It may be the fastest small cetacean for short bursts. A keen bow-rider – indeed, the only porpoise that often bow-rides – it prefers fast-moving vessels (more than 20km/h) and will lose interest in slower ones; it often

A Dall's porpoise bow-rides in front of a boat on a calm day.

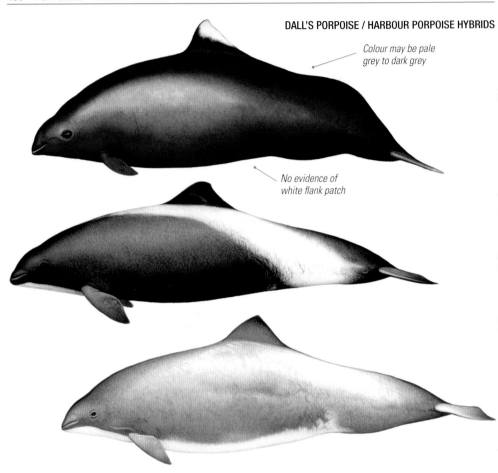

DALL'S PORPOISE / HARBOUR PORPOISE HYBRIDS

Colour may be pale grey to dark grey

No evidence of white flank patch

DIVE SEQUENCE

Fast swimming
- Most common: fast, slicing through surface and creating characteristic V-shaped 'rooster tail' of spray (supposedly resembles rooster's tail – spray formed by cone of water coming off head as it rises to breathe).
- In calm seas, spray is so distinctive it enables positive ID at great distance (even though little of body can be seen through walls of water).
- Indistinct blow.

Slow swimming
- Slow, rolling motion like harbour porpoise.
- Lifts tailstock higher above surface than harbour porpoise, with distinctive squarish profile.
- Creates little or no disturbance with indistinct blow.
- Typically 10–15 short, shallow dives in rapid succession (each lasting less than 15 seconds) before a longer, deeper dive.

FOOD AND FEEDING

Prey Opportunistic feeder, taking a range of surface to mid-water fish (including lanternfish and various sardines, pollock, anchovies, hake, sand lance, capelin, herring and mackerel) and squid (especially gonatid squid and magistrate armhook squid), mostly smaller than 30cm; may rarely take krill, shrimps and other crustaceans.
Feeding Mostly at night; recent research suggests daytime feeding in some areas.
Dive depth Recent tagging studies suggest most foraging in less than 100m; however, capable of deep diving and may forage at 500m-plus.
Dive time Typically 1–2 minutes, but some feeding dives may last more than five minutes.

---

appears suddenly from nowhere and disappears equally quickly. It even bow-rides in front of large whales and will also ride the stern waves of fast boats. Aerial behaviour such as breaching, tail-slapping or porpoising is extremely rare. Often associates with Pacific white-sided dolphins (from 50°N southwards) and short-finned pilot whales (from 40°N southwards) along the North American coast.

TEETH

dalli-type
Upper 46–56
Lower 48–56

truei-type
Upper 38–46
Lower 40–48

Teeth are spatulate, as in all porpoises. The smallest teeth of any cetacean – like grains of rice – separated by horny, rigid protrusions called 'gum teeth'.

GROUP SIZE AND STRUCTURE

Usually in fluid groups of 2–10 (usually fewer than five). Larger temporary aggregations around prey concentrations but these lack the cohesion of dolphin schools); largest groups in oceanic populations. One report suggests that single adult males often maintain close associations with adult females that have recently given birth (mate guarding) and will react aggressively towards other adult males.

PREDATORS

Killer whales; Dall's porpoises can tell killer whale ecotypes apart – they will often approach and swim among residents, but flee from Bigg's (transients) at high speed. Possibly also large sharks.

PHOTO-IDENTIFICATION

May be possible with dorsal fin pigmentation and deformities, combined with colour pattern anomalies.

POPULATION

The total population is possibly 1.2 million. The most recent regional estimates include 554,000 in the Okhotsk Sea, 104,000 in Japan, 100,000 off the US west coast, and a further 86,000 in Alaska.

CONSERVATION

IUCN status: Least Concern (2017). May have been hunted more than any other small cetacean. Since records began, during the period 1979–2016, 323,013 were taken for human consumption and pet food in the Japanese hand-harpoon fishery. The peak annual catch was 40,367, in 1988. A catch quota was introduced in 1993 (the 2015–16 quotas were 6,212 for *dalli*-type and 6,152 for *truei*-type), making it currently the largest direct hunt of any cetacean species in the world (one *dalli*-type and 6,152 *truei*-type were taken, respectively). Most are harpooned as they ride the bow waves of catcher boats. At least 10,000–20,000 were also killed incidentally in Japanese and Russian high-seas driftnet fisheries for salmon and squid, mainly in the 1950s and 1980s (these are now banned). Nowadays, low thousands die incidentally in fisheries in Japan and Russia, and low hundreds in the US and Canada every year. The other main threat is pollutants (especially organochlorines and mercury).

VOCALISATIONS

Echolocation clicks at frequencies many times higher than the range of human hearing (peaking in a narrow band of 120–140kHz, with some almost reaching 200kHz); this is above the hearing limit of killer whales.

LIFE HISTORY

Sexual maturity Females 4–7 years, males 3.5–8 years (great geographic variation).
Mating Mainly summer, but known year-round; male may compete directly for female, then guard her from other potential suitors.
Gestation 10–12 months.
Calving Every 1–3 years (varies with population); single calf born mainly in late spring or summer (June–August); female often ready to breed again within a month of birth.
Weaning Many different times reported, but possibly after 11–12 months.
Lifespan Less than 15 years (oldest recorded 22 years).

HARBOUR PORPOISE
Phocoena phocoena

(Linnaeus, 1758)

The harbour porpoise may be the most widespread and commonly seen of all the porpoises, but it can be surprisingly difficult to observe properly. It surfaces briefly, shows little of itself and rarely approaches boats, so a typical sighting is not much more than a fleeting glimpse.

Classification Odontoceti, family Phocoenidae.
Common name Reflects its habit of entering bays, estuaries, fjords, tidal channels and harbours.
Other names Harbor porpoise (American spelling), common porpoise; rarely – herring hog (especially Maine), puffing pig (especially Atlantic Canada) or puffer, after its sneeze-like blow.
Scientific name *Phocoena* from the Latin *phocaena* or Greek *phokaina*, meaning 'porpoise'.
Taxonomy Five subspecies are recognised: Atlantic harbour porpoise (*P. p. phocoena*), Black Sea harbour porpoise (*P. p. relicta*), Eastern Pacific harbour porpoise (*P. p. vomerina*), Western Pacific harbour porpoise (unnamed subspecies), and Afro-Iberian harbour porpoise (unnamed subspecies but possibly *P. p. meridionalis*, from the southern Iberian Peninsula and Mauritania). The main differences are in the DNA and skull and jaw morphology.

ADULT

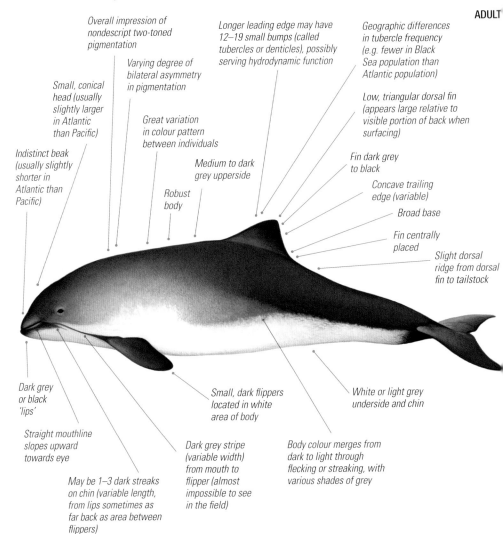

Overall impression of nondescript two-toned pigmentation

Longer leading edge may have 12–19 small bumps (called tubercles or denticles), possibly serving hydrodynamic function

Geographic differences in tubercle frequency (e.g. fewer in Black Sea population than Atlantic population)

Varying degree of bilateral asymmetry in pigmentation

Small, conical head (usually slightly larger in Atlantic than Pacific)

Great variation in colour pattern between individuals

Low, triangular dorsal fin (appears large relative to visible portion of back when surfacing)

Indistinct beak (usually slightly shorter in Atlantic than Pacific)

Medium to dark grey upperside

Fin dark grey to black

Concave trailing edge (variable)

Robust body

Broad base

Fin centrally placed

Slight dorsal ridge from dorsal fin to tailstock

Dark grey or black 'lips'

Small, dark flippers located in white area of body

White or light grey underside and chin

Straight mouthline slopes upward towards eye

May be 1–3 dark streaks on chin (variable length, from lips sometimes as far back as area between flippers)

Dark grey stripe (variable width) from mouth to flipper (almost impossible to see in the field)

Body colour merges from dark to light through flecking or streaking, with various shades of grey

AT A GLANCE

- Cool temperate and sub-Arctic waters of the northern hemisphere
- Small size and robust body
- Dark back and low, triangular dorsal fin
- No beak
- Usually shy and undemonstrative
- Usually alone or in small, loose groups
- Slow, forward-rolling motion on surfacing

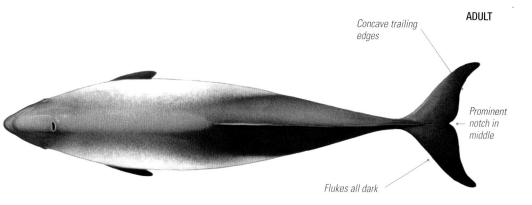

ADULT

Concave trailing edges

Prominent notch in middle

Flukes all dark

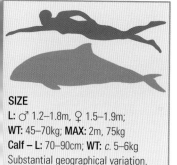

SIZE

L: ♂ 1.2–1.8m, ♀ 1.5–1.9m;
WT: 45–70kg; **MAX:** 2m, 75kg
Calf – L: 70–90cm; **WT:** c. 5–6kg
Substantial geographical variation.

SIMILAR SPECIES

Considerably smaller than most other cetaceans in the northern hemisphere and there are no other porpoises in the North Atlantic. May be confused with Dall's porpoise in the North Pacific, especially when backlit and at a distance, but the different surfacing behaviours should be enough to tell them apart much of the time (although Dall's porpoises sometimes exhibit a similar forward-rolling motion when swimming slowly). Female Dall's and male harbour porpoise hybrids are known, especially in British Columbia; they are reproductively viable, usually seen with Dall's porpoises, and typically behave like Dall's porpoises.

DISTRIBUTION

Discontinuous range in cool temperate and sub-Arctic waters of the northern hemisphere (mainly over the continental shelf). Favours coastal waters and frequents relatively shallow bays, estuaries, fjords, tidal channels and even harbours (and will also swim a considerable distance upriver in some areas). Rarely in seas deeper than 200m – although it is known in deep waters in some inshore regions (such as south-east Alaska, the fjords of western Norway and in deep waters off Greenland), and has been recorded

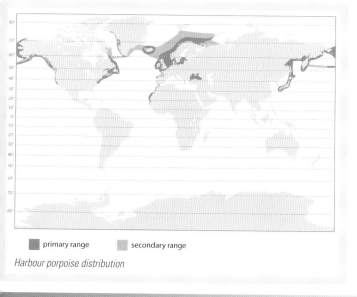

■ primary range   ■ secondary range

Harbour porpoise distribution

ADULT VARIATIONS

Many subtle differences in pigmentation between individuals

Slimmer than adult

Duller, more muted in colour than adult (often brownish on upperside)

No tubercles on dorsal fin

CAL

Variable dark grey stripe from mouth to flipper

ADULT HARBOUR/DALL'S HYBRIDS

Banding varies from
individual to individual

between land masses. Favours areas of strong tidal currents, usually near islands or headlands, where the currents combine with seafloor topography to create conditions where prey is aggregated. Some populations are resident (especially in enclosed waterways); others have seasonal movements related to food supply, sea temperature or ice cover (inshore or north in summer, offshore or south in winter). May have a home range as large as thousands of square kilometres.

North Atlantic In the west, from southeastern USA (about 34°N in North Carolina) to southeastern Baffin Island and southern and western Greenland; it does not appear to enter Hudson Bay. In the east, from Senegal discontinuously to Novaya Zemlya; it is the only cetacean found regularly in the Baltic Sea (where it has declined dramatically in the past century). An important breeding site has recently been discovered in and around the offshore banks in the Baltic Proper.

Black Sea There is an isolated population in the Black Sea and neighbouring waters (Azov Sea, Kerch Strait, Bosphorus and Marmara Sea); this population is separated from the nearest conspecifics in the north-east Atlantic by the Mediterranean Sea (apart from small numbers in the northern Aegean Sea, it is generally absent from the Mediterranean). Many individuals make annual migrations: northwestern Black Sea and Sea of Azov in summer, southeastern Black Sea in winter.

North Pacific From the southern Beaufort and Chukchi Seas to central California, USA, in the east and northern Honsho, Japan, in the west; there are limited bycatch records from Korean waters.

BEHAVIOUR
Usually avoids boats, or is indifferent, so it can be difficult to approach and follow (although it is more approachable in some areas, such as the San Francisco Bay area and in the Bay of Fundy, eastern Canada). Most approachable during extended periods of inactivity, especially on calm days, when resting motionless at the surface (with the body tilted slightly backwards and the blowhole the most elevated part of the body). Very rarely bow-rides or wake-rides. Acrobatics are uncommon, although it sometimes makes arc-shaped leaps when chasing prey and very occasionally tail-slaps when socialising. Rarely found in association with other cetaceans (although may feed in the same area as some species, such as common minke whales) and will actively avoid bottlenose dolphins in some areas (due to aggressive and sometimes lethal interactions).

TEETH
Upper 38–56
Lower 38–56
Teeth are spatulate, as in all porpoises.

GROUP SIZE AND STRUCTURE
Usually in mother–calf pairs or loose, fluid groups of 1–3 (larger groups of 6–8 are not uncommon in some areas); may be some segregation by sex and age; several hundred have been observed at good feeding grounds.

A typical view of a harbour porpoise: notice the nondescript colouring and low, triangular dorsal fin.

PREDATORS

Great white sharks (especially in the Bay of Fundy and Gulf of Maine) and other large sharks and killer whales; also, to some extent, grey seals.

PHOTO-IDENTIFICATION

Very difficult; mainly dorsal fin scars and nicks, but also body scarring and subtle variations in pigmentation.

POPULATION

The minimum global population is *c.* 700,000, despite substantial declines in some areas. Harbour porpoise numbers are notoriously difficult to assess, but very approximate regional estimates include 345,000 in the North Sea, including 41,000 in the English Channel;

LIFE HISTORY

Sexual maturity Both sexes three to four years; some geographic and density-dependent variation.
Mating Promiscuous (each individual mates with several other individuals); sperm competition may be primary way males compete to inseminate females.
Gestation *c.* 10–11 months.
Calving Every 1–2 years (usually every year in Atlantic, every two years in Pacific); single calf born mostly May–August.
Weaning After 8–12 months; may begin to eat solid food when a few months old.
Lifespan 8–10 years (oldest recorded 24 years).

DIVE SEQUENCE

- Typically surfaces 3–4 times quickly in a row before diving (usually for less than one minute) with little or no splash.
- When surfacing has slow, forward-rolling motion (as if dorsal fin is mounted on revolving wheel and lifted briefly above surface, then withdrawn).
- Rarely shows more than top of head, front portion of back and dorsal fin above surface (except in some regions).
- Tailstock not raised as high out of water as Dall's porpoise during forward roll.
- When feeding (swimming fast and erratically) may produce spray (known as 'pop-splashing' – very different to rooster's tail produced by Dall's porpoise).

BLOW

- Indistinct blow (can sometimes be heard on a calm day – a sharp puffing sound, like a sneeze).

FOOD AND FEEDING

Prey Wide variety of prey; varies between regions and seasons (diet in any one area, at a particular time of year, likely to be dominated by just a few species); mainly small schooling fish (e.g. herring, capelin, sprat, mackerel, sandeel, hake); some squid and octopuses; may consume benthic invertebrates (perhaps ingested involuntarily); calves will eat small crustaceans during early phase of weaning.
Feeding Opportunistic, taking prey mainly from near seabed, but will also forage in water column and close to surface; normally feeds independently, but groups of up to 20 have been observed collaborating to keep schools of fish together.
Dive depth Typically 20–130m (maximum 410m).
Dive time Most dives *c.* one minute; maximum six minutes.

102,500 in the Gulf of Maine–Bay of Fundy–Gulf of St Lawrence; 89,000 in Alaska (11,000 in south-east Alaska, 30,500 in the Gulf of Alaska and 47,500 in the Bering Sea), 27,000 off Iceland; 18,500 in the Kattegat and Great Belt areas; 25,000 in Norwegian coastal waters; 24,000 off west Scotland; 3,000–12,000 in the Black Sea and Sea of Azov; and 500–600 in the Baltic Sea.

CONSERVATION

IUCN status: Least Concern (2008); Baltic Sea subpopulation Critically Endangered (2008); Black Sea subspecies Endangered (2008); other subspecies have not been evaluated separately. Harbour porpoises were once hunted intensively for their meat and blubber in Europe (especially in the Black Sea, the Baltic Sea and the Danish Belt Seas, Iceland and Greenland) and in Canada (especially Puget Sound, the Bay of Fundy, the Gulf of St Lawrence, Labrador and Newfoundland). In the Black Sea alone, 163,000–211,000 were killed as recently as 1976–83. The species is now protected in most of its range, though there is still an active and unregulated hunt in west Greenland, where hundreds or low thousands are killed each year; and smaller kills probably occur unrecorded in other parts of the range. The biggest threat today is incidental capture in gillnets, as well as trammel nets, cod traps and other fishing equipment, in which many thousands drown every year. The main problem areas include Southeast Alaska, Japan, Russia, Turkey, Ukraine and the Baltic Sea (where the population is already critically low). The use of acoustic alarms ('pingers') and other mitigation measures have successfully reduced mortality in some areas. Other threats include: vessel traffic, various forms of pollution, prey depletion through overfishing, noise pollution, climate change (which, in particular, adversely affects sand eel availability), and habitat deterioration and destruction. The recent development of offshore wind farms is a possible new threat, especially in the North Sea.

Harbour porpoises rarely show much of themselves at the surface, though in some areas – such as here in the Bay of Fundy, eastern Canada – they sometimes leave the water completely.

VAQUITA
Phocoena sinus

Norris and McFarland, 1958

In imminent danger of extinction, the vaquita is the most endangered marine mammal in the world. Unless last-ditch conservation efforts are successful, it will not survive for much longer. Very little is known about its life and habits.

Classification Odontoceti, family Phocoenidae.
Common name Spanish for 'little cow', name used by local fishermen (pronounced 'vuh-*key*-tuh'); sometimes called vaquita marina ('little sea cow').
Other names Gulf of California (harbour) porpoise, cochito ('little pig'), Gulf porpoise, desert porpoise.
Scientific name *Phocoena* from the Latin *phocaena* or Greek *phokaina*, meaning 'porpoise'; *sinus* from the Latin for 'gulf' or 'bay' (referring to the restricted distribution in the Gulf of California).
Taxonomy No recognised forms or subspecies.

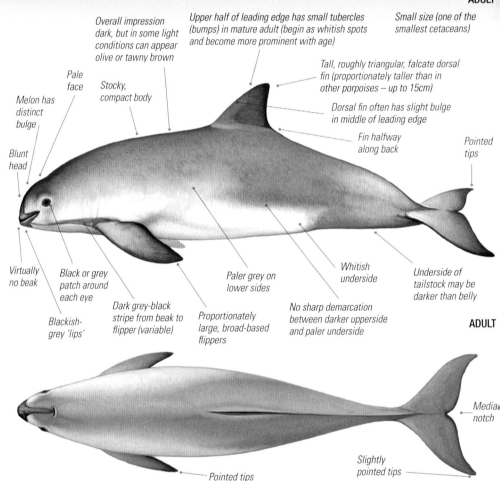

ADULT

Overall impression dark, but in some light conditions can appear olive or tawny brown

Upper half of leading edge has small tubercles (bumps) in mature adult (begin as whitish spots and become more prominent with age)

Small size (one of the smallest cetaceans)

Pale face

Stocky, compact body

Tall, roughly triangular, falcate dorsal fin (proportionately taller than in other porpoises – up to 15cm)

Melon has distinct bulge

Dorsal fin often has slight bulge in middle of leading edge

Blunt head

Fin halfway along back

Pointed tips

Virtually no beak

Black or grey patch around each eye

Paler grey on lower sides

Whitish underside

Underside of tailstock may be darker than belly

Blackish-grey 'lips'

Dark grey-black stripe from beak to flipper (variable)

Proportionately large, broad-based flippers

No sharp demarcation between darker upperside and paler underside

ADULT

Media notch

Slightly pointed tips

Pointed tips

AT A GLANCE
- Extreme northern end of Gulf of California
- Very small size
- Appears all grey or grey-brown in good light
- Prominent dorsal fin
- Lack of prominent beak
- Dark lips and eye patch
- Group size usually 1–3
- Typically surfaces slowly and inconspicuously

CALF

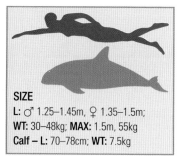

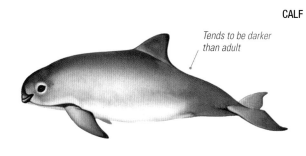

Tends to be darker than adult

SIZE
L: ♂ 1.25–1.45m, ♀ 1.35–1.5m;
WT: 30–48kg; **MAX:** 1.5m, 55kg
Calf – L: 70–78cm; **WT:** 7.5kg

SIMILAR SPECIES
There are no other porpoises in the vaquita's range, though bottlenose dolphins and common dolphins are seen regularly and may look similar at a distance (care should be taken because of the vaquita's tall dorsal fin). The lack of a prominent beak, smaller group size and elusive behaviour should be distinctive.

DISTRIBUTION
Extreme northern end of the Gulf of California, western Mexico (mainly north of 30°45'N and west of 114°20'W). Prefers shallow, murky, sediment-laden offshore waters with strong tidal mixing (it is rarely in water deeper than 40m). This is the most restricted distribution of any cetacean, and there is no evidence to suggest that it has retracted in historical times (reports from Islas Marías, 375km south-east of Cabo San Lucas, are unverified). The entire range is less than 65km across and is centred around Roca Consag, a 90m-high granite outcrop 27km east-north-east of San Felipe. Most recent sightings have been between Roca Consag and San Felipe (almost all within sight of the outcrop) and less than 25km from shore.

BEHAVIOUR
Shy and retiring, typically surfacing away from vessels. Tends to avoid large motorised boats, but may occasionally approach quiet drifting boats. Does not bow-ride and aerial displays such as breaching are unknown. Most sightings are fleeting and once only.

TEETH
Upper 32–44
Lower 34–40
Teeth are spatulate, as in all porpoises.

GROUP SIZE AND STRUCTURE
Most vaquita sightings are of 1–3 individuals together, but up to 10 have been observed in short-lived, loose aggregations; small groups often consist of several mother–calf pairs.

PREDATORS
Vaquita have been found in the stomachs of at least six large shark species (great white, shortfin mako, lemon, black-tipped, bigeye thresher and broadnose sevengill); killer whales are also likely predators.

PHOTO-IDENTIFICATION
A significant portion of adult vaquitas have distinctive scars and other markings on their backs and dorsal fins, which may allow photo-identification in the future.

POPULATION
The vaquita is probably a naturally rare species. There have been a number of attempts to estimate approximate numbers through visual and acoustic surveys: 885 in 1988–89; 567 in 1997; 245 in 2008; and 59 in 2015. The latest estimate was 6–22 (probably 10) in 2018, but there have been more deaths since.

Vaquita distribution

primary range   secondary range

DIVE SEQUENCE

- Surfaces slowly and inconspicuously (almost impossible to see in anything but flat-calm conditions).
- Beak usually does not break surface, and body appears and disappears with slow, arching roll.
- Eyes rarely appear above surface (except when individual is curious).
- Typically surfaces 3–5 times, followed by longer dive lasting 1–3 minutes.
- Indistinct, invisible blow (but makes loud, sharp puffing sound reminiscent of harbour porpoise).

FOOD AND FEEDING

Prey 21 small (mainly bottom-feeding) fish species known, especially grunts and croakers; also takes squid and some crustaceans.
Feeding Unknown.
Dive depth Shallow (rarely in water deeper than 40m).
Dive time Maximum at least three minutes.

CONSERVATION

IUCN status: Critically Endangered (2017). The biggest threat for decades has been entanglement and accidental drowning in near-invisible gillnets, which are set by fishermen from three small towns (San Felipe, El Golfo de Santa Clara and, to a lesser extent, Puerto Peñasco). Gillnets are set for a variety of species, including sharks and blue shrimp, but the main concern recently has been those set for a 2m-long sea bass-like fish, the totoaba (pronounced 'toe-twa-buh'). Endemic to the Gulf of California, and Critically Endangered itself, the totoaba is highly prized for its swim bladder, used in Chinese traditional medicine. Conservation efforts have included establishing a vaquita refuge, developing alternative fishing gear, promotion of 'vaquita-safe' seafood, fishing boat buyouts, better enforcement of existing legislation and compensation for fishermen for lost income as a result of vaquita protection. Despite an emergency gillnet ban, introduced in May 2015, and a ban on totoaba fishing, illegal fishing activity has continued at a very high level. Conservation efforts for the vaquita were slow to start and minimal action taken by the Mexican government since 2007 may be too little, too late. A programme to capture some of the last survivors alive, to evaluate the possibility of captive breeding, tragically resulted in a female dying; this has largely dashed hopes that captive breeding might save the species. Without proper enforcement of suitable fishery regulations in the upper Gulf of California, the vaquita will likely go extinct in the next few years.

LIFE HISTORY

Sexual maturity 3–6 years.
Mating Presumed to be May–June.
Gestation 10–11 months.
Calving Probably every two years; single calf born March–April (peak late March and early April).
Weaning Unknown, but probably after 6–8 months.
Lifespan Oldest recorded 21 years (female).

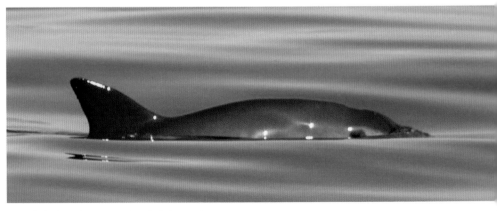

Probably the best picture ever taken of a living vaquita.

BURMEISTER'S PORPOISE
Phocoena spinipinnis

Burmeister, 1865

Burmeister's porpoise is inconspicuous and easy to overlook. There have been relatively few scientific observations of live animals, yet it may be fairly common and widespread along the coasts of South America.

Classification Odontoceti, family Phocoenidae.
Common name After the German-Argentinian zoologist Karl Hermann Konrad Burmeister (1807–92), who described the first live specimen in 1865 (caught in the mouth of the La Plata River, Argentina).
Other names Black porpoise (a misnomer – reflecting the fact that most specimens are seen only after they are dead and their colour has darkened).
Scientific name *Phocoena* from the Latin *phocaena* or Greek *phokaina*, meaning 'porpoise'; *spinipinnis* from the Latin *spina* for 'with spines' and *pinna* for 'fin' or 'wing' (referring to the spiny bumps on the leading edge of the dorsal fin).
Taxonomy No recognised subspecies, but recent genetic studies indicate two sub-populations: Peruvian and Chilean-Argentinian (which differ in body size).

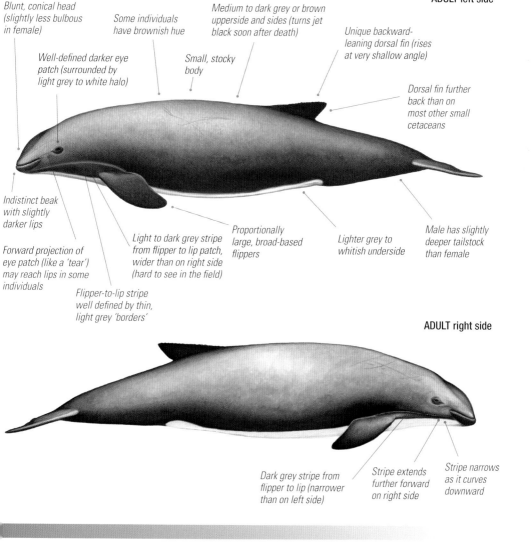

ADULT left side

Blunt, conical head (slightly less bulbous in female)

Some individuals have brownish hue

Medium to dark grey or brown upperside and sides (turns jet black soon after death)

Unique backward-leaning dorsal fin (rises at very shallow angle)

Well-defined darker eye patch (surrounded by light grey to white halo)

Small, stocky body

Dorsal fin further back than on most other small cetaceans

Indistinct beak with slightly darker lips

Forward projection of eye patch (like a 'tear') may reach lips in some individuals

Light to dark grey stripe from flipper to lip patch, wider than on right side (hard to see in the field)

Proportionally large, broad-based flippers

Lighter grey to whitish underside

Male has slightly deeper tailstock than female

Flipper-to-lip stripe well defined by thin, light grey 'borders'

ADULT right side

Dark grey stripe from flipper to lip (narrower than on left side)

Stripe extends further forward on right side

Stripe narrows as it curves downward

AT A GLANCE
- Coastal waters of South America
- Small size
- Stocky body
- Appears very dark at sea
- Unique backward-leaning dorsal fin well behind midline
- Tends to be inconspicuous, with little disturbance of water

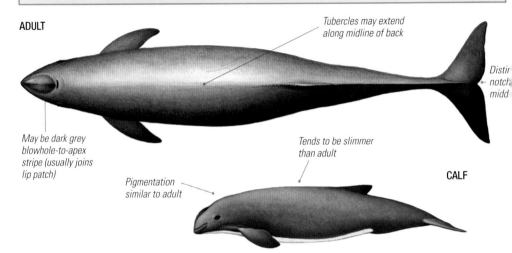

ADULT

Tubercles may extend along midline of back

Distir notch midd

May be dark grey blowhole-to-apex stripe (usually joins lip patch)

Pigmentation similar to adult

Tends to be slimmer than adult

CALF

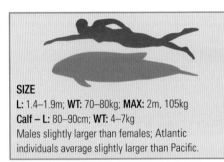

SIZE
L: 1.4–1.9m; **WT:** 70–80kg; **MAX:** 2m, 105kg
Calf – L: 80–90cm; **WT:** 4–7kg
Males slightly larger than females; Atlantic individuals average slightly larger than Pacific.

SIMILAR SPECIES
Unmistakable when the dorsal fin is seen at close range. At a distance, confusion is possible with the Chilean dolphin, spectacled porpoise and Commerson's dolphin. The long beak of the franciscana is sufficiently different. Beware fleeting glimpses of South American sea lions (when swimming at the surface, they roll exactly like a Burmeister's porpoise, and their flippers can look remarkably like Burmeister's porpoise dorsal fins).

DISTRIBUTION
Coastal waters of South America, over the continental shelf, possibly more common in the Pacific than the Atlantic. Most of the 120-plus sightings in southern Chile have been in water depths greater than 40m (favouring deeper channels) and at least 500m from shore. May be present further offshore – up to 50km recorded in Argentina. Range extends from Bahía de Paita, northern Peru (5°01'S), south to Cape Horn on the Pacific coast, and north to the La Plata River basin, Argentina (c. 37°S), on the Atlantic coast. The northern boundaries coincide with the westward turn of the northward-flowing Humboldt Current (in the Pacific) and the eastward turn of the northward-flowing Falklands Current (in the Atlantic). Occasionally recorded as far north as Rio Uruçanga, Brazil (28°48'S), usually in association with the sporadic intrusion of colder waters associated with the Atlantic Subtropical Convergence. At least some populations are likely to be resident (e.g. in the Beagle Channel) but elsewhere there is evidence of an inshore movement in summer and offshore in winter.

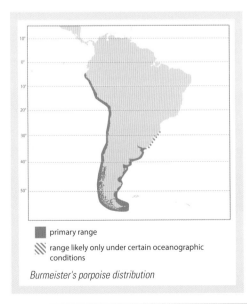

■ primary range

▨ range likely only under certain oceanographic conditions

Burmeister's porpoise distribution

ADULT FIN VARIATIONS

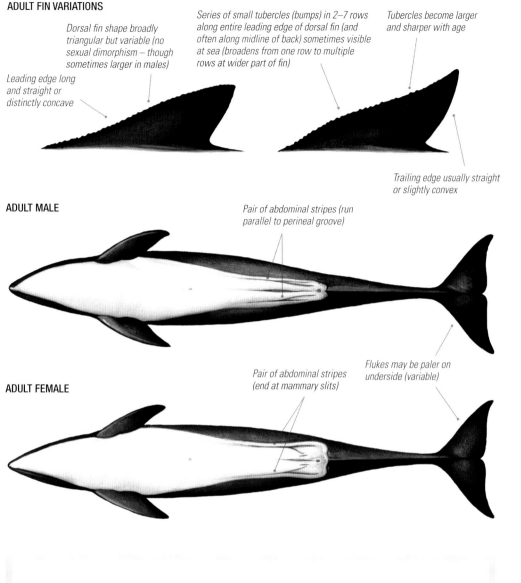

Dorsal fin shape broadly triangular but variable (no sexual dimorphism – though sometimes larger in males)

Series of small tubercles (bumps) in 2–7 rows along entire leading edge of dorsal fin (and often along midline of back) sometimes visible at sea (broadens from one row to multiple rows at wider part of fin)

Tubercles become larger and sharper with age

Leading edge long and straight or distinctly concave

Trailing edge usually straight or slightly convex

ADULT MALE

Pair of abdominal stripes (run parallel to perineal groove)

Flukes may be paler on underside (variable)

ADULT FEMALE

Pair of abdominal stripes (end at mammary slits)

DIVE SEQUENCE
- Surfaces causing little disturbance.
- Shows little of body (though dorsal fin usually clearly visible).
- Slow, forward-rolling motion (not unlike harbour porpoise).
- In Chile, typically surfaces 3–4 times in a small area, then dives for three minutes or more, reappearing 50–100m away.
- In Argentina, limited evidence suggests typically surfaces 7–8 times in a small area, then dives for 1–3 minutes, reappearing at least 17m away.
- Overall impression may be like an undulating sea lion.

BLOW
- Indistinct blow, but short 'puff-puff' can be heard in calm weather.

FOOD AND FEEDING
Prey Mainly fish such as anchovy, hake, silverside, sardine and jack mackerel; also some squid, shrimp and krill.
Feeding Unknown.
Dive depth Usually in water shallower than 200m.
Dive time Limited records average 1–3 minutes.

BEHAVIOUR
Tends to be inconspicuous, and rarely engages in aerial activity such as porpoising or breaching (although some individuals have been reported riding coastal breakers and occasionally leaping as part of this surfing behaviour). Almost impossible to see in rough weather. Bursts of speed associated with feeding are common. Groups will often scatter and accelerate when frightened (especially if approached by a boat).

TEETH
Upper 20–46
Lower 28–46
Teeth are spatulate, as in all porpoises. Young tend to have higher tooth counts than adults (they lose 12–20 barely visible and poorly anchored small teeth).

GROUP SIZE AND STRUCTURE
Typically seen alone, in pairs or in small groups (1–4, occasionally up to eight), though temporary larger aggregations have been reported (likely the result of concentrated food sources). There is one record of *c.* 70 in the Bay of Mejillones, northern Chile, in 1982, and another of *c.* 150 near Isla Guañape Sur, off north-central Peru, in 2001 (scattered over several sq km).

PREDATORS
Possibly killer whales and large sharks, but there are no records.

PHOTO-IDENTIFICATION
Difficult, since it bears few individually identifying marks and is tricky to photograph.

POPULATION
Unknown, but strandings, hunting and fisheries bycatch data indicate that it may be more abundant than the limited numbers of sightings suggest.

CONSERVATION
IUCN status: Near Threatened (2018). Hunted with nets and harpoons in Peru (and, to a lesser degree, elsewhere); the meat is sold for human consumption and for shark and crab bait. Hunting small cetaceans was banned in Peru in 1996, but enforcement is poor. Also caught incidentally in a variety of fishing nets (especially gillnets) throughout its range (in Peru, at least, the bycatch is used extensively for human consumption). The current mortality from hunting and bycatch throughout the range could be in the thousands annually.

LIFE HISTORY
Sexual maturity Unknown.
Mating Presumed mid summer to early autumn.
Gestation 11–12 months.
Calving Probably every year (records of pregnant females simultaneously lactating); single calf born mainly late summer to early autumn.
Weaning Unknown.
Lifespan Unknown (oldest recorded 12 years).

An extremely rare view of Burmeister's porpoise, showing its overall dark body, unique backward-leaning dorsal fin and distinct tubercles.

SPECTACLED PORPOISE
Phocoena dioptrica

Lahille, 1912

The spectacled porpoise is instantly recognisable, with its striking black-and-white colour pattern and the male's enormous dorsal fin. However, it is rarely seen and is one of the least known of all cetaceans.

Classification Odontoceti, family Phocoenidae.
Common name From the distinctive white 'spectacles' around the eyes.
Other names None.
Scientific name *Phocoena* from the Latin *phocaena* or Greek *phokaina*, meaning 'porpoise'; Greek *dioptra* (meaning 'optical instrument') gives *dioptrica*, referring to the double eye rings.
Taxonomy No recognised forms or subspecies; briefly (1985–95) put in its own genus, *Australophocaena*, but genetic and morphometric studies put it back in *Phocoena*.

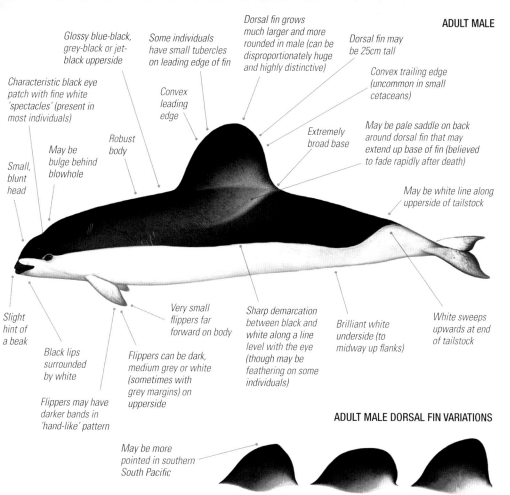

ADULT MALE

Glossy blue-black, grey-black or jet-black upperside

Some individuals have small tubercles on leading edge of fin

Dorsal fin grows much larger and more rounded in male (can be disproportionately huge and highly distinctive)

Dorsal fin may be 25cm tall

Convex trailing edge (uncommon in small cetaceans)

Characteristic black eye patch with fine white 'spectacles' (present in most individuals)

Convex leading edge

Extremely broad base

May be pale saddle on back around dorsal fin that may extend up base of fin (believed to fade rapidly after death)

Robust body

May be bulge behind blowhole

Small, blunt head

May be white line along upperside of tailstock

Slight hint of a beak

Very small flippers far forward on body

Sharp demarcation between black and white along a line level with the eye (though may be feathering on some individuals)

Brilliant white underside (to midway up flanks)

White sweeps upwards at end of tailstock

Black lips surrounded by white

Flippers can be dark, medium grey or white (sometimes with grey margins) on upperside

Flippers may have darker bands in 'hand-like' pattern

ADULT MALE DORSAL FIN VARIATIONS

May be more pointed in southern South Pacific

AT A GLANCE
- Cool waters of the southern hemisphere
- Two-toned: black upperside, brilliant white underside (with sharp demarcation)
- Small size
- Absurdly large, rounded dorsal fin of male
- Strong sexual dimorphism
- White 'spectacles' distinctive at close range

May be no, one or two light grey stripes running from blowhole to apex of melon

May be pale saddle on back around dorsal fin

Some individuals have relatively light (grey/brown) dorsal colour

Upperside of flukes usually grey but may be white (underside usually white but may be grey)

ADULT MALE

Distin̶ medi̶ notcl̶

Small flukes with fairly straight trailing edge

ADULT FEMALE

Usually lighter on back than male (more noticeable under good lighting conditions)

Usually slightly convex on leading and trailing edges

Dorsal fin smaller (up to 12cm), lower and more triangular (cf. male)

Both sexes may have one or two indistinct grey stripes (or wider stripe) leading from around lips to flippers (may fade with age and be absent in some individuals)

The only strongly sexually dimorphic porpoise species

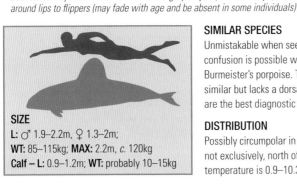

SIZE
L: ♂ 1.9–2.2m; ♀ 1.3–2m;
WT: 85–115kg; **MAX:** 2.2m, *c.* 120kg
Calf – L: 0.9–1.2m; **WT:** probably 10–15kg

SIMILAR SPECIES

Unmistakable when seen well and at close range. At a distance, confusion is possible with Commerson's dolphin, Chilean dolphin and Burmeister's porpoise. The southern right whale dolphin is superficially similar but lacks a dorsal fin. Dorsal fin shape and colour differences are the best diagnostic features.

DISTRIBUTION

Possibly circumpolar in cool temperate to polar waters (mostly, but not exclusively, north of the Antarctic Convergence). Preferred water temperature is 0.9–10.3°C (most sightings in 4.9–6.2°C). Known mainly from strandings, especially along the east coast of Tierra del Fuego and southern Argentina. Also known from widely scattered offshore islands of the Antarctic Circumpolar Current (the Falkland Islands, South Georgia, Kerguelen Islands, Heard Island and Macquarie Island, and the Auckland Islands). There are a few records from New Zealand's South Island and sub-Antarctic islands, South Australia and Tasmania. The northernmost sighting was 32°S (Santa Catarina, southern Brazil), the southernmost 64°33'S (between New Zealand and Antarctica).

■ probable range   ▨ possible range

Spectacled porpoise distribution

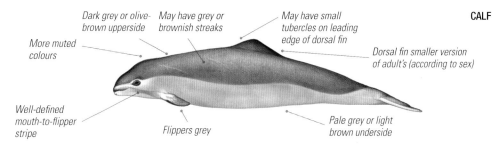

Dark grey or olive-brown upperside

May have grey or brownish streaks

More muted colours

May have small tubercles on leading edge of dorsal fin

CALF

Dorsal fin smaller version of adult's (according to sex)

Well-defined mouth-to-flipper stripe

Flippers grey

Pale grey or light brown underside

Known mainly from coastal waters (also in some rivers and turbid channels near the shore) but the primary habitat is believed to be deep offshore waters. Nothing is known about migrations.

BEHAVIOUR

There are only a few dozen confirmed sightings at sea. It is not known to be acrobatic and does not bow-ride. Usually avoids boats (though it has approached research vessels).

TEETH

Upper 32–52

Lower 34–46

Teeth are spatulate, as in all porpoises, or peg-shaped; they are often hidden in the gums.

GROUP SIZE AND STRUCTURE

Typical group size is 1–3 (average two), but as many as five have been seen together; most strandings are of solitary animals. Mother–calf pairs are often accompanied by one or two adult males (unlikely to be biological fathers of calves – more indicative of a mate-guarding mating system, as seen in Dall's porpoises).

PREDATORS

Possibly killer whales, leopard seals and sharks.

FOOD AND FEEDING

Very little information, but known to eat anchovies and other small schooling fish, mantis shrimps and squid.

PHOTO-IDENTIFICATION

No research to date.

POPULATION

There is no global estimate, but the high genetic diversity and abundance of strandings (more than 300 specimens in Tierra del Fuego) suggests a reasonable population size similar to better-known porpoises.

CONSERVATION

IUCN status: Least Concern (2018). The greatest threat is believed to be incidental capture in coastal gillnets, especially in Tierra del Fuego. In the past, it has been harpooned for crab bait and food off southern Chile and Argentina, but the numbers involved, the impact and the current situation are unknown. Other threats may include further incidental capture in expanding Southern Ocean fisheries, oil and mineral exploration, and pollution.

LIFE HISTORY

Sexual maturity Females *c.* two years, males *c.* four years.

Mating Unknown.

Gestation Possibly 8–11 months.

Calving Probably every year; single calf born in southern spring and summer (November–February).

Weaning Possibly after 6–15 months.

Lifespan Maximum known 27 years.

DIVE SEQUENCE

- Usually inconspicuous when surfacing (slow forward roll, not unlike that of harbour porpoise).
- Tip of snout breaks surface first, then strongly arches back on each dive.
- Top of white sides may just be visible when arching back.
- Capable of porpoising fast (sometimes clearing the water).

BLOW

- Indistinct blow.

NARROW-RIDGED FINLESS PORPOISE
Neophocaena asiaeorientalis
(Pilleri and Gihr, 1972)

In 2009 it was officially agreed that, instead of one species of finless porpoise, there are actually two – now called the narrow-ridged finless porpoise and the Indo-Pacific finless porpoise – which are reproductively isolated and can look sufficiently different to be told apart in the wild. There may ultimately be a third distinct species, living in the Yangtze River.

Classification Odontoceti, family Phocoenidae.
Common name Reflects the relatively narrow dorsal ridge and the lack of a dorsal fin.
Other names Yangtze finless porpoise, East Asian finless porpoise, sunameri, black finless porpoise (resulting from descriptions of dead animals – the colour darkens rapidly after death).
Scientific name *Neos* from the Greek for 'new', *phocaena* from Greek *phokaina* or Latin *phocaena*, meaning 'porpoise'; *asiaeorientalis* refers to the geographical range.
Taxonomy Two subspecies are currently recognised: East Asian finless porpoise or sunameri (*N. a. sunameri*), and Yangtze finless porpoise (*N. a. asiaeorientalis*). However, recent genetic research (using whole-genome sequencing) strongly suggests that the Yangtze finless porpoise is genetically and reproductively isolated from its marine counterpart, and should be considered a unique species; in this case, the narrow-ridged finless porpoise would be split into the East Asian finless porpoise (*N. sunameri*) and the Yangtze finless porpoise (*N. asiaorientalis*).

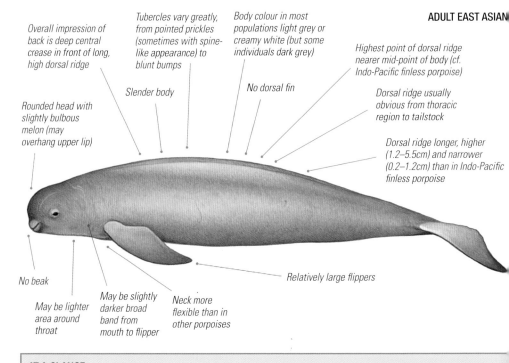

ADULT EAST ASIAN

Overall impression of back is deep central crease in front of long, high dorsal ridge

Tubercles vary greatly, from pointed prickles (sometimes with spine-like appearance) to blunt bumps

Body colour in most populations light grey or creamy white (but some individuals dark grey)

Highest point of dorsal ridge nearer mid-point of body (cf. Indo-Pacific finless porpoise)

Slender body

No dorsal fin

Dorsal ridge usually obvious from thoracic region to tailstock

Rounded head with slightly bulbous melon (may overhang upper lip)

Dorsal ridge longer, higher (1.2–5.5cm) and narrower (0.2–1.2cm) than in Indo-Pacific finless porpoise

No beak

Relatively large flippers

May be lighter area around throat

May be slightly darker broad band from mouth to flipper

Neck more flexible than in other porpoises

AT A GLANCE
- Shallow coastal waters of western North Pacific and Yangtze River
- Small size
- Great individual, geographical and age-related differences in colour (from creamy white to nearly black), but overall coloration usually lighter than in Indo-Pacific finless porpoise
- Distinctive high dorsal ridge instead of dorsal fin
- Lighter individuals superficially resemble small beluga whales
- Rounded head with no beak
- Little disturbance of water (nearly invisible if water rough)
- Usually alone or in small groups

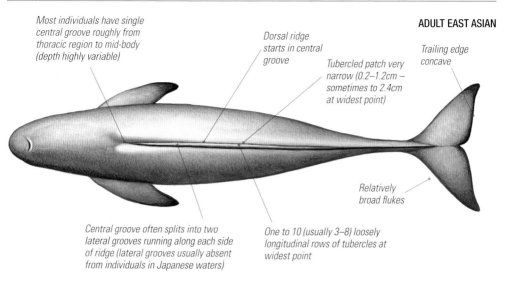

Most individuals have single central groove roughly from thoracic region to mid-body (depth highly variable)

Dorsal ridge starts in central groove

Tubercled patch very narrow (0.2–1.2cm – sometimes to 2.4cm at widest point)

ADULT EAST ASIAN

Trailing edge concave

Relatively broad flukes

Central groove often splits into two lateral grooves running along each side of ridge (lateral grooves usually absent from individuals in Japanese waters)

One to 10 (usually 3–8) loosely longitudinal rows of tubercles at widest point

SIZE

L: 1.6–2.3m; **WT:** 40–70kg; **MAX:** 2.27m, 110kg (East Asian), 1.77m (Yangtze)
Calf – L: 75–85cm; **WT:** 5–10kg
Larger of the two finless porpoise species (except around the Matsu Islands, in the Taiwan Strait); East Asian substantially larger than Yangtze; males larger than females on average.

SIMILAR SPECIES

The lack of a dorsal fin makes it relatively easy to distinguish this species from other cetaceans in the region. To tell it apart from the Indo-Pacific finless porpoise, use the more temperate geographical range (the only overlap is around the Taiwan Strait), narrower dorsal area, position of the apex of the dorsal ridge (further forward), frequently lighter colour and differences in surfacing behaviour. Confusion is most likely with the dugong (which is best identified by the lack of a dorsal ridge, the double nostrils at the tip of the snout, and the very different mouth shape). Bear in mind that the colour darkens quickly after death.

DISTRIBUTION

Yangtze subspecies Middle and lower reaches of the Yangtze River, China. Until recently it was found from the estuary near Shanghai to 1,600km upstream, but the range has contracted dramatically and it no longer occurs beyond Yichang, about 1,000km upstream. Range includes Poyang and Dongting Lakes and Gan and Xiang Rivers. The only porpoise restricted to freshwater (there are no confirmed records from marine waters) and the only extant cetacean in the Yangtze. Preferred habitats include confluences of rivers and lakes, areas adjacent to sand bars and close to riverbanks in the main channel. Distribution changes seasonally.

East Asian subspecies Shallow, cool temperate coastal and estuarine waters of the western North Pacific. Range includes the Taiwan Strait

extralimital record from Okinawa

▓ Yangtze subspecies   ▓ overlap with Indo-Pacific finless porpoise

Narrow-ridged finless porpoise distribution

ADULT EAST ASIAN JAPANESE COLOUR MORPH

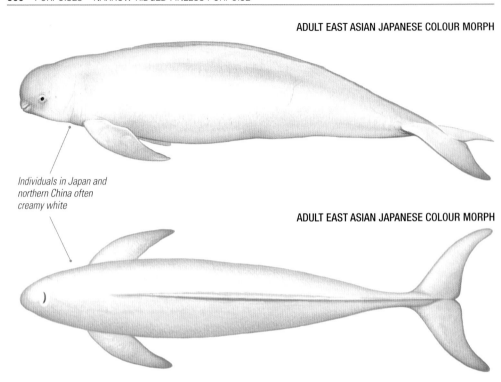

Individuals in Japan and northern China often creamy white

ADULT EAST ASIAN JAPANESE COLOUR MORPH

(especially the Matsu and Kinmen archipelagos), through the East China Sea and Yellow Sea (including the Bohai Sea) north to Korea and Japan. Five distinct populations in the coastal waters of Japan: Omura Bay, Sendai Bay–Tokyo Bay, Inland Sea–Hibiki Nada, Ise Bay–Mikawa Bay and Ariake Sound–Tachibana Bay; one extralimital record from Okinawa Island, southern Japan. Absent from the central Korean Strait, which effectively separates Chinese-Korean populations from Japanese populations. Greatest densities tend to be in shallow bays and near the estuaries of large rivers; may also enter mangrove swamps. Normally in water less than 50m deep, but it has a greater tendency than the Indo-Pacific finless porpoise to occur offshore; populations in the Bohai and Yellow Seas are frequently seen up to 240km from the coast, especially in winter, where the water is less than 200m deep. There appears to be a strong preference for sandy or soft seafloors – relatively small local sub-populations are separated by unsuitable habitats of deep water or rocky bottoms. Seasonal shifts in abundance are reported in some regions. Overlaps in range with the Indo-Pacific finless porpoise only in the Taiwan Strait.

DIVE SEQUENCE
- Surfaces briefly and quietly (for slightly less time than Indo-Pacific finless porpoise), causing little disturbance of water.
- Shows little of body (head occasionally appears above surface in some populations).
- Limited evidence that back tends to maintain a very rounded appearance and continues to roll into dive with little or no discontinuity in movement (cf. Indo-Pacific finless porpoise).
- Typically breathes 3–4 times, then dives for average 30 seconds.

BLOW
- Indistinct blow.

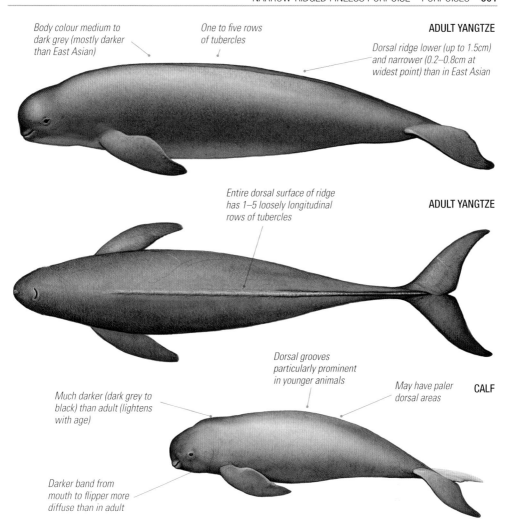

ADULT YANGTZE

Body colour medium to dark grey (mostly darker than East Asian)

One to five rows of tubercles

Dorsal ridge lower (up to 1.5cm) and narrower (0.2–0.8cm at widest point) than in East Asian

ADULT YANGTZE

Entire dorsal surface of ridge has 1–5 loosely longitudinal rows of tubercles

Dorsal grooves particularly prominent in younger animals

May have paler dorsal areas

CALF

Much darker (dark grey to black) than adult (lightens with age)

Darker band from mouth to flipper more diffuse than in adult

BEHAVIOUR

The East Asian subspecies tends to avoid boats in many areas (although it is readily approached by some commercial porpoise-watching trips in Japan), while the Yangtze subspecies is less shy and more used to heavy boat traffic. Does not bow-ride and rarely breaches (although individuals in the Yangtze have been observed leaping from the water and performing 'tail stands'). Generally unobtrusive, but when startled it may escape with splashes not dissimilar to those produced by Dall's porpoises; and, when chasing fish at high speed, it makes sharp turns and rapid accelerations below the surface. Unconfirmed reports of calves riding on the backs of their mothers (apparently lying on the roughened dorsal surface).

TEETH

Upper 32–42

Lower 30–40

Teeth are spatulate, as in all porpoises.

GROUP SIZE AND STRUCTURE

Usually seen as singles, pairs (mother and calf or two adults) or in groups of up to 20. Loose aggregations of up to 50 individuals have been reported in areas with good feeding opportunities.

PREDATORS

Probably killer whales and large sharks.

PHOTO-IDENTIFICATION

No work to date.

FINLESS PORPOISES' FINLESS BACKS

The dorsal surface of finless porpoises is unique – there is nothing else like it on any other living cetacean. Instead of a dorsal fin, there is a structure on the back that runs from just forward of the mid-back to the tailstock. It comprises three key features, which are highly variable between species, populations and individuals (and sometimes absent):

FOOD AND FEEDING
Prey Wide variety of fish, squid, cuttlefish and crustaceans; mainly fish and shrimp in the Yangtze River.
Feeding Unknown.
Dive depth Most populations rarely in water deeper than 50m.
Dive time Maximum four minutes.

1. Dorsal ridge: a long, thin, almost fin-like projection running along the centre of the back.
2. Dorsal grooves: there may be a 'central groove' running along the centre of the back (in front of the dorsal ridge); when a dorsal ridge is clearly present, the central groove splits into separate 'lateral grooves' that run along either side of the ridge.
3. Tubercled patch: the skin along the centre of the dorsal surface may be covered in an extensive area of wart-like protuberances called tubercles (which vary greatly from blunt bumps to pointed prickles and sometimes prickles with a spine-like appearance). These are arranged loosely into longitudinal rows, and more or less run along the entire length of the ridge (if it is present) and onto the tailstock, and sometimes on the skin either side. The purpose of these structures is still unclear.

POPULATION
The total population is unknown. There are rough estimates for the Yangtze River (*c.* 1,000), Japan (*c.* 19,000 in five different populations) and the South Korea–Yellow Sea population (21,500-plus offshore, 5,500-plus inshore).

CONSERVATION
IUCN status: Endangered (2017); Yangtze subspecies Critically Endangered (2012); East Asian subspecies not evaluated separately. Particularly vulnerable to incidental capture in fishing nets – especially gillnets, but also trammel nets and rolling hook longlines – and electro-fishing is a hazard. Other threats include coastal development (especially rampant harbour construction),

extensive modification of coastlines for shrimp farming, disturbance from vessel traffic and vessel strikes, intensive and widespread sand dredging, water development projects, and various forms of pollution (there is evidence of very high levels of toxic contaminants in some individuals). Incidentally caught animals in South Korea (and possibly elsewhere) are sold and consumed fairly widely in some fishing ports. Substantial numbers have also been captured alive for display in marine parks and aquaria. Overall, there has been a decline of at least 30 per cent in the past 50 years (much worse in some areas – there was a decline of 70 per cent from 1978 to 2000 in the Sea of Japan) and this may be threatening the viability of some populations.

The Yangtze subspecies was deliberately exploited for a short period in the late 1950s, but there is no evidence of a large direct hunt today. However, there are fears that it could follow the Yangtze river dolphin to extinction within a decade. Heavy shipping, sand mining, pollution, illegal fishing, dam-building and other threats in the river continue to worsen, and the population has declined from 2,550 in 1991 to fewer than 1,225 in 2006, and to about 1,000 at the last count in 2012; numbers continue to decline by 14 per cent per year. The population is also becoming increasingly fragmented. A translocation project has been underway since 1990, moving captured individuals to safer waterways in Tian-e-zhou (since 1990) and Ji-cheng-yuan (since 2015) oxbows, in an effort to establish secure and self-sustaining populations; there are currently 60 individuals in Tian-e-zhou and eight in Ji-cheng-yuan.

LIFE HISTORY
Sexual maturity Both sexes 3–6 years.
Mating Unknown.
Gestation *c.* 11 months.
Calving Every two years; single calf born mostly March–August, with regional variations (e.g. April–May in Yangtze River, November–December in Kyushu, Japan).
Weaning After 6–7 months.
Lifespan 18–25 years (oldest recorded 33 years).

Close-up of an East Asian finless porpoise's dorsal ridge and tubercled patch.

A rare picture of a Yangtze finless porpoise, photographed in Poyang Lake, China.

INDO-PACIFIC FINLESS PORPOISE
Neophocaena phocaenoides (G. Cuvier, 1829)

The Indo-Pacific finless porpoise is cryptic by nature. Its range overlaps with the similar narrow-ridged finless porpoise, but only in the region in and around the Taiwan Strait, where the two species have been observed within tens of metres of each other.

Classification Odontoceti, family Phocoenidae.
Common name Reflects the main distribution and the lack of a dorsal fin.
Other names Wide-ridged finless porpoise, black finless porpoise (resulting from descriptions of dead animals – the colour darkens rapidly after death).
Scientific name *Neos* from the Greek for 'new', *phocaena* from Greek *phokaina* or Latin *phocaena*, meaning 'porpoise'; *oides* from the Greek *eides*, meaning 'like'.
Taxonomy No recognised subspecies, but regional differences in body size and morphology. Officially split from narrow-ridged finless porpoise in 2009 (intermediates between the two new species have never been reported – they have not interbred since the last major glaciation period 18,000 years ago). Further taxonomic work may reveal as yet unnamed forms, subspecies or even species.

ADULT

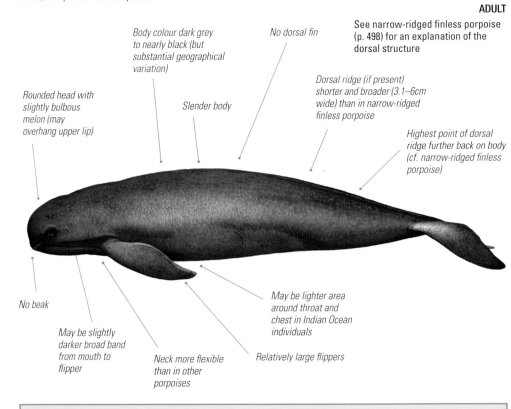

Body colour dark grey to nearly black (but substantial geographical variation)

No dorsal fin

See narrow-ridged finless porpoise (p. 498) for an explanation of the dorsal structure

Dorsal ridge (if present) shorter and broader (3.1–6cm wide) than in narrow-ridged finless porpoise

Rounded head with slightly bulbous melon (may overhang upper lip)

Slender body

Highest point of dorsal ridge further back on body (cf. narrow-ridged finless porpoise)

No beak

May be slightly darker broad band from mouth to flipper

Neck more flexible than in other porpoises

May be lighter area around throat and chest in Indian Ocean individuals

Relatively large flippers

AT A GLANCE
- Shallow, warm coastal and estuarine waters of Indian Ocean and Southeast Asia
- Dark grey to nearly black colour (overall coloration usually darker than narrow-ridged finless porpoise)
- Small size
- No dorsal fin
- Overall impression of back is flattened area in front of short, low dorsal ridge
- Rounded head with no beak
- Little disturbance of water (nearly invisible if water rough)
- Usually alone or in small groups

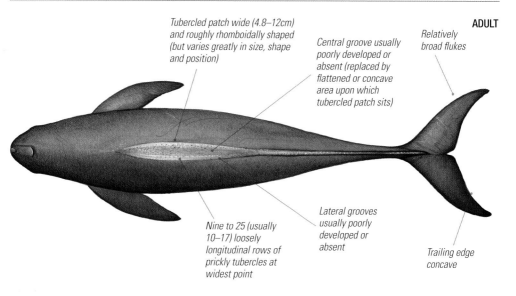

ADULT

Tubercled patch wide (4.8–12cm) and roughly rhomboidally shaped (but varies greatly in size, shape and position)

Central groove usually poorly developed or absent (replaced by flattened or concave area upon which tubercled patch sits)

Relatively broad flukes

Nine to 25 (usually 10–17) loosely longitudinal rows of prickly tubercles at widest point

Lateral grooves usually poorly developed or absent

Trailing edge concave

SIZE
L: 1.4–1.7m; **WT:** 45–50kg; **MAX:** 1.71m, 60kg
Calf – L: 75–85cm; **WT:** 5–10kg
Smaller of the two finless porpoise species (except around the Matsu Islands, in the Taiwan Strait); northern individuals larger than southern; males slightly larger than females on average.

SIMILAR SPECIES
The lack of a dorsal fin makes it relatively easy to distinguish this species from other cetaceans in the region. To tell it apart from the narrow-ridged finless porpoise, use the more tropical geographical range (the only overlap is around the Taiwan Strait), wider dorsal area, position of the apex of the dorsal ridge (further back), predominantly dark colour and differences in surfacing behaviour. Confusion is possible with the dugong (which is best identified by the lack of a dorsal ridge, the double nostrils at the tip of the snout, and the very different mouth shape). Bear in mind that the colour darkens quickly after death.

DISTRIBUTION
Wide (albeit discontinuous) range in a narrow strip of shallow tropical to warm temperate coastal waters in the Indian Ocean and Southeast Asia. More tropical and wide-ranging than the narrow-ridged finless porpoise. The type specimen supposedly came from South Africa (described by Cuvier in 1829), but there are no other records from Africa and its original location was probably mislabelled (more likely, it was from the Malabar coast, India). Likely to occur in Oman and the Philippines, but there are no records to date. Seasonal

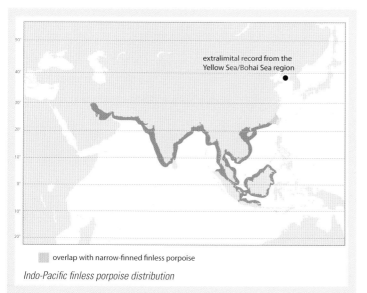

extralimital record from the Yellow Sea/Bohai Sea region

overlap with narrow-finned finless porpoise

Indo-Pacific finless porpoise distribution

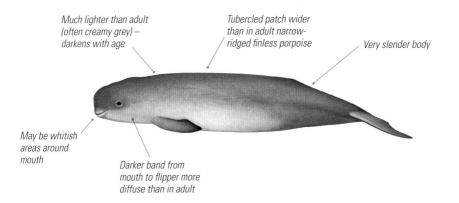

CALF

Much lighter than adult (often creamy grey) – darkens with age

Tubercled patch wider than in adult narrow-ridged finless porpoise

Very slender body

May be whitish areas around mouth

Darker band from mouth to flipper more diffuse than in adult

FOOD AND FEEDING
Prey Wide variety of fish, squid, cuttlefish and crustaceans.
Feeding Unknown.
Dive depth Rarely in water deeper than 50m.
Dive time Typically less than one minute, maximum four minutes.

---

movements are known in some regions (including most Chinese waters) but some populations appear to be predominantly resident. The greatest densities tend to be in shallow bays and the lower reaches of some large rivers, usually in water less than 50m deep. Will enter mangrove swamps and major river systems (up to 40km upstream in the Brahmaputra and 60km upstream in the Indus). There appears to be a strong preference for sandy or soft seafloors – relatively small local sub-populations are separated by unsuitable habitats of deep water or rocky bottoms.

BEHAVIOUR
Tends to avoid boats in many areas and does not bow-ride (though it will occasionally ride in the wake of fast vessels). Rarely breaches. Generally unobtrusive, but when startled it may escape with splashes not dissimilar to those produced by Dall's porpoises; and, when chasing fish at high speed, it makes sharp turns and rapid accelerations below the surface. Unconfirmed reports of calves riding on the backs of their mothers (apparently lying on the roughened dorsal surface).

TEETH
Upper 30–44
Lower 32–44
Teeth are spatulate, as in all porpoises.

GROUP SIZE AND STRUCTURE
Usually seen as singles, pairs (mother and calf or two adults) or in groups of up to 20 (2–5 is most typical). Loose aggregations of 50-plus individuals have been reported in areas with good feeding opportunities (specifically in China).

PREDATORS
Probably killer whales and large sharks.

PHOTO-IDENTIFICATION
No work to date.

DIVE SEQUENCE
- Surfaces briefly and quietly (though for slightly longer than narrow-ridged finless porpoise), causing little disturbance of water and showing little of body.
- Limited evidence that back tends to flatten out and then hang in water briefly before diving (cf. narrow-ridged finless porpoise).
- Typically breathes 3–4 times, then dives for average 30 seconds.

BLOW
- Indistinct blow.

POPULATION

The total population is unknown, but it is likely more than 10,000. There are estimates for Hong Kong (at least 217) and Bangladesh (*c.* 1,400).

CONSERVATION

IUCN status: Vulnerable (2017). No large-scale hunting of this species is known to occur, but it is often killed incidentally in fishing gear – particularly gillnets – throughout its range. There is clear evidence of dramatic declines that may be threatening the viability of some populations (overall, there has been a decline of at least 30 per cent in the past 50 years). Also affected by loss and degradation of habitat, pollution and vessel traffic.

Substantial numbers have been captured alive for display in marine parks and aquaria.

LIFE HISTORY

Sexual maturity Females 5–6 years, males 4–5 years.
Mating Unknown.
Gestation *c.* 11 months.
Calving Every two years; single calf born mainly June–March (October–January in Hong Kong and South China Sea).
Weaning After 6–7 months.
Lifespan 18–25 years (oldest recorded 33 years).

Close-up of an Indo-Pacific finless porpoise's dorsal ridge and tubercled patch.

CARING FOR WHALES, DOLPHINS AND PORPOISES

Human impact has now reached every square kilometre of the Earth's oceans. In particular, commercial whaling and other forms of hunting, entanglement in fishing nets and myriad other conflicts with fisheries, overfishing, pollution, habitat degradation and disturbance, underwater noise, ingestion of marine debris, ship strikes and climate change are some of the main threats being faced by whales, dolphins and porpoises around the world.

The IUCN Red List gives no fewer than 20 species a threatened rating – Critically Endangered, Endangered, Threatened or Vulnerable. A further 43 species (nearly half of all cetaceans) are classified as Data Deficient – we simply do not know enough to judge whether they are in trouble or not (revealing how much remains to be learnt). Two species are not listed, and the remaining minority are either Near Threatened or believed to be relatively safe (classified as Least Concern).

To the best of our knowledge, one cetacean has become extinct in modern times: the Yangtze river dolphin, or baiji, from China. But a frightening number of species are in serious trouble, while others have all but disappeared from many of their former haunts. The vaquita, a tiny porpoise from the extreme northern end of the Gulf of California in western Mexico, could be the next to go; there are probably just 10 survivors clinging on against all the odds.

We nearly lost many of the larger whale species – if we had not stopped killing them at the 11th hour, we could have driven grey whales, blue whales, right whales, bowhead whales and several other species to extinction.

Whalers have killed millions of great whales for profit.

It is estimated that nearly 2.9 million great whales were killed during the period 1990–1999 (276,442 in the North Atlantic, 563,696 in the North Pacific and 2,053,956 in the southern hemisphere). By the time the worst of the slaughter was over, we were left merely with the tattered remains – in many cases, no more than 5–10 per cent of their original populations. Some may never recover. There are still only about 430 North Atlantic right whales, for example, and recent population trends and ongoing threats are so dire that the species could become functionally (reproductively) extinct within 20 years.

Protecting cetaceans is no easy task: they are mobile and ignore political boundaries, and they face many quite complex, insidious and cumulative threats. These days the odds are firmly stacked against them and, for some at least, the future is undoubtedly bleak.

A killer whale lobtailing next to a huge tanker in British Columbia.

Overfishing and fisheries bycatch are major threats to cetaceans.

The Yangtze river dolphin, or baiji, is now extinct.

A humpback whale swims through an oil slick off Iceland.

HOW TO HELP

Volunteer Most conservation groups – large and small – could not survive without the invaluable help of dedicated volunteers. If you have some spare time, there are many ways to lend your support. You could offer half a day, a day or even several days a week to work in your favourite conservation charity's office. Whether you're photocopying, helping to answer letters from enthusiastic children or using your skills as an electrician to rewire the office for free, you'll be helping enormously. How about training to become a marine mammal medic and being on call to help rescue stranded, injured or lost whales, dolphins and porpoises, or helping to clear a beach of all its rubbish? Or, if you are a photographer, for example, donate some pictures to save the organisation the cost of buying them commercially.

Raise urgently needed funds Every conservation group is short of funds. Quite simply, if they had more money they could do more good work. You can raise funds to go into the general money pot (known as 'free funds') or for one particular species, place or project that you feel passionately about. Alternatively, if you don't have the time to organise fundraising events, why not consider adopting a whale or dolphin through one of the many excellent adoption schemes, or make a regular monthly donation by standing order?

Campaign Another great way to help is to support conservation campaigns. Your favourite charities will be able to give you some specific ideas about current campaigns and their websites are usually a good starting point. They might ask you to write a letter or sign a petition, for example, or you could take action about any other issue that is close to your heart.

Raise awareness The more people who are aware of conservation issues – and ultimately care about them – the better. It takes only one individual to educate hundreds of people and to affect the way they see the world. Here are a few ideas: write letters to the national press about environmental stories and issues you feel strongly about, write an article for your local newspaper, offer yourself for an interview on local radio, or give talks or lectures to local clubs and organisations.

Live a green life There are many relatively easy ways to reduce your impact on the world's oceans. For example, ensure that any fish you eat comes from a sustainable fishery with minimal bycatch, reduce the amount of plastic you use and choose who you do business with (don't buy goods that are overpackaged and don't support companies that are involved in harmful practices).

Get involved with research Depending on where you live, there may be opportunities to help directly with conservation or research work. One easy way is to help researchers by sending suitable photographs for their photo-identification catalogues. Fieldwork is expensive, and the larger the catalogues, the more information they can provide. For example, the Antarctic Humpback Whale Catalogue, which investigates the movements of humpbacks from the Southern Ocean to lower-latitude waters, relies on many photographs taken by tourists on expedition cruise ships. A brilliant place to submit ID photographs – and an excellent source of information on what is required – is happywhale.com. Images are forwarded on to relevant regional catalogues, and photographers are informed of any matches made with the whales in their pictures. Check how the species needs to be photographed – the underside of its tail, for example, or one particular side of its body – and do not forget to include your name and address, the date, the location of the sighting (ideally, the exact coordinates), the name of the vessel from which the photographs were taken and any other relevant information.

Whatever you are able to do, it all helps.

GLOSSARY

abyssal plain Ocean floor beyond the continental shelf, where the sea is generally more than 1,000m deep. Usually flat or gently sloping.

aerial behaviour Any behaviour that involves part or all of the animal leaving the water.

ambergris Dark greyish waxy substance formed in the intestines of sperm whales, once widely used in perfumes.

amphipod Small shrimp-like crustacean that is a food source for some whales.

anchor patch Variable grey or white anchor- or W-shaped patch on the chest of some smaller toothed whales.

Antarctic Convergence Natural oceanic boundary in the Antarctic, where cold, less saline waters from the south sink below warmer, more saline waters from the north; considered the northern limit of 'biological Antarctica'; lying roughly between 50°S and 60°S, its position varies according to location, and shifts from year to year and with the seasons. Otherwise known as the 'Polar Front'.

balaenopterid Member of the baleen whale family Balaenopteridae, otherwise known as a 'rorqual'.

baleen plate Dense comb-like structure hanging down from the upper jaws of most large whales (baleen whales in the Mysticeti); formerly known as 'whalebone'. Made of keratin (the same protein that makes hair, nails and rhino horn). Hundreds of baleen plates are packed tightly together, with fibrous fringes along the inner surfaces, to form a giant sieve for filter-feeding small prey.

baleen whale Member of the Mysticeti; a predominantly large whale with baleen plates instead of teeth.

bathypelagic Inhabiting the deepwater portion of the open ocean, 1,000–4,000m below the surface.

beak Elongated snout of many cetaceans; anterior portion of the skull that includes both the upper and lower jaws.

benthic Living in, on or just above the ocean floor.

benthic amphipod Shrimp-like crustacean that lives buried in seabed sediment.

blackfish Colloquial term for a group of six superficially similar members of the dolphin family (killer whale, false killer whale, pygmy killer whale, melon-headed whale, short-finned pilot whale and long-finned pilot whale).

blaze Light streaking, usually grey or white, on the side of a cetacean's body; it usually starts below the dorsal fin and points up into the cape.

blow Refers both to the act of breathing – the explosive exhalation followed immediately by an inhalation – and to the visible misty cloud of water droplets (condensed water, a fine spray of mucus from inside the lungs, and seawater trapped in the blowholes) formed when a whale breathes; also known as a spout.

blowhole Respiratory opening, or nostril, on the top of the head of a cetacean; baleen whales have two blowholes, toothed whales have one.

blubber Layer of fatty tissue between the skin and underlying muscle of most marine mammals; important for insulation, instead of (or as well as) fur.

bow-riding Swimming or 'riding' on the pressure wave created in front of a boat or ship (or, sometimes, a large whale).

breaching Leaping completely (or almost completely) out of the water. Officially, if more than 40 per cent of the whale's body leaves the water, it is termed a 'breach', otherwise it is a 'lunge'.

bubble-netting Feeding technique used by humpback whales in which they produce fishing nets by blowing bubbles underwater.

bycatch Animals that are caught accidentally or incidentally during fishing operations (when they are not the target species of the fishery).

callosity Area of roughened, keratinised tissue on the head of a right whale, inhabited by large numbers of whale lice.

caudal fin Tail fin.

caudal peduncle *See* 'tailstock'.

cephalopod Member of a group of benthic or swimming molluscs, including squid, cuttlefish and octopuses; the shell can be external, internal or absent.

cetacean Any mammalian member of the Cetacea, a group of aquatic mammals that includes all whales, dolphins and porpoises.

chevron V- or U-shaped light-coloured marking on the back or sides of a cetacean.

continental shelf Area of the seafloor around the edge of a continent; it slopes gently from the coastline to a drop-off point called the 'shelf break' or 'shelf edge' (from there, the seafloor drops steeply, via the 'continental slope', to the ocean bottom). The width of continental shelves varies greatly from less than 1km to 1,290km (with an average of about 65km); water depth averages 60m and is rarely more than 200m. The actual boundary of a continent is the edge of its continental shelf (not its coastline).

continental slope Stretch of the ocean floor that drops steeply between the 'shelf break' and the 'abyssal plain'; like a giant cliff or ridge, it is often where cetaceans (and other wildlife) concentrate in greater numbers.

cookiecutter shark Small shark (up to 50cm) normally found in sub-tropical and tropical waters that takes bites out of marine mammals (each about the size of an ice-cream scoop – typically 4–8cm in diameter); the resulting bite wounds (sometimes dubbed 'crater wounds') appear as round or oval lacerations.

copepod Minute shrimp-like crustacean (usually planktonic) that occurs in great abundance in the sea and is an important food source for some whales; dubbed the 'fleas of the sea'.

crustacean Member of a group of nearly 70,000 invertebrates (animals without backbones), and including lobsters, crabs, shrimps and barnacles, that breathes via gills (or similar structures); characterised by a segmented body, chitinous exoskeleton, jointed limbs and two pairs of antennae. Mostly aquatic, crustaceans are an important source of food for many marine animals.

decapod Literally '10-legged'; member of a group of more than 8,000 species of crustaceans, including crayfish, crabs, lobsters, prawns and shrimp.

delphinid Member of the oceanic dolphin family Delphinidae.

deep scattering layer (DSL) A dense layer up to 200m thick of huge numbers of small fish, squid, crustaceans and plankton, occurring in open oceans worldwide, which migrate up and down the water column within a single 24-hour period. They rest and float in mid-water at great depth (typically 400–600m) during the day, then rise closer to the surface around sunset and sink back down at dawn; they generally avoid light (the layer is deeper when the moon is bright). It is so called because it reflects, or scatters, the signals of echo sounders (sometimes giving the impression of a false seafloor).

demersal Lives near the seafloor.

diatom Microscopic single-celled algae, abundant in marine and freshwater environments, with cell walls made of silica; they often form a film that coats the bodies of some cetaceans, giving them a yellowish, brownish or even greenish tinge.

dorsal Pertaining to the upper surface or the back (or the upper surface of any other body part).

dorsal cape Distinct dark region on the backs of some toothed whales, dolphins and porpoises, mostly in front of the dorsal fin (sometimes stretching to behind it) and dipping onto the sides to varying degrees; not to be confused with the saddle patch.

dorsal fin Raised structure on the back of most (but not all) cetaceans (and various other, unrelated, marine and freshwater vertebrates); not supported by bone.

dorsal ridge Ridge on the back as well as, or instead of, a dorsal fin; may refer to the ridges on the top of the rostrum in many baleen whales.

driftnet Fishing net that hangs in the water vertically, virtually unseen and undetectable, and is carried freely with the ocean currents and winds; a gillnet that is not anchored. Dubbed a 'wall of death', it is notorious for catching everything in its path, from seabirds and turtles to whales and dolphins.

drive fishery Technique used to capture dolphins and other small toothed whales, usually using speedboats to herd them into a bay or shallow water; a net is then drawn across the mouth of the bay to prevent their escape, before the fishermen/hunters wade into the water to kill the animals.

eastern boundary current Found on the eastern side of oceanic basins, adjacent to the western coasts of continents, and flowing from high latitudes towards the tropics; relatively cold, shallow, broad and slow-flowing. They tend to have more nutrient-rich upwellings than western boundary currents, making them more productive.

echolocation Process of sending out high-frequency sounds and interpreting the returning echoes to build up a 'sound picture', as in sonar; used by many cetaceans to orientate, navigate and find food.

ecotype Term used to recognise scientific uncertainty with regard to systematics and speciation in killer whales (and, to a lesser degree, some other species); it recognises a work in progress, avoiding the immediate need to declare subspecies or species.

El Niño Complex global weather pattern marked by rising sea temperatures in the central and eastern tropical Pacific Ocean; South American fishermen coined the term to describe the appearance of warmer than normal coastal waters every few years around Christmas (El Niño means 'boy child' in Spanish – a reference to baby Jesus).

epipelagic Living within 200m of the surface in pelagic waters.

estrous *See* 'oestrous'.

euphausiid Any member of the order Euphausiacea, which comprises 86 known species of shrimp-like creatures called krill.

extirpated Ceasing to exist in a geographical area that a species formerly occupied (while continuing to exist elsewhere).

extralimital Occurrence of a species outside its normal range.

falcate Sickle-shaped or back-curved; often used to describe the shape of a dorsal fin with a concave rear margin.

fast ice Stable sea ice attached to land; sometimes extends out from shore for many kilometres.

filter-feeding Technique used by baleen whales to strain small prey animals from the water, using baleen plates.

flipper Variably shaped, flattened, paddle-like forelimb of a cetacean (also known as the 'pectoral fin' or 'pec fin').

flipper pocket Depression on each side of a beaked whale, where it tucks its flippers; sperm whales have less pronounced pockets; the feature might be linked with deep diving (probably to reduce drag).

flipper-slapping Lying on the back or side, raising one or both flippers out of the water and then slapping it/them onto the surface. Otherwise known as 'flipper-flopping', 'flippering', 'pectoral-slapping' or 'pec-slapping'.

fluke (noun) Horizontally flattened tail of a cetacean (in contrast to the vertically flattened tail of a fish); two flukes comprise a cetacean's tail.

fluke (verb) *See* 'fluking'.

fluking Natural extension of a deep or sounding dive – the whale bends its body towards the seabed and, as it rolls forward and down, the tail flukes automatically rise above the surface; larger, more rotund whales, such as humpback, right, bowhead, grey and sperm (and some blue) fluke regularly; slimmer whales never fluke, or do so only rarely.

flukeprint A circular swirl of smooth water that looks rather like a sheen of oil – made by the downward movement of the tail creating a vortex – which is left on the surface after a whale has dived.

fluke-slapping *See* 'lobtailing'.

gillnet A fishing net that is suspended vertically in the water and ensnares fish by the gill covers (or other parts of their body) as they try to back out of its meshes; usually used near the coast or in a river. Responsible for a huge amount of bycatch of dolphins and porpoises.

great whale Any large whale (including all the baleen whales and the sperm whale).

gulp-feeding Technique used by some baleen whales, lunging at prey patches and taking a mouthful at a time; especially effective when feeding on schooling fish and krill.

head-slap When a whale lunges partially out of the water and forcefully slaps its throat onto the surface with a large splash; also known as a 'chin-slap'.

home range Area that an animals patrols regularly.

hydrophone Waterproofed underwater microphone used to detect whale (and other) sounds.

infrasonic Low-frequency sound, below the normal range of human hearing (lower than 20Hz).

interspecific Between individuals of different species.

intraspecific Between individuals of the same species.

isobath Imaginary line on a chart connecting all the points with the same depth underwater (rather like an underwater contour line); e.g. the 200m isobath connects all points with a depth of 200m.

IWC International Whaling Commission; in 1946, whalers adopted the International Convention for the Regulation of Whaling for the 'orderly development of the whaling industry'; the IWC was established at the same time, as the convention's decision-making body, and it has attempted to regulate whaling (and, more recently, conserve whales) ever since.

keel Distinctive bulge (a deepening or thickening) on the tailstock near the flukes; it can be dorsal, ventral or both. On the underside, it is also known as a 'post-anal hump'.

kleptoparasitism Literally, parasitism by theft; it frequently involves stealing captured prey.

krill Small shrimp-like crustacean, making up a large proportion of the ocean's zooplankton, which is a major food source for many large whales; there are about 86 different species, ranging from 8–60mm in length. Also known as a 'euphausiid'.

lactation Production of milk by a female mammal to feed its young.

lamprey Primitive jawless fish, resembling an eel, with a permanently open mouth and a great number of teeth. There are 43 known species, 18 of which are parasitic (they bore into the flesh of cetaceans and other animals and suck their blood); mainly in temperate waters.

La Niña Complex global weather pattern marked by falling sea temperatures in the central and eastern tropical Pacific Ocean; often follows an 'El Niño'.

lateral On the side of the body.

latitude Measure of the relative position of a place on Earth north or south of the equator; measurements range from 0° at the equator to 90°N at the North Pole and 90°S at the South Pole; one degree of latitude is about 111km. 'High latitudes' are generally poleward of *c.* 60°N or 60°S, 'low latitudes' are within *c.* 30°N or 30°S of the equator.

leaping Breaching (leaping out of the water) when performed by dolphins and other smaller toothed whales.

lobtailing Lifting the tail clear of the water and then slapping it down onto the surface, usually repeatedly and often quite forcibly; also known as 'tail-lobbing' or 'fluke-slapping'. 'Tail-slapping' is a similar behaviour, though normally associated with smaller cetaceans.

logging Lying at or just below the surface, inactive and usually horizontally, to rest.

longline Very long fishing line, armed with multiple baited hooks on shorter branch lines attached at intervals along its length; set to catch large pelagic fish such as swordfish, tuna, halibut and sharks. It can be tens of kilometres long, with several thousand hooks, and is responsible for significant bycatch of dolphins and other species.

lunging Officially, if less than 40 per cent of the whale's body leaves the water, it is termed a 'lunge', otherwise it is a 'breach'; lunges are sometimes called 'half-breaches' or 'belly-flops' – which describe the behaviour perfectly.

mandible Entire lower jaw.

matrilineal A relationship, behaviour or other characteristic that can be traced along the female (maternal) line.

maxillary Bone in the upper jaw that bears teeth.

melon Bulging fatty tissue that forms the 'forehead' of toothed cetaceans, believed to be used to focus and modulate sounds for echolocation.

mesopelagic Inhabiting the intermediate depths of the open ocean, typically at 200–1,000m; because food is scarce in this zone, most mesopelagic organisms migrate to the surface to feed at night or live off falling detritus from the upper zone. It is beneath the 'epipelagic' zone and above the 'bathypelagic' zone.

mesoplodont Beaked whale belonging to the genus *Mesoplodon*.

mouthline From the front tip of the jaws to the corner of the mouth.

mysid Small shrimp-like crustacean in the order Mysida (with *c.* 1,200 species); also known as an 'opossum shrimp', because the female carries the fertilised eggs in a pouch; mostly benthic, and eaten by some whales, such as grey and bowhead.

Mysticeti One of two major groups of cetaceans, containing all the toothless or baleen whales (known as mysticetes).

nektonic Marine (and freshwater) animals that can swim freely and are generally independent of the currents and waves; includes fish, turtles and cetaceans.

oceanic Open sea environment beyond the edge of the continental shelf.

Odontoceti One of two major groups of cetaceans, containing all the toothed whales, dolphins and porpoises (known as odontocetes).

oestrous Regularly occurring period of sexual receptivity in most female mammals (including cetaceans, but not including humans), during which ovulation occurs and copulation can take place; 'in oestrous' is the same as 'in heat'.

offshore Well away from the coast.

parasite Organism that lives in or on another organism (the host) at the other's expense (usually without going so far as to cause the host's death); it obtains nourishment and protection, while offering no benefit in return.

PCBs Otherwise known as polychlorinated biphenyls. PCBs are a group of artificially-made chemicals resistant to extreme temperature and pressure, with many industrial applications. Despite being banned in many countries since the 1970s and 80s, about 10 per cent of the two million tonnes of PCBs produced still remains in the environment (it does not readily break down) where it is harmful to wildlife and people.

pectoral fin *See* 'flipper'.

pectoral slap *See* 'flipper-slapping'.

peduncle *See* 'tailstock'.

peduncle slapping *See* 'tail breaching'.

pelagic Inhabiting offshore waters of the open ocean beyond the continental shelf, and usually used to describe animals and plants that live in upper portions of the water column; neither near to the coast, nor close to the bottom.

pelagic trawl Bag-like cone-shaped net that is towed through the mid- and upper part of the water column (away from the seafloor).

photo-identification (photo-ID) Technique for studying cetaceans using photographs as a permanent record of identifiable individuals.

phytoplankton Plant form of 'plankton'.

pinger Acoustic deterrent designed to alert cetaceans to the presence of fishing nets, to limit bycatch; usually a small battery-powered device attached at intervals along a net that emits a repeated signal.

plankton Passively floating, or weakly swimming, plant and animal life that occurs in swarms, usually near the surface of open waters.

pod Coordinated group of closely related killer whales; the term is also used for any group of socially affiliated, medium-sized toothed whales.

polar Region around either the North Pole or South Pole (i.e. the Arctic or Antarctic); characterised by cold and often ice-covered waters.

Polar Front *See* 'Antarctic Convergence'.

polygynous Breeding system in which dominant males usually mate with multiple females.

polynya Russian word for 'open water surrounded by ice'; large area of water within the pack ice that remains open throughout the year; often provides refuge for air-breathing cetaceans.

polychaete Tube-dwelling marine worm in the class Polychaeta that lives in dense colonies in the upper few centimetres of seabed sediments; a favourite prey of grey whales, and some other cetaceans.

porpoising When members of the dolphin family (and, less commonly, some other cetaceans) travel at high speed and make low, arcing leaps clear of the water every time they take a breath, before re-entering headfirst; it is sometimes called 'running'.

purse-seine net Vertical curtain of netting set around a shoal of fish, then gathered at the bottom and drawn in to form a 'purse' to prevent the fish from escaping; responsible for killing more dolphins in the past 50 years than any other human activity (though new rules and regulations have reduced bycatch substantially).

rake marks Scarring produced by teeth during intraspecific fighting (usually between males) or from attacks by killer whales (recognisable by three or more parallel lines or marks in close proximity, usually on the flukes, flippers or dorsal fin); sharks produce more arc-shaped, jagged scars.

remora Type of fish that has modified its dorsal fin into a sucker (thus the alternative names 'sharksucker', 'whalesucker' or 'suckerfish') to attach onto large marine animals such as whales and dolphins (and anything else in the water, from turtles to submarines).

rorqual Baleen whale in the family Balaenopteridae, characterised by a variable number of pleats or grooves that run longitudinally from the chin towards the navel; the pleats expand during feeding to increase the capacity of the mouth; the name comes from the Norwegian word rørkval, meaning 'the whale with pleats' (after the grooves); otherwise known as a 'balaenopterid'.

rostrum Beak-like projection at the front of the head of a cetacean; also used specifically to describe the upper jaw.

saddle patch Light-coloured, more-or-less saddle-shaped marking that straddles the back behind the dorsal fin of some cetaceans, extending to a variable degree onto the sides; sometimes just called the 'saddle'; not to be confused with the dorsal cape.

school Term for a coordinated group, normally used in association with dolphins, that swims and socialises together; often used synonymously with 'herd'.

seamount Underwater mountain, typically rising more than 1,000m above the surrounding deep-sea floor; usually an extinct volcano, with the summit some way beneath the surface; attracts an abundance of marine life.

sexually dimorphic When males and females of the same species differ in size or appearance; the sperm whale is an extreme example.

shelf break Drop-off point at the edge of the continental shelf (from there, the seafloor drops steeply, via the 'continental slope', to the ocean bottom); also called the 'shelf edge'.

shelf seas Seas over the 'continental shelf'.

skim-feeding Technique used by some baleen whales that involves swimming slowly with the mouth open and constantly filtering food from the water, typically along or just below the surface; especially effective when feeding on small zooplankton such as copepods (only a few millimetres in size).

slope waters Seas over the 'continental slope'.

snout *See* 'beak'.

sonar *See* 'echolocation'.

sounding dive Deep (and usually longer) dive after a series of shallow dives; also known as the 'terminal dive'.

splashguard Elevated fleshy ridge immediately in front of the blowholes of a baleen whale, which helps to prevent water from pouring in when the blowholes are open; it is strikingly large on a blue whale.

spout *See* 'blow'.

spyhopping When a whale raises its head vertically out of the water, usually exposing the eyes to the air, before sinking smoothly below the surface without much splash. The animal will sometimes rotate slowly, apparently to scan the surrounding area visually; it is sometimes known as a 'head rise' or an 'eye-out'.

stranding The act of coming ashore, intentionally or accidentally, alive or dead.

submarine canyon Underwater canyon; deep, narrow, steep-sided valley cut into the seabed.

tail breaching Throwing the rear portion of the body, including the flukes, high out of the water and sideways across the surface, creating a huge splash; otherwise known as a 'peduncle-throw', 'peduncle slap' or 'rear-body throw'.

tail extending Raising the tail slowly into the air (usually high enough that the genital area is above the surface) and holding it there for some time; right, bowhead and grey whales may do this for several minutes at a time.

tail lobbing *See* 'lobtailing'.

tail-slapping *See* 'lobtailing'.

tailstock Muscular region of the tail between the dorsal fin and the flukes; also called the 'caudal peduncle' or 'peduncle'.

temperate Mid-latitude regions of the world, between the sub-tropical and sub-polar regions, characterised by a mild, seasonally changing climate; cold temperate regions are towards the poles, warm temperate regions towards the tropics.

throat grooves V-shaped grooves (deep folds in the skin and blubber) on the throat, characteristic of beaked whales and grey whales.

throat pleats Longitudinal parallel furrows or grooves on the underside of many baleen whales (backward from the chin) that allow the throat to expand when engulfing huge quantities of water to capture prey; also known as 'ventral pleats'.

toothed whale *See* 'Odontoceti'.

tropical Low-latitude regions of the world, between the Tropic of Capricorn (23°27'S) and the Tropic of Cancer (23°27'N), characterised by a warm climate and with just two seasons (wet and dry).

tubercle Circular raised protuberance, or bump, found on some cetaceans (usually along the edges of pectoral and dorsal fins, but also on a humpback whale's head).

turbid Term used to describe water with poor visibility because of the presence of sediment or other suspended matter.

ultrasonic High-frequency sound, above the normal range of human hearing (higher than 20kHz).

upwelling Process by which ocean water rises from the depths, forced by currents, winds or density gradients; this brings nutrients (the result of ocean animals and plants dying, sinking to the seabed and decaying to form marine compost) to the surface; water near the surface is relatively devoid of nutrients but is exposed to sunlight (the other key ingredient in photosynthesis); the combination of sunlight and nutrients leads to growth of phytoplankton and increased production; it occurs most dramatically along the edges of continental shelves and submarine canyons.

urogenital area Portion of the underside around and near the excretory and genital orifices.

wake-riding Swimming in the frothy wake of a boat or ship.

water column Anywhere between the surface and the seafloor.

western boundary current Found on the western side of oceanic basins, adjacent to the eastern coasts of continents and flowing from the tropics to high latitudes; relatively warm, deep, narrow and fast-flowing; tends to have fewer nutrient-rich upwellings than eastern boundary currents, making it less productive.

whalebone See 'baleen plate'.

whale louse An amphipod crustacean (not an insect) adapted to living on the skin of cetaceans.

zooplankton Animal form of 'plankton'.

SPECIES CHECKLIST

MYSTICETI (BALEEN WHALES)

Right and bowhead whales (family Balaenidae)

❏ North Atlantic right whale (*Eubalaena glacialis*)

❏ North Pacific right whale (*Eubalaena japonica*)

❏ Southern right whale (*Eubalaena australis*)

❏ Bowhead whale (*Balaena mysticetus*)

Pygmy right whale (family Neobalaenidae)

❏ Pygmy right whale (*Caperea marginata*)

Grey whale (family Eschrichtiidae)

❏ Grey whale (*Eschrichtius robustus*)

Rorquals (family Balaenopteridae)

❏ Blue whale (*Balaenoptera musculus*)

❏ Fin whale (*Balaenoptera physalus*)

❏ Sei whale (*Balaenoptera borealis*)

❏ Bryde's whale (*Balaenoptera edeni*)

❏ Omura's whale (*Balaenoptera omurai*)

❏ Common minke whale (*Balaenoptera acutorostrata*)

❏ Antarctic minke whale (*Balaenoptera bonaerensis*)

❏ Humpback whale (*Megaptera novaeangliae*)

ODONTOCETI (TOOTHED WHALES)

Sperm whale (family Physeteridae)

❏ Sperm whale (*Physeter macrocephalus*)

Pygmy and dwarf sperm whales (family Kogiidae)

❏ Pygmy sperm whale (*Kogia breviceps*)

❏ Dwarf sperm whale (*Kogia sima*)

Narwhal and beluga (family Monodontidae)

❏ Narwhal (*Monodon monoceros*)

❏ Beluga whale (*Delphinapterus leucas*)

Beaked whales (family Ziphiidae)

❏ Baird's beaked whale (*Berardius bairdii*)

❏ Arnoux's beaked whale (*Berardius arnuxii*)

❏ Dwarf Baird's beaked whale (*Berardius* sp.)

❏ Cuvier's beaked whale (*Ziphius cavirostris*)

❏ Northern bottlenose whale (*Hyperoodon ampullatus*)

❏ Southern bottlenose whale (*Hyperoodon planifrons*)

❏ Shepherd's beaked whale (*Tasmacetus shepherdi*)

❏ Longman's beaked whale (*Indopacetus pacificus*)

❏ Perrin's beaked whale (*Mesoplodon perrini*)

❏ Peruvian beaked whale (*Mesoplodon peruvianus*)

❏ Deraniyagala's beaked whale (*Mesoplodon hotaula*)

❏ Gray's beaked whale (*Mesoplodon grayi*)

❏ Ginkgo-toothed beaked whale (*Mesoplodon ginkgodens*)

❏ Hector's beaked whale (*Mesoplodon hectori*)

❏ Hubbs' beaked whale (*Mesoplodon carlhubbsi*)

❏ Blainville's beaked whale (*Mesoplodon densirostris*)

❏ Sowerby's beaked whale (*Mesoplodon bidens*)

❏ True's beaked whale (*Mesoplodon mirus*)

❏ Stejneger's beaked whale (*Mesoplodon stejnegeri*)

❏ Gervais' beaked whale (*Mesoplodon europaeus*)

❏ Andrews' beaked whale (*Mesoplodon bowdoini*)

❏ Strap-toothed beaked whale (*Mesoplodon layardii*)

❏ Spade-toothed whale (*Mesoplodon traversii*)

Marine dolphins (family Delphinidae)

❏ Killer whale (*Orcinus orca*)

❏ Short-finned pilot whale (*Globicephala macrorhynchus*)

❏ Long-finned pilot whale (*Globicephala melas*)

❏ False killer whale (*Pseudorca crassidens*)

❏ Pygmy killer whale (*Feresa attenuata*)

❏ Melon-headed whale (*Peponocephala electra*)

❏ Risso's dolphin (*Grampus griseus*)

❏ Fraser's dolphin (*Lagenodelphis hosei*)

❏ Atlantic white-sided dolphin (*Lagenorhynchus acutus*)

❏ Pacific white-sided dolphin (*Lagenorhynchus obliquidens*)

❏ Dusky dolphin (*Lagenorhynchus obscurus*)

❏ Hourglass dolphin (*Lagenorhynchus cruciger*)

❏ White-beaked dolphin (*Lagenorhynchus albirostris*)

❏ Peale's dolphin (*Lagenorhynchus australis*)

❏ Chilean dolphin (*Cephalorhynchus eutropia*)

❏ Commerson's dolphin (*Cephalorhynchus commersonii*)

❏ Heaviside's dolphin (*Cephalorhynchus heavisidii*)

❏ Hector's dolphin (*Cephalorhynchus hectori*)

❏ Northern right whale dolphin (*Lissodelphis borealis*)

❏ Southern right whale dolphin (*Lissodelphis peronii*)

❏ Australian snubfin dolphin (*Orcaella heinsohni*)

❏ Irrawaddy dolphin (*Orcaella brevirostris*)

❏ Rough-toothed dolphin (*Steno bredanensis*)

❏ Atlantic humpback dolphin (*Sousa teuszii*)

❏ Indo-Pacific humpback dolphin (*Sousa chinensis*)

❏ Indian Ocean humpback dolphin (*Sousa plumbea*)

❏ Australian humpback dolphin (*Sousa sahulensis*)

❏ Common bottlenose dolphin (*Tursiops truncatus*)

❏ Indo-Pacific bottlenose dolphin (*Tursiops aduncus*)

❏ Pantropical spotted dolphin (*Stenella attenuata*)

❏ Atlantic spotted dolphin (*Stenella frontalis*)

❏ Spinner dolphin (*Stenella longirostris*)

❏ Clymene dolphin (*Stenella clymene*)

❏ Striped dolphin (*Stenella coeruleoalba*)

❏ Common dolphin (*Delphinus delphis*)

❏ Tucuxi (*Sotalia fluviatilis*)

❏ Guiana dolphin (*Sotalia guianensis*)

South Asian river dolphin (family Platanistidae)

❏ South Asian river dolphin (*Platanista gangetica*)

Amazon river dolphin (family Iniidae)

❏ Amazon river dolphin (*Inia geoffrensis*)

Franciscana (family Pontoporiidae)

❏ Franciscana (*Pontoporia blainvillei*)

Yangtze river dolphin (family Lipotidae)

❏ Yangtze river dolphin (*Lipotes vexillifer*)

Porpoises (family Phocoenidae)

❏ Dall's porpoise (*Phocoenoides dalli*)

❏ Harbour porpoise (*Phocoena phocoena*)

❏ Vaquita (*Phocoena sinus*)

❏ Burmeister's porpoise (*Phocoena spinipinnis*)

❏ Spectacled porpoise (*Phocoena dioptrica*)

❏ Narrow-ridged finless porpoise (*Neophocaena asiaeorientalis*)

❏ Indo-Pacific finless porpoise (*Neophocaena phocaenoides*)

CONVERSION UNITS

°C	°F
0	32.0
1	33.8
2	35.6
3	37.4
4	39.2
5	41.0
6	42.8
7	44.6
8	46.4
9	48.2
10	50.0
11	51.8
12	53.6
13	55.4

°C	°F
14	57.2
15	59.0
16	60.8
17	62.6
18	64.4
19	66.2
20	68.0
21	69.8
22	71.6
23	73.4
24	75.2
25	77.0
26	78.8
27	80.6

°C	°F
28	82.4
29	84.2
30	86.0
31	87.8
32	89.6
33	91.4
34	93.2
35	95.0
36	96.8
37	98.6
38	100.4
39	102.2
40	104.0

METRES	FEET
1	3.3
2	6.6
3	9.8
4	13.1
5	16.4
6	19.7
7	23.0
8	26.2
9	29.5
10	32.8
11	36.1
12	39.4
13	42.7
14	45.9
15	49.2
16	52.5
17	55.8

METRES	FEET
18	59.1
19	62.3
20	65.6
30	98.4
40	131.2
50	164.0
100	328.1
200	656.2
300	984.3
400	1,312.3
500	1,640.4
600	1,968.5
700	2,296.6
800	2,624.7
900	2,952.8
1,000	3,280.8

KM	MILES
1	0.6
2	1.2
3	1.9
4	2.5
5	3.1
6	3.7
7	4.4
8	5.0
9	5.6
10	6.2
20	12.4
30	18.6
40	24.9
50	31.1
100	62.1
200	124.3
300	186.4

KM	MILES
400	248.6
500	310.7
600	372.8
700	435.0
800	497.1
900	559.2
1,000	621.4

KG	LBS
1	2.2
2	4.4
3	6.6
4	8.8
5	11.0
6	13.2
7	15.4
8	17.6
9	19.8
10	22.0
20	44.1
30	66.1
40	88.2
50	110.2
60	132.3
70	154.3
80	176.4
90	198.4
100	220.5

TONNE	TON (IMPERIAL)	TON (US)
1	1.0	1.1
2	2.0	2.2
3	3.0	3.4
4	3.9	4.4
5	4.9	5.5
6	5.9	6.6
7	6.9	7.7
8	7.9	8.8
9	8.9	10.0
10	9.8	11.0
20	19.7	22.0
30	29.5	33.0
40	39.4	44.1
50	49.2	55.1
60	59.1	66.2
70	68.9	77.2
80	78.7	88.1
90	88.6	99.2
100	98.4	110.2

SOURCES AND RESOURCES

I am very grateful to the innumerable scientists who have spent countless hours, days, months and years at sea, and in the laboratory, progressing our knowledge of cetaceans. I have read many thousands of their scientific papers during the preparation of this field guide, which represents the combined work of all these remarkable people. A comprehensive catalogue of so many references would more than double the size of the book so, unfortunately, it is impossible to list them all. But here is a small and varied selection of good websites and books for further reading.

WEBSITES

Society for Marine Mammalogy – marinemammalscience.org (Committee on Taxonomy 2018 List of Marine Mammal Species and Subspecies)

American Cetacean Society – acsonline.org

European Cetacean Society – europeancetaceansociety.eu

ORCA – orcaweb.org.uk

Whale and Dolphin Conservation – uk.whales.org

Marine Conservation Society – mcsuk.org

Red Data List – iucnredlist.org

NOAA Fisheries – fisheries.noaa.gov/whales

Happy Whale – happywhale.com

BOOKS

Baird, R. W. 2016. *The Lives of Hawai'i's Dolphins and Whales: Natural History and Conservation.* University of Hawaii Press.

Berta, A., J. L. Sumich and K. M. Kovacs. 2015 (Third Edition). *Marine Mammals: Evolutionary Biology.* Academic Press.

Bortolotti, D. 2009. *Wild Blue: A Natural History of the World's Largest Animal.* Thomas Allen Publishers.

Brakes, P. and M. P. Simmonds. 2011. *Whales and Dolphins: Cognition, Culture, Conservation and Human Perceptions.* Earthscan.

Burns, J. J., J. J. Montague, and C. J. Cowles (eds). 1993. *The Bowhead Whale.* Society for Marine Mammalogy.

Carwardine, M. 2016 (Second Edition). *Mark Carwardine's Guide to Whale Watching in Britain and Europe.* Bloomsbury.

Carwardine, M. 2017. *Mark Carwardine's Guide to Whale Watching in North America: USA, Canada, Mexico.* Bloomsbury.

Darling, J. 2009. *Humpbacks: Unveiling the Mysteries.* Granville Island Publishing.

Ellis, R. 2011. *The Great Sperm Whale: A Natural History of the Ocean's Most Magnificent and Mysterious Creature.* University Press of Kansas.

Ellis, R. and J. G. Mead. 2017. *Beaked Whales: A Complete Guide to their Biology and Conservation.* Johns Hopkins University Press.

Fitzhugh, W. W. and M. T. Nweeia (eds). 2017. *Narwhal: Revealing an Arctic Legend.* IPI Press & Arctic Studies Center, National Museum of Natural History, Smithsonian Institution.

Ford, J. K. B. *Marine Mammals of British Columbia.* Royal BC Museum, 2014.

Heide-Jørgensen, M. P. and K. Laidre. 2006. *Greenland's Winter Whales.* Greenland Institute of Natural Resources.

Hoyt, E. 2011 (Second Edition). *Marine Protected Areas For Whales, Dolphins and Porpoises: A World Handbook for Cetacean Habitat Conservation and Planning.* Earthscan.

Hoyt, E. 2017. *Encyclopedia of Whales, Dolphins and Porpoises.* Firefly Books.

Jefferson, T. A., M. A. Webber and R. J. Pitman. 2015 (Second Edition). *Marine Mammals of the World: A Comprehensive Guide to Their Identification.* Academic Press.

Kraus, S. D. and R. M. Rolland (eds). 2007. T*he Urban Whale: North Atlantic Right Whales at the Crossroads.* Harvard University Press.

Laist, D. W. 2017. *North Atlantic Right Whales: From Hunted Leviathan to Conservation Icon.* John Hopkins University Press.

McLeish, T. 2013. *Narwhals: Arctic Whales in a Melting World*. University of Washington Press.

Reynolds, J. E. III, R. S. Wells and S. D. Eide. 2000. *The Bottlenose Dolphin: Biology and Conservation*. University Press of Florida.

Ridgway, S. H. and R. Harrison (eds). 1985. *Handbook of Marine Mammals, Vol. 3: The Sirenians and Baleen Whales*. Academic Press.

Ridgway, S. H. and R. Harrison (eds). 1989. *Handbook of Marine Mammals, Vol. 4: River Dolphins and the Larger Toothed Whales*. Academic Press.

Ridgway, S. H. and R. Harrison (eds). 1994. *Handbook of Marine Mammals, Vol. 5: The First Book of Dolphins*. Academic Press.

Ridgway, S. H. and R. Harrison (eds). 1999. *Handbook of Marine Mammals, Vol. 6: The Second Book of Dolphins and the Porpoises*. Academic Press.

Ruiz-Garcia, M. and J. M. Shostell (eds). 2010. *Biology, Evolution and Conservation of River Dolphins Within South America and Asia*. Nova Science Publishers.

Sumich, J. 2014. E. robustus: *Biology and Human History of Gray Whales*. James Sumich at Amazon.

Swartz, S. L. 2014. *Lagoon Time: A Guide to Gray Whales and the Natural History of San Ignacio Lagoon*. The Ocean Foundation.

Turvey, S. 2008. *Witness to Extinction: How We Failed to Save the Yangtze River Dolphin*. Oxford University Press.

Whitehead, H. 2003. *Sperm Whales: Social Evolution in the Ocean*. University of Chicago Press.

Wilson, D. E. and R. A. Mittermeier. 2014. *Handbook of the Mammals of the World: 4. Sea Mammals*. Lynx Edicions.

Würsig, B., J. G. M. Thewissen and K. M. Kovacs (eds). 2018. *Encyclopedia of Marine Mammals*. Academic Press.

Würsig, B. and M. Würsig (eds). 2010. *The Dusky Dolphin: Master Acrobat of Different Shores*. Academic Press.

ARTISTS' BIOGRAPHIES

Martin Camm, from Bedfordshire, UK, is one of the world's most renowned illustrators of aquatic life, specialising in cetaceans. He has contributed to hundreds of books, magazines and journals, and his work is widely published by many organisations, including the United Nations, the BBC, Greenpeace, IFAW (International Fund for Animal Welfare), WDC (Whale and Dolphin Conservation Society), and The Wildlife Trusts.

Toni Llobet, from Catalonia, Spain, thinks of himself more as a naturalist than an artist. He is rigorous in both disciplines, as his intricate work shows. He has worked as a wildlife illustrator for some 20 years, and his work includes massive projects such as illustrating the prestigious *Handbook of the Mammals of the World* (published by Lynx Edicions).

Rebecca Robinson, from Tasmania, Australia, graduated with a BSc in Zoology. In a bid to marry her passion for art and nature, she completed a Bachelor of Fine Arts degree (with Honours) in Wildlife Illustration. She then worked in the design department at the Marine Science Institute at the University of California Santa Barbara, and has been a freelance natural science illustrator ever since.

ACKNOWLEDGEMENTS

Many wonderful people have helped with this book – answering my endless questions, providing as yet unpublished information and commenting on early tentative drafts – and it couldn't have been written without them. Their generous contributions have helped me to make fewer mistakes than I would have made on my own and I'd like to thank them all for their time, enthusiasm, generosity and support. It is very much appreciated. All these whale biologists – friends and colleagues – are listed separately.

Special thanks go to the brilliant wildlife artists Martin Camm, Toni Llobet and Rebecca Robinson, who worked tirelessly on many more than 1,000 illustrations between them. Martin and I have collaborated on more whale books than either of us can remember, over more years than we dare admit, and it's always a great pleasure. And it has been wonderful working with Toni and Rebecca for the first time. A very big thank you to Rachel Ashton, my outstandingly efficient manager, for her never-ending patience, perseverance, encouragement, enthusiasm and general brilliance. I couldn't do it without you, Rachel. My literary agent, Doreen Montgomery, was a huge support, as always over the past quarter of a century; very sadly, she passed away while I was writing, and I will miss her terribly. Doreen's daughter, Caroline Montgomery, kindly took the reins and carries on the Montgomery tradition with aplomb. I am particularly indebted to Jim Martin at Bloomsbury (without whom this book wouldn't have happened at all) for his unwavering belief in the whole idea and for his genuine love and passion for the natural world; even when the project took five times longer than we had all anticipated, he never stopped smiling and (at least seemed to) take it all in his stride. Thanks for everything, Jim. Thank you, also, to Alice Ward (Commissioning Editor, Bloomsbury Wildlife), who smoothed the way so calmly; it's been a pleasure working with you, Alice. I was very lucky to have Emily Kearns as copy-editor, and Julie Dando as designer – two outstanding professionals who went above and beyond the call of duty; thank you – I really appreciate it.

I'd like to thank my dear friends and family, who have enthused with me when things have been going well and cheered me on when I've been flagging: in particular, Peter Bassett and John Ruthven, for those welcome interludes over coffee in the Clifton Lido; John Craven, Nick Middleton and Marc Riley for putting up with my relentless chatter about field guides, whales, dolphins, porpoises, distribution maps, illustrations, scientific papers, etc., etc.; and Roz Kidman Cox, for her knowing sympathy and good counsel. I'd also like to give my wonderful, kind, encouraging parents, David and Betty, a special mention: without their never-ending support and encouragement, life would have been so different. My brother Adam, sister-in-law Vanessa, nieces Jessica and Zoe, Beryl, Al and Jude, Florence and Miller have all kindly put up with my mind-bendingly long hours and preoccupation with what became known as 'the-project-that-never-seems-to-end'. Last, but by no means least, a huge heartfelt thank you for everything to my co-conspirator in life, Debra Taylor, who always makes things better.

At the end of the day, despite a phenomenal effort to make this field guide as accurate and complete as possible, I take full responsibility for any mistakes, oversights and inconsistencies that may have crept in. I'd welcome any thoughts, comments and suggestions – via www.markcarwardine.com – to incorporate in new, improved future editions. Thank you very much.

WITH SPECIAL THANKS TO:

Robert L. Pitman
Charles Anderson

… AND ALL THE SCIENTISTS WHO KINDLY ADVISED ON INDIVIDUAL SPECIES

Àlex Aguilar
Wojtek Bachara
Robin W. Baird
Isabel Beasley
Chiara Giulia Bertulli
Arne Bjørge
Nancy Black
Moira Brown
Salvatore Cerchio
William Cioffi
Phillip J. Clapham
Diane Claridge
Rochelle Constantine
Barbara E. Curry
Merel Dalebout
Jim Darling
Natalia Dellabianca
David M. Donnelly
Simon H. Elwen
Ruth Esteban
James Fair
Ivan D. Fetudin
Andrew Foote
R. Ewan Fordyce
Ari Friedlaender
Sonja Heinrich
Denise Herzing
Sascha Hooker
Erich Hoyt
Miguel Iñíguez
Maria Iversen
Thomas A. Jefferson
Eve Jourdain
Catherine Kemper
Iain Kerr
Jeremy Kiszka

Kristin Laidre
Jack Lawson
Rob Lott
Donald McAlpine
Colin D. MacLeod
Amanda Madro
Anisul Islam Mahmud
Silvia S. Monteiro
Hilary Moors-Murphy
Dirk R. Neumann
Stephanie A. Norman
Giuseppe Notarbartolo di Sciara
Gregory O'Corry-Crowe
William F. Perrin
Cindy Peter
Róisín Pinfield
Andrew J. Read
Victoria Rowntree
Filipa Samarra
Jarrod A. Santora
Marcos César de Oliveira Santos
Richard Sears
Keiko Sekiguchi
Tammy L. Silva
Tiu Similä
Ravindra Kumar Sinha
Elisabeth Slooten
Kate Rose-Ann Sprogis
Steven Swartz
Jessica K. D. Taylor
Outi Tervo
Kirsten Thompson
Paul Thompson
Fernando Trujillo
Grigory A. Tsidulko
Samuel Turvey
Koen Van Waerebeek
Caroline R. Weir
Hal Whitehead
Tonya Wimmer
Bernd Würsig

IMAGE CREDITS

With the exception of the photographs listed on the page below, all photographs in this book remain © Mark Carwardine.

p52 (top) p121 (bottom) © Nick Hawkins/naturepl.com; p52 (bottom) Sea to Shore Alliance, NOAA Permit 15488; p53 (top) Allison Henry/NOAA, MMPA Permit 17335; p53 (bottom) © Peter Flood; p59 (top) Robert Pitman/NOAA; p59 (bottom) Brenda K Rone/NOAA/AFSC/NMML Permit 782-1719; p65, p126, © Gabriel Rojo/natuepl.com; p66, p335, p479 Hiroya Minakuchi/Minden Pictures; p67 (top left) © Buteo/shutterstock.com; p67 (top right) © Mogens Trolle/shutterstock.com; p67 (bottom), p424 © Gérard Soury/Biosphoto; p73 (top right) © NOAA/Alamy Stock Photo; p73 (bottom), p167, p451 © Flip Nicklin/Minden Pictures; p98 © Verborgh-CIRCE.INFO; p99 (top right) © Luis Quinta/naturepl.com; p99 (bottom) NOAA Fisheries/Brenda Rone; p104 NOAA Fisheries/Peter Duley/ MMPA Permit 17355; p105 (top) NOAA Fisheries/ Christin Khan/ MMPA Permit 17355; p105 (bottom) © Falklands Conservation/Caroline R Weir; p111 (top), p145 © Tony Wu/naturepl.com; p115 © Alex Lindbloom; p127 (top) © Graeme Snow/shutterstock.com; p127 (bottom), p287 (bottom), p441 (bottom) © robertharding/Alamy Stock Photo; p151 © Patrick Griffin/Ocean Sounds – Marine Mammal Research & Conservation; p168 © New Sue Productions/naturepl.com; p169 © Brandon Cole/naturepl.com; p174, p351, p371 (top), p418, p425 (top), p437 © Todd Pusser/naturepl.com; p178 © James Kemp; p181 © Reid Brewer; p186, p235 (top) © Robin W Baird/Cascadia Research; p195 © Robert L Pitman/SeaPics.com (top); p195 (bottom) © Matt Eade; p199 © Allan Cronin; p203, p419 © Anthony Pierce/Alamy Stock Photo; p215 © Charles Anderson; p219 © Michael S Nolan; p225 © Nick Gales; p234 Brittany D Guenther/Cascadia Research, NMFS ESA/MMPA Permit 20605; p235 (bottom) © BIOSPHOTO/ Alamy Stock Photos; p251 © Brian Patteson; p279 © Malcolm Schuyl/Alamy Stock Photo; p282 © Kathryn Jeffs/naturepl. com; p285 © Robert Pitman; p287 (top) © Jean-Pierre Sylvestre; p297, p325 © Heike Vester/Ocean Sounds – Marine Mammal Research & Conservation; p299 © Jan Baks/NiS/Minden Pictures; p307 © David Fleetham/naturepl.com; p311 © Cyril di Bisceglie/Wikimedia Commons; p356 © Mike Read/naturepl.com; p357 (top) © Solvin Zankl/naturepl.com; p357 (bottom) © Pete Oxford/Minden Pictures; p371 (bottom) © Richard Herrmann/Minden Pictures; p375 © Dennis Buurman Photography; p378, p507 © Carefordolphins/Alamy Stock Photo; p379 © Alex Brown, Murdoch University/WWF-Australia; p383 © aDam Wildlife/shutterstock.com; p391 Caroline R Weir/Ketos Ecology; p399 © Danielle S Conry/ORCA Foundation; p425 (bottom) © Alex Mustard/naturepl.com; p441 (top) © Jordi Chias/naturepl.com; p461 (top) © Grant Abel; p461 (bottom) © Zahoor Salmi/WWF-Pakistan; p470, p471 © Projeto Toninhas/UNIVILLE; p490 © Thomas Jefferson; p494 © Sonja Heinrich; p503 (top) © Jean-Pierre Sylvestre/Biosphoto; p503 (bottom) © Grant Abel.

With the exception of the artworks listed on the page below, all artworks in this book remain © Martin Camm (www.markcarwardine.com).

© Rebecca Robinson (www.markcarwardine.com): all dive sequences and whale blows.
© Toni Llobet: p28, p29, p63, p118 (top two), p122, p123, p124, p125, p259, p260, p385, p386, p422 (top), p423 (top); flukes on p11, p30, p31, p48, p56, p64 (left), p70, p81, p90, p96, p133, p142, p266; p63.
© Toni Llobet from: Wilson, D.E. & Mittermeier, R.A. eds. (2014). *Handbook of the Mammals of the World. Vol. 4. Sea Mammals.* Lynx Edicions, Barcelona: p11 (second from top), p60, p63 (top), p100, p102, p164, p312, p314 (top), p328 (second from top), p384, p392, p448, p452, p462, p463, p464, p465 (middle).
© Jack Ashton: p25 (bottom), p26, p27 (lice).
© Marc Dando, Fluke Art: p19 (top).

INDEX

INDEX ಅ